SECRECY AND LIBERTY: NATIONAL SECURITY, FREEDOM OF EXPRESSION AND ACCESS TO INFORMATION

International Studies in Human Rights

VOLUME 58

The titles published in this series are listed at the end of this volume.

SECRECY AND LIBERTY: NATIONAL SECURITY, FREEDOM OF EXPRESSION AND ACCESS TO INFORMATION

Edited by

SANDRA COLIVER
Legal Adviser, International Crisis Group (Bosnia); former Law Program Director, Article 19, the International Centre Against Censorship, United Kingdom

PAUL HOFFMAN
Member, International Board, Article 19; Chair of the Board of Amnesty International, U.S.A.; and Civil Rights Attorney, U.S.A.

JOAN FITZPATRICK
Professor of International Law, University of Washington, U.S.A.

STEPHEN BOWEN
Barrister; Program Director of the International Human Rights Law Group, Washington, U.S.A.

MARTINUS NIJHOFF PUBLISHERS
THE HAGUE / BOSTON / LONDON

A C.I.P. Catalogue record for this book is available from the Library of Congress.

ISBN 90-411-1191-3

Published by Kluwer Law International,
P.O. Box 85889, 2508 CN The Hague, The Netherlands

Sold and distributed in North, Central and South America
by Kluwer Law International,
675 Massachusetts Avenue, Cambridge, MA 02139, USA

In all other countries, sold and distributed
by Kluwer Law International, Distribution Centre
P.O. Box 322, 3300 AH Dordrecht, The Netherlands

Printed on acid-free paper

Printed in the Netherlands.

TABLE OF CONTENTS

APPENDICES

Acknowledgments

Stephen Bowen

Stephen Bowen gratefully acknowledges the assistance and support of the International Human Rights Law Group, Program and Research Associate Todd Freier, and Legal Fellow Alison Steward. He also wishes to thank the numerous interns that assisted on the project, particularly Jahna Hartwig, Sharon Maerten, Caroline Santa-Cruz, Amanda Vig, Erin Boggs, and Jörg Steinhauer.

Sandra Coliver

Sandra Coliver would like to acknowledge the support from a grant for Research and Writing from the John D. and Catherine T. MacArthur Foundation. An earlier version of her chapter was published in the *Human Rights Quarterly*, Vol. 20 (Feb. 1998).

Joan Fitzpatrick

Joan Fitzpatrick thanks Dorothy Liu for her editorial assistance and Gloria Strickland and Robert Kelly for their work on preparation of the manuscript.

Paul Hoffman

Paul Hoffman thanks Denise Williamson for her enormous skill and patience in transforming the manuscript into camera-ready copy.

FOREWORD

This study on secrecy and liberty arose out of an international gathering of experts which took place in South Africa in late 1995. Jointly convened by ARTICLE 19, the International Centre Against Censorship, and the Centre for Applied Legal Studies (CALS) at the University of the Witwatersrand, the gathering was a highly significant one. After three days of intensive debate, it resulted in the Johannesburg Principles on National Security, Freedom of Expression and Access to Information, a new and compelling set of standards for safeguarding the public's right to know in one of the most contentious of contexts foreseen under international law. The Principles have since been recommended to governments by the United Nations' Special Rapporteur on freedom of opinion and expression as providing "guidance for protecting adequately the right to freedom of opinion, expression and information".

ARTICLE 19 and CALS convened the South Africa conference in order to address one of the most sensitive questions of international law affecting freedom of expression - to what extent may governments withhold information from public disclosure and prohibit expression for reasons of national security. Both organizations had become concerned in the course of their respective work, internationally and in apartheid South Africa, that governments were exploiting the imprecision of international law on this question in order to withhold information that should properly be in the public domain, to deter investigative journalism and to stifle political opposition. A main purpose of the conference, therefore, was to examine the development of international law on this issue taking into account the findings reached by national courts and the international treaty bodies when dealing with relevant cases. Such findings, it was expected, and the reasons adduced in their support, would provide an important resource for charting the most appropriate standards to be followed by governments when balancing the interests of national security against the vitally important right to freedom of expression.

There can be no doubt, of course, that governments are permitted under international law to legislate for the protection of state secrets. The International Covenant on Civil and Political Rights specifically identifies the protection of national security as a legitimate ground for restricting freedom of expression and access to information, and this is echoed by the European Convention for the Protection of Human Rights and Fundamental Freedoms and other regional human rights instruments. Nor is it difficult to imagine the sort of contexts - for example, an imminent threat of foreign military aggression or invasion - to which such restrictions on individual rights were clearly intended to apply. In practice, however, as this volume underlines, many governments have found it useful to define the concept of national or state security much more broadly. By doing so, they have been able to justify prohibiting discussion of, or withholding information about, matters which would prove inconvenient or politically damaging if placed in the public domain. *Raison d'etat*, indeed, has often been the notional shield behind which those wielding power have sought to conceal their actions from the less powerful in whose name they rule and to whom they are theoretically accountable. Nor has this merely been a practice of tyrannies and dictatorships: governments in longstanding democracies have also tended all too easily to sacrifice their citizens' rights to freedom of expression on the widely framed altar of national security.

This report seeks to restore that balance and to do so, unashamedly, in favor of freedom of expression and the public's right to know. It argues strongly that governments have a heavy obligation to promote and protect these key rights, and that any restriction of those rights should only occur in the narrowest and clearest circumstances, and according to law. It is not enough for governments simply to contend that national security will be jeopardized as grounds for censorship: to be legitimate any such restriction must be capable of justification against more precise criteria such as those already available within emerging international human rights law. It is to this end that the Johannesburg Principles are devoted.

Frances D'Souza, Executive Director
ARTICLE 19
April 1998

INTRODUCTION

The tension between national security and freedom of expression and information is both acute and multifaceted. Stifling of dissent and secretiveness are the hallmarks of repression. Free voicing of diverse political opinions and "sunshine" policies exposing governmental operations to public and media scrutiny, conversely, are indicators of a vigorously effective democracy.

At the same time, armed conflict and espionage pose significant security threats that may justifiably result in restrictions upon the free flow of information. National security concerns will be heightened when the state undergoes a state of emergency, and free expression rights will frequently be among those subjected to derogation or increased restriction. However, the tendency of governing elites to confuse "the life of the nation" with "the survival of the regime" creates a grave risk that derogations and limitations on expression and information rights will be excessive. A proper balance between secrecy and liberty cannot be struck without review of executive and legislative measures by an independent national judiciary, supplemented by the oversight and monitoring activities of international human rights bodies, non-governmental organizations and a vigilant press.

Reconciliation of these tensions, with a strong emphasis upon preservation of fundamental freedoms and genuine democracy, was the objective of the drafters of the Johannesburg Principles on National Security, Freedom of Expression and Access to Information, convened in October 1995 by Article 19, the International Centre Against Censorship. The Johannesburg Principles explicate the dimensions of the freedoms of expression and opinion, the right of access to information, and the scope of permissible limitations on these rights based upon grounds of national security. The Principles further address important structural and procedural protections that may hamper the misuse of state security laws for improper and antidemocratic purposes.

The Commentary by Sandra Coliver elaborates upon the Principles and traces their roots in progressive interpretations of both international and national standards, noting where the Principles reflect an existing consensus and the points at which they attempt to elicit a more rights-regarding approach. Moreover, she explains the potential of the Principles as a guide both to governments and to inter-governmental bodies seeking to reconcile the inevitable tensions between national security and free expression.

Following this distillation and analysis of the general normative framework, we examine the approaches taken by competent inter-governmental bodies in monitoring state compliance with free expression standards, where their limitation on grounds of national security is in question. Here we find valuable cross-fertilization among UN and regional bodies, while also noting distinct regional challenges posed by security regulations. One can discern the emergence of an analytical framework emphasizing that restrictions on expression and information must be prescribed by law; must have both the purpose and effect of protecting a genuine national security interest; and must be proportional, meaning that they are necessary in a democratic society and adopt the least restrictive means to protect the asserted national security objective.

Elizabeth Evatt describes the experience of the Human Rights Committee in applying Article 19 of the International Covenant on Civil and Political Rights, as well as the Committee's consideration of the national security grounds for restriction of other rights protected by the Covenant. Paul Mahoney and Lawrence Early analyze the influential jurisprudence of the European Commission on Human Rights and the European Court of Human Rights under Article 10 of the European Convention for the Protection of Human Rights and Fundamental Freedoms. They also describe the broader role of the Council of Europe in the fields of expression and information, noting the challenges faced by the Council in absorbing its new members from Eastern and Central Europe, whose traditions of reconciling expression and security differ significantly from those of the Western European democracies.

Viviana Krsticevic, José Miguel Vivanco, Juan Méndez and Drew Porter explore the challenge posed by the all-consuming "national security" ideology of autocratic Latin American states during the 1970s and 1980s that ruthlessly suppressed dissent under an expansive concept of necessity. They note the ways in which expression and information have continued to be restricted during the redemocratization process, with the asserted objective of post-crisis national reconciliation. Further, they explore specific Western Hemisphere problems such as "desacato" laws penalizing insult to high officials, analyzing the response of the human rights organs of the Organization of American States under the especially protective standards of the American Convention on Human Rights. Claude Welch examines the challenges faced by the African Commission on Human and People's Rights in implementing the less explicit standards of the African Charter under daunting resource and logistical limits, as well as the evolution of national security concepts between the eras of colonization, decolonization and contemporary armed conflict and political instability. Welch also notes the importance of NGOs as monitors of respect for expressive rights. The European Union poses an interesting contrasting model, as Andrew Nicol notes its modest efforts to promote access to information, while consciously maintaining a fairly low profile in the promotion of fundamental human rights and grappling with its own set of tensions between conformity to EU standards and the national security interests of its member states.

In a series of country studies, we display the tremendous diversity of conceptions of national security, the variety of penal measures states have adopted to stamp out allegedly subversive or dangerous speech, the treatment of journalistic freedoms, the relative openness or closure of government files to public scrutiny, and the central role of an independent and depoliticized judiciary as a check upon obsessive concern over dissent and criticism of government policy. Among the states profiled are those facing significant and persistent threats of international armed conflict, such as Israel and South Korea. Ruth Gavison and Kyo Ho Youm cogently examine legislative and judicial developments in Israel and South Korea relating to the regulation of speech, the maintenance or gradual flourishing of democracy, and the definition of a role for a critical and free press, in contexts where government must also cope with significant (but sometimes overbroadly defined) external security threats.

The developed Western democracies, such as France, Germany, Norway, the United States and the United Kingdom, have been preoccupied by the risk of espionage, enacting many broad-reaching measures that are frequently applied by deferential judiciaries under diluted procedural standards, while also battling internal enemies with a range of questionable measures punishing sedition or aggressive speech and placing impediments in the path of an inquiring press. Roger Errera reviews developments in French law and practice, finding a trend toward increased accessibility to government information and greater precision in penal laws affecting expression. Ulrich Karpen explains the approach of the German courts, which apply a balancing test strongly favoring free expression as vital to the maintenance of democracy and, consequently, to the genuine protection of national security, while permitting modest limitations on journalists and others engaged in expressive activities. Nils Petter Gleditsch provides a detailed analysis of state secrecy in Norway during the Cold War, noting that national security is likely to recede from prominence in discussions of the role of the media in society, as public attention turns to issues such as privacy and socially divisive speech. Laurence Lustgarten critiques the doctrine of sedition in the United Kingdom, the problematic role of the British judiciary in the protection of expression and the weak tradition of access to information, including the lack of protection for "whistleblowers". Paul Hoffman and Kate Martin provide a detailed guide to statutory and case law in the United States, regarding both freedom of expression and access to information, explaining the central importance of the First Amendment, the influence of the Freedom of Information Act and the vital role of independent judicial review.

In Central Europe, control of the media has emerged as a prime strategy of the regimes taking power in the aftermath of the Cold War in Albania and the Federal Republic of Yugoslavia. Louise Krabbe examines in detail the struggle for journalistic freedom and access to information in Albania. Branislav Milinkovic describes Slobodan Milosevic's manipulation of the mass media to inflame Serb nationalistic fervor, fueling the conflict in Bosnia-Herzegovina and tensions in Kosovo and the Sandzak, and the failure of the judiciary to check severe constraints upon expression.

In Turkey, a tradition of authoritarian rule and an overarching commitment to a secular and unified national identity have resulted in severe repression of Kurdish and Islamist activists. Kerim Yildiz describes the national security and anti-terrorist laws, the role of the National Security Council and state security courts, and a pattern of punitive measures against politicians, activists and journalists. Egypt also has experienced significant internal unrest as well as international armed conflict, resulting in an elaborate array of security measures restricting expression and information, analyzed by Nagad Al-Boray.

In addition to South Korea, four other Asian states are profiled (China, Hong Kong, India and Japan), presenting a variety of interesting contrasts. Sofia Woodman and Yu Ping examine the role of the Chinese Communist Party in defining state security, the range of legislative measures that suppress dissent and control the media, restrictions on access to official information, the gradual substitution of "endangering state security" for "counterrevolution" as the premise for punishing expressive activity, recent procedural developments toward greater legal formality and the Government's strategy of discouraging dissent by means of targeted prosecutions of prominent critics of its policies. Yash Ghai and Jennifer Van Dale describe efforts to entrench basic liberties in the Hong Kong Special Administrative Region, in a context of Chinese concerns that Hong Kong might become the locus of dissent and against an historical background of substantial restrictions on expression during the colonial era. K.S. Venkateswaran traces the jurisprudence of the Indian judiciary concerning the national security and public order exceptions to India's constitutional protection of free expression, noting the impact of derogations during states of emergency and sensitivity to the threat posed by regional separatist movements. Lawrence Beer argues that the demilitarization of post-War Japan has produced a new and potentially influential reinterpretation of the concept of national security, which is conducive to unfettered expression.

Two states (Chile and South Africa) offer case studies in the evolution of security-based restrictions on expression and information during the transition from non-democratic to democratic rule. Cecilia Medina and Felipe Gonzalez note how the expansive doctrine of "national security" held by the military regime focused repression on perceived internal enemies, the impact of the state of emergency, the lingering effects of restrictive legislation, the continued influence wielded by the military and the reluctance of the Chilean courts to scrutinize national security and public order justifications asserted by the Government. Gilbert Marcus describes South Africa's apartheid security policy and its pervasive web of censorship, expansive secrecy laws and state controlled media, and also examines the impact of South Africa's extended state of emergency. He analyzes the 1994 Constitution and its present and potential effects upon South Africa's entrenched culture of secrecy, and notes how the work of the Truth and Reconciliation Commission may bring to light covert actions by the security forces of the apartheid regime.

Through presentation of the Johannesburg Principles, the Commentary, critiques of inter-governmental bodies and these country studies, we have attempted to offer a framework for striking a proper balance between legitimate concerns for peace and security and the fundamental, but not unlimited, rights of free expression and access to information.

Joan Fitzpatrick
May 1998

THE JOHANNESBURG PRINCIPLES ON NATIONAL SECURITY, FREEDOM OF EXPRESSION AND ACCESS TO INFORMATION

These Principles were adopted on 1 October 1995 by a group of experts in international law, national security, and human rights convened by ARTICLE 19, the International Centre Against Censorship, in collaboration with the Centre for Applied Legal Studies of the University of the Witwatersrand, in Johannesburg.

The Principles are based on international and regional law and standards relating to the protection of human rights, evolving state practice (as reflected, *inter alia*, in judgments of national courts), and the general principles of law recognized by the community of nations.

These Principles acknowledge the enduring applicability of the Siracusa Principles on the Limitation and Derogation Provisions in the International Covenant on Civil and Political Rights and the Paris Minimum Standards of Human Rights Norms In a State of Emergency.[1]

PREAMBLE

The participants involved in drafting the present Principles:

Considering that, in accordance with the principles proclaimed in the Charter of the United Nations, recognition of the inherent dignity and of the equal and inalienable rights of all members of the human family is the foundation of freedom, justice and peace in the world;

Convinced that it is essential, if people are not to be compelled to have recourse, as a last resort, to rebellion against tyranny and oppression, that human rights should be protected by the rule of law;

Reaffirming their belief that freedom of expression and freedom of information are vital to a democratic society and are essential for its progress and welfare and for the enjoyment of other human rights and fundamental freedoms;

Taking into account relevant provisions of the Universal Declaration of Human Rights, the International Covenant on Civil and Political Rights, the UN Convention on the Rights of the Child, the UN Basic Principles on the Independence

---

[1] The Siracusa Principles were adopted in May 1984 by a group of experts convened by the International Commission of Jurists, the International Association of Penal Law, the American Association for the International Commission of Jurists, the Urban Morgan Institute for Human Rights, and the International Institute of Higher Studies in Criminal Sciences. The Paris Minimum Standards were adopted in April 1984 by a group of experts under the auspices of the International Law Association.

of the Judiciary, the African Charter on Human and Peoples' Rights, the American Convention on Human Rights and the European Convention on Human Rights;

Keenly aware that some of the most serious violations of human rights and fundamental freedoms are justified by governments as necessary to protect national security;

Bearing in mind that it is imperative, if people are to be able to monitor the conduct of their government and to participate fully in a democratic society, that they have access to government-held information;

Desiring to promote a clear recognition of the limited scope of restrictions on freedom of expression and freedom of information that may be imposed in the interest of national security, so as to discourage governments from using the pretext of national security to place unjustified restrictions on the exercise of these freedoms;

Recognizing the necessity for legal protection of these freedoms by the enactment of laws drawn narrowly and with precision, and which ensure the essential requirements of the rule of law; and

Reiterating the need for judicial protection of these freedoms by independent courts;

Agree upon the following Principles, and recommend that appropriate bodies at the national, regional and international levels undertake steps to promote their widespread dissemination, acceptance and implementation:

I. GENERAL PRINCIPLES

Principle 1: Freedom of Opinion, Expression and Information

(a) Everyone has the right to hold opinions without interference.

(b) Everyone has the right to freedom of expression, which includes the freedom to seek, receive and impart information and ideas of all kinds, regardless of frontiers, either orally, in writing or in print, in the form of art, or through any other media of his or her choice.

(c) The exercise of the rights provided for in paragraph (b) may be subject to restrictions on specific grounds, as established in international law, including for the protection of national security.

(d) No restriction on freedom of expression or information on the ground of national security may be imposed unless the government can demonstrate that the restriction is prescribed by law and is necessary in a democratic society to protect a legitimate national security interest.[2] The burden of demonstrating the validity of the restriction rests with the government.

Principle 1.1: Prescribed by Law

(a) Any restriction on expression or information must be prescribed by law. The law must be accessible, unambiguous, drawn narrowly and with precision so as to enable individuals to foresee whether a particular action is unlawful.

(b) The law should provide for adequate safeguards against abuse, including prompt, full and effective judicial scrutiny of the validity of the restriction by an independent court or tribunal.

Principle 1.2: Protection of a Legitimate National Security Interest

Any restriction on expression or information that a government seeks to justify on grounds of national security must have the genuine purpose and demonstrable effect of protecting a legitimate national security interest.

Principle 1.3: Necessary in a Democratic Society

To establish that a restriction on freedom of expression or information is necessary to protect a legitimate national security interest, a government must demonstrate that:

(a) the expression or information at issue poses a serious threat to a legitimate national security interest;

---

[2] For the purposes of these Principles, a democratic society is one which has a government that is genuinely accountable to an entity or organ distinct from itself; genuine, periodic elections by universal and equal suffrage held by secret ballot that guarantee the free expression of the will of the electors; political groups that are free to organize in opposition to the government in office; and effective legal guarantees of fundamental rights enforced by an independent judiciary. This formulation is based on a definition of constitutionalism provided by Professor S A de Smith in *The Commonwealth and its Constitution* (London: Stevens & Sons, 1964), 106, augmented by reference to Article 25 of the International Covenant on Civil and Political Rights.

(b) the restriction imposed is the least restrictive means possible for protecting that interest; and

(c) the restriction is compatible with democratic principles.

Principle 2: Legitimate National Security Interest

(a) A restriction sought to be justified on the ground of national security is not legitimate unless its genuine purpose and demonstrable effect is to protect a country's existence or its territorial integrity against the use or threat of force, or its capacity to respond to the use or threat of force, whether from an external source, such as a military threat, or an internal source, such as incitement to violent overthrow of the government.

(b) In particular, a restriction sought to be justified on the ground of national security is not legitimate if its genuine purpose or demonstrable effect is to protect interests unrelated to national security, including, for example, to protect a government from embarrassment or exposure of wrongdoing, or to conceal information about the functioning of its public institutions, or to entrench a particular ideology, or to suppress industrial unrest.

Principle 3: States of Emergency

In time of public emergency which threatens the life of the country and the existence of which is officially and lawfully proclaimed in accordance with both national and international law, a state may impose restrictions on freedom of expression and information but only to the extent strictly required by the exigencies of the situation and only when and for so long as they are not inconsistent with the government's other obligations under international law.

Principle 4: Prohibition of Discrimination

In no case may a restriction on freedom of expression or information, including on the ground of national security, involve discrimination based on race, colour, sex, language, religion, political or other opinion, national or social origin, nationality, property, birth or other status.

II. RESTRICTIONS ON FREEDOM OF EXPRESSION

Principle 5: Protection of Opinion

No one may be subjected to any sort of restraint, disadvantage or sanction because of his or her opinions or beliefs.

Principle 6: Expression That May Threaten National Security

Subject to Principles 15 and 16, expression may be punished as a threat to national security only if a government can demonstrate that:

(a) the expression is intended to incite imminent violence;

(b) it is likely to incite such violence; and

(c) there is a direct and immediate connection between the expression and the likelihood or occurrence of such violence.

Principle 7: Protected Expression

(a) Subject to Principles 15 and 16, the peaceful exercise of the right to freedom of expression shall not be considered a threat to national security or subjected to any restrictions or penalties. Expression which shall not constitute a threat to national security includes, but is not limited to, expression that:

(i) advocates non-violent change of government policy or the government itself;

(ii) constitutes criticism of, or insult to, the nation, the state or its symbols, the government, its agencies, or public officials,[3] or a foreign nation, state or its symbols, government, agencies or public officials;

(iii) constitutes objection, or advocacy of objection, on grounds of religion, conscience or belief, to military conscription or service, a particular conflict, or the threat or use of force to settle international disputes;

---

[3] "Public officials", for the purpose of these Principles, include the Head of State; the Head of Government; all government officials including Ministers; all officers of the military, security forces and police; and all people who hold elected office.

(iv) is directed at communicating information about alleged violations of international human rights standards or international humanitarian law.

(b) No one may be punished for criticizing or insulting the nation, the state or its symbols, the government, its agencies, or public officials, or a foreign nation, state or its symbols, government, agency or public official unless the criticism or insult was intended and likely to incite imminent violence.

Principle 8: Mere Publicity of Activities That May Threaten National Security

Expression may not be prevented or punished merely because it transmits information issued by or about an organization that a government has declared threatens national security or a related interest.

Principle 9: Use of a Minority or Other Language

Expression, whether written or oral, can never be prohibited on the ground that it is in a particular language, especially the language of a national minority.

Principle 10: Unlawful Interference With Expression by Third Parties

Governments are obliged to take reasonable measures to prevent private groups or individuals from interfering unlawfully with the peaceful exercise of freedom of expression, even where the expression is critical of the government or its policies. In particular, governments are obliged to condemn unlawful actions aimed at silencing freedom of expression, and to investigate and bring to justice those responsible.

III. RESTRICTIONS ON FREEDOM OF INFORMATION

Principle 11: General Rule on Access to Information

Everyone has the right to obtain information from public authorities, including information relating to national security. No restriction on this right may be imposed on the ground of national security unless the government can demonstrate that the restriction is prescribed by law and is necessary in a democratic society to protect a legitimate national security interest.

Principle 12: Narrow Designation of Security Exemption

A state may not categorically deny access to all information related to national security, but must designate in law only those specific and narrow categories of information that it is necessary to withhold in order to protect a legitimate national security interest.

Principle 13: Public Interest in Disclosure

In all laws and decisions concerning the right to obtain information, the public interest in knowing the information shall be a primary consideration.

Principle 14: Right to Independent Review of Denial of Information

The state is obliged to adopt appropriate measures to give effect to the right to obtain information. These measures shall require the authorities, if they deny a request for information, to specify their reasons for doing so in writing and as soon as reasonably possible; and shall provide for a right of review of the merits and the validity of the denial by an independent authority, including some form of judicial review of the legality of the denial. The reviewing authority must have the right to examine the information withheld.[4]

Principle 15: General Rule on Disclosure of Secret Information

No person may be punished on national security grounds for disclosure of information if (1) the disclosure does not actually harm and is not likely to harm a legitimate national security interest, or (2) the public interest in knowing the information outweighs the harm from disclosure.

Principle 16: Information Obtained Through Public Service

No person may be subjected to any detriment on national security grounds for disclosing information that he or she learned by virtue of government service if the public interest in knowing the information outweighs the harm from disclosure.

---

[4] Additional grounds for obtaining and correcting personal information in files about oneself, such as the right to privacy, lie beyond the scope of these Principles.

Principle 17: Information in the Public Domain

Once information has been made generally available, by whatever means, whether or not lawful, any justification for trying to stop further publication will be overridden by the public's right to know.

Principle 18: Protection of Journalists' Sources

Protection of national security may not be used as a reason to compel a journalist to reveal a confidential source.

Principle 19: Access to Restricted Areas

Any restriction on the free flow of information may not be of such a nature as to thwart the purposes of human rights and humanitarian law. In particular, governments may not prevent journalists or representatives of intergovernmental or non-governmental organizations with a mandate to monitor adherence to human rights or humanitarian standards from entering areas where there are reasonable grounds to believe that violations of human rights or humanitarian law are being, or have been, committed. Governments may not exclude journalists or representatives of such organizations from areas that are experiencing violence or armed conflict except where their presence would pose a clear risk to the safety of others.

IV. RULE OF LAW AND OTHER MATTERS

Principle 20: General Rule of Law Protections

Any person accused of a security-related crime[5] involving expression or information is entitled to all of the rule of law protections that are part of international law. These include, but are not limited to, the following rights:

(a) the right to be presumed innocent;

(b) the right not to be arbitrarily detained;

(c) the right to be informed promptly in a language the person can understand of the charges and the supporting evidence against him or her;

---

[5] For the purposes of these Principles, a "security-related crime" is an act or omission which the government claims must be punished in order to protect national security or a closely related interest.

(d) the right to prompt access to counsel of choice;

(e) the right to a trial within a reasonable time;

(f) the right to have adequate time to prepare his or her defence;

(g) the right to a fair and public trial by an independent and impartial court or tribunal;

(h) the right to examine prosecution witnesses;

(i) the right not to have evidence introduced at trial unless it has been disclosed to the accused and he or she has had an opportunity to rebut it; and

(j) the right to appeal to an independent court or tribunal with power to review the decision on law and facts and set it aside.

Principle 21: Remedies

All remedies, including special ones, such as habeas corpus or amparo, shall be available to persons charged with security-related crimes, including during public emergencies which threaten the life of the country, as defined in Principle 3.

Principle 22: Right to Trial by an Independent Tribunal

(a) At the option of the accused, a criminal prosecution of a security-related crime should be tried by a jury where that institution exists or else by judges who are genuinely independent. The trial of persons accused of security-related crimes by judges without security of tenure constitutes a prima facie violation of the right to be tried by an independent tribunal.

(b) In no case may a civilian be tried for a security-related crime by a military court or tribunal.

(c) In no case may a civilian or member of the military be tried by an *ad hoc* or specially constituted national court or tribunal.

Principle 23: Prior Censorship

Expression shall not be subject to prior censorship in the interest of protecting national security, except in time of public emergency which threatens the life of the country under the conditions stated in Principle 3.

Principle 24: Disproportionate Punishments

A person, media outlet, political or other organization may not be subject to such sanctions, restraints or penalties for a security-related crime involving freedom of expression or information that are disproportionate to the seriousness of the actual crime.

Principle 25: Relation of These Principles to Other Standards

Nothing in these Principles may be interpreted as restricting or limiting any human rights or freedoms recognized in international, regional or national law or standards.

COMMENTARY ON THE JOHANNESBURG PRINCIPLES ON NATIONAL SECURITY, FREEDOM OF EXPRESSION AND ACCESS TO INFORMATION[1]

Sandra Coliver

I. Introduction

National security and freedom of expression and information are often viewed as pulling in opposite directions. On the one hand, governments, particularly those that feel threatened by external or internal violence, maintain that disclosure of "secret" information or airing of critical opinions can undermine the very institutions that protect the security and well-being of law-abiding citizens. On the other hand, human rights defenders point to government suppression of speech on national security and related grounds as having paved the way for some of the worst human rights violations, subversions of democracy, and threats to peace experienced in the last half of this century.

While there is an undeniable tension between national security and freedom of expression and information, a clear-eyed review of recent history suggests that legitimate national security interests are, in practice, better protected when the press and public are able to scrutinize government decisions than when governments operate in secret.[2] Freedom of expression and access to information, by enabling public scrutiny of government action, serve as safeguards against government abuse

---

[1] This chapter is an updated version of an article published in the Human Rights Quarterly, Vol. 20, No. 1 (Feb. 1998). Support for the article was provided by a grant for Research and Writing from the John D. and Catherine T. MacArthur Foundation. The author wrote the first drafts of the article while serving as the Law Programme Director of Article 19, the International Center Against Censorship. The author thanks Stephen Bowen, Joan Fitzpatrick, Paul Hoffman, and Malcolm Smart for their helpful comments on earlier drafts, and Alison Stewart for her accomplished research assistance.

[2] *See, e.g.*, the "Pentagon Papers" case, New York Times Co. v. United States, 403 U.S. 713 (1971) (discussing the disclosure by Daniel Ellsberg of 47-volume Pentagon study entitled "History of Decision-Making Process on Viet Nam Policy"); Laurence Lustgarten, "United Kingdom," *infra* this volume, at 457 (describing how Clive Ponting, a senior civil servant in the UK Ministry of Defence, supplied information to an Opposition Member of Parliament which demonstrated that information provided by the Government concerning the presence of an Argentine destroyer near the Falklands/Malvinas Islands - which had been used to justify Britain's entry into war - was misleading if not outright false).

and thereby form a crucial component of genuine national security.[3] Equally, national security is a pre-condition for the full enjoyment of all human rights, including freedom of expression.

There are, without doubt, circumstances in which national security and freedom of expression clash head on. For instance, protection of a genuine national security interest may require the suppression of sensitive defense information or speech likely to promote violence against the state. However, most claimed conflicts arise because national security and related concepts (such as "state security", "internal security", "public security", and "public safety") are so imprecise that they may be, and frequently have been,[4] invoked by governments to suppress precisely the kinds

---

[3] As stated by Prof. Chevigny, "The problem with the 'national security state' is not so much that it violates [fundamental] rights, although it sometimes does just that, but that it can lead to the repetition of irrational decisions." Paul G. Chevigny, "Information, the Executive and the Politics of Information," in Shimon Shetreet, ed., *Free Speech and National Security*, at 138 (1990).

[4] For instance, the Malawian Preservation of Public Security Act defines public security to include the securing of the safety of persons and property, the maintenance of supplies and services essential to the life of the community, the preservation and suppression of violence, intimidation, disorder and crime, the maintenance of the administration of justice and the prevention and suppression of mutiny, rebellion and concerted defiance of and disobedience to lawfully constituted authority and the laws in force in Malawi. Laws of Malawi, Chapter 14:02, § 2.

Turkey's Anti-Terror Law defines terrorism to include any use of "pressure" to change "the characteristics of the Republic . . . [or] its political, legal, social, secular and economic system." Anti-Terror Law, art. 1, § 1. Article 8 of the law specifically penalizes the publication of propaganda that threatens the "indivisible unity of the state." *Id.* art. 8. Prior to 1995, people could be charged and convicted "regardless of the method, intention and ideas behind" what they wrote. In 1995, Article 8 was revised to ban only writings that "aim[] at damaging the State." *Id.* The excesses of enforcement of the prior law are demonstrated by the release, in the first eighteen months following the revision, of 269 prisoners, and reduction in sentences of another 1,408. US State Department, "Turkey," *Country Reports on Human Rights Practices for 1996*, at 1163-64 (Feb. 1997). Despite amendment to the law, in 1996 at least 135 journalists were detained. A well-known musician was arrested and charged with "aiding members of an armed organization" when he participated in a discussion on a TV station associated with the Kurdish terrorist PKK. In March 1996, novelist Yasar Kemal was convicted under the revised Article 8 and Article 312 of the Criminal Code (for inciting to racial or ethnic enmity) for publishing a book in which he accused the Turkish Government of waging a "campaign of lies" in its censorship of reporting on the Kurdish question. Another ninety-nine individuals were charged as accomplices. Four pro-Kurdish former Members of Parliament were convicted and sentenced to prison under the revised Article 8 for peaceful advocacy of greater autonomy for the Kurdish region. *Id.* at 1163-66.

The Constitution of Guinea allows restrictions on fundamental rights to protect the "security of the realm," "the economic well-being of the people" and "the defence of national interests." Report of the Human Rights Committee, U.N. GAOR, 48th Sess., ¶ 547, UN Doc. A/48/40 (Part I) (1993).

The Committee to Protect Journalists reported that, as of March 1994, "at least 126

of speech that provide protection against government abuse, such as information or expression exposing circumvention of the democratic process, attacks on opposition parties, damage to the environment, corruption, wasting of public assets, and other forms of wrongdoing by government officials and their associates.[5]

Courts in countries around the world tend to demonstrate the least independence and greatest deference to the claims of government when national security is invoked. This deference is reinforced by provisions in the security laws of many countries that trigger exceptions to ordinary rules of evidence and due process upon a minimal showing by the government of a national security risk.[6] A government's claim of a security threat can deal a knock-out blow to the main institutional safeguards against government abuse: independence of the courts, due process of law, freedom of the press, and open government.

The tension between expression and national security is particularly vexing because there is little margin for error and much at stake. Quick action often is necessary to thwart a genuine threat to national security but restraints on political speech can trigger an inexorable slide into tyranny. The more fragile the democracy, the less likely it is to be able to tolerate either a threat to its genuine security or the suppression of legitimate political debate.

It is this profound tension that led Article 19, the International Center Against Censorship, to convene a group of independent experts to draft a set of principles that would adequately safeguard both the right to freedom of expression and information as well as the prerogative of governments to limit the right when necessary to protect a legitimate national security interest. The result was the Johannesburg Principles on National Security, Freedom of Expression and Access to Information.

---

journalists were held in prison for their reporting . . . under charges such as 'separatist propaganda,' 'treason,' 'counterrevolutionary activities,' or 'undermining national security;' sometimes there were no charges. The only crime committed by these journalists, 71 of whom ha[d] been in prison for more than two years, was to have written something that their governments disliked." Committee to Protect Journalists, *Attacks on the Press in 1993*, at 16 (1994).

[5] *See* Rodney A. Smolla, *Free Speech in an Open Society*, at 319 (1992): "History is replete with examples of governmental efforts to suppress speech on the grounds that emergency measures are necessary for survival that in retrospect appear panicky, disingenuous, or silly."

[6] *See, e.g.*, Reports by Amnesty International on China (1995 and 1997); India (1997), Kenya (1995, 1996, 1997), Nigeria (1995, 1996) South Korea (1991, 1995, 1996) and Sri Lanka (1997). Violations sanctioned under national security laws include administrative detention without charge or trial, *incommunicado* detention, closed trials, trials before military tribunals or other tribunals lacking independence, denial of the right to counsel, admission at trial of confessions extracted under torture or duress, denial of right to call witnesses, denial of right of *habeas corpus* and other processes by which to challenge legality of detention, and denial of right of appeal to an independent court.

The Principles are based on international and regional law and standards relating to the protection of human rights, evolving state practice (including judgments of national courts), and general principles of law. While some of the Principles undoubtedly are more protective of freedom of expression than widely accepted international norms, they reflect the drafters' views of the direction in which international law is, or should be, developing.

Thirty-seven experts participated in the drafting, representing expertise in the relevant areas of law and practice of nineteen countries from all regions of the world, the United Nations, the Council of Europe, the European Union, the Organization of American States, and the Organization of African Unity.[7] This commentary sets forth the law, standards, and practice that support the Principles, as well as the discussion that informed the drafting.

II. National Security, Freedom of Expression, and Access to Information: General Principles

A. Freedom of Expression: *Preamble to the Johannesburg Principles and Principle 1*

Freedom of expression and access to information are indispensable to the protection of all other human rights as well as to a democratic society governed by the rule of law. As declared by the UN General Assembly at its first session: "Freedom of information is a fundamental human right and . . . the touchstone of all of the freedoms to which the United Nations is consecrated."[8] The Inter-American Court of Human Rights ("Inter-American Court") elaborated:

> Freedom of expression is a cornerstone upon which the very existence of a democratic society rests. It is indispensable for the formation of public opinion . . . . It represents, in short, the means that enable the community, when exercising its options, to be sufficiently informed. Consequently, it can be said that a society that is not well informed is not a society that is truly free.[9]

The European Court of Human Rights ("European Court") has called attention to the importance of freedom of expression to self-fulfillment, in addition to the progress of a democratic society:

---

[7] The participants are listed in Appendix C.

[8] G.A. Res. 59(I), *adopted* 14 Dec. 1946, U.N. GAOR, 1st Sess., U.N. Doc. A/RES/59/1/1946, *reprinted in U.N. Year Book*, at 176 (1948).

[9] Compulsory Membership in an Association Prescribed by Law for the Practice of Journalism, Advisory Opinion OC-5/85 of 13 Nov. 1985, Inter-Am. Ct. Hum. Rts. (ser. A) ¶ 70 (1985) [hereinafter Compulsory Membership].

> Freedom of expression . . . constitutes one of the essential foundations of a democratic society and one of the basic conditions for its progress and for each individual's self-fulfillment. . . . [I]t is applicable not only to "information" or "ideas" that are favorably received or regarded as inoffensive or as a matter of indifference, but also to those that offend, shock or disturb the State or any sector of the population. Such are the demands of that pluralism, tolerance and broadmindedness without which there is no "democratic society".[10]

The Universal Declaration of Human Rights ("Universal Declaration")[11] includes a strong protection of the right to freedom of expression and information.[12] That protection was codified and elaborated in Article 19 of the International Covenant on Civil and Political Rights ("International Covenant").[13] Paragraph 1 asserts the absolute right to hold opinions "without interference"[14] Paragraph 2 states the positive content of the right to freedom of expression:

> Everyone shall have the right to freedom of expression; this right shall include freedom to seek, receive and impart information and ideas of all kinds, regardless of frontiers, either orally, in writing or in print, in the form of art, or through any other media of his choice. [15]

The right may be subject to certain enumerated and narrowly circumscribed restrictions, including as necessary to protect national security.[16] The right to

---

[10] Lingens v. Austria, 103 Eur. Ct. H.R. (ser. A) ¶ 41 (1986); Handyside v. United Kingdom, 24 Eur. Ct. H.R. (ser. A) ¶ 49 (1976); The Sunday Times v. United Kingdom, 30 Eur. Ct. H.R. (ser. A) ¶ 64 (1979).

[11] Universal Declaration of Human Rights, *adopted* Dec.10, 1948, G.A. Res. 217A (III), U.N. GAOR, 3d Sess., (Resolutions, part 1), U.N. Doc. A/810 (1948), *reprinted in* 43 *Am. J. Int'l L. Supp.* 127 (1949) (adopted without dissent) [hereinafter Universal Declaration].

[12] *See id.* art. 19. ("Everyone has the right to freedom of opinion and expression; this right includes freedom to hold opinions without interference and to seek, receive and impart information and ideas through any media and regardless of frontiers.").

[13] International Covenant on Civil and Political Rights, *adopted* 16 Dec. 1966, G.A. Res. 2200 (XXI), U.N. GAOR, 21st Sess., Supp. No. 16, U.N. Doc. A/6316 (1966), 999 U.N.T.S. 171 (*entered into force* 23 Mar. 1976) [hereinafter ICCPR].

[14] *Id.* art. 19(1).

[15] *Id.* art. 19(2).

[16] *See id.* art. 19(3) which reads:

> The exercise of the rights provided for in paragraph 2 of this article carries with it special duties and responsibilities. It may therefore be subject to certain restrictions, but these shall only be such as are provided by law and are necessary: (a) for respect of the rights or reputations of others; (b) for the protection of national security or of public order (*order public*), or of public health or morals.

Id. art. 19(3).

freedom of expression and information, and permissible restrictions, are set forth in similar terms in the European Convention for the Protection of Human Rights and Fundamental Freedoms ("European Convention")[17] and the American Convention on Human Rights ("American Convention").[18] The right is phrased more restrictively in the African Charter on Human and Peoples' Rights: individuals are granted the right to receive information but not necessarily opinions, and to express and disseminate opinions, but only consistent with national law; restrictions, moreover, are permitted in the "common interest" as well as for purposes stated in the other treaties.[19]

As of January 1, 1997, 136 countries had ratified or acceded to the International Covenant;[20] 110 countries had accepted the obligations of one of the three regional human rights treaties, including twelve that are not party to the International Covenant.[21] Thus, in total, 148 countries are parties to the International Covenant and/or one of the regional treaties.

Moreover, all countries are bound by the Universal Declaration, which "constitutes an obligation for the members of the international community"[22] and

---

[17] European Convention for the Protection of Human Rights and Fundamental Freedoms, *opened for signature* 4 Nov. 1950, 213 U.N.T.S. 221, Eur. T.S. No. 5 (*entered into force* 3 Sept. 1953) [hereinafter European Convention].

[18] American Convention on Human Rights, *signed* 22 Nov. 1969, O.A.S.T.S. No. 36, O.A.S. Off. Rec. OEA/Ser.L/V/II.23, doc. 21, rev. 6 (1979) (*entered into force* 18 July 1978), *reprinted in* 9 I.L.M. 673 (1970) [hereinafter American Convention].

[19] *See* African Charter on Human and Peoples' Rights, *adopted* 27 June 1981, O.A.U. Doc. CAB/LEG/67/3 Rev. 5, *reprinted in* 21 I.L.M. 58 (1982) (*entered into force* 21 Oct. 1986) [hereinafter African Charter]. Article 9 of the African Charter reads:

> (1) Every individual shall have the right to receive information.
> (2) Every individual shall have the right to express and disseminate his opinions within the law.

Article 9 grants the right to receive information but not necessarily opinions, and to express and disseminate opinions but not necessarily information. More importantly, the phrase "within the law" gives governments wider discretion than they have under the other human rights treaties to impose restrictions on freedom of expression and information. *See* Claude E. Welch, Jr., *The African Charter*, *infra* this volume at 145. Article 27(2) permits restrictions in the "common interest" in addition to the grounds stated in the other treaties.

[20] *See* Jean-Bernard Marie, *International Instruments Relating to Human Rights: Classification and Status of Ratification as of 1 Jan. 1997*, 18 *Hum Rts. L. J.* 79, 84 (1997).

[21] *See id.* at 84-86. The twelve states are Andorra, Lichtenstein, and Turkey (which are bound by the European Convention); and Botswana, Burkina Faso, Comoros, Djibouti, Ghana, Guinea-Bissau, Mauritania, and the Saharawi Arab Democratic Republic (which are bound by the African Charter); and Honduras (which is bound by the American Convention). *See id.* at 93-95.

[22] *The Proclamation of Tehran*, U.N. GAOR, U.N. Doc. A/CONF/32/41, endorsed by the General Assembly in G.A. Res. 2442, U.N. GAOR, 23rd Sess., Supp. No. 18 at 49, U.N. Doc. A/7218.

"applies to every member of the human family, everywhere, regardless of whether or not his Government accepts its principles or ratifies the Covenants."[23] Provisions protecting freedom of expression in the constitutions and laws of dozens of countries reflect the influence of the Universal Declaration, and courts around the world have endorsed the importance of freedom of expression in language that resonates with the sentiments expressed by the international bodies.[24]

A logical corollary of the fundamental relationship between democratic society, human rights, and freedom of expression is that restrictions on freedom of expression weaken the foundations of a democratic society. As noted by the European Court, restrictions imposed on freedom of expression and other rights in the name of national security pose a genuine danger "of undermining or even destroying democracy on the ground of defending it".[25]

B. National Security: *Johannesburg Principle 2*

Although the right to freedom of expression is fundamental, it is not absolute.[26] All of the main human rights treaties recognize that the right may be subject to restrictions, including in the interest of protecting national security.[27] Yet, none of the international bodies charged with interpreting and applying these treaties has provided a definition of national security, and few have even offered meaningful guidance in limiting its scope.[28]

---

[23] *United Nations Action in the Field of Human Rights*, UN Doc. ST/HR/2/Rev. 2, ¶ 68, UN Sales No. E.83.XIV.2 (1983). The manual further emphasizes that "the very existence of the Covenants [on Civil and Political Rights, and Economic, Social and Cultural Rights], and the fact that they contain the measures of implementation required to ensure the realization of the rights and freedoms set out in the Declaration, give greater strength to the Declaration." *Id.* ¶ 67.

[24] *See* Sandra Coliver, *The Article 19 Freedom of Expression Handbook: International and Comparative Law, Standards and Procedures* 9-11, 51-54 (1993) [hereinafter *Handbook*].

[25] Klass v. Germany, 28 Eur. Ct. H.R. (ser. A) ¶ 49 (1978).

[26] Rights that are absolute include (but are not limited to) the right not to be arbitrarily deprived of life; the right not to be subjected to torture or other cruel, inhuman or degrading treatment or punishment; the right not to be held in slavery or servitude; and the right to freedom of religious belief (though not observance).

[27] *See* ICCPR, *supra* note 13, art. 19(3) ("national security," "public order"); American Convention, *supra* note 18, art 13(2)(b) ("national security," "public order"); African Charter, *supra* note 19, art. 27(2) ("collective security") and art. 29(3) (duty of individual "not to compromise the security of the state whose national or resident he is"); European Convention, *supra* note 17, art. 10(2) ("national security, territorial integrity and public safety").

[28] *See* Elizabeth Evatt, *The International Covenant on Civil and Political Rights, infra* this volume at 83; *see also* Erica-Irene A. Daes, *Special Rapporteur of the UN Sub-Commission on Prevention of Discrimination and Protection of Minorities, Freedom of the Individual Under Law: A Study on the Individual's Duties to the Community and the Limitations on Human Rights and*

1. Components of a Legitimate National Security Interest

The most thoughtful contribution to the inquiry was made in 1985 by a group of experts, convened by the International Commission of Jurists and partner organizations, who drafted the Siracusa Principles on the Limitation and Derogation Provisions in the International Covenant on Civil and Political Rights.[29] These Principles have been widely endorsed by international law scholars and UN experts.[30] Principles 29-32 address national security:

> 29. National security may be invoked to justify measures limiting certain rights only when they are taken to protect the existence of the nation or its territorial integrity or political independence against force or threat of force.[31]
>
> 30. National security cannot be invoked as a reason for imposing limitations to prevent merely local or relatively isolated threats to law and order.[32]
>
> 31. National security cannot be used as a pretext for imposing vague or arbitrary limitations and may only be invoked when there exist adequate safeguards and effective remedies against abuse.[33]
>
> 32. The systematic violation of human rights undermines true national security and may jeopardize international peace and security.[34] A state responsible for such violation shall not invoke

---

Freedoms Under Article 29 of the Universal Declaration of Human Rights, Center for Human Rights, U.N. Human Rights Study Series 3, UN Sales No. E.89.XIV.5 (1990). This report states:

> The terms "public safety" and "national security" are not sufficiently precise to be used as a basis for limitation or restriction of the exercise of certain rights and freedoms of the individual. On the contrary, they are terms with a very broad meaning and application. Therefore they can be used by certain States to justify unreasonable limitations or restrictions.

Id. ¶ 227.

[29] *The Siracusa Principles on the Limitation and Derogation Provisions in the International Covenant on Civil and Political Rights*, U.N. Doc. E/CN.4/1985/4, Annex, ¶ 30 (1985), *reprinted in 7 Hum. Rts. Q.* 3 (1985) [hereinafter Siracusa Principles].

[30] *See Introduction, 7 Hum. Rts. Q.* 1 (1985). The Principles were endorsed by the UN Sub-Commission Special Rapporteurs, Mssrs. Danilo Türk & Louis Joinet, in *The Right to Freedom of Opinion and Expression: Final Report by Mr. Danilo Türk and Mr. Louis Joinet, Special Rapporteurs*, U.N. ESCOR, Comm'n on Hum. Rts., 44th Sess., ¶ 77, UN Doc. E/CN.4/Sub.2/1992/9 (14 Jul. 1992).

[31] Siracusa Principles, *supra* note 29, at 6.

[32] *Id.*

[33] *Id.* This Principle is endorsed and amplified in Johannesburg Principle 1.1(b), discussed *infra* at 24-26.

[34] This key point is expanded upon in the Preamble of the Johannesburg Principles.

> national security as a justification for measures aimed at suppressing opposition to such violation or at perpetrating repressive practices against its population.[35]

Principles 29 and 30 reflect, and contributed to the further development of, what is now a broad consensus among independent experts that any restriction justified on national security grounds must respond to a threat to the country as a whole, and must be necessary to protect the country's political independence or territorial integrity from the use, or threatened use, of force.[36] To pose a threat to the entire country, it is not necessary that public disturbances threaten to erupt throughout the country, but their *effects* must be felt throughout, and the threats cannot be merely to the ruling party nor relatively isolated.[37]

Johannesburg Principle 2(a) expands on Siracusa Principles 29 and 30 in three ways. First, it provides that restrictions on national security grounds are justifiable only if necessary to protect the existence of a "country" rather than a "nation". Although the term "nation" may convey more strongly than the word "country" the sense of a population connected to a territory, the Principles do not use the term because of the too frequent abuse by governments of their authority to

---

[35] Siracusa Principles, *supra* note 29, at 6. Johannesburg Principles 7-9 expand upon this principle as it relates to the protection of freedom of expression.

[36] For instance, Abid Hussein, the Rapporteur on Freedom of Expression appointed by the UN Commission on Human Rights in 1993, wrote in his 1995 report:

> For the purpose of protecting national security, the right to freedom of expression and information can be restricted only in the most serious cases of a direct political or military threat to the entire nation.

Question of the Human Rights of All Persons Subjected to Any Form of Detention or Imprisonment: Report of the Special Rapporteur on Promotion and Protection of the Right to Freedom of Opinion and Expression, Mr. Abid Hussein, Submitted Pursuant to Commission on Human Rights Resolution 1993/45, U.N. ESCOR, Comm'n on Hum. Rts., 51st Sess., ¶ 48, U.N. Doc. E/CN.4/1995/32 (1994); *see also* Bert B. Lockwood, Jr. et al., *Working Paper for the Committee of Experts on Limitation Provisions*, 7 *Hum. Rts. Q.* 35, 70-71 (1985); Alexandre Kiss, *Commentary by the Rapporteur on the Limitation Provisions*, 7 *Hum. Rts. Q.* 15, 21 (1985); Manfred Nowak, *UN Covenant on Civil and Political Rights: CCPR Commentary* 355 (1993) (citing Karl Josef Partsch, "Freedom of Conscience and Expression, and Political Freedoms," *in The International Bill of Rights* 211, 216-27 (Louis Henkin, ed., 1981)).

[37] *See, e.g.*, Alexandre Kiss, "Permissable Limitations on Rights," *in The International Bill of Rights*, *supra* note 36, at 290, 296-97. Professor Kiss argues:

> [R]estrictions on human rights can be adopted under this concept only if the interest of the whole nation is at stake. This excludes restrictions in the sole interest of a government, regime or power group. Limitations are not based on "national security," moreover, if their only purpose is to avoid riots or other troubles, or to frustrate revolutionary movements which do not threaten the life of the whole nation."

Id. at 296; *see also* Lockwood, *supra* note 36, at 56-63, 70-76.

defend the "nation" to justify measures aimed at entrenching the hegemony of the majority national group, its culture, or heritage.[38]

Second, Principle 2(a) permits restrictions on freedom of expression to the extent necessary to protect not only a country's existence or its territorial integrity against the use or threat of force, but also "its capacity to respond to the use or threat of force." This latter phrase was added in recognition of the legitimate prerogative of governments to limit the disclosure of information about particular weapons systems or troop movements.

Third, Principle 2(a) makes explicit that not only must the genuine purpose of a restriction be to protect national security, but the restriction must have the "demonstrable effect" of doing so. These added words require that any restriction, before it is imposed, must be judged to be *likely* to be effective in enhancing national security, and, in order to be maintained, must be shown in fact to have been, and continue to be, effective.

"Territorial integrity" was included in Principle 2(a) (and is also in the Siracusa Principles) because protection of territorial integrity is expressly recognized by the European Convention on Human Rights to be a legitimate state interest closely linked to national security,[39] and is generally understood to be implicitly recognized as such by the other main human rights treaties. Although the interest in protecting territorial integrity may justify restrictions aimed at suppressing violent secessionist movements, it may not justify restrictions on peaceful advocacy of minority rights, self-determination, or arguably even secession.[40]

---

[38] For instance, several of the new democracies of Central and Eastern Europe have adopted laws that make "defamation of the nation" a crime on the ground that such crimes are necessary to promote respect for the culture and honor of the ruling ethnic or "national" group. *See generally* Ana Arana, "The Americas," *in* Committee to Protect Journalists, *Attacks on the Press in 1995*, at 69 (1996); David Satter, "Central Europe and the Republics of the Former Soviet Union," *in Attacks on the Press in 1995*, *supra* at 36.

[39] European Convention, *supra* note 17, art. 10(2).

[40] International law does not recognize a right of peoples or groups to secede (at least, outside of the decolonization context), but neither does it recognize a duty not to secede. Rather, secession is a matter for domestic law, and international law becomes relevant only if international peace and security are threatened. *See* T.M. Franck, "Postmodern Tribalism and the Right to Secession," *in Peoples and Minorities in International Law* 3, 12-13 (Catherine Brölman et al. eds., 1993) (international law is implicated "when the secessionist struggle is fomented from external sources, . . . has caused large numbers of casualties, when no decisive military outcome is in sight, and when the struggle creates a flood of refugees and threatens to involve or engulf neighbouring states."). Professor Hurst Hannum adds: "[U]nless a group has no option but to secede in order to protect itself from massive violations of human rights, self-determination must be sought within the framework of existing states." Hurst Hannum, "Minorities, Indigenous Peoples and Self-Determination," *in Human Rights: An Agenda for the Next Century* 1, 10-11 (Louis Henkin & John Lawrence Hargrove eds., 1995).

In sum, Principle 2(a) envisages that legitimate national security interests are limited to preventing violence aimed at changing a country's government, institutions, or borders; preventing espionage; and protecting genuine military secrets, such as the movement of troops and details of weapons design.[41] This list is narrower than the range of national security interests that may justify restrictions under the Siracusa Principles,[42] reflecting the sense of the Johannesburg drafters that the widescale abuse of the concept over the intervening ten years warranted an even further tightening of its definition.

2. Illegitimate Grounds for Invoking National Security

A restriction sought to be justified on grounds of national security is clearly not legitimate if it is used as a pretext to protect interests unrelated to national security imperatives. Johannesburg Principle 2(b) provides an illustrative list of interests that are illegitimate. In particular, Principle 2(b) states that it is illegitimate to use national security as a pretext for protecting the government from "embarrassment or exposure of wrongdoing," including diplomatic embarrassment. This proposition finds support in the European Court's ruling in the *Spycatcher* case,[43] which held that an injunction on the publication of the memoirs of a retired high-ranking official of the British Security Service MI-5 could not be sustained on national security grounds after publication in the United States. This was so even though the injunction might well have promoted

> the efficiency and reputation of the Security Service, notably by: preserving confidence in that Service on the part of third parties; making it clear that the unauthorized publication of memoirs by its former members would not be countenanced; and deterring others who might be tempted to follow in [the official's] footsteps.[44]

Too many governments consider that, because good relations with foreign governments form part of their national security, they are entitled to keep secret a

---

[41] This definition comports with Professor Kiss's interpretation of "national security" restrictions. *See* Kiss *supra* note 37, at 297. Similarly, Thomas Emerson, an American professor and author of an early and influential article on the right of the public to have access to government information, was of the view that governments legitimately may keep information secret on national security grounds only if it concerns "tactical military movements, design of weapons, operation of espionage or counterespionage, and similar matters." Thomas Emerson, “Legal Foundations of the Right to Know,” 1976 *Wash. U.L.Q.* 1, 17 (1976).

[42] *Compare* Kiss, *supra* note 37, at 297.

[43] Observer and Guardian v. United Kingdom, 216 Eur. Ct. H.R. (ser. A) ¶ 69 (1991).

[44] *Id.* ¶ 69.

broad spectrum of foreign relations information.[45] The economic well-being of a country is undoubtedly a component of its stability and, therefore, its security. This does not mean, however, that a government is entitled to impose restrictions on freedom of expression and information in order to conceal information about the country's economic situation.[46] Nor may a government justify suppressing a country-wide strike of all workers on the ground that a strike of such scale necessarily threatens national security and public order.[47]

Also illegitimate is the elevation of an official ideology or religion to a position where it is beyond challenge.[48] As stated by Professor Nowak, "[n]ational laws and bills of rights that permit freedom of expression only in the interest of a certain purpose or a sole belief or religion (e.g., socialism or Islam) violate th[e] international minimum standard [of protection of freedom of expression], even when this belief or religion constitutes the *ordre public* of the State concerned."[49]

---

[45] *See id.* For instance, the UK government has contended that national security includes action "in support of the Government's defence and foreign policies," as well as actions to combat terrorism, espionage, and major subversive activities. Graham Zellick, "Spies, Subversives, Terrorists and the British Government: Free Speech and Other Casualties," 31 *Wm. & Mary L. Rev.* 773, 794 (1990) (quoting and discussing Home Office, The Interception of Communications in the United Kingdom, Cmnd. 9438, annex 2 (1985)).

[46] *See* Kiss, *supra* note 37, at 296. A particularly outrageous case involved Xi Yang, a Chinese reporter who was convicted in 1994 by a Chinese court and sentenced to 12 years imprisonment for "spying and stealing state secrets." His crime was to publish a story in a Hong Kong paper on official Chinese plans to sell gold and raise interest rates. The conviction and sentence were strongly criticized by the UN Human Rights Committee. UN Human Rights Committee, *Annual Report, 1996*, §§ 60-61 (Concluding Observations on Fourth Periodic Report of the UK, Supplementary Report on Hong Kong).

[47] Jong-Kyu Sohn v. Republic of Korea, App. No. 518/1992, U.N. GAOR, Hum. Rts. Comm., (views adopted July 1995.) Under a law which prohibited third parties from intervening in labor disputes, the applicant in this case was convicted for persuading a solidarity group to issue a statement that supported a nation-wide strike and condemned the government's threats to send in troops. The government contended that the statement incited the strike and moreover that a national strike in any country would threaten national security and public order. The applicant was convicted and sentenced to jail for a term of one and a half years. The Committee concluded that his right to freedom of expression had been violated and that he was entitled to a remedy, including compensation. See Evatt, *infra* this volume, at 89.

[48] *See* Türk & Joinet, *supra* note 30, ¶ 32; *see also* Viviana Krsticevic, et al., "The Inter-American System of Human Rights Protection," *infra* this volume, at 167, note 23 (condemning Cuba's constitutional commitment to "the socialist objectives of the State"). For another example of a constitution that elevates an ideology to a position where it is beyond challenge, see Kerim Yildiz, "Turkey," *infra* this volume, at 445, esp. note 13.

[49] Nowak, *supra* note 36, at 357 (citing Partsch, *supra* note 36, at 224).

C. Legitimacy of Restrictions on Freedom of Expression: *Principle 1*

Not all restrictions on freedom of expression justified by reference to a legitimate national security interest are therefore legitimate. As stated by the UN Human Rights Committee (which interprets and monitors compliance with the International Covenant), "a restriction on freedom of expression may never jeopardize the right itself."[50] Freedom of expression is the principle, and any exception must be narrowly interpreted.[51] The two UN Sub-Commission Rapporteurs on Freedom of Expression, Danilo Türk and Louis Joinet, elaborated:

> In interpreting the legal norms, the principle [of freedom of expression] must be interpreted broadly and the permissible restrictions restrictively. . . .
>
> The presumption is always in favour of freedom of expression, i.e., in favour of the principle. The proponent of a restriction bears the burden of proof regarding the necessity and legality of the proposed restriction, as well as regarding its compatibility with the principle of the right to freedom of expression.[52]

The main human rights treaties and declarations all set forth essentially the same three-part test for assessing the legitimacy of restrictions on the right to freedom of expression (and other human rights): to be permissible a restriction must (1) be prescribed by law, (2) aim to protect one of a short list of legitimate purposes, including national security, expressly enumerated in the text, and (3) be necessary to protect that purpose.[53]

---

[50] *General Comment on Article 19*, General Comment No. 10, U.N. GAOR, Hum. Rts. Comm., 38th Sess., A/38/40, ¶ 1 (1983) [hereinafter *General Comment No. 10*], *reprinted in* Compilation of General Comments and General Recommendations adopted by Human Rights Treaty Bodies, U.N. Doc. HRI/GEN/1/Rev.1 of 29 July 1994 [hereinafter Compilation of General Comments].

[51] *See* Sunday Times v. United Kingdom, 30 Eur. Ct. H.R. (ser. A) ¶ 64 (1979) (evaluating a particular restriction, the Court is faced "not with a choice between two conflicting principles but with a principle of freedom of expression that is subject to a number of exceptions which must be narrowly interpreted").

[52] Türk & Joinet, *supra* note 30, ¶¶ 20, 25.

[53] The standard used by the Human Rights Committee in interpreting Article 19 of the ICCPR is stated in General Comment 10. *General Comment No. 10*, *supra* note 50, Annex VI.

The European Court first elaborated its standard in the case of Sunday Times v. United Kingdom, 30 Eur. Ct. H.R. (ser. A) ¶¶ 49, 63-66 (1979).

The Inter-American Court applied the test to freedom of expression for the first time in Compulsory Membership. Compulsory Membership, *supra* note 9, ¶¶ 39, 42-46. It expressly stated that it followed the jurisprudence of the European Court on this point. *Id.* (citing Sunday Times v. United Kingdom, 30 Eur. Ct. H.R. (ser. A) ¶¶ 59, 62). The documents adopted by the states participating in the Organization for Security and Cooperation in Europe (OSCE) generally refer to the same standard. *See, e.g.*, Conference on Security and Cooperation

1. Principle of Legality: *Principle 1.1*

To be "prescribed by law", a restriction must either be codified in legislation or else set forth in unwritten law such as the common law.[54] An administrative practice, even if made public and approved by the legislature, is not sufficient because it is not legally binding on the public authorities.[55] Nor is it sufficient that the restriction complies with domestic law; in addition, the law must meet minimum standards of the rule of law, so as to provide "legal protection . . . against arbitrary interferences by public auhorities".[56] This requires that the law be "adequately accessible," that is, there must be notice of what the law requires.[57] The law must also meet the tests of "legal certainty" and "foreseeability," that is, it must be "formulated with sufficient precision" to enable individuals to (a) understand their obligations and (b) foresee whether particular action is unlawful.[58]

If it confers discretionary power on public authorities, the law must indicate the scope and manner of exercise of any such discretion with sufficient clarity to protect individuals against arbitrary interference with their rights and must afford adequate safeguards against abuse.[59] Furthermore, the government carries the burden of showing that the law clearly applies in the circumstances of the particular case.[60]

The restriction (whether codified or unwritten) must not be vague or over-broad. As stated by the Inter-American Commission of Human Rights ("Inter-

---

in Europe: Document of the Copenhagen Meeting of the Conference on the Human Dimension, 29 June 1990, ¶ 24, *reprinted in* 29 I.L.M. 1305 (1990) [hereinafter Document of the Copenhagen Meeting].

[54] Sunday Times v. United Kingdom, 30 Eur. Ct. H.R. (ser. A) ¶ 49 (1979).

[55] *E.g.*, Malone v. United Kingdom, 82 Eur. Ct. H.R. (ser. A) ¶ 67 (1984); *see also* Paul Mahoney and Laurence Early, "The European Convention on Human Rights and Other Council of Europe Instruments," *infra* this volume, at 113-114.

[56] Mahoney and Early, *supra*.

[57] *See Sunday Times*, 30 Eur. Ct. H.R. (ser. A) ¶ 49.

[58] *Sunday Times*, 30 Eur. Ct. H.R. (ser. A) ¶ 49; *see also* LJM de G v. Netherlands, App. No. 578/1994, U.N. GAOR, Hum. Rts. Comm., ruled inadmissible, Oct. 1995 (*cited in* Evatt, *infra* this volume, at 87, note16).

[59] *See, e.g.*, Kruslin v. France, 176-B Eur. Ct. H.R. (ser. A) ¶¶ 27, 30 (1990); Huvig v. France, 176-B Eur. Ct. H.R. (ser. A) ¶¶ 26, 29 (1990) (stating that several vital conditions concerning police discretion in carrying out telephone surveillance were not sufficiently specified in law to ensure against arbitrary interference with privacy). *See also* Klass v. Germany, 28 Eur. Ct. H.R. (ser. A) ¶¶ 49-50 (1978) (concluding that secret surveillance by the German security service violated the privacy rights of those subjected to surveillance).

[60] *See* Monja Jaona v. Madagascar, Communication No. 132/1982, U.N. GAOR, Hum. Rts. Comm., views adopted 1 Apr. 1985, *reprinted in* 2 *Selected Decisions of the Human Rights Committee Under the Optional Protocol,* Sess. 17-32, at 161; Mpaka-Nsusu v. Zaire, Communication No. 157/1983, U.N. GAOR, Hum. Rts. Comm., views adopted 26 Mar. 1986, *reprinted in* 2 *Selected Decisions of the Human Rights Committee Under the Optional Protocol, Sess. 17-32,* at 187.

American Commission") in examining the incompatibility with the American Convention of various Nicaraguan decrees that imposed broad restrictions on the press in the interest of state security:

> [A] limitation on freedom of the press is justified only when the order and the security of the State are truly compromised. . . . The legislation currently in effect may give rise to serious abuses, because of its great ambiguity and breadth. When freedom of the press is at stake, any restrictions must be clearly established so that anyone may know precisely what activities are prohibited or may be subject to censorship.[61]

The Commission singled out for special criticism a number of vaguely stated grounds for limiting expression, including because a statement "in any way damage[s] or compromise[s] the economic stability of the nation," or "harm[s] the national defence."[62]

The UN Sub-Commission Special Rapporteurs on Freedom of Expression similarly condemned restrictions that are

> so broad in scope or drafted in such terms as to put the right itself in jeopardy. For instance, limitations which would otherwise be permissible under article 19, paragraph 3 (for instance laws relating to official secrecy) may be defined too vaguely or too broadly and thus jeopardize the right to freedom of expression.[63]

The UN Rapporteurs expressly condemned "*délits d'opinion* . . . which are broad, unclear, ambiguous or 'catch-all' in nature, . . . [such as] 'hostile propaganda' or 'agitation.'"[64] The danger, as noted by the Rapporteurs, is that "[i]n practice, such formulations sometimes provide the legal basis for the imposition of heavy penalties on people who have expressed opinions but have not resorted to or advocated violence."[65] Other offenses that suffer from ambiguity are "subversion," "disinformation," and "false rumours."[66] A law may not contain terms that are so vague or "over broad" that it could be used to suppress expression protected by international law.[67]

The UN Rapporteurs noted that the requirements of legality are particularly important regarding laws that provide for sanctions.[68] Such laws

---

[61] *Report on the Situation of Human Rights in Nicaragua*, Inter-Am. Comm'n. on Hum. Rts., O.A.S. Doc. OEA/Ser.L/V/II.53, doc.25 (1981), at 118, ¶ 6.

[62] *Id.*

[63] Türk & Joinet, *supra* note 30, ¶ 29.

[64] *Id.* ¶ 30.

[65] *Id.* ¶ 30.

[66] *Id.* ¶ 62.

[67] *See id.* ¶ 63.

[68] *See id.* ¶ 72.

> must be precise and specific with regard to all the constituent elements of the restriction and the offense, especially the element of intent . . . . [T]he laws should rule out any possibility of a presumption of bad faith, which is admissible under some national legislation on defamation. . . . If sanctions are based on laws that are vague or manifestly imprecise or formulated with clear intent to provide a "legal" basis for silencing people, they come close to "informal" or arbitrary sanctions.[69]

2. Principle of Legitimacy: *Principle 1.2*

All of the main human rights instruments recognize the protection of national security as a permissible ground for imposing restrictions on freedom of expression.[70] To be legitimate, a restriction must be genuinely directed towards achieving that aim.[71] The international human rights treaty bodies have rarely, if ever, challenged a government's assertion that a restriction was genuinely aimed at protecting national security.[72]

3. Principle of Democratic Necessity: *Principle 1.3*

The requirement that any restriction must be shown to be necessary is the prong of the tri-partite test that is most frequently violated. "Necessary" here does not mean what the government in power considers to be necessary, but rather what may reasonably be considered necessary "in a democratic society."[73] The European Convention expressly includes the phrase "in a democratic society" to modify the concept of necessity.[74] The Inter-American Court has also adopted this standard, as well as the pertinent jurisprudence of the European Court discussed below.[75] Likewise, the Universal Declaration of Human Rights requires that any restriction on a human right must meet "requirements of morality, public order and general welfare in a democratic society."[76]

---

[69] *Id.* ¶¶ 72, 74.
[70] *See* Universal Declaration, *supra* note 11, art. 29; ICCPR, *supra* note 13, art. 19(3); American Convention, *supra* note 18, art. 13(2); African Charter, *supra* note 19, art. 27 ("collective security"), art. 29(3) ("security of the State"), art. 29(5) ("national independence"); European Convention, *supra* note 17, art. 10.
[71] *See, e.g.*, Sunday Times v. United Kingdom, 30 Eur. Ct. H.R. (ser. A) ¶¶ 55-57 (1979).
[72] See Mahoney and Early on the European Court and Commission on Human Rights, and Evatt on the UN Human Rights Committee, *infra* this volume at 109.
[73] *See* Türk & Joinet, *supra* note 30, ¶ 64.
[74] European Convention, *supra* note 17, art. 10(2).
[75] *See* Compulsory Membership, *supra* note 9, ¶¶ 42, 44. For a discussion of the European Court's relevant jurisprudence, *see infra* sub-section (a) of the text.
[76] Universal Declaration, *supra* note 11, art. 29.

The International Covenant applies the standard of democratic necessity to restrictions on public access to trials, freedom of assembly, and freedom of association, but not to freedom of expression.[77] However, even if the drafters of the International Covenant intended to set a different standard for freedom of expression than for the other freedoms,[78] the Human Rights Committee has indicated in recent decisions that it now applies the "democratic necessity" test to restrictions imposed on any fundamental right, including the right to freedom of expression.[79] Although the drafters of the International Covenant did not agree on what they meant by "democratic necessity," several country representatives expressed their opinion that a "democratic society was one that respected the principles of the UN Charter and the Universal Declaration."[80]

The European Court has amplified that a democratic society is built on a foundation of freedom of expression,[81] and is characterized by "pluralism, tolerance and broadmindedness," including tolerance for information and ideas "that offend, shock or disturb the state or any sector of the population."[82] Moreover, "[i]n a democratic system the actions or omissions of the government must be subject to the close scrutiny not only of the legislative and judicial authorities but also of the press and public opinion."[83]

The requirements of "democratic necessity" as elaborated by the European Court and the UN Human Rights Committee are set forth in sub-sections (a) and (b), below. Sub-sections (c) and (d) examine additional requirements based on comparative law and practice as well as evolving international standards.

a. Any restriction must be supported by specific evidence that it is necessary.

In a series of decisions, the UN Human Rights Committee has made clear that governments bear the burden of proving, with *specific* evidence, that restrictions on freedom of expression and other rights are *necessary* to protect state security or

---

[77] *See* ICCPR, *supra* note 13, arts. 14, 19, 21, 22.

[78] Professor Nowak argues that at least some significance should be attached to the fact that ICCPR Articles 21 and 22 expressly require that restrictions on the rights to peaceful assembly and freedom of association be "necessary in a democratic society" while Article 19 requires only that restrictions on freedom of expression be "necessary." Nowak, *supra* note 36, at 350.

[79] *See* Evatt, *infra* this volume, at 83.

[80] *See* Lockwood, *supra* note 36, at 50-51, *citing* 10 U.N. GAOR Annexes (Agenda Item 28) at 42, U.N. Doc. A/2929 (1955); *see also* Kiss, *supra* note 37, at 294.

[81] *See* Lingens v. Austria, 103 Eur. Ct. H.R. (ser. A) ¶ 41 (1986).

[82] *Id.*

[83] Castells v. Spain, 236 Eur. Ct. H.R. (ser. A) at 23 § 46 (1992).

some other legitimate interest.[84] For instance, in a case against Uruguay, the Committee found a violation because the applicant had been "arrested, detained and tried for his political and trade union activities" and the prosecutor had not presented specific evidence of activities that could legitimately be treated as criminal.[85] Courts around the world have adopted the Committee's approach.[86]

The European Court has held that reasons given by a government to justify a restriction must be "relevant and sufficient".[87] When a government refuses, on national security grounds, to reveal information that it claims justifies restrictions on fundamental rights, it must nevertheless "furnish at least some facts or information" to support the need for the restrictions and for keeping the evidence secret, even if the information concerns a serious terrorist threat.[88] Moreover, the Court has required governments that seek to justify restrictions on matters of "undisputed public concern" (including information and opinions critical of government policies and actions) to demonstrate that they are "absolutely certain" that dissemination would have "identifiable, adverse consequences".[89]

b. Any restriction must be proportionate to the legitimate aim pursued.

The European Court has stated that, to be "necessary", a restriction does not have to be "indispensable" or "strictly required," but it must be more than merely "reasonable" or "desirable"; a "pressing social need" must be demonstrated, and the

---

[84] Evatt, *infra* this volume, at 82-88. *See, e.g.*, L. Weinberger Weisz v. Uruguay, Communication No. 28/1978, U.N. GAOR, Hum. Rts. Comm., *reprinted in* 1 *Selected Decisions of the Human Rights Committee Under the Optional Protocol, Sess. 2-16*, at 60, ¶ 14; L. Buffo Carballal v. Uruguay, Communication No. 33/1978, U.N. GAOR, Hum. Rts. Comm., *reprinted in* 1 *Selected Decisions of the Human Rights Committee under the Optional Protocol, Sess. 2-16*, at 64, ¶ 12 (stating that a general charge of "subversive activities" did not suffice).

[85] Pietroroia v. Uruguay, Communication No. 44/1979, U.N. GAOR, Hum. Rts. Comm., (views adopted 27 Mar. 1981), *reprinted in Selected Decisions of the Human Rights Committee under the Optional Protocol, Sess. 2-16*, at 79, ¶ 17 (1985). The Committee explained: "[B]are information from the State party that [the applicant] was charged with subversive association and conspiracy to violate the Constitution, followed by preparatory acts thereto, is not in itself sufficient, without details of the alleged charges and copies of the court proceedings." *Id.* ¶ 15.

[86] *See, e.g.*, Josephat v. Republic, High Court of Malawi, Misc. Civil App. No. 28 of 1992 (holding that the state must adduce evidence to support claims that the exercise of a fundamental liberty is prejudicial to national security).

[87] Handyside v. United Kingdom, 24 Eur. Ct. H.R. (ser. A) ¶¶ 48-50 (1976); Sunday Times v. United Kingdom, 30 Eur. Ct. H.R. (ser. A) ¶ 62 (1979).

[88] Murray v. United Kingdom, 300-A Eur. Ct. H.R. (ser. A) ¶¶ 59, 60 (1994) (holding that the UK government was required to provide some concrete information to justify the detention of a person suspected of assisting IRA terrorists).

[89] *Sunday Times*, 30 Eur. Ct. H.R. (ser. A) ¶¶ 65-66; *see also* The Observer & Guardian v. United Kingdom, 216 Eur. Ct. H.R. (ser. A) ¶ 59(c) (1991).

restriction must be proportionate to the legitimate aim pursued.[90] A court should not approve an interference with expression unless the court is "satisfied that the interference was necessary having regard to the facts and circumstances prevailing in the specific case before it."[91] Similarly, the Human Rights Committee, in its General Comment on freedom of religion, stated: "[L]imitations may be applied only for those purposes for which they were prescribed and must be directly related and proportionate to the specific need on which they are predicated."[92] The Committee has applied that standard to freedom of expression and other Covenant rights as well.[93]

The practice of states that are party to a common human rights treaty may be relevant in assessing a restriction's proportionality. For instance, the European Court, in ruling in 1979 that the Belgium Government's unequal treatment of children born in and out of wedlock violated the European Convention, relied in part on the fact that the law of most of the states parties to the European Convention had, by the time of the decision, evolved towards requiring greater equality in the treatment of such children.[94] Similarly, the European Court cited evolving standards throughout Western Europe in disapproving laws in Northern Ireland, Ireland, and Cyprus that made it a crime for consenting male adults to engage in homosexual activity.[95] The two UN Sub-Commission Rapporteurs on Freedom of Expression

---

[90] *Handyside*, 24 Eur. Ct. H.R. (ser. A) ¶¶ 48-50; *Sunday Times*, 30 Eur. Ct. H.R. (ser. A) ¶ 62.

[91] *Observer & Guardian*, 216 Eur. Ct. H.R. (ser. A) ¶ 63. For instance, the European Court ruled that the Irish Supreme Court's ban on information about where to obtain legal abortions outside of Ireland was "disproportionate" and therefore unnecessary because it was "absolute" and failed, e.g., to take account of the woman's age, state of health, or reasons for seeking to terminate her pregnancy. Open Door & Dublin Well Woman v. Ireland, 246-A Eur. Ct. H.R. (ser. A) ¶¶ 73, 74 (1992).

[92] *General Comment on Article 18*, General Comment No. 22, U.N. GAOR, Hum. Rts. Comm., 48th Sess., ¶ 8, U.N. Doc. CCPR/C/21/Rev.1/Add.4 (1993), *in* Compilation of General Comments, *supra* note 50.

[93] *See, e.g.*, Pietraroia v. Uruguay, Communication No. 44/1979, U.N. GAOR, Hum. Rts. Comm., views adopted 27 Mar.1981, *reprinted in* 2 *Selected Decisions of the Human Rights Committee under the Optional Protocol, Sess. 2-16*, at 76, ¶ 17 (1985) (finding that a fifteen year sentence for political and trade union activities was disproportionate); Toonen v. Australia, Communication No. 488/1992, U.N. GAOR, Hum. Rts. Comm., views adopted Mar. 8, 1994, U.N. Doc. CCPR/C/50/D/488/1992 (holding that the criminalization of homosexual activity constituted disproportionate interference with privacy). *See also* Evatt, *infra* this volume, at 83.

[94] *See* Marckx v. Belgium, 31 Eur. Ct. H.R. (ser. A) ¶¶ 38-43 (1979).

[95] *See, e.g.*, Modinos v. Cyprus, 259 Eur. Ct. H.R. (ser. A) (1993); Norris v. Ireland, 142 Eur. Ct. H.R. (ser. A) (1988); Dudgeon v. United Kingdom, 45 Eur. Ct. H.R. (ser. A) (1981). For an excellent discussion of this principle, *see* P. Mahoney, *Judicial Activism and Judicial Self-Restraint in the European Court of Human Rights: Two Sides of the Same Coin*, 11 *Hum. Rts. L.J.* 57, 61 (1990).

noted that "comparative law . . . helps in developing evidence of democratic necessity."[96]

c. Any restriction must be the least restrictive means possible.

Principle 1.3(b) of the Johannesburg Principles states that, to be legitimate, a restriction must not only aim to protect a legitimate national security interest, but in addition, it must be "the least restrictive means possible for protecting that interest." This requirement is more demanding than the proportionality tests applied by the European Court and the UN Human Rights Committee, which in general require only that a restriction be reasonably proportionate to the legitimate aim pursued.

The European Court, however, has ruled that a "strict proportionality" test is appropriate for measures, such as secret surveillance, that "characterize the police state."[97] The states participating in the Organization for Security and Cooperation in Europe have also adopted a "strict proportionality" standard, agreeing in 1990 that "any restriction on rights and freedoms must, in a democratic society . . . be strictly proportionate to the aim of that law."[98]

The Inter-American Court applied the "least restrictive means" standard in its leading freedom of expression case. Stated the court:

> [T]he "necessity" and, hence, the legality of restrictions imposed . . . on freedom of expression depend upon a showing that the restrictions are required by a compelling governmental interest. Hence, if there are various options to achieve this objective, that which least restricts the right protected must be selected.[99]

The standard is also applied by the US Supreme Court which holds that any content-based restriction on freedom of expression must be "narrowly tailored" to achieve a compelling state interest, and that a restriction will not satisfy the test if "a less restrictive alternative is readily available."[100]

---

[96] Türk & Joinet, *supra* note 30, ¶ 67.

[97] Klass v. Germany, 28 Eur. Ct. H.R. (ser. A) ¶ 42 (1978); Malone v. United Kingdom, 82 Eur. Ct. H.R. (ser. A) ¶¶ 69-70 (1984).

[98] Document of the Copenhagen Meeting, *supra* note 53, ¶ 24 (emphasis added). *Cf.* ICCPR, *supra* note 13, art. 4(1). Article 4(1)(a) provides that any derogations from the Covenant's obligations must be "strictly required by the exigencies of the situation." *Id.* 4(1)(a).

[99] Compulsory Membership, *supra* note 9, ¶ 46.

[100] Boos v. Barry, 485 U.S. 312, 329 (1988). *See also* Carey v. Brown, 447 U.S. 455, 461-62 (1980). "Content-based" speech restrictions are those that are "justified only by reference to the content of speech." *Boos*, 485 U.S. at 321. In *Boos*, the Supreme Court concluded that a law which made it a crime to display signs "tending to bring a foreign government into . . . public disrepute" was content based and was not narrowly tailored because there existed a substantially narrower law that adequately accomplished the state's legitimate interest in discharging its international law obligations towards foreign officials. *Id.*

The decision of the Johannesburg drafters to adopt the "least restrictive means" test reflects their awareness of the all-too-common tendency of courts to accord excessive deference to executive claims of national security. Experience has shown that judicial independence is often compromised in national security cases, even in "mature" democracies. Additionally, the speech that is most at risk is precisely the sort which is entitled to the greatest protection, namely, political speech that exposes government wrongdoing or ineptitude and may thereby alter government policy or even the government itself.[101] For these reasons, the Johannesburg drafters required that restrictions on such speech meet the most exacting standard of necessity.

d. Governments should not be afforded a margin of appreciation.

The Johannesburg Principles do not allow governments a "margin of appreciation" or other measure of discretion in determining the necessity of restrictions imposed on the ground of national security. The "margin of appreciation" doctrine, developed by the European Court, affords governments a measure of discretion in determining the necessity of restrictions, subject to a "European supervision."[102] Governments are granted a broad margin concerning the demands of "public morals," which differ widely among European states.[103] In contrast, governments are afforded only a narrow margin regarding such concepts as the independence of the judiciary, which have a relatively uniform understanding across Europe.[104] At least as of 1978 the Court was prepared to afford governments a fairly wide margin of appreciation regarding matters affecting national security, so long as the applicable laws provided "adequate and effective guarantees against abuse."[105]

However, according to one judge of the European Court, the Court does not and should not apply a "margin of appreciation" to restrictions on freedom of expression, especially where political debate is involved.[106] Judge Martens wrote in a concurring opinion to the 1992 *Schwabe* judgment:

> As in [two prior] judgments, the Court makes it clear in its present judgment that, where the right to freedom of expression is at stake, there is no room for leaving to the national courts a margin of appreciation as to the assessment of the relevant statements, but that it will effect a full review of such assessments. Rightly so, for

---

[101] *See, e.g.*, Zellick, *supra* note 45.
[102] Sunday Times v. United Kingdom, 30 Eur. Ct. H.R. (ser. A) ¶ 59 (1979).
[103] *See id.*
[104] Klass v. Germany, 28 Eur. Ct. H.R. (ser. A) ¶¶ 49-50 (1978).
[105] *See id.*
[106] *See* Schwabe v. Austria, 242-B Eur. Ct. H.R. (ser A.) at 40, ¶ 2 (1992) (Martens, J., concurring).

> such control is indispensable, especially where freedom of public debate on political issues is at stake.[107]

The majority of the Court did not comment on Judge Marten's statement or otherwise address the issue of the margin of appreciation. Recent judgments involving political expression and press freedom seem to confirm his views.[108]

Despite the fact that the "margin of appreciation" has occupied a significant place in the jurisprudence of the European Court, the doctrine has not been embraced by the UN Human Rights Committee. The Committee applied a "margin of discretion" in a 1982 decision upholding the permissibility of a restriction on freedom of expression justified on the ground of public morals,[109] but since then has not applied the doctrine, and indeed expressly rejected it in at least two cases.[110] The Johannesburg Principles, in rejecting the "margin of appreciation" doctrine, place the burden on national authorities to establish the necessity of restrictions, and recognize that international bodies may and should scrutinize the conclusions of national authorities concerning both fact and law.

D. States of Emergency: *Principle 3*

Circumstances that justify restrictions on human rights in the interest of national security may constitute a state of emergency,[111] but they need not rise to

---

[107] *Id.*

[108] *See, e.g.*, Goodwin v. United Kingdom, 7 Eur. Ct. H.R. App. 16/1994/463/544, 22 EHRR 123, ¶ 40 (1996-II). ("[T]he national margin of appreciation is circumscribed by the interest of democratic society in ensuring and maintaining a free press. . . . In sum, limitations on the confidentiality of journalistic sources call for the most careful scrutiny by the Court."). *See also* R. St. J. Macdonald, "The Margin of Appreciation," *in The European System for the Protection of Human Rights* 83, 93 (R. St. J. Macdonald et al. eds., 1993) (agreeing with Judge Martens that it is certainly arguable that, at least concerning freedom of political debate, the Court has moved away from applying a margin of appreciation).

[109] Hertzberg v. Finland, App. 61/1979, views adopted 2 Apr. 1982, ¶ 10.3.

[110] *See* Toonen v. Australia, Communication No. 488/1992, views adopted Mar. 1994, U.N. GAOR, Hum. Rts. Comm., U.N. Doc. CCPR/C/50/D/488/1992 (1994), and Ilmari Lansman v. Finland, App. No. 511/1992, views adopted Oct. 1994, *cited in* Evatt, *infra* this volume, at 89-90.

[111] The European Court has applied the following test to assess whether a situation meets the requirements of a "public emergency":

> (1) It must be actual or imminent.
> (2) Its effects must involve the entire nation.
> (3) The continuance of the organized life of the community must be threatened.
> (4) The crisis or danger must be exceptional, in that the normal measures or restrictions, permitted by the Convention for the maintenance of public safety, health and order, are plainly inadequate.

The Greek Case, 12 *Year Book Eur. Conv. H.R.* ¶ 153 (1969). *See also* P. van Dijk & G.J.H. van

that level. Thus, for example, governments may impose restrictions even during peacetime that are necessary to prevent espionage or to protect genuine military secrets.[112]

International law, as codified, *inter alia* in Article 4 of the International Covenant, recognizes that, during times of emergency, states may derogate from a number of fundamental human rights including the right to freedom of expression. However, this derogation is only allowable when (a) the emergency "threatens the life of the nation," (b) the emergency "is officially proclaimed," (c) the measures are "strictly required by the exigencies of the situation" and are "not inconsistent with [the state's] other obligations under international law," and (d) the measures "do not involve discrimination solely on the ground of race, color, sex, language, religion or social origin."[113]

While this emergency standard may appear sufficiently precise to guard against misuse, in practice it has been frequently and massively abused.[114] Governments claim emergency powers even when only the life of the regime rather than "the life of the nation" is under threat; they frequently fail to proclaim the emergency officially, let alone meet their treaty obligations to notify other states parties; and they often suspend derogable rights completely rather than limit them only as "strictly required."[115] Moreover, as noted by the UN Sub-Commission

---

Hoof, *Theory and Practice of the European Convention on Human Rights* 348 (2d ed. 1990). *See generally* Ireland v. United Kingdom, 25 Eur. Ct. H.R. (ser. A) (1978).

[112] *See* Kiss, *supra* note 37, at 297.

[113] ICCPR, *supra* note 13, art. 4(1). The Article reads:

> In time of public emergency which threatens the life of the nation and the existence of which is officially proclaimed, the States Parties to the present Covenant may take measures derogating from their obligations under the present Covenant to the extent strictly required by the exigencies of the situation, provided that such measures are not inconsistent with their other obligations under international law and do not involve discrimination solely on the ground of race, colour, sex, language, religion or social origin.

Id.; see also European Convention, *supra* note 17, art. 15.

[114] *See, eg.*, Amnesty International, *Annual Report 1996* (1997) (entries on Algeria, Egypt, India, Myanmar, Pakistan, Peru, Sri Lanka, and Turkey). See generally the annual reports of Amnesty International and Human Rights Watch. For a systematic analysis of the ways in which states of emergency impact human rights see International Commission of Jurists, *States of Emergency: Their Impact on Human Rights* (1983) (discussing Argentina, Canada, Colombia, Eastern Europe, Ghana, Greece, India, Malaysia, Northern Ireland, Peru, Syria, Thailand, Turkey, Uruguay, and Zaire).

[115] Joan Fitzpatrick, *Human Rights in Crisis: The International System for Protecting Rights During States of Emergency* 10, 37 (1994); Daniel O'Donnell, "Commentary on the Siracusa Principles by the Rapporteur on Derogation," 7 *Hum. Rts. Q.* 1, 24 (1985); Leandro Despouy, Special Rapporteur on States of Emergency of the Sub-Commission on Prevention of Discrimination and Protection of Minorities, *Eighth annual report and list of states which, since 1 January 1985, have proclaimed, extended or terminated a state of emergency*, UN Doc.

Rapporteurs on Freedom of Expression, "Freedom of opinion and expression are generally among the first victims when derogations from human rights are imposed in a state of emergency."[116]

For these reasons, Johannesburg Principle 3 on States of Emergency does not refer to the possibility of derogation. Rather, it treats emergencies as a sub-category of the general standard and narrows the circumstances in which emergency restrictions may be imposed. The emergency must not only be "officially" proclaimed, it must also be "lawfully proclaimed in accordance with both national and international law." Derogations are not envisaged; any restrictions on freedom of expression must be "strictly required" by the exigencies of the situation, and may be imposed "only when and for so long as they are not inconsistent with the government's other obligations under international law."

E. Prohibition of Discrimination: *Principle 4*

The drafters of the Johannesburg Principles considered the principle of non-discrimination to be so important, even during states of emergency, that they devoted a separate principle to it. Principle 4 differs in several respects from the non-discrimination provision in the "emergency" clause of the International Covenant (which provides that measures may not be taken even during emergencies if they involve "discrimination solely on the ground of race, color, sex, language, religion or social origin").[117] The word "solely" has been dropped and several categories, including "national origin," have been added. The *travaux preparatoires* of the International Covenant's emergency clause disclose that inclusion of the word "solely" and exclusion of "national origin" reflected a compromise between country delegates who wanted to permit discriminatory treatment of enemy aliens during wartime and those who wanted non-discrimination to be a non-derogable right.[118] Inclusion of the word "solely" was understood by the delegates to permit differential

---

E/CN.4/Sub.2/1995/20 (1995). In 1995, the UN Sub-Commission on Prevention of Discrimination and Protection of Minorities adopted a resolution in which it "[n]ote[d] with deep concern that to deal with certain situations, including internal unrest or the threat of such unrest, some states do not hesitate to take emergency measures without officially proclaiming a state of emergency . . . in accordance with national law and international rules and principles." Resolution 1995/33, at ¶ 7, in *Report of the Sub-Commission on Prevention of Discrimination and Protection of Minorities, 47th Sess.*, UN Doc. E/CN.4/1996/2, E/CN.4/Sub.2/1995/51.

[116] Türk & Joinet, *supra* note 30, ¶ 36.

[117] For text of the emergency clause, *see supra* note 113.

[118] *See* Joan Fitzpatrick Hartman, "Working Paper for the Committee of Experts on the Article 4 Derogation Provision," 7 *Hum. Rts. Q.* 89, 118 (1985). Those who wanted the authority to discriminate against enemy aliens included the delegates of Belgium, India, the Philippines, and the United States. *See id.* at 118 & n.189.

measures against "a minority which poses a singular threat to the nation, but not against a minority which is simply unpopular."[119] As genuine as may have been the delegates' belief that governments in emergency situations would distinguish between minorities who were merely unpopular and those who posed a singular threat, the word "solely" provides a loophole that has severely undermined the non-discrimination principle.

By omitting the word "solely" from Johannesburg Principle 4, the drafters did not create a standard that prohibits all differential treatment. Rather, Principle 4 prohibits differential treatment only if based on one of a list of enumerated grounds. In addition to the grounds listed in the International Covenant's emergency clause (race, color, sex, language, religion, and social origin), the drafters added all of the other prohibited grounds for discrimination in the International Covenant's general non-discrimination clauses; namely, "national origin," "political or other opinion," "property," and "birth or other status."[120] The Johannesburg drafters added one more category, "nationality," so as to make clear that non-citizens may not be subjected to discrimination on the ground of lack of citizenship. Principle 4's protections are narrower than those of the International Covenant's main non-discrimination clauses in one regard, however: Principle 4 omits the words "such as" before the list of grounds of prohibited discrimination, thus making the list inclusive rather than illustrative. The drafters omitted these words to limit the Principle's divergence from the International Covenant's emergency clause.

III. Requirements for Restrictions on Freedom of Expression Based on National Security

Part II of the Johannesburg Principles begins by emphasizing, in Principle 5, the absolute nature of the right to freedom of opinion, which admits of no restriction of any kind.

Principle 6 defines the limited category of expression that legitimately may be punished as a threat to national security.[121] The Johannesburg drafters considered it important to affirm that a category of expression may indeed be punishable, as well as to define that category narrowly and with precision.

Principles 7-10 set forth in some detail the two main obligations of governments regarding expression or information they deem threatening to national security. First, governments must respect, and may not punish, expression, however

---

[119] *Id.* at 118.

[120] ICCPR, *supra* note 13, arts. 2, 26.

[121] *See id.* ("Expression may be punished as a threat to national security only if a government can demonstrate that: . . . the expression is intended to incite imminent violence; . . . it is likely to incite such violence; and . . . there is a direct and immediate connection between the expression and the likelihood or occurrence of such violence.").

challenging to the regime in power, that falls short of incitement to violence. Second, governments must take reasonable measures to prevent third parties from interfering with protected expression.

A. Right to Hold Opinions: *Johannesburg Principle 5*

The right to hold opinions under the International Covenant is absolute,[122] in contrast to the right to express opinions and, indeed, in contrast to treatment of the right to hold opinions under the regional treaties.[123] While it is certainly the case that the Inter-American and European treaty bodies generally interpret the rights set forth in their Conventions to be at least as protective as corresponding rights in the International Covenant,[124] the European Court has declined to extend absolute protection to the right to hold opinions,[125] and neither the Inter-American Court nor the Commission has directly addressed the issue.[126]

Principle 5's absolute protection of the right to hold opinions or beliefs is premised on the International Covenant's protection as well as on the understanding that the mere holding of opinions or beliefs cannot threaten legitimate national security interests.[127]

---

[122] *See* ICCPR, *supra* note 13, art. 19(1).

[123] *See* American Convention, *supra* note 18, art. 13(1); European Convention, *supra* note 17, art. 10; African Charter, *supra* note 19, art. 9(2).

[124] *See, e.g.*, Müller v. Switzerland, 133 Eur. Ct. H.R. (ser. A) ¶ 27 (1988) (referring to ICCPR Article 19 in concluding that freedom of expression under the European Convention includes artistic expression); Groppera Radio, 173 Eur. Ct. H.R. (ser. A) ¶ 61 (1990) (referring to the text and history of Article 19 in concluding that European Convention Article 10(1) permits states to regulate technical aspects of broadcasting but otherwise requires that content regulation comply with the requirements of Article 10(2)).

[125] *See, e.g.*, Glassenapp v. Germany, 104 Eur. Ct. H.R. (ser A.) (1986) (ruling that a teacher could be dismissed from her probationary civil service job for refusing to dissociate herself from the German Communist Party, of which she was not a member); Vogt v. Germany, 323 Eur. Ct. H.R. (ser. A) ¶¶ 75-82 (1995) (concluding that a civil servant may be dismissed for membership in a group "the aims of which are inimical to the constitutional order" if the job entails access to sensitive information).

[126] *See* Viviana Krsticevic, et al., inf*ra* this volume, at 166.

[127] This Principle does not, however, preclude the dismissal of a government servant from a job granting him or her access to sensitive information based on membership in a group "the aims of which are inimical to the constitutional order," coupled with words or deeds demonstrating an inclination to act in furtherance of those aims. *Cf. Vogt*, 323 Eur. Ct. H.R. (ser. A) ¶ 75, *supra* note 125.

B. Incitement to Violence that Threatens National Security: *Johannesburg Principle 6*

Principle 6 states that, subject to Principles 15 and 16 concerning the disclosure of secret information,[128] expression may be punishable as a threat to national security only if it is intended and likely to incite imminent violence. No one may be punished for "mere advocacy" of violence. Advocacy rises to the level of incitement when those to whom the advocacy is addressed are urged to commit violence now or in the near future, and are reasonably likely to do so.[129] Principle 6 further provides that no one may be punished on national security grounds for incitement to non-violent activity, even if the activity is unlawful under national law. The Johannesburg drafters included this last prohibition reasoning that to allow punishment under national security laws for incitement to "unlawful activity" would open a loophole that would eviscerate the principle: governments could escape the application of Principle 6 simply by pronouncing various activities to be unlawful under national law.

It may indeed be that Principle 6 protects a small range of speech that legitimately could be prohibited under even the most liberal interpretations of international free speech law. Arguably, the Principle could adequately protect freedom of expression and yet prohibit incitement to actions, though non-violent, that violate legitimate national security interests as defined in Principle 2. Such acts might, for instance, involve disobedience of lawful military orders necessary for the protection of legitimate interests.[130] In addition, a footnote could usefully be added to Principle 6 clarifying that it does not prevent governments from conditioning employment in jobs that involve handling classified information on loyalty to the state and the constitutional order.[131]

---

[128] *See infra* Section III.D.

[129] This definition is based upon the reasoning of the United States Supreme Court in Brandenburg v. Ohio, 395 U.S. 444, 447 (1969).

[130] The UN Human Rights Committee and the European Court and Commission have all authorized restrictions on fundamental rights, including freedom of expression, in the interest of protecting a state's authority to raise an army. The UN Human Rights Committee upheld Finland's denial of a passport to a man who had failed to report for military service, reasoning that a state may legitimately determine that prohibiting conscripts from leaving the country during their period of military service is necessary for the defense of national security. *See* Lauri Peltonen v. Finland, App. No. 492/1992, views issued 21 July 1994, ¶ 8.4; *see also* X v. United Kingdom, 3 Eur. Comm'n H.R. 62, 64 (1975); Arrowsmith v. United Kingdom, 19 Eur. Comm'n H.R. 5 (1978); *infra* at 48.

[131] *See* discussion of the European Court's decision in *Vogt*, 323 Eur. Ct. H.R. (ser. A), *supra* note 125, at ¶ 75. See also Ulrich Karpen, "Germany," *infra* this volume, at 295, note 24 and accompanying text, discussing a judgment (*Dienstpflicht von Offizieren*, 28 FCC 36, 47 (1970)) in which the Federal Constitutional Court upheld a law requiring civil servants to display loyalty to the state in both words and deeds.

Principle 6 is not yet an accepted norm of international law. However, the core principle that political speech should not be subject to criminal sanctions unless it is likely to cause violence has been embraced by a number of international bodies, and also finds support in the case law of several countries and the writings of distinguished experts.[132] While most of the precedents do not concern speech that allegedly threatens national security, the principle is equally valid in the security context: speech that is neither aimed at nor likely to incite violence (and does not disclose national secrets or incite others to do so) simply cannot threaten legitimate national security interests (with the possible exception of speech that incites disobedience of lawful military orders and similar actions). Of course, all speech that incites violence does not thereby threaten national security; the government must also establish that the violence is likely to endanger national security. Equally, speech that falls short of incitement to violence may be restricted in the interest of protecting other legitimate interests (but any sanctions must be proportionate and, arguably, should not involve imprisonment).[133]

The closest precedent for Principle 6 is the US Supreme Court's unanimous 1969 judgment in *Brandenburg v. Ohio*.[134] In that case the Court held that speech that advocates unlawful conduct may only be punished where two conditions are satisfied.[135] First, the speech must be "directed to inciting or producing imminent lawless action"[136] (often referred to as the "clear and present danger" test[137]). Second, the speech must be "likely to incite such action."[138] This part of the standard makes the important distinction between support for an abstract doctrine or principle on the one hand, and incitement to concrete, unlawful action on the other. In a previous case, the Court explained that "[t]he essential distinction is that those to whom the advocacy is addressed must be urged to *do* something, now or in the future, rather

---

[132] *See infra* notes 135-53.

[133] *See* Türk & Joinet, *supra* note 30, ¶ 83. Similarly, Article 19, the International Center Against Censorship, maintains that speech that does not promote violence should not be punished with imprisonment; rather, expression that violates a private right (e.g., defamation, invasion of privacy) or a public interest (e.g., protection of public health) is better redressed by fines, rights of reply, required retractions, or other remedies. *See* Article 19, "Policy Statement on Incitement to Hatred or Discrimination," *in Striking a Balance: Hate Speech, Freedom of Expression and Non-Discrimination* 315-18 (Sandra Coliver ed., 1992).

[134] Brandenburg v. Ohio, 395 U.S. 444 (1969).

[135] *See id.* at 447.

[136] *Id.*

[137] This test was first stated by Justice Oliver Wendell Holmes, on behalf of a unanimous court, in affirming the conviction of a Socialist Party leader who urged draft age men to avoid conscription, in Schenck v. United States, 249 U.S. 47, 52 (1919).

[138] Brandenburg, 395 U.S. at 447.

than merely to *believe* in something."[139] Principle 6 "internationalizes" the Brandenburg ruling.[140]

Providing additional and strong support for Principle 6 is the Inter-American Commission's conclusion that speech "particularly in the political arena" may be criminalized only if likely to result in "lawless violence":

> [P]articularly in the political arena, the threshold of State intervention with respect to freedom of expression is necessarily higher because of the critical role political dialogue plays in a democratic society. The Convention requires that this threshold be raised even higher when the State brings to bear the coercive power of its criminal justice system to curtail expression. Considering the consequences of criminal sanctions and the inevitable chilling effect they have on freedom of expression, criminalization of speech can only apply in those exceptional circumstances where there is an obvious and direct threat of lawless violence.[141]

As strong a protection of freedom of expression as that is, Principle 6 is stronger in at least one respect: It opposes all punishment for advocacy of unlawful conduct, not merely criminal sanctions. This aspect of Principle 6 is based on the reasoning that civil penalties can be as onerous as some criminal penalties, and that the harm to legitimate public interests which could result from speech short of incitement to violence is far less than the risk of harm due to excessive punishment, whether civil or criminal. In addition, it is not clear whether "an obvious and direct threat" is as demanding as Principle 6's "incitement" standard. Conceivably, a "direct threat" of violence could be satisfied by speech that is likely to *provoke* violence by a hostile crowd or lead to violence unintentionally.

The two UN Sub-Commission Special Rapporteurs endorsed a standard very similar to that put forward by the Inter-American Commission:

---

[139] Yates v. United States, 354 U.S. 298, 324-25 (1957). For instance, in 1969 the Supreme Court ruled that even a public threat to murder President Johnson could not be punished where it was clear from all the circumstances that the speaker intended to convey strong criticism of the President and not to advocate violence. *See* Watts v. United States, 394 U.S. 705, 708 (1969). The speaker, an anti-war activist, declared in a public speech: "If they ever make me carry a rifle, the first man I want to get in my sights is L.B.J." *Id.* at 706. Relevant to the Court's conclusion was that the threat was conditional and the audience responded with laughter. *Id.* at 707.

[140] Principle 6 extends *Brandenburg* to the extent that it protects all speech short of incitement to violence from restrictions based on national security (though not other) grounds, including speech that incites unlawful action. Thus, for instance, *Brandenburg*.would allow prosecution of incitement to draft evasion, while Principle 6, as written, would not.

[141] Inter-American Commission on Human Rights, Organization of American States, *Annual Report of the Inter-American Commission on Human Rights* 1994, at 211 (1995) (discussing the compatability of laws that prohibit defamation of or insult to government officials, known as *descato* laws, with the American Convention).

> In the Special Rapporteurs' opinion, deprivation of liberty [as a punishment for the unlawful expression of opinion] is clearly a disproportionate sanction. Moreover, deprivation of liberty carries the inherent risk of leading to numerous violations of human rights. In principle it should not be provided for as a penalty save in wholly exceptional cases in which there is a clear and present danger of violence.[142]

The Rapporteurs' inclusion of the term "clear and present danger" suggests incorporation of the U.S. requirement of incitement.

Courts of several countries have adopted tests similar to the *Brandenburg* standard, prohibiting the punishment of speech that constitutes mere advocacy of opinions or action absent a showing that the speech is likely to cause violence or other unlawful action. However, few if any of these courts apply the standard as rigorously as do U.S. courts, and few require that the speech must intend to incite violence (and thus may restrict speech that provokes a hostile reaction). For example, India's Supreme Court stressed the requirement of a direct, causal relationship between a statement and the feared unlawful consequences:

> The anticipated danger should not be remote, conjectural or far-fetched. It should have a proximate and direct nexus with the expression . . . [which] should be inseparably locked up with the action contemplated like the equivalent of a 'spark in a powder keg'.[143]

Using similar reasoning, the Nagoya High Court of Japan overturned a conviction for distributing politically inflammatory printed material supportive of crimes of insurrection.[144] The Court reasoned that there was a distinction between the abstract and concrete danger of inciting the encouraged crimes, and ruled that the establishment of foreknowledge of a clear and present danger to public safety on the part of the accused was an essential element of the offense.[145]

In Pakistan, the Lahore High Court, expressly adopting the U.S. Supreme Court's "clear and present danger" test, stated that "criticism of the government does not always indicate an intention to bring about disorder."[146] The Peshawar High

---

[142] Türk & Joinet, *supra* note 30, ¶ 83. *See also id.* ¶ 30 (condemning "the imposition of heavy penalties on people who have expressed opinions but have not resorted to or advocated violence").

[143] *Handbook*, *supra* note 24, at 135 (quoting Rangarajan v. Jagjivan Ram, [1990] LRC (Const) 412, 427; Union of India v. Jagjivam Ram, 2 SCR 204, 226, decided on 30 Mar. 1989).

[144] *See id.* at 136 (discussing Japan v. Kanemoto, 396 Hanrei Jiho 19 (S. Ct. 21 Dec. 1964), *translated and discussed in* Hiroshi Itoh & Lawrence W. Beer, *The Constitutional Law of Japan* 242 (1978)).

[145] *Id.* at 136-37

[146] *See id.* at 137 (quoting Maluvi Farid Ahmad v. Government of West Pakistan, PLD 1965 (WP) Lahore 135).

Court ruled that criticism of the government may only be restricted if it encourages the use of force or violence.[147]

In several cases, the Supreme Court of Sri Lanka ruled that expression of views short of advocacy of violence or other unlawful conduct may not be restricted.[148] In a 1987 case, the Chief Justice emphasized that "what is prohibited is advocacy of action and not advocacy of ideas."[149]

The courts of England which developed the common law crime of seditious libel have made clear in recent decades that the crime is limited to punishing speech that is both *likely* and *intended* to incite violence aimed at disturbing "constituted authority" (that is, authority which is lawful and based on some manifestation of the will of the people). In 1991, the Queen's Bench Divisional Court (England), in the most authoritative, modern statement of the crime of sedition,[150] expressly endorsed the following statement of a Canadian court:

> It cannot be that words which, for example, are intended to create ill-will even to the extent of violence between any two of the innumerable groups into which society is divided, can, without more, be seditious. In my opinion, to render the intention seditious, there must be an intention to incite to violence or resistance or defiance for the purpose of disturbing constituted authority. I do not think there is any basis in the authorities for defining the crime on any lower plane.[151]

Similarly, the Supreme Court of India ruled that speech, to be seditious, must be likely to incite violence.[152]

C. Protected Expression: *Johannesburg Principles 7, 8, and 9*

Governments around the world subject people to long prison terms for exercising their rights to freedom of expression (or association or assembly) on the ground that their peaceful expression--from forming an opposition party, to

---

[147] *See id.* at 136 (discussing Hussain Bakhsh Kasuar v. the State, PLD 1958 (WP) Peshawar 15).

[148] *See id.* at 138-39 (discussing Amaratunga v. Sirimal, SC App. No. 468/92, decided on 6 Mar. 1993; The Democratic Socialist Republic of Sri Lanka v. P. V. Nallanayagam, HC Colombo, Case No. 1715/85, decided on 17 July 1986; Ratanasara Thero v. Udugampola, SC App. No. 125/82, decided on 8 Feb. 1983).

[149] *See id.* at 141 (quoting M. Joseph Perera v. Attorney-General, SC App. Nos. 107-109/86, decided on 25 May 1987, at 15).

[150] *See id.* at 128 (discussing R v. Chief Metropolitan Stipendiary Magistrate, *ex parte* Choudhury, 1 Q.B. 429, 453 (1991)).

[151] *See id.* at 127-28 (quoting Boucher v. The King [1951] 2 D.L.R. 369, 389).

[152] *See id.* at 129 (discussing Kedar Nath Singh v. State of Bihar, (1962) 2 S.C.R. Supp. 769, 807).

criticizing the government, to advocating minority rights--is aimed at removing the government in power. It is a bedrock principle of democratic society that there must be a process by which an undemocratic government can be removed by peaceful means. People are entitled to call (or at least cannot be condemned under international law for calling) for the overthrow of a tyrannical government. As proclaimed in the preamble of the Universal Declaration of Human Rights: "[I]t is essential, if man is not to be compelled to have recourse, as a last resort, to rebellion against tyranny and oppression, that human rights should be protected by the rule of law."[153]

Johannesburg Principles 7-9 enumerate six categories of expression (discussed below in subsections 1-6) that have been the most frequent targets of government censure.

1. Advocacy of Non-Violent Change of Government: *Johannesburg Principle 7(a)(i)*

Johannesburg Principle 7(a)(i) asserts that people are entitled to advocate non-violent change of government policy or the government itself, including calling for self-determination, even if prohibited under national law. This Principle finds support in several statements of the UN Human Rights Committee and bodies of the Council of Europe. For instance, the UN Human Rights Committee concluded in its General Comment on the prohibition of war propaganda and hate speech:

> The provisions of article 20 [of the International Covenant] . . . do not prohibit advocacy of the sovereign right of self-defence or the right of peoples to self-determination and independence in accordance with the Charter of the United Nations.[154]

In several cases, the Human Rights Committee has made clear that leadership of an opposition political party and other efforts to change the government through peaceful means, even if in violation of national law, are protected forms of political expression or association that may not properly be punished.[155] For instance, in a

---

[153] Universal Declaration, *supra* note 11, pmbl. ¶ 3.

[154] *General Comment on Article 20*, General Comment No. 11, U.N. GAOR, Hum. Rts. Comm., ¶ 2, (1983), *reprinted in Compilation of General Comments*, *supra* note 50. *See also* Hannum, *supra* note 40; Franck, *supra* note 40.

[155] *See, e.g.*, Mpandanjila v. Zaire, Communication No. 138/1983, views adopted Mar.26, 1986; Mpaka-Nsusu v. Zaire, Communication No. 157/1983, U.N. GAOR, Hum. Rts. Comm. (views adopted Mar. 26, 1986), *reprinted in* 2 Selected Decisions of the Human Rights Committee Under the Optional Protocol, Sess. 17-32, at 187; Muteba v. Zaire, Communication No. 124/1982, views adopted July 24, 1984; Pietroroia v. Uruguay, Communication No. 44/1979, U.N. GAOR, Hum. Rts. Comm. (views adopted Mar. 27, 1981), *reprinted in* Selected Decisions of the Human Rights Committee under the Optional Protocol, Sess. 2-16, at 79, ¶ 17 (1985); L. Buffo Carballal v. Uruguay, Communication No. 33/1978, U.N. GAOR, Hum. Rts. Comm., *reprinted in* 1 *Selected Decisions of the Human Rights Committee under the*

1984 decision, the Committee examined the application of a Zairean political activist who had been imprisoned, held *incommunicado*, and subjected to torture on charges that he had "attack[ed] the internal and external security of the State [by means of] having established a clandestine political party and of having, while abroad [in France], sought ways of changing the established institutions -- acts which are . . . punishable by death under Zairean law."[156] The Committee concluded that the charges, as well as the detention and mistreatment, amounted to persecution on grounds of political opinion, signaling that leadership of a political party, even one which seeks to change the government, is entitled to full protection.[157]

Similarly, in a case against Cameroon, the Committee concluded that the applicant was unjustly punished for having given an interview to the BBC in which he criticized the government and advocated multi-party democracy.[158] While the government's stated objective--to safeguard and indeed strengthen national unity under difficult political circumstances--was legitimate, the objective could not be advanced by muzzling advocacy of multi-party democracy and respect for human rights.[159]

The Parliamentary Assembly of the Council of Europe declared its view that peaceful advocacy of at least some degree of autonomy for a region of a country is entitled to the protection of Article 10 of the European Convention.[160] Accordingly, it roundly condemned the detention and prosecution of six members of the Turkish Grand National Assembly for charges "solely based on the public statements and writings of these members claiming recognition of a Kurdish identity and advocating some form of (cultural) autonomy for the region."[161] The Assembly concluded that advocacy of changes to the Constitution, even though prohibited by the Constitution itself, fell "within the limits of free speech."[162]

In a 1994 judgment, the European Court upheld the right of a German Member of the European Parliament to make statements in French Polynesia calling for its independence from France (as well as for an end to nuclear testing), given that she did not advocate violence or disorder.[163] The French government, invoking its interest in territorial integrity, expelled the MEP from Polynesia and refused to let her leave the airport upon arrival in New Caledonia.[164] The Court ruled that the

---

Optional Protocol, Sess. 2-16, at 64, ¶ 12.

[156] Muteba v. Zaire, Communication No. 124/1982, ¶ 8.2, U.N. GAOR, Hum. Rts. Comm.

[157] *Id.*

[158] *See* Mukong v. Cameroon, App. No. 458/1991, U.N. GAOR, Hum. Rts. Comm. (views adopted July 21, 1994), discussed in Evatt, *infra* this volume, at Sec. II.B.2, notes 30-31.

[159] *Id.*

[160] *See* Council of Europe, Parliamentary Assembly, Res. 1030 (1994), ¶ 6, (text adopted by the Assembly on Apr. 13, 1994 (13th Sitting)).

[161] *Id.* ¶ 6.

[162] *Id.* ¶ 7(iii).

[163] *See* Piermont v. France, 314 Eur. Ct. H.R. (ser. A) (1995).

[164] *See id.* ¶¶ 12, 18-20.

French government's measures were disproportionate, even though "the political atmosphere was tense and [the applicant's] arrival [in New Caledonia] led to a limited demonstration of hostility,"[165] because "[a]t no time did the MEP call for violence or disorder."[166]

2. Criticism of, or Insult to, the Government, Foreign Governments or Officials: *Johannesburg Principle 7(a)(ii)*

Prosecutions for insult to the government, leaders of state, or public officials often are motivated by the same illegitimate concerns that motivate national security prosecutions, and often pose similar threats to freedom of political expression. As the U.S. Supreme Court observed, in its landmark 1964 judgment in *New York Times v. Sullivan*, defamation actions by public officials concerning their public functions pose a threat of discouraging robust criticism of government institutions and policies just as surely as had the sedition laws which were condemned a century earlier.[167] The Court emphasized that freedom of expression requires "breathing space" to survive, and that even some false speech had to be shielded from sanction in order to ensure free political debate.[168] Accordingly, the Supreme Court ruled that public officials, to sustain an action for defamation, must prove by clear and convincing evidence that an allegedly libelous statement was published with actual knowledge of its falsity or with reckless disregard for its truth.[169]

The Supreme Court of India endorsed the *Sullivan* reasoning and adopted its holding.[170] The UK House of Lords, citing *Sullivan*, ruled that it was "contrary to the public interest [to allow governmental institutions to sue for libel] because to admit such actions would place an undesirable fetter on freedom of speech."[171] The highest court of Australia and a South African trial court have also adopted the main points of the *Sullivan* judgment.[172]

The European Court ruled in a series of judgments that individuals have a broad right to criticize political leaders, public officials, governments, and institutions of state. In the landmark *Lingens* case, the Court established that the "limits of acceptable criticism are . . . wider as regards a politician as such than as regards a

---

[165] *Id.* ¶ 85.
[166] *Id.* ¶ 77.
[167] *See* New York Times Co. v. Sullivan, 376 U.S. 254, 270-74 (1964).
[168] *Id.* at 271-72.
[169] *See id.* at 279-80.
[170] *See* Rajagopal v. State of Tamil Nadu, JT 1994 (6) SC 514.
[171] *See also Handbook, supra* note 24, § 7.1.4 (discussing Derbyshire County Council v. Times Newspapers [1993] 2 W.L.R. 449).
[172] *See* Theophanous v. Herald & Weekly Times Ltd, (1994) 68 A.L.R. 713; Holomisa v. Argus Newspapers Ltd (Witwatersrand Local Div.) Case No. 94/1983.

private individual."[173] In *Castells v. Spain*,[174] the European Court ruled that governments are required to tolerate an even greater degree of scrutiny than politicians:

> The limits of permissible criticism are wider with regard to the Government than in relation to a private citizen, or even a politician. In a democratic system the actions or omissions of the Government must be subject to the close scrutiny not only of the legislative and judicial authorities but also of the press and public opinion. Furthermore, the dominant position which the Government occupies makes it necessary for it to display restraint in resorting to criminal proceedings, particularly where other means are available for replying to the unjustified attacks and criticisms of its adversaries or the media.[175]

This ruling is all the more significant in light of the government's claim that Mr. Castells had, in essence, threatened its security and territorial integrity by having "insulted a democratic government in order to destabilize it, and during a very sensitive, indeed critical, period for Spain, namely shortly after the adoption of the Constitution, at a time when groups of differing political persuasions were resorting to violence concurrently."[176] Mr Castells, a senator who represented a Basque separatist coalition, had published an article condemning murders and attacks committed by armed groups against Basque citizens and accusing the government, through its failure to investigate any of the crimes, of actually encouraging them.[177] The European Court suggested that a government may prohibit criticism of itself only in extraordinary circumstances, such as when necessary to protect public order and when the accusations are "devoid of foundation or formulated in bad faith."[178]

Defamation actions have long been used by public officials and institutions to suppress criticism of the government. The practice became more common throughout Eastern Europe and much of Africa following the thawing of the Cold War owing to the pressure placed by some donor governments on recipient states to hold elections and become "democratic". For the first time, former single-party regimes had to contend with competition at the polls. Many responded by jailing their opponents without charges; then, when donors objected, they brought such

---

[173] Lingens v. Austria, 103 Eur. Ct. H.R. (ser. A) ¶ 41 (1986). *See also* Oberschlick v. Austria, 204 Eur. Ct. H.R. (ser. A) ¶ 59 (1991); Schwabe v. Austria, 242-B Eur. Ct. H.R. (ser. A) ¶ 34 (1993).

[174] Castells v. Spain, 236 Eur. Ct. H.R. (ser. A) (1992).

[175] *Id.* at 46.

[176] *Id.* at 41.

[177] *See id.* at 6, 7.

[178] *Id.* at 46. The Court based its ruling that the government had violated Article 10 of the European Convention on the narrow ground that the government had prevented Castells from offering evidence as to the truth of his allegations. *See id.* at 47-50.

charges as seditious libel, "spreading false rumors likely to bring the government into contempt," and defamation.[179]

Clearly, the characterization of a statement as defamatory (rather than, for example, seditious) should not remove its prosecution from international scrutiny or censure. Although governments maintain that defamation charges are justified in the interest of protecting the rights and reputations of government institutions or officials, consensus is developing in international and comparative law that their rights and reputations must give way to the right of the press and public to engage in robust political debate and criticism.

For instance, the Czech Parliament adopted an amendment to the Penal Code, effective 1 January 1998, which abolished the crime of defamation of the Czech Republic or its president.[180] That law had been used against Vaclav Havel and other dissidents before the democratic transition, and thereafter by President Havel against his sharpest critics. In 1987 the Supreme Court of South West Africa set aside a Cabinet order directing the *Namibian* newspaper to pay a high registration fee before it could lawfully engage in publishing.[181] The Cabinet's order was based on its finding that the *Namibian*'s editor had written articles critical of various Cabinet members which tended to lower the esteem in which its members were held by the

---

[179] For instance, Chikufwa Chihana, the leading candidate challenging President Banda in Malawi's first presidential election, was convicted and jailed for sedition during the campaign period. Multi-Party Republic of Malawi vs. Chikufwa Chihana, High Court of Malawi, Criminal Case No. 1 of 1992 (on file with the author). In March 1996, two editors of "The Post," Zambia's leading opposition publication, were held in a maximum security jail under an order that allowed indefinite detention for publishing a "contemptuous" article about the Vice-President's statements in Parliament. A high court later quashed the sentences, but only after the two editors had spent several weeks in prison. U.S. Department of State, "Zambia," *Country Reports on Human Rights Practices for 1996* (Feb. 1997). The Republic of Slovakia passed an antisubversion law in March 1996 that allows prison sentences to be imposed for the crime of "disseminating false information abroad damaging to the interests of the Republic." Adrian Bridge, "Slovaks Protest as Their Freedoms are Whittled Away," *The Independent* (London), 1 Apr. 1996. Two Ghanaian editors and a publisher stood trial beginning in February 1996 for "publishing false information likely to injure the reputation of the Government of Ghana," the first time that anyone had been prosecuted under that law, which carries a penalty of up to ten years imprisonment. *See* Letter from Nana Akufo Addo, Counsel for the editors and publisher, to Article 19, (15 Mar. 1996) (on file with author); Letter from Nana Akufo Addo, Counsel for the editors and publisher, to Article 19, (22 Mar. 1996) (on file with author).

[180] ICFJ Clearinghouse on the Central and East European Press, published by the International Center for Journalism, Washington, D.C., editor@icf.org. Under the new law, the president may still file a defamation suit under the Civil Code.

[181] *See Handbook*, *supra* note 24, §§ 4.5.1, 8.2 (discussing Free Press of Namibia (Pty) Ltd. v. Cabinet, Interim Gov. WA, 1987 (1) SA 614).

public, and thus was likely to endanger the security of the state.[182] The Court criticized the Cabinet for contending that attacks upon Cabinet members could endanger state security matters and, accordingly, set aside the decision.[183]

South African courts, even during the apartheid era, recognized the right of citizens in a democracy to level criticism at the government, its policies, or actions:

> [I]t would involve a serious interference with the free expression of opinion hitherto enjoyed in this country if the wealth of the State, derived from the State's subjects, could be used to launch against those subjects actions for defamation because they have, falsely and unfairly it may be, criticized or condemned the management of the country.[184]

Similarly, the Privy Council ruled that protection of freedom of expression requires tolerance of statements critical of the government, even if false and even if they undermine public confidence in the government.[185] In *Hector v. Attorney General of Antigua and Barbuda*, a newspaper editor was convicted of publishing a false statement "which was likely to cause fear or alarm in or to the public or to disturb the public peace or to undermine public confidence in the conduct of public affairs."[186] The Privy Council, finding for the editor, declared the law unconstitutional, reasoning that it was a grave impediment to a free press:

> In a free, democratic society, it is almost too obvious to need stating that those who hold office in government and who are responsible for public administration must always be open to criticism. Any attempt to stifle or fetter such criticism amounts to political censorship of the most insidious and objectionable kind. At the same time it is no less obvious that the very purpose of criticism levelled at those who conduct . . . public affairs by their political opponents is to undermine public confidence in their stewardship and to persuade the electorate that the opponents would make a better job of it than those presently holding office. In the light of these considerations, their Lordships cannot help viewing a statutory provision which criminalises statements likely

---

[182] *See id.* The court observed:

> Because people (or a section thereof) may hold their government in contempt does not mean that a situation exists which constitutes a danger to the security of the State or to the maintenance of public order. In fact, to stifle just criticism could as likely lead to these undesirable situations.

Id.

[183] *See id.*

[184] *See id.* at § 7.1.4. (discussing 1946 SA 999, 1013 (A)).

[185] *See* Hector v. Privy Council, [1990] 2 AC 312 (PC) [1991] LRC (Cons) 237.

[186] *Id.*

> to undermine public confidence in the conduct of public affairs with the utmost suspicion.[187]

3. Objection to Military Service: *Johannesburg Principle 7(a)(iii)*

Johannesburg Principle 7(a)(iii) states that protected expression includes "objection, or advocacy of objection . . . to military conscription or service, a particular conflict, or the threat or use of force to settle international disputes." The Principle protects advocacy of, not incitement to, such objection.[188] This Principle finds support in U.S. jurisprudence and in the reasoning of the European Commission of Human Rights, although its protection exceeds that currently provided by the Strasbourg case law.

In a 1975 decision, the European Commission considered a UK applicant's conviction under the Incitement to Disaffection Act for disseminating copies of two documents, one of which invited soldiers to turn their guns on their officers.[189] Although the Commission concluded that the conviction did not violate the right to freedom of expression, it made clear its opinion that not all speech aimed at persuading soldiers to disobey orders could be made criminal.[190] As the Commission stated:

> If any lesson can be drawn from the Judgment of the International Military Tribunal at Nuremburg, it is that soldiers must not be permitted to be used as mindless machines. To prevent this they must be permitted to be exposed to the kind of political and philosophical propaganda that may very well conflict with the military aims of the government that commands them.[191]

Three years later the European Commission, in the *Arrowsmith* case, concluded that a British court legitimately could convict a person of a national security offense for distributing leaflets to British soldiers in Northern Ireland that encouraged them to desert.[192]

In 1994, the European Court ruled that the Austrian government's refusal to allow a soldier to distribute a satirical magazine in his barracks violated his freedom of expression.[193] The government asserted that the magazine, which included

---

[187] *Id.*

[188] In contrast, Principle 6 (which states that expression may be punishable on national security grounds only if it is intended and likely to incite imminent violence) implicitly protects incitement to objection to military service. See text accompanying note 130 for discussion of the difference between advocacy and incitement.

[189] *See* X v. United Kingdom, 3 Eur. Comm'n H.R. 62 (1975).

[190] *See id.* at 64-65.

[191] *Id.* at 64.

[192] *See* Arrowsmith v. United Kingdom, 19 Eur. Comm'n H.R. 5, 17-26 (1978).

[193] *See* Vereinigung Demokratischer Soldaten Osterreichs & Gubi v. Austria, 302 Eur. Ct. H.R. (ser. A) (1995).

stories critical of the armed forces and calling for reforms, represented a threat to discipline and to the army's effectiveness.[194] The Court concluded that the Government had not substantiated its claim because the articles "did not call into question the duty of obedience or the purpose of service in the armed forces . . . [and therefore] could scarcely be seen as a serious threat to military discipline."[195]

In 1966 the US Supreme Court ruled that exclusion of Julian Bond from membership in the Georgia House of Representatives violated his constitutional rights.[196] Bond, an opponent of the Vietnam War, had joined a statement of "sympathy with, and support, [for] the men in this country who are unwilling to respond to a military draft."[197] The Court held that Bond could not be penalized for that statement because it did not constitute a call for unlawful draft resistance but was merely a general, abstract declaration of opposition to the war, and Bond in other statements had explicitly denied advocating the breaking of the draft laws.[198] The Court emphasized that in order "to give freedom of expression the breathing space it needs to survive, . . . statements criticizing public policy and the implementation of it must be . . . protected."[199]

4. Information about Violations of International Human Rights or Humanitarian Law: *Johannesburg Principle 7(a)(iv)*

The right to communicate information about violations of international human rights forms one of the crucial, and much debated, Articles of the "UN Draft Declaration on the Rights and Responsibilities of Individuals, Groups and Organs of Society to Promote and Protect Universally Recognized Human Rights and Fundamental Freedoms."[200] Article 4 reads, in part:

> Everyone has the right, individually and in association with others,
>
> (a) To know, seek, obtain, receive and hold information about all human rights and fundamental freedoms . . .;
>
> . . .
>
> (c) To study, discuss, form and hold opinions on the observance, both in law and practice, of all human rights and fundamental freedoms, and,

---

[194] *See id.* at 54, 68-70, 100, 104 (references to the decision of the European Commission on Human Rights).

[195] *Id.* at 49.

[196] *See* Bond v. Floyd, 385 U.S. 116, 137 (1966).

[197] *Id.* at 120.

[198] *See id.* at 133-34.

[199] *Id.* at 136.

[200] *Draft Declaration on the Right and Responsibility of Individuals, Groups and Organs of Society to Promote and Protect Universally Recognized Human Rights and Fundamental Freedoms: Report of the Working Group on its twelfth session,* U.N. ESCOR, Com. on Hum. Rts., 53rd Sess., Agenda Item 20, U.N. Doc. E/CN.4/1997/92, Annex I (1997).

through these and other appropriate means, to draw public attention on these matters.[201]

The UN General Assembly is expected to adopt the Draft Declaration in 1998, marking the fiftieth anniversary of its adoption of the Universal Declaration of Human Rights.

Human Rights Watch provided copious documentation of the extent to which this right is violated around the world in its *World Report* publications which, since 1991, have included a separate section in each country report on violations of "The Right to Monitor."[202]

5. Publicity of Activities that May Threaten National Security: *Johannesburg Principle 8*

Principle 8 states that "[e]xpression may not be prevented or punished merely because it transmits information issued by or about an organization that a government has declared threatens national security or a related interest." This Principle responds to laws in several countries that make it a crime to republish communiqués of, or information about, proscribed organizations, on the theory that these organizations draw vitality from the "oxygen of publicity."[203]

The Principle is based on the press's right to publish information and ideas on matters of public interest and the public's right to receive them.[204] Governments may restrict that right only if they can prove that the statements threaten legitimate public interests or private rights. The activities and statements of terrorist organizations are undoubtedly matters of considerable public interest.

---

[201] *Id.* art. 4. As useful as this Article is in reaffirming and elaborating upon the right to seek and obtain information about human rights violations, the language represents a retreat from language that earlier had been accepted by all countries of the working group save Cuba and China. The earlier draft made more explicit the right to "study, discuss and form opinions as to whether these rights and freedoms are observed, both in law and in practice *in their own country* and elsewhere." *Drafting a Declaration on the Right and Responsibility of Individuals, Groups and Organs of Society to Promote and Protect Universally Recognized Human Rights and Fundamental Freedoms*, U.N. ESCOR, Comm'n on Hum. Rts., 50th sess., at 50, U.N. Doc. E/CN.4/1994/81 (1994).

[202] *See, e.g.*, Human Rights Watch, *World Report 1996* (1997).

[203] Prime Minister Margaret Thatcher justified the imposition in 1988 of the infamous "Broadcasting Ban" on the ground that it was necessary to deprive various organizations of "the oxygen of publicity." The Ban, issued by the Home Secretary, ordered all broadcasters to refrain from broadcasting the direct spoken words of members of Sinn Fein and a list of proscribed organizations, as well as words spoken by anyone who supported or solicited support for such organizations.

[204] *See, e.g.*, Sunday Times v. United Kingdom, 30 Eur. Ct. H.R. (ser. A) ¶ 65 (1979); Lingens v. Austria, 103 Eur. Ct. H.R. (ser. A) ¶ 41 (1986).

The Constitutional Court of Spain ruled that a state's interest in countering terrorism cannot justify restrictions on information about statements by terrorist groups except where the expression *intends* to build support for terrorism:

> [B]oth the right of the journalist to inform and the rights of his readers to receive full and accurate information constitute, in the last resort, an objective institutional guarantee, which effectively prevents the imputation of any criminal will on the part of those who only transmit information.[205]

In the 1980s, the UK and Irish governments imposed bans on the broadcast of interviews with members of various proscribed groups and also Sinn Fein (a lawful political party that supports the aims of the outlawed IRA). Because the European Commission on Human Rights ruled challenges to these bans inadmissible, the European Court did not have the opportunity to assess their compatibility with international law. However, the Supreme Court of Ireland, in a unanimous 1993 judgment, placed some limits on the Irish ban.[206] It ruled that a mere member of Sinn Fein, who was also a union spokesperson, could not be excluded from talking about the union's grievances on RTE, Ireland's national broadcasting service.[207] It made clear that, while access to broadcasting is not a right, access could not be denied on arbitrary grounds.[208] Moreover, the UN Human Rights Committee, examining Ireland's broadcasting ban in 1993, observed that the prohibition on broadcasting interviews with members of certain groups, in the absence of a particularized showing that the broadcasts would threaten legitimate state interests, infringed on freedom to receive and impart information.[209]

The Supreme Court of Israel applied a similar test in 1985 in striking down a directive that prohibited TV interviews with "public personalities identified with those who see the PLO as the exclusive or legitimate representative of Arabs living

---

[205] *See Handbook*, *supra* note 24, § 6.1 (discussing STC 159/86, (Egin case) Boletin de Jurisprudencia Constitucional 68, 1447 ¶ 8).

[206] *See id.* § 6.1 (discussing O'Toole v. Radio Telefís Éireann, [1993] I.L.R.M. 458 (Ir. 30 Mar. 1993)).

[207] *See id.*

[208] *See id.* The court stated:

> [S]omeone speaking on an innocuous subject on the airwaves, even though he is a member of an organisation which includes in its objects a desire to undermine public order or the authority of the State, is [not] . . . outside the constitutional guarantee . . .. [H]e should be treated equally with others when his views do not transgress either the Constitution or the law.

Id. (O'Flaherty, J., concurring).

[209] Report of the Human Rights Committee, July 1993, U.N. GAOR, 48th Sess., ¶¶ 593-613, U.N. Doc. A/48/40 (1993), discussed in Evatt, *infra* this volume, at 103, note 75.

in the Judea and Samaria Region and in the Gaza Strip."[210] The Court ruled that the directive was over-broad and, accordingly, could be applied only if the Israeli Broadcasting Authority issued "a clear and unequivocal definition for the terms 'public personalities' and 'identifying themselves with the PLO.'"[211]

The European Court ruled, in its 1994 *Jersild* judgment, that a journalist's conviction and fine for broadcasting the racist statements of others violated his right to freedom of expression and information. The journalist had not endorsed the sentiments and indeed was motivated by a good faith desire to inform the Danish public about the existence in their country of racist groups.[212] The Court stated that journalists should not be hampered in the exercise of their editorial judgment about matters of public interest absent "particularly strong reasons for doing so."[213] The reasoning is equally applicable to statements about terrorist groups and other matters affecting national security.

6. Use of a Minority or Other Language: *Johannesburg Principle 9*

A number of countries faced with movements for autonomy or separation of part of the territory have banned or restricted the use of minority languages on grounds that their use threatens national security or unity. Most notably, until 1991 Turkey banned all publications or communication in Kurdish; still today, all discussion that takes place at political meetings must be in Turkish, and Kurdish may not be spoken in court proceedings or in other official government settings.[214]

Principle 9 declares that expression can never be prohibited on the ground that it is in a particular language. The Principle is based on the right to use one's own language, at least outside of official proceedings, which is a fundamental aspect of freedom of expression. The UN Human Rights Committee, affirming this right, concluded that Quebec's "French only" sign law (which prohibited the posting of government or commercial signs in languages other than French) violated the International Covenant's protection of freedom of expression.[215] As it stated: "A State may choose one or more official languages, but it may not exclude, outside the spheres of public life, the freedom to express oneself in a language of one's choice."[216]

---

[210] *See Handbook, supra* note 24, § 6.1 (discussing Zikhrony v. (a) Management Committee of the Broadcasting Authority, (b) Broadcasting Authority, 15 ISR. Y.B.H.R. 201, 201 (1985), H.C. 243/82 37(1) P.D. 757 (1985)).
[211] *See id.* at 284 § 6.1.
[212] Jersild v. Denmark, 298 Eur. Ct. H.R. (ser. A.) ¶¶ 1, 27-30 (1994).
[213] *Id.* ¶ 35.
[214] *See* Kerim Yildiz, "Turkey," *infra* this volume, at 453, note 36.
[215] *See* U.N. GAOR, Hum. Rts. Comm., 47th Sess., Annex, ¶ 11.4, U.N. Doc. CCPR/C/47/D/359/1989 and 385/1989 (1993) (discussing Ballyntine & Davidson v. Canada and McIntyre v. Canada).
[216] *Id.*

The Council of Europe's Convention on the Protection of Regional and Minority Languages also protects this principle.[217]

D. Unlawful Interference with Expression by Third Parties: *Johannesburg Principle 10*

Principle 10 states the obligation of governments to take reasonable measures to ensure that private parties do not violate the rights of others to freedom of expression, even where the expression advocates non-violent change of government. Reports and precedent-setting decisions issued by human rights bodies in the past decade provide a solid foundation for this principle.

In one 1988 judgment, the European Court reviewed an application from an association of Austrian doctors opposed to Austria's relatively liberal abortion laws.[218] The association complained that the police had not taken adequate measures to prevent two of its demonstrations from being disrupted by counter-demonstrators. The Court held that governments must take "reasonable and appropriate measures" to prevent private groups or individuals from violating the free expression rights of others, but concluded that the Austrian government had discharged its duty by deploying a reasonable number of police.[219] Also in 1988, the Inter-American Court of Human Rights ruled that the government of Honduras was responsible for the disappearance and presumed murder of a man in light of findings that his was but one of many disappearances that the government had done nothing to "prevent, investigate [or] punish."[220] The Court stated:

> An illegal act which violates human rights and which is initially not directly imputable to a State (for example, because it is the act of a private person or because the person responsible has not been

---

[217] *See* The European Charter for Regional or Minority Languages, *opened for signature* 5 Nov. 1992, Council of Europe, Eur. T.S. No. 148 (1992), *reprinted in* Council of Europe, *Explanatory Report--European Charter for Regional or Minority Languages* 41 (1993).

[218] *See* Platform "Ärzte für das Leben" v. Austria, 139 Eur. Ct. H.R. (ser. A) (1988).

[219] *Id.* at 34. The court reasoned:

> The participants [in a demonstration] must . . . be able to hold the demonstration without having to fear that they will be subjected to physical violence by their opponents; such a fear would be liable to deter associations or other groups . . . from openly expressing their opinions on highly controversial issues affecting the community. In a democracy the right to counter-demonstrate cannot extend to inhibiting the exercise of the right to demonstrate.

Id. at ¶ 32. The court, however, ruled that states are obliged only "to take reasonable and appropriate measures" and were not obliged to guarantee freedoms "absolutely." *Id.* at ¶ 34.

[220] Velásquez Rodríguez v. Honduras, 1988 Inter-Am. Y.B.H.R. 914, ¶ 166 (Inter-Am. Ct. on H.R.).

identified) can lead to international responsibility of the State, not because of the act itself, but because of the lack of due diligence to prevent the violation or to respond to it as required by the [American] Convention [on Human Rights].[221]

In a 1993 report on Guatemala, the Inter-American Commission applied the above doctrine of state responsibility to violations of freedom of expression committed by non-state actors.[222] The Commission declared that "State authorities must not only provide proper protection, but must explicitly denounce and repudiate [a campaign by individuals against those who expressed opposition to the government] and investigate and bring to trial or administratively censure those responsible."[223]

IV. Restrictions on Freedom of Information

The right to freedom of information is central to the concept of democratic accountability. James Madison, a leading figure in the drafting of the US Constitution, eloquently described the importance of an informed citizenry to democratic governance:

> A popular Government, without popular information, or the means of acquiring it, is but a prologue to a farce or a tragedy; or, perhaps, both. Knowledge will forever govern ignorance; and a people who mean to be their own governors must arm themselves with the power which knowledge gives.[224]

The right to freedom of information increases with the importance of the information at issue to the individual or society.[225] Matters of particular importance include the competency for public service of public officials and candidates,[226] the functioning of government and public agencies,[227] and public health issues.[228]

---

[221] *Id.* at ¶ 172.

[222] *See Fourth Report on the Situation of Human Rights in Guatemala*, Inter-Am. Comm'n. on Hum. Rts., O.A.S. Doc. OEA/Ser.L/V/II.83, doc.16, (1993) at 79.

[223] *Id.* at 85.

[224] Letter from James Madison to William T. Barry (4 Aug. 1822), *in* 3 *Letters and Other Writings of James Madison* 276 (R. Worthington ed., 1884). *See also supra* notes 8-15 and accompanying text.

[225] *See* Sunday Times v. United Kingdom, 30 Eur. Ct. H.R. (ser. A) ¶¶ 65-66 (1979); Gaskin v. United Kingdom, 160 Eur. Ct. H.R. (ser. A) ¶ 49 (1989).

[226] *See, e.g.*, Lingens v. Austria, 103 Eur. Ct. H.R. (ser. A) (1979); Oberschlick v. Austria, 204 Eur. Ct. H.R. (ser. A) (1993); Schwabe v. Austria, 242-B Eur. Ct. H.R. (ser. A) (1993).

[227] *See, e.g.*, Thorgeir Thorgeirson v. Iceland, 239 Eur. Ct. H.R. (ser. A) (1992); Castells v. Spain, 236 Eur. Ct. H.R. (ser. A) (1992).

[228] *See, e.g.*, *Sunday Times*, 30 Eur. Ct. H.R. (ser. A) ¶ 66.

A. Access to Information: *Johannesburg Principle 11*

Most of the main human rights instruments protect the right "to seek, receive and impart" information as an integral aspect of the right to freedom of expression.[229] Traditionally, the right has been understood to be limited to the right to receive and impart information free from government interference, and not to establish a general right to receive information from the government or others.[230] In recent years, however, developments at the international, regional and national levels suggest the emergence of a positive duty on governments to provide information necessary for the enjoyment of fundamental rights.[231] Johannesburg Principle 11, reflecting this trend, declares the right of everyone to obtain information from public authorities, including information relevant to national security, subject only to the restrictions on freedom of expression discussed above regarding Priinciple 1.[232]

In 1981, the Committee of Ministers of the Council of Europe, the Council's highest political body, issued a Recommendation to the member states on access to information held by public authorities.[233] The Committee called on member states to ensure to "everyone" within their jurisdictions "the right to obtain, on request, information held by the public authorities other than legislative bodies and judicial authorities" and to provide "[e]ffective and appropriate means . . . to ensure access to information."[234] The right to obtain information should be "subject only to such limitations and restrictions as are necessary in a democratic society for the protection of legitimate public interests (such as national security . . .) and for the protection of privacy and other legitimate private interests."[235] The relevant public authority should decide a request for information "within a reasonable time" and should state

---

[229] Universal Declaration, *supra* note 11, art. 19; ICCPR, *supra* note 13, art. 19; American Convention, *supra* note 18, art. 13; European Convention, *supra* note 17, art. 10 (establishes the right to "receive and impart" information); African Charter, *supra* note 19, art. 9 (protects the right of every individual to receive information).

[230] *See, e.g.*, Open Door & Dublin Well Woman v. Ireland, 246-A Eur. Ct. H.R. (ser. A) ¶¶ 71, 72 (1992); Leander v. Sweden, 116 Eur. Ct. H.R. (ser. A) ¶ 74 (1987); *Annual Report of the Inter-American Commission on Human Rights 1980-81,* Inter-Am. Comm'n on Hum. Rts., O.A.S. Doc. OEA/Ser.L/V/II.54, doc. 9, rev. 1 (1981) at 121 ("[F]reedom of information is . . . universal and embodies the collective rights of everyone to receive information without any interference or distortion.").

[231] *See, e.g.*, Gaskin v. United Kingdom, 160 Eur. Ct. H.R. (ser. A) ¶ 49 (1989).

[232] Section II.C., *supra.*

[233] *See* Council of Europe, Committee of Ministers, Recommendation No. R (81) 19 of the Committee of Ministers to Member States on the Access to Information Held by Public Authorities, *adopted* 25 Nov. 1981 by the Committee of Ministers at the 340th meeting of the Ministers' Deputies, 1949-1987, O.J. at 96-97 (1989).

[234] *Id.* at 97.

[235] *Id.*

the reasons for any denial, which should be subject to review.[236] In the application of these principles "every endeavor should . . . be made to achieve the highest degree of access to information."[237]

In a 1982 Declaration, the Committee of Ministers confirmed the above Recommendation.[238] The member states of the Council of Europe declared their commitment to strive to achieve the protection of the right of everyone to seek and receive information from whatever source and to pursue "an open information policy in the public sector, including access to information, in order to enhance the individual's understanding of, and his ability to discuss freely, political, social, economic and cultural matters."[239]

The European Court has recognized the right of individuals to obtain vital personal data held by the government,[240] and the right of the public to information relevant to public health held by a private company that a newspaper obtained and sought to publish.[241] The UN Human Rights Committee and the Inter-American Commission have concluded that governments have a positive duty to protect the rights to life and health, which reasonably should include an obligation to publish information that could assist people in protecting their life or health.[242] The right also arguably applies to information relevant to the environment, including impacts caused by the development of weapons systems, and to information necessary for effective public oversight of government institutions.[243]

These decisions and declarations by the Inter-American and European bodies have been matched by legislative and judicial developments at the national level. According to a 1994 survey of the legal guarantees of access to government-held information in forty-five countries, twelve provided constitutional guarantees, fourteen had a law that stated a presumption of public access to government information (three of which also had constitutional guarantees), and in an additional

---

[236] *Id.*
[237] *Id.* at 96.
[238] Council of Europe, Committee of Ministers, Declaration on the Freedom of Expression and Information, *adopted* 29 Apr. 1982 by the Committee of Ministers at its 70th Session, 1982 O.J. at 214 (1989).
[239] *Id.*
[240] Gaskin v. United Kingdom, 160 Eur. Ct. H.R. (ser. A), ¶ 49 (1989); Leander v. Sweden, 116 Eur. Ct. H.R. (ser. A), ¶ 84 (1987).
[241] Sunday Times v. United Kingdom, 30 Eur. Ct. H.R. (ser. A) ¶¶ 65-66 (1979).
[242] *See, e.g.*, UN Human Rights Committee, General Comment No. 6, 16th Sess., 1982, ¶ 5 (concluding that "the inherent right to life" recognized in Article 6 "requires that states adopt positive measures"); Case 7615, Inter-Am. C.H.R. 24, 33-34, OEA/Ser.L/V/II.66, doc. 10, rev. 1 (1985) (regarding the positive obligation to protect health).
[243] *See, e.g.*, European Union Council Directive 90/313 of 7 June 1990 (requiring greater access to information held by public authorities relevant to the environment). *See also* Stefan Weber, "Environmental Information and the European Convention on Human Rights," 12(5) *Hum. Rts. L.J.* 177, 179 (1991).

nine countries, legislation was under consideration.[244] In a few countries, the public is granted a right of access to information (albeit qualified) held by corporations in addition to government bodies.[245] The presumption of access to government information is strongest in the United States[246] and Northern Europe, and finds solid support throughout western Europe and in India. Hungary was the first of the formerly Soviet Bloc countries to adopt a freedom of information act in 1992, and Latvia adopted one in 1994.[247] Laws granting access to some categories of government information are common throughout Latin America, and access laws are actively being considered in, among other countries, South Africa, Hong Kong, and Japan.[248]

Sweden provides one of the strongest and oldest constitutional protections of the right. The core of the principle, dating from the Constitution of 1766, is that all government documents are public in the absence of a statute which expressly regulates otherwise.[249] This presumption of openness is considered one of the most important foundations of Swedish democracy.[250]

---

[244] *See* Giny Scuttrups, *International Freedom of Information Acts* (The Nat'l Sec. Arc., Oct. 1994). Countries that have constitutional guarantees (explicit or articulated in case law) include Austria, Costa Rica, Germany, Guatemala, India, Mexico, Portugal, South Africa, South Korea, Spain, Sweden, and the United States. Countries that have laws on the books include Australia, Austria, Canada, Colombia, Denmark, Finland, France, Greece, Hungary, Netherlands, New Zealand, Norway, Sweden, and the United States. As of 1994, draft legislation was under consideration in Belgium, Czech Republic, Hong Kong, Iceland, India, Ireland, Japan, Latvia, and the United Kingdom.

[245] For instance, Article 20(4) of the Federal Constitution of Austria reads, in relevant part: "All federal, state and local government bodies and all corporations under public law must give information on affairs within their responsibility unless laws protecting confidentiality provide for non-disclosure . . . ." *See* Walter Berka, "Austria," *in* S. Coliver, ed., *Press Law and Practice: A Comparative Study of Press Freedom in European and Other Democracies* 32, § 14 (Article 19, 1993) [hereinafter *Press Law and Practice*]. Article 20(3) states that the right is restricted by the need to protect official secrets. *Id.* (citing Austrian Const., ch. 2, art. 20(3)).

[246] It is not clear whether the First Amendment of the Constitution guarantees some measure of a right of access to government information. There have been few cases because most claims are made pursuant to the Federal Freedom of Information Act, 5 U.S.C. § 552(b) (1966), adopted in 1966 and amended substantially in 1974. The Act exempts from disclosure information properly classified as secret in the interest of "national defense or foreign policy". When a classification is challenged, the government is required to give detailed reasons supporting the classification, and the courts may examine the classified documents. *See* Paul Hoffman & Kate Martin, "United States," *infra* this volume, at 487 on the Freedom of Information Act.

[247] Information received on 23 Apr. 1996 from the National Democratic Institute of International Affairs (Washington, D.C.) (on file with the author).

[248] *See* Scuttrups, *supra* note 244.

[249] Const. of Sweden (The Freedom of the Press Act) ch. 2: "The Principle of Public Access to Official Records."

[250] Hans-Gunnar Axberger, *Freedom of the Press in Sweden*, *in Press Law and Practice*, *supra* note 245, at 160.

A number of modern constitutions expressly mention the public's right of access to government information and the constitutional courts of several countries have declared that the "public's right to know" is an implicit aspect of freedom of expression or representative democracy or both.[251] For instance, the Supreme Court of India, in a 1975 judgment, offered the following reasoning:

> In a government of responsibility like ours, where all the agents of the public must be responsible for their conduct, there can be but few secrets. The people of this country have a right to know every public act, everything that is done in a public way, by their public functionaries. They are entitled to know the particulars of every public transaction in all its bearing. The right to know, which is derived from the concept of freedom of speech, though not absolute, is a factor which should make one wary when secrecy is claimed for transactions which can, at any rate, have no repercussion on public security.[252]

B. Exceptions to Access: *Johannesburg Principles 12 and 13*

The right to freedom of information is subject to the same restrictions as are applicable to the broader right to freedom of expression.[253] Principles 12 and 13 state two specific limits on permissible government restrictions in addition to those discussed above regarding Principle 1. First, a state may not categorically deny access to all information related to national security but must designate in law those narrow categories the disclosure of which could harm legitimate national interests. Second, the public interest in obtaining the information requested must be given substantial weight in assessing the need for secrecy.

These Principles are based on a small, but nonetheless steadily growing, trend among national courts and legislatures to place constraints on the executive's discretion to classify information as secret. For instance, in 1990 the Constitutional Court of the Republic of Korea ruled that a law that penalized unauthorized

---

[251] *See, e.g.*, Constitutional Court of South Korea, Judgment of 13 May 1991, 90 Honma 133, 3 Honbop Chaepanso Panraejip [Constitution Court Case Report] 234, at 237-38 and 246 (1992), in which the Court referred to the UDHR as well as the Constitution in support of its conclusion that the right to know is "naturally included in the freedom of expression," and that the essence of the right lies in the "people's right to know about information in the possession of the government."

[252] State of Uttar Pradesh v. Raj Narain, A.I.R. 1975 S.C. 865, 884. Accordingly, despite the fact that tensions within the country were growing, the Court ordered the government to disclose documents regarding security arrangements for the Prime Minister's travels within the country so long as they did not endanger his security or public order. *See also Handbook*, *supra* note 24, § 6.2.4 (discussing this case).

[253] *See supra* at 14, Commentary to Principle 1.

collection and intentional or negligent disclosure of military secrets could only be constitutional if the term "military secrets" were defined more narrowly.[254] In a subsequent case, the Constitutional Court concluded that "the boundary of military secrets should be as minimal as necessary to extend the parameters of people's freedom of expression or 'right to know' to a maximum possible degree."[255]

The Dutch Act on Public Access to Information imposes an "active" obligation to transfer information "when it is 'in the interest of a just and democratic government.'"[256] Exemptions are provided for information the disclosure of which would endanger the unity of the Crown or state security, information imparted confidentially to the government by private parties, and "internal" documents (those that include personal views on policy matters).[257] Information may be designated as secret only pursuant to regulations promulgated by the Minister of Home Affairs. These provide that only a small category of officials are authorized to designate information as a state secret; each ministry, in consultation with the Minister of Home Affairs, must specify categories of data that are secret; and these classifications generally are valid only for a limited time.[258] French law imposes similarly strict requirements on the classification of information.[259]

In several countries, the press is granted a more powerful right of access to government information than is the public, based on the "public function" of the press to inform the public about matters of public concern. In Germany, the "*Länder* press laws provide . . . access to government information . . . [and] Federal government information is protected by Article 5 of the Basic Law."[260] Information

---

[254] The Court stated:

> The definition of military secrets is ambiguous and misleading enough to restrict the freedom of information and expression. [Accordingly,] there needs to be a more exact and detailed specification. Everything related to military affairs cannot be defined as a military secret.

Case 89 Honka 113, Constitutional Court, Judgment of Apr. 2, 1990), discussed in *Handbook*, *supra* note 24, at 119. *See generally* Kyu Ho Youm, "South Korea," *infra* this volume, at 424-425, notes 84-85 and accompanying text.

[255] Kyu Ho Youm, "Press Freedom and Judicial Review in South Korea," 30 *Stan. J. Int'l L.* 1, 14 (1994) (quoting the case reviewing the Military Secrets Protection Act, Judgment of Feb. 25, 1992, 89 Honka 104, which was also reprinted in *Naewoe Popyul News* [Domestic and Foreign Legal News] July 15,1992, at 5).

[256] Francine van Lenthe & Ineke Boerefijn, "Press Law in the Netherlands," *in Press Law and Practice, supra* note 245, at 98 § 14.1 (quoting the Netherlands' Act on Public Access to Information, Stb. 1991, 703 *entered into force* May 1, 1992).

[257] *See id.* (discussing, in particular, Articles 10 and 11 of the Act on Public Access to Information).

[258] *See id.* § 14.2.

[259] Penal Code art. 413-9 and the Decree of May 12, 1981, discussed in Roger Errera, "France," *infra* this volume, at 286-287.

[260] *See* Ulrich Karpen, "Press Law in Germany," *in Press Law and Practice*, *supra* note 245, at 78 § 14.

may be refused "only if disclosure would interfere with judicial proceedings; 'the rules of secrecy stand in the way'; an overriding public or private interest would be infringed; or the amount of information requested is excessive."[261] "The press may apply to the courts for a ruling in the event of a refusal."[262]

The International Criminal Tribunal for the former Yugoslavia set a precedent concerning government-held information needed by the UN for a war crimes prosecution. The Tribunal ruled, in October 1997, that the Government of Croatia could not refuse to provide information on national security grounds that the Tribunal's prosecutor had subpoenaed in a case against a Bosnian Croat general. The Appeals Chamber of the Court deemed that the validity of such claims were to be examined during *in camera, ex parte* proceedings.[263]

C. Right to Review on the Merits of Denial of Information: *Johannesburg Principle 14*

Principle 14 states that individuals must be able to seek review of a government's refusal to release information on national security grounds from an authority independent of the agency that denied the request, and that the reviewing authority must have the right to examine the information withheld. In addition, individuals must be able to seek some form of judicial review of the legality of any such denial. The Principle is crucial; however broadly stated may be the right of access to government information, the ability of people actually to obtain information is only as strong as their right to have denials of such information reviewed by an independent authority.

This Principle finds support in the law and jurisprudence of several countries, although it offers stronger protection than most of them in that it directs courts to review the merits of a denial of information including, where necessary, to examine the withheld information. It also affords stronger protection than the European Court of Human Rights, which requires review by an administrative authority independent of the agency that denied access, but does not require judicial review.[264]

In the *Leander* case, the European Court considered the application of a person who sought access to information in a police register which, allegedly,

---

[261] *See id.*
[262] *See id.*
[263] *The Prosecutor of the Tribunal v. Blaskic*, ruling of the Appeals Chamber, Oct. 29, 1997, on the Government of Croatia's appeal against the decision of Trial Chamber II affirming the Tribunal's power to issue subpoenas duces tecum.
[264] *See* Leander v. Sweden, 116 Eur. Ct. H.R. (ser. A) ¶ 84 (1987); Gaskin v. United Kingdom, 160 Eur. Ct. H.R. (ser. A) ¶ 49 (1989).

rendered him unfit for a civil service job that required a security clearance.[265] The Government refused to disclose the information on national security grounds. The European Court stated that, although it had concluded in a previous case that there is no right to a civil service job, "in view of the risk that a system of secret surveillance for the protection of national security poses of undermining or even destroying democracy on the ground of defending it, the Court must be satisfied that there exist adequate and effective guarantees against abuse."[266] Accordingly, the applicant was entitled to "a remedy that is as effective as can be, having regard to the restricted scope for recourse inherent in any system of secret surveillance for the protection of national security."[267] The Court decided that the system of administrative review at issue in the case was adequate.[268]

In several countries, refusal of information is subject to administrative review either by a body specially constituted to oversee compliance with the disclosure laws or else by a general administrative body.[269] Decisions of these bodies may then be appealed to the courts.[270] In a number of countries, an administrative

---

[265] *See Leander*, 116 Eur. Ct. H.R.

[266] *Id.* ¶ 60.

[267] *Id.* ¶ 84.

[268] *See id.* ¶¶ 83-84; *see also* Gaskin v. United Kingdom, 160 Eur. Ct. H.R. (ser. A) ¶ 49 (1989). In *Gaskin*, the European Court ruled that the UK government had not violated the applicant's right to freedom of information by refusing to let him see his personal data files on the ground that they contained information given in confidence, but the court did hold that the UK government had violated the applicant's right to private and family life by failing to establish an authority to decide on requests for information that was independent of the agency that held the information. *See id.* ¶ 49.

[269] *See generally* Sandra Coliver, "Comparative Analysis of Press Law in European and Other Democracies," *in Press Law and Practice, supra* note 245, at 255:

> In France, a special commission, the *Commission d'acces aux documents administratifs* (CADA) examines complaints and difficulties concerning access. Most problems are resolved at this level. An applicant dissatisfied with CADA's decision may seek review by an administrative court. In Sweden, a Justice Ombudsman, appointed by the Parliament, supervises disclosure and tries to resolve disputes. Australia allows appeals to an ombudsman or an administrative appeals tribunal, and Canada allows appeals to a special commissioner. However, only the Australian tribunal can order disclosure; the ombudsman and commissioner are limited to recommendations. In the US, an appeal may be made to the head of the agency which denied the request.

Id. at 276 § 14.3.

[270] *Id.* at 275. For example, in Spain, individuals may challenge the "administrative classification of a matter as secret or reserved" as a violation of the constitutionally guaranteed right to freedom of information "through a speedy and preferential procedure before the ordinary courts, and from there to the Constitutional Court via a recourse *de amparo*." Blanca Rodriguez Ruiz, "Freedom of the Press in Spain," *in Press Law and Practice, supra* note 245, at 131, 144 (citing Law 48/78, art. 48.1, Law 17 July 1958 "de Procedimiento Administrativo"

body that refuses to grant disclosure must specify its reasons in writing, and must inform the applicant of the right to appeal.[271] Courts in most countries, however, will reverse a decision of an administrative body only if it is based on an incorrect application of the law (rather than an incorrect weighing of the facts) or if, for other reasons, it is patently unreasonable.

A notable exception is the United States. A 1974 amendment to its Freedom of Information Act (FOIA) provides that (a) courts should have the final say as to whether documents are properly classified and therefore exempt from disclosure, and (b) the government has the burden of proving that information is exempt from disclosure.[272] To meet that burden, the government must submit sworn statements by appropriate officials explaining with some particularity why the disclosure of each item of classified information would pose a threat to national security. Courts are authorized to review the documents themselves and to decide on the merits whether the government's classification was substantively correct.[273] Similarly, in Canadian deportation hearings, including where exclusion is sought on grounds of a national security threat, judges are entitled to review all of the evidence and the alien is entitled to a summary of the evidence.[274]

In France, courts may not challenge an administrative decision to classify a document as secret.[275] However, if the Administration refuses to disclose a document on national security grounds that has not been classified, the applicant may request review by an independent commission established for that purpose; one of the Commission's members, after receiving a security clearance, must be able to see the document.[276]

(Law of Administrative Procedures)). *See also* David Flint, "Australia," *in Press Law and Practice, supra* note 245, at 1, 14; Jan Bauer, "Canada," *in Press Law and Practice, supra* note 245, at 38, 48; Roger Errera, "France," *in Press Law and Practice, supra* note 245, at 57, 69 (explaining that a dissatisfied seeker of information may petition the local administrative court pursuant to the *recours pour exces de pouvoir*); Steingrim Wolland, "Norway," *in Press Law and Practice, supra* note 245, at 116, 124; Hans-Gunnar Axberger, "Sweden," *in Press Law and Practice, supra* note 245, at 150, 160.

[271] Examples include Australia, France, Norway, and Sweden. *See* Coliver, *supra* note 268, at 257 § 14.3; Errera, "France," infra this volume, at 272.

[272] *See* 5 U.S.C. § 552(a)(4)(B) (1994).

[273] *See* Hoffman & Martin, "United States," *infra* this volume, at 487-493.

[274] *Canadian Immigration Act 1976*, as amended by *the Immigration Act* 1988.

[275] Errera, "France," *infra* this volume, at 287.

[276] Errera, *supra*, at 271.

D. No Punishment for Disclosure of Secret Information in the Public Interest

1. The General Rule: *Johannesburg Principle 15*

In a growing number of countries that recognize the importance to a democracy of access to government information, journalists and other members of the media are not liable for publishing government information, even if classified, so long as the disclosure did not risk serious damage to national security or, in some countries, international relations.[277] In several countries, the fact that disclosure was in the public interest provides a defense even if the disclosure risked, but did not actually cause, serious damage. There is a developing trend to refrain from punishing or even prosecuting the media unless disclosure actually harmed a legitimate national security interest and the harm resulting from the disclosure outweighed the public interest in knowing the information. Johannesburg Principle 15 reflects this trend and goes one step further by extending the protection to all persons (not merely the press), other than those who received the secret information in the course of government service. (The standard applicable to government servants is set forth in Principle 16, discussed below.) The extension is based on the notion that researchers who discover information of public interest should have the same right as the press to publish the information.

In the United States, the media have not, in recent memory, been held liable for publishing secret information. Several narrowly drawn laws criminalize the release of certain categories of information by people who have come into possession of the information by virtue of their government service; however, only one, the Intelligence Identities Protection Act, expressly makes it a crime to publish such information.[278] Even when people in government service have been convicted for "leaking" information, the media publishers have not been prosecuted.[279]

---

[277] For instance, in the United Kingdom, even where there is an enforceable duty of confidence, the courts will not apply it to information the disclosure of which would be in the public interest. *See* British Steel v. Granada TV, 3 W.L.R. 780 (House of Lords 1980). *See generally* Y. Cripps, *The Legal Implications of Disclosure in the Public Interest* (2d ed. 1994).

[278] Intelligence Identities Protection Act, 50 U.S.C. § 421 (1982). The Act penalizes the publication of the names of intelligence agents when publication is part of a pattern of activities intended to expose covert agents and is done with knowledge that such activities would impair intelligence activities. See Hoffman & Martin, "United States," *infra* this volume, at 494, re criminal penalties for public disclosure.

[279] *See id.*

In Austria,[280] Germany,[281] the Netherlands,[282] and Sweden,[283] journalists and editors are not subject to prosecution for publishing official secrets, unless the disclosure risked severe damage to national defense or international relations. The courts make the determination as to whether a disclosure risked, or was likely to risk, such damage; the administrative classification of information as "secret" is not decisive.[284] The courts tend to scrutinize government claims of secrecy with considerable independence. In Austria, "within the last decades, only a very few charges have been filed against the mass media."[285] In Sweden, only one case in recent years resulted in prison terms: a member of the Investigation Bureau and two journalists received sentences from nine months to one year for publishing secret information about the security services.[286]

In Germany, courts will scrutinize whether published information should have been labeled secret in the first place, so long as the information was not an "absolute secret."[287] Journalists will not be punished if the information should not have been labeled secret. "Absolute secrets" include facts, objects, or information that are accessible only to a limited number of persons and must be kept secret from foreign powers to avert serious damage to the external security of the Federal Republic.[288] Moreover, the Federal Constitutional Court (FCC) has ruled that publication of secret information may be excused if the interest in disclosure was strong and outweighed the interest in keeping the information from the public.[289] This constitutional doctrine has been codified in various statutes.[290]

Of considerable interest is the policy of the European Union to require states applying for membership to provide a defense in their criminal law for

---

[280] *See* Walter Berka, "Press Freedom in Austria," *in Press Law and Practice*, *supra* note 245, at 22 § 14 (discussing section 255 of the Austrian Criminal Code).
[281] *See* Karpen, "Germany," *infra* this volume, at 296.
[282] *See* van Lenthe & Boerefijn, *supra* note 256, at 98 § 14.1.
[283] *See* Const. of Sweden (The Freedom of the Press Act) ch. 7, art. 3, *discussed in* Hans-Gunnar Axberger, "Freedom of the Press in Sweden," *in Press Law and Practice*, *supra* note 245, at 150 § 14.2 (discussing also the Secrecy Act, chap. 16, art. 1).
[284] *See, e.g.*, van Lenthe & Boerefijn, *supra* note 256, § 14.2 (citing HR May 14, 1974).
[285] Berka, *supra* note 245, at 22 § 14.
[286] *See* Axberger, *supra* note 250, at 150 §§ 14.2, 18.
[287] *See* Karpen, "Germany," *infra* this volume, at 296; C. Starck, *Archiv fur Presserecht* 177 (1978).
[288] *See* § 93 StPO (German Criminal Code).
[289] *See* 61 FCC 1, 11 (1982) (Christlich Soziale Union).
[290] *See* Karpen, "Germany," *infra* this volume, at 296. He notes two provisions of the Criminal Code in particular: § 93(2) StPO, which states that "[f]acts which are in contradiction to the free democratic order or which are kept secret from treaty partners in violation of arms limitation agreements are not state secrets," *id.*; and § 97 B, which states that publication of a genuine secret by one who, however erroneously, believed that the information was not entitled to be kept secret, is not a crime if the person acted with the intent to stop an activity that he believed to be illegal. *Id.*

journalists who publish military or state secrets in order to reveal irregularities, provided the disclosure does not harm the state. In November 1997, the Slovenian Justice Minister announced his government's intention to amend the Criminal Code in response to the EU's request.[291]

In several countries, including Australia, Germany, and Norway, the fact that disclosure serves the public interest provides a defense for publication of information collected by illegal means.[292]

The European Court, in a 1995 judgment, indicated that it might not follow this liberal trend.[293] In dictum, it suggested that it might find unobjectionable the prosecution of two journalists who published classified information.[294] However, even in such a case, the Court might well weigh the public's interest in the information; in its landmark *Sunday Times* judgment, it made clear that, in assessing whether an interference with freedom of information was "necessary in a democratic society," it would consider "any public interest aspect of the case."[295]

2. Information Obtained through Government Service: *Johannesburg Principle 16*

While there is a cognizable trend among democracies not to punish publication of classified information so long as the information does not endanger national security, support for a norm protecting government employees who "leak" such information is considerably weaker.

Nonetheless, Johannesburg Principle 16 calls for protection for people who disclose information learned in the course of government service, so long as "the public interest in knowing the information outweighs the harm from disclosure." This Principle provides less protection for government servants than Principle 15 provides for the press and members of the general public: persons engaged in government service are entitled to protection *only* if there is a public interest in the information they disclosed, whereas the press and general public are also entitled to

---

[291] Reuters, 13 Nov. 97, "Slovenia to liberalise journalist legislation".

[292] *See* David Flint, "Press Law in Australia," *in Press Law and Practice*, *supra* note 245, at 1 § 14; Karpen, *supra* note 261, at 78 § 14; Steingrim Wolland, "Press Law in Norway," *in Press Law and Practice*, *supra* note 245, at 116 § 14 ("The law does not explicitly permit disclosure of information of legitimate public interest, but the public interest principle is likely to be taken into consideration both by prosecutors when deciding whether to file charges as well as by judges when formulating their opinions.").

[293] *See* Vereniging Weekblad Bluf! v. Netherlands, 306-A Eur. Ct. H.R. (ser. A) ¶¶ 39-46 (1995) (ruling that seizure of a publication containing classified information that had already been distributed in limited numbers violated the European Convention).

[294] *See id.* ¶ 45; *see also* Hadjianastassiou v. Greece, 252 Eur. Ct. H.R. (ser. A) ¶¶ 39, 44-47 (1992) (noting that members of the armed forces have certain "duties" and "responsibilities" and, accordingly, their freedom to impart information is more limited than private individuals).

[295] Sunday Times v. United Kingdom, 2 Eur. Ct. H.R. (ser. A) ¶ 65 (1979).

protection if the disclosure does not actually, and is unlikely, to harm a legitimate national security interest.

Principle 16 is premised on the recognition that the public often has a particularly strong interest in knowing about the information that governments seek to keep secret on bogus national security grounds. Clearly, there is some information that the public has no interest in knowing (*e.g*, particulars about the movement of troops, weapons systems, and military capacity). However, there have been few instances anywhere in the world in recent memory where information disclosed by a government servant damaged a vital state interest. To the contrary, most information that governments have sought to suppress disclosed government ineptitude or wrongdoing, sometimes on a grand scale. One of the most notorious cases was Daniel Ellsberg's disclosure that the US government had lied to the US Congress and the American people about its bombing of Cambodia.[296] More recent cases abound.[297]

When governments commit violations of human rights or humanitarian law, disclosure by government servants (the only people who usually have access to information about the violations) can and has in many situations led to the stopping of the violations. Moreover, disclosures stimulate open debate which in turn generally results in the adoption of better decisions and policies.[298] Principle 16 reflects the view that human rights and indeed national security are better protected

---

[296] Russo v. Byrne, 409 U.S. 1219 (1972).

[297] For instance, in 1995, US Congressman Robert Torricelli published a letter to President Clinton informing him that the CIA had known for years that one of its paid informants in Guatemala had ordered the killings of an American citizen and a guerilla leader married to Jennifer Harbury, an American lawyer. Tim Weiner, "Guatemalan Agent of CIA Tied to Killing of American," *N.Y. Times*, Mar. 23, 1995, at 1. Because Torricelli had obtained the information by virtue of his position on the House Intelligence Committee, he was investigated for possible violation of the House oath not to disclose classified information. He was cleared of the charge on the ground that publication of the information served the public interest. Adam Clymer, "Congressman Is Cleared of Breaking Oath," *N.Y. Times*, July 13, 1995, at 9. The CIA station chief in Guatemala was removed from his post and an investigation was launched into CIA violations of a 1980 law that requires the CIA to keep Congress "fully and currently informed" about its activities. *See* Tim Weiner, "More is Told About CIA in Guatemala," *N.Y. Times*, Apr. 25, 1995, at 6; Tim Weiner, "Senators Seek Legal Inquiry on CIA in Guatemala," *N.Y. Times*, Sept. 30, 1995, at 5. In February 1996, Alexander Nikitin, a retired Russian submarine captain, was arrested on charges of treason and disclosing state secrets based on a book he was writing for a Norwegian non-governmental organization about the dangers of nuclear waste contamination caused by Russia's Northern fleet. He was held in prison for a year and, as of October 1997, continued to face charges that carried penalties of up to 15 years' imprisonment. Amnesty International, "Urgent Action Appeal", Feb. 9, 1996; Bellona Foundation, "The Nikitin Case", Oct. 1997.

[298] Paul G. Chevigny, "Information, the Executive and the Politics of Information," in Shimon Shetreet, ed., *Free Speech and National Security* (1990), at 138.

by giving government servants immunity for disclosing information in the public interest than by permitting governments to demand of them complete secrecy.[299]

Principle 16 finds support in German law,[300] although it offers stronger protection by providing that people who disclose information of substantial public interest learned in the course of government service may not be dismissed from their posts or indeed subjected to *any* detriment, whereas German law protects people in such positions only from criminal prosecution. Section 97B of Germany's Criminal Code provides that publication of a genuine secret by one who, however erroneously, believed that the information was not entitled to be kept secret, is not a crime if the person acted with the intent to stop an activity that he or she believed to be illegal.[301]

Principle 16 also finds a degree of support in US law. A US statute protects federal employees who disclose information of government wrongdoing confidentially to members of Congress or to the Inspector General of the relevant agency.[302] Although statutory protection does not extend to public disclosures, "the Supreme Court has held that the First Amendment protects government employees' speech about matters of public concern in circumstances where the free speech interests outweigh the government's interest in promoting an efficient workforce."[303] The reasoning of those cases would seem to apply as well to information in the public interest relevant to national security. However, government employees are prohibited from disclosing classified information as a condition of their employment and may be dismissed for doing so.[304] They may also be subject to criminal penalties if they disclose the names of intelligence agents when done with "reason to believe that such disclosure would impair the US government's foreign intelligence activities."[305]

More problematically, government employees may be subject to criminal penalties under the general espionage statute[306] and the theft of government property

---

[299] For an excellent discussion of this strong form of the public's right of access to government information, see Mary M. Cheh, "Judicial Supervision of Executive Secrecy: Rethinking Freedom of Expression for Government Employees and the Public Right of Access to Government Information," 69 *Cornell L. Rev.* 690, 720-34 (1984) (volume dedicated to a symposium on National Security and Civil Liberties).

[300] *See* Ulrich Karpen, "Germany," *infra* this volume, at 296.

[301] *See id.*, at 297.

[302] *See* 5 U.S.C. § 2302.

[303] Nadine Strossen, "Press Freedom in the United States," *in Press Law and Practice, supra* note 245, § 14.4 (citing in particular Connick v. Myers, 461 U.S. 138 (1983) and Pickering v. Board of Educ., 391 U.S. 563 (1968)).

[304] Hoffman and Martin, *infra* this volume, at 493, re civil and administrative penalties for public disclosure of information by government employees.

[305] *See id.* § 14.3.

[306] *See* 18 U.S.C. § 793.

statute,[307] which have been used on occasion as surrogates for an Official Secrets Act.[308] The first government contractor prosecuted under the general espionage law for leaking information of public interest was Daniel Ellsberg, but the prosecution was dismissed for government misconduct.[309] The first government servant convicted under the law was a Navy employee, prosecuted by President Reagan's Justice Department for leaking a classified photograph of a Russian aircraft carrier to *Jane's Defence Weekly*.[310] The employee was convicted despite demonstrating that publication of the photograph did not reveal any secret information and did not harm the national security of the United States. The government has since successfully prosecuted a handful of government officials.[311]

E. Information in the Public Domain: *Johannesburg Principle 17*

Principle 17 states that, once information has been published, its further re-publication cannot be prevented, even if the initial disclosure was unlawful. The Principle is based on the notion that the government loses whatever interest it had in keeping information secret once the information has been made available to some portion of the public.

The Principle reflects the holding of the European Court in the *Spycatcher* cases.[312] These twin cases followed publication by a number of U.K. newspapers of extracts from *Spycatcher*, the unauthorized memoirs of a retired member of the British security service. The Crown obtained permanent injunctions restraining publication of any further Spycatcher material, which remained in force even after the book had been pubished in the United States. The Court concluded that restraint prior to publication in the U.S. lay within the Government's margin of appreciation regarding measures necessary to protect national security and its role as a litigant in pending litigation. However, following U.S. publication, the Government's interest in promoting "the efficiency and reputation of the Security Service" was overridden by the public's right to know.[313] The Court applied similar reasoning in ruling that the Dutch Government had exceeded its margin of appreciation when it enjoined

---

[307] *See* 18 U.S.C. § 641.
[308] *See* Hoffman & Martin, *infra* this volume, at 494, re criminal penalties.
[309] *See* Russo v. Byrne, 409 U.S. 1219 (1972) (granting a stay against the prosecution).
[310] *See* United States v. Morison, 844 F.2d 1057 (4th Cir. 1988), *cert. denied*, Morison v. United States, 488 U.S. 908 (1988).
[311] *See* Hoffman & Martin, *supra* note 308.
[312] The Observer and Guardian v. UK and The Sunday Times v. UK (No. 2), *supra* note 43, Judgments of November 26, 1991, Series A, No. 216 and 217, 216 Eur. Ct. H. R. (ser. A), para. 69 (1991).
[313] *Id.* at paras. 66-70 (Observer and Guardian), and paras. 52-56 (The Sunday Times (No.2)).

further publication of a 6-year old confidential report of the internal security service.[314] Several national courts have reached similar results.[315]

F. Protection of Journalists' Sources: *Johannesburg Principle 18*

Principle 18 states that protection of national security may not be used as a reason to compel a journalist to reveal a confidential source. This Principle reflects the law of Austria and France, and the reasoning of Norway's Supreme Court. Courts of several other countries, as well as the European Court of Human Rights, have recognized the crucial need for the press to be able to protect the confidentiality of its sources if it is to fulfill effectively its public function as a watchdog of government.

In Austria and France, a journalist may not be compelled to reveal the source of information, even concerning matters relevant to national or state security, if the information was received in confidence in the course of his or her journalistic activity.[316]

The Supreme Court of Norway established the principle that "the more important the interest violated, the more important it will be to protect the sources."[317] A Parliamentary oversight body sought to compel the authors of a book to reveal their source of information about connections between the Norwegian Labour party and the intelligence agency. In rejecting the petition of the Parliamentary body, the Supreme Court reasoned: "It must be assumed that a broad protection of sources will lead to more revelations of hidden matters than if the protection is limited or not given at all."[318]

In Germany, Sweden, and the majority of states of the United States, a journalist may not be compelled to reveal the source of information concerning matters relevant to national or state security unless publication of the information actually harmed a legitimate security interest, the party seeking the information convincingly establishes that the identity of the source is necessary to prove a central claim in a court proceeding, and there is no alternative way to obtain the necessary

---

314 *Vereniging Weekblad Bluf! v. Netherlands*, Judgment of 9 Feb. 1995, Series A, No. 306-A.
315 *See, e.g., Lord Advocate v. The Scotsman Publications and Ors* [House of Lords] AC (1990) 812 (the "Scottish *Spycatcher* case").
316 *See* Berka, *supra* note 245, § 19; Roger Errera, "Press Law in France," *in Press Law and Practice, supra* note 245, at 57 § 19 (citing Article 109(2), added to the French Code of Criminal Procedure by the Act of Jan. 4, 1993, which reads: "Any journalist who appears as a witness concerning information gathered by him in the course of his journalistic activity is free not to disclose its source").
317 Kontrolluvalget v. Johansen [1992] 1 L.N.R. 39, *quoted in* Steingrim Wolland, "Press Law in Norway," *in Press Law and Practice, supra* note 245, at 116 § 19.
318 *Id.*

information.[319] This right to refuse in turn provides considerable protection for public sector employees who "blow the whistle" on governmental misconduct.

Germany's Federal Constitutional Court (FCC) reasoned that the Basic Law's constitutional guarantee of press freedom permits journalists to protect confidential sources if the interest in promoting press freedom is found to outweigh the interest in the enforcement of justice.[320] The constitutional right to protect confidential sources is intended primarily to protect the role of a free press in controlling government abuse.[321]

The Sapporo District Court of Japan, sustained by the appellate courts, held that journalists may refuse to divulge, even to a court, information about a source as "an occupational secret" unless the information is necessary for a fair trial.[322] The High Court of Lagos State (Nigeria) ruled that protection of the journalistic privilege must be all the stronger where the published information concerns a matter of general public interest.[323]

The European Court concluded that the UK authorities violated the free expression rights of a journalist when they ordered him to reveal the confidential source of a story which, if published, could have damaged a private company's business.[324] The Court reasoned:

> Protection of journalistic sources is one of the basic conditions for press freedom, as is reflected in the laws and the professional codes of conduct in a number of Contracting States and is affirmed in

---

[319] *See* Karpen, *supra* note 260, at 92-93; Axberger, *supra* note 250, at 164; Strossen, *supra* note 303, at 212-13.

[320] *See* 64 FCC 108 (1983).

[321] *See id.* In this case, the FCC rejected the journalist's effort to protect the confidentiality of the source of an advertisement because the matter did not touch public affairs at all.

[322] Lawrence W. Beer, "Freedom of Expression: The Continuing Revolution," 53 *L. & Contemp. Probs.*, Spring 1990, at 39, 59 (discussing Sasaki v. The Hokkaido News, Inc., 930 Hanrei Jihô 44 (Sapporo D. Ct., May 30, 1979) (interpreting Article 281 of the Code of Civil Procedure), *aff'd* 937 Hanrei Jihô 16 (Sapporo H. Ct., Aug. 31, 1979), *aff'd* 30 Minshû 403 (Sup. Ct., Mar. 8, 1980).

[323] *See* Oyegbemi v. Attorney-General of the Federation and Others [1982] FNLR (Federation of Nigeria Law Reports) 192. The Court stated:

> [W]hen a newspaper has investigated a matter of general public interest or concern (such as it ought to make known to the public), the publication of an article upon the matter is so much in the public interest that the newspaper ought not to be restrained or "interfered" with by any person or authority, solely on the ground that the information in the article originated in confidence. . . . Nor should a newspaper be compelled (except in grave and exceptional circumstances . . .) to disclose the source of the information.

Id. at 208.

[324] *See* Goodwin v. United Kingdom, 7 Eur. Ct. H.R. App. 16/1994/463/544, 22 EHRR 123, holding ¶¶ 1-3.

> several international instruments on journalistic freedoms . . . Without such protection, sources may be deterred from assisting the press in informing the public on matters of public interest. As a result, the vital watchdog role of the press may be undermined and the ability of the press to provide accurate and reliable information may be adversely affected. Having regard to the importance of the protection of journalistic sources for press freedom in a democratic society and the potentially chilling effect an order of source disclosure has on the exercise of that freedom, such a measure cannot be compatible with . . . the Convention unless it is justified by an overriding requirement in the public interest.[325]

The Court concluded that the UK had not established such an overriding interest, particularly given that the company had already obtained an injunction against publication of the damaging information.[326]

G. Access to Restricted Areas: *Johannesburg Principle 19*

Principle 19 states that any restrictions on the free flow of information should not be of such a nature as to thwart the purposes of humanitarian law. In particular, governments may not prevent journalists from entering into conflict zones, except where their presence would pose a clear risk to the safety of others. Governments may not harass journalists found within or seeking entry into conflict zones, such as by confiscating their equipment, or interrogating or detaining them. This Principle finds solid support in the four Geneva Conventions of 1949, as well as in statements of UN rapporteurs and the UN Secretary General.

Pursuant to Article 1 of the four Geneva Conventions, the High Contracting Parties undertake not merely to respect those conventions but also to ensure that all other High Contracting Parties respect them in all circumstances.[327]

---

[325] *Id.* at 39.

[326] *See id.* at ¶ 46.

[327] *See* Geneva Convention for the Amelioration of the Condition of the Wounded and Sick in Armed Forces in the Field (Geneva I), art. 1, adopted Aug. 12, 1949, 6 U.S.T. 3114, T.I.A.S. No. 3362, 75 U.N.T.S. 31, (*entered into force* Oct. 21, 1950) (*entered into force for U.S.* Feb. 2, 1956); Geneva Convention for the Amelioration of the Condition of Wounded, Sick and Shipwrecked Members of Armed Forces at Sea (Geneva II), art. 1, *opened for signature* Aug. 12, 1949, 6 U.S.T. 3217, T.I.A.S. No. 3363, 75 U.N.T.S. 85 (*entered into force* Oct. 21, 1950)(*entered into force for U.S.* Feb. 2, 1956); Geneva Convention Relative to the Protection of Civilian Persons in Time of War (Geneva IV), art. 1, *adopted* Aug. 12, 1948, 6 U.S.T. 3516, T.I.A.S. No. 3365, 75 U.N.T.S. 287 (*entered into force* Oct. 21, 1950) (*entered into force for U.S.* Feb. 2, 1956); Geneva Convention Relative to the Treatment of Prisoners of War (Geneva III), art. 1, *adopted* Aug. 12, 1949, 6 U.S.T. 3316, T.I.A.S. No. 3364, 75 U.N.T.S. 135 (*entered into*

These obligations include, for example, respect for various measures to protect the civilian populations and in particular the prohibition of indiscriminate attacks.[328] Clearly, each Contracting Party needs information if it is to satisfy itself that other parties are indeed respecting the Conventions.[329] Moreover, as the two UN Rapporteurs on Freedom of Expression recognized, informed public opinion is one of the most effective means of preventing violations of international norms.[330] For these reasons, any restrictions that affect the free flow of information during wartime cannot be such as to block efforts to monitor compliance with, or publicize violations of, humanitarian law obligations by the High Contracting Parties.[331]

Once a military operation is over, restrictions on freedom of expression and information about the operation may be maintained only if necessary to protect the security of troops and civilians.[332] There can be no justification for a government authority to deny journalists access to, for example, prisoner-of-war camps, shelters and hospitals when there no longer is any risk to their lives.[333] Concern not to disclose strategic information to the enemy is justifiable, but can only be temporary.

In 1994, when UN Secretary-General Kofi A. Annan was Under-Secretary General for Peacekeeping Operations, he offered a compelling rationale for his policy of allowing journalists access to areas of recent conflict:

> This new policy recognizes the need for assisting journalists in obtaining access to areas of conflict. Peacekeeping operations in particular depend for their support on widespread public awareness of the conflicts they have been deployed to resolve, and we are committed to doing everything we can to facilitate the work of the media to this end.[334]

In several armed conflict situations, coverage by journalists has helped generate support for peacekeeping operations or other forms of humanitarian intervention and, indeed, journalists have uncovered or drawn attention to mass violations of human rights and humanitarian law.[335] Conversely, where journalists

---

force Oct. 21, 1950) (*entered into force for U.S.* Feb. 2, 1956).

[328] *See id.* at 114.

[329] *See Update of the Preliminary Report Prepared for the UN Sub-Commission on Prevention of Discrimination and Protection of Minorities*, D. Türk & L. Joinet, ¶¶ 114-15, UN Doc. E/CN.4/Sub.2/1991/9 (1991).

[330] *See id.* at 134.

[331] *See id.* at 131.

[332] *See id.* at 127.

[333] *See id.* at 128.

[334] Committee to Protect Journalists, *U.N. to Allow Journalists on Aircraft to Sarajevo* (Press Release: New York, Dec. 21, 1994).

[335] Roy Gutman of Newsday was the first journalist, on July 3, 1992, to enter one of the transit camps run by Bosnian Serbs near Banja Luka and report on the atrocities he witnessed. As stated by two chroniclers of the Yugoslav conflict, "his detailed series of interviews blaz[ed] a trail that would rouse international public opinion about the nature of Bosnia's war." Laura

have been excluded, either by government orders or by random violence, reporting has dropped and international scrutiny, even of massive violations, has waned.[336]

V. Rule of Law and Other Matters

Part IV of the Johannesburg Principles addresses various procedural protections for freedom of expression. These become particularly important in the context of prosecutions for security-related offenses owing to the greater likelihood in such cases of government interference with judicial independence, and the increased powers of governments to withhold "sensitive" information from the courts thus further reducing their ability to assess independently the merits of the government's claims. A court that is reluctant to second-guess the government's asserted need to impose restrictions in the name of national security may, nevertheless, be willing to insist that it must at least comply with internationally recognized due process requirements.

The first three parts of the Principles discuss restrictions on freedom of expression and access to information imposed in the interest of national security, and thus define the term narrowly. Part IV, in contrast, addresses procedural protections against abuse of the concept. Thus, its scope is wider, encompassing prosecutions for all "security-related crimes" defined by Principle 20 to comprise acts or omissions "which the government claims must be punished in order to protect national security or a closely related interest." This wider definition ensures that targets of government

---

Silber & Alan Little, *The Death of Yugoslavia: a Companion to the BBC Television Series* 274 (1995). Penny Marshall of ITN and Ed Vulliamy of the Guardian were the first journalists to enter the infamous Omarska camp. The international community had information about the camps beginning in May but took no action until the media captured the horrors on film. The chain of events "reveal[ed] a recurring characteristic of the foreign policy-making of the main western powers with regard to Bosnia: that it was driven substantially by television coverage." *Id.* at 278.

[336] According to the Committee to Protect Journalists, the murders in 1993 by an angry mob of four reporters and photographers working for Western media in Somalia "brought to a halt the on-going coverage of the conflict." Committee to Protect Journalists, *Attacks on the Press in 1993*, at 36 (1994). In Algeria, a campaign of terror against journalists launched by Islamic extremists in May 1993 (including the murders of at least fifty-two journalists through the end of 1995), has been effective in minimizing international attention to the widespread human rights abuses committed there. *See* Committee to Protect Journalists, *supra* note 38, at 9. "The 'blackout,' as many editors call it, has eclipsed the profile of a war that is victimizing an increasing number of innocent civilians." Youssef Ibrahim, "Algeria is Too Risky for Press: Civil War's Extent and Horror Little Known," *Int'l Herald Trib.*, Dec. 29, 1994. Laurent Kabila, the new president of the Democratic Republic of the Congo, has been able to conceal evidence of massacres in eastern Congo by refusing access to journalists as well as UN investigators. Farhan Haq, "Congo: Human Rights Groups Say Kinshasa Hiding Massacre Evidence," *Inter Press Service*, Oct. 9, 1997.

repression do not lose the protections of this Part merely because a government's prosecution does not in fact implicate legitimate national security concerns.

A. General Rule of Law Protections: *Johannesburg Principles 20-22*

Principle 20 states the general principle that persons accused of security-related crimes involving expression or information are entitled to all of the rule of law protections that are part of international law, and lists the most important ones. In particular, it emphasizes that a person convicted of a security-related crime has the right to have the conviction reviewed by a court or tribunal which is independent of the lower tribunal as well as the government and which is authorized to review decisions on law for error and decisions on facts for substantial evidence. This standard of review is more demanding than that required by international or regional law[337]; it was adopted by the Johannesburg drafters for the same reasons they endorsed, in Principle 14, an exacting standard of review of denials by the government of requests for information.

Principle 21 emphasizes that persons accused of security-related crimes are entitled to apply for all available remedies, including *habeas corpus* or *amparo*, even during public emergencies.

Principle 22 sets forth particular safeguards for the independence of the judiciary, in recognition of the fact that no cases place greater pressure on judicial independence than those that raise claims of national or state security. Principle 22 amplifies that where there has been a pattern of governmental interference with the independence of the judiciary, the trial of persons accused of security crimes by judges without security of tenure constitutes a prima facie violation of the right to be tried by an independent tribunal.[338] The Principle notes that trial by jury can be an effective means of ensuring a measure of independence.[339] It further insists that

---

[337] For example, Article 14(5) of the ICCPR states that "[e]veryone convicted of a crime shall have the right to his conviction and sentence being reviewed by a higher tribunal according to law." It does not require that the higher tribunal be authorised to review decisions on law for error and decisions on facts for substantial evidence.

[338] The European Court has noted several factors to be considered in assessing a court's independence, including the "manner of appointment of its members and the duration of their term of office, . . . the existence of guarantees against outside pressures . . . and the question whether a body presents an appearance of independence." Campbell & Fell v. United Kingdom, 7 EHRR 165 (1984), Series A, No. 80, ¶ 78. The European Court has also said that the irremovability of judges by the executive during their term of office must in general be considered as a corollary of their independence although the absence of a formal recognition of this irremovability in the law does not in itself imply lack of independence provided that it is recognized in fact and the other necessary guarantees are present. *Id.*

[339] *See* Laurence Lustgarten, "United Kingdom," *infra* at 457.

civilians may not be tried by military courts.[340] This point reflects the views of the UN Human Rights Committee, which has concluded that, under the International Covenant, military courts may only try cases concerning offenses committed by members of the armed forces in the course of their duties.[341] The Principle also reflects the jurisprudence of the European Court which has stated that "the irremovability of judges by the executive during their term of office must in general be considered as a corollary of their independence."[342] The court added, however, that "the absence of a formal recognition of this irremovability in the law does not in itself imply lack of independence provided that it is recognised in fact and the other necessary guarantees are present."[343] Other factors relevant to assessing a court's independence include "the manner of appointment of its members and the duration of their term of office, . . . the existence of guarantees against outside pressures . . . and . . . whether a body presents an appearance of independence."[344]

Although Principles 20-22, and indeed also 23 and 24, apply directly only to prosecutions for security-related crimes, their rationales apply equally to deportation proceedings. The consequences of a deportation decision are often as onerous as criminal punishment, entailing separation from family and risk of persecution upon return, and yet the government's discretion in many countries is virtually unchecked. The Johannesburg drafters did not expressly extend Principles 20-24 to deportation proceedings primarily owing to a shortage of time and the difficulty of crafting an appropriate standard given the broad discretion international law affords governments concerning admission and exclusion of aliens.

Nevertheless, various precedents suggest the development of greater protections for aliens facing deportation actions, even when they are alleged to be a risk to the host country's national security. For instance, in 1987, the UN Human Rights Committee concluded that the government of Madagascar violated the Covenant when it expelled an alien on national security grounds without demonstrating that there were compelling reasons for doing so.[345] The Canadian Immigration Act 1976, as amended by the Immigration Act of 1988, authorizes judges in deportation cases to hold *in camera* hearings of all the evidence, at which

---

[340] *See id.*

[341] *See* Evatt, *infra* this volume, at 105, referring, *e.g.*, to Committee's discussion of Egypt's report, *in Report of the Human Rights Committee*, U.N. GAOR, 48th Sess., ¶ 706, U.N. Doc. A/48/40 (Part I) (1993).

[342] Campbell & Fell v. United Kingdom, 7 EHRR 165 (1984), Series A, No. 80, ¶ 80.

[343] *Id.*

[344] *Id.* ¶ 78.

[345] *Eric Hammel v. Madagascar*, App. No. 155/1983, views adopted April 3, 1987, *Selected Decisions, Vol. 2*, at 11 and 179. *But see* Celepi v. Sweden, App. No. 456/1991, views adopted July 18, 1994, in which the Human Rights Committee ruled that the state could expel the applicant, a Turkish Kurd, on grounds that it had substantial evidence suggesting that he had played an active role in planning or executing terrorist activities, without providing him with any evidence.

the applicant is provided with a statement summarizing, as far as possible, the case against him or her and has the right to be represented and to call evidence.[346] The confidentiality of security material is protected by the requirement that such evidence may be examined only in the absence of both the applicant and his or her representative, who are instead represented by a security-cleared counsel instructed by the court. The applicant is entitled to a summary of the evidence obtained by this procedure.[347]

The European Commission on Human Rights, in a 1995 report, gave its unanimous opinion that the power of review of deportation decisions on national security grounds by UK courts "was too restrictive to satisfy the requirements of . . . [the European Convention]."[348] The Commission concluded that there were two areas in which the UK's system of review was deficient.[349] First, the Home Secretary was not required to present to the court any information concerning the evidence supporting his view of the perceived threat to national security posed by the person subject to deportation. Second, the court was not empowered to carry out its own assessment of the respective risks. The European Court agreed with the Commission that the UK had failed to provide an adequate remedy, but on different grounds, and thus did not reach the national security issue.[350]

---

[346] *See* Chahal v. United Kingdom, Eur. Ct. H.R., Judgment of Nov. 15, 1996, App. No. 70/1995/576/662, ¶ 144 (summarizing Canadian law).

[347] *See id.*

[348] The Chahal Family v. the United Kingdom, Report adopted on June 27, 1995, App. No. 22414/93, ¶ 152. The Commission described the process of review by UK courts as follows:

> [W]here national security considerations are invoked as a ground for the deportation decision, the powers of review of domestic courts are limited to determining, first, whether the decision of the Home Secretary that the deportation was required for reasons of national security was irrational, perverse or based on a misdirection and, secondly, whether there was sufficient evidence that the Home Secretary balanced the gravity of the national security risk against all other circumstances, including the likely risk of persecution if the person were deported.

[349] *See id.* at 150-51.

[350] *See* Chahal v. United Kingdom, Eur. Ct. H.R., Judgment of Nov. 15, 1996, App. No. 70/1995/576/662, ¶ 151. The Court concluded that the United Kingdom's judicial review was inadequate because it failed to require independent scrutiny of the claim that there existed substantial grounds for fearing that the applicant would face ill-treatment if deported to his home country. *See id.* at 160.

B. Prior Censorship: *Johannesburg Principle 23*

Principle 23 reflects the near-absolute ban on prior censorship set forth in the American Convention.[351] Although the International Covenant does not expressly preclude prior censorship, the *travaux preparatoires* indicate that at least a majority of its drafters shared the understanding that it did.[352] As summarized by Professor Nowak:

> Whereas the Human Rights Committee generally took the view that none of the grounds for interference provided for in Art. 19(3) authorized pre-censorship, several delegates in the 3d Committee of the General Assembly were of the opinion that in exceptional cases, such as subversive propaganda by foreign newspapers, pre-censorship should be permitted. Nevertheless, 11 Latin American States moved that every form of pre-censorship be absolutely prohibited. They then withdrew this motion subject to the express understanding that the text drafted by the Human Rights Committee already precluded prior censorship.[353]

Concluding the debate, drafters emphasized that "appropriate forms for restricting freedom of expression were . . . limited to subsequent criminal or civil prosecution."[354]

The UN Sub-Commission Rapporteurs on Freedom of Expression have similarly condemned "all forms of prior censorship," noting:

> The principle of legality requires the elimination of all informal sanctions and all forms of prior censorship, which in practice are usually informal. . . . Similarly, "preventive sanctions" (censorship, banning and seizure) raise serious questions of legality, especially having regard to the inherent imprecision and arbitrariness in the definition of the material element and element of intent and of the injury likely to be caused. The inherent imprecision and arbitrariness of preventive sanctions also raise the question of the legitimacy of laws providing for such sanctions.[355]

---

[351] *See* American Convention, *supra* note 18, art. 13(2). Article 13(2) reads, in part: "[T]he exercise of the right [to freedom of thought and expression] . . . shall not be subject to prior censorship but shall be subject to subsequent imposition of liability . . . expressly established by law to the extent necessary in order to ensure [*inter alia,*] . . . the protection of national security." *See also* Krsticevic, *et al.*, "The Inter-American System," *infra*, at 172.

[352] *See* Nowak, *supra* note 36, at 349 (citing, *inter alia*, the Declaration of the Peruvian Delegate to the Third Committee of the General Assembly, *in* U.N. Doc. A/C.3/SR/1077, ¶ 32).

[353] *Id.* (citations omitted).

[354] *Id.*

[355] Türk & Joinet, *supra* note 30, ¶ 73.

While the laws of many countries, and the constitutions of some, prohibit prior restraints on publication of printed matter, most courts interpret the prohibition to apply only to administrative censorship.[356] The two outstanding examples of countries that have, in practice, echewed prior restraints are Sweden and the United States. The Swedish Constitution admits no exceptions whatsoever to the ban on pre-publication censorship, and no form of prior censorship has been upheld in recent memory.[357]

The US Supreme Court has stated that prior restraints are presumptively unconstitutional; the presumption may be overcome only upon a showing that: (1) the publication would pose a clear threat of immediate and irreparable damage to a "near sacred right"; (2) the prior restraint would be effective; and (3) no other measures, less restrictive of freedom of expression, would be effective.[358] The Court has amplified that a prior restraint could be tolerated on national security grounds only concerning an exceedingly narrow range of publications and only under exceptional circumstances, such as "when a nation is at war," information that amounts to "actual obstruction to its recruiting service or the publication of the sailing dates of transports or the number and location of troops."[359] The Court has never upheld a restraint on national security grounds.

The Johannesburg Principles recognize the legitimacy of restraints on publication based on national security grounds only during a declared state of emergency and only under the circumstances stated in Principle 3.[360] The drafters adopted this approach for the above reasons and also because of their assessment that the dangers posed by prior restraint far outweigh the risk that information substantially harmful to national security might be published. The drafters noted the frequency with which governments suppress information of no legitimate security consequence on national security grounds, compared to the smattering of cases where national security could reasonably be said to have been harmed, and in no case seriously.

---

[356] *See generally* Coliver, *supra* note 268, at 280.

[357] *Id.* A case from the early 1970s illustrates the absolute nature of the prohibition. A member of the Investigation Bureau (IB), a secret part of the security services, disclosed information about the IB to two journalists who published a series of articles in a magazine and later in a book that was translated into English. The IB agent and the two journalists were convicted of espionage and sentenced to prison for terms of up to one year. No attempt was ever made to restrain publication of the articles or the book, nor could any such attempt have succeeded. *Id.* at 280-81.

[358] *See* Nebraska Press Assoc. v. Stuart, 427 U.S. 539, 565-66 (1976); Matter of Providence Journal Co., 820 F.2d 1342, 1351 (1st Cir. 1986).

[359] Near v. Minnesota, 283 U.S. 697, 716 (1931).

[360] Principle 3 states that for restrictions justified by a state of emergency to be legitimate, the emergency must threaten the life of the country and must be officially and lawfully proclaimed, and the restrictions must be strictly required by the exigencies of the situation and last only for so long as necessary.

It should be noted that the European Court has taken a more conservative approach. It has made clear that publications may be seized and withdrawn from circulation upon an *ex parte* judicial order, provided that (a) the information has not already been published and (b) the publisher has an opportunity to have the order promptly reviewed in a judicial proceeding at which he or she is represented.[361] In its judgments in the two *Spycatcher* cases, the Court reiterated that the European Convention does not "prohibit the imposition of prior restraints on publication, as such."[362] It continued:

> On the other hand, the dangers inherent in prior restraints are such that they call for the most careful scrutiny on the part of the Court. This is especially so as far as the press is concerned, for news is a perishable commodity and to delay its publication, even for a short period, may well deprive it of all its value and interest.[363]

The Court upheld the restraint on publication of *Spycatcher*, the memoirs of a retired official of the British Security Services, until its publication in the United States. At that point, the balance of interests shifted; the injunction became ineffective and thus could no longer be justified.[364]

Similarly, in a 1995 judgment, the Court ruled that an order to withdraw from circulation copies of a magazine that reprinted a classified report of the Dutch internal security services violated the European Convention because a few thousand copies had already been distributed, the report was six years old, and the head of the security service had admitted that the various items of information taken separately were no longer state secrets.[365]

C. Disproportionate Penalties: *Johannesburg Principle 24*

Principle 24 amplifies Principle 1(d)'s requirement that any restriction on freedom of expression or information on the ground of national security must be "necessary in a democratic society," and thus proportionate. The Johannesburg drafters added Principle 24 to drive home the points that (a) civil fines and injunctions must be proportionate no less than sentences of imprisonment, and (b) any sanction must be proportionate to the *actual* crime committed and may not, for example, be based simply on the severity of the crime charged.

---

[361] *See, e.g.*, Vereniging Weekblad "Bluf!" v. the Netherlands, 306-A Eur. Ct. H.R. (ser. A) ¶ 32 (1995); Observer & Guardian v. United Kingdom, 216 Eur. Ct. H.R. (ser. A) (1991); Sunday Times v. United Kingdom (no. 2), 217 Eur. Ct. H.R. (ser. A) ¶ 51 (1991).

[362] Observer & Guardian, 216 Eur. Ct. H.R., ¶ 60; Sunday Times, 217 Eur. Ct. H.R., ¶ 60.

[363] *Id.*

[364] *See* Observer & Guardian, 216 Eur. Ct. H.R., ¶¶ 66-69.

[365] *See* Vereniging Weekblad "Bluf!" v. the Netherlands, 306-A Eur. Ct. H.R. (ser. A) ¶¶ 41-45 (1995).

The drafters considered including an express prohibition of imprisonment for speech-related crimes short of incitement to violence, based on authorities discussed in support of Principle 6, but decided not to do so on the grounds that heavy fines may be even more onerous than light prison sentences and that the requirement of proportionality to the actual crime sufficed. Nonetheless, it is worth noting the strong trend in international and comparative law towards shielding speech offenses from sanctions of imprisonment except where violence is threatened. The UN Sub-Commission Rapporteurs on Freedom of Expression concluded in their 1992 final report that, "In principle [deprivation of liberty] should not be provided for as a penalty save in wholly exceptional cases in which there is a clear and present danger of violence."[366] They reasoned that (a) "deprivation of liberty is clearly a disproportionate sanction" for most speech offenses and (b) reports of UN human rights bodies show that imprisonment for free expression "crimes" places the detained person at high risk of torture or other cruel, inhuman or degrading treatment.[367] For the latter reason, only in a situation where freedom of expression can be exercised without risk is it "possible to discuss the question of the proportionality of sanctions against persons who, in the course of expressing their opinions, break the laws protecting [interests recognized to be legitimate under international law]."[368]

The UN Human Rights Committee has frequently criticized countries for retaining laws that authorize imprisonment for speech crimes. For instance, the Committee indicated that Iceland's libel law was inconsistent with Article 19 of the International Covenant because it permitted "[t]he possibility of a sentence of up to one year's imprisonment for libel."[369] The Committee similarly criticized Norway for maintaining "certain obsolete laws . . ., in particular with regard to penal sanctions against defamation."[370]

VI. Looking Forward: Developing Widespread Acceptance

Abid Hussain, the UN Special Rapporteur on Freedom of Opinion and Expression, attached the Johannesburg Principles to his report to the UN Commission on Human Rights for its March/April 1996 session and recommended

---

[366] Türk & Joinet, *supra* note 30, ¶ 83.
[367] *See id.* The Rapporteurs note that, of the cases examined by the Human Rights Committee between its second through sixteenth sessions, four out of nine cases of alleged torture related to exercise of the right to freedom of expression. *See id.* ¶ 81. In addition, the Working Group on Arbitrary Detention has estimated that some 90 percent of the cases of arbitrary detention involved freedom of expression. *See id.*
[368] *Id.*
[369] *Report of the Human Rights Committee*, U.N. GAOR, 49th Sess., Supp. No. 40, ¶ 78, U.N. Doc. A/49/40/Vol. 1 (1994).
[370] *Id.* at 91.

that the Commission endorse them.[371] As a result, the Principles have been disseminated widely. Mr. Param Cumaraswamy, the UN Commission's Special Rapporteur on the Independence of Judges and Lawyers "welcomed" the Principles in his 1996 Report to the Commission and stated that he would "from time to time refer to these standards to the extent that they are applicable to his mandate."[372]

A member of the UN Human Rights Committee said that the Principles would be of great value in interpreting standards concerning freedom of expression and movement under the Covenant on Civil and Political Rights. Article 19 has sent copies of the Principles to all Committee members, as well as to all judges of the European Court of Human Rights. Two experts who frequently work with the Inter-American Commission and Court of Human Rights said that they would bring the Principles to the attention of the Inter-American bodies as appropriate. The Principles have been translated by human rights organizations into several languages, including Arabic, Croatian, Indonesian, Japanese, Korean, Romanian, Serbian, Sinhalese and Slovakian.[373]

By these activities, and with the publication of this book, it is hoped that the Principles will win increasing acceptance as a guide to the interpretation of the provisions of the International Covenant and regional human rights treaties concerning national security, freedom of expression and access to information.

---

[371] *See Promotion and Protection of the Right to Freedom of Opinion and Expression, Report of the Special Rapporteur, Mr. Abid Hussain, Pursuant to Commission on Human Rights Resolution 1993/45*, U.N. ESCOR, Comm'n on Hum. Rts., 52nd Sess., Provisional Agenda Item 8, at 26 ¶ 154, 28-35 (Annex), U.N. Doc. E/CN.4/1996/39 (1996).

[372] *Question of the Human Rights of All Persons Subjected to Any Form of Detention or Imprisonment: Report of the Special Rapporteur on the Independence of Judges and Lawyers, Dato'Param Cumaraswamy, Submitted Pursuant to Commission on Human Rights Resolution 1995/36*, U.N. ESCOR, Comm'n on Hum. Rts., 52nd Sess., Provisional Agenda Item 8, ¶¶ 81-82, U.N. Doc. E/CN.4/1996/37 (1996).

[373] Translations may be obtained from Article 19 (e-mail: article19@gn.apc.org). The Japanese translation by Mamoru Jino is reprinted along with an introduction by Prof. L.W. Beer in *Horitsu Jiho (The Law Review)*, Vol. 68, No. 12 (Nov. 1996, Tokyo), at 73.

THE INTERNATIONAL COVENANT ON CIVIL AND POLITICAL RIGHTS: FREEDOM OF EXPRESSION AND STATE SECURITY

Elizabeth Evatt

I. Introduction

This chapter outlines the approach taken by the Human Rights Committee (hereafter "Committee" or "HRC") concerning restrictions on freedom of expression on the ground of national security or public order under Article 19 of the International Covenant on Civil and Political Rights (hereafter "Covenant" or "ICCPR").[1] It is based on the following sources: (a) views adopted by the Committee under the procedure set forth in the first Optional Protocol to the ICCPR,[2] pursuant to which the Committee examines individual complaints, determines whether a State party has committed a violation and, where appropriate, recommends remedial measures; (b) the Committee's General Comments on relevant articles of the Covenant; (c) observations on State reports made by individual Committee members pursuant to Article 40,[3] and, since 1992, by the full Committee in its Concluding Observations adopted by consensus.

The chapter includes reference to other articles of the Covenant which permit restrictions of rights on the grounds of national security or public order and which give rise to parallel issues, namely: Article 12(3) (liberty of movement); Article 13 (rights of aliens prior to expulsion); Article 14(1) (fair and public hearing); Article 21 (right of peaceful assembly); Article 22 (right to freedom of association).

While the focus of this paper is on national security, the decisions and comments of the Committee sometimes couple public order (*ordre public*) with national security. The Covenant also permits restrictions of some rights on the ground of "public safety".[4] A distinction should be made between these concepts,

---

[1] ICCPR, adopted and opened for signature, ratification and accession by U.N. General Assembly res. 2200A (XXI) on 16 Dec. 1966, entered into force on 23 March 1976.

[2] Optional Protocol to the ICCPR, adopted and opened for signature, ratification and accession by U.N. General Assembly res. 2200A (XXI) on 16 Dec. 1966, entered into force 23 March 1976.

[3] Art. 40 of the ICCPR establishes the obligation of States parties to "submit reports on the measures they have adopted which give effect to the [Covenant's] rights ... and on the progress made in the enjoyment of those rights ... within one year of the entry into force of the ... Covenant ... and thereafter whenever the Committee so requests". The Committee has requested States parties to submit reports at least every five years.

[4] These include Arts. 18(3), 21 and 22. Arts. 21 and 22 are discussed in Section III.B, *infra*. Art. 18(3) permits restrictions on freedom of thought, conscience and religion if necessary "to protect public safety". In its General Comment on Art. 18, the Committee made clear that it would construe paragraph (3) strictly, and that restriction on grounds not specified, such as national security, are not allowed. General Comment on Art. 18, no. 22, 48th Session, July

but there is little guidance on how this should be done. For the purposes of this chapter, the protection of national security is taken to cover measures to prevent or respond to serious threats to the country as a whole, whether from an external source, such as a military threat, or an internal source, such as incitement to violent overthrow of the government.[5] Measures could also legitimately be directed to ensuring that the defense and security systems are able to identify and be prepared to respond to a potential threat or to minimize the risk of such a threat.[6]

Measures to protect public safety or public order (*ordre public*) overlap national security measures at the point where civil disorder may escalate beyond a local temporary affair to become a threat to the country. Issues relating to public safety or public order are mentioned where they may throw light on the Committee's approach to restrictions on the basis of national security.

Article 4 of the ICCPR provides for certain derogations of rights in the circumstances of a national emergency. This is discussed in Section IV, below.

II. Article 19 of the ICCPR: Freedom of Opinion and Expression

Article 19 reads as follows:

> 1. Everyone shall have the right to hold opinions without interference.
> 2. Everyone shall have the right to freedom of expression; this right shall include freedom to seek, receive and impart information and ideas of all kinds, regardless of frontiers, either orally, in writing or in print, in the form of art, or through any other media of his choice.
> 3. The exercise of the rights provided for in paragraph 2 of this Article carries with it special duties and responsibilities. It may therefore be subject to certain restrictions, but these shall only be such as are provided by law and are necessary:
>   a) For respect of the rights or reputations of others;
>   b) For the protection of national security or of public order (*ordre public*), or of public health or morals.

1993, at para. 8, in Compilation of General Comments Adopted by U.N. Treaty Bodies, U.N. Doc. HRI/GEN/1/Rev.2, 29 July 1994.

[5] *See, e.g.*, Professor Nowak: "Restrictions on freedom of expression and information to protect national security are permissible only in serious cases of political or military threat to the entire nation. Publication of a direct call to violent overthrow of the government in an atmosphere of political unrest or propaganda for war ... as well falls within this ground for restriction." Manfred Nowak, *U.N. Covenant on Civil and Political Rights: CCPR Commentary* (Engel 1993), at 355.

[6] *The Johannesburg Principles on National Security, Freedom of Expression and Access to Information* reflect a similar interpretation of legitimate national security interests. *See* Johannesburg Principle 2.

Article 19(1) protects the right to freedom of opinion, without interference. The Covenant does not permit any restrictions to be imposed on the right to hold opinions.[7] National security grounds have no relevance as a defense to an alleged violation of paragraph (1) of Article 19, though they have sometimes been raised by States. In a number of cases where government opponents were arrested and detained (and in some cases tortured) without being charged or tried, the Committee found that they had suffered persecution because of their political opinions in violation of paragraph (1).[8] In one case the State alleged that this was done because of subversive activities, but without providing any supporting evidence.[9]

Paragraph (2) of Article 19 protects the right to freedom of expression. The scope of this right is broad. While it is generally thought to create obligations on the State in regard to access to public information ("freedom of information"), this has not been tested in communications.

The issues raised most frequently concern the scope of the restrictions on the right which are permissible under paragraph (3). That paragraph provides that the exercise of the rights provided for in paragraph (2) carries with it special duties and responsibilities and that it may therefore be subject to certain restrictions. An important observation made by the Human Rights Committee in its General Comment on Article 19 is that those restrictions may not put in jeopardy the right itself.[10] The reference to special duties and responsibilities does not seem to have played a role in expanding the scope of restrictions permissible on the ground of national security.[11]

Restrictions on freedom of expression generally take the form of penalties for offenses, though a number of cases have involved detention and seizure of publications. Where restrictions are imposed to protect respect of the rights and reputations of others, civil responsibility may result.

---

[7] General Comment on Article 19, no. 10, 19th Session, in *Compilation*, *supra* note 4, at para. 1: "This is a right to which the Covenant permits no exceptions or restrictions."

[8] *Mpaka-Nsusu* v. *Zaire*, Communication No. 157/1983, views adopted 26 March 1986, *reprinted in* HRC, *Selected Decisions under the Optional Protocol, Vol. 2, 17th to 32nd Sessions* (1990), at 187. *Primo Jose Essono Mika Miha* v. *Equatorial Guinea*, Communication No. 414/1990, views adopted 8 July 1994, in *HRC Report 1994, Vol. II*, Annex IX.O, G.A.O.R., 49th Sess., Supp. No. 40, U.N. Doc. A/49/40.

[9] *Monja Jaona* v. *Madagascar*, Communication No. 132/1982, views adopted 1 April 1985, *Selected Decisions, Vol. 2*, *supra* note 8, at 161. *See also Ngalula Mpandanjila v. Zaire*, Communication No. 138/1983, views adopted 26 March 1986, *Selected Decisions*, *Vol. 2*, *id.*, at 164.

[10] General Comment on Article 19, *supra* note 7, at para. 4.

[11] Prof. Nowak has suggested that the phrase may add weight to the validity of measures considered necessary to prevent concentration of media power or abuse of that power. Nowak, *supra* note 5, at 349.

A. General Rules Regarding Permissible Restrictions

In regard to restrictions imposed for the purpose of protecting national security, the key issues under Article 19(3) are the following: (1) whether the restrictions are provided by law; (2) whether there is an established need for the restrictive measures to protect national security; and (3) whether the restrictions are kept to the minimum necessary for that purpose.

1. Restrictions on freedom of expression must be "provided by law" and must be compatible with the aims and objectives of the Covenant.

Article 19(3) permits only those restrictions of freedom of expression which are provided by law. For example, a State may not rely on paragraph 3(b) to justify the detention of persons who advocate ideas considered subversive, or the seizure of publications, unless it can point to the application of specific laws providing for such detention or seizure.

It is up to the State to show the legal basis for any restrictions imposed on the right to freedom of expression. If the Human Rights Committee has to determine in a communication procedure whether a particular restriction is imposed by law, the State should provide details of the law, of the actions said to constitute the offense or to fall within the scope of the law, and of the actual application of the law in that case. Whether a particular law applies to the circumstances of the case is essentially a matter for the State authorities or the domestic courts to determine.[12] The State party must, however, give full information to the Committee about the law and its application.

If the State fails to provide details of the law restricting freedom of expression (or other rights) or fails to show how the law applies to the circumstances of the particular case, the Committee will be unable to conclude that the restrictions were provided by law or that they comply with the Covenant. It is not enough for the State merely to argue that action was taken under a law applicable to persons who have been convicted, for example, of subversive activity.[13]

In *Monja Jaona* v. *Madagascar*,[14] the State party submitted that the author had been detained under a law relating to the dissolution of certain associations and to the

---

[12] *Maroufidou* v. *Sweden*, Communication No. 58/1979, *HRC Report 1981*, U.N. Doc. A/36/40, at 160, reprinted in *Yearbook of the Human Rights Committee 1981-1982, Vol. 2*, at 318.

[13] *E.g.*, *Luciano Weinberger Weisz* v. *Uruguay*, Communication No. 28/1978, views adopted 29 Oct. 1980, HRC, *Selected Decisions under the Optional Protocol, Vol. 1, 2nd to 16th Session* (1985), at 57; *Leopoldo Buffo Carballal* v. *Uruguay*, Communication No. 33/1978, 27 March 1981, *Yearbook, Vol. 2, supra* note 12, at 305.

[14] Communication No. 132/1982, *supra* note 9. *See also Mpaka-Nsusu* v. *Zaire*, Communication No. 157/1983, 26 March 1986, *Selected Decisions, Vol. 2, supra* note 8, at 187; *Ngalula Mpandanjila* v. *Zaire*, Communication No. 138/1983, *supra* note 9.

placing under house arrest of persons convicted of subversive activities. No evidence was adduced that this law applied to the victim, who had not been charged or put on trial. The Committee stated that the allegation of subversive activity had to be substantiated by reference to specific laws. The Committee could not conclude that the author had engaged in any activities prohibited by the law. His rights were violated because he suffered persecution on account of his political opinions.

Laws restricting Covenant rights must themselves be compatible with the aims and objectives of the Covenant.[15] Whether they consist of legislation or common law, they must be sufficiently clear to enable individuals to understand their obligations and to foresee whether particular action is unlawful. If a law is too vague and general, the restriction may not satisfy the description of "provided by law" and may be incompatible with other provisions of the Covenant. For instance, Article 15 precludes the retrospective operation of penal law. If a person is convicted as a result of an interpretation of a law that is so vague and broad-ranging that no one could know reasonably that his/her actions were criminal, then this could violate Article 15.[16] The Committee will not find a violation in an individual case, however, if a law, which may be too broad in scope to be a justifiable restriction in itself, is nevertheless applied compatibly with the Covenant in the particular case.[17]

---

[15] *Toonen* v. *Australia*, Communication No. 488/1992, views adopted 8 March 1994: "Even interference provided for by the law should be in accordance with the provisions, aims and objectives of the Covenant and should be, in any event, reasonable in the circumstances." Article 12(3) specifically requires that restrictions be consistent with the other rights recognized in the Covenant.

[16] Observation in *Leonardus J. M. de Groot* v. *the Netherlands*, Communication No. 578/1994, declared inadmissible October 1995. This requirement is similar to the requirement formulated by the European Court of Human Rights in the *Sunday Times* case: "A norm cannot be regarded as a 'law' unless it is formulated with sufficient precision to enable the citizen to regulate his conduct: he must be able, if need be with appropriate advice, to foresee, to a degree that is reasonable in the circumstances, the consequences which a given action may entail." *Sunday Times* v. *United Kingdom*, Judgment of April 26, 1979, Series A, no. 30, at para. 49, discussed in Mahoney and Early, elsewhere in this volume, at Section II.C.1.

[17] *Faurisson* v. *France*, Communication No. 550/1993, views adopted 8 Nov. 1996, discussed *infra* at note 39.

2. Restrictions on freedom of expression must be necessary for a legitimate purpose.

Article 19(2) provides that restrictions may be imposed on freedom of expression only if *necessary* to achieve one of a short list of aims, including national security or public order (*ordre public*). Other articles state expressly that certain rights may be subject to restrictions only where "necessary in a democratic society;"[18] this has led some commentators to suggest that at least some significance should be given to the omission of this phrase from Article 19.[19] However, in its consideration of individual communications, the Human Rights Committee has tended to apply the more demanding standard of "democratic necessity" to restrictions on Article 19 rights.[20]

To satisfy the Committee that a particular restriction on freedom of expression is necessary, a State must make a three-part showing. The State must establish that: (1) there exists a threat to the nation as a whole; (2) the expression at issue has caused or contributed to that threat; and (3) the restrictive measures are necessary to prevent the threat and proportional to it.

Emergency measures leading to derogation of rights have to be independently justified under Article 4 (concerning public emergencies "which threaten[] the life of the nation").[21] []Even in an emergency falling within the definition of Article 4, derogations are permitted only to the extent strictly required.

3. Restrictions must be proportional to the legitimate aim pursued.

In a number of cases the Human Rights Committee has applied a test of proportionality in determining whether a particular measure was necessary. The Committee asks whether the restriction is necessary for the particular purpose and whether the limitation of rights is proportional to that purpose, bearing in mind that exceptions from rights are to be strictly construed.[22] Although the Committee has

---

[18] Article 14 provides that the "press and the public may be excluded from all or part of a trial" for various enumerated reasons, including national security "in a democratic society". Articles 21 and 22 permit restrictions on the freedoms of association and assembly only when "necessary in a democratic society" in the interest of national security or other listed interests.

[19] Nowak, *supra* note 5, at 350.

[20] For instance, in *M.A.* v. *Italy*, the Committee declared a communication inadmissible because it found that the restriction on freedom of expression and association was "clearly . . . necessary . . . in a democratic society for the protection of national security and public order." Communication No. 117/1981, *Selected Decisions, Vol. 2, supra* note 8, at 31.

[21] *See* Section IV, *infra* at 93.

[22] The interference must be proportional to the legitimate aim pursued. See, e.g., Pietraroia *Zapala* v. *Uruguay*, Communication No. 44/1979, views adopted March 27, 1981, *Selected Decisions, Vol. 1, supra* note 13, at 76. The Committee commented that the principle of proportionality would require that a measure as harsh as the deprivation of all political rights

not applied the proportionality test in cases involving restrictions on freedom of expression for the purpose of protecting national security or public order, it may be assumed that the requirement that restrictions be "necessary" includes the standard of proportionality.

4. Governments are not afforded a margin of appreciation.

In most of the cases discussed in this chapter the Committee reserved to itself the question whether there were circumstances which made the restriction of freedom of expression necessary.[23] []This has been its approach in recent years. However, in a 1982 decision, the Committee concluded that it could not question the decision of the national authorities to impose penalties against a broadcaster for airing a program about homosexuality.[24] It observed:

> Public morals differ widely. There is no universally applicable common standard. Consequently, in this respect, a certain margin of discretion must be accorded to the responsible national authorities.

Since that decision, the Committee has not applied a "margin of discretion" or "appreciation" and it has expressly rejected the doctrine more than once, even in cases concerning moral values. For instance, where it was alleged that the right to privacy was violated by laws outlawing homosexual conduct, the Committee rejected the government's argument that moral issues must be deemed a matter for domestic decision.[25]

In a recent case from Finland concerning mining activities which posed a threat to the economic rights of members of an indigenous minority, the State party argued that a certain margin of discretion must be allowed to the national authorities

---

for a period of 15 years be specifically justified. No such attempt had been made in that case. In *Toonen* v. *Australia*, March 1994, *supra* note 15, the Committee determined that restrictions on the right to privacy were not proportional to the end sought and, accordingly, not necessary. In its General Comment on freedom of religion, the Committee observed that limitations must be directly related and proportionate to the specific need on which they are predicated. General Comment on Article 18, *supra* note 4, at para. 8.

[23] *Jong-Kyu Sohn* v. *Republic of Korea*, Communication No. 518/1992, views adopted July 1995, discussed *infra* note 33.

[24] *Hertzberg, et al.* v. *Finland*, Communication No. 61/1979, views adopted 2 April 1982: "The Committee finds that it cannot question the decision of the responsible organs of the Finnish broadcasting corporation that radio and TV are not appropriate forums to discuss issues related to homosexuality".

[25] *Toonen* v. *Australia*, March 1994, *supra* note 15.

in the application of Article 27 to the regulation of economic activities. The Committee did not accept this submission.[26]

The Committee has not applied the "margin of discretion" in relation to national security restrictions or to the right to freedom of expression. The Committee's current approach appears to be that it is for the State to establish the circumstances said to make a restriction on freedom of expression necessary to protect national security and for the Committee to determine whether the particular restriction is compatible with the Covenant.

B. Decisions Finding National Security Restrictions Unnecessary

1. The Uruguayan Anti-Subversion Cases

In a series of Uruguayan cases, alleged victims claimed, *inter alia*, that their freedom of expression had been violated by their conviction on charges of "subversive association". The military government of Uruguay did not co-operate with the Committee. It provided no information concerning the legal or factual bases of the offenses or the reasons which might make the laws in question necessary, even though it was generally known that the country was experiencing internal disorder and conflict at the time. These cases were decided by the Committee in the late 1970s and early 1980s. When Uruguay reported to the Committee in 1982 under Article 40, the Government argued that it had been necessary to suspend certain rights because of civil conflict. The Committee observed that Uruguay had failed, in the Optional Protocol procedure, to provide information to justify the restrictions it had imposed on individuals. It had also failed to fulfill its obligation to investigate alleged abuses and to provide the Committee with information about charges, orders and judgments concerning alleged victims.

Uruguay took the view that there was a conspiracy against it in the international arena, noting in one case that "some paragraphs of the author's submission were identical to another communication before the Committee and that this proves that there is an organized campaign aimed at preparing complaints for submission to international organizations".[27]

In the absence of information to support Uruguay's argument justifying restrictions on national security grounds, the Committee was unable to conclude in

---

[26] *Ilmari Lansman, et al.* v. *Finland*, Communication No. 511/1992. The Committee concluded that the scope of a State's discretion to encourage economic activity is "not to be assessed by reference to a margin of appreciation, but by reference to the obligations it has undertaken in Article 27." However, under the particular circumstances of the case, the Committee did not find a violation.

[27] *Maria A. Cabreira d'Estradet* v. *Uruguay*, Communication No. 105/1981, views adopted 21 July 1983, *Selected Decisions, Vol. 2, supra* note 8, at 133, para. 8.2.

most of the cases that the action taken against the complainants was necessary on any of the grounds mentioned in Article 19(3)(b). In many cases, the Committee found violations of several provisions of the Covenant. For example in *Pietraroia Zapala* v *Uruguay*[28] the alleged victim was charged with subversive association, and conspiracy to violate the Constitution followed by acts preparatory thereto. The State failed to provide information as to the facts of the alleged offense, details of the charges or copies of the proceedings. The Committee could not be satisfied that grounds existed to justify the arrest, detention and trial of the victim on any grounds mentioned in Article 19(3). It concluded that the author's rights under Article 19(2) were violated because he had been penalized for political and trade-union activities.[29]

In none of the cases referred to above did the State provide legal or factual information which would enable the Committee to consider whether the restrictions imposed on freedom of expression or other rights were imposed by law, or were necessary, or to enable the Committee to set standards for what is a "necessary" restriction in these or similar situations.

2. Complaint from Cameroon

In *Mukong* v. *Cameroon*, the first communication filed against Cameroon, decided in 1994,[30] the author was a journalist, writer and long-time opponent of the one-party system. He had been arrested after an interview with the BBC in which he had criticized the President and the Government. He was ill-treated during his detention and later released. He was arrested again after a meeting in which he advocated multi-party democracy. The author claimed a violation of his right to freedom of expression and opinion, contending that he had been persecuted for his advocacy of multi-party democracy and the expression of opinions inimical to the government.

The government replied that restrictions on the author's freedom of expression were justified on grounds of national security and/or public order under paragraph (3)(b) because the author had exercised his right to freedom of expression

---

[28] Communication No. 44/1979, views adopted 27 March 1981, *supra* note 22, at 76. *See also Alberto Grille Motta* v. *Uruguay*, Communication No. 11/1977, views adopted 2 April 1980, *Selected Decisions*, Vol. 1, *supra* note 13, at 54; *Anna Maria Garcia Lanza de Netto, Beatriz Weismann and Alcides Lanza Perdomo* v. *Uruguay*, Communication No. 8/1977, views adopted 3 April 1980, *Selected Decisions*, Vol. 1, *id.*, at 45; *Weinberger Weisz* v. *Uruguay*, *supra* note 13, *Selected Decisions*, *id.*, at 57; *Leopoldo Buffo Carballal* v. *Uruguay*, *supra* note 13, Yearbook 1981-1982, Vol. 2, at 305.

[29] The Committee also rejected the possibility that the application of "prompt security measures" to the complainant could be justified as a derogation under Article 4 in the absence of any submission on that issue. *See also Delia Saldias de Lopez (on behalf of Sergio Ruben Lopez Burgos)* v. *Uruguay*, Communication No. 52/1979, views adopted 29 July 1981, *Selected Decisions*, Vol. 1, *supra* note 13, at 88.

[30] Communication No. 458/1991, views adopted 21 July 1994, *HRC Report for 1993-94*, at 171.

without regard to the country's political context and continued struggle for unity. He had been charged with subversion in respect of statements said to be untrue under an ordinance criminalizing statements which intoxicate national or international public opinion.

The Committee accepted that the restrictions on the author's freedom of expression were provided for by law. As to the question whether the measures taken against him were necessary to safeguard national security and/or public order, the Committee considered that it was not necessary to safeguard an allegedly vulnerable state of national unity by subjecting the author to arrest, continued detention and treatment in violation of Article 7. The legitimate objective of safeguarding and indeed strengthening national unity under difficult political circumstances could not be achieved, concluded the Committee, by attempting to muzzle advocacy of multi-party democracy, democratic tenets or human rights. In this regard the question of deciding which measures might meet the "necessity" test in such situations did not arise.

The Committee focused on the restrictive law itself and on its effect in suppressing any criticism of government or advocacy of multi-party democracy. The Committee was not willing to consider such restrictions as necessary as they would completely undermine the purpose of freedom of expression. Despite the "difficult political circumstances" acknowledged by the Committee the restrictions could not be shown to be necessary.[31]

3. Advocacy of Labor Rights in Republic of Korea

In *Jong-Kyu Sohn* v. *Republic of Korea*, decided in 1995,[32] the author was a trade union official. In February 1991 during a shipyard strike in Guhjae Island, the government announced that it would send in police troops to break the strike. The author called a meeting of the Solidarity Forum in Seoul, 400 kilometers away. The meeting issued a statement supporting the strike and condemning the government's threat to send in troops. The statement was sent to the workers at the shipyard.

The author and others were arrested and charged with contravening Article 13(2) of the Labor Disputes Law.[33] That law prohibited persons other than the concerned employer, employees or trade union, or persons having legitimate authority attributed to them by law, to intervene in a labor dispute for the purpose of manipulating or influencing the parties concerned. The author was found guilty and sentenced to one and a half years' imprisonment. His appeal was dismissed.

---

[31] *Id.* at 181, para. 9.7.

[32] Communication No. 518/1992, *supra* note 23. As of April 1998, two further cases were pending before the Committee raising issues concerning Korea's national security laws.

[33] *Art 13(2) of the Labor Disputes Adjustment Act, Law No. 1327 of 13 April 1963, amended by Law No. 3967 of 28 Nov. 1987.*

The author argued that the law denied the right to freedom of expression to supporters of laborers or trade unions. He referred to the Labor Union Act, which prohibited third party support for the organization of a trade union. He submitted that any support to laborers or trade unions could thus be punished by the Labor Dispute Adjustment Act at the time of strikes and by the Labor Union Act at other times.

The Committee considered that the author, by joining others in issuing a statement supporting the strike and criticizing the government, had exercised his right to impart information and ideas within the meaning of Article 19(2) of the Covenant. The State party had invoked national security and public order to justify the restriction of the author's rights. It made reference to the general nature of the labor movement, alleging that the statement issued by the author was a disguise for the incitement to a national strike. It argued that a national strike, in any country, would be a threat to national security and public order. However, the State party did not specify the alleged threat posed by the author's exercise of his right to freedom of expression. The information before the Committee did not show that, in the circumstances of the instant case, the restriction was necessary within the meaning of Article 19(3). Accordingly, the Committee found a violation of Article 19(2). The author was entitled to a remedy, including compensation, for his conviction, and the State party was invited to review Article 13(2) of the Labor Disputes Adjustment Act.

The Committee based its conclusion on the absence of any threat to security justifying the need for the restrictions. The State party had argued that the labor movement in Korea was politically oriented, and that labor activists had led workers to extreme actions to fulfill their political aims. The State party's contention was that a nation-wide strike of all workers would of itself present a threat to national security and public order. The Committee did not accept that contention and concluded instead that no threat existed which could justify the restrictive measures applied to the author.

C. Examples of Restrictions Found Necessary

In a few cases, the Committee has declared inadmissible a communication alleging a violation of freedom of expression, with the practical result of upholding the restrictions at issue.

In *M.A.* v. *Italy*,[34] decided in 1984, the author was prosecuted for participation in an illegal organization and was sentenced to four years' imprisonment. The Italian government relied, *inter alia*, on Article 19(3) of the Covenant, arguing that M.A. had been indicted for "reorganizing the dissolved fascist

---

[34] Communication No. 117/1981, *supra* note 20, *Selected Decisions*, Vol. 2, at 31.

party", that is, for organizing a movement which had as its object the elimination of democratic freedoms and the establishment of a totalitarian regime.

The Committee took the view that the acts of which M.A. had been convicted (reorganizing the dissolved fascist party) were of a kind which were removed from the protection of the Covenant by operation of Article 5[35] and which were in any event justifiably prohibited by Italian law having regard to the limitations and restrictions applicable to the right to freedom of expression as well as the rights to manifest one's beliefs, to freedom of association, and to take part in the conduct of public affairs.[36] Accordingly, the Committee found the complaint inadmissible.

The Committee did not consider at any length the issue of "necessity" in terms of Article 19(3)(b), although the State party had expressly referred to national security and public order in its submissions. The Committee's reasons do not explain in what way paragraph (3) was thought to apply or whether its concern was with national security or public order.

In *J.R.T. and the W.G. Party* v. *Canada*,[37] decided in 1983, the Western Guard had used public telephone services to warn of the dangers of international finance and international Jewry leading the world into wars, unemployment and inflation and the collapse of world values and principles. They circulated particularly serious anti-Semitic messages by transmitting tape-recordings over the telephone. They were precluded from using the telephone services under the Canadian Human Rights Act which declared it a discriminatory practice to communicate telephonically any matter likely to expose a person or persons to hatred or contempt by reason, *inter alia*, of their religion or race. The communication, which alleged a violation of freedom of expression under Article 19(2) was declared inadmissible. In the Committee's view, the opinions being disseminated "clearly constitute[d] the advocacy of racial or religious hatred which there is an obligation under Article 20(2) to prohibit."[38]

Somewhat similar issues arose in the case of *Faurisson* v. *France*,[39] which concerned the French "holocaust denial" or "Gayssot" law. The law prohibited the questioning of the existence of crimes which were the subject of the judgment of the International Military Tribunal at Nuremberg. France sought to justify the Gayssot Law on the ground that Holocaust denial is a contemporary expression of racism

---

[35] Art. 5(1) reads: "Nothing in the present Covenant may be interpreted as implying for any State, group or person any right to engage in any activity or to perform any act aimed at the destruction of any of the rights or freedoms recognized herein, or at their limitation to a greater extent than is provided for in the present Covenant."

[36] The articles that had been violated were Articles 18(3), 19(3), 22(2) and 25 of the Covenant.

[37] Communication No. 104/1981, views adopted 6 April 1983, in *Selected Decisions*, Vol. 2, at 25.

[38] Article 20 reads: "(1) Any propaganda for war shall be prohibited by law. (2) Any advocacy of national, racial or religious hatred that constitutes incitement to discrimination, hostility or violence shall be prohibited by law."

[39] Communication No. 550/1993, views adopted 8 Nov. 1996, *supra* note 17.

and anti-Semitism. The Committee was of the view that the law was a restriction on freedom of expression and far exceeded the permissible scope of restrictions under Article 19(3). The essential issue before the Committee, however, was not the law itself, but whether the application of the law to the author could in the circumstances be seen as a necessary limitation on his rights.[40]

France argued that the clear implication of statements made by Faurisson was that the Jews had concocted the "myth" of the gas chambers for their own purposes.[41] The denial of the Holocaust was, France argued, a principal vehicle for anti-Semitism and the restriction was necessary to protect the rights of others, in particular, the right to be free from an atmosphere of that kind of racism. The Committee accepted this argument and concluded that the restriction was permissible under Article 19(3)(a). This case is notable for the number of individual opinions, an indication of the difficulty in reconciling freedom of expression with the provisions of Article 20(2)[42] and the right to be free from incitement to racism or anti-Semitism.

So far as national security is concerned, the important point to note is that the law which in itself was regarded as too wide in scope to satisfy the requirements of Article 19(3) nevertheless, in the particular case, was validly applied. The case concerned restrictions which were argued to be necessary for respect of the rights or reputations of others. The Committee might take a narrower view of laws which the State sought to justify as necessary to protect national security.

III. Parallel Restrictions on Other Rights and Freedoms

A. National Security in Relation to Articles 12 and 13

Article 12 protects the "right of everyone lawfully within the territory of a State" to have, within that territory, "the right to liberty of movement" including the freedom "to leave any country, including his own". Restrictions are not permitted, "except those which are provided by law, are necessary to protect national

---

[40] *Id.* at para. 9.3: "Although it does not contest that the application of the terms of the Gayssot Act, which, in their effect, make it a criminal offense to challenge the conclusions and the verdict of the International Military Tribunal at Nuremberg, may lead, under different conditions than the facts of the instant case, to decisions or measures incompatible with the Covenant, the Committee is not called upon to criticize the abstract laws enacted by States parties. The task of the Committee is to ascertain whether the conditions of the restrictions imposed on the right to freedom of expression are met in the communications which are brought before it."

[41] In the interview for which he had been convicted, the author referred to the "magic gas chamber" and to "the myth of the gas chambers" that had been a "dirty trick" *("une gredinerie")* endorsed by the victors in Nuremberg.

[42] For text of Art. 20(2), *see* note 38, *supra*.

security, public order, (*ordre public*), public health or morals or the rights and freedoms of others, and are consistent with the other rights recognized in the ... Covenant." Article 13 gives aliens who are lawfully in the territory of a State party certain protections; any decision to expel must be in accordance with law and there is a right of review "except where compelling reasons of national security otherwise require."

In several cases the Committee found violations of Article 12 or 13 in the absence of any explanation from the State as to the need for the restrictions which had been imposed. For example, Uruguay was found to have violated Article 12(2) by refusing or revoking a passport without providing reasons to justify its action.[43] In another case, the Dominican Republic denied the author a right of review, as required under Article 13, prior to his expulsion. The Government argued that its action was justified on the ground of national security. The Committee rejected this submission because the government failed to give details of the relevant law or to put forward reasons why the denial was necessary.[44] The Committee similarly concluded that Madagascar violated Article 13 when it expelled an alien without showing that there were compelling reasons of national security for doing so.[45]

In *Lauri Peltonen* v. *Finland*, decided in 1994,[46] the Committee upheld the government's denial of a passport to the applicant because he had failed to report for military service. Conscripts were not permitted to leave the country during the period of military service. No proceedings were taken against the author who lived abroad. He claimed that the denial of a passport was a punishment. The Committee found that the restrictions on the author's freedom of movement were provided by law and were necessary for the protection of national security and public order.[47]

---

[43] *E.g., Lichtensztejn* v. *Uruguay,* Communication No. 77/1980, views adopted 31 March 1982, *Selected Decisions,* Vol. 2, *at 102.*
[44] *Giry* v. *Dominican Republic,* Communication No. 193/1985, views adopted 20 July 1990, HRC 1990 Report, at 38.
[45] *Eric Hammel* v. *Madagascar,* Communication No. 155/1983, views adopted 3 April 1987, *Selected Decisions,* Vol. 2, at 11 and 179.
[46] Communication No. 492/1992, views adopted 21 July 1994, at 238.
[47] *Id.,* at 243, para. 8.4: "Restrictions of the freedom of movement of individuals who have not yet performed their military service are, in principle, to be considered necessary for the protection of national security and public order. The Committee notes that the author has stated that he needs his passport for holiday traveling, that he has not claimed that the authorities' decision not to provide him with a passport was discriminatory or that it infringed any of his other rights under the Covenant. In the circumstances of the present case, therefore, the Committee finds that the restrictions placed upon the author's right to leave any country are in accordance with Article 12(3) of the Covenant." *But see* dissent by Wennergren, who considered that the denial of the right to leave any country is also at issue and that the refusal of a passport infringes that right.

In *Celepli* v. *Sweden*, decided in 1994,[48] the author was an alien who was the subject of an expulsion order. Restrictions had been placed, *inter alia*, on his place of residence under a law giving power to expel, or prescribe restrictions on the movement of, an alien, where required for reasons of national security. The author, a Turkish Kurd, claimed that he had never been charged with any offense, and that he had had no opportunity to challenge the reasons for the restriction, which was later revoked. The State explained that measures against aliens suspected of belonging to terrorist organizations were applied in exceptional cases where there were substantial grounds to fear that the person in question played an active role in planning or executing terrorist activities. No arguments were advanced specifically linking the author to these issues. The Committee ruled the author's complaint under Article 13 inadmissible.

In regard to Article 12, the Committee accepted the argument that the restrictions imposed on the author's movements were justifiable on the ground that they had been imposed for compelling reasons of national security and were compatible with Article 12(3). The Committee did not look behind the State's assessment of the security risk posed by the author or the need for the restrictions to be imposed on him.

In a case concerning arbitrary detention alleged to violate Article 9, the Committee declined to question a State's evaluation of the security rating of an alien who was detained pending deportation.[49] In an earlier case from Uruguay, which also related to Article 9, the Committee observed that administrative detention of an individual under "prompt security measures" might be justified if the State were able to show that the person concerned constituted "a clear and serious threat to society which cannot be contained in any other manner."[50] That test does not appear to have been applied substantively in any case.

B. National Security and Freedom of Assembly and Association: Articles 21 and 22

Articles 21 (right of peaceful assembly) and 22 (right to freedom of association) allow only those restrictions which are imposed by law and which are necessary "in a democratic society" in the interests of national security, public safety, public order (*ordre public*), the protection of public health or morals or the protection of the rights and freedoms of others.

---

[48] Communication No. 456/1991, views adopted 18 July 1994, at 165.
[49] *J.R.C.* v. *Costa Rica*, Communication No. 196/1988, 30 March 1989, at 293.
[50] *Olga Machado de Campora Schweizer* v. *Uruguay*, Communication No. 66/1980, 12 Oct. 1982, *Selected Decisions*, Vol. 2, at 90.

For instance, in *de Lopez* v. *Uruguay*,[51] the alleged victim, a trade union organizer, was arrested and detained under "prompt security measures". He was charged with subversive association, convicted and sentenced to seven years' imprisonment, reduced on appeal to four and a half years. The Government did not put forward any material to support the view that the restrictions were justified. The Committee found violations of several articles of the Covenant, including Articles 22 and 19(1) and (2), because the author had suffered persecution in his trade union activities.

C. National Security and the Right to a Public Trial: Article 14(1)

Article 14(1) provides for the right to a public hearing of a criminal charge. The press and the public may be excluded "for reasons of morals, public order (*ordre public*) or national security in a democratic society". The Committee has commented on the importance of a public hearing and observed that even in cases in which the public is excluded from the trial, the judgment must, except in certain strictly defined circumstances, be made public.[52]

In several Uruguayan cases authors were sentenced to prison terms in secret trials before military tribunals in violation of the right to a public hearing. The military government did not attempt to justify the exclusion of the public for the reasons listed in Article 14.[53] Its reference to "prompt security measures" was not backed up by substantive submissions justifying any restriction or derogation of rights. The Committee found violations of Article 14(1) in these cases.

In a Zairian case, eight former members of Parliament were convicted in secret by the State security court.[54] The Committee found a violation of Article 14, because they were denied a fair and public hearing. Significant security issues were not argued by the State.

---

[51] *Delia Saldias de Lopez* v. *Uruguay* 52/1979, *supra* note 29, *Selected Decisions,* Vol. 1, at 88.

[52] General Comment on Article 14, at para. 6, in Compilation of General Comments, *supra* note 4.

[53] *Luciano Weinberger Weisz* v *Uruguay,* Communication No. 28/1978, *supra* note 13; *Pietraroia Zapala* v. *Uruguay,* Communication No. 44/1979, *supra* note 22 (violation of Article 14(1) because the applicant had no fair and public hearing and because the judgment rendered against him was not made public); Altesor v. Uruguay, Communication No. 10/1977, views adopted 29 March 1982, Select Decisions, Vol. 1, at 105.

[54] *Ngalula Mpandanjila* v. *Zaire,* Communication No. 138/1983, *supra* note 9. *See* D. McGoldrick, *The Human Rights Committee: Its Role in the Development of the International Covenant on Civil and Political Rights* (Clarendon Press 1991), at 418-19. To date, no state has raised any of the exceptions to the public hearing requirement in answer to an allegation against it.

IV. Restrictions During States of Emergency under Article 4

Article 4 sets forth the circumstances in which a state of emergency may be declared, and permits certain Covenant rights to be derogated from where such circumstances exist. This provision is strictly construed by the Committee. Derogations from Covenant rights (other than those rights in respect of which no derogation is permitted) may be made and will be recognized by the Committee only if the conditions specified in Article 4 are met. Following are the main principles which the Committee has developed and which it applies in reviewing country reports as well as deciding communications under the Optional Protocol procedure.

First, a State may not derogate from rights unless it can establish that there is in fact "a public emergency which threatens the life of the nation". In the reporting process, the Committee has observed in respect of several States that the laws under which an emergency may be proclaimed exceed the circumstances envisaged by Article 4; the mere resort to emergency powers does not lead to the conclusion that the circumstances envisaged by Article 4 exist. Unless the State puts before the Committee information establishing that there is in fact an emergency threatening the life of the nation, the Committee is unlikely to recognize the derogations.

The Committee has pursued a similar approach in cases under the Optional Protocol.[55] Unless the State provides full and comprehensive information, the Committee will not conclude that valid reasons exist to legitimize a departure from the normal legal regime prescribed by the Covenant.

Second, the existence of an emergency must be officially proclaimed for derogations to be permissible. The proclamation must be made in accordance with established legal provisions and with Article 4. Preferably, the courts should have power to review the legality of the declaration and of measures taken under it.[56] The Committee reserves its position to examine the declaration of emergency for its consistency with the provisions of the Covenant.

Third, the State must immediately notify other States through the U.N. Secretary-General of the provisions from which it has derogated and of the reasons

---

[55] Prof. Nowak has pointed out that the Committee has followed the Strasbourg institutions (which apply the European Convention on Human Rights) in emphasizing that it is empowered to review the legitimacy of a State's claim of a state of emergency in individual and inter-State applications. For instance, *in* Jorge Landinelli Silva v Uruguay, the Committee refused to accept that the conditions of Article 4(1) had been met where the State merely invoked the existence of exceptional circumstances. Communication No. 34/1978, views adopted 8 April 1981, in *Selected Decisions*, Vol. 1, *supra* note 13, at 65, para. 8.3.

[56] The Committee expressed its concern, in relation to Sri Lanka, that the courts did not have power to examine the legality of the declaration and of the measures taken in respect of Covenant rights. *Concluding Observations on Sri Lanka's 3rd periodic report*, U.N. Doc. CCPR/C/79/Add.56, 27 July 1995, at para. 17.

for having done so. The Committee has criticized States which have failed to do so.[57] Under the Optional Protocol procedure the Committee will not recognize any derogation in respect of rights which have not been included in the notification.[58]

Fourth, any derogation may be only to the extent strictly required by the exigencies of the situation, and must not be inconsistent with other obligations under international law, or discriminatory.[59]

Fifth, no derogations are permitted in respect of the Covenant articles set out in Article 4, paragraph (2). The Committee has criticized the emergency laws of many States which allow for derogations which exceed those permitted by the Covenant.[60] The right to freedom of expression (Article 19) is not listed as one of the non-derogable rights.

Sixth, in its General Comment on Article 4 in 1981, the Committee noted the exceptional and temporary nature of measures taken under Article 4, and appealed to all States parties concerned to inform the other States parties without delay of any declaration of an emergency, to fulfill their reporting obligations to the Committee, and in particular to ensure that non-derogable rights are observed.[61] In keeping with this view, the Committee invited Ireland in 1993 to examine critically

---

[57] *See* Jaime Oráa, *Human Rights in States of Emergency in International Law* (Clarendon Press 1992), at 77. Recent examples of States which have notified include: Venezuela, 7 July 1994, re Arts. 9, 12, and 17; Azerbaijan, 7 Feb. 1994, re Arts. 9(1) and (2), 19, 21, 22; Russia, in respect of the events of October 1993; the United Kingdom re Art. 9. Countries which have not notified include: Peru, *HRC Report*, July 1992, U.N. G.A.O.R. Supp. 40, U.N. Doc. A/47/40, at 338-45; Egypt, *HRC Report*, 7 Oct. 1993, U.N. Doc. A/48/40, Vol. I, at para. 704; Senegal, *HRC 1993 Report, id.*, at para. 113; Ireland, *HRC 1993 Report, id.*, at para. 603; Cameroon, *HRC 1994 Report*, U.N. Doc. A/49/40, Vol. I, at para. 189; Togo, *HRC 1994 Report, id.*, at para. 253; Sri Lanka, *Concluding Observations on Sri Lanka's 3rd periodic report*, U.N. Doc. CCPR/C/79/Add.56, 27 July 1995, at para. 36.

[58] *See, e.g., Consuelo Salgar de Montejo* v. *Colombia*, Communication No. 64/1979, views adopted 24 March 1982, and *Orlando Fals Borda et al.* v. *Colombia*, Communication No. 46/1979, in *Yearbook 1981-1982*, Vol. 2, *supra* note 12, at 421.

[59] General Comment on Art. 4, in Compilation of General Comments, *supra* note 4.

[60] *E.g.*, Algeria, *HRC Report*, July 1992, U.N. G.A.O.R, Supp. 40, U.N. Doc. A/47/40, at paras. 292, 299; Peru, *HRC 1992 Report, id.*, at para. 338 ff.; Mongolia, *HRC 1992 Report, id.*, at paras. 595, 601; Tanzania, *HRC Report*, July 1993, Supp. 40, U.N. Doc. A/48/40, at paras. 178, 184; Dominican Republic, *HRC 1993 Report, id.*, at paras. 457, 459; Uruguay, *HRC 1993 Report, id.*, at paras. 496, 503; Ireland, *HRC 1993 Report*, at paras. 593, 603; Jordan, *HRC Report*, July 1994, Supp. 40, U.N. Doc. A/49/40, at paras. 227, 231; Nepal, *Concluding Observations*, April 1995, at para. 9; Sri Lanka, *Concluding Observations*, at para. 17, July 1995. *See also Luciano Weinberger Weisz* v. *Uruguay*, Communication No. 28/1978, *supra* note 13.

[61] General Comment on Art. 4, *supra* note 59, at para. 3: "The Committee holds the view that measures taken under Article 4 are of an exceptional and temporary nature and may only last as long as the life of the nation concerned is threatened and that, in times of emergency, the protection of human rights becomes all the more important, particularly those rights from which no derogations can be made."

its long standing state of emergency.[62] Also, the United Kingdom was invited in 1995 to keep under review whether a situation of public emergency still existed.[63] In its comments on Egypt, the state of emergency was identified as one of the main obstacles impeding implementation of the Covenant.[64]

Seventh, States are expected in any event to fulfill their reporting obligations; there can be no reservation or derogation in respect of this obligation.[65] In practice, many States have reported while in a state of emergency.[66]

V. Restrictions on National Security Grounds Examined by the Committee in the Reporting Process

In the Optional Protocol procedure, the Committee's function is to determine whether a particular individual is a victim of a violation of the Covenant within the meaning of Articles 1 and 2 of the Optional Protocol. The Committee has stated that it "cannot review in the abstract whether national legislation contravenes the Covenant."[67] Nevertheless, where the Committee has found a violation of rights it might ask the State to review the law which gave rise to the violation as part of the remedy. For instance, in the Korean labor rights case,[68] it was implicit in the Committee's decision that the law at issue exceeded the scope permissible for its legitimate purpose. Accordingly, the Committee invited the State party to review the law in question.[69]

In the reporting procedure, the Committee is able to express its views on the compatibility of particular laws with the Covenant. The Committee's concluding observations, which are adopted by consensus, should carry considerable weight on such issues. The problem for the Committee is that it may not have sufficiently detailed information about particular restrictions imposed by law on rights or freedoms. The constitutional or legal provisions allowing for restrictions may be drawn up in broad and general terms, and their application to particular cases may

---

[62] *Ireland, HRC Report, July 1993, supra* note 60, at paras. 593, 603, 611. Uruguay was asked to review and to repeal derogating measures when the threat from the Tupamaros movement had diminished substantially. Summary Record 356, paras. 20 and 26; Summary Record 357, para. 20. The Committee recommended to the Republic of Korea that it should phase out its national security law as it was an obstacle to the full realization of rights. *HRC Report*, July 1992, Supp. 40, U.N. Doc. A/47/40, at paras. 511, 514, 518.

[63] *Concluding observations on U.K. Report, July 1995,* at para. 13.

[64] *Egypt, HRC 1993 Report, supra* note 57, at 704.

[65] General Comment on Art. 4., *supra* note 59, at para. 3.

[66] *See, e.g.*, Sri Lanka, Concluding Observations, *supra* note UN Doc. CCPR/C/79/Add.56.

[67] *Hertzberg* v. *Finland*, Communication No. 61/1979, *supra* note 24, *Selected Decisions,* Vol. 1, at 124, 126; *Faurisson* v. *France*, Communication No. 550/1993, *supra* note 39.

[68] *Jong-Kyu Sohn* v. *Republic of Korea*, Communication No. 518/1992, *supra* note *23.*

[69] *See also Faurisson* v. *France, supra* note 39.

not have given rise to precise interpretations in domestic law, or to communications under the Optional Protocol. As a result, the Committee may not be able to give more than a general view about the compatibility of particular legal measures with the Covenant. Examples illustrating the Committee's approach to this question follow. They involve situations where application of measures restricting freedom of expression gives rise to national security or public order issues.

A. Constitutional Provisions Allowing Broad Limitations of Freedom of Expression

Some constitutions define very broadly the limitations which may be imposed on rights and freedoms, including freedom of expression.[70] The grounds for limitation may not fit within the grounds permitted by paragraph 3(b) of Article 19. For example, the Constitution of Guinea permits restrictions to protect "the security of the realm", "the economic well-being of the people", and "national interests".[71] Under Japan's constitution, limitations are permitted on the ground of "public welfare", and it was not clear to the Committee that this provision would always be applied in conformity with the Covenant.[72]

B. Particular Laws Limiting Freedom of Expression on National Security or Related Grounds

Some laws create vaguely defined offenses or confer powers which may be exercised in ill-defined circumstances. In such cases it may not be clear whether the restrictions on rights are for a permitted purpose or are necessary for that purpose. It does not follow that those laws are applied in particular cases in violation of the Covenant. However, the Committee will question the State to ascertain how these limits are interpreted and applied in practice, and whether they authorize restrictions going beyond the Covenant.[73] The Committee sometimes comments on such laws in its concluding observations and calls for their repeal or amendment. Examples follow.

---

[70] *Iran, HRC Report*, July 1993, Supp. 40, U.N. Doc. A/48/40, at paras. 248-62; Romania, *HRC Report*, July 1994, Supp. 40, U.N. Doc. A/49/40, at paras. 132-39.
[71] *Guinea, HRC Report*, July 1993, id., at paras. 543-47.
[72] *Japan, HRC Report*, July 1994, at paras. 98, 105.
[73] *See, e.g.*, *Faurisson* v. *France*, *supra* note 17.

1. Laws Prohibiting Criticism of Parliament: Sri Lanka

The Committee expressed concern that Article 15(2) of the Sri Lankan Constitution allowed the right to freedom of expression to be restricted in relation to statements made during sessions of Parliament or its official committees (parliamentary privilege), particularly in view of the fact that the Parliament (Power and Privileges) Act as amended in 1978 gave Parliament the power to impose penalties for breaches of this Act. The Committee recommended the removal of these provisions.[74]

2. Sedition and Incitement to Public Disorder: Cyprus and Australia

The Criminal Code of Cyprus allowed restrictions to be imposed on the press, particularly with regard to seditious intent. The Committee noted that freedom to criticize the authorities and challenge government policies is a normal and essential component of a functioning democracy. Accordingly, the Committee recommended that restrictions on freedom of expression should be amended to conform with the Covenant's requirements.[75]

The Committee questioned whether Australia's sedition law, which criminalizes "advocacy and promotion of ill-will and hostility between classes of citizens", was genuinely necessary to protect national security or public order.[76]

3. Restrictions on Publishing Statements by Members of Proscribed Organizations: Ireland

Ireland's Broadcasting Authority Act 1960, Section 31, empowered the Minister to prohibit the national broadcasting organization from airing any matter that might undermine State security or promote crime. Orders of prohibition were made forbidding interviews or reports of interviews with members of several proscribed organizations as well as Sinn Fein, a registered political party that supports the aims of the outlawed IRA. The Human Rights Committee observed that the prohibition of interviews with certain groups by broadcast media infringed the freedom to receive and impart information under Article 19(2). The Committee recommended that the Government take necessary measures to ensure enjoyment of freedom of expression.[77]

---

[74] *Concluding Observation on Sri Lanka's 3rd periodic report,* July 1995, at para. 44.
[75] *Cyprus, HRC Report,* July 1994, at paras. 312-22, 327; Concluding Observations on Cyprus, 2nd periodic report.
[76] *HRC, Summary Record 402,* at para. 6.
[77] *HRC Report,* July 1993, at paras. 593-613.

4. Restrictions Relating to State Secrets: Russia, Belarus and Korea

In Russia, the concept of "state secret" still operates as a potential restriction on freedom of expression and on other Covenant rights. The Constitution provides under Article 29(4):[78]

> Everyone shall have the right to seek, receive, transfer, produce and disseminate information by any lawful means. The list of kinds of information constituting state secrets shall be established by federal law.

Laws on state secrets are applied to certain citizens by virtue of their positions. For example, members of the armed services must not disclose state or military secrets, and must not discuss or criticize the orders of commanders. Trials are held *in camera* when an open court hearing would be prejudicial to the protection of state secrets.[79] Restrictions on leaving the country still apply to persons who are said to hold state secrets.

In considering Russia's fourth report in 1995, the Human Rights Committee recommended that further steps be taken to bring the law concerning the right to leave the country into full compliance with its obligations under Article 12 paragraphs (2) and (3) of the Covenant and that in particular the restrictions related to holders of State secrets be removed.[80]

A number of other States formerly part of the Eastern bloc still deny exit visas to those holding State secrets. The Human Rights Committee considered such a law in Belarus to be incompatible with Article 12(3) of the Covenant,[81] and also Article 19(2), because it infringed the right to receive information of all kinds.

The Committee criticized laws of the Republic of Korea which defined State secrets broadly in connection with espionage, and recommended that the relevant laws be amended.[82]

5. Self-Censorship: Iran

In extreme authoritarian societies, freedom of expression is limited by forms of self-censorship. The Committee raised the question of self-censorship in dealing with a report by Iran.[83]

---

[78] *Russia, 4th periodic report, at* paras. 225-26, 246.

[79] *Id.* at para. 189.

[80] *Id.* at para. 178; Concluding Observations of the Committee, July 1995, at para. 34.

[81] *Belarus, HRC Report*, July 1992, Supp. 40, U.N. Doc. A/47/40, at paras. 553-60; Hungary, *HRC Report*, July 1993, Supp. 40, U.N. Doc. A/48/40, at paras. 655, 662.

[82] *HRC Report*, 1991-1992, at paras. 516, 518.

[83] *Iran, HRC Report*, July 1993, at paras. 248-262: "Self-censorship also seems to be widespread in the media and severe limitations appear to have been placed upon the exercise of freedom of assembly and of association."

6. Use of Military Courts to Try Cases Involving Civilians: Uruguay, Egypt and Ireland

Some of the cases from Uruguay, Egypt and Ireland mentioned above involved trial by military courts or military judges. The Committee often expresses its concern over the existence of such special courts. Its view is that military courts should not have the authority to try cases which do not refer to offenses committed by members of the armed forces in the course of their duties.[84] For legal consistency and procedural guarantees it is important that special courts exist as an exceptional measure if at all.[85]

7. Hong Kong

The sensitive nature of national security has made it one of the chief concerns in Hong Kong's reversion to Chinese rule. Issues reflecting on freedom of expression in Hong Kong were considered by the Committee in 1995 and 1996. For example, the Emergency Regulation Ordinance gives power to the executive to deal with a state of emergency and, *inter alia*, to make regulations providing for censorship.[86] However, as of June 1997, no detailed laws covering emergencies had yet been adopted. Another concern is that while the Joint Declaration makes the maintenance of public order a responsibility of the Hong Kong Special Administrative Region ("HKSAR"), Article 18 of the Basic Law gives the Chinese government power to apply its national laws in a state of emergency arising "by reason of turmoil which endangers national unity or security". The Committee is concerned that these provisions do not correspond with Article 4 of the Covenant.[87]

Article 23 of the Basic law requires the HKSAR to enact laws to prohibit acts of secession, subversion, or theft of state secrets. One fear is that subversion would be regarded as including counter-revolutionary propaganda which would preclude advocacy of other forms of government. Another is that there is no definition of state secrets. In 1994 a reporter in China working for a Hong Kong paper was sentenced by a Chinese court to 12 years for "spying and stealing state secrets".[88] He had reported on official Chinese plans to sell gold and raise interest rates. This kind of action by China is regarded as an ominous warning of the kinds of risks to human rights which could arise after 1 July 1997.

---

[84] *Egypt, HRC Report*, July 1993, supra note 57, at paras. 698, 706.

[85] *Ireland, HRC Report*, July 1993, at paras. 593-603; Jordan, *HRC Report*, July 1994, at paras. 227-31.

[86] *See* 4th Periodic Report of the U.K., Supplementary Report on Hong Kong, U.N. Doc. CCPR/C/95/Add.5, at paras. 228-230.

[87] *Concluding Observations on 4th Periodic Report of the U.K., Supplementary Report on Hong Kong, Annual Report 1996*, at paras. 60-61.

[88] *Id.* at para. 246.

VI. Summary and Conclusions

The Committee has had the opportunity in only a few cases to examine, on the merits, the necessity of restrictions on freedom of expression justified by reference to national security or public order. In the several cases concerning repressive measures adopted in Uruguay at a time of civil unrest and conflict, and in a handful of other cases from countries including Zaïre, Madagascar and Equatorial Guinea, the non-co-operation of the States parties precluded the Committee from analyzing the need for restrictions. For these reasons it is difficult to draw comprehensive conclusions about the factors which would be considered relevant to the question whether restrictions on freedom of expression to protect national security are "necessary" in various circumstances.

Nevertheless, it is possible to draw some conclusions by bringing into account decisions under other articles and by reference to the Committee's General Comments and its observations in the reporting procedure. For instance, although the Committee has not dealt with any cases involving sedition, it has criticized, in the reporting procedure, the sedition laws of Cyprus. While it has not examined any case concerning administrative or penal restrictions on the media or others for publishing or disclosing classified information, it has been critical of restrictions imposed on holders of state secrets in Russia and other countries. Following are several principles drawn from the Committee's comments made in the course of the reporting procedure and its "case-law" on individual communications.

Reporting Procedure

1. The Committee will express its view that constitutional and legal provisions which permit restrictions on freedom of expression exceeding those permitted by paragraph (3) of Article 19 are incompatible with the Covenant, even if they have not been applied improperly in a particular case.

Communications Procedure

2. The Committee will apply strictly the requirement that restrictions on freedom of expression are not permissible under the Covenant unless imposed by law. It will insist that details of the law be provided by the State and that the law itself must be compatible with the Covenant.

3. The Committee will insist that the State party explain how a law which restricts freedom of expression is said to apply to the actions of the alleged victim, and must provide details of the law and the alleged offense.

4. The Committee will consider the necessity of a restriction only when the above conditions are met. It will insist that the State party explain the circumstances which make necessary the restriction in law and its application to the alleged victim, and the ways in which the actions of the alleged victim pose a threat to national

security. The existence of an identifiable internal or external threat to security is not conclusive; it is necessary, in addition, to show (a) how the exercise by an individual of his or her right to freedom of expression contributed to that threat or otherwise put national security at risk, and (b) why it was necessary to restrict that right to protect national security.

Where there are no clear threats to security, internal or external, the burden on the State to establish the need for restrictive measures is a heavy one. The terms "pressing" or "imperative social need" have been suggested as a test in other contexts,[89] but these terms have not been used by the Committee.

5. In considering the question whether a particular restriction is necessary, the Committee will apply the proportionality test by asking the State whether the restriction is necessary for the particular purpose and proportional to that purpose, bearing in mind that restrictions on rights are to be strictly construed. The fact that particular kinds of restrictions have been adopted in many democratic countries may lend some support to the view that they are necessary and proportional, but is not conclusive.

6. The Committee will reserve to its own consideration whether a particular restriction is necessary in the light of the circumstances and submissions put to it by the State.

7. Restrictions may be found justifiable in terms of paragraph 3(a) of Article 19 if they are an appropriate implementation of Article 20 (concerning propaganda for war and incitement to hatred)[90] or if they support Article 5 by preventing actions which are likely to destroy rights and freedoms. The only case in which the Committee upheld a restriction on freedom of expression in the interest of protecting national security was *M.A.* v. *Italy*, which involved a perceived threat to democracy in re-establishing the Fascist party.

8. The Committee will scrutinize with particular care any restrictions on the peaceful advocacy of different forms of government, criticism of government or speech that supports labor rights.

---

[89] *Paul Sieghart, The International Law of Human Rights* (Clarendon Press 1993): "The notion 'necessary' implies the existence of a 'pressing social need' which may include the 'clear and present danger' test [articulated by the U.S. Supreme Court, see chapter on the United States, elsewhere in this volume] and must be assessed in the light of the circumstances of a given case." *See also* European Court of Human Rights, *Handyside* v. *United Kingdom*, Judgment of 7 Dec. 76, Series A, no. 24, at 49 (stating that the word "necessary" in the ECHR implies the existence of a "pressing social need").

[90] For the text of Art. 20, *see supra* note 38.

Freedom of Expression and National Security: Judicial and Policy Approaches under the European Convention on Human Rights and Other Council of Europe Instruments

Paul Mahoney and Lawrence Early[1]

I. Introduction

Democracy is built on a paradox: by guaranteeing freedom of expression and information, it gives its opponents the means to undermine its existence. Unlike closed authoritarian systems which are characterized by the suppression of the free flow of ideas and opinions and interpret dissent as an overt attack on the security of their power structures, democracy must, by definition, be tolerant of the opposing view.

The freedom to hold opinions and to receive and impart information and ideas without interference by public authorities is of central importance to the functioning of the *Rechtstaat* (the state governed by the rule of law), as is the existence of a free and inquiring press system. The guarantee, and development, of these freedoms are at the heart of the value system espoused by the Council of Europe.[2] At the Vienna Summit Conference held in October 1993, the Heads of State and Government of the member States of the Council of Europe solemnly reaffirmed that: "guaranteed freedom of expression and notably of the media ... must remain, in our view, decisive criteria for assessing any application for membership."

The legal and political culture of the Council of Europe on freedom of expression and information is, not surprisingly, rooted in the European tradition. It is precisely this tradition which enables democracies in Europe to resolve the dilemmas created by the above-mentioned paradox. Unlike the approach favored by the authors of the First Amendment to the United States Constitution, the Council of Europe system does not view freedom of expression and information as an unyielding absolute. As is put in stark relief by the case law under the European Convention on Human Rights (ECHR), this system acknowledges the need to reconcile the exercise of this freedom with the protection of other lawful rights and legitimate interests, including national security.

---

[1] The ideas and opinions expressed in this report are those of the authors alone and do not reflect the official standpoint of the institutions of the European Convention on Human Rights or of the Council of Europe as a whole.

[2] There are now 40 member States of the Council of Europe, including the following 16 Central and East European countries: Albania, Bulgaria, Croatia, Czech Republic, Estonia, Hungary, Latvia, Lithuania, Moldova, Poland, Romania, Russia, Slovenia, Slovakia, "the former Yugoslav Republic of Macedonia" and Ukraine. The following Central and East European countries have applied for membership: Armenia, Azerbaijan, Belarus, Bosnia and Herzegovina and Georgia.

Article 10 of the ECHR reads as follows:

1. Everyone has the right to freedom of expression. This right shall include freedom to hold opinions and to receive and impart information and ideas without interference by public authority and regardless of frontiers. This article shall not prevent States from requiring the licensing of broadcasting, television or cinema enterprises.

2. The exercise of these freedoms, since it carries with it duties and responsibilities, may be subject to such formalities, conditions, restrictions or penalties as are prescribed by law and are necessary in a democratic society, in the interests of national security, territorial integrity or public safety, for the prevention of disorder or crime, for the protection of health or morals, for the protection of the reputation or rights of others, for preventing the disclosure of information received in confidence, or for maintaining the authority and impartiality of the judiciary.

The following analysis seeks to highlight the ways in which the European Commission and European Court of Human Rights have dealt with attempts by governments to restrict Article 10 freedoms on grounds of national security (Part II).[3] In addition to an overview of the judicial approach under the ECHR to the reconciliation of free speech and national security imperatives, the analysis also focuses on the Council of Europe's standard-setting instruments in the media field which are of relevance to the impact of national security (Part III). A final section is devoted to the monitoring mechanisms recently introduced within the framework of the Council of Europe as well as to the treatment of the issue of national security in the context of the organization's co-operation and assistance Programs for Central and East European countries in the media and human rights field (Part IV).

II. Substantive Norms

A. Rationale of Freedom of Expression as Protected under the ECHR

The guiding philosophy which the European Court and Commission of Human Rights have consistently applied was enunciated in the 1976 landmark judgment in *Handyside* v. *UK*[4]:

---

[3] Thirty-two of the 40 member States are Contracting Parties to the European Convention on Human Rights, and have accepted the right of individual petition to the Commission under Article 25 ECHR as well as the compulsory jurisdiction of the Court under Article 46.

[4] Judgment of December 7, 1976, Series A vol. 24, § 49. The applicant was a left-wing publisher convicted of publishing obscene material. The British courts had found that one of his publications, an anti-authoritarian handbook on living primarily addressed to children and adolescents, tended to "deprave and corrupt" its intended readership and was therefore

> Freedom of expression constitutes one of the essential foundations of [a 'democratic society'], one of the basic conditions for its progress and for the development of every man. Subject to paragraph 2 of Article 10, it is applicable not only to 'information' or 'ideas' that are favorably received or regarded as inoffensive or as a matter of indifference, but also those that offend, shock or disturb the State or any sector of the population. Such are the demands of that pluralism, tolerance and broadmindedness without which there is no 'democratic society'.

The most frequently cited rationale for free speech in the Strasbourg case law is that derived from citizen participation in the democratic process.[5] In particular, judicial recognition has been given to freedom of the media as an indispensable motor for ensuring the functioning of political democracy. In the 1986 case of *Lingens* v. *Austria*[6] the Court affirmed the capital role of the press in imparting information and ideas on political issues as on other topics of public interest and, as a corollary, the right of the public to receive such information and ideas. An open discussion of political issues is essential to ensure the efficacy of the elective process, the Court noted. The press was described as having the task of purveyor of information and "public watchdog".

From 1976 onwards the argument that free speech is an integral part of each individual's self-fulfillment—its so-called "emotive" role—may also be found in several judgments. However, the free-market-place-of-ideas doctrine, which has influenced much of the thinking in the United States, has hardly figured, if at all, in the Strasbourg scheme. In general, the European Court and Commission have opted for a much more community-oriented view of freedom of speech in comparison with the individual-autonomy perspective now largely favored in the United States.[7] As the *Handyside* reference to pluralism, tolerance and broadmindedness presaged, the

---

criminally obscene. The Strasbourg Court found no violation of Article 10 on the facts (protection of morals). The principle quoted has been repeatedly reaffirmed, most recently in the Court's *De Haes and Gijsels* v. *Belgium* judgment of February 24, 1997.

[5] *See* Rolv Ryssdal (current President of the Strasbourg Court and former President of the Norwegian Supreme Court), *Freedom of Expression under the European Convention on Human Rights*, public lecture given at University College Galway, Ireland, April 11, 1994.

[6] Judgment of July 8, 1986, Series A vol. 103. The case concerned the private prosecution and conviction for criminal libel of a journalist for having written a highly critical article on the political stance of the then Austrian Chancellor, Bruno Kreisky. The Strasbourg Court found a violation of ECHR art.10 , largely because there was not available under Austrian libel law any defense of fair comment. Most recently, the Court's *Worm* v. *Austria* judgment of August 29, 1997 reaffirmed the *Lingens* doctrine on the critical role of a free press in a democracy.

[7] *See* Eric Barendt, *Freedom of Speech in an Era of Mass Communication*; Christopher McCrudden, *Freedom of Speech and Racial Equality*; and Paul Mahoney, *Emergence of a European Conception of Freedom of Speech*, in P.B.H. Birks, ed. *Pressing Problems in the Law, vol. 1: Criminal Justice and Human Rights*, (1995).

Strasbourg rationale has treated freedom of speech as a vital tool of democratic society not only for facilitating the political process, public debate, and individual and group self-fulfillment—the procedural/functional framework, if you like -- but also for furthering the democratic health, ideals and values of the community. To this extent the European conception of free speech is not "content-neutral" in the way that the current American approach (if not the Canadian approach) is. This possible difference of philosophy and of result in concrete contexts between the two sides of the Atlantic should not be overlooked in the following account.

B. Text of Article 10 ECHR

As a consequence of the generality and vagueness of the wording of Article 10 ECHR, an inherent characteristic of "constitutional" provisions guaranteeing fundamental rights, it is not only the text of the article that determines the content of the freedom guaranteed in specific contexts but also the accumulated case law of the Strasbourg Commission and Court.

Further, Article 10 ECHR expressly contemplates in its paragraph 2 that restrictions on an individual's free speech may be justified in a democratic society for the common good. This paragraph is unique in the ECHR, since it is the only clause that speaks explicitly of the duties and responsibilities of the holder of the right or freedom guaranteed. The Strasbourg Court has recognized that freedom of expression as safeguarded under Article 10 involves a balance of interests between the liberty of the individual to receive and impart information, on the one hand, and the need to protect the community and other individuals against the perceived harm that can be inflicted by speech, on the other. As noted above, under the European approach there is no brutal dichotomy between protected and unprotected speech: "even admitted interferences with a protected form of expression may be legitimately justified under paragraph 2".[8] The balance between liberty and restriction is not entirely neutral, however, in that one of the accepted canons of construction of the ECHR is that clauses permitting exceptions to the protected rights and freedoms should always be narrowly interpreted.[9]

---

[8] *See* Ryssdal, *supra* note 5.

[9] *Klass and Others* v. *Germany*, Judgment of September 6, 1978, Series A vol. 28, § 42. *But see*, Steven Greer, *Public Interest and Human Rights in the ECHR*, Council of Europe document H(95) 1 at 8-9, who considers that "choosing between the 'priority-to-rights' or 'balance' tests has become a key source of confusion" in determining the boundaries of European review.

C. Conditions for Justifying an Interference with Freedom of Expression

Broadly speaking, for any interference with the exercise of freedom of expression to be justified under paragraph 2 of Article 10 ECHR (whatever interest of the community is said to have prompted it), it must
(a) be prescribed by law,
(b) pursue one or more of the listed legitimate aims,
(c) and be necessary in a democratic society for the attainment of that aim.

1. Prescribed by Law

The expression "prescribed by law" means that the interference in question must have some basis in, and comply with, the law of the country concerned, which may be a statute but also unwritten law such as the common law. However, it was made clear in the first *Sunday Times* v. *UK* judgment (where the subject-matter of complaint was the British contempt-of-court rules aimed at preventing trial by newspaper) that the expression did not merely involve a reference back to domestic law.[10] As it was put in later cases involving the equivalent expression in Article 8 ECHR (which guarantees, *inter alia*, the right to privacy), over and above compliance with domestic law it also requires that domestic law itself be compatible with the minimum standards of the rule of law.[11] It thus implies that there must be a measure of legal protection in domestic law against arbitrary interferences by public authorities with freedom of expression so that the quality of the domestic law is also in issue. Two of the implications of proper legal protection were specified in the *Sunday Times* judgment:

> Firstly, the law must be adequately accessible: the citizen must be able to have an indication that is adequate in the circumstances of the legal rules applicable to a given case. Secondly, a norm cannot be regarded as a `law' unless it is formulated with sufficient precision to enable the citizen to regulate his conduct: he must be able -- if need be with appropriate advice -- to foresee, to a degree that is reasonable in the circumstances, the consequences which a given action may entail.[12]

---

[10] Judgment of April 26, 1979, Series A vol. 30. The background to this case was that between 1958 and 1961 a pharmaceutical company manufactured and marketed a drug called *Thalidomide*, which was taken by a number of pregnant women who later gave birth to children suffering from serious deformities. In late 1972 *The Sunday Times* newspaper was restrained by injunction from publishing an article on the *Thalidomide* tragedy on the ground that the article would involve prejudgment of a pending civil action for damages brought by the victims against the pharmaceutical company.

[11] See *Malone* v. *UK*, Judgment of August 2, 1984, Series A vol.82, §67; *Kruslin* v. *France*, Judgment of April 24, 1990, Series A vol. 176-A, §§ 27 and 30; *Huvig* v. *France*, Judgment of April 24, 1990, Series A vol. 176-B, §§ 26 and 29.

[12] *Supra* note 10 at § 49.

This requirement of legal certainty was explained in the context of Article 8 cases on interception of communications as meaning that the public is entitled to know in advance the limits on and the conditions of what is allowed and, in addition, to have the assurance that those conditions are contained in obligations that are legally binding on the surveillance agencies. In the British case of *Malone*[13] an administrative practice, although made public and approved by Parliament, was held not to be sufficient to make the impugned tapping of the applicant's telephone "prescribed by law" since it was not legally regulated.

A discretionary element and unresolved grey areas in the governing law will not prevent an interference from being "prescribed by law".[14] However, the national law, whether it be written or unwritten, must indicate the scope and manner of exercise of any discretion conferred on the public authorities with sufficient clarity to give the individual adequate protection against arbitrary interference.[15] This was found not to be so in two French cases (*Kruslin* and *Huvig*[16]), where several vital conditions concerning the carrying out of telephone tapping measures by the police under the Penal Code and the subsequent use made of the results were not specified in legal provisions. Because of this lacuna, the Court concluded, the system did not afford adequate safeguards against possible abuse, and the interference with the right to respect for correspondence and private life was not "prescribed by law".

The guarantee of adequate legal protection in relation to freedom of speech under Article 10 takes on further significance in the ECHR scheme when taken together with Article 6(1), which guarantees the right of access to the domestic courts in the determination of one's "civil rights and obligations".

---

[13] *Supra* note 11. The opposite conclusion was reached in the Swedish case of *Leander* (Judgment of Mar. 26, 1987, Series A vol. 116) - where the interests of national security were invoked as a justification by the respondent Government - since the conditions governing the security vetting of government employees were set out in some detail in an official ordinance. However, in the recent case of Halford v. the United Kingdom which concerned, *inter alia,* an alleged tapping of a senior police officer's office telephone by her employers, the Merseyside Police, the Court found that the relevant legislation governing interception of telephone communications did not apply to internal communications systems. There was accordingly no provision in domestic law to regulate interception of such systems. The interference at issue was therefore not "in accordance with the law."(*see* Judgment of June 25, 1997, §51).

[14] *See e.g., The Sunday Times* (No. 1), *supra* note 10 at §§ 49-52; *Barthold* v. *Germany*, Judgment of March 25, 1985, Series A vol. 90, §§46-47; and *Open Door and the Dublin Well Woman* v. *Ireland,* Judgment of 29 October 1992, Series A vol. 246, §§ 59-60.

[15] *See Tolstoy Miloslavsky* v. *UK,* Judgment of 13 July 1995, Series A vol. 323, § 37, for the most recent reaffirmation of this principle in relation to freedom of expression.

[16] *Supra* note 11.

2. Legitimate Aim

The list of legitimate aims given in paragraph 2 of Article 10 ECHR is exhaustive, not merely illustrative.[17] The purposes are reasonably clear in what they mean and in what they cover and have not generated much case law. An obvious point is that not only must the purpose invoked by the respondent government be one that falls within the limitative list in paragraph 2, but also the concrete measures must have been genuinely directed towards achieving that aim.[18] The "interests of national security" represent one of the listed legitimate aims, capable of justifying a restriction on freedom of expression.

3. Necessity in a Democratic Society

As one commentator has written of the democratic necessity condition, "one of the key tasks for the Court and the Commission, and one of the most difficult, is to test the persuasiveness of any [public interest] defense to ensure that it complies with the genuine interests of democracy and is not merely political expediency in disguise".[19] The word "necessary" in the ECHR, so the European Court held in *Handyside*, implies the existence of a "pressing social need".[20] In this context, the Strasbourg enforcement bodies have to examine whether the reasons adduced by the national authorities to justify the interference are "relevant and sufficient" and whether the interference caused was proportionate to the legitimate aim pursued.

The requirement of democratic necessity formulated in such terms would at first sight appear to involve a strict test. However, it was recognized in *Handyside* that in identifying a "pressing social need" and then adopting appropriate remedial measures in a given case, the national authorities enjoy what is termed a "margin of appreciation," in other words a degree of discretion.[21]

This deference to national choice follows from the underlying philosophy of the ECHR. By virtue of Article 1, the ECHR leaves to the national authorities the primary responsibility for securing the guaranteed rights and freedoms within the national legal order.[22] The machinery of protection set up under the ECHR is subsidiary to the national systems safeguarding human rights. Furthermore, the ECHR does not so much

---

[17] It should be noted, however, that the licensing of broadcasting may lead to interferences whose aims, although not corresponding to any of those listed in paragraph 2, will be legitimate under the third sentence of paragraph 1 (for example cultural or language quotas). The justification of such interferences must nevertheless be reviewed in the light of the other requirements of paragraph 2. *See Informationsverein Lentia and Others* v. *Austria,* Judgment of November 24, 1993, Series A vol. 276.

[18] *See e.g., Handyside, supra* note 4 at § 52.

[19] Greer, *supra* note 9 at 8.

[20] *Supra* note 4 at §48.

[21] *Id.*

[22] Article 1 provides: "The High Contracting Parties shall secure to everyone within their jurisdiction the rights and freedoms defined in Section 1 of this Convention."

impose uniform rules as set standards to which a Contracting State may conform in a variety of different ways, depending on its legal, political and social traditions and structures. The Contracting States have available to them a spectrum of choices for fulfilling their duty of implementation; and choice implies discretion and even a certain scope for trial and error in dealing with "pressing social needs". The national authorities' assessment of a "pressing social need" will not be found to give rise to a violation of the ECHR merely because the judges on the Strasbourg Court would not personally have come to the same decision had they been acting in the place of the national authorities, or even because the judges consider that the ECHR's objectives could have been better achieved in another way. For there to be a violation, the national authorities' assessment must fall outside the range of permissible options open to them, outside their "margin of appreciation".

The doctrine of the "margin of appreciation" is a legitimate expression of judicial self-restraint; it serves to trace the dividing line between judicial law-making in Strasbourg and the proper responsibility of the democratic institutions of the ECHR countries.[23]

The following pattern as regards the "margin of appreciation" under Article 10 ECHR can be inferred from the case law to date: whilst all actionable interferences with freedom of expression have to be justified as necessary in a democratic society, the level of protection afforded to the individual and, conversely, the area of discretion open to the state will vary according to the context. The Convention institutions would appear to apply a sliding scale of protection. At the top end of the scale political speech and political comment by the press undoubtedly enjoy the highest level of protection. The state must make out especially convincing grounds if it is to justify restricting the flow to the public of information and opinion on matters in the political arena. As one goes down the scale from political speech in its pure form, the degree of public interest involved will be a material factor in determining the limits of what is a "necessary" restriction in a democratic society. Thus, as illustrated by the first *Sunday Times* case, risk of trial by newspaper may well not suffice to muzzle the press during a whole decade from commenting or even campaigning on a national tragedy.[24] The Strasbourg Court, in finding a violation of Article 10 ECHR, reaffirmed that freedom of expression embraces not only the press's right and duty to comment on matters of public concern, but also the public's right to be properly informed. A more detailed study is beyond the remit of this chapter, but doubtless even the existing case law would allow some attempt to be made to situate with more certainty on this sliding scale of protection areas such as problems of concern to a local community alone; debate in the scientific, technical and educational sphere; debate on religious and philosophical issues; the expression of ideas through cultural endeavors and the arts; productions of the entertainment industry; commercial speech; and not ignoring the personal or trivial information of everyday discourse.

---

[23] *See* Paul Mahoney, "Judicial Activism and Judicial Restraint in the European Court of Human Rights: Two Sides of the Same Coin", 11 *Human Rights Law Journal* 57, 78-88 (1990).
[24] *Supra* note 10.

As regards the interests of national security in particular, although the state is recognized as enjoying a "certain discretion", that discretion is not unfettered. This was stressed by the Court in *Klass and Others* v. *Germany*[25] when reviewing the compatibility with Article 8 ECHR of the German system of secret surveillance by the security service. To begin with, the Court stated, whatever system of surveillance the state chooses to adopt, there must exist adequate and effective safeguards against abuse. Consequently, to pick up a point addressed earlier, even if the conditions governing a national security interference are spelled out with sufficient clarity in domestic law, so that the "prescribed-by-law" requirement is satisfied, the issue of safeguards against abuse will also enter the picture in the context of the "democratic necessity" requirement. Furthermore, Strasbourg bodies will not simply accept without more the assertions by a respondent government of facts to justify a restriction. However, in a recent right-to-liberty case concerning Article 5 (1) ECHR, where an impugned power of arrest "represented a *bona fide* attempt by a democratically elected parliament to deal with terrorist crime under the rule of law", the Court was "prepared to attach some credence" to the respondent government's declaration concerning the existence of reliable but confidential information which could not be revealed in the interests of protecting lives and personal safety. Nevertheless, the respondent government had to "furnish at least some facts or information capable of satisfying the Court" that the particular arrest was justified.[26] It is not inconceivable that a similar approach might be taken in relation to reluctance on the part of a respondent government to reveal all the facts prompting a decision to restrict information flow on the ground of national security.

D. National Security Defense under Article 10 ECHR

The issue of national security has not often been litigated before the Strasbourg enforcement bodies.

In two decisions from the early 1990s the Commission rejected as inadmissible, on the ground of being manifestly ill-founded,[27] two applications brought respectively against Ireland and the United Kingdom in which the applicants, journalists or radio and television producers, challenged governmental restrictions on broadcasts involving persons

---

[25] Judgment of September 6, 1976, Series A vol. 28, §§ 49-50.

[26] *Murray Family* v. *UK*, Judgment of 23 October 1994, Series A vol. 300-A, §§ 59-60. The most recent authority is the *Chahal* v. *UK*, Judgment of 15 November 1996, wherein the Court recognized that the use of confidential material may be unavoidable as a basis for the detention of an individual. However, the Court stressed that this does not mean that the national authorities can be free from effective control by the domestic courts whenever they choose to assert that national security and terrorism are involved. For the Court, habeas corpus or judicial review proceedings to challenge the lawfulness of detention must not be undermined simply on the basis of the authorities' appeal to the national security considerations at stake in a particular case (*see* §§ 130-133 of the judgment).

[27] § 2 ECHR, art. 27, §2.

or organizations deemed to be linked to terrorism. In *Purcell and Others* v. *Ireland*[28] the statutory order objected to was an outright ban on interviews with spokespersons from a number of listed organizations and on broadcasts by or on behalf of Sinn Fein; whereas in *Brind and Others* v. *UK*[29] the ministerial directive was somewhat narrower, prohibiting the broadcasting of the voices of those speaking on behalf of or supporting terrorist groups in Northern Ireland.

In each case the Commission found that the objective of the contested measures was to combat terrorism and that this came within the legitimate aims listed in Article 10 (2) ECHR, namely protecting the interests of national security and preventing disorder and crime. In *Purcell* the Commission noted that the order "prohibit[ed] the use of the broadcast media for the purpose of advocating support for organizations which seek to undermine, by violence and other illegal means, the constitutional order and the fundamental rights it guarantees".

In each case the Commission also concluded that the resultant interference with journalistic freedom of expression could not be regarded as disproportionate to the legitimate aim pursued.[30] Having regard to the special problems experienced in combating terrorism, the Commission "ha[d] no doubt as to the difficulties involved in striking a fair balance between the requirements of protecting freedom of information, especially the free flow of information from the media, and the need to protect the State and the public against armed conspiracies seeking to overthrow the democratic order which guarantees this freedom and other human rights". These difficulties evidently persuaded the Commission to accept that the range of policy options available to the state for fighting against the violence of terrorism, that is the state's "margin of appreciation", was wide enough to include the contested restrictions on journalistic freedom of expression.

These decisions have not been greeted with unanimous approval by commentators. David Pannick, a British barrister and ECHR expert, has stressed that, along with the individual speaker's right to be allowed the maximum degree of freedom to express himself or herself, the public's right to know, to be fully and intelligently informed about matters of concern for society, also lies at the heart of freedom of speech. "It does not fit easily with those important values for the Commission to tolerate restrictions on how news and current affairs programs may be presented to the public."[31] Similar thinking colors the recent judgment in *Jersild* v. *Denmark*,[32] where the Strasbourg

---

[28] Application no. 15404/89, admissibility decision of April 16, 1991, reported in 70 *Decisions and Reports* (of the European Commission of Human Rights) 262 (1991).

[29] Application no. 18714/91, admissibility decision of May 9, 1994, as yet unreported.

[30] The Commission arrived at a similar conclusion in *McLaughlin* v. *UK*, Application no. 18759/91, admissibility decision of May 9, 1994, as yet unreported, where the challenge against the UK directive was brought not by a member of the media but by an active member of Sinn Fein who was an elected local councillor in Northern Ireland.

[31] *See* David Pannick,"ECHR, art.10,", in *Pressing Problems in the Law*, *supra* note 7; and *also* David Pannick QC, *The Times*, August 2, 1994.

[32] 298 Eur.Ct.H.R. (Ser. A)(1994).

Court placed much reliance on the notion of editorial freedom in the presentation of news and current affairs. The conviction and fining of a television journalist under anti-racist criminal legislation for good-faith reporting of racist speech, albeit with little or no accompanying commentary, was held not to be justified under paragraph 2 of Article 10 ECHR. It is not unreasonable to infer from *Jersild* that the performance by journalists of their normal job of informing the public about significant (and, in particular, disturbing or dangerous) phenomena in society cannot, in the absence of strong justificatory grounds, constitute a breach of freedom of expression under the ECHR.

The leading analysis of the Court in this sphere is to be found in the two judgments rendered in 1991 in the *Spycatcher* case.[33] A number of newspapers in the United Kingdom printed extracts from the unauthorized memoirs of a retired member of the British security service. The book (entitled *Spycatcher*) included allegations by the author that his former employers had engaged in illegal activities. The Crown instituted proceedings for breach of confidence and obtained permanent injunctions restraining the newspapers from any further publication of *Spycatcher* material. These injunctions remained in force even after the book had been published in the United States and become available in the United Kingdom. The Court had no difficulty in finding that the interference with the applicant newspapers' freedom of expression was "prescribed by law" and pursued aims that were legitimate under paragraph 2 of Article 10 ECHR, namely the maintenance of the authority of the judiciary (which includes the protection of the rights of litigants) and the protection of national security. The main point in contention was whether the interference could be regarded as necessary in a democratic society. The analysis of the "necessity" issue was prefaced with a statement of principle of some importance:

> [Whilst] Article 10 . . . does not in terms prohibit the imposition of prior restraints on publication, as such . . ., the dangers inherent in prior restraints are such that they call for the most careful scrutiny on the part of the Court. This is especially so as far as the press is concerned, for news is a perishable commodity and to delay its publication, even for a short period, may well deprive it of all value and interest.[34]

The Vice-President of the Court, Rudolph Bernhardt, went even further when writing in his personal capacity: in his view, "censoring in the sense that all or certain publications must be subjected to public control prior to publication is not . . . permitted" in peacetime, even in situations of tension when public order may be under threat.[35]

---

[33] The *Observer and Guardian* v. *UK* and *The Sunday Times* v. *UK* (No. 2), Judgments of November 26, 1991, Series A vols. 216 and 217.

[34] *The Observer and Guardian*, *supra*, note 32; *The Sunday Times*, No.2, *supra* note 32 at §51.

[35] "The Role of Public Powers vis-à-vis the Activities of the Media in Situations of Conflict and Tension", *in Proceedings of the Seminar on the Media in Situations of Conflict and Tension*, Strasbourg, November 29 - December 1, 1993 (Council of Europe document DH-MM (94) 11).

On the facts in *Spycatcher* the Court, sitting in its plenary formation, held that up till the date of the book's publication in the United States the British courts were entitled, in the exercise of the "margin of appreciation" available to them, to consider a prior restraint in the form of injunctive relief as being necessary. The circumstances which persuaded the Court to this conclusion were the nature and contents of the book, the interests of national security in preserving the secret character of information that ought to be kept secret, and the potential prejudice to the Crown as a litigant (the substance of the actions for breach of confidence, and hence the Crown's prospect of a fair trial, would have been destroyed by publication before trial).[36] On the other hand, there was no longer judged to be a "sufficient" reason for preventing disclosure in the United Kingdom following the US publication since the confidentiality of the contents of the book had been destroyed. In particular, as regards national security interests, the purpose of the restrictions had become confined to promotion of the efficiency and reputation of the security service. "Above all," the Court said, "continuation of the restrictions after [U.S. publication] prevented newspapers from exercising their right and duty to purvey information, already available, on a matter of legitimate public concern."[37] The intervening loss of confidentiality had shifted the balance away from protection of national security in favor of journalistic freedom of expression.

Similar reasoning was subsequently applied in a recent case against the Netherlands in which the respondent government relied on protection of information as a State secret (*Vereniging Weekblad Bluf!* v. *Netherlands*).[38] The object of complaint was a court order withdrawing from public circulation an issue of a left-wing magazine reprinting a confidential report which the Dutch internal security service had drawn up on its activities. The interference with freedom of expression was unquestionably designed to protect national security, the Court found. It recognized that the proper functioning of a democratic society based on the rule of law may call for institutions like the Dutch internal security service which, in order to be effective, must operate in secret and be afforded necessary protection [as regards disclosure of information about its activities]. In this way a state may protect itself against the activities of individuals and groups attempting to undermine the basic values of a democratic society.[39]

The withdrawal order had, however, been obtained by the public prosecutor after the publishers had already distributed and sold a large number of copies of the offending issue in the streets of Amsterdam. Further, the report in question was six years old at the time, was of a fairly general nature and contained items of information which,

---

[36] The *Observer and Guardian*, *supra* note 32 at § 63.

[37] The *Observer and Guardian*, §§ 66-70 and *The Sunday Times*, No. 2, §§ 52-56.

[38] Judgment of February 9, 1995, Series A vol. 306-A.

[39] *Id.* at § 35. *See also Klass and Others*, *supra* note 9 §§ 55 and 58, where in relation to Article 8 ECHR the Court gave judicial recognition to the fact that at least a degree of secrecy is essential, and hence justified under the ECHR, in order to ensure the efficacy of the democratic state's activities in combating underground threats such as espionage and terrorism for the common good of society.

taken on their own, were no longer state secrets. The Court was not convinced of the necessity of preventing the disclosure of information of such low sensitivity, especially seeing that it had already been made public and commented on in the media. That being so, there had ceased to be any justification for the continued protection of the information as a state secret and the withdrawal order could not be regarded as necessary to achieve the legitimate aim of protecting national security.[40]

The 1992 judgment of *Hadjianastassiou* v. *Greece*[41] illustrates the obvious point that the constraints imposed by national security interests may be greater for serving members of the armed forces than for journalists reporting on "matters of legitimate public concern". The applicant serviceman had been court-martialled and convicted on a charge of disclosing to a private arms manufacturer "general information" on a military arms project classified as secret. Whilst military personnel are not excluded from the protection afforded by Article 10 ECHR[42], the judgment observed, specific "duties" and "responsibilities" are incumbent on them, in the applicant's case, an obligation of discretion in relation to anything concerning the performance of his duties as an officer in the Greek Army. In view of this and the possible damage to national security resulting from the applicant's disclosure, the Greek military courts could not be said to have strayed outside the national "margin of appreciation".

E. Suspension of the Guarantee of Free Speech in Time of War or Public Emergency

The foregoing discussion has been concerned with the acceptability or not of censorship for reasons of national security in time of peace. The ECHR also permits even greater inroads on free speech to be made in the interests of national security in time of war or public emergency: by virtue of Article 15,[43] a Contracting State may purely and simply suspend the guarantee of free speech for a specified, but renewable, duration. In that event, gone therefore is the state's obligation to observe to the full all the various requirements of Article 10. The consequence of this is not, however, total liberty for the state or immunity from review by the Strasbourg Commission and Court, since Article 15 lays down a number of strict conditions for the exercise by the state of this power of derogation:

(i) the public emergency must be one "threatening the life of the nation";

---

[40] The Court accepted, however, that it would have been quite possible to prosecute the offenders without contravening Article 10 ECHR: *supra* note 36 § 45 *in fine*.

[41] Judgment of December 16, 1992, Series A vol. 252.

[42] *See also Engel and Others* v. *Netherlands*, Judgment of June 8, 1976, Series A vol 22, § 100.

[43] Article 15 ECHR provides that, subject to a number of conditions, "in time of war or other public emergency threatening the life of the nation any High Contracting Party may take measures derogating from its obligations under this Convention".

(ii) the derogation must not go beyond "the extent strictly required by the exigencies of the situation";
(iii) the measures of derogation must not be "inconsistent with [the state's] other obligations under international law";
(iv) no derogation may be made from certain listed obligations (not including the obligation to secure freedom of expression, however);
(v) a state may not avail itself of the right to derogation unless it has given prior notification of the measures to the Secretary General of the Council of Europe.

Although a wide "margin of appreciation" is evidently left to the national authorities in this matter, the Strasbourg Commission and Court have not taken their duty of review under Article 15 lightly and merely accepted at face value all assertions made by the respondent Government. To take a recent example, in the 1993 judgment in *Brannigan and McBride* v. *UK* (which concerned detention of suspects under anti-terrorism legislation in Northern Ireland) the issues considered under heading (ii) included whether the derogation was a response to an emergency situation, whether the derogation was premature, whether the absence of judicial control of extended detention was justified, and safeguards against abuse.[44]

F. Conclusions

"Limited exceptions [to freedom of speech] are only permitted to protect other values of equal importance."[45] European judicial supervision ensures that national security is not a blanket exemption from the rights set forth in paragraph 1 of Article 10 ECHR. The ECHR's enforcement bodies are attentive to the circumstances in which the exception is invoked, and the strict conditions laid down by the Strasbourg Court and Commission circumscribe appreciably the scope which Contracting States enjoy to interfere with paragraph 1 rights. Although the relevant case law on Article 10 ECHR is sparse, it is nevertheless possible, with the help of some extrapolation from the Article 8 judgments, to draw the existing strands together so as to formulate a number of general propositions regarding freedom of expression and the defense of national security under the ECHR.

1. *Suspension of free speech in time of war or public emergency.* The most extreme instance of the muzzling of free speech for reasons of national security - namely suspension, in time of war or public emergency, of the normal guarantees attaching to

[44] Judgment of May 26, 1993, Series A vol 258-B. In its *Aksoy* v. *Turkey* judgment of December 18, 1996, the Court also noted its competence to examine whether a derogation lodged by the respondent State complied with the formal requirements of Article 15 § 3 of the Convention, for example whether the notice of derogation contained sufficient information about the measures taken in application of the derogation (*see* §§ 85-86).
[45] *See* Bernhardt, *supra* note 35.

freedom of expression – is nonetheless attended by safeguards and the action taken at national level is susceptible of review by the Strasbourg enforcement bodies.

2. *Legitimacy of national security measures.* The ECHR bodies have recognized, as a matter of principle, the legitimacy of restrictions placed, even in peacetime, on the exercise of freedom of expression in the interests of national security: democratic states need to have effective tools to combat the threat posed to their institutions and population by violent and subversive forces such as terrorism and espionage, and secrecy and non-disclosure of sensitive information are essential to ensure the effectiveness of those tools. This legitimacy is of course based on the assumption – which one should be able to make of states that have secured membership of the Council of Europe – that the society in question is a democratic one, with all that that entails.

3. *Wide but not unfettered discretion for national authorities.* In the nature of things the national authorities are better placed than the international judge in Strasbourg to assess both the degree of threats to the state's vital interests of national security and the appropriate measures for dealing with those threats. Hence, a wider "margin of appreciation" pertains here than in some other spheres. The national authorities do not, however, have *carte blanche* to suppress free speech whenever they choose to assert that interests of national security are at risk.

4. *Legal protection.* Any encroachment on free speech must be authorized under the law, and the national legislation empowering the state to limit free speech in the interests of national security must meet the minimum standards of the rule of law: accessibility, foreseeability (*i.e.* legal certainty) and adequate, legally binding safeguards against abuse.

5. *Legitimate aim.* It must be shown to the satisfaction of the Strasbourg enforcement bodies that the restriction is genuinely aimed, both in theory and in practice, at the protection of some aspect of the interests of national security and is not, for example, merely an excuse for saving the government in power or the civil service from embarrassing revelations.

6. *Democratic necessity and the balancing of interests.* The mere principle of protection of state secrets will not suffice to justify in all circumstances prevention or punishment of disclosure of information, even in relation to state security services. The less vital the particular interest of national security to be protected, the higher the level of detailed justification required. In particular, the absence or intervening loss of confidentiality of the information in issue will usually destroy the justification. The "necessity" of restrictions will always be evaluated in the light of the fundamental values underpinning "democratic society". And in this connection, especially once the veil of confidentiality has been pierced, the right of the public to know, to be fully and properly informed on matters of common concern, as well as the media's duty to act as public watchdog, may well tip the balance away from the protection of national security in favor of free speech. The rationale of free speech in a democratic society is after all based on the notion that human progress depends on people being able as far as possible to question the established order.

III. Norms Beyond the ECHR

A. Standard Setting Instruments in the Media Field: the Issue of National Security

The Committee of Ministers and the Parliamentary Assembly of the Council of Europe have, over the years, sought to give greater precision to the rights and freedoms set out in Article 10 ECHR, especially in the context of legal and policy instruments designed to offer arrangements for the reconciliation of media freedoms with other lawful rights and interests. In line with the judicial approach of the European Commission and European Court of Human Rights, the standard-setting instruments are rooted in the "European approach" to freedom of expression, and unequivocally treat the issue of free speech as a crucial element in the configuration of a democratic society.

To date, the issue of national security has not been a specific focus of the recommendations and conventions elaborated within the framework of the Council of Europe. This being said, the texts that have been adopted are premised on the understanding that the governments of the member states may invoke the national security proviso in accordance with the terms of paragraph 2 of Article 10 ECHR.

Thus, for example, Recommendation NE R (81) 19 of the Committee of Ministers on access to information held by public authorities provides that access to information by the public:

> shall apply subject only to such limitations and restrictions as are necessary in a democratic society for the protection of a legitimate public interest (such as national security, public safety, public order . . .).

The Declaration on Freedom of Expression and Information adopted by the Committee of Ministers on April 29, 1982 implicitly accepts that freedom of expression and information may, in well-defined circumstances, yield to the need to protect the range of imperatives laid down in paragraph 2 of Article 10 ECHR. However, this acknowledgment of the justifications for restricting freedom of expression must not conceal the fact that the member states of the Council of Europe, in adopting the Declaration, undertook to prioritize free speech and the free flow of information and to take positive steps to deepen and develop these cardinal values. To illustrate, the Declaration states categorically that the governments shall pursue information and media policies so as to achieve "the absence of censorship or any arbitrary controls or constraints on participants in the information process, on media content or on the transmission and dissemination of information."

The various texts adopted by the Parliamentary Assembly on media freedom pursue a similar approach to the national-security proviso. Thus, the Parliamentary Assembly's Resolution 428 (1970) containing a Declaration on mass communication media and human rights is formulated as follows:

> There shall be no direct or indirect censorship of the press, or of the contents of radio and television programs, or of news or information conveyed by other media such as news reels shown in cinemas.

> Restrictions may be imposed within the limits authorized by Article 10 of the European Convention on Human Rights. There shall be no control by the state of the contents of radio and television programs, except on the grounds set out in paragraph 2 of that Article.

The general approach is thus to make a *renvoi* to the provisions of paragraph 2 of Article 10 of ECHR without further elaboration. Nor have attempts been made to spell out in the standard setting legal and policy instruments the conditions which must be fulfilled before any of the derogations, including national security, can be successfully invoked.

It is, however, possible to perceive a development in the way in which the possibilities for derogation from Article 10 rights have been treated up to now. Of key relevance is the approach pursued to the elaboration of the texts on media freedoms, which were adopted at the 4th European Ministerial Conference on Mass Media Policy (Prague, December 7-8, 1994).

Significantly, the Declaration on Media in a Democratic Society adopted at the Prague Conference highlights, *inter alia*, that the member States of the Council of Europe must defend and promote media freedoms and media pluralism in accordance with Article 10 ECHR, as interpreted by the Convention's institutions. This is clear recognition of the need to read Article 10 in the light of the case law of the Court and Commission. This "fleshing out" of Article 10 is given increased emphasis in the Resolution on Journalistic Freedoms and Human Rights, also adopted by the Ministers at the Prague Conference. It is noteworthy that one of the key principles of this Resolution picks up on the principles defined by the ECHR enforcement bodies for testing the legality of measures which infringe freedom of expression. Principle 4 evidently reflects these case law principles:

> Bearing in mind the fundamental role of journalistic freedom of expression in a genuine democracy, any interference by public authorities with the practice of journalism must:
> a) be foreseen in the complete and exhaustive list of restrictions set out in paragraph 2 of Article 10 of the European Convention on Human Rights;
> b) be necessary in a democratic society and reply to a pressing social need;
> c) be laid down by law and formulated in clear and precise terms;
> d) be narrowly interpreted;
> e) be proportional to the aim pursued.

This approach is to be welcomed, since it circumscribes the invocation of the national security proviso by drawing the attention of policy makers to the strict conditions which must be fulfilled before this can be prayed in aid. It has recently been confirmed in two important legal texts adopted by the Committee of Ministers on May 3, 1996 which address the protection of journalists in situations of conflict and tension. Taking as their point of departure the concern expressed by the Ministers participating in the above-mentioned Prague Conference about the dangers which confront journalists when operating in situations of war, conflict and social and political tension, government experts working in close collaboration with media professionals drew up, firstly, a

Declaration of the protection of journalists in situations of conflict and tension and, secondly, a supplementary Recommendation (Recommendation No. R. (96) 4) giving greater precision to the terms of the Declaration and advising the governments of the member States on how to transpose their international obligations, including ECHR obligations, into their domestic media law and practice. Without prejudice to the legal and policy importance of both texts as a whole, it is relevant for present purposes to pinpoint the content of principle 7 of the Recommendation which postulates that notwithstanding the fact that the protection of national security may be invoked as a legitimate aim for interfering with journalists' rights and freedoms, this notion cannot be understood or used as a blanket ground for restricting fundamental rights and freedoms.

B. The European Convention on Transfrontier Television

The European Convention on Transfrontier Television (currently undergoing revision) was conceived as a sectoral application of Article 10 freedoms in the context of the transfrontier delivery of program services made possible by the exponential developments in cable and satellite technologies in the 1980s.[46] Given the ECHR Commission's and Court's views on the power of the audio-visual media,[47] the Television Convention is of particular relevance to discussions on national security.

The aim of the Television Convention is set out in Article 4:

> Parties shall ensure freedom of expression and information in accordance with Article 10 of the Convention for the Protection of Human Rights and Fundamental Freedoms and they shall guarantee freedom of reception and shall not restrict the retransmissions on their territories of program services which comply with the terms of this Convention.

Although the instrument admits of a number of possibilities for interfering with the freedom of retransmissions of transfrontier program services, the authors did not include any reference to the possibility of interfering with this freedom for reasons of national security.[48] The absence of a national security proviso could be read as implying that a receiving Party would not be entitled to restrict retransmissions on its territory of a program service uplinked from another contracting Party which is alleged to contain program material undermining a vital national interest of the former. The interaction between Article 10 ECHR and the Television Convention has not yet been tested on the issue of national security. Significantly, Article 4 of the Television Convention provides

---

[46] The European Convention on Transfrontier Television (ETS 132) entered into force in May 1993. To date, it has been ratified by 15 states: Cyprus, Finland, France, Germany, Hungary, Holy See, Italy, Malta, Norway, Poland, San Marino, Slovakia, Switzerland, Turkey, United Kingdom.

[47] *See e.g., Purcell, supra* note 30; and *Jersild, supra* note 32.

[48] *Cf.* Article 24 of the Television Convention.

that the Contracting Parties shall ensure freedom of expression and information in accordance with Article 10 ECHR. This acknowledgment of the higher normative value of Article 10 ECHR might lead the Strasbourg Court to conclude that the national security proviso may still be invoked in well-defined circumstances despite the silence of the Television Convention on this matter.

IV. New Developments

A. Monitoring of Compliance with Commitments: New Possibilities for Supervising Recourse by Governments to the National Security Proviso

As noted in the introduction, the Heads of State and Government of the member States of the Council of Europe reaffirmed that respect for freedom of expression, including media freedoms in general, is a condition *sine qua non* of membership of the Council of Europe. The Heads of State and Government also declared their resolve "to ensure full compliance with the commitments accepted by all member States within the Council of Europe".

The mechanism of judicial control operated by the European Commission and the European Court of Human Rights for ensuring compliance by governments with Article 10 has been examined at length *supra*. Recently, a new political initiative has been launched within the Council of Europe which may help ensure compliance by governments with Article 10 freedoms, including observance of the strict conditions which justify recourse to use of derogations based on the protection of national security. On November 10, 1994, the Committee of Ministers adopted a Declaration on Compliance with the Commitments Accepted by Member States of the Council of Europe. These commitments are not confined to the statutory conditions of membership of the organization, namely respect for democracy, human rights and the rule of law. The commitments also embrace respect for basic freedoms guaranteed by legal instruments of the Council of Europe as well as, evidently, the ECHR. Under this Declaration, and without prejudice to the jurisdictional role of the ECHR enforcement bodies, the Committee of Ministers is empowered to consider any issues which arise in any member State concerning respect for commitments. These issues may be referred to the Committee of Ministers by member States, the Secretary General or the Parliamentary Assembly. The Declaration provides that the Secretary General will forward to the Committee of Ministers information deriving from contacts and co-operation with member States that are liable to call for the Ministers' attention. The Committee of Ministers will consider in a constructive manner any such matters brought to its attention and will encourage the governments of member States, through dialogue and co-operation, to take all appropriate steps to conform with their commitments.

The follow-up procedure under the Declaration has not yet been tested in practice. It does, however, offer the potential to call member states to account for the way in which they have restricted information flow by introducing censorship, interfering with the activities of media professionals, curtailing individual access to official information, and so on in the name of national security.[49]

B. Assistance to the Democratic Reform Process in Central and East European Countries: Clarification of the Issue of National Security for the Benefit of Policy Makers

The enlargement process which has characterized the Council of Europe since 1989 has led the Organization to develop specific programs to assist Central and East European countries to bring, *inter alia*, their constitutional and legislative machinery into line with accepted European standards, especially the human rights guarantees laid down in the ECHR.[50] Particular attention has been given in these programs to ensuring that information law and policy in the countries applying for membership of the Organization reflect the values of Article 10 ECHR. To this end, the programs include the provision of counseling and advice on the preparation of press and broadcasting legislation, as well as legislation on freedom of information. These legislative expertises, which are carried out at the request of governments, provide important opportunities for independent media law experts recruited by the Council of Europe to review constitutional and legislative provisions which seek to limit information flow or the activities of the media for reasons of national security. The experts have been particularly anxious to date to highlight that it is not sufficient *per se* to repeat verbatim the wording of paragraph 2 of Article 10 ECHR relating to national security, but to take due account of the legal culture which the ECHR enforcement bodies have developed thereon.

[49] The adoption of this Declaration complements the monitoring procedures (as regards both member States and candidate States) introduced since 1993 by the Parliamentary Assembly of the Council of Europe. *See*, Resolution 1115 (1997), consolidating and replacing previous texts.
[50] In the pre-membership stage the Parliamentary Assembly of the Council of Europe also conducts a detailed review of the democratic health of the applicant country. To this end, the competent Assembly committees investigate the conformity of the constitutional, legal and political order of the applicant country with ECHR standards, including the free flow of information in the face of national security restrictions. It is not uncommon for reforms to be sought and undertaken before entry into the organization.

THE EUROPEAN UNION: NATIONAL SECURITY RESTRICTIONS, HUMAN RIGHTS AND INFORMATION IN THE PUBLIC INTEREST

Andrew Nicol, Q.C.

I. Introduction

The European Union ("EU" or "Union") represents a highly sophisticated undertaking to develop supranational institutions without (as yet) a single federated government. The authority of these institutions derives ultimately from the treaties establishing the Union and the consent of the Member States that are parties to those treaties.[1] In addition, the Council of Ministers and the Commission (though not the Parliament) have been given powers to make subsidiary legislation in the form of regulations and directives. Regulations, directives and the treaties themselves are intended to produce a common framework throughout the Union in the spheres in which the Member States have surrendered a measure of their own sovereignty.

Although EU law takes precedence over conflicting national laws, the precise effect of the various types of Community measures differs. Regulations apply directly without the need for implementing national legislation. They are therefore binding on everyone as soon as they come into force. Directives are addressed primarily to the Member States which are required to bring their domestic laws into conformity with the directives. The directives do not, themselves, impose obligations on private persons. However, even before implementing legislation has been adopted, the directives or parts of them may be "directly effective", that is they may be relied upon as against the Member State which has failed to implement it and against any public body (or in Euro-speak any "emanation of the State"). In order to have this effect, directives must be sufficiently clear and precise and be intended to benefit private persons (against the State) immediately upon the directive's entering

---

[1] The original Member States were France, Germany, Italy, Netherlands, Luxembourg and Belgium. They formed the European Coal and Steel Community (ECSC) by the Treaty of Paris in 1951 and, by two treaties of Rome in 1957, the European Atomic Energy Commission (EAEC) and the European Economic Community (EEC). The merger of the institutions of these three communities began in 1957 and was carried forward in 1965. The UK, Denmark and Ireland joined the EEC in 1973, Greece in 1979 and Spain and Portugal in 1986. In 1986 by a further treaty, the Single European Act, various measures were adopted for closer co-operation between the Member States. This was extended by the Treaty of European Union signed at Maastricht in 1993. The TEU substantially amended the Treaty of Rome which had established the EEC. The organization was renamed the European Union and the term European Economic Community was revised by omitting the word "Economic". In 1995 Austria, Finland and Sweden joined the Union, bringing total membership to 15 states. Negotiations continue concerning the further expansion of the Union.

into force. Particular provisions of the treaties can also have direct effect if they fulfill these criteria.

II. Permissible Exceptions to Community Obligations on National Security Grounds

Because the surrender of sovereignty by States that join the EU is only partial and because Member States have made clear that protection of national security remains an exclusive function of the States, it is unsurprising that EU rights and powers include important qualifications where they might impinge on national security.

The bedrock of the Union is often said to be the "four freedoms" of movement: freedom of movement of persons, capital, goods and services. Nonetheless, each "freedom" may be curtailed in the interest of national security as well as several other public interests. Thus, for instance, freedom of movement for workers, guaranteed by Article 48 of the Treaty,[2] is "subject to limitations justified on grounds of public policy, public security or public health."

In addition, Member States have wide powers to protect their national security interests under Article 223(1) of the Treaty:

> The provisions of this Treaty shall not preclude the application of the following rules:
>
> (a) No Member State shall be obliged to supply information the disclosure of which it considers contrary to the essential interests of its security;
>
> (b) Any Member State may take such measures as it considers necessary for the protection of the essential interests of its security which are connected with the production of or trade in arms, munitions and war material; such measures shall not adversely affect the conditions of competition in the common market regarding products which are not intended for specifically military purposes.

The last proviso concerning the effect of measures on competition in the common market reflects a constant concern, further developed in the case-law, that national security should not be used as a mantra to permit wholesale disregard of European requirements.

Article 224 recognizes that Member States are free to take measures contrary to the common market where necessary owing to "serious internal disturbances affecting the maintenance of law and order, in the event of war or serious

---

[2] Except where indicated otherwise, references to the Treaty are to the EC Treaty of Rome, as amended from time to time, most recently by the Treaty of the European Union (Official Journal of the EC, OJL 293, 27 Nov. 1993, at 61).

international tension constituting a threat of war, or in order to carry out obligations that a Member State has accepted for the purpose of maintaining peace and international security." Even here, the recognition is a by-product of the positive obligation on Member States to "consult with each other with a view to taking together the steps needed to prevent the functioning of the common market being affected" by the measures. The European Court of Justice ("ECJ") has said that these are to be regarded as "wholly exceptional situations" and has shown itself willing to review critically a Member State's purported reliance on them.[3]

In the *Johnston* case, the ECJ rejected an argument by the United Kingdom Government that there was inherent in the Treaty a general proviso allowing Member States to take all measures deemed necessary for reasons of public safety. The House of Lords (in its judicial capacity, the highest court of the United Kingdom) had come very close to adopting just such a principle as a matter of English public law.[4] While the ECJ might have been tempted to follow the same course as a means of reassuring Member States that Community membership would not jeopardize what they considered to be their essential national security interests, it was alive to the countervailing dangers, namely, that such a principle "might impair the binding nature of Community law and its uniform application".[5]

III. A Human Rights Approach to Restrictions on Community Rights

The Treaty, which serves as a Constitution of the Union, does not include a statement of individual rights, such as is found in most national constitutions.

The ECJ from an early stage was conscious of the dangers which this lacuna could pose. Many of the Member States are required by their constitutions to guarantee certain basic rights. If these are not respected by the Community, national courts might feel compelled to qualify their application of Community law. The ECJ's solution was to declare that it would recognize and be guided by the constitutional principles common to the Member States.[6] Once again, the interest in

---

[3] ECJ, *Johnston* v. *Chief Constable of the Royal Ulster Constabulary (Case 222/84)* [1986] ECR 1651, at paras. 27 and 60.

[4] *Council of Civil Service Unions* v. *Minister for the Civil Service* [1985] AC 374. This case concerned a challenge to the Conservative government's decision to ban trade unions from the Government Communications Headquarters (GCHQ), an intelligence base for monitoring radio and telecommunications signals.

[5] *Johnston, supra* note 3, at para. 26. For the facts of this case, see text accompanying notes 24-26, *infra*. Similarly, Member States cannot rely on national security exemptions in Community instruments if other Community rules provide for the necessary measures to ensure protection of these interests. *R.* v. *H.M. Treasury and Bank of England ex parte Centro-Com SRO* (Case C-124/95) [1997] 1 CMLR 555.

[6] *International Handelgesellschaft gmbh* v. *Einführ und Vorratsstelle für Getreide und Füttermittel* (Case 11/70) [1970] ECR 1125.

assuring the supremacy of European law became a channel for protecting individual rights.

While the Court, on occasion, has consulted the constitutions of the individual Member States, it treats the European Convention on Human Rights ("Convention" or "ECHR"), to which all Member States of the Union are party, as a ready guide to those common principles.[7] The EU is not itself a party to the Convention.[8] However, the Treaty of European Union, agreed at Maastricht, does include an express reference to the Convention:

> The Union shall respect fundamental rights, as guaranteed by the European Convention for the Protection of Human Rights and Fundamental Freedoms ... and as they result from the constitutional traditions common to the Member States, as general principles of Community law.[9]

Although this is not the same as formal incorporation of the Convention into Community law, "it confirms and consolidates the court's case law, underlining the paramount importance of respect for fundamental rights."[10]

Community rights sometimes directly involve the rights guaranteed by the Convention. For instance, restrictions sought to be imposed on workers from other Member States in the interest of public security, if connected with their speech or writings, could be ruled impermissible on grounds that they entail an interference with the right to freedom of expression under Article 10 of the European Convention on Human Rights.

The ECJ has not only had recourse to the Convention in such circumstances, but indeed has treated certain Community rights as analogous to the rights contained in the Convention. Free movement of workers, for instance, is treated as a fundamental right under Community law.[11] This is important because it means that Member States, in imposing restrictions on Community rights, can be

---

[7] There are many examples of the E.C.J.'s acceptance of principles enunciated in the E.C.H.R., including the following: the freedom to choose and practice a trade or profession, First Protocol to ECHR, Art. 1 (*Nold K.G.* v. *Commission* (Case 4/73) [1974] ECR 491); the right to an effective judicial remedy, ECHR, Arts. 6 and 13 (*Johnston, supra* note 3, [1986] ECR 1651); non-retroactivity of penal provisions, ECHR, Art. 7 (*Kirk* [1984] ECR 2689). Others are listed in A.G. Toth, e.d., *Oxford Encyclopedia of European Community Law, Vol. 1*, "Institutional Law," at 286-87 (1990).

[8] The Community does not have competence under its own law to accede to the E.C.H.R.. *See* E.C.J., *Re the Accession of the Community to the European Human Rights Convention* [1996] 2 CMLR 265.

[9] Treaty of European Union, Art. F(2).

[10] *Bosphorus Hava Yollari Turizm Ve Ticaret AS* v. *Minister for Transport, Energy and Communications, Ireland* (Case C-84/95) [1996] 3 CMLR 257, opn. of Advocate-General Jacobs.

[11] *See, e.g., R.* v. *Bouchereau* (Case 30/77) [1977] ECR 1999.

required to comply with principles developed by the European Court of Human Rights through its case-law.[12]

Thus, because the free movement of workers is treated as a fundamental right, any restriction on this right must be narrowly construed.[13] Even though a restriction is imposed in order to promote a permitted aim, it will not be found to be justified unless the person's presence or conduct constitutes "a genuine and serious threat to public policy".[14] The ECJ saw this standard as a

> specific manifestation of the more general principle enshrined in articles 8, 9, 10 and 11 of the Convention for the Protection of Human Rights and Fundamental Freedoms ... which provide in identical terms, that no restrictions in the interests of national security or public safety shall be placed on the rights secured by the above-quoted articles other than such as are necessary for the protection of those interests 'in a democratic society'.[15]

Part of this principle is that any curb on a fundamental right must be proportionate to the legitimate purpose sought to be achieved. The concept of "proportionality" is somewhat elusive. On some occasions, it appears to be similar to the English concept of "irrationality",[16] but on many others it seems to allow a much closer degree of judicial scrutiny and judges applying the European tradition (here meant to embrace both that of the European Court of Human Rights and the European Court of Justice) appear far readier to strike down an administrative (or legislative) measure as disproportionate than would an English court used to the *Wednesbury* tests of unreasonableness.

---

[12] These include that any restriction must be provided for in law, must be necessary to promote a vital public or private interest, and must be proportionate to the legitimate end sought to be achieved. *See* chapter on the European Convention on Human Rights by Paul Mahoney and Lawrence Early, Section II.C., elsewhere in this volume.

[13] *See, e.g.*, *Rutili* v. *Minister for the Interior* (Case 36/75) [1975] ECR 1219, at para. 27.

[14] *Rutili, id.*, at para. 28.

[15] *Rutili, id.*, at para. 32. Arts. 8, 9, 10 and 11 set forth the rights to respect for private and family life, home and correspondence (Art. 8); freedom of thought, conscience and religion (Art. 9); freedom of expression and opinion (Art. 10); and freedom of peaceful assembly and association with others (Art. 11).

[16] In English administrative law (in common with many other national systems) judicial scrutiny of administrative action will distinguish between the merits of the decision (which is for the administrators and not the courts) and the legality of the decision (as to which the courts are the final arbiter). A decision may be unlawful for many reasons, including that it is "irrational" or "perverse" and so regarded as beyond the administrator's legal power. The irrationality test has become associated indelibly with an early case in which it was articulated, *Associated Provincial Picture Houses Ltd* v. *Wednesbury Corporation* (1948) 1 KB 223. The House of Lords considered that so far as the concept of "proportionality" in the case-law of the European Court of Human Rights went beyond the concept of "irrationality", it was not yet part of English administrative law. *Brind* v. *Secretary of State for the Home Department* (1991) 2 AC 696.

The principle of proportionality was discussed by the ECJ in a 1996 case concerning the enforcement of UN sanctions against the Federal Republic of Yugoslavia ("FRY"). In *Bosphorus Hava Yollari AS* v. *Minister for Transport, Energy and Communications, Ireland*,[17] an airplane owned by the FRY national airline but leased for four years by a Turkish airline (Bosphorus) was seized by the Irish authorities. Bosphorus argued that its lease had been made in good faith and was not entered into in order to circumvent sanctions, that the lease rentals were being paid into blocked accounts and that the seizure was contrary to its fundamental rights to enjoy property and pursue economic activities. The ECJ said that although these rights were fundamental, they were not absolute and could, thus, be subject to restrictions "justified by objectives of general interest pursued by the Community". The ECJ concluded that the seizure was not disproportionate. It stated:

> As compared with an objective of general interest so fundamental for the international community, which consists in putting an end to a state of war in the region and to the massive violations of human rights and humanitarian international law in the Republic of Bosnia-Herzegovina, the impounding of the aircraft in question, which is owned by an undertaking based in or operating from FRY, cannot be regarded as inappropriate or disproportionate.[18]

The human rights approach has influenced the ECJ's attitude to procedure as well as substance. In particular, administrators are now expected to give reasons for any decisions that impinge on essential rights. In the case of freedom of movement rights, Directive 64/221/EC expressly requires administrators to provide reasons for any restrictions on grounds of public security:

> The person concerned shall be informed of the grounds of public policy, public security, or public health upon which the decision taken in his case is based, unless this is contrary to the interests of the security of the State involved.[19]

The qualification for national security reflects Article 223(1)(a) of the Treaty, quoted above.[20]

When Gerry Adams, the President of Sinn Fein, was prevented by an exclusion order from traveling to London to address a meeting at the House of Commons, he sought judicial review on domestic and European grounds. One of his challenges was to the failure of the Home Secretary to give reasons for the order. However, the English Divisional Court concluded that the national security proviso to the Directive and the Treaty gave a straightforward answer to this complaint; it made no real attempt to examine the Secretary of State's contention that national

---

[17] [1996] 3 CMLR 257.
[18] *Id.* at para. 26.
[19] Art. 6. The person concerned must have at least the same legal remedies as are open to nationals of the Member State who wish to challenge an administrative act. *Id.*, Art. 8.
[20] *See* Section II, *supra*.

security would be prejudiced by giving reasons.[21] Moreover, the court refused to refer the issue to the ECJ.

The court did, however, agree to refer a number of questions concerning Article 8a of the Treaty[22] to the ECJ, including: "What are the precise requirements of the principle of proportionality in a case such as this which, in relation to limitations on rights of free movement, involves freedom of speech and national security?"[23] The ECJ never had the opportunity to answer the question because the reference was aborted when the government canceled the exclusion order following the IRA's 1994 cease-fire in Northern Ireland.

The Divisional Court's approach to national security issues in *Adams* stands in marked contrast to that of the ECJ in the *Johnston* case. Mrs. Johnston had challenged her dismissal from the Royal Ulster Constabulary (RUC) as being due to her sex, contrary to the prohibition against sex discrimination in Article 119 of the Treaty. Domestic law provided that discrimination was not unlawful if committed to safeguard national security or public order, and that a certificate from the Secretary of State to this effect was final. The ECJ examined and dismissed the government's claim that internal disturbances in Northern Ireland made judicial review impossible.[24]

The *Johnston* case illustrates the importance of having a judicial remedy to test whether a restriction has been properly imposed. As Advocate-General Darmon stated in that case:

> Although the principle of legality is the cornerstone of the rule of law, it does not exclude consideration of the demands of public order. Indeed, they must be accommodated in order to ensure the survival of the State, whilst at the same time arbitrary action must be prevented. Review by the courts is a fundamental safeguard against such action: the right to challenge a measure before the courts is inherent in the rule of law.
>
> Formed of States based on the rule of law, the European Community is necessarily a community of law. It was created and

---

[21] *R.* v. *Secretary of State for the Home Department ex parte Adams* [1995] All ER (EC) 177.

[22] Article 8a states that every citizen of the Union shall have the right to move and reside freely within the territory of the Member States, subject to the limitations laid down by the Treaty and by measures adopted to give it effect. It is far from clear whether this provision creates new rights additional to those found elsewhere in the Treaty and, if it does, whether they are directly effective (*i.e.*, enforceable against the government of a Member State even though the directive has not been implemented by national legislative measures). These questions were among the questions the Divisional Court referred to the ECJ in the *Adams* case. In two cases, the Court of Appeal of England did not think that Article 8a created new, directly effective rights: *R.* v. *Secretary of State for the Home Department ex parte Phull* [1996] Imm AR 72; and *R.* v. *Secretary of State for the Home Department ex parte Vitale* [1996] Imm AR 275.

[23] *Ex parte Adams, supra* note 21.

[24] *Johnston, supra* note 3, at para. 60.

> works on the understanding that all Member States will show equal respect for the Community legal order.
>
> Consequently, and subject to review by the courts, the Community legal order expressly incorporates the concept of public order so as to reconcile the proper functioning of the common market with the necessity for the Member States to cope with emergencies which threaten their vital interests.
>
> The Treaty, like the case-law of the Court of Justice, therefore lays down the fundamental rule - a corollary of the principle of legality - that, whilst the demands of public order may be allowed to modify the scope of judicial review, they cannot override the actual right to obtain a judicial determination.[25]

The ECJ reached a similar view, buttressing its decision by reference to the European Convention on Human Rights:

> The requirement of judicial control stipulated by [Article 6 of Council Directive 76/207/EEC] reflects a general principle of law which underlies the constitutional traditions common to the Member States. That principle is also laid down in Articles 6 and 13 of the European Convention on Human Rights ... . As the European Parliament recognized in their joint declaration of 5th April 1977 (OJ 1977 No. C 103 p.1) and as the court has recognized in its decisions, the principles on which that Convention is based must be taken into consideration in Community law.[26]

Accordingly, the ECJ concluded that Mrs. Johnston's rights had been violated by the UK's failure to enable her to seek judicial review of the decision dismissing her from employment.

For EU Member States, like the UK, which have not yet incorporated the Convention into domestic law by specific legislation,[27] the ECJ's approach is extremely important; it has rendered the Convention directly enforceable at least regarding Community rights. The ECJ's approach also may be expected to have a significant indirect impact: the more judges are required to grapple with the jurisprudence of the ECJ and the European Court of Human Rights and the more familiar they become with concepts such as "proportionality", the more strained it will become for them to exclude such considerations when addressing parallel conflicts between individual rights and national security in domestic law.

---

[25] *Id.*, paras. 3-4.

[26] *Id.*, para 18. In particular, the ECJ referred to Art. 6 of the European Convention, concerning fair trial rights, and Art. 13, stating the right to an effective remedy.

[27] In early 1998, the Labor Government introduced legislation to incorporate the Convention into UK law.

IV. The Limitations of the Human Rights Approach

The ECJ is not a surrogate for the European Court of Human Rights. It has no mandate to review the policies or actions of Member States merely on the ground that they may infringe the ECHR. The complaint must be linked in some way to a right conferred, or an area of activity governed, by Community law. This was confirmed by the ECJ in a 1997 case in which it held that it could not give interpretative guidance necessary for a national court to determine whether national legislation was in conformity with fundamental rights such as those derived from the ECHR in a situation which did not fall within the field of Community law.[28]

There is also potential for conflict between the two jurisdictions. The ECJ has final responsibility for adjudicating claims arising from the Treaty and its subordinate legislation. The European Court of Human Rights has the last word on the Convention. Yet there is no mechanism whereby the ECJ can obtain the opinion of the ECHR and there is therefore potential for conflict in the approach of the two courts to the Convention. The likely consequence of this is that the ECJ will follow only a clear line of jurisprudence and will be reluctant to place itself at the cutting edge of human rights development. If this prediction is right, European law will suffer doubly from the delay which at the moment bedevils procedures under the Convention.

V. Access to Information

A. Right of Access to Information

In several areas, albeit limited, the EU has been a positive force in expanding the categories of information that must be made available to the public. A series of

---

[28] *Kremzow* v. *Republik of Osterreich* (Case C-299/95), 29 May 1997, reported in *The Times,* 11 August 1997. A retired Austrian judge had successfully complained to the European Court of Human Rights that the denial of his appeal against his conviction for murder violated Article 6 of the ECHR. He brought an action for damages in the Austrian court which sought the ECJ's ruling on whether the ECJ could give rulings on the interpretation of the Human Rights Convention. He alleged that his life sentence of imprisonment meant that he could not exercise his right to freedom of movement under Article 8a of the Treaty. The Court ruled that this purely hypothetical prospect of exercising the right did not establish a sufficient connection with Community law to justify the application of Community provisions, and that Mr. Kremzow's conviction was, accordingly, purely a national matter.

measures, for instance, has harmonized the information that companies must make publicly available.[29]

The EU has also adopted a directive requiring greater access to information held by public authorities relevant to the environment.[30] Consistent with Article 223 of the Treaty, Member States are allowed to make exceptions where the information affects international relations, national defense or public security.[31] The UK's regulations implementing this directive predictably also incorporate exceptions along the same lines.[32] The EU directive requires Member States to allow a person who considers that his or her request for information has been unreasonably refused or ignored or has been inadequately answered by a public authority to seek a judicial or administrative review of the decision in accordance with the relevant national legal system.[33] The UK regulations require a request to be answered as soon as possible and no later than two months after it has been made. Reasons must be given for any refusal.[34] The regulations do not expressly provide a mechanism for review, but they do categorically place a duty on the person holding the information to comply with them. Presumably, a person aggrieved by a refusal or inadequate answer would be able to seek judicial review.

It will be interesting to see what standard of review the UK courts will apply. In particular, if the government or other public authority relies on an exception, will the courts apply a "rationality" standard of review or the stricter "proportionality" test? For that matter, will the ECJ treat the public's right of access to environmental information as a "fundamental right", such that any limitations would have to be narrowly construed, necessary and proportionate to the legitimate aim to be achieved? In the national security context, will either the English courts or the ECJ require a government to say more than that the refusal was on grounds of national security? *Adams* suggests that an English court would require nothing more. *Johnston* suggests that the ECJ might not be satisfied with such an answer.

---

[29] *E.g.*, Council Directive on the co-ordination of safeguards for the protection of the interests of members and others required by Member States of companies, 68/151/EEC (1968) OJ Spec.Ed. (I), at 41; 2nd Company Directive 77/911 [1977] OJ L26/1, re public liability companies; 4th Company Law Directive 78/660 [1978] OJ L222/11, re: annual accounts of companies; 7th Directive 83/349 [1983] OJ L193/1, re presentation of consolidated accounts for groups of companies; amendment to 4th and 7th Directives 90/604 [1990] OJ L317/57; extensions of 4th and 7th Directives to certain partnerships 90/605 [1990] OJ L317/60; Directive 86/635 [1986] OJ L372/1, re accounts of banks; 11th Directive on branches of companies from other Member States 89/666 [1989] OJ L395/36; Directive 82/121/1982 OJ L48/26 on information to be published on a regular basis by companies with a listing on a stock exchange in a Member State.

[30] Council Directive 90/313 of 7 June 1990.

[31] *Id.* Art. 3(2), 2nd and 3rd indents.

[32] The Environmental Information Regulations, S.I. 1992, No. 3240, Reg. 4.

[33] Directive 90/313, *supra* note 30, Article 4.

[34] S.I. 1992, No. 3240, Reg. 3(2).

The Community's own institutions have come under increasing pressure to respect the principle of freedom of information. The Inter-Governmental Conference which signed the Treaty on European Union also made the following declaration:

> The Conference notes that transparency of the decision-making process strengthens the democratic nature of the institutions and the public's confidence in the administration. The Conference accordingly recommends that the Commission submit to the Council no later than 1993 a report on measures designed to improve public access to the information available to the institutions.[35]

The Council of Ministers and the Commission have each adopted a Code of Conduct to further these objectives.[36] Both begin with a statement of general principle that the public is to have a right of access (the Commission's Code's specifies "the widest possible access") to documents held by the Commission/ Council. Both then qualify this by two exceptions, which are framed in very similar terms.

The first exception is mandatory and extends to cases where disclosure of the document could undermine

> the protection of the public interest (public security, international relations, monetary stability, court proceedings, inspections and investigations), the protection of the individual and of privacy, the protection of commercial and industrial secrecy, the protection of the Community's financial interests, the protection of confidentiality as requested by the natural or legal persons that supplied the information or as required by the legislation of the Member State that supplied the information.[37]

The second exemption is discretionary and allows the Commission or Council to refuse access "to protect the confidentiality of the [Council's/ Commission's] proceedings"[38].

As of 1997, the European Court of First Instance had considered the substance of these provisions in two cases. In *Carvel* v. *Council*,[39] it held that the Council could not take a blanket decision to refuse access to its documents under the discretionary exemption. Accordingly, it was not sufficient for the Council to respond to a request by simply saying that the documents "contain confidential

---

[35] Declaration 17, annexed to the Final Act of the Treaty on European Union [1992] OJ C191/101.

[36] Council Decision 93/731 on public access to Council documents; and Commission Decision 94/90 on public access to Commission documents.

[37] *See* Art. 4(1) of Council Decision 93/731, and the corresponding provision of the Commission's Code of Conduct.

[38] *Id.*, Art. 4(2).

[39] *Carvel* v. *EU Council* (Case T-194/94) [1996] All ER (EC) 53.

information relating to the position taken by the members of the Council during its deliberations", as the Council had done in its letter of response to the applicants in *Carvel*.[40] Instead, the Council had to balance in each case its own interests in protecting confidentiality and the public's interest in access to Council documents.

This approach was followed in the second case, *WWF-UK* v. *Commission*.[41] The World Wide Fund for Nature had challenged the refusal of the Commission to allow it to have access to documents relating to the Commission's examination of a project of the Irish Government, funded in part by the Commission, to build a visitors' Centre in an Irish national park. The Commission had investigated allegations that the project contravened environmental law and was thus ineligible for structural funds, but decided not to initiate infringement proceedings. The Court annulled the decision because the Commission had not carried out the proper balancing exercise. So far as documents which the Commission claimed were shielded by the mandatory "public interest" exemption, the Court agreed that the Commission was not required to give "imperative reasons" to justify the application of this exception and thereby risk jeopardizing its essential function. However, the Commission *was* required to indicate to which subject-matter the documents related and particularly whether they involved inspections or investigations relating to a possible procedure for infringement of Community law. In the *WWF* case, the Commission had not given adequate reasons even in the attenuated form that are sufficient for the mandatory exemption.

B. European Law Limiting Free Access to Information: Commercial and Official Secrets

A further exception to the right of access to environmental information arises when disclosure would compromise commercial or industrial confidentiality.[42] This exclusion appears to be unqualified. In England, the law of breach of confidence similarly protects commercial and industrial confidentiality (as well as other types of confidence ranging from the personal to governmental). Yet the courts have recognized that the preservation of confidence cannot always claim priority. Starting from the proposition that "there is no confidence in iniquity", the principle has developed a wider base so that the courts will not now enjoin a breach of confidence where the public interest in disclosure outweighs the public interest in preserving

---

[40] *See id.*, para. 72.
[41] [1997] All ER (EC) 300.
[42] Directive 90/313, *supra* note 30, Art. 3(2), 4th indent.

confidences.[43] Although EU law contains no comparable provision in express terms, the ECJ might well soon be inclined to find an implied limitation on similar lines.

The ECJ took some tentative steps in this direction in *AKZO Chemi BV* v. *EC Commission*,[44] a case in which the Commission had been investigating potential abuse of a dominant market position. Information which the Commission had obtained from AKZO was disclosed to an intervenor in the proceedings. AKZO alleged that this was contrary to the Commission's duty to preserve its business secrets. It relied on two provisions: (a) Article 214 of the Treaty, which requires officials and servants of the Community not to disclose information in their possession of the kind covered by the obligation of professional secrecy; and (b) Article 20 of Regulation 17/62, which imposes a similar obligation in the context of a Commission investigation of the type in question. The Regulation qualified this duty so as to permit the intervenor to exercise its right to be heard.[45] However, this qualification did not extend to documents containing "business secrets". These could never be disclosed to the intervenor. The Commission had to make its own decision as to whether particular documents contained "business secrets" but before doing so it was required to give the business concerned the opportunity to make representations, notify the business of its decision and give the business an opportunity to challenge the legality of the decision. On the facts of the case, the ECJ criticized the Commission, not for having decided that the documents did not contain professional secrets, but for having failed to give AKZO sufficient opportunity to challenge the decision before it was implemented.

The opinion of Advocate-General Lenz in this case is interesting in a number of respects. First, he reasoned that the term "professional secrets" connoted the obligations of secrecy under which the "liberal professions" operated, and that the notion at which the Treaty was directed could better be described as "official secrecy."[46] Second, he foresaw that in exceptional circumstances the preservation of professional or official secrecy might stymie the Commission's investigation and that a balance might have to be struck between the aims of different parts of the Treaty.[47] Although this falls well short of a general public interest exception, it illustrates the somewhat plastic nature of EC law and the potential for the development of implied limitations.

Of course, not even the most demanding campaigner for freedom of information would expect or wish the right of access to be without any qualification. Journalists who often champion most loudly the values of freedom of information

---

[43] *See Attorney-General* v. *Guardian Newspapers* (No.2) [1990] 1 AC 109, 282-83; *Lion Laboratories Ltd* v. *Griffiths* [1985] QB 526, 550; and *Woodward* v. *Hutchins* [1977] 1 WLR 760, 763-64.

[44] Case 53/85 [1987] 1 CMLR 231.

[45] Regulation 17/62, Arts. 19 and 21.

[46] AKZO, *supra* note 44, at 246.

[47] Id., at 249.

will guard with great zeal the identity of their sources who have provided information only on a promise of anonymity. Governments, too, are sometimes quite rightly protective of their sources of information. The ECJ was called on to decide the extent of protection due a confidential source in a case brought by Hoffman-La Roche. An "insider", Stanley Adams, provided information to the Commission which suggested that the company was abusing a dominant market position. In the course of its investigation, the Commission provided information to the company which allowed it to identify Adams as the source. He was prosecuted in Switzerland and suffered great personal hardship as a result. The ECJ held that Article 214 of the Treaty required the Commission to preserve his anonymity, and its failure to do so was a wrong for which the Commission was required to compensate him.[48]

In general the European obligations of confidence operate within the civil law: they may give rise to claims for damages (as in the *Adams* case), or proceedings for a declaration of nullity (as in the *AKZO* case). Comparable obligations are contained in the staff regulations which apply to EU officials.[49] The obligations of confidence continue after termination of the official's service. Officials are prohibited from publishing any matter dealing with the work of the Community without the approval of the appointing authority. Interestingly, this is subject to a "damage" proviso: that is, permission is to be refused only where the proposed publication is liable to prejudice the Community's interests.[50] The official who receives instructions he finds unacceptable is given little succor. If he considers the instructions to be irregular or likely to give rise to serious difficulties, he must report the matter to his immediate superior, but if the instructions are confirmed in writing, he is obliged to carry them out unless they constitute a breach of the criminal law or relevant safety standards.[51] Refusal to carry out lawful instructions may result in dismissal or other employment penalties but will not (in general) expose the official to criminal prosecution.

A rare exception to this proposition is the security regime created by the EURATOM Treaty for information the disclosure of which is likely to harm the defense interests of one or more Member States.[52] It appears that this Treaty may require criminal penalties for unauthorized disclosure. For instance, when the UK joined the EC, it needed to include in the enabling legislation a provision making it a crime to disclose European classified information under the EURATOM regulations.[53]

---

[48] *Adams* v. *Commission* (Cases 145/83 and 53/84) [1985] ECR 3539.

[49] Council Regulation 31 (European Economic Community) and 11 (European Atomic Energy Commission), of December 18, 1961, Art. 17.

[50] *Id.*

[51] *Id.*, Article 21.

[52] EURATOM Treaty, Arts. 24-27, and Council Regulation 3 (EURATOM) of July 31, 1958.

[53] European Communities Act 1972, s.11.

VI. Conclusion

If the EU moves further towards integration and if, in particular, defense and foreign policies become more and more the policies of the Union rather than the individual Member States, the concept of "national security" may well be adapted to protect what the institutions of the Union view as its "supra-national security". Will then the EURATOM system of security classification backed by penal provisions be enlarged? When collisions occur between these efforts and the probing of investigative journalists, how robust will the ECJ's defense be of fundamental rights of free speech and access to information?

The African Charter and Freedom of Expression in Africa

Claude E. Welch, Jr.

I. Introduction

The Johannesburg Principles, although drafted in Africa and addressing issues of pressing relevance there, bear little resemblance to current reality north or south of the Sahara. The fifty-plus states of the continent have long been characterized by governments intolerant of criticism, by restrictions on media coverage said to be justified by situations of national emergency, and by severe limitations on freedom of expression.

A cynic might ask, "What's new?" Widespread flouting of constitutional guarantees and unwillingness to honor commitments to international human rights treaties have characterized the majority of African states in their thirty-five or more years of independence. Continuities rather than contrasts are striking. Freedom of expression was subjected to significant restraints when Africa was divided among various colonial powers. The limits imposed in the colonial period were in many respects enhanced following independence, rather than relaxed or abolished. The veneer of democratization that had accompanied the achievement of self-government was rapidly stripped away by leaders anxious to preserve their version of national unity, and/or by military elites who shot their way into power. Multi-party systems were consolidated into single-party systems, then into one-man systems. With the "second independence" of the 1990s, in which open political competition returned to many countries, freedom of expression seemed to obtain a new lease on life. The overall climate for civil and political rights, however, remains inhospitable.

The question that arises here is whether international pressures and the activities of non-governmental organizations (NGOs), both domestic and international, can help overcome the obstacles to freedom of expression erected in the name of national security. Treaties such as the African Charter on Human and Peoples' Rights (African Charter), accepted by fifty-one of the fifty-three Member States of the Organization of African Unity (OAU), and the International Covenant on Civil and Political Rights (ICCPR) have been widely ratified,[1] yet their impact has been limited. Governmental willingness to employ a variety of pressures against the

[1] As of January 1, 1997, the African Charter had been ratified by 51 countries of Africa (the exceptions being Ethiopia and Morocco, which withdrew from the OAU following its recognition of the Saharawi Arab Democratic Republic). The ICCPR had been ratified by 136 countries (the exceptions in Africa being Botswana, Burkina Faso, Comoros, Djibouti, Ghana, Guinea-Bissau, Liberia, the Saharawi Arab Democratic Republic (not considered a state by the United Nations), South Africa and Swaziland). Jean-Bernard Marie, "International Instruments Relating to Human Rights," 18 *Human Rights L.J.* 79, 84, 86 (No. 1-4,1997).

media and individuals on grounds of "national security" has been a long-term feature of the African scene.

This chapter complements the case studies published elsewhere in this volume in two respects. First, it adopts a continent-wide approach, rather than concentrating on a single country. Because Africa was subjected to a particularly strong, intense form of colonial rule, post-independence governments inherited powerful means of restraining the media and restricting freedom of expression; these can aptly be studied by looking at the continent as a whole. Second, this chapter provides more of a political perspective on freedom of expression throughout Africa than a legal one. This approach is warranted given that, where the rule of law is not firmly established, considerations of power dominate. While legal strategies for enhancing freedom of expression are important, they must be pursued within a framework that takes cognizance of, and seeks to address, the political realities.

There are at least two reasons for the parlous condition of freedom of expression in many African countries. They involve, paradoxically, both the strength and the weakness of African governments and the societies over which they attempt to rule. The state is in crisis; civil society is weak. The "patrimonial administrative state" of tropical Africa created under colonial rule and continued after independence became what one expert aptly deemed a "lame leviathan."[2] In theory, it disposed of vast powers; in reality, it existed as a means of transferring resources to small groups of the politically privileged. Government activities south of the Sahara catered to the "politics of the belly."[3] Self-serving rulers sought to maintain their privileges by clamping down on opposing points of view.

National leaders were not, however, merely driven by an interest in self and group enrichment. They also responded to (and often sought to manipulate and/or inflame) growing disjunctures between state and society. Concern about secession or ethnically-inspired unrest marked many countries. Civil society has cohered more around ethnic group or region than around putative nation, a development with deep historic roots.[4] As a result, the specter of "tribalism" haunts Africa. Major building blocks of civil society in the view of many Western scholars remain weak, and hence the protection of freedom of expression remains limited. Human rights NGOs and privately-owned media in Africa confront enormous obstacles to their functioning. Political leaders remain intent on maintaining their control, despite (and because of) their weaknesses. Governments possess multiple means of restraint on freedom of expression. Poor, and in many respects worsening, economic conditions constrain the development of the press; radio, which serves as the most important means of

---

[2] Thomas M. Callaghy, "The State as Lame Leviathan: The Patrimonial Administrative State in Africa," *in* Zaki Ergas., ed., *The African State in Transition*, 87-116 (1987).

[3] Jean-François Bayart, *The State in Africa: The Politics of the Belly* (1993) (originally published in 1989 as *L'État en Afrique: la politique du ventre*).

[4] Peter P. Ekeh, "Colonialism and the Two Publics in Africa: A Theoretical Statement," 29 *Comparative Studies in Society and History*, 106-31 (1975).

communication, has almost without exception remained under direct government control; political dissidents have found their liberties circumscribed, and many have been killed for their beliefs. Irrespective of liberal, constitutional guarantees, the domestic reality has been characterized by severe restrictions on freedom of expression. Domestically, accordingly, civil society is fragmented, while governments are narrowly based and fearful. There should be little wonder that major limits on freedom of expression exist, and that these limits have yet to be effectively challenged from within most African countries.

These phenomena within individual African states have been exacerbated in important respects by modest international initiatives. Neither international treaties, nor entreaties from important NGOs, nor even pressure from major aid-givers, have cracked the panoply of national security legislation that restricts freedom of expression throughout much of the continent. The African Charter contains very limited protection for freedom of expression. The African Commission on Human and Peoples' Rights, established pursuant to the African Charter, has given little serious attention to freedom of expression, for a variety of reasons explored below.

International NGOs have focused attention on problems, but can claim only limited successes to date. Despite rhetoric about linking foreign assistance to greater openness on the part of governments, such conditionalities have been irregularly applied. On the other hand, pressures for democratization (internal and external) have started to expand attention and protection given to freedom of expression. NGOs should and will play an increasing role in this effort. It will be a lengthy struggle, requiring profound changes in attitudes about national security and significant alterations in the functioning of human rights treaty bodies. Strengthening of civil society, constitutional and legal protections, and freedom of expression should go hand-in-hand in this process.

In this chapter, I examine the following four topics:

- the armature of the "colonial state", which laid the basis historically for restrictions on freedom of expression throughout the African continent;
- increased use of emergency powers to bolster post-independence governments in Africa, a process that proved unsuccessful as military *coups d'état* and domestic conflict roiled the political cauldron;
- problems both in the wording of the African Charter and in the limited powers of, and support for, the African Commission on Human and Peoples' Rights, complemented by the weakness of political institutions and the tendency of political leaders to resort to claims of national security to restrict freedom of expression;
- limited efforts by donor governments and domestic and international human rights groups to pressure newly-emergent African governments to provide effective guarantees for freedom of expression.

II. Colonial Roots of National Security Restrictions

The roots of national security legislation lie in colonial history. The precedent for extensive governmental involvement in media regulation was set prior to 1960. As stated by Professor Howard, "[t]he idea that the African press should not be critical of the established government is thus a direct legacy of the colonial period."[5] Whether by *arêté* (French colonial edict), ordinance, decree or act of a colonial assembly, the various administrations were endowed with sweeping regulatory powers. Whether the overlords were Belgian, British, French, Italian, Portuguese or Spanish, the results were identical. Freedom of expression was legally circumscribed by censorship, sedition and other laws.

The colonial state in Africa differed in some fundamental respects from earlier historical examples of colonial government.[6] The implantation of European rule occurred with extraordinary rapidity; it coincided with the height of racist beliefs; and it sought dramatic transformation of societies to overcome chronic economic underdevelopment. (The colonial overlords believed firmly that the new possessions should finance their own development, with blood as well as taxes.) Administrators imposed their versions of the *pax britannica*, and did not welcome dissent. From early in the colonial period, security legislation quelled criticism. Powers legitimized by these laws were used frequently against "nationalists" who sought self-government and against the small, late-developing press linked to post-World War II nationalist parties.[7]

When independence came, many foreign-owned media were taken over by the state. For example, the Nigerian government acquired a majority share in the *Daily Times* of Nigeria by 1975, when the indigenization decree mandated national ownership. In other countries, such steps came earlier. As a result, the press came to reflect the interests of the political elite.[8] Few African states could boast a vigorous fourth estate – in the sense of watching closely over government actions – within a few years of independence. Why? The reasons can be found not only in colonial history, but also in the perceptions of African leaders. Freedom of

---

[5] Rhoda Howard, *Human Rights in Commonwealth Africa*, 121 (1986).

[6] Crawford Young, *The African Colonial State in Comparative Perspective* (1994).

[7] Note should be taken, however, of Ghana (Gold Coast), Nigeria and Sierra Leone, where relative economic affluence, the early spread of education along the coast, and the development of English-speaking African elites facilitated the rise of newspapers well before the period of nationalist politics. In Hachten's words, "An exception [to the journalist traditions of European influence or African nationalist influence], and a bright exception at that, was British West Africa where a firm tradition of African-run, owned and read newspapers preceded similar developments elsewhere on the continent by half a century or more." William A. Hachten, *Muffled Drums: The News Media in Africa*, 5 (1971). *See also* Gunilla L. Faringer, *Press Freedom in Africa*, 2-9 (1991).

[8] Hachten, *id*; Faringer, *id*.

expression was a casualty of their emphasis on the central importance of national unity.

III. Post-Independence: Heydays of Authoritarianism

Kwame Nkrumah, the first African Prime Minister and President of Ghana (itself the first tropical African colony to gain independence, in 1957) wrote a striking comment in his autobiography:

> What other countries have taken three hundred years or more to achieve, a once dependent territory must try to accomplish in a generation if it is to survive. Unless it is, as it were, "jet-propelled", it will lag behind and thus risk everything for which it has fought. ... But even a system based on social justice and a democratic constitution may need backing up, during the period following independence, by *emergency measures of a totalitarian kind.* Without discipline, true freedom cannot survive.[9]

The sentiments expressed by Nkrumah became commonplace. A contradictory sense of optimism and crisis permeated African presidential palaces. On the one hand, euphoria generated by the unexpected ease with which independence had been gained in most states by the mid-1960s (with the exceptions of Portuguese colonies and the white minority redoubts of Namibia, Rhodesia (Zimbabwe) and South Africa) gave African leaders a sense they could, and must, compress stages of "nation-building".[10] Progress toward unity, they felt, was absolutely essential. The advent of home rule raised the complex question, "Who shall rule at home?" Ethnic sentiments became more acute. In a process recognized by all students of African politics, force rather than consent became the currency of change. Government weakness rather than strength led to increased authoritarianism and an acceleration of one-man rule. Centralized political institutions declined in their effectiveness. "Presidents-for-life" became increasingly common. Government bureaucracies declined in effectiveness. Using strikingly similar words, leading scholars opined that presidents such as Nkrumah worked within "an almost complete institutional vacuum at the central, national level";[11] and that "the most salient characteristic of political life in Africa is that it constitutes an almost institutionless arena with conflict and disorder as its most prominent features."[12]

---

[9] Kwame Nkrumah, *The Autobiography of Kwame Nkrumah* (1957) (emphasis added).

[10] William J. Foltz, "Building the Newest Nations: Short-Run Strategies and Long-Run Problems," *in* Karl W. Beutsch & William J. Foltz, eds., *Nation-Building*, 117-31 (1965).

[11] James M. Coleman & Carl G. Rosberg, Jr., *Political Parties and National Integration in Tropical Africa*, 2 (1964).

[12] Aristide Zolberg, "The Structure of Political Conflict in the New States of Tropical Africa," 40 *American Political Science Review* 70-87 (1967).

There is not space in this chapter or volume to examine the twists and turns of post-independence politics. Major post-independence events include the following:

- Rosy visions of rapid economic development were replaced, especially from the mid-1970s, with the reality of agricultural stagnation, declining per capita gross national product (GNP), rampant corruption, and growing gaps between African states and other "developing" countries.[13]
- Authoritarianism and personalized rule increased, with peaceful changes of government practically unknown.[14]
- Limitations on freedom of expression, and in particular of the press, were largely the result of government actions, such as censorship, harassment of editors and reporters, and state takeovers.[15]
- One of the basic principles of the Organization of African Unity, non-interference in the internal affairs of states, was and continues to be used to justify a *noli me tangere* attitude among African leaders, for whom protection of domestic sovereignty and retention of position have been paramount values.

Many African national leaders (whether elected, self-proclaimed, or beneficiaries of military seizures of power) used national security legislation to restrict freedom of expression; others ensured inclusion of restrictive provisions in their countries' constitutions.[16] The results were bleak. Although there have been

---

[13] For example, in 1960 Ghana and South Korea were characterized by roughly similar GNPs per capita. By 1992, an extraordinary gap had opened: South Korea, ranked 31 of 174 countries by the United Nations Development Program, had a per capita GNP of $7,220, while Ghana, mired at 129 in the same ranking, had a per capita GNP of $460. When "real" GNP per capita was used as the basis of comparison, the gap narrowed to a still substantial gap of four to one ($9,250 compared to $2,110). U.N. Development Program, *Human Development Report 1995*, at 158-59 (1995).

[14] Between 1965 and 1990, more than 75 successful *coups d'état* were staged in Africa, most notably in West Africa (Benin, Burkina Faso, Ghana, Mauritania and Nigeria each experienced at least four); peaceful change (through elections) of government and of the dominant party occurred only in the unusual island state of Mauritius (in 1982). Not included in this assessment are transitions within the same party following resignation or death of a president, such as the changes in Somalia (1967), Kenya (1978) and Cameroon (1982). That Ghana and Nigeria were centers of both a vigorous pre-independence press and significant military intervention in politics is coincidental. Some countries avoided overt takeovers by the armed forces by having troops of the former colonial power stationed there (for example, Côte d'Ivoire and Senegal).

[15] Howard, *supra* note 5, at 120.

[16] Clawback clauses constitute a particularly insidious way of weakening international human rights obligations. For instance, the 1974 Constitution of the former Republic of Zaire (now the Democratic Republic of Congo) contains a provision which exemplifies the ease with which national security could be invoked in proclaiming a state of emergency, as well as the predilections of then-President Mobutu:

> If serious circumstances imminently threaten the Nation's independence or integrity *or cause an interruption in the regular functioning of the organs*

exceptions, the decades following independence were heydays of authoritarianism. Some noteworthy changes came in the early 1990s, when a "second independence" swept through parts of the continent. The end of the Cold War reduced external involvement in several countries; more important, it bolstered already-extant trends towards greater political freedoms. Democratization and concomitant emphasis on media openness have, in the view of several observers, opened new opportunities for freedom of expression. As noted by one expert, "[T]he independent press which has emerged in recent years is, for most African countries, the first independent press that has been there."[17]

How has this emerging opportunity for greater freedom of expression been affected by NGOs and inter-governmental human rights institutions, including the African Commission on Human and Peoples' Rights?

IV. International Monitoring and Pressure

With the "second independence" and with ratification of human rights conventions, governments in Africa started to confront a new situation. Their long-standing assumptions of untrammeled domestic sovereignty and limited criticism of government activities were challenged.

As discussed above, the African political elite utilized, and continues to draw upon, restrictive national security legislation to limit freedom of expression. Leaders drew lessons from their colonial predecessors, and added new twists. Domestic voices of dissent were and continue to be stilled, although the conditions they document cannot be fully concealed. The majority of African governments have ratified international treaties in which they pledge to uphold freedom of expression. They thereby, at least in theory, accept external monitoring and expose themselves to new avenues of pressure. How effective have these mechanisms proven to be? In particular, what impact can be attributed to the African Charter on Human and Peoples' Rights, ratified by the overwhelming majority of African states?

Supervision of the Charter is carried out by the African Commission on Human and Peoples' Rights. Since its creation in 1987, the Commission has played a marginal role in protecting freedom of expression. In both legal and political terms,

---

> *of the Popular Movement of the Revolution or jeopardize vital State interests* ... the President of the Republic may proclaim a state of emergency, with the consent of the Political Bureau.

Constitution of 1974 of Republic of Zaire, *quoted in* Richard Gittleman, "The Banjul Charter on Human and Peoples' Rights: A Legal Analysis," *in* Claude E. Welch, Jr. & Ronald I. Meltzer, eds., *Human Right and Development in Africa*, at 160(Albany: State University of New York Press, 1984) (italics added).

[17] Richard Carver, *Truth From Below: The Emergent Press in Africa*, 12 (London: ARTICLE 19, 1991).

it appears to be a weak but not irrelevant player in efforts to achieve accountability of African leaders.

The African Charter gives the weakest formulation of freedom of expression of any of the major international human rights documents. According to Article 9:

1. Every individual shall have the right to receive information.
2. Every individual shall have the right to express and disseminate his opinion within the law.

The last three words reflect the cautious, state-centered approach found within the Charter, and pursued by the actions - and inactions - of the African Commission. The phrase, "within the law", opens the door to any sort of *raison d'état*. It is a clawback clause, restricting rights from the start.[18] Other major human rights treaties give considerably less scope to such restrictions.[19] For instance, the International Covenant on Civil and Political Rights (ICCPR), while permitting "certain restrictions" adds that "these shall only be such as are provided by law and are necessary: (a) For the respect of the rights or reputations of others; (b) For the protection of national security or of public order (*ordre public*), or public health or morals." The chapters elsewhere in this book on the ICCPR, the European Convention and the Inter-American Convention all depict treaties, and systems, more vigorous in protecting freedom of expression. Limitations are clear rather than vague; bodies of precedent and experience have developed; applications for remedies are numerous and carefully reviewed; well-qualified (albeit overworked) professionals provide staff support; and governments criticized by the treaty bodies usually modify the offending laws or practices. As of the time of writing (July 1997), these points, regrettably, did not apply to the African Charter or Commission. The reasons lie within the Commission, as well as in the Charter. A vague or weakly-worded treaty can be developed or interpreted over time, *if* the political will is present. The limitations of the African Charter are striking; equally important, in the case of freedom of expression, the political will necessary to interpret its protections broadly has been decidedly lacking.

In the two decades since the African Charter entered into force, a wave of democratization has swept over much of the continent. Far greater attention has been given generally to human rights since 1990 than in the preceding post-independence decades. Freedom of expression, however, has not received significant attention from the African Commission, nor has restrictive national security legislation been rescinded. The undoubted progress in South Africa since the freeing of Nelson Mandela, and the more limited changes in the countries of the Southern African Development Community (SADC) are encouraging but far from continent-wide in their scope. The "second independence" promised far more than thus far has been delivered. The African Commission's record to date has been spotty. It has

---

[18] Gittleman, *supra* note 16, at 158-62.

[19] *See, e.g.*, "Commentary on the Johannesburg Principles," *supra* this volume, at 15-16.

been hampered by the wording of the Charter, the caution of the Commission, and the inadequacies of government actions.

Why is the wording of the African Charter so cautious? In brief, because of the timing and circumstances of its preparation. As I have written elsewhere:

> The Charter was drafted on behalf of the Organization of African Unity [OAU] by persons sympathetic to governments' desires (perhaps interpreted as necessities and preconditions), and desirous of including African values. The OAU itself was far more concerned early in its history with ensuring stability for newly independent countries and self-determination for remaining colonial areas, than with protection of human rights within its member states.[20]

In order to ensure adoption by African heads of state gathered at the 1981 OAU summit, and ratification by governments subsequently, the language chosen by the drafters gave states wide discretion. The brief, government-centered wording of Article 9 of the African Charter should be contrasted with the comparable, lengthier sections of the American Convention and European Convention (respectively, Articles 13 and 10). It is highly unlikely that the African Charter will be amended to strengthen its provisions on freedom of expression, at least in the foreseeable future. Other means of strengthening, accordingly, must be sought.

Does the African Commission have the power, resources and willingness to enhance protection of freedom of expression within the narrow confines of Article 9 and other parts of the African Charter? Several commentators on the African Commission have urged it to become more active in interpreting the Charter. Slowly and hesitantly, it has taken a few steps.[21] For example, Commissioners have taken it upon themselves to examine reports from States Parties in public session, even though the Charter is by no means clear that this is what the framers intended. Non-governmental human rights organizations have attended Commission sessions in increasingly greater numbers, and have started to produce reports for its members' consideration. In my view, the most important changes in the activity level of the African Commission on free expression issues will come when (a) States Parties report seriously on freedom of expression in their particular countries, and 2) NGOs press both the African Commission and individual governments more vigorously for action.

The major responsibility of the African Commission lies in its examination of reports from the States Parties to the African Charter. Reporting to human rights treaty supervisory bodies such as the Commission is intended to serve at least seven functions:

---

[20] Claude E. Welch, Jr., *Protecting Human Rights in Africa: Strategies and Roles of Non-Governmental Organizations*, at 149 (1995).

[21] See commentaries on sessions of the African Commission, published periodically in *The Netherlands Human Rights Quarterly*.

- initial review, through which the supervisory body becomes aware of the relevant domestic law and practice;
- monitoring, based on detailed review of current developments, as a step toward identifying and remedying human rights problems;
- policy formulation, in which governments take steps to respond to the problems identified;
- public scrutiny, in which governmental accountability is enhanced both internationally and domestically;
- evaluation, in which both states and the supervisory body assess changes made over time;
- acknowledgment of problems, in which governments become more candid in their discussion of human rights issues;
- information exchange, perhaps most notably through general comments by the supervisory body.[22]

In almost all these respects, the African Commission has, to date, been hampered or deficient. Initial reviews of reports have been brief; more important, States Parties have submitted patently inadequate documentation.[23] It has thus proven difficult to establish a baseline of information. Monitoring has been impeded by sketchy reports, or utterly precluded by failure to submit any reports whatsoever.[24] The physical isolation of the African Commission in The Gambia has limited the extent to which Commissioners or governments can learn from each other; chronic staff shortages and problems have affected the Commission's efficiency; individual members hold other positions (often governmental), and can thus give only limited time to the Commission; general comments remain at a rudimentary stage. Even when the Commission has formulated comments, there is little evidence that governments have paid any serious attention to them. In contrast, the Human Rights Committee (which supervises compliance with the ICCPR) and other supervisory bodies have scored some successes.[25] Public scrutiny of reports

---

[22] Philip Alston, "The Purposes of Reporting," *in Manual on Human Rights Reporting*, UN Doc. HR/PUB/91/1/, at 14-16 (1991).

[23] The case of Nigeria, which I treat in greater detail in a recent book, is instructive. What can be kindly viewed as bureaucratic confusion meant that Nigeria's first attempt at a report consisted of nothing more than the table of contents of its suspended constitution! *Protecting Human Rights in Africa, supra* note 20, at 154-55.

[24] By the 19th session of the Commission, held in March 1996, the Commission had examined reports from barely a dozen states; the great majority of states parties had yet to furnish their initial reports, which are supposed to provide the baseline information on which subsequent discussions are to be based. On the other hand, lateness in submitting reports is hardly confined to Africa.

[25] *E.g.*, Cindy A. Cohn, "The Early Harvest: Domestic Legal Changes Related to the Human Rights Committee and the Covenant on Civil and Political Rights," 13 *Human Rights Quarterly* 295-321 (1993); Ineke Boerefijn, "Towards a Strong System of Supervision: The Human Rights Committee's Role in Reforming the Reporting Procedure under Article 40 of

submitted to the African Commission has been practically non-existent: reports by States Parties have been drafted by bureaucrats who rarely communicate with human rights activists; comments made by members of the African Commission disappear into filing cabinets. On the brighter side, some states (notably Senegal) have reported more than once, and their second reports have been more open in acknowledging problems. The record is thus not totally bleak.

The Commission's attention has been chiefly focused on reports from States Parties. As of mid-1996, the Commission had not devoted any lengthy attention to Article 9 of the Charter in analyzing these reports. When the Commission examines lacunae in, or non-compliance with, the Charter, more pressing issues, such as extra-judicial executions or the need for an African Court of Human Rights, have come to the fore.[26]

The Commission's limited attention to freedom of expression has also been due to the lack of information in the initial reports. Details have been limited. Governments often have not provided information on implementation of each article of the Charter, as requested by the Commission. A few examples will suffice. Though fifty pages in length, the initial report from Egypt, concerning freedom of expression, merely mentioned that the constitution contains the "freedom and the right of . . . journalism." Libya asserted, "Every one enjoys freedom of opinion, research and creativity," then added, "these rights are exercised without disturbing public order or morality." Neither Cape Verde, Rwanda nor Tanzania made any explicit mention of freedom of expression in their initial reports. Togo confidently proclaimed, without any detail, that "fundamental human rights and freedoms" are spelled out in its constitution. The Gambia, by contrast, quoted the relevant section of the country's constitution, whose wording was clearly inspired by Article 19 of the ICCPR; Senegal also made specific reference to its constitution and laws in discussing freedom of expression. I need not go further. With such sketchy information coming from most official sources, members of the African Commission (assuming they are interested) must seek details about freedom of expression from other sources. Reports from ratifying countries are necessary, but they are not sufficient, to examine the freedom of expression in individual African states.

The African Commission has the power to receive and make recommendations on communications. Communications (most of which have been generated by NGOs) call the Commission's attention to alleged violations of the

---

the Covenant on Civil and Political Rights," 17 *Human Rights Quarterly* 766-93 (1995).

[26] In 1995 a group of government experts met in Cape Town and adopted a draft protocol to the African Charter on the establishment of an African Court of Human and Peoples' Rights. The draft is reproduced in 8 *African Journal of International and Comparative Law* 493 (1996). The experts also proposed a number of measures to strengthen the powers of the African Commission. *See* Gino Naldi & Konstantinos Magliveras, "The Proposed African Court of Human and Peoples' Rights: Evaluation and Comparison," 8 *African Journal of International and Comparative Law* 944 (1996).

Charter not resolved through domestic courts or by other means. These must (as is common for international human rights treaty bodies) go through a lengthy, complex and often unsatisfactory process of consideration.[27] Until mid-1996, only one communication had been filed with the African Commission challenging a specific violation of freedom of expression; the communication, filed against the Government of Ghana by International PEN (an NGO comprised of writers who, among other functions, work to defend the human rights of writers under threat), was withdrawn before the Commission could take any action. Five other communications, all also filed by International PEN, dealt with alleged false imprisonment of writers or editors; PEN argued, implicitly, that freedom of expression had been denied. The fate of these may be instructive: one which was directed against Malawi, Ethiopia, Cameroon and Kenya, and another which was directed solely against Malawi, were declared inadmissible since the four states had not ratified the African Charter at the time of the alleged infringements.[28] A third, arising in Burkina Faso, was dismissed since the applicant had been released before the Commission could consider the communication.[29] The fourth, coming from Sudan, was not considered due to non-exhaustion of local remedies.[30] And in the last case, arising in Côte d'Ivoire, an amnesty had "extirpated the legal effects of detention" which two journalists critical of the President had suffered![31] In short, the Commission found excuses so as not to have to voice criticism against governments. A languorous pace and lack of anti-government comment have been typical of the African Commission, hampered through most of its history by a poorly-staffed secretariat and by a high degree of caution of many members.

I do not wish to conclude this chapter on a totally pessimistic note, however. It is my contention that, despite the inherent limitations of the African Charter and the African Commission, pressure from below can help effect a change in the Commission's seemingly limited interest in freedom of expression. NGOs must play an important role in this effort.

---

[27] Welch, *supra* note 20, at 157-61.

[28] African Commission on Human Rights, Comm. Nos. 19/88 and 42/90.

[29] African Commission, Comm. No. 22/88.

[30] African Commission, Comm. No. 92/93.

[31] African Commission, Comm. No. 138/94. I wish to thank Dr. Gerd Oberleitner of the Institute of International Law and International Relations, University of Graz, Austria, for information about these five communications.

V. Non-Governmental Organizations: Their Increasingly Important Role

There has been little active NGO involvement focused specifically on freedom of expression issues before the African Commission.[32] Where NGOs have discussed media in statements made to the Commission, this usually has been in terms of enhancing coverage of human rights issues. Communications dealing specifically with freedom of expression, as already noted, have been limited in number. But this record should not obscure the possibilities for change that exist, both legally and behaviorally.

What I have referred to elsewhere as the "NGO revolution"[33] has the potential to affect freedom of expression in Africa, as in other parts of the world. Here, the work of ARTICLE 19 merits special commendation; but since its accomplishments are known to readers of this volume, I shall concentrate on Africa-based organizations and networks circulating information about the continent.[34]

Significant international publicity has occurred through IFEX, the International Freedom of Expression Exchange. This watchdog group, whose electronic clearing house is based in Toronto, carries reports and action alerts from groups such as the Committee to Protect Journalists (New York), International Federation of Journalists (Brussels) and Reporters sans frontières (Paris). Most active among Africa-based groups has been MISA, the Media Institute of Southern Africa, based in Windhoek, Namibia. Founded by Namibia-based editor Gwen Lister,[35] David Lush, and others, MISA concentrates its attention on the largely English-speaking countries from Malawi and Kenya to Lesotho and South Africa. MISA prepared and published the "Declaration of Windhoek on Promoting an Independent and Pluralistic African Press" in May 1991.[36] This proclaims, *inter alia:*

> 1. Consistent with Article 19 of the Universal Declaration of Human Rights, the establishment and maintenance and fostering of an independent, pluralistic and free press is essential to the development and maintenance of democracy in a nation, and for economic development . . . .

---

[32] Christopher Hall, Legal Officer for Africa at Amnesty International, compiled a 35-page table of recommendations to the African Commission from major NGOs from late 1987 through 1993; none in his compilation involved freedom of expression, although there were several suggestions as to how the Commission might interpret the African Charter and improve the examination of States' reports.

[33] Welch, *supra* note 20, at 284-317.

[34] ARTICLE 19 has published reports or addressed specific comments to the U.N. Human Rights Committee, among others, on Cameroon, Central African Republic, Congo, Egypt, Guinea, Mauritius, Morocco, Rwanda, Togo, Tunisia, Zaire and Zambia. Reports from Human Rights Watch/Africa occasionally give attention to freedom of expression; a noteworthy recent example is its study of Sudan (Human Rights Watch/Africa 1996, at 142-63).

[35] For brief biographical details, see Welch *supra* note 20, at 189-90.

[36] The Declaration is reprinted in Carver, *supra* note 17, at 80-84.

> 4. The welcome changes that an increasing number of African states are now undergoing towards multi-party democracies provide the climate in which an independent and pluralistic press can emerge . . . .
> 9. African states should be encouraged to provide constitutional guarantees of the freedom of the press and freedom of association.

MISA has kept a watchful eye on the hesitant democratization steps taken south of the Equator. The task has proven complex. As perhaps should be expected, the resurgence of competitive party politics has reawakened long-repressed tensions in many African states. Even governments elected on the basis of promises of full democracy have been liable to backsliding when it comes to freedom of expression. Although the formal institutions of democracy exist on paper, the habits of mind necessary to support them have not marked many African countries. Eternal vigilance is the price of liberty. MISA has circulated numerous, vigorous challenges to abridgements of freedom of expression. Among the issues MISA publicized in the first half of 1996 were the dismissal of the editor of the *Times of Zambia* for political reasons,[37] the indefinite imprisonment in Zambia of two newspaper editors (an action criticized by the U.N. Human Rights Committee, but not considered by the African Commission, since Zambia had not yet submitted its report under the African Charter),[38] a proposed bill in Namibia to outlaw deliberate or unintentional publication of "false information" about Parliament and its proceedings,[39] and an attempt by the President of Malawi to use sedition laws against politicians who insulted him.[40] The Committee to Protect Journalists and Reporters sans frontières reported during the same period, among others, on arrests and imprisonment of Gambian, Ghanaian, Guinean and Ivoirien editors and reporters.[41] Thus, although the African Commission was not included "in the loop" for these communications, other human rights groups and agencies received information, and could potentially apply pressure on the relevant governments.

There is, I believe, a major lesson here. A new pattern is emerging in international human rights. A trilateral rather than bilateral relationship can be discerned. While the first decades of reporting on the application of human rights involved States Parties to particular conventions and the relevant examining committee in a bilateral relationship (with governments preparing and submitting reports directly to the body set up by the particular human rights treaty), NGOs have now entered the scene. The exchange has become three-cornered. NGOs play critical roles: critical *to* the success of consultation, and critical *of* the governments that abuse human rights or submit incomplete or misleading reports. ARTICLE 19,

---

[37] IFEX alert of March 25, 1996.
[38] IFEX alerts of April 1 & April 12, 1996.
[39] IFEX alert of April 29, 1996.
[40] IFEX alert of June 26, 1996.
[41] IFEX alerts of April 23, 1996, April 30, 1996, May 8, 1996 and June 14, 1996.

MISA, International Federation of Journalists and other groups concerned with freedom of expression have the potential to influence the African Commission, albeit within limits. As one who has observed several meetings of the African Commission, I believe a stronger presence by such NGOs would pay long-term dividends.

However, I also recognize that non-governmental organizations of and by themselves cannot make up for serious deficiencies in international human rights documents. The weakly-worded Article 9 of the African Charter will not be strengthened because NGOs complain. On the other hand, NGOs can, by their documentation, their presence at meetings, and their pressure for change, influence *how treaty bodies operate.*[42] NGOs have the potential to push the protection of human rights generally to higher levels. They can exert pressure on individual countries, using multiple channels to convey their messages. Although freedom of expression remains weakly protected in the constitutions and laws of most African states, and although the African Commission has thus far given it limited attention, increased attention can and should be expected as a result of NGO efforts. ARTICLE 19 and similar groups will help create the future. What has emerged largely since 1991 should be seen as the first major international steps for freedom of expression to become a widespread feature of African societies.

---

[42] Welch, *supra* note 20, at 211-37.

THE INTER-AMERICAN SYSTEM OF HUMAN RIGHTS PROTECTION: FREEDOM OF EXPRESSION, "NATIONAL SECURITY DOCTRINES" AND THE TRANSITION TO ELECTED GOVERNMENTS

Viviana Krsticevic, José Miguel Vivanco, Juan E. Méndez and Drew Porter

I. Introduction

National security has been the justification for numerous infringements of basic rights in the Americas.[1] Governments, citing national security concerns to legitimize their actions, have imprisoned, raped and murdered political opponents; placed direct and indirect restrictions on freedom of thought and expression and on freedom of association; and violated guarantees of due process and fair trial. While under appropriate circumstances national security may be a valid reason to place some limitations on freedom of expression and other rights, in the recent history of Latin America, military elites have used national security to suppress rights far beyond the limitations allowed under international law.

Former *de facto* President Jorge Rafael Videla of Argentina provided an extreme example of this misuse of national security to justify the suppression of political or ideological opposition in an interview: when asked by foreign correspondents about the disappearance of a handicapped woman, he replied that she might be guilty of an "ideological crime" in the context of an ideological war that threatened the nation.[2] Because they are in a position of power, governments are able to misuse national security by identifying their interests as political actors with the greater interests of the state. They fail to distinguish the security of the state from the security of their particular government or political party. National security should not be used to justify limitations of rights in order to promote one particular political or ideological perspective.

Military regimes in Latin America have largely been replaced by elected governments in the 1980s and '90s and the result has been a considerable expansion

---

[1] National security has been a recurrent justification used by governments and the military in limiting or derogating from human rights. Since the 1960s, concerns about national security took the more developed shape of a "national security doctrine" - ideological support of the fight against a Communist "enemy within" - which influenced the role of the military in Latin American politics. *See* David Collier, *The New Authoritarianism in Latin America* (Princeton University Press 1989). The official Argentine report *Nunca Más*, on disappearances during the 1976-1983 military dictatorship, considered this doctrine the ideological framework of repression. *Nunca Más: informe de la comisión nacional sobre la desaparición de personas*, at 473 (EUDEBA 1984).

[2] J. Patrice McSherry, *Incomplete Transition: Military Power and Democracy in Argentina*, at 85 (1997).

in the exercise of rights, most notably the right to freedom of expression. Unfortunately, the ideology of national security did not necessarily die with the demise of the regimes that based their *raison d'etre* on national security. The misuse of national security to limit rights must be viewed in the context of the difficult debate regarding civilian-military relations in a democratic setting. Elected governments have inherited, and continue to work within, states and systems of governance deeply rooted in, and even dependent upon, authoritarian exercise of power. In the circumstances, elected governments have continued to misuse national security to justify violations of rights. In some cases they have done so explicitly, although in most cases national security has been presented under other guises.

In Mexico, national security was the justification for imprisoning Brigadier General Gallardo, whose case illustrates the need for a human rights ombudsman for the military. A journal printed an excerpt from Gallardo's master's thesis, documenting human rights abuses by the military and suggesting proposals for reform. The Ministry of Defense labeled Gallardo's discussion the "spreading of completely negative ideas about the Mexican military, with the object of dishonoring, offending and discrediting the military in the eyes of the public".[3] Gallardo has been held in a Mexico City military prison since November 1993, and is presently charged with defamation and crimes against military honor.[4] The Mexican army has also filed a civil suit against the editor of the magazine, a small monthly journal called *Forum*.[5]

In Peru, anti-terrorism laws enacted in 1992 have established several provisions which limit freedom of expression in violation of Peru's international obligations. Under the anti-terrorism laws, conduct that may constitute terrorism includes "provoking anxiety" and "affecting international relations". Such conduct also includes "apology of terrorism" - this appears to connote the excuse of, or even perhaps the mere failure to condemn, acts of guerrillas or terrorists. The death penalty can be imposed for terrorism.[6]

---

[3] *Proceso*, Dec. 27, 1993, at 1, 9-11, *quoted in* Minnesota Advocates for Human Rights, "Stifling Human Rights Advocacy in Mexico: the Censure of Brigadier General Jose Fransisco Gallardo Rodriguez," *Human Rights Observer* (May 1994).

[4] *Id.*, at 1, 5. Gallardo was charged under the Code of Military Justice, Articles 280 and 407, part IV. Article 280 is part of Title 8, "Crimes against the Existence and Security of the Military", and prohibits "insulting, defaming, or slandering or making libelous statements about the military or its institutions". Article 407 is part of Title 11, Chapter 7, "Crimes Against Military Honor". Para. 4 of Article 407 prohibits any act or omission "spreading information that could cause lukewarmness or dislike for the service". A complaint against Mexico was filed with the Inter-American Commission on Human Rights in 1996 . IACHR, *Annual Report 1996*, Report Number 43/96 (1997).

[5] "Despite Gains, Press Freedom in Mexico Still Limited," *New York Times*, 20 Nov. 1994, at A3.

[6] Human Rights Watch/Americas, "Peru: the Two Faces of Justice," at 3, Vol.7, No. 9 (July 1995).

Although elected democratically, governments in Latin America today remain semi-authoritarian - characterized by serious breaches of the principle of separation of powers. Frequently, the executive branch has been able to override the authority of the legislative and judicial branches.[7] While democracies normally respect freedom of expression, many elected governments in Latin America remain wary and stifle criticism. Governments continue to misuse national security to limit free expression, though under the guise of concerns for the respect owed to authorities, the need to protect state secrets or the promotion of an ill-defined "reconciliation" between civilians and military. The national security justification has become increasingly diffuse and vague.

Freedom of expression constitutes the backbone not only of a democratic society, but also of personal autonomy.[8] It stands to play a vital role in the strengthening of new Latin American democracies and in the expansion of autonomy and rights enjoyed by citizens in the newly democratic regimes. Absent freedom of expression, the notion of political choice becomes a fiction, and democracy becomes illusion. Yet Latin American governments show a poor understanding of the role of freedom of expression in promoting a democratic order. This manifests itself in misguided attempts to balance free expression with other "values" such as public order, honor of both public and private figures, and national security. Poorly drafted legislation and court judgments evidence this trend, but it is also apparent in extra-judicial means to restrict freedom of expression used by military and paramilitary officials.[9]

The Inter-American system of human rights protection has played a vital role in defending rights in the era of totalitarian dictatorships; in the new democratic period many Latin Americans look to it to help define the scope of freedom. Compared with universal standards, the substantive law on freedom of expression within the regional framework is more progressive in the protection of expression. The adjudicatory framework of the system is promising but still in an early stage of development. The Inter-American Commission on Human Rights (the IACHR or Commission) and the Inter-American Court of Human Rights (the IACtHR or Court) have made significant contributions to the advancement of international law

---

[7] Guillermo O'Donnell identifies these as "delegative democracies" in his paper *Delegative Democracy?*, Working Paper #172 (Helen Kellogg Institute for International Studies, March 1992). *See especially* at 2-3 and 6-10.

[8] *See, e.g.*, Danilo Türk and Louis Joinet, Special Rapporteurs of the UN Sub-Commission on Prevention of Discrimination and Protection of Minorities, *The Right to Freedom of Opinion and Expression: Final Report*, U.N.Doc. E/CN.4/Sub.2/1992/9, at 1 (July 14, 1992): "The right to freedom of expression is a decisive vehicle of social change and as such will always be at the centre of political struggles and discourse. . . ."

[9] Programa Venezolano de Educacion-Accion por los Derechos Humanos (PROVEA), *Situación de los derechos humanos en Venezuela* at 59-64 (Edisil 1993); Letter from Lawyers Committee for Human Rights, Lawyer-to-Lawyer Network, regarding Chilean attorney Héctor Salazar Ardiles, Apr./May 1994.

in sensitive areas of human rights protection. However, in regard to freedom of expression, they have developed only a limited jurisprudence to date. Specifically, there has been no occasion yet to interpret Article 13(2)(b) of the American Convention on Human Rights (the ACHR or Convention) that allows restrictions on freedom of expression on grounds of national security. Nevertheless, decisions and advisory opinions by the Court and reports by the Commission do offer glimpses of how that clause may be construed and applied in the future. This chapter analyzes the standards and relevant jurisprudence, offers some comparisons with the UN and other regional systems, and attempts to glean from these materials some guidance concerning the complex relationship between free expression and national security.[10]

II. Substantive Rules for Restricting the Right to Freedom of Expression in the Inter-American System

The drafters of the Convention sought to promote two objectives in protecting freedom of thought and expression: the autonomy of individuals (by protecting their right to seek, receive and impart information and ideas) and the effective functioning of the democratic system (by ensuring the free exchange of ideas within society). The Court has stressed this latter role:

> Freedom of expression constitutes the primary and basic element of the public order of a democratic society, which is not conceivable without free debate and the possibility that dissenting voices be fully heard.[11]

The drafters further aimed to reinforce the protection of free expression by including an absolute prohibition of prior censorship, a prohibition not expressly stated in any of the other major human rights treaties. Article 13 provides, in part:

> 1. Everyone has the right to freedom of thought and expression. This right includes freedom to seek, receive and impart information and ideas of all kinds, regardless of frontiers, either orally, in writing, in print, in the form of art, or through any other medium of one's choice.
>
> 2. The exercise of this right provided for in the foregoing paragraph shall not be subject to prior censorship but shall be subject to

---

[10] The authors, who work as lawyers for Human Rights Watch/Americas and the Center for Justice and International Law (CEJIL), are pursuing several cases before the Commission seeking pronouncements about Article 13. References to these cases and their likely outcome are included in this chapter.

[11] IACtHR, *Compulsory Membership in an Association Prescribed by Law for the Practice of Journalism* (Articles 13 and 29 *American Convention on Human Rights),* Advisory Opinion OC-5/85, Series A, No. 5, at para. 69 (Nov. 13, 1985). [Hereinafter Advisory Opinion].

> subsequent imposition of liability, which shall be expressly established by law and be necessary in order to ensure:
>
> a. respect for the rights or reputations of others; or
>
> b. the protection of national security, public order, or public health or morals.

The framework of the Convention maximizes the possibilities for public debate by protecting the right to be informed and seek information[12] as well as by protecting the right of reply.[13] States have an affirmative duty to provide an environment in which individuals feel secure in exercising their freedom of expression such that it will not result in any threat or harm to them, from either public authorities or private actors. In a report on the situation of human rights in Guatemala, the Commission stated that "State authorities must not only provide proper protection, but must explicitly denounce and repudiate [a campaign by individuals against those who express opposition to the government] and investigate and bring to trial or administratively censure those responsible."[14]

Freedom of expression receives stronger protection under the Convention than under the International Covenant on Civil and Political Rights (hereinafter ICCPR or Covenant), the European Convention for the Protection of Human Rights and Fundamental Freedoms (hereinafter ECHR) and the African Charter on Human and Peoples' Rights (hereinafter African Charter). As stated by the Court:

> A comparison of Article 13 with the relevant provisions of the European Convention (Article 10) and the Covenant (Article 19) indicates clearly that the guarantees contained in the American Convention regarding freedom of expression were designed to be more generous and to reduce to a bare minimum restrictions impeding the free circulation of ideas.[15]

First, Article 13(2) includes an express prohibition of prior censorship, a prohibition not expressly included in the other treaties. Second, freedom of expression may be limited only in order to protect the rights or reputations of others, national security, public order, public health or public morals. The ICCPR permits restrictions on these grounds as well as in the interest of protecting "*ordre public*", a term considered to cover a broader range of circumstances than "public order". The ECHR also permits restrictions in the interest of protecting territorial integrity or public safety, the confidentiality of information received in confidence, and the authority and impartiality of the judiciary. The African Charter permits restrictions on the free flow of information and ideas so long as they are stated in national law.

---

[12] ACHR, Art. 13(1).
[13] ACHR, Art. 14.
[14] IACHR, *Fourth Report on the Situation of Human Rights in Guatemala*, OEA/Ser.L/V/II.83, Doc. 16 rev. 1, June 1, 1993, at 85.
[15] Advisory Opinion, *supra* note 11, at para. 50.

However, the Convention may provide less protection to "freedom of thought" than does the ICCPR, which extends absolute protection to "freedom of opinion". The Convention attaches the same limitations clause to the freedom of thought as to the freedom of expression clause, while the ICCPR draws a textual distinction between them in its Article 19 and provides for limitations only as to the freedom of expression.

The Inter-American system permits some restrictions on freedom of thought and expression. In the *Journalists Association* Advisory Opinion,[16] the Court stated that freedom of expression and thought plays a crucial role in public debate. The Convention places an "extremely high value" on this right, and is skeptical of any restrictions. As will be developed below, the permissible limitations under the Convention are narrower than the ones allowed by either the ICCPR or the ECHR.

The Convention sets forth general rules for interpreting the applicable restrictions to the rights guaranteed by it. These include Article 32(2), which states that "(t)he rights of each person are limited by the rights of others, by the security of all, and by the just demands of the general welfare, in a democratic society".[17] Article 27 indicates that freedom of expression may be suspended during states of emergency.

The general rules are supplemented, concerning freedom of thought and expression, by the specific limitations set forth in Articles 13 and 14. These make clear that the right to freedom of expression, though fundamental, is not absolute and admits of restrictions. The general and specific rules for imposing restrictions on freedom of expression in the interest of protecting national security are discussed in the following sections.

A. General Rules for Restricting Rights

The Convention contains several general rules for the restriction of rights.

1. The restrictions cannot jeopardize the right itself.

As stated by the United Nations Special Rapporteurs on Freedom of Expression, "restrictions can . . . be considered acceptable only if they do not jeopardize the principle itself. In interpreting the legal norms, the principle must be interpreted broadly and the permissible restrictions restrictively."[18]

---

[16] *Id.*, at paras. 30-32.

[17] This general principle of international law is also supported by the jurisprudence of the Court, *inter alia*, in IACtHR, *The Word "Laws"*, American Convention on Human Rights, Art. 30, Advisory Opinion OC-6186 of May 9, 1986, Series A No. 6. [Hereinafter *The Word*].

[18] Türk and Joinet, *Freedom of Opinion and Expression: Final Report*, *supra* note 8, at para. 20.

This principle stems from the basic rule of treaty interpretation that mandates the interpretation of treaties in good faith and in light of their object and purpose.[19] Article 29 of the American Convention provides:

> No provision in this Convention shall be interpreted as:
> a. permitting any State Party, group, or person to suppress the enjoyment or exercise of the rights and freedoms recognized in this Convention or to restrict them to a greater extent than is provided for herein. This requirement has been repeatedly applied by the Court.[20] The Convention permits rights to be limited but not suppressed. The object and purpose of the Convention is "the protection of the basic rights of individual human beings irrespective of their nationality".[21] In the same spirit, the Court says that "under the Convention (Article 29(a)), all acts directed toward the suppression of any one of the rights set forth therein are illicit".[22]

This rule is crucial when applied to freedom of expression and has been repeatedly applied by the Commission and the Court. For instance, in its Seventh Report on Cuba, the Commission addressed the legitimacy of a provision of the Cuban Constitution which subordinates freedom of expression to "the objectives of socialist society":[23]

> Limitations on the exercise of human rights are always essential; . . . they obey the need to harmonize the exercise of different rights and thus to guarantee observance of all of them; the role of the State is to bring about this harmonization in concrete situations, restricting the exercise of rights only for that purpose. In the case

---

[19] Vienna Convention on the Law of Treaties, Art. 31. *See, The Siracusa Principles on the Limitation and Derogation Provisions in the International Covenant on Civil and Political Rights*, U.N.Doc. E/CN.4/1985/4, Annex, at para. 2 (1985), *reprinted in 7 Hum. Rts. Quarterly* 3 (1985).

[20] IACtHR, *"Other Treaties" Subject to the Advisory Jurisdiction of the Court (Art. 64 American Convention on Human Rights)*, Advisory Opinion OC-1/82 of Sept. 24, 1982, Series A, No. 1, at para. 33; *Restrictions to the Death Penalty* American Convention on Human Rights Arts. 4(2) and 4(4) , Advisory Opinion OC-3/83 of Sept. 8, 1983, Series A, No. 3, at paras. 48-49; OC-6/86, *supra* note 17; *Enforceability of the Right to Reply or Correction,* American Convention on Human Rights Arts. 14(1), 1(1) , 2 , Advisory Opinion OC-7/86 of August 29, 1986, Series A, No. 7, at para 21; *Habeas Corpus in Emergency Situations,* American Convention on Human Rights Arts. 27(2), 25(1) and 7(6), Advisory Opinion OC-8/87 of 30 Jan. 1987, Series A, No. 8, at paras. 14 and 21.

[21] IACtHR, *The Effect of Reservations over the Convention's effective date*, OC-2/82, Series A, No. 2, at para. 29 (Sept. 24, 1982).

[22] *The Word, supra* note 17, at para. 14. This general rule is also acknowledged in the Siracusa Principles, *supra* note 19, Principle 2.

[23] *Cuban Constitution*, Art. 52 (1976).

> of [Cuba] the perspective is otherwise: . . . it is the individual who must limit his rights in the face of the objectives pursued by the State.[24]

A constitutional commitment to a particular political philosophy endangers rights. It is a restriction which becomes more important than the right itself. In the view of the United Nations Special Rapporteurs, if "the right is to be effective, its exercise should not be tied to any particular public philosophy. Expression of ideas 'of any kind' . . . is an essential ingredient of genuine freedom of expression."[25]

In practice, Cuban laws have greatly undermined freedom of expression and political debate under a misguided application of the concept of national security. Authorities use legal and extralegal means to silence critics, including human rights monitors and pro-democracy activists. Stiff judicial penalties are applied for many "thought crimes" against the state:[26]

> Cuba lacks the laws and institutions that would protect basic civil and political rights on a permanent basis. There is no free press. Only state-owned media may operate legally. Self-censorship by journalists is the norm. The Communist Party's Department of Revolutionary Orientation provides guidance on the limits of expression. Free speech is curbed by laws that prohibit and penalize "enemy propaganda," "clandestine printing," and "defamation of public institutions." . . . For insulting President Fidel Castro, Cubans are imprisoned for up to three years.[27]

2. Restrictions must be set forth in law.

In discussing the duty of states to guarantee rights recognized in the Convention, the Court has distinguished the obligations of states when rights are restricted from the obligations of states when rights are ensured. States may only restrict rights by one particular means; namely, by law. The obligation of states to ensure rights is by contrast an obligation of result: any measure which accomplishes that result will suffice.[28] In cases involving the right to freedom of thought and

---

[24] IACHR, *The Situation of Human Rights in Cuba, Seventh Report*, OEA/Ser.L/V/II.61, Doc. 29 rev. 1, at 62, Oct. 4, 1983.

[25] Türk and Joinet, *Freedom of Opinion and Expression: Final Report, supra* note 8, at para. 32. *See also* IACHR, *Ten Years of Activities: 1971-1981,* at 332 (General Secretariat, Organization of American States 1982) (criticizing the criminalization of "the mere act of maintaining or disseminating a particular political doctrine ... [including] any expression of political, sociological, economic, historical, or philosophical thinking derived from the teachings of Karl Marx and his followers").

[26] Human Rights Watch/Americas, "Cuba: Stifling Dissent in the Midst of Crisis," Vol.6, No.2, at 4, February 1994.

[27] *Id.*

[28] IACtHR, *Enforceability of the Right to Reply or Correction, supra* note 20, at para. 33.

expression, the Court has used this distinction to afford maximum protection to individuals in the exercise of their rights.[29]

3. Restrictions on freedom of expression based on national security must be narrowly drawn.

This principle flows from the two preceding principles. Concerns about ambiguous and imprecise definitions have often been raised.[30] One narrowing approach asserts that national security is only genuinely imperiled by a general threat to the nation.[31]

The Commission has on several occasions evaluated restrictions on freedom of expression based on a strict definition of national security. In its 1981 *Report on the Situation of Human Rights in the Republic of Nicaragua* the Commission specifically addressed the issue of the need for a clear definition:

> In the Commission's view, a limitation on freedom of the press is justified only when the order and the security of the State are truly compromised. Such a limitation may be in effect only for a *limited and declared period of time* and under *certain specific circumstances.* The legislation currently in effect may give rise to serious abuses, because of its great ambiguity and breadth. When freedom of the press is at stake, any restrictions must be *clearly established* so that anyone may know precisely what activities are prohibited or must be subject to censorship. Expressions such as: "or that in any way damage or compromise the economic stability of the nation" or "harm the national defense" or "other similar case," that are found in Decrees Nos. 511 and 512 and currently incorporated into Decree No. 708 amending the Law on the Communications Media, give the Governmental authorities such discretion as to represent

[29] IACtHR, *Compulsory Membership in an Association, supra* note 11, at para. 52. This principle is also repeatedly mentioned by commentators as crucial in analyzing restrictions, and different aspects of it have been acknowledged in several of the Siracusa Principles, *supra* note 19, at Principles 1, 3, and 4. *See also* Johannesburg Principle 1.

[30] The U.N. Special Rapporteurs on Freedom of Opinion and Expression voiced their concern, speaking of "[r]estrictions with the purpose of protecting national security, such as restrictions relating to military and State secrets. In this connection, mention should be made of the problems arising from the ambiguity of provisions defining the concept of military or State secrets, etc. or the penalization of incitement to treason or sedition. Here again caution is called for; the term 'sedition' may be given a very broad interpretation and used to bar the exercise of the right to freedom of expression." U.N.Doc. E/CN.4/Sub.2/1992/9, *supra* note 8, at para. 7.

[31] Siracusa Principles, *supra* note 19, at Principles 29-32; Johannesburg Principle 2.

> a risk to the freedom of expression set forth in Article 13 of the American Convention on Human Rights.[32]

The Commission has applied these criteria in order to prevent abuses common to invocation of threats of national security and related concepts. For instance, in its *1973 Annual Report*, it criticized the existence of "crimes of opinion":

> It is also apparent that in some cases states of emergency have been perpetuated far longer than necessary to safeguard national security, or they have taken on the characteristics of a true, ideologically motivated persecution. In fact, some legal provisions have been issued establishing "crimes of opinion", that is, crimes stemming from a person's beliefs, without those beliefs necessarily taking the form of overt harmful acts.[33]

4. The State must provide "an effective judicial remedy" for violations of the right to freedom of expression.

Article 25(1) of the Convention declares the right to a "simple and prompt recourse, or any other effective recourse, to a competent court or tribunal for protection against acts that violate his fundamental rights . . . ." The Inter-American Court has amplified that, to fulfill this obligation, each state must provide "an effective judicial remedy for violations of fundamental rights".[34] Article 8(1) requires the judicial power to be "competent, independent and impartial". Judicial "[g]uarantees are designed to protect, to ensure or to assert the entitlement to a right or the exercise thereof".[35] Furthermore, certain judicial guarantees may not be suspended during states of emergency.[36]

5. States of emergency.

The right to freedom of expression may be suspended during states of emergency, as implied by Article 27(2).[37] Since this chapter attempts to develop

---

[32] IACHR, *Report on the Situation of Human Rights in the Republic of Nicaragua*, OEA/Ser.L/V/II.53, Doc. 25, 30 June 1981, at 118, para. 6 (emphasis in original). *See also* IACHR, *Annual Report 1972,* at 32.

[33] IACHR, *Annual Report*, OEA/Ser.L/V/II.30, Doc. 45 rev. 1, 12 Oct. 1973, at 34-35.

[34] IACtHR, Judicial Guarantees in States of Emergency (Arts. 27(2), 25 and 8 of the American Convention), OC-9/87 of 6 Oct. 1987, Series A, No. 9, at para. 23.

[35] *Habeas Corpus in Emergency Situations*, OC-8/87, *supra* note 20, at para. 25.

[36] *Id.* at para. 27; ACHR, Art. 27(2).

[37] Art. 27(1) states:

> In time of war, public danger, or other emergency that threatens the independence or security of a State Party, it may take measures derogating from its obligations under the present Convention to the extent and for the period of time strictly required by the exigencies of the situation,

principles governing the limitation of freedom of expression in general, limitations during states of emergency are not discussed in depth. Limitations during states of emergency do, however, provide insight as to the threshold required to justify limitations in exceptional situations.

In the context of states of emergency, in practice the Commission has used, albeit by default, the concept of national security in order to evaluate the existence of a real threat and assess the validity of derogations of rights.[38] The Commission has recognized that, in some circumstances, governments have an obligation to restrict rights in order to protect national security:

> In the life of any nation, threats to the public order or to the personal safety of its inhabitants, by persons or groups that use violence, can reach such proportions that it becomes necessary, temporarily, to suspend the exercise of certain human rights.[39]

B. Specific Rules Regarding Restricting the Right to Freedom of Expression

The American Convention lists specific rules for evaluating the permissible limitations to freedom of expression. Article 13(2) provides.

> The exercise of the right provided for in the foregoing paragraph shall not be subject to prior censorship but shall be subject to subsequent imposition of liability, which shall be expressly established by law to the extent necessary in order to ensure:
>
> a. respect for the rights or reputations of others; or
>
> b. the protection of national security, public order, or public health or morals.

The Inter-American Court has established three core principles to determine the validity of restrictions: first, prior censorship is absolutely prohibited; second, governments may use subsequent liability to control expression only where specific criteria are satisfied; and third, indirect restrictions of freedom of expression are absolutely prohibited.

> provided that such measures are not inconsistent with its other obligations under international law and do not involve discrimination on the ground of race, color, sex, language, religion, or social origin.

Art. 27(2) lists the rights from which no derogation is permitted; the right to freedom of expression and opinion is not included.

[38] Jaime Oraá cites several examples in *Human Rights in States of Emergency in International Law*, at 54 (Clarendon Press 1992). *See, e.g.*, IACHR, *Fourth report on the Situation of Human Rights in Guatemala*, *supra* note 14, at 80.

[39] IACHR, *Report on the Situation of Human Rights in Argentina*, OEA/Ser.L/V/II.49, Doc. 19 corr. 1, 11 April 1980.

1. Absolute Prohibition of Prior Censorship

The Convention prohibits prior censorship, with only two exceptions: (a) during a declared state of emergency where strictly required by the circumstances, and (b) when aimed at protecting the moral health of children and adolescents, and the expression regulated is public entertainment.[40] Such a near-absolute prohibition of prior censorship is not found in the ECHR, ICCPR or the African Charter. For instance, those treaties permit, and may indeed require, prior restraint of advocacy of national, racial or religious hatred.[41]

The prohibition of prior censorship has specific consequences for threats to national security: abuse of freedom of information cannot be controlled by preventive measures but only through the subsequent imposition of sanctions on those who are guilty of the abuses.[42] The radical consequence of the provisions of the Convention have not been fully understood by States Parties.

2. Imposition of Subsequent Liability only upon Satisfaction of Specific Criteria

According to the Convention, limitations on rights must be established by law, and must be necessary to protect the rights of others, national security, public order, or public health or morals. The Court uses the term "restrictions" to describe "liabilities imposed by law for the abusive exercise of freedom of expression".[43]

In order to determine the validity of sanctions imposed subsequently, the Inter-American Court uses a test similar to that formulated by the European Court of Human Rights in the *Sunday Times* case.[44] The criteria resemble those developed

---

[40] ACHR, Art. 27(2), *supra* note 37, and Art. 13(4). Art. 13(4) reads: "Notwithstanding the provisions of paragraph 2 above, public entertainment may be subject by law to prior censorship for the sole purpose of regulating access for the moral protection of childhood and adolescence."

[41] ICCPR Art. 20(2) provides: "Any advocacy of national, racial or religious hatred that constitutes incitement to discrimination, hostility or violence shall be prohibited by law. African Charter, Art. 28 reads: "Every individual shall have the duty to respect and consider his fellow beings without discrimination, and to maintain relations aimed at promoting, safeguarding and reinforcing mutual respect and tolerance." The European Court of Human Rights interpreted the requirements concerning prohibition of hate speech under ECHR Art. 10 in *Jersild* v. *Denmark* (1994), 298 Eur. Ct. H.R. 1 (ser. A.) (1994).

[42] IACtHR, *Compulsory Membership in an Association, supra* note 11, at para. 39.

[43] *Id.* at para. 35 *in fine.*

[44] ECHR, *The Sunday Times Case*, Judgment of April 26, 1979, Series A, No. 30, at para. 59. This general test for legitimacy of restrictions is threefold:(a) the restriction must be established by law and precisely defined; (b) the ends sought must be legitimate; and (c) the restriction must be shown to be necessary to ensure a legitimate aim (limited to the aims listed in the relevant treaties). Art. 13(2) of the ACHR allows restrictions only to ensure "respect for the rights or reputations of others" or "the protection of national security, public order, or public

by the U.N. Special Rapporteurs, which they "consider universal in nature and applicable in every situation in which restrictions of the right to freedom of expression are imposed", namely: "legality, legitimacy, proportionality, and democratic necessity".[45]

The Inter-American Court's formulation provides that any restrictions must meet the following four requirements, which correspond, with some slight differences, to those articulated by the U.N. Rapporteurs:

a. the grounds for liability must be precisely defined in a law duly adopted before the expression in question;

b. the ends sought to be achieved must be legitimate;

c. the grounds for liability must be "necessary to ensure" the aforementioned ends;[46] and

d. the restrictions must be the "least restrictive means" reasonably available to achieve the state's legitimate goals.[47]

a. Legality

The principle of legality is set forth in Articles 9 and 30 of the American Convention: the principle holds that restrictions may be placed on the exercise of rights or freedoms only pursuant to a duly enacted law (Article 30), and that criminal penalties may be imposed only pursuant to a law which makes clear the grounds for liability enacted *prior* to the conduct in question(Article 9).

Article 30 states that any restrictions placed on the rights recognized in the Convention "may not be applied except in accordance with laws enacted for reasons of general interest and for the purpose for which the restrictions have been established." The Court has concluded that the word "laws", as used in Article 30, refers only to formal laws - that is, laws passed by the legislature and promulgated by the Executive Branch, pursuant to the procedure set out in the domestic law of each State.[48] This requirement is more stringent than the requirements of legality under the ICCPR and European Convention, which consider the principle of legality to be satisfied by unwritten law, such as the common law.[49]

---

health or morals". *See also*, S. Coliver, *The Article 19 Freedom of Expression Handbook*, at 110-12 (London: Article 19, 1993); and Commentary to Johannesburg Principle 1(c), *supra* at 11.

[45] Türk and Joinet, *Freedom of Opinion and Expression: Final Report*, *supra* note 8, at 12-13. The rapporteurs derive this test from the Universal Declaration of Human Rights, the ICCPR and the three regional human rights treaties.

[46] IACHR, *Compulsory Membership in an Association*, *supra* note 11, at para. 39.

[47] *Id.*

[48] *The Word "Laws" in Article 30*, Adv. Opn OC 6/86, *supra* note 17, at para. 27 *in fine*.

[49] *See*, *supra*, at 109 (European Convention), and at 87 (ICCPR). See also Johannesburg Principle 1.1, *supra* at 1, and the Commentary thereto, *supra* at 23.

Concerning Article 9,[50] the Inter-American Court has explained that "(b)ecause the provision deals with restrictions as that concept has been used by the Court, the legal definition of the liability must be express and precise".[51] Without the prior specification of grounds of liability, the right to freedom of expression could be manipulated at the "sole discretion of governmental authorities".[52]

b. Legitimacy

The purpose of any law restricting freedom of expression must be legitimate according to the meaning of Article 13(2). The Commission has identified illegitimate objectives for restricting freedom of expression based on national security concerns. For example, as noted above, in its *Seventh Report on the Situation of Human Rights in Cuba*, it condemned the subordination of freedom of expression to the "objectives of a socialist society" in the Cuban Constitution.[53] Similarly, the Commission strongly opposed Paraguay's misuse of Article 71 of its Constitution (proscribing the defense of "hatred or class struggle among Paraguayans, or crime or violence") which "has been repeatedly used by the Government to silence simple statements of disagreement by the opposition".[54]

c. Necessity in a Democratic Society

According to the Court, Article 13(2) must be interpreted in light of Articles 29(b), 29(c) and 32. Thus:

> It follows from the repeated reference to 'democratic institutions', 'representative democracy' and 'democratic society' that the question whether a restriction on freedom of expression imposed by a state is 'necessary to ensure' one of the objectives listed in subparagraphs (a) or (b) must be judged by reference to the legitimate needs of democratic societies and institutions.[55]

According to the Convention the restriction has to be proportionate and closely tailored to the achievement of those ends.[56]

---

[50] Art. 9 reads, in relevant part: "No one shall be convicted of any act or omission that did not constitute a criminal offense, under the applicable law, at the time it was committed."

[51] IACtHR, *Compulsory Membership in an Association, supra* note 11, at para. 40.

[52] *Id.*

[53] *See* IACHR, *Report of the Situation in Cuba, supra* note 24.

[54] IACHR, *Report on the Situation of Human Rights in Paraguay*, OEA/Ser.L/V/II.71, Doc. 19 rev. 1, at 64, 67, Sept. 28, 1987.

[55] IACtHR, *supra* note 11, at para. 42.

[56] *Id. at* para. 46.

> The just demands of democracy must consequently guide the interpretation of the Convention and, in particular, the interpretation of those provisions that bear a critical relation and functioning of democratic institutions.[57]

The Commission has acknowledged specifically the illegitimacy of restrictions on freedom of expression based on national security concerns which are rooted in the lack of appropriate democratic checks.[58] Even during states of emergency, there must be appropriate means to control the measures taken, so that they are proportionate to the needs and do not exceed the strict limits imposed by the Convention or derived from it.[59]

d. Least Restrictive Means

The Inter-American Court has gone further than the European Court of Human Rights or the U.N. Human Rights Committee (created under the ICCPR) in stating explicitly that any restrictions imposed on freedom of expression must not only be necessary to achieve a legitimate aim but must actually be the "least restrictive means" available.[60] Stated the court:

> [T]he "necessity" and, hence, the legality of restrictions imposed . . . on freedom of expression depend upon a showing that the restrictions are required by a compelling governmental interest. Hence, if there are various options to achieve this objective, that which least restricts the right protected must be selected.[61]

3. Prohibition of Indirect Restrictions

Article 13(3) of the Convention prohibits the imposition of indirect restrictions on freedom of expression:

---

[57] *Id.* at para. 44 *in fine.*

[58] IACHR, *Report on the Situation of Human Rights in Chile,* OEA/Ser.L/V/II.66, Doc 17, 27 Sept. 1985, at 213-14: "Indeed, the broad discretionary powers the laws and the Constitution confer on the military chiefs of areas in the state of emergency, and on the President himself, to suspend and restrict the freedoms of opinion, expression, and dissemination of thought, have meant that in these 12 years those freedoms have been severely limited and in certain periods even eliminated by such measures as the closure of information media, censorship, prohibition of publishing specified news items and even illustrations, the need for authorization for establishing new publications, and other restrictions mentioned in this Chapter."

[59] ACHR, Art. 27(1). *See* IACtHR, *Judicial Guarantees in States of Emergency (Arts. 27(2), 25 and 8 American Convention on Human Rights),* OC-9/87 of October 6, 1987, Series A, No. 9, at para. 20.

[60] See Johannesburg Principle 1.3(b), and Commentary thereto, *supra* this volume at 30-31.

[61] IACtHR, *supra* note 11, at para. 39.

> The right of expression may not be restricted by indirect methods or means, such as the abuse of government or private controls over newsprint, radio broadcasting frequencies, or implements or equipment used in the dissemination of information, or by any other means tending to impede the communication and circulation of ideas and opinions.

The ICCPR and ECHR do not contain an explicit prohibition of indirect methods; particularly noteworthy is the American Convention's prohibition of restrictive measures by private parties.

III. Application of the Substantive Rules

The principles set forth above for limiting freedom of expression for reasons of national security are very much shaped and influenced by the procedure and practice of the monitoring bodies. In the case of the Inter-American system, the Commission and the Court have a very active and flexible view of their role.[62]

The Inter-American system of human rights protection has developed under circumstances different from those that influenced the development of its European counterpart. Much of the case law evolved during the era of poorly functioning or unresponsive domestic judicial systems. This has also influenced the manner in which the Commission and Court view their roles in the system. As a result, the Commission has become a flexible and responsive institution; it has effectively used, for example, *in loco* investigations and protective provisional measures.[63] When the limits of freedom of expression are adjudicated, three principal themes emerge: the allocation of burdens of proof; the principle of subsidiarity; and the margin of appreciation.

A. Burden of Proof

As affirmed in the Siracusa Principles, "[t]he burden of justifying a limitation upon a right guaranteed under the Covenant lies with the State".[64] In an

---

[62] Cecilia Medina Quiroga, *The Battle of Human Rights,* at 104 (1989).

[63] *Id.* at 71-76.

[64] Siracusa Principles, *supra* note 19, at Principle 12. *See also* Johannesburg Principle 1.3.

international legal proceeding, the burden and standards of proof are applied differently than they would be in a domestic proceeding.[65]

The Court has recognized that the State is generally in a better position to supply evidence than victims. In the *Velásquez* case, the Court was called on to determine whether the Government of Honduras bore responsibility for a series of disappearances of political opponents of the regime. The Court concluded that the Government had pursued a policy "designed to conceal and destroy evidence of the disappearance of the victims". Because of the difficulty of proving government responsibility for a person's disappearance, the Court stated that "the disappearance of a particular individual may be proved through circumstantial or indirect evidence or by logical inference. Otherwise, it would be impossible to prove."[66] Similarly, responsibility for establishing the need for restrictions to the freedom of expression falls to the State: it is in a better position to assess threats to national security than the applicant whose rights or freedoms have been restricted.

B. Subsidiarity

International mechanisms of human rights protection are by nature subsidiary mechanisms. International law and jurisprudence have acknowledged this principle.[67] Subsidiarity denotes a default check upon the maintenance of basic rights, where there is a failure to protect those rights domestically.[68] Subsidiarity is sensitive to national authorities' need for flexibility in formulating political and economic policies. Subsidiarity gives the system "great flexibility in dealing with the myriad problems of everyday life within the Contracting States that have come before it".[69]

The essence of the principle of subsidiarity is that domestic institutions retain primary competence and responsibility for protecting fundamental rights. Where they fail to do so, the international and regional oversight bodies should accord less deference to their decisions. As stated by leading authorities on the European human rights system:

---

[65] IACtHR, *Velásquez Rodriguez Case*. OEA/Ser.C, No. 4 (1988), at para. 128. (Judg. of July 29, 1988). The Court explained: "The international protection of human rights should not be confused with criminal justice. States do not appear before the Court as defendants in a criminal action. The objective of international human rights law is not to punish those individuals who are guilty of violations, but rather to protect the victims and to provide for the reparation of damages resulting from the acts of the States responsible." *Id.* at para. 134 .

[66] *Id.* at para. 124.

[67] R.St.J.MacDonald, et al., *The European System for the Protection of Human Rights*, at 49-50 (1993).

[68] Cecilia Medina Quiroga, *Derecho Internacional de los Derechos Humanos*, at 20 (La Union, 1989).

[69] MacDonald, *supra* note 67, at 122.

> The impact of the principle of subsidiarity is thus to a considerable extent dependent on the attitude and conduct of the national authorities and notably their judiciary. The greater their willingness to consider and take into account the provisions of the Convention, the more restraint and discretion can be expected from the Commission institutions when exercising their supervisory function.[70]

The doctrine of subsidiarity emphasizes the importance of a domestic judiciary which is independent, impartial and capable of giving effect to the right of individuals to due process of the law. In the Inter-American context, the human rights organs need to examine the extent to which rights and privileges established by the Convention are respected. Where a member state's judiciary has not been effective in protecting rights established by the Convention, the Inter-American Commission and Court should show less deference to the domestic institutions.

C. Margin of Appreciation

The margin of appreciation doctrine is a derivative of subsidiarity. Deference is given to local conditions and standards on certain issues for reasons of flexibility and in recognition of the diversity of the political, social, economic and other conditions in the various member states.[71] Subsidiarity as a practice in Europe developed from the manner in which the ECHR establishes certain rights and duties to be protected as obligations of result, without prescribing the means by which they are to be protected. Within the Inter-American system as well, States may similarly choose whichever policies allow them to achieve the standards mandated in the Convention. In the words of the Inter-American Court, "[t]he contents of the law may vary from one State to another, within certain reasonable limits and within the framework of the concepts stated by the Court".[72] In the case of limitations upon freedom of expression, Article 13 goes further than the ECHR or the ICCPR by specifying that States may not use prior censorship. By invalidating this means of restricting freedom of expression, the Convention allows for a narrower margin of appreciation.

In cases where the rights are more fundamental in nature, the margin of appreciation is narrower. Some rights, such as the right to a fair trial, are foundational to democracy and enable other rights to be secured domestically. Political and economic concerns should not weigh heavily in such circumstances. In any case where a fundamental right is found to be superseded by a purportedly public

---

[70] *Id.* at 62.

[71] *See, e.g.,* ECHR. *Handyside Case,* Judgment of Dec. 7, 1976, Series A, No. 24.

[72] *Enforceability of the Right to Reply or Correction,* OC-7/86, *supra* note 20, at para. 27.

interest, such as national security, a suspicion as regards the propriety of the limitation must arise.

In a European freedom of expression case (*Schwabe*), Judge Martens in his concurring opinion stated that

> the Court makes it clear in its present judgment that, where the right to freedom of expression is at stake, there is no room for leaving to the national courts a margin of appreciation as to the assessment of the relevant standards, but that it will effect a full review of such assessments examine.[73]

The majority in the *Schwabe* case did not discuss the issue or comment on Judge Marten's statement, but he may well have presaged a developing approach of the Court, at least as regards political expression.[74]

IV. Current Threats to Free Expression and the System's Response

Governments throughout Latin America today seldom seek to justify restrictions on free expression as necessary to safeguard national security. The national security doctrine is rightly out of fashion after the nightmare of repression it generated. But its authoritarian bent, its obsession with "social discipline", and its intolerance of dissent manifest in restrictions imposed by governments under other guises. The Inter-American system of protection has become the leading battleground to check these excesses and to protect the broadening space that Latin American journalists, writers and social activists are making for themselves. The following cases are examples of restrictions supported on other grounds that bear the mark of national security-inspired curbs.

A. Defamation of Public Officials

In Argentina, President Carlos S. Menem dusted off the old criminal statute of *desacato* to prosecute critics he deemed to have offended him and his aides or their offices. *Desacato* laws "criminalize expression which offends, insults, or threatens a public functionary in the performance of his or her official duties".[75] They protect public officials from criticism based on the presumption that, by leaving them unhindered by criticism, they are better able to perform their duties. This presumably prevents the destabilizing effect which is said to be caused by widespread

---

[73] ECHR, *Schwabe v. Austria*, Series A, No. 242-B (1992), *quoted in* MacDonald, *supra* note 67, at 93.

[74] *Id.*

[75] IACHR, *Report on the Compatibility of "Desacato Laws" With the American Convention on Human Rights* at 201 (Annual Report, 1994) OEA/Ser.L/V/II.88, Doc. 9 rev. 1, 17 Feb. 1995.

criticism of government officials. Such criticism supposedly not only tarnishes the official, but "reflects . . .on the office he or she holds and the administration he or she serves".[76] In some countries, truth does not provide a defense against such laws.[77]

Several charges were filed against Argentine journalists and human rights leaders on the basis of their expression of opinion. The first case to result in a conviction affected Horacio Verbitsky, Argentina's foremost investigative journalist and author of two best-selling books on corruption and manipulation of the judiciary.[78] Verbitsky was given a suspended sentence for his comments on the attitude of a Supreme Court justice towards Menem's successful packing of that body. After exhausting his domestic remedies, Verbitsky filed a complaint with the Commission, and participated in its hearings in Washington. With the assistance of the Commission, the representatives of the Argentine Government and Verbitsky entered into a "friendly settlement" procedure under Article 48(1)(f) of the Convention.

In the proposed settlement, the Government agreed to repeal the *desacato* statute and to apply the benefit of that repeal to Verbitsky's conviction. Verbitsky formally renounced any claim for damages, including costs and attorneys' fees. Both parties asked the Commission to conduct a study of the *desacato* laws in the region and their compatibility with the Convention. The Commission approved the settlement and the Argentine Congress amended the Penal Code to delete the offense of *desacato*. Verbitsky's conviction was vacated.

In December of 1994, the Commission published its *Report on the Compatibility of "Desacato" Laws with the American Convention on Human Rights*.[79] In the *Report*, it concluded that such laws are incompatible with the Convention and are not "necessary to ensure" public order in a democratic society.[80] Moreover, the laws violate the principles of non-discrimination and equality before the law, set forth in the Convention. As the Commission stated, "The use of *desacato* laws to protect the honor of public functionaries acting in their official capacities unjustifiably grants a right to protection to public officials that is not available to other members of society".[81] The adoption and application of these laws incorrectly suggests that order and reputation are more compelling interests than truth and the necessity of debate in a democratic society.[82]

---

[76] *Id.* at 202.

[77] *Id.*

[78] Horacio Verbitsky, *Robo para la Corona* (1992) and *Hacer la Corte* (1993). In 1995, Verbitsky published a third best-seller, *El Vuelo*, about atrocities during the "dirty war" and a current "conspiracy of silence" about them. Of the latter, there is an English version: Horacio Verbitsky, *The Flight: Confessions of an Argentine Dirty Warrior* (1996).

[79] *Desacato Report, supra* note 75.

[80] *Id.* at 197, 209.

[81] *Id.* at 207.

[82] *See, e.g.,* Eur. Court H.R., *Lingens Case*, Judgment of 8 July 1986, Series A, No. 103.

The Verbitsky case and the subsequent report of the Commission offer a basis for a campaign to repeal the regressive *desacato* statutes that still exist in several other Latin American countries. Unfortunately, the General Assembly of the Organization of American States, which received the report, has so far chosen not to act on it. It would greatly enhance the cause of freedom of expression if, at a future session, the region's highest political organ would express support for the Commission's conclusions and urge all countries to repeal *desacato* laws.[83]

In Argentina, the Menem administration persisted in its efforts to control the press. In early 1995, Minister of Justice Rodolfo Barra submitted a bill to Congress to (a) increase the prison terms for libel and (b) aggravate the crime if the victim is a public official or a public institution. The bill would also require publications to post bonds against possible libel lawsuits. Verbitsky filed a new complaint with the Commission and appeared at a preliminary hearing in Washington. While admission of the case was still under consideration, Barra backed down and withdrew his bill.

B. Prior Restraints and Self-Censorship

In Chile a court prohibited the circulation of a book published in Argentina by Chilean journalist Francisco Martorell.[84] The book describes the exploits of Menem's ambassador to Chile, Oscar Spinosa Melo, who allegedly organized parties at his ambassadorial residence and then blackmailed prominent Chileans. Chilean citizens mentioned in the book sued for slander and obtained an unjunction against sales or distribution of the book in Chile. Martorell was unable to have the injunction against circulation removed, and filed a complaint with the Commission. In his pleadings, Martorell claimed that the actions of the Chilean judiciary violated Chile's obligation under the Convention not to engage in prior restraints. The Government of Chile answered the complaint claiming that there was no violation because the court's decision constituted a valid balancing of two competing values protected by the Convention: freedom of expression and the honor of persons.[85] In 1996, the Commission issued a report condemning Chile for the violation of the prohibition on prior censorship in Article 13 of the Convention.[86] Although

---

[83] Charles Moyer, "Friendly Settlement in the Inter-American System: The Verbitsky Case," in IACtHR, *La Corte y el Sistema Interamericanos de Derechos Humanos* (Rafael Nieto N., ed. 1994.)

[84] Martorell Francisco, *Impunidad Diplomática* (1993).

[85] In representing Martorell before the Inter-American system, the authors of this chapter made it clear that they made no assertions about the veracity of the book's contents or about the importance of its theme. Instead, we stressed the importance of seeking a judgment against any form of prior censorship, even if judicially and not administratively imposed.

[86] IACHR, *Annual Report 1996*, Report Number 43/96 (Wash. D.C. 1997).

Martorell had specifically asked for the case to be submitted to the Inter-American Court, the Commission chose not to do so; Chile also declined to seek the Court's judgment, but instead submitted a request for an advisory opinion challenging the Commission's interpretation of its own powers as applied in *Martorell*. In November 1997, the Court issued an Advisory Opinion largely upholding the Commission's position.[87]

In August 1995, it was revealed that a video-clip by an Argentine rock group called *Los Fabulosos Cadillacs* had been altered for circulation in Chile. The clip features a song called *Mal Bicho* ("mean bug"), the general theme of which is an indictment of fascism. The video images include photographs of Hitler, Mussolini and Generals Videla and Pinochet. Pinochet was Commander-in-Chief of the Chilean Army; presumably the censorship was due to the fact that, under Chilean law, personal attacks on public figures may incur criminal liability. It is unclear whether any agency of the Chilean Government was involved in the censorship, which was strongly protested by the musicians. Rather, it may have been a case of self-censorship by the Sony Corporation, which distributed the video-clip.

C. State Secrets and the "Right to Truth"

In the aftermath of the military dictatorships, the human rights communities in Latin America have focused upon the issue of accountability for crimes perpetrated under those regimes. Owing to their efforts, the issue is a central part of the debate regarding the nature of democracy and the limits of the so-called "transitions" from dictatorship to democracy. The debate highlights the fact that accountability requires justice: States are obliged to investigate, prosecute and punish grave violations of human rights such as massive executions and forced disappearances. But accountability also requires "truth", and imposes an obligation on States to disclose all that can be known about those atrocities. For this purpose, truth Commissions have been formed and have produced important reports in Argentina, Chile and El Salvador (the last, with the support of the United Nations). A truth commission recently was set up in Haiti; under the auspices of the United Nations, the Guatemalan Government and the insurgent forces agreed to set up a "Commission on Clarification" of the events of the past decades.[88]

The Inter-American system of human rights protection has played a significant role in developing and asserting the emerging principle of international law that, where crimes against humanity are concerned, the state is obligated to investigate, prosecute and punish the perpetrators; to disclose to the victims, their families and society all that can be faithfully established about them; and to provide

---

[87] IACtHR, *Informes de la Comisión Interamericana de Derechos Humanos, Solicitada por Chile*, OC-15/97, (1997). (An English version will be issued in 1998.)

[88] *See* U.S. Institute of Peace, *Transitional Justice* (Neil Kritz, ed., 1995).

for appropriate reparations. The Inter-American Court, in a frequently quoted passage in the ground-breaking *Velasquez* decision, wrote:

> The State has a legal duty to take reasonable steps to prevent human rights violations and to use the means at its disposal to carry out a serious investigation of violations committed within its jurisdiction, to identify those responsible, impose the appropriate punishment and ensure the victim adequate compensation.[89]

Largely on the strength of this pronouncement, the Commission had occasion to elaborate on State obligations when it received challenges against laws in Uruguay and Argentina (in the latter case also presidential decrees) that had the effect of precluding prosecutions for the crimes of the military dictatorships. The Commission stated that those actions by democratic governments were incompatible with their obligations under the Convention, in particular because their effect was to make truth-seeking and truth-telling all but impossible.[90] The Commission had earlier articulated the rationale underlying this obligation (and the corresponding "right to truth") in 1986:

> Independently of the problem of proving guilt . . . every society has the inalienable right to know the truth about past events, as well as the motives and circumstances in which aberrant crimes came to be committed, in order to prevent repetition of such acts in the future. Moreover, the family members of the victims are entitled to information as to what happened to their relatives...[T]he Commission considers that the observance of the principles cited above will bring about justice rather than vengeance, and thus neither the urgent need for national reconciliation nor the consolidation of democratic government will be jeopardized.[91]

The struggle for the truth continues. Beyond securing official acknowledgment of the general structure of repression, Latin American human rights organizations now seek a complete, individualized "truth" in respect of each family affected, after thorough investigation and examination of all records. The interests of military establishments remain an obstacle. In some instances, the military have classified records of human rights violations as military secrets, or simply asserted that there are no records.

In August 1995, Argentine Senator Eduardo Vaca, of the ruling party, announced his intention to submit a bill to force journalists to reveal sources or face

---

[89] IACtHR, *Velásquez Rodríguez Case*, *supra* note 65, at para. 174. On this emerging principle, see also Diane Orentlicher, "Addressing Gross Human Rights Abuses: Punishment and Victim Compensation", in L. Henkin and J.L. Hargrove, eds., *Human Rights: An Agenda for the Next Century* (1994).

[90] IACHR, *Annual Report 1992*, Nos. 28 and 29.

[91] IACHR, *Annual Report 1985-86*, OEA/Ser.L/V/II.68, Doc. 8 rev. 1, at 192-93.

prison terms if they reveal "state secrets". The definition of what would constitute a state secret was left to the Executive Branch. The proposal received near-unanimous condemnation in journalistic and political circles and eventually died in the Argentine Congress.

In 1995, the Commission received a complaint which sought to force the Government of Brazil to disclose military records about the extermination of members of an insurgent force in an episode from the 1970s called the *Guerrilha do Araguaia*. Brazilian human rights lawyers had exhausted their domestic judicial remedies; the courts had allowed the Ministry of Defense to refuse to provide any information about the way in which dozens of persons died. In 1996, the Brazilian Government submitted a bill and Congress approved a law offering compensation to the families of the Araguaia victims. The law also created a procedure by which relatives of victims of similar abuses could claim compensation.

The Commission also received petitions from Argentine groups to reopen the file of a case regarding the concentration and extermination center run in the 1970s by the Naval Mechanical School (ESMA). This new petition was prompted by the revelations of Navy officer Adolfo Scilingo that he had participated in throwing prisoners from airplanes into the ocean.[92] In the controversy that ensued, Argentine courts ordered the Executive Branch to produce records or to reproduce the list of the "disappeared" held at ESMA. The Navy refused to cooperate. The head of the Army, General Martin Balza, made a historic public apology for the wrongs committed during the "dirty war" and asked his subordinates to come forward with information so that he could relay it to the families and to society. Although more than two years have passed, as of this writing not a single officer accepted the invitation of his commander. In the meantime, victims have asked the courts to order the Executive to investigate the fate and whereabouts of the "disappeared" and to provide the information to the families, even if prosecutions are barred by the amnesty laws and presidential pardons issued in the late 1980s. The Prosecutor-General has filed a favorable opinion, and the Supreme Court is expected to rule on it soon. The Commission is likely to revisit its historic opinion regarding the incompatibility of "impunity laws" with the Convention; it will certainly be asked to refer the cases to the Court.

V. Concluding Remarks

The Inter-American system provides progressive standards for protecting the right to freedom of expression. The standards set the Convention apart from the ICCPR and the ECHR by taking the protection of an individual's right to free expression, and the concomitant benefit to society, much further. The absolute

---

[92] Horacio Verbitsky, *El Vuelo*, *supra* note 78.

prohibition of prior censorship and the comparatively few permissible justifications for restricting the freedom of expression are powerful components of our human rights structure.

Nonetheless, many Latin American governments have unenviable records regarding the protection of free expression. While formally democratic, many states remain semi-authoritarian and have retained a culture of less-than-total respect for the rule of law and the rights and duties spelled out in the Convention. This is particularly the case where states rely upon vaguely defined notions of national security as a justification for their actions.

After many years of censorship and self-censorship of the media, persecution of "thought crimes", and other illegitimate restraints, it remains a challenge for newly democratic regimes to fulfill their obligations to the Convention. Measures such as the *desacato* laws, or the bans on news reporting during states of emergency, suggest that many governments do not fully comprehend the nature of freedom of expression.

FREEDOM OF EXPRESSION AND ACCESS TO INFORMATION IN RELATION TO NATIONAL SECURITY IN ALBANIA

Louise Krabbe

I. Background Information on Albanian Government

Albania gained independence and was formally recognized as an independent state by the international community in 1913. Between the Second World War and 1990 the ruling Albanian Communist Party maintained a strong isolationist policy. This policy ended abruptly when political reforms swept across Eastern Europe and the Albanian population claimed the right to democracy. The first democratic elections were held on March 31, 1991, and on April 29 an interim constitution was adopted[1] formally converting the state to a democracy based on the rule of law. During the parliamentary and local elections in May and October 1996, respectively, the ruling Democratic Party won overwhelming victories. The elections were roundly condemned as fraudulent by the Albanian opposition, international observers, the foreign media and human rights groups. In a demonstration on May 28, 1996, following the parliamentary elections, riot police ploughed into opposition groups protesting against systematic fraud in the elections.

In the beginning of 1997 the so-called pyramid investment schemes collapsed. With the collapse, most Albanians lost all their invested money and the country was drained of an estimated $2 billion. The collapse caused a massive popular uprising and requests for repayment as well as new parliamentary elections. The state administration collapsed totally, including the organs of public order and defense institutions. As a consequence, an emergency government was created to run the country until the next parliamentary elections scheduled for June 29, 1997.

Prior to the collapse, in November 1994, a new draft constitution was defeated in a referendum. The majority of the population rejected the draft mainly because it gave the President excessive powers to diminish the influence of parliament[2]. Pending a new constitution, fundamental rights and freedoms are guaranteed by the Law on Fundamental Human Rights and Freedoms of 1993[3] which supplements the interim constitution. The law provides protection of freedom of expression and access to information. Also, the Law on the Major Constitutional Provisions ensures respect for the fundamental human rights and freedoms provided for by international instruments. Albania ratified the International Covenant on Civil and Political Rights on October 4, 1991 and the European Convention on

---

[1] Law on the Major Constitutional Provisions, Law No. 7491 of April 29, 1991.

[2] Edwin Rekosh ed., *In the Public Eye: Parliamentary Transparency in Europe and North America* at 11 (1995).

[3] Law No. 7692 of March 31, 1993.

Human Rights in 1996. Albania became a member of the Organization for Security and Cooperation in Europe in June 1991.[4]

The fundamental principle of divided legislative, executive and judicial powers is set out in the Law on Major Constitutional Provisions. The People's Assembly, which is unicameral, seats 140 deputies who are elected for four-year terms. The Assembly holds legislative power, decides on peoples' referenda and lays down guidelines for the internal and foreign policy of Albania. The sittings of the Assembly are public, enabling the public as well as the media to attend. The Assembly may decide to hold sittings *in camera* in special cases.

The President of the Republic of Albania is elected by the People's Assembly by secret ballot and by a two-thirds majority of the votes of all deputies. The President holds the power to demand the reexamination by the People's Assembly of laws within fifteen days of their adoption and has the power to dissolve the People's Assembly when its composition does not allow the Assembly to perform, thereby hindering government. Furthermore, the President can declare states of emergency and states of war in cases when the Assembly cannot convene. The adoption and amendment of laws are based on a majority vote. Thus, laws are only adopted when voted for by the majority of the deputies present, who must form no less than one third of all deputies. The President does not have to approve the adoption of laws.

According to the Law on the Major Constitutional Provisions, the judicial power is exercised by courts which are independent and guided solely by law. The independence of the judiciary is set forth in the chapter on The Organization of the Judiciary and the Constitutional Court[5]. The judicial system comprises the courts of first instance (district courts), the Courts of Appeal and the Court of Cassation. These courts are all divided into three jurisdictions: criminal, civil and military. The Constitutional Court reviews cases involving interpretation of constitutional legislation. The judges of the Constitutional Court and the Court of Cassation are elected by the President and the People's Assembly conjointly. They can only be dismissed by the People's Assembly. All other judges are appointed or dismissed by the Supreme Judicial Council which is chaired by the President. According to the Code of Criminal Procedure[6] court hearings should normally be public. However, the courts have the power to decide to hold hearings *in camera* when it is in the interest of the state, morality or of witnesses.

---

[4] Albania is a signatory to the major international instruments protecting minorities' rights, including the Universal Declaration of Human Rights, the major conventions of the United Nations and the documents of the Organization on Security and Cooperation in Europe (OSCE). United Nations, *Human Rights: International Instruments, Chart of Ratifications as at 31 December 1994*, UN Doc. ST/HR/4/Rev.1 (1995). Further, Article 26 of the Law on Fundamental Rights and Freedoms contains a strong protection of minority rights.

[5] Law No. 7561 of April 29, 1992.

[6] Law of March 20, 1995. The law entered into force on August 1, 1995.

II. Disclosure of Classified Information

A. Restrictions on Access to Information

Throughout Albania's history there has never been a tradition of allowing access to government held information. Today, Article 2 of the Law on Fundamental Human Rights and Freedoms provides that "The right to be informed may not be denied to anyone". This constitutional right is not supported by any act on freedom of information; only the rather weak Article 4 of the Law on the Press[7] indicates that "the officials are obliged to give to the representatives of the press information which permits them to fulfill the public duty". The right to receive this information is limited by a fairly broad exception clause, however, stating that officials have no duty to provide the press with any information when: (1) conduct of a legal procedure would be hindered, made more difficult or jeopardized; (2) giving information would interfere with security interests or (3) when public or private interests which are protected by law would be injured. The exception clause is extremely wide and can be used to undermine the obligation the authorities have to disclose information to the press. These broad exceptions undermine the ability of the press to act as the watchdog of society.[8] The authorities do not have any obligation to state the reasons for refusing to grant access to requested information. Furthermore, the individual seeking information has no right to appeal the authorities' refusal to a court or an administrative tribunal.

Due to the lack of regulation of access to information, the authorities have not been obliged to break away from old procedures, but have been free to follow a policy that often results in arbitrary decisions. For example, there is a clear tendency for the authorities to reveal far more information to state media and the pro-governmental media than to independent and opposition media. During the emergency period in 1997 there has been an embargo on information to other than government media. Due to such discrimination, the independent media suffer from a lack of factual information (*e.g.*, about legislative proceedings, parliamentary records, draft laws and the like), obliging them to seek information from indirect sources.[9] There have been attempts to make the authorities set up press offices, thereby eliminating this discrimination. So far these attempts have not been successful.

---

[7] Law No. 7756 of October 11, 1993.

[8] In a series of judgments the European Court of Human Rights has iterated that the main role of the media is to act as the public's watchdog. *See e.g.*, *Sunday Times* v. *United Kingdom II*, Judgment of November 26, 1991, Series A no. 217, para. 50 (b) (referring to the media's vital role as "public watchdog"); and *Jens Olaf Jersild* v. *Denmark*, Judgment of 23 September 1994, Series A no. 298, paras. 31 and 35.

[9] Rekosh, *supra* note 2 at 11.

Besides the prevailing official information embargo, journalists are from time to time harassed by police and the National Information Service (SHIK) during their collection of daily news information from non-official sources. During the post-parliamentary election demonstration in Tirana on May 28, 1996 the police clubbed several journalists, including some foreign reporters, and confiscated their cameras and film. On September 6, 1995, two journalists from *Koha Jonë* were arrested while taking photographs outside the Court of Cassation where a press conference with Zef Brozi, former President of the Court, was to take place.[10] The journalists were detained, questioned and had their film confiscated.[11] The police cited no legal authority for this treatment.

In addition, deputies of the People's Assembly may encounter restrictions on access to information. Article 22 of the Law on Major Constitutional Provisions provides that the deputies can be prevented from obtaining information concerning state secrets, but does not specify the conditions for such denial of access.

According to Law on Human Rights and Fundamental Freedoms (Article 15, para.4), "No one may be denied the right to know the information collected about him [by the authorities], with the exception of cases when there is a judicial decision to protect the interests of the criminal process or national security". There is no other regulation on the public's right to access to documents containing matters of vital and personal interest to them.

B. Disclosure of Information by Government Agents and Employees

Albania does not have an Official Secrets Act, but the Penal Code[12] provides general regulation of information which may not be disclosed by civil servants. Thus, civil servants who disclose, disseminate or give information on facts, figures, documents or material contents which constitute state secrets according to law can be sentenced to fines or terms of five years imprisonment. According to Article 294[13]

---

[10] The issue of the press conference was the authorities' increasing harassment of Zef Brozi and the judiciary.

[11] This information was obtained from an interview on September 7, 1995 with Aleksandër Frangaj and Nikollë Lesi, editor-in-chief and general director respectively.

[12] Law No. 7895 of January 27, 1995.

[13] Article 294 reads:

> Disclosing, disseminating and informing on the facts, figures, document or material contents, constituting, according to the publicly familiar law, a state secret, in case committed by the authorized confidential person, or the person managing to have access to them, on account of his function and services, are punished with fines or a sentence by up to five years' imprisonment term.
>
> The same offence, committed publicly, is punished with fines or a sentence by up to ten years' imprisonment term.

of the Penal Code, the sentence for illegally disclosing information rises to a term of ten years imprisonment if the act is committed publicly. If secret documents are lost the defendant can be sentenced up to three years imprisonment, according to Article 296.[14] So far, the latter provision has never been invoked. The provisions do not contain any demand for a balancing of the national security interest and the public interest. Neither do they make possible a public interest defense.

Persons providing or procuring secret information of military character for a foreign power with the intention to violate the country's independence can be sentenced to terms of imprisonment of 10-20 years and 3-10 years, according to Articles 213[15] and 214[16] respectively.

A major problem in relation to classifying information as a "state secret" is that Albanian law does not contain any definition of the term. The People's Assembly which holds the legislative power has not used its competence to reduce the margin of appreciation of the executive power in this respect. Thus, within the scope of law the executive is free to decide the extent of the term "state secrets" and thereby what information should be classified.

The leading case relating to illegal disclosure of information was initiated on January 31, 1994 when Alexandër Frangaj and Martin Leka, editor-in-chief and journalist of the independent and critical paper *Koha Jonë*, were arrested for publishing military information. *Koha Jonë* had published a government document which spoke of the disarming of off-duty military officers. The information was leaked to the paper by two military officers, Romeo Licaj and Bashkim Feta. Proceedings were instituted against the journalists and the military officers as the Government alleged that the information was classified information and therefore could not be disclosed.

Martin Leka was charged with revealing a state secret, defamation and conspiracy with the government official who leaked the information and sentenced to eighteen months of prison on February 25, 1994. Aleksandër Frangaj was charged with not keeping his paper free of punishable violations but was acquitted in the first

---

[14] Article 296 reads:

> Loss of documents or other materials, constituting, according to the publicly familiar law, a state secret, in case committed by the authorized confidential person, trusted with safeguarding or using them, is punished with fines or a sentence by up to three years' imprisonment term.

[15] Article 213 reads:

> Providing secret information of military character or whatever to a foreign power, with a view to violating the country's independence, is punished with a sentence varying from ten to twenty years' imprisonment term.

[16] Article 214 reads:

> Procuring secret information of military character or whatever, with a view to offering it to a foreign power, intended to violate the country's independence, is punished with a sentence varying from three to ten years' imprisonment term.

instance. In the Appeal Court his acquittal was reversed and he was sentenced to five months in prison on March 21, 1994. He was sentenced in absentia for divulging state secrets, charges on which he had previously been acquitted.[17] Following heavy national and international criticism of the decisions, both journalists were pardoned by President Sali Berisha on May 3, 1994, International Press Freedom Day, and were subsequently acquitted on May 31, 1994 by the Court of Cassation.[18] The case against them serves as a warning to other journalists from independent and opposition media to be more careful about publishing information perceived as sensitive by the Government.[19]

The two military officers, Romeo Licaj and Bashkim Feta, were sentenced for leaking military information to the press. In the first two instances Romeo Licaj was sentenced to four years of imprisonment for collaboration to disseminate a state secret. The sentence was reduced to two years by the Court of Cassation. His superior, Bashkim Feta, was sentenced to six months of imprisonment for negligence in the performance of duty for ordering Romeo Licaj to reveal the information.

C. Publication of Information by News Media

The publication of information by the press is subject to the regulation of the Press Law[20] which was adopted in November 1993 by the People's Assembly. The law only regulates the written media; no specific law regulates the electronic media. However, the People's Assembly has been working on the adoption of a broadcasting law which has not as yet entered into force. In the meantime information disseminated by the electronic media is subject to assessment according to general Albanian laws. According to the Press Law the press is free and limited only by the interim constitutional provisions and the law itself.[21] The law indicates that the press has a public duty to provide information for the public and to influence public opinion, but not necessarily to provide information of public interest.

There is no registration requirement for the press. According to Article 8 of the Press Law the editorship must comply with formal requirements, however, such as having residency in Albania, having reached the age of eighteen, identification of editors on the publication and a prohibition on editors being the subject of verdict

---

[17] The new trial was initiated after the President publicly condemned the acquittal of the first instance and the public prosecutor therefore appealed the decision.

[18] Penal question no. 67 of the Court of Cassation.

[19] Interview with Marc Pelumbi, Aleksander Frangaj and Martin Leka's lawyer, September 5, 1995.

[20] Law No. 7756 of October 11, 1993.

[21] The law is based on a German law which was enacted in Westphalia in 1966 and presupposes the existence of a constitutionally guaranteed freedom of the press.

banning them from public posts. Furthermore, the law sets out a very wide obligation for the editor to publish refutations of false information.

The Press Law imposes large fines on editors for failing to comply with the formal requirements of the law (100,000 to 800,000 leks which equals $1,000 to $8,000, enough to ruin any newspaper[22]). Commission of criminal offenses, such as publishing material which the authorities consider secret or sensitive, is dealt with under the Penal Code. The law has been widely criticized by Albanians as well as the international community. It is the general view that the law limits the possibility of the press to publish freely and that the restrictive measures provided for are disproportionate to the aims they pursue.[23]

In June 1995 the Albanian Government set forth a proposal to ban the sale of newspapers in the streets and to restrict distribution to state owned kiosks and bookshops. The opposition and independent press feared that this would restrict their sales and went on strike. The Government retreated from its proposal.

Several journalists have taken action against publication restrictions. Seven journalists from the Democratic Party's newspaper *Rilindja Demokratike* resigned on August 24, 1992 in response to what they described as the increasing weight of censorship. They said they were "refusing to be obedient, blind soldiers of the Democratic Party or any of its clans".[24]

Foreign journalists have also encountered difficulties when reporting about Albania. During the Omonia trial against five alleged ethnic Greek spies in 1994 some Greek journalists who followed the trial were harassed, and a few of them were even briefly detained. Some were accused of being Greek nationalists who wanted to slander the Albanian court system while others were accused of being spies. Most of them were released upon showing their press credentials.[25] When broadcasting on the same issue, the British Broadcast Corporation (BBC) was accused of bringing out communist messages and the Albanian Government consequently deprived the station of its FM-licence in Albania. Furthermore, when covering the trial of socialist leader Fatos Nano, the BBC was treated as a supporter of the former communist regime and named "the Bolschevik Broadcasting Service" by the Albanian Government newspaper.

---

[22] The average income of a journalist is presently between $50-100 per month.

[23] When the law was adopted seven major Albanian newspapers protested against it during a one day strike. The newspapers were published with blank pages saying only, "This is what our articles will look like under the suppression of this law".

[24] *Index on Censorship*, No. 1/93.

[25] Committee on the Protection of Journalists (CPJ), *Attacks on the Press in 1994* at 150 (1995).

III. Expression Deemed Threatening to National Security, State Security or Territorial Integrity

A. Incitement to National, Racial Hatred and Disputes and Dissemination of False or Panicking Information

The Albanian Penal Code punishes incitement to national, racial and religious hatred with fines or imprisonment for terms of up to ten years. Equally, the dissemination of false information which is intended to arouse a feeling of panic is subject to fines or imprisonment for terms of up to five years.[26]

On April 17, 1995 Ilir Hoxha, the eldest son of former communist leader Enver Hoxha, was placed under house arrest. He was arrested for having given an interview to the independent newspaper *Modeste* in which he defended his father's reputation and record and in which he seriously criticized the present Government. He was accused of "calling for national hatred" and was consequently charged under article 56 of the former Penal Code.[27] He was sentenced to a term of one year imprisonment in May 1995, which was upheld on appeal. Among Albanian critics it is generally felt that this harsh judgment arises from politically motivated charges and that any act of leniency now towards Ilir Hoxha would be conceived as supportive of the communist past.[28]

Under the former Penal Code Aleksandër Frangaj, editor-in-chief of *Koha Jonë*, was charged for "spreading false information liable to cause panic" and placed under house arrest for five weeks on 26 March 1993. On 24 March 1993 *Koha Jonë* had published an article saying that dozens of tanks had recently been moved towards the country's northern border. The charges against him were later withdrawn.[29]

B. Political Parties

According to Article 6 of the Law on Major Constitutional Provisions[30] "political pluralism is one of the fundamental conditions of democracy in the

---

[26] Articles 265-267 of Law No. 7895 of January 27, 1995.

[27] The article reads:

> A person endangering public peace by inciting hatred against parts of the population by insults or slander, encouraging violence or arbitrary acts against them, is liable to imprisonment from one to five years.

[28] In April 1995, Amnesty International declared Ilir Hoxha to be a prisoner of conscience. AI INDEX: EUR 11/02/95.

[29] This information is derived from Amnesty International, *International Report 1994,* and interview with Fatos Lubonja, Secretary of the Albania Helsinki Committee, on September 5, 1995.

[30] Law No. 7491 of April 29, 1991.

Albanian state". The only exception to political pluralism has been the banning in 1992 of the Communist Party.[31] The party was considered a threat to the safety of the state and to the introduction of democracy.

In 1991 the Law on the Political Parties was passed.[32] Article 6 of the law outlines the aims, structure and/or activity of any party which is considered illegitimate. These include: (1) the use of weapons or any other anti-democratic means; (2) the use of incitement of racist, totalitarian or anti-national activity; (3) advocacy of anti-democratic principles; (4) the use of undemocratic principles within the party; (5) the creation of organizations of military character and (6) the establishment of parties founded on religious or local activities.

Omonia, the Democratic Union of the Greek Minority, was founded in early 1991 in order to represent the political, social and cultural demands of the Greek minority during the elections in March 1991. As a result of the enactment of the Law on Political Parties, Omonia was not permitted to put forward candidates during the elections in 1992. Therefore, the Omonia leaders founded the Union of Human Rights Party which includes Albanians and other minorities in order to dilute its ethnic character. The Minister of Justice approved the formation of this party before the elections and currently two members of the Party hold chairs in the People's Assembly.[33]

The Law on Political Parties does not itself set out penal provisions for non-compliance with its regulations. These are to be found in Article 224[34] of the Penal Code which penalizes the establishment or membership of unconstitutional parties, organizations and associations which aim at overthrowing the constitutional order by violent means. The maximum punishment is five years imprisonment. Equally,

---

[31] Election Law, Law No. 7556 of February 4, 1992.

[32] Law No. 7502 of July 25, 1991.

[33] Human Rights Watch Helsinki, *Albania: The Greek Minority* 10f (Feb. 1995).

[34] Article 224 reads:

> Establishing membership in anti-constitutional parties, organizations or associations, intending the violent overthrow of the constitutional order, is punished with fines or a sentence by up to three years' imprisonment term.
>
> Establishing a new party, organization or association banned as anti-constitutional, or continuing the activity overtly or covertly, is punished with a sentence varying from one to five years' imprisonment term.

Article 225[35] provides that the distribution of unconstitutional material from these parties can be punished with fines or imprisonment of up to three years.

On September 22, 1995 the Albanian Parliament passed the Law on Genocide and Crimes Against Humanity Committed in Albania During Communist Rule for Political, Ideological and Religious Motives,[36] only half a year before the next parliamentary elections. The law was followed by the Law on the Verification of the Moral Character of Officials and Other Persons Connected With the Defense of the Democratic State on November 30, 1995. The law provides for opening the Segurimi files (files of the former National Intelligence Service). Until November 1995 the files were kept officially closed, although occasionally some opponents of the government found that their files were used against them and published in the pro-government newspapers.[37] Both laws aim at cleansing Albanian public offices of ex-communists in order for Albania to proceed with a democratic transition. The laws were designed to exclude from public office all those who held major political positions before March 1991, until the year 2002. The opposition parties took part in the parliamentary hearing of the laws but abstained from voting, alleging that the measures would end the political careers of leaders of the main opposition parties.[38] This proved to be true in May 1996 when a Verification Commission[39] banned 139 individuals from standing for the parliamentary elections. Only three of these candidates belonged to the ruling Democratic Party and most of the opposition candidates were prominent political figures. Most of the individuals affected by the Verification Commission's decisions were denied a fair review of the decisions.

In spite of the introduction of political pluralism, opposition parties have experienced various hardships. A number of former political leaders, including Ramiz Alia from the present Socialist Party, have been sentenced on charges of

---

[35] Article 225 reads:

> Distributing writings or employing symbols belonging to an anti-constitutional party, organization or association, or disbanded as such, is punished with fines or sentence by up to three years' imprisonment term.
>
> Distributing or introducing materials, writings or symbols, made available in the Republic of Albania from abroad, intending the overthrow of the constitutional order or violating the country's territorial integrity, is punished with fines or sentence by up to three years' imprisonment term.

[36] Law No. 8001 of September 22, 1995.

[37] International Helsinki Federation, *Annual Report 1995*, at 19.

[38] According to the governing Democratic Party, the enactment should be seen as justice rather than revenge.

[39] The Commission consisted of seven individuals, primarily appointed by government or pro-government individuals: two members were appointed by the Council of Ministers; one member was appointed by the Minister of Justice, the Minister of Defense, the Minister of the Interior, and the head of the National Intelligence Service, respectively; and one member was elected by Parliament.

corruption, embezzlement of State funds or abuse of power.[40] Fatos Nano, the Chairman of the Socialist Party and former deputy prime minister of the reformist communist government at the end of 1990, has been subject to various types of political harassment. On April 3, 1994 he was sentenced to serve twelve years in prison and to pay a sum equivalent to $720,000 to the state. He was found guilty of falsification of official documents, embezzlement of state property, and diverting emergency aid from Italy. Amnesty International declared him to be a prisoner of conscience in April 1995.

On July 14, 1995 the President of the Court of Cassation, Zef Brozi, decided that the case of Fatos Nano should be reexamined by the Court of Cassation. Following this decision, as well as other politically sensitive decisions, Zef Brozi was dismissed by the People's Assembly on September 21, 1995. The vote in the People's Assembly, which was based on a decision of the Constitutional Court,[41] was boycotted by all opposition parties. The Constitutional Court held that the Court of Cassation had no jurisdiction to reexamine the Nano case according to the new Code on Criminal Procedure.[42] It is widely believed that this decision was a political move to control the judiciary in Albania.

On January 1, 1996 President Berisha reduced Fatos Nano's sentence when announcing a New Year's partial amnesty for eighty prisoners.[43] The sentence was reduced again on December 29, 1996. Fatos Nano was released in the beginning of 1997 following the uprising which took place after the collapse of most of the Albanian pyramid investment schemes.

C. Advocacy of Self-Determination

So far no minority group in Albania has publicly advocated self-determination. There has, however, been some tension between Albanians and ethnic Greeks who mainly live in the southern part of Albania. The Greek Government, which supports the latter, has claimed back parts of southern Albania from time to time.[44] In June 1993 the Greek Orthodox cleric Chrysostomos Maidonis was expelled from the southern town of Gjirokaster, allegedly for

---

[40] Inter-Parliamentary Union, *Report on the Mission of the Committee on the Human Rights of Parliamentarians to Albania, Regarding the Case of Mr Fatos Nano*, December 19 to 22, 1994.

[41] The Constitutional Court decided that Zef Brozi by suspending the execution of a number of court decisions had acted unconstitutionally. The hearing on the legitimacy of Zef Brozi's procedural acts in the Constitutional Court was requested by the Minister of Justice.

[42] Benet Koleka, Reuters News Service, September 19, 1995.

[43] The amnesty left Fatos Nano with two more years to serve.

[44] According to the Albanian Government approximately 60,000 ethnic Greeks live in Albania. The Greek Government alleges that there are around 250,000.

distributing maps and leaflets calling for the annexation of southern Albania to Greece.[45] No similar incidents have been reported since.

D. Criticism of Government or Government Officials

Under the former Communist regime, criticism of official institutions was not surprisingly rare. The state was the only financial sponsor of the activities of journalists, writers and artists and equally their sole censor. Thus, there were no dissidents in Albania and the self-censorship was pervasive. Any dissenting opinion led to severe punishment.[46]

Since gaining formal freedom of expression with the Law on Major Constitutional Provisions, the independent and opposition media have tried to take up their task as the public's watchdog.[47] The Government, sensitive to criticism, has taken legal action against journalists by means of the Penal Code provisions on insult or defamation.

The Penal Code, which was substantially revised in 1995, regulates criticism of Government. Articles 239,[48] 240[49] and 241[50] are set forth in the section regarding penal acts committed by the citizens against state activity. These provisions provide

---

[45] *Index on Censorship,* No. 8 and 9/1993.

[46] Jane Kokan, "Albania: Sex, lies and foreign video", *Index on Censorship*, 1/1991, at 13; and Perikli Yargoni, "Dead poets translation society", *Index on Censorship*, 9/1992, at 17.

[47] According to the European Court of Human Rights, freedom of the press includes the dissemination of information which might even "offend, shock or disturb". *Lingens* v. *Austria,* Judgment of July 8, 1986, Series A no. 103, para 41.

[48] Article 239 reads:

> Insulting behavior, deliberately effected on the state administration or public service employee, on account of his state activity or service, constitutes penal contravention, hence punished with fines or a sentence by up to six months' imprisonment term.
>
> The same act, in case committed in public, constitutes penal contravention, hence punished with fines or a sentence by up to one year's imprisonment term.

[49] Article 240 reads:

> Deliberate slander, effected on the state administration or public service employee, on account of his state activity or service, constitutes penal contravention, hence punished with fines or a sentence by up to one year's imprisonment term.
>
> The same act, in case committed in public, constitutes penal contravention, hence punished with fines or a sentence by up to two year's imprisonment term.

[50] Article 241 reads:

> Deliberate slander, effected against the President of the Republic, is punished with fines or a sentence by up to three years' imprisonment term.

specific punishment for insult and defamation of public officials and the President of the Republic. The provisions are slightly stricter than the general provisions on insult and defamation contained in Articles 119[51] and 120.[52] Insult of the state administration or public service employees may be punished with fines or sentences of up to one year imprisonment. Intentional defamation against the same category of individuals may be punished with fines or sentences of up to two years imprisonment. If intentional defamation is committed against the President of Albania the punishment rises to an imprisonment term of up to three years. The provisions are clearly not in compliance with international law, according to which politicians have to tolerate greater criticism than other individuals.[53]

The provision on defamation against public officials has been used to sentence at least three important journalists. On August 1, 1995 the editor-in-chief of *Populli Po*, Arban Husani, was sentenced to pay a fine of more than $1,000 for alleged defamation of the head of the SHIK, Mr. Bashkim Gazidede. The charges against him related to an article published in March 1995 asserting that the SHIK was responsible for the murder of a politician, Gjovani Cekini, in Shkoder in January 1994.[54] During the trial Arban Husani refused to reveal his source of information, which was believed to be within the Shkoder Police Commissariat. He was found guilty of defamation, although the duty log of the Police Commissariat in Shkoder was declared a "state secret" and consequently could not be used as evidence in the trial.

In August and September 1995, respectively, Blendi Fevjiu, editor of the Democratic Alliance Party's daily *Aleanca*, and Gjergj Zefi, editor of *Lajmeteri* and a high-ranking person within the Democratic Alliance Party, were both convicted of defamation for articles they wrote about official corruption. Mr. Fevjiu was given a fine of $2,000, but was pardoned on 8 December by President Berisha. Mr. Zefi

---

[51] Article 119 reads:

> Deliberate insulting behavior towards a person constitutes a penal act punished with fines or by up to six months' imprisonment term.
>
> In case the above is committed blatantly, it constitutes a penal act punished with fines or by up to one year's imprisonment term.

[52] Article 120 reads:

> Slander, respectively deliberate defamatory statements, likewise any other type of information, known to be false, consequently affecting and lowering the person's reputation and dignity, constitutes a penal act punished with fines or by up to one year's imprisonment term.
>
> In case of libel, committed blatantly, it constitutes a penal act punished with fines or by up to two years' imprisonment term.

[53] According to the European Court of Human Rights, the "freedom of political debate is at the very core of the concept of a democratic society which prevails throughout the Convention". *Oberschlick* v. *Austria*, Judgment of May 23, 1991, Series A no. 204, para 58.

[54] Fatos Lubonja, Secretary of Albanian Helsinki Committee, "Report on Hate Speech in Albanian Print Media - August 1995".

was sentenced to one month of imprisonment with credit for the time he had served before the sentence. As a complementary punishment, Gjergj Zefi was excluded from public office for one year under Article 30 of the Penal Code.

Unlike most democracies, defamation and insults against national and foreign symbols in Albania may result in punishment by imprisonment of up to two years, according to Articles 229[55] and 268[56] respectively. In September 1995 three people, two members of the Socialist Party and a former local communist official, were arrested for criticism of the United States Government. They were charged with distributing anti-American leaflets which read "Down with the United States" while the Albanian President was on an official visit to the United States. The Government newspapers allege that the two socialists are former collaborators of the Sigurimi, the former secret police.[57]

The authorities have not only used legal actions for silencing criticism against them, they have attempted to arouse hatred against independent and opposition journalists, against opposition parties and against intellectuals and activists of human rights groups. This incitement to hatred has often been directed through the government media.[58] A considerable number of the people targeted have been accused of being former agents for the Sigurimi or of somehow being hostile and threatening to the Republic of Albania. Thus, in August 1995 the reaction against the statement of the leader of the Democratic Alliance, Neritan Ceka, that Albania should accept Serb refugees rather than sending them to Kosovo, led the Government media to treat him as a spy and a traitor with pro-Serb feelings. Neritan Ceka alleged that his statement was meant as a message of peace and solidarity.[59] Equally, in August 1995 the Government media attacked Carlo Bollino, the Italian director of the independent and critical paper *Gazeta Shqiptare*. Mr. Bollino was accused of

---

[55] Article 229 reads:

> Employing words or committing actions insulting publicly, the respective flag, emblem and national anthem of foreign states or of the prominent international organizations, likewise removing, demolishing or rendering useless the flag, emblem, displayed in the official institution premises, constitutes penal contravention, hence punishable with fines or sentence by up to one year's imprisonment term.

[56] Article 268 reads:

> Humiliating the Republic of Albania and the constitutional order, the flag, the emblem, the national anthem, the nation's martyrs, in public or through publications or through disseminating writings, removing, damaging, demolishing, rendering indiscernible or useless the flag or the emblem of the Republic of Albania, when exhibited by the official institutions and bodies, constitute penal contravention punished with fines or a sentence by up to two years' imprisonment term.

[57] Benet Koleka, Reuters News Service, September 23, 1995.

[58] Examples include the Democratic Party press and the State Radio and Television.

[59] Lubonja, *supra* note 54.

being a member of the mafia, a racist, and violating the Albanian language, to which he responded that "the freedom of press is not freedom of defamation".[60] Along with the media attacks, the police have warned the journalists of *Gazeta Shqiptare* to be more prudent with critical information and to give the readers the "right image of Albania".[61]

E. Public Order and State of Emergency

During the democratic transition and until the beginning of the public uprisings in 1997, public order and security were mainly a matter of concern of the police and the National Intelligence Service (SHIK). Following the uprisings the President for the first time used his constitutional powers to declare a state of emergency to stop the violent actions of the public which brought most state institutions to collapse. The state of emergency was lifted shortly afterward when an emergency government was created. However, the country is still suffering from the crisis which is of a profound political, economic and social nature. Reestablishment of public order requires the building up of state institutions, an effective administration, economic and social change, as well as a rekindling of trust between the population and their political system.

IV. Extraordinary Procedures for Determining National Security Issues

A. Scope of Judicial Review of Decisions Restricting Information or Expression on National Security Grounds

Despite the division of the three state powers set forth in the Law on the Major Constitutional Provisions, the Albanian judiciary is not fully autonomous. Due to the judiciary's traditional lack of independence from the executive, its lack of judicial skills[62] and also severe political harassment of judges who have passed

---

[60] *Gazeta Shqiptare*, August 4, 1995.

[61] Interview on September 7, 1995 with deputy editor of *Gazeta Shqiptare*, Fatos Baxhaku; and Marianne Sullivan, "Albanians Still Struggle for Information", *Transition*, Vol.1 No.18 of October 6, 1995.

[62] Due to a lack of trained judges, prosecutors and investigators, the Ministry of Justice ran a six month legal course in March 1993. Approximately 470 students have been trained and are now holding major legal positions, although the original plan was that they should only be inserted for an interim period. Most of these people had no legal background and many of them had been politically persecuted under the communist regime. The major part of them were chosen by the ruling Democratic Party.

judgments that collide with the interests of the Government, the judiciary tends not to challenge the executive's interpretation of Albanian laws. This clearly endangers the freedom of expression in Albania as the judiciary fails to implement international standards regarding freedom of expression set out in Article 10 of the European Convention on Human Rights and Article 19 of the International Covenant on Civil and Political Rights.

Albanian law generally lacks legal definitions of terms such as "national security", "state secret", "public order" and the like. As the People's Assembly has not used its legislative power to narrow down these terms, there is no limit to the executive's interpretation of them. As there is no tradition for altering the assessment of the executive in cases of political character, it is very rare that a court would question the use of these legal terms. The only exception is a dissenting opinion by Judge Brozi to the judgment of the Court of Cassation regarding five alleged ethnic Greek spies.[63] Judge Brozi reversed the assessment of the authorities that the information provided by the defendants constituted secret information, but without offering an alternative definition of what would constitute a state secret.

Very few courts have access to or updated versions of the laws according to which they judge. The lack of copies of the laws in the courts has been so striking that the Council of Europe and foreign non-governmental organizations are working with the Government to print and distribute the Penal Code and other laws throughout Albania. Moreover, the courtrooms and lawyers suffer from the absence of clear standards for review of lower court decisions. Thus, none of the decisions taken by the Appeal Courts are or have been published, which means that there is no written precedent regarding second instance rulings. The Albanian Judges' Association has published the first edition of a law journal in Albanian including the most significant decisions of the Court of Cassation (around thirty decisions).[64]

From the Albanian Code of Criminal Procedure it is unclear to what extent it is possible to suspend the execution of court decisions which have been appealed. Article 417 of the Code foresees suspensions in all other cases than decisions regarding imprisonment. As prison sentences are possible for defamation, for instance, persons who have been convicted of such charges may serve their sentence even during appeal.

The Code of Criminal Procedure does not give defendants the right to be tried by a jury. According to Article 438, however, cases brought before the Court of Cassation can be tried by a double set of panels each consisting of three judges, when the case is considered of great importance. Only the President of the Court of Cassation is empowered to assess the importance of individual cases. This procedure was not used in the case against Aleksandër Frangaj, Martin Leka, Romeo Licaj and Bashkim Feta, concerning information about disarming of off-duty military officers.

---

[63] Decision of the Court of Cassation of February 8, 1995.

[64] *Jurisprudenca Shqiptare*, Volume 1, Issue 1, Spring 1995.

The establishment of extraordinary courts in Albania is prohibited according to Article 5 of the Law on the Organization of the Judiciary and the Constitutional Court.[65]

B. Use of Military Courts to Try Cases Involving Civilians

Military Courts of first and second instance are provided for by the constitutional chapter on the organization of the judiciary and the Constitutional Court as well as the Code of Criminal Procedure. These courts have no jurisdiction in cases involving civilians. The courts will judge according to the provisions concerning the military in the former Penal Code, until a Military Code has been adopted.

Awaiting the adoption of a Military Code and establishment of separate Military Courts, the jurisdiction in cases involving military is placed under the ordinary courts.

C. Prior Restraint of Publication

Before the fall of the Communist regime, prior censorship and arbitrary persecution were commonly used to keep writers and intellectuals under control. The intellectual community was kept in a constant state of fear.[66] The use of prior censorship has now been formally prohibited.[67] However, a case from June 1995 demonstrated that prior censorship is still in use. Thus, on June 20, 1995 police arrested the editor-in-chief and a journalist of the magazine *Hosteni 2000* and confiscated an entire print run of a forthcoming issue. It was argued that the director, Filip Cakuli, intended to use a front page showing two naked women on either side of President Sali Berisha. Both journalists were detained and questioned and released uncharged later the same day. The journalists never used the front page.[68]

Notwithstanding the ban on prior censorship, the Press Law contains a range of measures which may be taken prior to the publication by the news media

---

[65] Law No. 7561 of April 29, 1992.

[66] "Visar Zhiti: Victim of the surreal", *Index on Censorship*, No. 4/1993.

[67] Article 2 of the Law on Fundamental Rights and Freedoms.

[68] In a protest letter which was sent to President Sali Berisha in July, ARTICLE 19, The International Centre Against Censorship, said: "The European Court of Human Rights has specifically warned that `the dangers inherent in prior restraints are such that they call for the most careful scrutiny on the part of the Court', and has noted that this is so especially as regards the press as `news is a perishable commodity and to delay its publication, even for a short period, may well deprive it of all its value and interest'". ARTICLE 19 never received a response to its communication.

and which may effectively hinder the publication of the information concerned. Thus, Article 12 permits confiscation of press publications by court order. Article 18 further empowers the prosecutor or his officials to remove publications from public circulation or to prohibit their issuance temporarily without court order when publication would constitute an illegal act, such as "risk to peace, high treason, treason against the country, risk to the democratic juridical state and risk to external security". As is the case with many other legal terms, these illegal acts are defined nowhere in Albanian law. Article 18 recognizes the danger inherent in applying the temporary security measures to daily newspapers and consequently forbids such use.

The protection of journalists' sources in Article 23 of the Press Law extends to all individuals involved in the publication of information. Where the person who holds the right to refuse to give evidence about his source of information is suspected of having committed a criminal offense, protection can be lifted. Persons who take part professionally in the preparation and publication of information via electronic media do not enjoy the same strong protection of their sources. The electronic media, which are not yet governed by a *lex specialis* do not enjoy the same protection for their sources of information. The right to professional secrecy of this part of the media is governed by a *lex generalis*, the new Code of Criminal Procedure which was passed in 1995. Unlike Article 23 of the Press Law, Article 159 of the Code of Criminal Procedure limits the right to professional secrecy to professional journalists. These have the right to refuse to give evidence regarding the names of the persons from whom they have collected information. In case the information is indispensable to prove a criminal offense, the court may order the journalist to reveal his source.

Apart from legal restrictions the independent and opposition press has encountered practical obstacles during the printing process, as the two main Albanian printing houses are owned by the governing Democratic Party.[69] Only the opposition and independent press pay the full price for publishing with the printing houses, and this price is very high. Furthermore, the opposition and independent media allege that they are subject to a discriminatory system of taxation. They are obliged to pay a 15% circulation tax which is levied by the printing houses as part of the production costs. As the Albanian Parliament has not yet taken steps to lower the taxes and levies, some independent and opposition press have submitted an application to the European Union for a credit in order to purchase a printing house themselves.[70] Others have resorted to receiving subsidies from political parties, trade unions, private businesses and the like. On 4 August 1994 nine major newspapers decided to suspend the publication of their papers for three days as a protest against what they call "economical censorship".

---

[69] The Albanian media is generally very politicized as most of the important newspapers are owned or affiliated with political parties.

[70] According to interview on September 7, 1995 with Aleksandër Frangaj and Nikollë Lesi, Editor-in-Chief and General Director of the newspaper *Koha Jonë* respectively.

The ongoing harassment of journalists from independent and opposition media has had a great effect on the degree of self-censorship which prevails. *Koha Jonë* has been particularly affected by harassment which has included physical harassment of employees, higher taxes and increased printing charges, confiscation of eight cars and disconnection of telephones from 14 April to 8 December 1996. As a result, journalists are very careful about publishing sensitive information.[71]

V. Conclusions and Recommendations

The present chaotic situation in Albania necessitates not only legal, but also political, economic and social reform. The striking lack of access to information is of major concern and gives rise to calls for an Act on Freedom of Information under which the authorities would be obliged to provide information on equal terms to all journalists. An initiative to set up a press office with the ministries would be a step forward in this regard and could further the process of breaking down the embargo on the free flow of information. It is particularly urgent that the files of former secret service, the Sigurimi, be made accessible to the Albanian population as there seems to be a clear misuse of this information.

Several of the legal terms in Albanian law which are related to security are overbroad. Their breadth is aggravated by the fact that the legislature has provided inadequate legal definitions, and because elements of the judiciary are neither sufficiently experienced to interpret them nor politically willing to do so. This leaves the executive with a virtually unlimited margin of appreciation. Furthermore, the state organs seem to be very sensitive to criticism and therefore use the Penal Code regulation on insult and defamation widely in order to silence any political criticism. These factors pose a severe threat to the continuation of the democratic transition process. In order to ensure compliance with the international standards which Albania is obliged to respect, it is therefore most urgent that the Albanian legislature provide clear legal norms.

A strong political commitment is necessary for legal reform to succeed. Albania has previously shown its will to transform itself from a totalitarian into a democratic society, most significantly by becoming a signatory to the International Covenant on Civil and Political Rights and the European Convention on Human Rights. In order to honor these commitments politicians need to set an example and commit themselves to greater openness and transparency.

---

[71] Interview on September 5, 1995 with Secretary of the Albanian Helsinki Committee, Fatos Lubonja, and defense lawyer in the Aleksandër Frangaj and Martin Leka-case, Marc Pelombi.

CHILE: NATIONAL SECURITY, FREEDOM OF EXPRESSION AND THE LEGACY OF THE MILITARY DICTATORSHIP

Cecilia Medina and Felipe González[1]

I. Introduction

Current regulations and practices on freedom of expression are a mixture of Chile's authoritarian heritage and more recent democratic influences. Freedom of expression and access to information were severely restricted in Chile on national security grounds during the former military regime (1973-1990). A broad, non-democratic concept of national security was utilized to prevent citizens from enjoying freedom of expression and other basic rights. National security was seen by the military regime as the most important component of a society; its ideology considered communism to be both an external aggression and a cancer that tried to penetrate the country from the inside, through the unions, the political parties, the universities and the churches. As a consequence, the main role of the Armed Forces shifted from defending the country from external aggression to defending it from its internal enemies. Due to the importance of their role, the Armed Forces considered themselves to be at the top of the hierarchies of the country.[2]

Although this chapter focuses on the current Chilean situation, the former military regime is discussed in several sections in order to establish the context in which some of the legislation was enacted.

II. Constitutional Provisions

A. Non-Emergency Periods

Article 19.12 of the 1981 Constitution recognizes the right of everyone to freedom of opinion and information without prior censorship. Nevertheless, everyone must answer for offenses and abuses committed in the exercise of these

---

[1] The authors wish to thank Mr. Nicolás Espejo for his research assistance.

[2] In a speech on the occasion of the third anniversary of the coup, General Pinochet stated that "National security emerges as a concept oriented not only to protect the State's territorial integrity, but also, and particularly, to defend the essential values constituting the national soul or tradition, because otherwise the very same national identity would be destroyed." *El Mercurio* newspaper, 12 September 1976. For further analysis of the national security doctrine under the military regime, *see* Felipe Gonzalez, Jorge Mera & Juan Enrique Vargas, *Protección Democrática de la Seguridad Interior: Estados de Excepción y Derecho Penal Político*, 141-221 (1991).

freedoms, according to the rules specified by the law.[3] An exception is provided regarding motion pictures, as the Constitution states that the law will establish a system of censorship for their exhibition and publicity. Access to information is not explicitly enshrined in the Constitution.

International human rights standards were elevated to a constitutional status as a result of a reform to the Constitution in 1989.[4] The revised Article 5.2 states that "[t]he exercise of sovereignty recognizes as a limitation the respect for the fundamental rights emanating from human nature. It is a duty of the organs of the State to respect and promote these rights, guaranteed by this Constitution and by international treaties ratified by Chile and in force."[5] As a consequence, the human rights provisions contained in these treaties now have constitutional status in Chile.

Chile is currently party to the International Covenant on Civil and Political Rights ("Covenant"), its Optional Protocol and the American Convention on Human Rights. To these three treaties, Chile made reservations to the effect that the jurisdiction of the Human Rights Committee (both under Article 41 of the Covenant and the Optional Protocol) and of the Inter-American Commission and Court of Human Rights does not extend to alleged violations of human rights which commenced before March 11, 1990. These reservations were made with the aim of preventing international scrutiny of disappearances and other human rights violations committed during the military dictatorship, although naturally the Inter-American Commission is competent to consider claims of such violations by virtue of Chile's membership in the Organization of American States. Chile is also a party to the International Covenant on Economic, Social and Cultural Rights and the Convention on the Rights of the Child, among other international human rights treaties.

However, to date, domestic tribunals have rarely used provisions of these treaties as a basis for deciding freedom of expression cases. One such case was that of *Megavision*, when the courts invoked Article 13 of the American Convention on Human Rights, which forbids prior censorship, to dismiss a penalty of US $6,150 against a television network. The penalty had been imposed by the National Television Council (a state agency) for broadcasting a surreptitiously recorded political conversation. The courts declared that the broadcast was not imputable to the TV network. Despite the fact that it was the President of Megavision who played the recording, he did so in the context of a live program in which he had participated

---

[3] The current Constitution entered into force in 1981, that is, during the military regime. Subsequently, it has been reformed in several areas.

[4] This reform was introduced as a result of an agreement between the military government and the democratic opposition and approved in a plebiscite.

[5] "El ejercicio de la soberanía reconoce como limitación el respeto a los derechos esenciales emanados de la naturaleza humana. Es deber de los órganos del Estado respetar y promover tales derechos, garantizados por esta Constitución, así como por los tratados internacionales ratificados por Chile y que se encuentren vigentes."

as a private citizen, without having given prior notice to the network. The courts concluded that to sanction the network for this situation would amount to prior censorship in violation of the American Convention.[6]

B. States of Exception

States of Exception provisions in Articles 39 through 41 of the Constitution allow harsh limitations on freedom of expression. Under State of Assembly, the Constitution allows the Executive Branch to suspend or restrict freedom of opinion. Under powers conferred by State of Siege and by State of Catastrophe, freedom of information and opinion can be restricted (but not suspended). A State of Assembly can be declared in case of an external war; internal war or internal commotion are the basis to declare a State of Siege. A State of Catastrophe can be declared in case of a public calamity (this has usually been applied to earthquakes and other kinds of natural disasters).

The above-mentioned provisions on States of Exception are inconsistent with international standards. Article 4 of the International Covenant on Civil and Political Rights provides that a threat to the life of the nation is required to take measures derogating from the right to freedom of opinion and expression. However, the Chilean Constitution does not require such a high standard to be met.

In addition, the Covenant states that such measures may be taken "to the extent strictly required by the exigencies of the situation", that is, it requires that the factual conditions be analyzed. In contrast, Chilean courts are prevented by the Constitution from analyzing the facts surrounding the application of derogating measures. Article 41.3 of the Constitution provides that the courts are not allowed to challenge the factual circumstances invoked by the authorities to justify derogating measures.[7] As a consequence, judges may only review legal formalities of derogating

---

[6] This case was highly controversial, since the recorded conversation consisted of a discussion, in crude language, between a potential presidential candidate, Senator Sebastián Piñera, and a journalist about ways to harass Evelyn Matthei, another potential presidential candidate of the same party, on issues about which she might be inconsistent, such as a draft law on divorce. Ms. Matthei obtained the tape from an army telecommunications officer and handed it over to Megavision's President, Ricardo Claro. The army officer later argued that he had recorded the conversation at random. As a result of this scandal, both Mr. Piñera and Ms. Matthei withdrew from the presidential race. Proceedings were started against the TV network, but no charges on personal liability were pursued against Mr. Claro. *See Red Televisa Megavisión S.A. con Consejo Nacional de Televisión*, Supreme Court, 18 March 1993, upholding the decision of the Court of Appeals of Santiago of 18 November 1992.

[7] The original in Spanish states as follows: "Los tribunales de justicia no podrán, en caso alguno, entrar a calificar los fundamentos ni las circunstancias de hecho invocadas por la autoridad para adoptar las medidas en el ejercicio de las facultades excepcionales que le confiere esta Constitución."

measures, but not "the exigencies of the situation", as the Covenant requires. What previously had been a jurisprudential practice (judges' self-restraint to analyze factual conditions surrounding derogating measures) acquired constitutional status.[8]

III. Access to Information and Protection of National Security Secrets

A. The Armed Forces

1. Legislation

The Code of Military Justice and a series of regulations contain norms about access to information and restrictions on national security grounds. Article 436 of the Code of Military Justice defines secret documents as those directly related by content to State security, national defense, internal public order or the security of persons.

Articles 144 and 144 bis of the Code of Military Justice regulate the disclosure of secret documents during judicial investigations. According to Article 144, the military prosecutor in charge of an investigation is the only person who can request the submission of secret documents. In judicial cases where the Prosecutor deems it necessary to request secret documents, he will have to ask the respective Commander-in-Chief, who can refuse to submit the document on the grounds that state security, national defense, internal public order or the security of persons would be affected. Should the prosecutor consider it indispensable to obtain the document, the Supreme Court, in addition to the Legal Counsel of the Army, will decide on the matter.[9] In any event, individuals who are the subject of an investigation conducted by a military prosecutor are not allowed access to any secret documents, not even in cases where the secret document is relevant to the individual's defense.

Similarly, in cases within civilian jurisdiction, a civilian judge in charge of a criminal investigation who thinks that a secret document may be relevant to the case, must lodge a request for the document with the respective Commander-in-Chief, who may deny the request without stating reasons.[10]

---

[8] In view of the fact that international human rights treaties have been incorporated by the Chilean Constitution, it could be asserted that the above mentioned domestic provisions regarding States of Exception have automatically been repealed. So far, however, this issue has not been brought before a court and this paradoxical situation persists.

[9] According to art. 70-A of the Military Code, in cases under military jurisdiction, the Legal Counsel of the Army sits with the Supreme Court, even when none of the parties is a member of the military.

[10] Criminal Procedural Code, art. 53, in connection with Military Code, arts. 144 and 144 bis.

Further provisions about the protection of secrecy within the Armed Forces are contained in the Regulations on Intelligence and Military Security. These regulations provide, as a general rule, that all matters concerning the Armed Forces are public. It adds, however, that such matters become classified when their disclosure would actually or potentially harm the Army or the State, either within the country or abroad. These provisions have usually been construed as establishing a sort of objective responsibility, that is, a person will be considered responsible solely on the basis of having had knowledge of a classified document regardless of whether or not he had any intent to cause harm.

These Regulations contain detailed provisions about the formalities required to gain access to secret documents. To obtain and to handle classified information, a member of the military has to have an authorization, which is given by assigning him a "*grado de acceso*" (degree of access). The type of classified documents that he may examine will depend on the degree of access he is granted.

The Administrative Regulations on Correspondence and Documentation go further by establishing a classification of the potential harm caused by unauthorized disclosures and by ruling on degrees of secrecy. Some regulations on secrecy about matters related to the Armed Forces, such as the Regulations of the Garrison Service of the Army, are also applicable to former military officers.

2. The Humberto Palamara Case

The case of Humberto Palamara illustrates the current domestic standards concerning restrictions on access to information and freedom of expression on national security grounds. Mr. Palamara, a former member of the Intelligence Services of the Navy, attempted to publish a book on intelligence matters in 1993. Although he was already retired from the Navy by the time he wrote the book, the Military Courts declared the case to fall within their jurisdiction. There were two different trials in connection with this matter, both under military jurisdiction.

In one trial, Mr. Palamara was charged with two criminal offenses: first, for not having requested authorization from the Navy to publish the book *Ethics and Intelligence Services* (*Etica y Servicios de Inteligencia* in the Spanish original), causing danger to national security and defense; and second, for having refused to give the book to the authorities when requested to do so.[11] In the end, he was convicted, and received two suspended sentences, each of them of 61 days. In addition, his book was confiscated.

The case was tried by a military tribunal; reviewed by a Martial Court, which operates as a Court of Appeals within the military jurisdiction, and has a

---

[11] Additionally, Mr. Palamara was convicted of a third charge by the military tribunal but was later declared innocent by the Martial Court and the Supreme Court. This charge was for publicly criticizing the Navy in connection with the prohibition to publish the book, despite having been warned not to do so.

mixed civilian/military composition, with the military predominating (three military justices and two civilians); and decided by a panel of five Supreme Court justices augmented by a representative of the Armed Forces. The case is currently pending before the Inter-American Commission on Human Rights.

As to the first charge, Mr. Palamara's failure to request authorization was considered to be contrary to the Ordinance of the Navy of Chile, which states in Article 89:

> It is forbidden to all members of the Navy or persons in its service to publish or to facilitate the publication in the press of articles involving criticism of the Navy services, of other armed institutions, of public organs, or of the government.
>
> It is likewise forbidden to publish, directly or indirectly, articles concerning matters of a secret or confidential nature, matters of a political or religious nature, as well as others that could lead to controversies in which the good name of the Navy could be involved.
>
> Taking into account the above mentioned restrictions, Navy personnel can make publications in the press, in their personal capacity, with the prior knowledge and authorization of their Commandant or the Competent Navy Authority.
>
> In times of war or when circumstances so require, the Commander in Chief of the Navy can suspend or limit this authorization.[12]

As to the charge of disobedience, the judicial decision was based on Article 337.3 of the Military Code. The grounds of the charge were that Mr. Palamara had

---

[12] The original in Spanish reads as follows:

> Estará prohibido a todo miembro de la Armada o persona que se encuentre a su servicio, publicar o dar facilidades para que se publiquen en la prensa, artículos que envuelvan una crítica a los servicios de la Armada, de otra institución armada, de organismos públicos o de gobierno.
>
> Igualmente estará prohibido publicar, directa o indirectamente, artículos que se refieran a asuntos *de carácter secreto, reservado o confidencial*, temas políticos o religiosos u otros que puedan dar margen a una polémica o controversia en la cual se pueda ver envuelto el buen nombre de la institución.
>
> Teniendo en cuenta las anteriores restricciones, el personal de la Armada podrá hacer publicaciones a la prensa, a título personal, previo conocimiento y autorización de su Comandante o de la Autoridad Naval competente.
>
> En tiempo de guerra o cuando las circunstancias así lo exijan, la Comandancia en Jefe de la Armada podrá suspender o limitar esta autorización.

been forbidden to give any information to the press, and that despite this prohibition he had done so.

In responding to these charges, Mr. Palamara disputed the facts and challenged the military jurisdiction over his case. However, military jurisdiction is typical in Chile for this type of case, so it was not unexpected that the military tribunal kept its jurisdiction.

It should be noted that Mr. Palamara's book had not been published when the military tribunal began the investigation of the case. The military became aware that the book was going to be published without the required authorization, and the military court (*Fiscalía Naval*), even before reviewing the contents of the book, searched the printing facilities where the book was being prepared and seized all copies found. Mr. Palamara's home was also searched, and his computer's hard drive containing the book was deleted. Mr. Palamara was not given the chance to dispute whether what he had written fell under Article 89, quoted above.

At some latter point during the procedure, the court ordered the book to be reviewed by two experts to obtain their expert opinions as to whether it threatened national security. It is striking in this case that the military experts who reviewed the book concluded that it contained no confidential information or analysis affecting national security or defense. This development led to a new request by the court for the military experts to express an opinion on whether the book "affected the institutional interests" of the Navy. In this second report the experts concluded that the book did affect the Navy's institutional interests, but in no way did they state that the Navy might be harmed as a result of the book's publication. They based their statement on the fact that "in his [Mr. Palamara's] statement that his writing responds 'to the moral obligation that a person has to disseminate his knowledge and experiences to others', it is implicit that the author's capacity to write on the topic is based on his Navy training as an intelligence specialist".[13]

In fact, Mr. Palamara's book contains no description about Chilean or foreign intelligence activities, past or present. Instead, it describes the main standards of intelligence, emphasizing the need for these to be adapted to ethical criteria. Although not explicitly stated by Navy authorities, what might have aroused some suspicions about Mr. Palamara's book is the fact that in it he stresses the necessity of keeping intelligence activities in accordance with human rights standards, opposes torture, and states that it is not the role of intelligence services to detain or interrogate persons.[14]

---

[13] For more information on this case, *see* C. Medina, "La Libertad de Expresión", in C. Medina and J. Mera (eds.), *Sistema Jurídico y Derechos Humanos. El derecho nacional y las obligaciones internacionales de Chile en materia de derechos humanos*, at 145-216 (Sociedad de Ediciones de la Universidad Diego Portales, Santiago, Chile, 1996).

[14] While Mr. Palamara has never openly criticized intelligence activities undertaken during the military regime, in broadcast appearances he has kept his distance from the intelligence agencies' role during those years, recognizing the Truth Commission Report as a valuable

In the second trial, Mr. Palamara was convicted of libel (*desacato*[15]) against the Navy Prosecutor, and received a third suspended sentence of sixty-one days' imprisonment. This process started because of statements Mr. Palamara made to the press following the seizure of the book ordered by the prosecutor. In particular, Mr. Palamara said to the press that "there are reasons to presume that the Office of the Navy Prosecutor forged legal documents and lied to the Court of Appeals when consulted about who had made the complaint that initiated the summary process as well as about the case number".[16]

In the first instance, the military tribunal absolved Mr. Palamara of the charge of libel, on the ground that his statement had not been directed against the Navy Prosecutor (*Fiscal Naval*) nor to any other individual, but to the Office of the Navy Prosecutor (*Fiscalía Naval*), thus lacking a key element of libel. This ruling, however, was changed by the Martial Court in a divided decision, condemning Mr. Palamara to serve sixty-one days of imprisonment. On July 20, 1995, the Supreme Court, also in a divided decision, confirmed the Martial Court's decision. This case was brought before the Inter-American Commission on Human Rights, where it is pending. It is expected that the Commission will decide the case in favor of Mr. Palamara, since the Commission has stated that *desacato* laws are incompatible with the American Convention on Human Rights.[17]

As of February 1998, Mr. Palamara's book, *Ethics and Intelligence,* had not been published. The judicial investigation focused on the issue of the required authorization, while the issue of the book's contents themselves was placed in a secondary position. The case represents the extent to which Chilean law as implemented falls well below the minimum standards set by the Inter-American Court and Commission of Human Rights. First, the courts upheld prior censorship even though the material was not found to threaten national security. Second, Mr. Palamara was convicted of *desacato* even though criticism of public officials is recognized to be a key aspect of freedom of expression in a democratic society.[18]

B. Public Administration

In Chile, it is largely the public administration which decides about confidentiality issues. There is no tradition of bringing cases before the courts to dispute public administration decisions on these matters.

---

source of information. (The Navy, on the contrary, publicly criticized this report.)

[15] "*Desacato*" means contempt of, or libel against, any State authority.

[16] *La Prensa Austral* newspaper, May 7, 1993.

[17] *See* Inter-American Commision of Human Rights, *Report on the Compatibility of "Desacato Laws" with the American Convention on Human Rights,* at 197 (Annual Report 1994), OEA/Ser.L/V/II. 88, Doc. 9 rev. 1, February 17, 1995.

[18] *See id.* See also Krsticevic, et al., The Inter-American System, *supra* this volume, at 179.

The Regulations of the Administration (*Estatuto Administrativo*) establish the obligation of public employees to keep secret issues considered confidential by law, by executive regulations, by their nature or according to special instructions.[19] Public employees who do not comply with this obligation may be held administratively as well as criminally responsible. Penalties include the suspension from their position for up to 540 days and/or a fine; in the case of grave harm being done to the public cause (*causa pública*) as a consequence of the disclosure, imprisonment from five years and one day to twenty years is provided.

In addition to the severity of the potential penalties, it is surprising that no explicit warning of the confidential character of a document is required: a document may be confidential by nature, and it is the duty of public employees to recognize this confidential character. The Comptroller General of the Republic has made extensive use of the category "confidential by nature" to keep documents secret.[20]

IV. Limitations on Grounds of National Security and Public Order During Non-Emergency Periods

In addition to the regulations on States of Exception, Chilean legislation establishes limitations to freedom of expression based on grounds of national security and public order that are applicable during normal (non-emergency) periods. Throughout the 20th Century, Chile has had a series of laws on this matter. Currently, the most important piece of legislation in this regard is Law N° 12,927, called the Law on State Security (*Ley de Seguridad del Estado*).

Law 12,927 was enacted in 1958. Over the last four decades, this legislation has been subject to many transformations and has been applied in very different contexts. In particular, the military regime used this legislation as a key tool to repress its opponents, perverting its purpose to protect a dictatorial regime. The most repressive provisions introduced to this law by the military regime were repealed during the transition to democracy,[21] although a number of provisions

---

[19] *Estatuto Administrativo*, art. 55.

[20] The General Comptrollership of the Republic (*Contraloría General de la República*) is an organ of the Executive Branch which determines whether or not Executive decrees and regulations are in accordance with the law. Regarding causes for confidentiality, *see, e.g.*, Dictamen N°50.907 of 1978, Dictamen N°30.790 of 1989, Dictamen N°28.977 of 1993, and Dictamen N°20.680 of 1994.

[21] For instance, the military regime created a new crime against public order, consisting of "promoting or convoking public and collective demonstrations without authorization, and promoting or inciting to demonstrations of any other nature that permit or facilitate the disturbance of public tranquility." The penalty was up to five years during peace time, and up to twenty years in times of war. According to this legislation, the Regime punished those who acted without prior authorization. At that time the Government had absolute discretion regarding whether or not to issue a permit for a demonstration and, in fact, until the date of

introduced by the dictatorship are still in force. Regarding freedom of expression, the current regulations are basically the same as existed prior to the military regime.

The originally declared aim of Law 12,927 was to protect the democratic system. However, from the very beginning, this legislation lacked adequate consideration for human rights and, in applying it, the tribunals have expanded the limitations on rights that the law permits.

First, given the traditional reluctance of the courts in Chile to confront issues of a political character, the fact that special legislation on national security remains without being incorporated into the Criminal Code, in and of itself undermines protection for human rights. In practice, the courts usually do not take the general principles of the Criminal Code into consideration when applying national security regulations.

One basic problem of Law 12,927 is that many of its provisions are vague and overly broad. For instance, Article 4, which regulates crimes against Internal State Security, punishes a person who *in any way* attempts to act, or in fact acts, against the "established government".

Second, Law 12,927 is not clear enough in the protection of the democratic system, although this was reportedly its basic purpose. Many of its provisions refer to the protection of the "established government" (Gobierno Constituido). In Spanish, this is an ambiguous expression, which means both the political organization of the State and the Executive Branch of power. Many provisions of the law, including several concerning freedom of expression, use the words "established government", and the courts have often considered the words to protect only the regime in power.

In applying the provisions of the Law on State Security, the courts have consistently declared that it is beyond their powers to determine whether national security or public order were indeed affected in a specific case. As a consequence, freedom of expression and other rights have been further limited. In regulating offenses against public order, Article 6 provides: "In the following cases an offense against public order is committed", and enumerates eight situations. This has led to a sort of unassailable assumption of criminal responsibility, despite the fact that public order may not have been actually affected in a specific case. The courts have stated:

> Article 6 of the Law [12,927] establishes that those who engage in any of the acts that the law describes 'commit a crime against the public order'. In this way, it is the law itself that assumes that this crime causes a disturbance of the public order in some way.

---

the establishment of this act as a crime, a permit for a demonstration for the Opposition had been issued *on only one occasion.* Concerning the disturbance of public tranquility, through this provision the Government tried to make its opponents responsible for the violence that they themselves were the victims of during the demonstrations, coming from military and paramilitary groups.

> Therefore, it is not proper for the judge to rule contrary to the explicit wording of the law, which is clear, reaching a different conclusion by way of interpretation.[22]

In a high profile case during the sixties, socialist Senator Carlos Altamirano was accused of advocacy of violence. Although he claimed in his defense that his words were not able to cause harm to the public order, the court did not consider this argument at all.[23] The court ruled that "[i]t is a matter for the legislator, who promulgates the law, and not for the judge, whose role is limited to its application, to protect that right [freedom of expression]."[24]

Moreover, the Courts have failed to implement the Constitution's Bill of Rights whenever national security and public order have been invoked by the government as grounds for restricting rights. The list of rights contained in the Constitution provides a guide for an appropriate reading of the law. However, the courts have tried to implement national security and public order regulations without regard to the constitutional context, rendering the constitutional norms meaningless in this respect.

On the few occasions when courts have dismissed charges in national security or public order cases, they have used legal technicalities to do so rather than applying an interpretation of the law consistent with Chile's human rights commitments. For instance, in the case *Against Sergio Onofre Jarpa and others* (1967), the board members of the Partido Nacional, a right wing party, were accused of defaming the Christian-Democrat Government of Eduardo Frei Montalva. Jarpa and the other board members were acquitted on legal technicalities; the court thus avoided having to address the issue of freedom of speech clearly involved.[25] The court similarly avoided the freedom of expression issue in a 1969 case against the firector of the newspaper *La Segunda*; it made no reference to freedom of expression or speech at all.[26]

During the military regime, Law 12,927 was systematically used to repress the opposition. Although after that period it has not been widely used, some cases of a political nature have been initiated. The most publicized of them concerned the accusation in 1995 against Francisco Javier Cuadra, a former Minister of the military regime, who publicly stated that there were members of Congress who used cocaine,

---

[22] *Against Jose Antonio Gómez*, Revista de Derecho y Jurisprudencia, T.LXIX, 2ª p., Secc. 4ª, pp.4 ss. Jose Antonio Gómez was the director of the leftist newspaper *Puro Chile*. The process against him took place prior to the military regime. This jurisprudence has been reaffirmed on many occassions.

[23] *Against Carlos Altamirano*, Revista de Derecho y Jurisprudencia, T.LXV, 2a. parte, sección 4a, 9 ss. See also Revista de Derecho y Jurisprudencia, T.LXIV, 2a parte, sección 4a, 272 ss.

[24] "Incumbe al legislador, que dicta la ley, y no al juez, que se limita a aplicarla, precaver que aquella garantía no sea desvirtuada injustificadamente."

[25] *See* Revista de Derecho y Jurisprudencia T.LXIV, 2a parte, sección 4a, 266 ss., and T.LXV, 2a parte, sección 4a, 95 ss.

[26] *See* Revista de Derecho y Jurisprudencia T.LXVI, 2a parte, sección 4a, 302 ss.

though he refused to identify who they were. The House of Representatives and the Senate, by near-unanimous votes, accused Cuadra of violating the State Security Law.

In the first instance, Mr. Cuadra was condemned to a suspended sentence for disturbing public order. This decision was later overturned by the Court of Appeals, which declared that Mr. Cuadra's statements in no way affected public order. The decision quoted the Minister of Interior, Mr. Carlos Figueroa, who said to the press before charges were presented against Mr. Cuadra that public order had not been affected. This opinion was relevant because the Minister of Interior is precisely the authority whose role it is to protect public order.

The Court of Appeal's decision arguably should have been final, since Congress had just passed legislation restricting access to the Supreme Court in order to reduce its case-load, including cases like Mr. Cuadra's. However, the very same members of Congress who had passed that legislation submitted the Cuadra case to the Supreme Court. The Court found a very particular ground to affirm its jurisdiction over the case, stating that the legislation restricting its powers with regard to its competence was partially unconstitutional. It was unprecedented for the Supreme Court to declare a law unconstitutional without a prior request by the complainant, as the Court did in this case. Of course, Congressmen could not make such a petition, since they had just approved the legislation. In 1996, the Supreme Court condemned Mr. Cuadra for an offense against public order, based on the doctrine that it is beyond its powers to determine whether or not public order has been in fact affected.

Ironically, one year later, Mr. José Antonio Viera-Gallo, a member of the Socialist Party who, as President of the Chamber of Deputies, had been one of the leaders of the accusation against Mr. Cuadra, was himself accused before the courts of violating the same Law 12,927 on State Security by the Army Commander-in-Chief and former dictator General Augusto Pinochet. In a TV program, Mr. Viera-Gallo said in the context of a live discussion on corruption that, during his government, General Pinochet had "dirtied his hands". This was interpreted by Gen. Pinochet as an accusation of corruption. The judicial proceedings were quickly closed after Mr. Viera-Gallo publicly apologized, stating that in no way had he intended to accuse General Pinochet. As a result of this incident, Mr. Viera-Gallo changed his opinion about the State Security Law, saying it should be repealed.

Another well publicized case was that against Mr. Arturo Barrios, President of the Youth of the Socialist Party, who said that General Pinochet was an assassin. He was convicted under the State Security Law to a 541 days' suspended sentence for disturbing public order. As of February 1998, Mr. Barrios was under parole and a complaint was being prepared for presentation to the Inter-American Commission.

In a very similar case, Ms. Gladys Marín, Secretary General of the Communist Party, was accused by General Pinochet of disturbing public order under the State Security Law for having called him an assassin. After governmental authorities intervened, however, General Pinochet withdrew the charges.

In a fourth case presented by General Pinochet on state security grounds, this time against Mr. Nolberto Díaz, then-President of the Youth of the Christian Democratic Party, the court ended up dismissing the charges. In a broadcast program, Mr. Díaz stated in 1996 that "they want us [the youngsters] to serve in the Armed Forces [when drafted] having the same elderly, former dictator, as the Commander-in-Chief of the Armed Forces."[27] He also said that he thought that links existed between Chilean army officers and the killing of a former Chilean intelligence officer in Uruguay, and raised questions about the purpose of a trip made by General Pinochet to Uruguay when a judicial investigation of this killing was being carried out. The judge in charge of the case against Mr. Díaz closed the case, stated that he would re-open it if sufficient proof were provided. The Court of Appeals confirmed this decision, and the Supreme Court, in late 1996, refused to review the case arguing lack of jurisdiction. The case has not been re-opened.

In early 1998, TV comedian Rafael Gumucio and journalist Paula Coddou were charged under the State Security Law for an offense against public order.[28] In responding to a humorous survey about the year 1997 prepared by Ms. Coddou for a magazine, Mr. Gumucio featured Mr. Servando Jordán, former President of the Supreme Court and still a Justice on that Court, as "old, ugly and with a turbid past". It has to be noted that while Mr. Jordán was serving as President of the Court, the Chamber of Deputies moved to impeach him on grounds of corruption and links with drug dealers. The petition for impeachment was rejected by a very close margin.

The use of Law 12,927 in this and other cases during the transition to democracy shows that it is being used in basically the same way as it was during the democratic period prior to the dictatorship, that is, without consideration for the protection of human rights. Although no longer used as a mechanism for systematic repression, this legislation is still a powerful tool for restricting freedom of expression beyond the limits imposed by the Constitution and international human rights treaties.[29]

---

[27] Mr. Díaz's words in Spanish were as follows: "Pretenden que ahora hagamos el servicio militar teniendo al mismo anciano, ex-dictador, como Comandante en Jefe de las Fuerzas Armadas."

[28] A few days after they had been charged, and after spending a night in jail, Pinochet withdrew the charges and the case was closed.

[29] For a more detailed revision of the jurisprudence on national security and public order in Chile, *see* González, Mera and Vargas, *Protección Democrática de la Seguridad Interior: Estados de Excepción y Derecho Penal Político*.

V. Use of Military Courts to Try Cases Involving Civilians

The military justice system has not experienced significant transformations during the transition to democracy and it currently fails to meet some basic rule of law standards. A few isolated reforms have been introduced over the last years, but the military courts still have jurisdiction over a wide range of cases, including many involving civilians. These include cases on freedom of expression. Grave problems of lack of independence of the military courts and of insufficient recognition of the rights of the accused persist.

A reform introduced to the Military Code in 1991 reduced the jurisdiction of military courts regarding freedom of expression. As a result of this reform, military courts are no longer competent in cases involving civilians accused of libel or defamation against military personnel or police officers.

However, by different means, the military courts have managed to circumvent this restriction. The best-known case in this regard is that of Hector Salazar, a human rights lawyer, who was accused of improper sedition (*sedición impropia*) and submitted to military jurisdiction in 1994. Mr. Salazar was at that time the lawyer representing the relatives of three members of the Executive Committee of the Communist Party assassinated by *carabineros* (police officers) in 1985. A civilian judge condemned several police officers to life imprisonment for assassination and declared that General Rodolfo Stange, director of the *carabineros* had obstructed the investigation by recommending to his subordinates that they lie to the judge. The Government then repeatedly and publicly called on General Stange to resign from his position, but he refused.[30] The civilian judge sent the documentation on General Stange's obstruction of the investigation to a military tribunal.

In this context, attorney Salazar declared to the television: "I ask any *carabinero* of Chile if he/she is in a position to obey an order given by General Stange, risking, like others have already risked, life imprisonment".[31] Mr. Salazar was referring to General Stange's intervention in the case of the triple assassination. As a consequence of these statements, a military prosecutor charged Mr. Salazar with improper sedition, defined by the Military Code in Article 276:

> The incitement to any disturbance or disorder, either orally, in writing or by any other means, or the transmission of ideas to the troops intended to cause them annoyance or lack of enthusiasm for the [military] service, or to encourage gossip about the service.

For civilians, the penalty ranges from sixty-one days to five years of imprisonment.

---

[30] Under the current Constitution, the Executive does not have the power to remove the Commanders-in-Chief of the Armed Forces or the *Carabineros*, a legacy of the military regime.

[31] In Spanish: "Yo le pregunto a cualquier carabinero de Chile si está en condiciones de cumplir una orden emanada del general Stange, corriendo el riesgo, como lo han corrido otros, de enfrentar cadena perpetua."

The charges against Mr. Salazar were confirmed by a martial court in a split decision, with the three military justices voting to uphold the charges and the two civilian justices, to dismiss them. The six judges of the Supreme Court initially reached a tie vote, with three (including the representative from the Army) voting to uphold the charges, and the three others, voting to dismiss them. Neither side explained its reasoning at any length, with the three judges who voted to uphold the decision stating only that the proof was sufficient to charge Mr. Salazar, and the three other judges stating that the proof was insufficient. To break the tie, the acting Supreme Court President was called to vote and he voted for dismissal of the charges, on the ground that attorney Salazar's statements were not, of themselves, likely to cause the *carabineros* to feel annoyance or lack of enthusiasm for their service, since the President of the Republic had publicly asked General Stange to resign in connection with the same facts. This case shows the broad reach of the jurisdiction of the military courts and the negative impact of this broad jurisdiction on freedom of expression.[32]

VI. Conscientious Objection

In Chile, there is no right to conscientious objection on religious or any other grounds. Recently some debate has arisen about the possibility of establishing a system parallel to the draft, but it is not envisioned that reforms on this matter will take place in the near future. Indeed, the Committee of National Defense of the House of Representatives voted unanimously against this reform on national security grounds.

Jehovah's Witnesses are in a special position regarding the draft. Although an exemption does not exist for them in the law, in practice, following an informal process of selection, Jehovah's Witnesses are usually not recruited into the military because of their beliefs. The same applies to those who are in the process of becoming priests.

VII. Conclusion

A non-democratic concept of national security has been widely used in Chile to restrict freedom of expression and access to information. This situation was seriously aggravated during the military regime, and some legal provisions dating from that period are still in force. The deficiencies of legislation are not overcome by

---

[32] No charges against General Stange were issued in the end. However, attorney Salazar's statement was made while the situation of Gen. Stange was uncertain. Gen. Stange resigned about a year later, making clear that this was his decision and that he was not following a governmental order.

judicial supervision. As said above, when dealing with national security problems judges tend to apply legal criteria more loosely than in other cases.

It is very unlikely that the pertinent legislation will be amended in the near future. The military maintains an important share of political power and, due to laws enacted just before the change of government from General Pinochet to President Aylwin, Congress does not reflect the majorities obtained in the polls by the coalition of political parties supporting the Government. As long as these factors do not change, legislation in this area will most surely remain as it is.

Beyond the issue of the military, there seem to be certain authoritarian components that pervade Chilean culture, placing additional obstacles in the way of development of a democratic concept of national security, compatible with the protection of freedom of expression. Therefore, in order to overcome the current restrictions there must be not only a change of political will, but also cultural transformations.

In this sense, perhaps one cause for hope is that Chile has become a party to several human rights treaties. The most important ones are the American Convention on Human Rights and the International Covenant on Civil and Political Rights, because they subject Chile to the scrutiny of the Inter-American Commission and Court of Human Rights and the UN Human Rights Committee. Opinions and decisions of these organs will significantly aid those who are committed to the task of eliminating both the authoritarian elements of Chilean culture and the legacy of the military regime.

"KILLING THE CHICKEN TO FRIGHTEN THE MONKEYS": THE USE OF STATE SECURITY IN THE CONTROL OF FREEDOM OF EXPRESSION IN CHINA[1]

Sophia Woodman and Yu Ping[2]

When your goal is to warn the monkeys, you don't care what attitude the chicken has. Wei Jingsheng, explaining in a 1981 letter to his siblings why it would not have made any difference to the outcome of his case if he had expressed regret for his actions during the 1978-79 Democracy Wall Movement.[3]

I. Introduction

Since its founding, the Chinese Party-state has carried out routine, pervasive suppression of freedom of expression. Despite the existence of constitutional provisions guaranteeing freedom of speech, the press and publication, like other communist parties, the Chinese Communist Party (CCP) has always claimed the sole right to speak on behalf of the people and to determine the "correct" view of history, policy and social reality. The CCP considers the principal role of the mass media as "guiding public opinion" to support Party policy. On the level of individual expression, the CCP has characterized the suppression of its critics as a necessary aspect of the "class struggle" carried out to protect the socialist revolution.

According to the PRC State Council's 1991 White Paper, *Human Rights in China*, however, people in China cannot be punished solely for having opinions which do not accord with those of the authorities. "[I]deas alone, in the absence of action which violates the criminal law, do not constitute a crime; nobody will be sentenced to punishment merely because he holds dissenting political views. So-called political prisoners do not exist in China."[4] In reality many people have been sent to prison merely for expressing their ideas, either verbally or in writing. Authoritative legal opinions and documents confirm that whereas thought which is "reactionary" or "counter-revolutionary" according to the standards of the leaders of

---

[1] The Chinese saying, "killing the chicken to frighten the monkeys" (*sha ji xia hou*), means to punish someone as a warning to others.

[2] The authors conducted the research for this paper as part of their work for the organization, Human Rights in China, in particular for the report, *Whose Security? "State Security" in China's New Criminal Code*, issued jointly with Human Rights Watch/Asia in April 1997. Sophia Woodman is Human Rights in China's Hong Kong Representative; Yu Ping is the group's Legal Consultant and a Ph.D. Candidate at the University of Washington.

[3] Wei Jingsheng, *The Courage to Stand Alone: Letters from Prison and Other Writings* 7 (1997).

[4] Information Office of the PRC State Council, *Human Rights in China* (1991).

the day cannot be punished, speech is generally considered an "action" (*xingwei*) and therefore potentially subject to prosecution.[5]

Until the reform era beginning in the late 1970s, the struggle against counter-revolutionaries was mostly conducted through a process of political mobilization with little reference to legal procedures. Following the return to power of Deng Xiaoping in 1978, there was a shift towards more legalistic methods in the suppression of the critics of the Party-state; provisions on counter-revolution were incorporated into the nation's first Criminal Code, promulgated in 1979.[6]

However, with the current leadership mostly downplaying the importance of class struggle domestically[7] and seeking greater acceptance internationally, during the 1990s the idea of "endangering state security" has gradually replaced the politically-loaded term counter-revolution. This process culminated in the revision of the Criminal Code in March 1997, when the chapter laying out crimes of counter-revolution was replaced with one on "Crimes Endangering State Security".[8]

This change did not take effect until the revised Criminal Code entered into force on 1 October 1997, but the first formal legal expression of "endangering state security" as the new organizing principle for the suppression of dissent had come with the enactment of the 1993 PRC State Security Law (hereafter "State Security Law"). This had been preceded by a law on a closely-related matter, the concept of "state secrets": the 1988 PRC Law on the Preservation of State Secrets (hereafter "State Secrets Law") is also extensively used to suppress information and restrict expression.

The evolution of the concept of state security in these laws also demonstrates the effects of the events of 1989: it is part of the hardening of official attitudes towards dissent which followed the brutal crackdown on the nationwide

---

[5] Marina Svensson, Counter-Revolutionary Crimes in 20th Century China: Judicial Theory and Legal Praxis, (July 1997) (unpublished paper on file with the authors) contains a review of various such opinions and documents from the 1980s.

[6] For a recent overview of the use of counter-revolution charges, *see Whose Security?, supra* note 2 at 27-35.

[7] Publicly, the CCP's line is that class struggle is no longer necessary to protect the revolution. However, privately some officials have indicated that it continues. For example, Minister of Public Security Tao Siju was quoted by a Hong Kong newspaper recently as saying that class struggle would exist for a long time to come within a certain scope. He warned that following the death of Deng Xiaoping, "hostile forces" inside and outside China's borders would clamor for a reassessment of the 1989 Democracy Movement and create disturbances surrounding controversial issues such as unemployment, poverty and the payment of pensions. *See* "Minister of Public Security: Class Struggle Still Exists," *Ming Pao*, July 22, 1997.

[8] Criminal Code of the People's Republic of China (1997), Special Provisions, Chapter 1. The term "state security" is commonly used to translate the Chinese *guojia anquan*, but "national security" would be an equally appropriate translation, since the Chinese *guojia* means both state and nation and in some sense incorporates both these words. In this paper, we use state security and national security interchangeably, as is the case in Chinese publications.

Democracy Movement that year and which also entailed a radical diminution of the "space" for public and scholarly discussion of sensitive issues, whether political, economic, social or even historical. Thus the characterization of opposition views as threats to state security is the most extreme manifestation of a broader freeze on public freedom of expression which has continued since 1989.

At certain times during the last 48 years, counter-revolutionary cases made up the majority of all criminal cases in China, but in the reform era prosecutions under this rubric have declined substantially. According to Chinese officials, several thousand such prisoners are currently serving prison terms, constituting less than half of one percent of all convicted prisoners.[9] Although there are few available statistics and some are contradictory, it is clear that a substantial proportion of such individuals were tried for freedom of expression-related offenses.[10]

The declining numbers do point to the less politicized atmosphere which has prevailed since the beginning of the reform era, including a relatively tolerant attitude to the private expression of critical views. There have been crucial exceptions to this overall trend, in particular the suppression of the 1978-79 Democracy Wall Movement between 1979 and 1981 and the period of widespread purges and trials immediately following the June Fourth Massacre in 1989.

The relative rarity of prosecutions for counter-revolution does not mean the Party-state has decided to abandon the criminal prosecution of its critics or end restrictions on freedom of expression.[11] The Party-state now uses its repressive powers in a more targeted manner, needing to convict only a relatively small number of "chickens" of state security crimes in order to serve its purpose of frightening the "monkeys" - the population at large. Although news reports on such cases usually contain minimal information - if they are reported at all - citizens are regularly

---

[9] Information on numbers of counter-revolutionaries has been released sporadically, if at all. In April 1997, Chinese officials said 2,026 prisoners convicted on counter-revolutionary charges remained in jail. A comprehensive overview of available information, as well as some from internal sources, is contained in Svensson, *supra* note 5.

[10] Most were charged under Article 102 of the 1979 Criminal Code on "counter-revolutionary propaganda and incitement". An official law journal article noted that by 1990, 80% of such cases were brought under Article 102. *See Whose Security?*, *supra* note 2 at 27-35; *see also* Svensson, *supra* note 5.

[11] Many religious and political dissidents have been sentenced administratively or convicted for purely criminal offenses (such as "hooliganism" and "swindling", for example) on trumped up charges which would not normally merit prosecution, and thus the number of counter-revolutionaries does not reflect the full picture of political imprisonment. Under the Reeducation Through Labor regulations, individuals can be sent to labor camps without trial for periods of up to four years. *See* Human Rights in China, *Detained at Official Pleasure: Arbitrary Detention in the PRC* (June 1993); Amnesty International, *China - Punishment Without Crime: Arbitrary Detention* (Sept. 1991). On the issue of the use of criminal charges, *see* Human Rights in China and Human Rights Watch/Asia, *China - Use of Criminal Charges Against Political Dissidents* (Oct. 1994).

reminded that they have a responsibility to "protect state security" and "state secrets". The indeterminate nature of these concepts combined with the example of the "chickens" creates a climate of fear and intimidation which has a serious impact on freedom of expression for all.

This chapter examines the concept of state security in Chinese law and how it is used to suppress critics of the Party-state and its policies, then attempts to draw some conclusions about the implications of this legal regime. It briefly reviews constitutional provisions regarding expression, and the lack of protections for freedom of expression. It then looks at how the elements of the above-mentioned chapter of the revised Criminal Code and the State Security and State Secrets Law may be used to restrict freedom of expression, showing how the vague and expansive nature of the legal provisions allows for arbitrary, politically-driven decisions just as the concept of counter-revolution did in the past. This is demonstrated by a number of individual cases, primarily involving human rights, labor and minority activists and journalists.[12]

II. Constitutional Provisions

The PRC's fourth constitution, promulgated in 1982, appears unequivocal in providing for freedom of expression for Chinese citizens, and for their right to criticize the government and its officials. Article 35, which is part of the section entitled "The Fundamental Rights and Duties of Citizens", reads: "Citizens of the People's Republic of China enjoy freedom of speech, of the press, of assembly, of association, of procession, and of demonstration".[13] Article 41 states: "Citizens of the People's Republic of China have the right to criticize and make suggestions regarding any state organ or functionary. Citizens have the right to make to relevant state organs complaints or charges against, or exposures of, any state organ or functionary for violation of the law or dereliction of duty".[14] Article 47 provides for "the freedom to engage in scientific research, literary and artistic creation and other cultural pursuits".[15]

However, this section follows the Preamble and Chapter 1, which clearly serve to limit the scope for the actual exercise of these freedoms. The former provides that all Chinese citizens and their activities must adhere to the "Four Basic

---

[12] This paper does not cover religious expression. For an overview of current restrictions on religion, *see* Human Rights Watch/Asia, *China: State Control of Religion* (Oct. 1997); for the situation in Tibet, *see* Human Rights Watch/Asia and Tibet Information Network, *Cutting Off the Serpent's Head: Tightening Control in Tibet 1994-1995* (Mar. 1996).

[13] *Constitution of the People's Republic of China*, adopted by the National People's Congress on December 4, 1982 (1987), ch. 2.

[14] *Id.*

[15] *Id.*

Principles" which include keeping to the socialist road, upholding CCP leadership, following Marxism-Leninism-Mao Zedong Thought and submitting to the people's democratic dictatorship.[16] The latter states that socialism is the "basic system" of the PRC, and details state involvement in all spheres of life, including the economy, work, education, academia, the media and culture.[17]

Further specific restrictions on the exercise of rights are envisaged by articles detailing the "duties" of Chinese citizens. Citizens are bound to "safeguard the unification of the country and the unity of all its nationalities", to "keep state secrets ... and respect social ethics" and "to safeguard the security, honor and interests of the motherland".[18] Article 51 sharply restricts individual rights: "Citizens of the People's Republic of China, in exercising their freedoms and rights, may not infringe upon the interests of the state, of society or of the collective, or upon the lawful freedoms and rights of other citizens".[19]

Citizens have virtually no recourse in cases in which their constitutional rights are violated. The highest organs of state power, the National People's Congress (NPC) and its Standing Committee, have responsibility to see that the constitution is enforced,[20] but no formal mechanism has been established for them to carry this out. Despite some signs in recent years that the NPC is gradually becoming more autonomous, in practice it is mainly a rubber-stamp body which enacts laws and endorses policies already approved by the CCP.[21] China has neither a constitutional court charged with overseeing the implementation or interpretation of constitutional provisions, nor any institution of judicial review by ordinary courts, which means that it is impossible to seek a ruling on a constitutional controversy from a court.

The Administrative Litigation Law (ALL) which came into force in 1990 has been presented as a panacea for citizens with grievances about violations of laws or regulations committed by officials or government bodies; it appears to give courts broad discretion to review administrative decisions, including those involving rights

---

[16] *Id.* at 3-7.

[17] *Id.* at 11-25.

[18] *Id.* at Arts. 52-54.

[19] *Id.* at Art 51.

[20] *Id.* at Art. 62.

[21] CCP documents make this abundantly clear. *See, e.g.*, CCP Central Committee, "Notice that All Party Members Must Firmly Defend the Socialist Legal System," *zhong fa* [1986], July 10, 1986, *in Judicial Handbook* at 94-95. This document states:

> Party Committees at all levels should strengthen their leadership over the work of the People's Congresses and firmly uphold [the principle] of the People's Congresses and their Standing Committees exercising their duties in accordance with law. In principle, the decisions or resolutions to be made or passed by the People's Congresses and their Standing Committees must be approved in advance by the corresponding Party Committees at all levels.

violations. [22] In reality, however, its scope is severely limited. The ALL provides courts with virtually unlimited discretion to reject suits on procedural grounds, does not allow for actions against CCP organs and specifically exempts decisions made under regulations which allow for final determination by an administrative body. Also, it limits a court's review to the "lawfulness" of a specific law or administrative act, which means that unless an agency has violated a written law or regulation, the court may not rule against it.

Despite these barriers, in cases which are not politically sensitive, plaintiffs have sometimes prevailed against official bodies. Some of these cases involved arbitrary detention under measures for "Shelter and Investigation" and "Reeducation Through Labor."[23] However, we are not aware of any case brought by a political or religious dissident in which a court has ruled in favor of the plaintiff, and generally courts have refused to hear such suits. Many dissidents have attempted to bring suits under the ALL, including against administrative labor camp terms imposed under Reeducation Through Labor. Since the latter is specifically included under the remit of the ALL, the plaintiffs have been granted hearings in such cases, but none has ever resulted in a reversal of the original decision. Moreover, in cases brought by dissidents or their families regarding other types of abuses, courts have invariably exercised their discretion to refuse a hearing.

In cases in which "state security" is cited, courts are especially likely to deny relief. Article 12(1) of the ALL states that courts "shall not accept and hear" cases involving "acts of state pertaining to such matters as national defense or diplomatic relations".[24]

With all the above-mentioned limitations, citizens have little chance of exercising their constitutional right to freedom of expression in any realistic sense, or of achieving any kind of redress if this right is violated, particularly if the expression is in any way critical of the powers-that-be. In the current system, it is the

---

[22] *See* Pitman B. Potter, "Administrative Litigation and Political Rights in China," and Richard Dicker, "A Law for Change ... With Loopholes," *both in Human Rights Tribune*, Vol. III, No.2 (Human Rights in China, eds., 1992).

[23] Shelter and Investigation was a major form of arbitrary detention until 1996, when it was abolished by the Criminal Procedure Law revisions. In a number of cases, plaintiffs detained under the measures for Shelter and Investigation or Reeducation Through Labor prevailed against the authorities. For example, in a case cited in *Law Book of the People's Courts, 1992* at 745-47 (1995), Wang Yinchun brought suit against the Public Security Bureau of Lishi County, Shanxi Province, for detaining her in March 1991 under Shelter and Investigation on suspicion of having committed a criminal offense. The court found in her favor and awarded compensation for the wrongful detention.

[24] *See also* H. L. Fu & Richard Cullen, "National Security Law in China," 34 *Colum. J. Transnat'l L.* 449, 466 (1996). Fu and Cullen argue that this clause "provides that the only issues excluded from judicial review are those concerning 'national defense'." However, the wording of the law clearly views "acts of state" as including national defense, diplomatic relations and other unspecified matters.

CCP which ultimately decides what are the "interests" of the state, society and the collective, and those interests invariably coincide with its own.

III. Legitimizing Repression

The gradual emergence of "state security" as a primary justification in Chinese law for the suppression of dissent and a rationale for the control of information is a part of the Party-state's project of "ruling the country by means of law". As the use of the concept of state security described below shows, there are fundamental differences between this project and the establishment of a "rule of law".

The concept of the rule of law, which is fundamental to the functioning of many modern societies, provides that all are equal before the law; that a legal system established through transparent procedures is superior to any other social norms; and that effective, independent and just judicial organs perform a crucial role in implementing these legal rules. By contrast, the system long advocated by China's leadership - ruling the country by means of law (*yi fa zhi guo*) - concentrates overwhelmingly on legal rules and the obedience of citizens to those rules. Law is regarded as a pure instrument parallel to other methods of social control, and does not have the nature of supremacy. This view derives partly from the "legalist" tradition of imperial China.

This concept was what President Jiang Zemin identified at the 15th CCP Congress as the central objective of his version of political reform, summed up by the following slogan: "ruling the country by means of law and building a socialist country ruled by law". The rationale for this is primarily maintaining party rule: "Ruling the country by means of law joins together upholding the leadership of the CCP, giving full play to people's democracy and doing things strictly in accordance with law, thus guaranteeing the full implementation of the Party's basic line and its basic policies as well as ensuring that the Party is in command of the overall situation from beginning to end and serves as the coordinating leadership core".[25]

In China's system of rule *by* law, repression is carried out according to published rules and through established procedures which provide a veneer of legitimacy for what still amount to systematic denials of basic rights. In cases involving dissidents, the legal process is merely a show which reflects the government's preference for using "law" to deal with such issues, but compared with previous more overtly "political" methods, the results are hardly different - and equally predictable.

A glaring example is provided by the stock response to questions about imprisoned dissidents, such as Wei Jingsheng and Wang Dan, sentenced to prison

---

[25] *See* "In his Report to the 15th Party Congress, Jiang Zemin Proposes: Push Forward Reform of the Political Structure, Strengthen Construction of Democracy and the Legal System," *Legal Daily*, September 14, 1997.

terms of fourteen and eleven years respectively, having both been convicted of "conspiracy to subvert the government".[26] "Their cases were handled not because of their political views or religious beliefs, but because they violated the criminal law of China", said Jiang, on the eve of his landmark visit to the United States.[27] But the "crimes" Wei and Wang committed, as detailed by the prosecution indictments and the courts' verdicts in their cases, involved only such acts as publishing articles, making statements, collecting money for victims of political persecution and discussing "the struggle" with friends, all clearly within the scope of the internationally protected rights to freedom of expression and association.[28] The official line on Wei and Wang is that their non-violent advocacy of human rights and democracy constituted a "conspiracy to subvert the government" and a threat to national security.

Such a misuse of law, justified by invoking national security concerns, has been highlighted by the U.N. Special Rapporteur on States of Emergency, Leandro Despouy. His 1994 report to the U.N. Commission on Human Rights stated:

> A particularly disturbing development is that these laws [citing national security and similar concerns] introduce, under normal circumstances, restrictions on rights which may be suspended only during formally declared states of emergency. What is more, the ordinary legislation in question occasionally affects even inalienable rights from which no derogation is possible, even under exceptional circumstances.[29]

As the Special Rapporteur's report shows, China is far from the only state to abuse the concept of national security in this way. As in many other countries, in the Chinese legal system, state security and what constitutes harm to it are poorly defined and the authorities have ample scope to employ whatever interpretations suit their purposes. As mentioned above, Chinese courts are not authorized to review the legality of laws or regulations, and thus no review of such interpretations is provided for. Chinese legal scholars barely dare to touch on the subject of state security or state secrets, let alone to propose limits to the reach of these concepts. All the laws relating to state security and state secrets suffer from a crucial omission: there is no effort whatsoever in any of them to establish clear-cut standards to determine that any act has actually proved harmful or could have done so. Prosecutors in individual

---

[26] As this paper went to press, in November 1997 Wei Jingsheng was suddenly released from prison on medical parole on condition that he went into exile in the United States.

[27] Tom Korski, "Jiang in UN Charter Vow," *South China Morning Post*, October 26, 1997.

[28] On the prosecution of Wei, *see* Human Rights in China, *A Travesty of Justice: The Show Trial of Wei Jingsheng* (Mar. 4, 1996); and on the case of Wang, *see* Human Rights Watch/Asia, *China: Slamming the Door on Dissent, Wang Dan's Trial and the New "State Security" Era* (Oct. 29, 1996).

[29] *Annual Report of the Special Rapporteur on States of Emergency*, UN Doc. E/CN.4/Sub.2/1994/23 at para. 40 (1994).

cases have not attempted to demonstrate harm and judges have not requested any such showing. An authoritative statement supports this attitude:

> According to ... the law, where activities involving conspiracy to subvert the government, splitting the nation or the overthrow of the socialist system are concerned, it is not necessary that any actual harmful consequences should ensue; provided only that such actions have been performed, then legal responsibility must be pursued.[30]

In practice, therefore, the concept of state security is as much a political construct as was counter-revolution. The various pieces of legislation which provide for its use were enacted over a number of years. The State Security Law and the State Secrets Law in particular were important steps in this process.

IV. State Secrets Law

Despite the fact that there was little legislation in existence governing state secrets and thus no agreed definition of the concept itself, during the drafting of the State Secrets Law in the late 1980s, a period of relative liberalism in terms of academic debate, there was virtually no public discussion over how the scope of state secrets should be legally defined. However, some legal scholars expressed concern over this privately.

Even so, in many ways the 1988 State Secrets Law, while still containing serious ambiguities, was a significant improvement over the previous system, in that it recognized that there should be a formal classification system for secret materials restricting their circulation to specific categories of people and subject to specific time limits.[31] Under the 1951 Provisional Regulations on the Protection of State Secrets which the new law superseded, almost anything could be classified as a state secret: "Indeed, a 'presumption of secrecy' might be said to pervade the PRC's approach to the flow of information", wrote one scholar of the pre-1988 regime.[32] These regulations contained no procedure for determining whether or not a particular item was a state secret.

But under the State Secrets Law the scope of classified information remained vast and infinitely expandable. While covering many of the obvious areas – national defense, diplomatic affairs, science and technology and criminal investigations – the State Secrets Law's definition also includes questionable categories such as "major policy decisions on state affairs", "secret matters in national economic and social

---

[30] NPC Standing Committee's Legislative Commission, Criminal Law Section, *An Explanation of the PRC State Security Law* (1993).
[31] *See* Timothy A. Gelatt, "Recent Development: The New Chinese State Secrets Law," 22 *Cornell Int'l L.J.* 255 (1989).
[32] *Id.* at 255.

development", "those secret matters of political parties .... [that] concern the security and interests of the state" and a catch-all clause, "other state secret matters that the state secrecy preservation departments determine should be preserved".[33]

The tentative move towards a more restricted and formalized system represented by the passage of the State Secrets Law, however, was reversed with the implementing regulations and other corresponding rules for the law, passed after the 1989 crackdown, which failed to duplicate even the minimal level of specificity of the law itself.[34] These rules delegated the power to ascertain the classification level[35] of state secrets to a range of different departments and let them decide independently what should be considered a secret.[36] Although various procedures are established in these regulations for the specific marking of secret materials and for time limits on their classification, these allow the authorities enormous latitude. But they have been ignored in a number of important cases.

For example, documents about Party meetings which the prosecution claimed were "top secret" were not marked with such a designation when she read them, said freelance journalist Gao Yu, arrested in 1993. The official who showed her the documents wrote "top secret" on them in handwriting after she had read them, which her lawyers argued did not comply with the formal classification procedures. Furthermore, the defense demonstrated that the information contained in the documents, which Gao used in a political commentary for a pro-Beijing Hong Kong news magazine, had been widely reported elsewhere *before* she used it. But the court ignored all these arguments and sentenced Gao to six years' imprisonment for "leaking important state secrets".[37]

---

[33] PRC Law on the Preservation of State Secrets, adopted by the NPC Standing Committee on September 5, 1988, Article 8.

[34] *S ee* particularly Implementation Regulations for the PRC Law on the Preservation of State Secrets (1990).

[35] The State Secrets Law recognizes three categories of classification: "secret" (*mimi*), "highly secret" (*jimi*) and "top secret" (*juemi*). The duration of classification for "secret" items is generally ten years, that of the "highly secret" twenty years, while for "top secret" materials the period is thirty years. Furthermore, material in any of the three categories may also be labeled a "long-term" (*changqi*) secret – in other words, indefinitely classified.

[36] The law itself confers classification authority very broadly, stating in Art. 10:

> The specific scope of state secrets and their grades of secrecy shall be stipulated by the state secrecy preservation departments in conjunction respectively with the foreign affairs, public security or state security and other relevant central organs. Provisions on the specific scope of state secrets and their grades of secrecy shall be promulgated within the relevant spheres.

[37] Human Rights in China and Human Rights Watch/Asia, *China – Leaking State Secrets: the Case of Gao Yu* (July 1995), contains translations of documents from Gao's trial, as well as an examination of the application of the State Secrets Law more generally.

Another case demonstrates that the information in question need not even be contained in classified documents or be disclosed by any official to be considered secret. Human rights activist Li Hai was found guilty by a Beijing court, according to its verdict, of "prying into and gathering the following information about people sentenced for criminal activities during the June 4, 1989, period: name, age, family situation, crime, length of sentence, location of imprisonment, treatment while imprisoned". The court ultimately rejected the prosecution's argument that Li's crime involved "leaking state secrets", since no evidence was presented that he had disseminated the prisoner list he had compiled through house-to-house visits with the families of the individuals concerned. Nevertheless, the court ruled that facts concerning the outcome of what were supposed to be public trials were "high-level state secrets". In December 1996, Li was sentenced to nine years' imprisonment.[38]

As these cases indicate, the scope of what is considered secret under the regulations issued by different authorities is enormous. In a set promulgated jointly by the State Secrets Administration and the Supreme People's Procuratorate, subjects ranked "top secret" include information about the Strike Hard Anti-Crime Campaign, the number of people sentenced to death or charged with counter-revolutionary crimes and reports about cases involving cadres of above-provincial level or members of ethnic minority groups.[39] According to regulations issued by the Ministry of Public Security, virtually all information relating to crime and law enforcement is "state secrets" unless the Public Security organs have specifically permitted its publication.[40] Information on cases of torture and drug smuggling are in the category of "highly secret", in regulations of both the procuratorates and the public security departments.

Other regulations enacted before the State Secrets Law but remaining in effect keep secret such absurd items as "the actual cost of commodities exported to earn foreign currency",[41] accidents occurring in the course of industrial production and the situation of epidemic diseases. Even the curriculum in university courses within the minor concentration in state secrets is itself secret.[42] Other official documents demonstrate clearly that the CCP routinely suppresses potentially

---

[38] *See* Mark Goellner, "Li Hai" (prisoner profile), *China Rights Forum* (Human Rights in China, eds., 1997).

[39] Regulations on the Scope and Classification Level of State Secrets Concerning the Work of the Procuratorates, promulgated by the Supreme People's Procuratorate and the National Secrets Protection Administration, October 23, 1989, at Art. 2(1).

[40] *See, e.g.*, Provisional Regulations on the Scope and Classification Level of State Secrets Concerning the Work of the Public Security Organs, passed by the Ministry of Public Security, January 18, 1986.

[41] State Statistical Bureau, The Practical Administration of Statistical Materials Concerning State Secrets, March 15, 1985, Art. 2 (5).

[42] *Id.* at Arts. 3(6) & 3(7).

embarrassing information, an effort in which it has also enlisted the concept of state secrets.[43]

One regulation still conflates the terms "internal use only" (*neibu*) and "domestic publication" (*guonei faxing*)[44] with state secrets despite the fact that these terms do not appear in either the law or its implementing regulations. Many people have been convicted, both before and after enactment of the State Secrets Law, of leaking state secrets for disclosing such information.

In 1993 a couple, Bai Weiji and Zhao Lei, were sentenced to ten- and six-year terms respectively on the charge of "leaking state secrets" merely for translating materials from magazines marked "internal use only" for *Washington Post* correspondent Lena Sun. Bai and Zhao, both unemployed because of their involvement in the 1989 Democracy Movement, had been doing freelance translation for Sun. Two others, Wang Jun and Tang Yi, also received two- and four-year sentences in the same case.[45]

Since the early 1990s, the majority of known cases involving secrets prosecutions have involved Chinese journalists, although many prosecutions of officials may have occurred which were not reported. In all cases, regardless of

---

[43] *See, e.g.*, CCP Central Committee Propaganda Department, "Notice on Doing a Good Job of News Reports and Propaganda on the Rectification of Party Work Styles," *zhong xuan fa wen* [1986] No. 5, March10, 1986, *in Judicial Handbook*, at 783-84 (1989), which states:

> [We] should differentiate between internal and public reports and defend the image of the judicial organs. All reporting which could possibly damage the image of the People's Liberation Army, the public security organs, the procuratorates, the courts, the judicial administration, the state security organs, the customs office, or our diplomatic image must not be made public without prior approval from the central leadership.

See also, CCP Central Committee Propaganda Department, "Several Opinions on Propaganda Relating to Phenomena in the Anti-Corruption Campaign," *zhong xuan fa wen* [1989], No. 11, September 9, 1989, *in IV Collection of Party Documents on Propaganda Work*, at 1889 (1994), which reads in part:

> Negative reports should be strictly controlled and should not be excessively publicized or become a focus all at once. For those cases to be reported nationwide, approval should be sought from the Central Discipline Inspection Commission, the Ministry of Supervision and the judicial departments. If local reports are to be publicized nationwide, this should be done only by Xinhua News Agency.

[44] The Practical Implementation by the State Secrets Protection Administration and the State Customs Bureau of Regulations on the Administration of Exit of Documents, Materials And Other Items Concerning State Secrets, Ministry of Justice, June 20, 1990. Art. 1 (4) states that if internal documents and materials bearing designations such as "internal use only" or "domestic publication" are to leave the country, permission must be granted in advance from the Ministry of Justice's Committee on the Preservation of State Secrets.

[45] For more information on this and other cases involving secrets, *see* Amnesty International, *State Secrets: A Pretext for Repression*, AI Index: ASA 17/037/1996 (Nov. 1996).

whether the information concerned had subsequently been made public, trials were held *in camera* and usually even family members were not permitted to attend.[46] In some cases, the "secret" information had been published only in the domestic press.[47] In many of these cases, as in that of Bai Weiji and Zhao Lei, the courts demonstrated an extreme lack of proportionality in their sentencing, meting out heavy penalties for "crimes" which could only be defined as minor, if criminal at all, according to the relevant laws and regulations.[48] Such prosecutions were widely interpreted as being aimed particularly at Hong Kong journalists and mainlanders who choose to assist foreign correspondents. According to a 1989 publication, in 50 percent of cases involving illegal disclosure of state secrets journalists were responsible, while government officials revealing such material in their articles accounted for 40 percent and disclosures connected with dereliction of duty by government officials were only 10 percent of cases.[49] Unfortunately, more recent figures are not available.

Another major target of prosecutions on secrets charges has been Chinese nationals working for foreign companies, who, as part of their work, have disclosed economic information which in most countries would generally be considered public knowledge.[50]

The evolution of the legal regime relating to secrets in the reform period shows the gradual expansion of the types of persons subject to ever heavier penalties for revealing information officials wish not to be disclosed. In the 1979 Criminal Code, two types of offenses relating to secret materials were defined: "stealing, secretly gathering and providing intelligence for an enemy" (Article 97), punishable by life imprisonment or death; and violation of laws and regulations governing

---

[46] For example in the case of Wu Shishen, a Xinhua News Agency journalist sentenced to life in prison in 1993 for allegedly selling an advance copy of Jiang Zemin's political report to the 1992 14th CCP Congress to a Hong Kong journalist. Obviously nothing about the material in question was secret by the time of the trial, since the report had been presented publicly to the Congress.

[47] For several such cases, *see* Zhang Weiguo, "Sealing in Dissent: Secrets Laws Aim at Scaring Internal Critics into Silence," *China Rights Forum*, (Human Rights in China, eds., 1995).

[48] Another notable example is the case of Xi Yang, sentenced in 1994 to a 12-year term for reporting on China's plans to sell gold on international markets and on interest rate policies, information given him by a People's Bank of China clerk, Tian Ye, who received a 15-year sentence. The information in question could only be considered as the lowest level of classification ("secret"), yet Xi was prosecuted under the State Security Law. Xi was released on parole in early 1997.

[49] "Secrets Law and News Reporting," 5 *China Reporter*, 1989, *cited in* H. L. Fu & Richard Cullen, *Media Law in the PRC* (Aug. 1996).

[50] *See, e.g.*, "Oil giant employee released after year," *South China Morning Post*, March 14, 1997. In this instance, a Chinese employee of Royal Dutch/Shell, Xiu Yichun, was detained for a year on charges of "stealing state secrets". Although she was not prosecuted (and her employers said they had kept the case quiet trying to find a resolution), Xiu's counterpart at the China National Offshore Oil Corporation is thought to be still in detention and may face prosecution. Nothing is publicly known of what "secrets" the case allegedly involved.

secrets (Article 186), punishable by a maximum of seven years in prison. Article 186 of the Code made clear that "state personnel" were the main targets of the prohibition on violating the laws and regulations on secrecy and disclosing secrets, although "consideration [could] be given according to the circumstances" to prosecution of people who were not state employees. Despite its establishment of formal classification procedures, however, the 1988 State Secrets Law implies that all Chinese people may have an obligation to guard secrets: "All state organs, armed forces, political parties, social organizations, enterprises, institutions and citizens have the duty to preserve state secrets" (Article 3). Commentaries have appeared in newspapers reminding members of the public of their responsibility to "protect state secrets".

At the same time as it promulgated the State Secrets Law, the NPC Standing Committee issued regulations that essentially created a new category of offense, identifying the target of prosecutions as: "Anyone who steals, secretly gathers, buys or illegally provides state secrets for institutions, organizations or individuals outside the country". These regulations also drastically increased the available penalties for offenses under the State Secrets Law.[51] These 1988 regulations filled in what the government perceived as a blank in the secrets regime, by allowing the authorities to punish *anyone* for leaking state secrets to *anyone else*. Thus, a third category of secrets offense was formed, which did not necessarily involve either an enemy or an official breaking the rules. These regulations also introduced the expansive formulation "institutions, organizations and individuals outside the country" which would later become such a key element of the State Security Law. Consequently, this change laid the groundwork for the conceptualization of secrets and other offenses in the State Security Law, and ultimately, the new Criminal Code.

V. State Security Law

By definition, an offense under the State Security Law involves some foreign element. On its face much of this law appears little different from laws of other countries on protecting national security interests. According to some commentators:

> The National Security Law was passed to strengthen the anti-espionage powers of the government and to counter, through specific enforcement mechanisms, the perceived adverse increase in foreign involvement in China's political and social affairs. National security threats are, by definition, limited to those involving some

---

[51] Supplementary Decision of the NPC Standing Committee Concerning Punishing Crimes of Leaking State Important Secrets, passed by the Third Plenary Meeting of the Standing Committee of the Seventh National People's Congress, September 5, 1988.

> links outside of China. Purely internal subversive activities fall within the jurisdiction of the regular police.[52]

While such a view could be taken from a literal reading of the law and its implementing regulations, it seems over-generous, given the way the authorities have actually used the law. Those regarded as contributing to the "adverse increase in foreign involvement in China's political and social affairs" have included human rights organizations, for example. The State Security Bureau forces and its facilities have been deployed in a number of cases involving expression of opinion.

An offense may either be carried out by "organizations, groups and individuals outside the territory, or [be] instigated and financed by them but carried out by others" or it may involve acts carried out by parties inside the country "in collusion with organizations, groups and individuals outside the territory". Five types of crimes are envisaged: "plotting to subvert the government, dismember the state and overthrow the socialist system"; espionage; "stealing, secretly gathering, buying and illegally providing state secrets for an enemy"; instigating state personnel to defect or rebel; and "engaging in other sabotage activities against state security".[53] This last catch-all clause is a common feature of Chinese laws, and essentially leaves the definition of the act to the discretion of the authorities concerned.[54]

However, the detailed implementing regulations go far beyond legitimate national security concerns into outright prohibition of political or religious advocacy.[55] The State Security Law is a direct product of the suppression of the 1989 protests. The political motive was obvious: the government wanted to preempt any possibility of the kind of "peaceful evolution"which had occurred in the former Eastern Bloc countries, while also seeking to make prosecution of dissenters appear

---

[52] Fu & Cullen, *supra* note 24 at 467.

[53] PRC State Security Law, adopted by the NPC Standing Committee on 22 February 1993, Art. 4.

[54] Fu & Cullen, however, state: "The positive contribution of the [State Security Law] is that, together with the [implementing regulations], it defines, in some detail, what constitutes a threat to national security". *Supra* note 24 at 467. While they do point out a number of problems with the law and with lack of supervision of agencies enforcing it, overall they present a fairly optimistic view which, we believe, is not borne out by the reality of its implementation and the subsequent use of the term "state security".

[55] Fu & Cullen, *id.* at 455-57, claim that the sweeping powers conferred on the authorities under this law caused some disquiet, even within the system. This was demonstrated, they write, by the fact that the NPC Standing Committee amended the original draft to restrict the scope of the law somewhat, in particular changing the catch-all clause from "other activities endangering state security" to the final "other sabotage activities endangering state security" (Art. 4(5)). However, these formulations are little different, since the term "sabotage" is not defined in the law.

more acceptable internationally.[56] Furthermore, the State Security Law is linked to what the authorities tacitly agree are the provisions on political offenses,[57] since it does not contain any sentencing guidelines but refers for enforcement principally to the counter-revolution clauses of the 1979 Criminal Code.

The clearest indications of the State Security Law's intended role in suppressing freedom of expression are contained in the implementing regulations for the law,[58] in particular Article 8 which contains a laundry list of activities which may be considered as falling under "other sabotage activities". These include "fabricating or distorting facts, publishing or disseminating written or verbal speeches, or producing or propagating audio and video products", "establishing social organizations or business institutions", "using religion", "creating national disputes or inciting national splittism" and "activities of individuals outside the country who disregard dissuasion and meet with personnel in the country who have endangered state security, or who are seriously suspected of endangering state security".

The key to whether the types of actions listed in the implementing regulations contravene the law appears to be an administrative determination, to be made by the State Security Bureau or the Public Security Bureau, that the person or group in question is "endangering state security".[59] Thus, the central issue in determining whether an act is criminal becomes whether or not its author has been determined to be a "danger" to state security, a question to be decided solely by the powerful State Security Bureau and Public Security Bureau, which are not accountable to any other state body, including the NPC.[60]

> Where the implementing regulations indicate the basis for determinations about what agencies or persons are harmful to state

---

[56] "Peaceful evolution" is a term coined by the CCP leadership in the wake of the 1989 movement to describe an alleged campaign by Western governments to bring down China's socialist system. Part of this "strategy" involved sponsorship of dissident forces both inside and outside China, the Party claimed.

[57] One of the most recent examples of such an acknowledgment is an explanation of the proposals for the 1997 revisions to the Criminal Code by NPC Vice-Chairman Wang Hanbin. He said of the draft revisions: "Counter-revolutionary activities stipulated in the current [1979] Criminal Law are still all considered as crimes, with the exception that some of the activities will be dealt with as *ordinary criminal acts*". (Emphasis added). "Changes to Criminal Law 'Mostly Cosmetic'," *South China Morning Post*, December 26, 1996.

[58] The Detailed Implementation Regulations for the State Security Law were drafted by the Ministry of State Security, issued by the State Council and signed into law by Premier Li Peng on June 4, 1994, the fifth anniversary of the military crackdown on the 1989 demonstrations and thus a date which clearly indicated that the law's main target was dissenters of all kinds.

[59] *See* State Security Law, Arts. 2 & 33; Implementation Regulations for the Law, Art.5.

[60] Under the State Security Law, Arts. 6-12, the State Security Bureau is given enormous powers, ranging from stop and search to commandeering vehicles, using surveillance equipment and controlling entry into the country. *See also* Fu and Cullen, *supra* note 24 at 458-63.

security, they are largely circular. As Wang Dan wrote in 1994:

> These Detailed Implementation Regulations are supposed to be practical interpretations of the State Security Law, but the basic premise of such definition is that repeating the concept does not provide a sufficient interpretation.... But when it comes to the practical explanation of the concept we would all most like to see defined, namely 'endangering state security,' it is apparent that the definitions are nothing but tautologies. For instance, actions defined in the Regulations as 'harmful to state security' include giving speeches and producing writings which harm state security. Obviously, this way of doing things makes it very easy to carry out what is essentially 'rule by man' in the process of law enforcement....[61]

In the case of the "hostile institutions" and "agents of espionage institutions" mentioned in the State Security Law,[62] the implementing regulations refer respectively to "institutions hostile to the PRC government and socialist system characterized by the people's dictatorship, as well as institutions which endanger state security" and "those people engaging in activities which endanger the People's

---

[61] Wang Dan, "Tightening the Net Around Dissidents," *China Rights Forum,* (Human Rights in China, eds., 1994).

[62] The term "hostile organizations" (*didui zuzhi*) appears only in Art. 25 of the State Security Law, which reads: "Provided a person who has been coerced or entrapped by hostile organizations into participating in activities which harm the state security of the People's Republic of China explains the facts to an institution of the People's Republic of China abroad in a timely fashion ... he or she should not be prosecuted". However, the term likely applies to all the organizations mentioned in the law which are considered to carry out actions "harmful" to state security. Human rights organizations, among other groups, have been described by Chinese officials as being "hostile". The implementing regulations appear to have expanded the term beyond the scope envisaged for it in the text of the law itself, a tactic which has often been used by administrative agencies to dilute any safeguards present in specific legislation.

The term "espionage organization" (*jiandie zuzhi*) appears in Art. 4(2) of the law, which states:

> All organizations and individuals carrying out acts which harm the state security of the People's Republic of China must be prosecuted under the law.... Acts which harm the state security of the People's Republic of China referred to in this law are the following acts harming the state security of the People's Republic of China carried out by institutions, organizations and individuals outside the borders, or instigated and subsidized by them but carried out by others, or carried out by organizations and individuals inside the borders in collusion with institutions, organizations and individuals outside the borders: ... Joining an espionage organization or accepting an assignment from an espionage organization or its representative.

Republic of China at the instigation of or commission of an espionage institution or its members".[63] Thus if an organization outside China is deemed to be "hostile", any act it performs, or any contact it may have with anyone inside China, could be labeled as "endangering state security". No definition of an "espionage institution" is contained in the regulations. Further, the State Security Bureau may designate any individual as being "suspected" of endangering state security, and under the implementing regulations even meeting with such a person could constitute an offense.

The implementing regulations describe an entirely opaque and arbitrary process for making these crucial determinations. There is no requirement that decisions that individuals and groups inside and outside the country pose a danger be made known to the people in question, or that any opportunity be provided for the individuals and groups so labeled to challenge that designation.

While the scope of the State Security Law and its implementing regulations has undoubtedly shaped the work of the State Security Bureau, it has not been frequently cited in actual prosecutions. This is partly because the law contains no sentencing guidelines, and thus any prosecutions have had to be based on a relevant provision of the 1979 Criminal Code. For example, while the State Security Law was cited in the indictments brought against Gao Yu and Wang Dan, it was not mentioned in the verdicts for those cases. References to "state security" in individual cases have continued to increase, however, thus suggesting the law's growing influence. A number of dissidents and others charged with related offenses have been held pre-trial in the Beijing State Security Bureau Detention Center, rather than in a detention center run by the regular police (the Public Security Bureau), indicating that their cases are being dealt with by the State Security Bureau.[64]

Another such person is Beijing native Han Chunsheng, sent to jail for sending letters to Voice of America. In its 1996 verdict, a Beijing court found that the twenty "reactionary" letters, which Han denied having written or sent, "attacked our country's socialist system and the current policies of the Chinese Communist Party, railed against and defamed the leaders of the Party and government and incited the overthrow of the people's democratic dictatorship". No evidence was presented that the letters ever reached Voice of America, let alone that they were broadcast, or that anyone was "incited" to action by them. Han's wife has not been able to find out what the letters actually said, or anything else about the case, and was not permitted to attend her husband's ostensibly public trial. In order to "seriously apply national law, uphold the people's democratic dictatorship and protect state

[63] Detailed Implementation Regulations, Arts. 4 & 5.

[64] For example, both Gao Yu (mentioned above) and Xiao Biguang, a religious dissident eventually sentenced to an administrative labor camp term under Reeducation Through Labor, were detained there.

security", the court sentenced Han to eight years of imprisonment. Prior to his conviction, he had been held in the Beijing State Security Bureau Detention Center.[65]

This is not the only case in which Chinese people's contacts with foreign media organizations have been cited as threats to state security. For example, in 1996, after Xinna, the wife of imprisoned Inner Mongolian dissident Hada, accepted an interview with Voice of America on a mobile phone belonging to her elder brother, the provincial Public Security Bureau confiscated the phone on the grounds that it was "an instrument used for carrying out activities harmful to state security". The phone has still not been returned to its owner.[66]

Like the State Secrets Law, the State Security Law contains the presumption that all citizens have a role in protecting the security of the state. The latter states that all citizens are "duty-bound to safeguard national security, honor and interests".[67] Individuals can be punished if they refuse to answer questions or provide evidence relating to the acts covered in the law.[68] "Offices, institutions and other organizations" are also required to "educate" their staff about protecting state security and "should mobilize and organize personnel in preventing and checking acts of harming state security".[69]

VI. The Criminal Code

Outside China, reporting on the NPC's March 1997 revisions to the 1979 Criminal Code focused on the removal of "counter-revolution" from China's statute book.[70] While in the 1980s, many of those who proposed eliminating the term counter-revolution sought an end to prosecutions for political offenses, in the 1990s the principal aim of the change was to enhance the legitimacy of China's legal system, diffusing the intense international criticism which had followed the suppression of the 1989 Democracy Movement and reflecting the Party-state's new priorities in the categorization of its "enemies".[71] Thus the change proved to be more cosmetic than real.

---

[65] The quotes are translated from Beijing No.1 Intermediate People's Court Criminal Case Verdict No. 2436 (1996) (unpublished Chinese document, on file with the authors); for more details, *see* George Wehrfritz, "The Case of '8964'," *Newsweek*, September 29, 1997.
[66] Human Rights in China Press Release No. 36, October 16, 1997.
[67] State Security Law, Art. 3.
[68] *Id.* Art. 26.
[69] *Id.* Art. 15.
[70] By contrast, a front page commentary in China's major newspaper hailing the revisions did not even mention this change. "The New Criminal Code Should Strike Root in the Hearts of the People," *Legal Daily*, March 19, 1997.
[71] For more on the background to the revisions of the Criminal Code, *see Whose Security?*, *supra* note 2 at 7-13.

The fact that the authorities do not intend to release any of the thousands of convicted "counter-revolutionaries" who remain in prison is the most telling indication that the change in terminology does not mean a departure from past practice.[72] Indeed, the gradual linguistic shift towards referring to political prisoners as "criminals who endangered state security" began long before the revisions were passed, as some of the cases mentioned below demonstrate.[73] Of course, it remains to be seen how the law is actually used, but these factors, as well as the evolution of the State Secrets and the State Security Laws, give little cause for optimism. All the indications are that the authorities intend continue using such legislation to imprison their critics.

The 1979 counter-revolution provisions and their 1997 replacement, the section entitled "Crimes Endangering State Security", have pride of place in the Criminal Code. Both occupy Chapter One of the Code's "Special Provisions" which describe specific offenses and the sentencing ranges, thus emphasizing the social significance the authorities attach to this part of the Code.

In the revised Criminal Code, expression may be restricted under provisions prohibiting secession and subversion (Articles 103 and 105 respectively), and those relating to state secrets and espionage (Articles 111 and 110 respectively). Articles 102, 106 and 113 provide for heavier punishments of these offenses in certain situations.

Expanding the provision in the old law on "splitting the nation" (Article 91) into a separate article, Article 103 is clearly aimed at pro-independence movements and activists in restive ethnic minority regions such as Tibet, Xinjiang and Inner Mongolia. Article 103(1) allows penalties of up to life imprisonment or even death for the crime of "organizing, scheming and carrying out activities to split the nation and sabotage national unity". Article 103(2) permits sentences of over five years, up to the statutory maximum of fifteen years for sentences of "fixed term imprisonment",[74] for "ringleaders" in acts of "incitement to split the nation and sabotage national unity", an echo of the "counter-revolutionary propaganda and incitement" charge in the old law. China has consistently interpreted incitement to

---

[72] "The punishment meted out for crimes of counter-revolution in the past will remain valid and cannot be altered", said Wang Hanbin, NPC Standing Committee Vice-Chairman, when introducing the new Criminal Code on Mar. 6, 1997.

[73] For a discussion of this, *see* Human Rights Watch/Asia, *China: Slamming the Door on Dissent, Wang Dan's Trial and the New "State Security" Era* (Oct. 29, 1996). A September 1997 news report on sentence reductions in Tibet stated that one woman prisoner, released one year early, had been convicted of "endangering state security". This charge did not yet exist formally, since the revised Criminal Code had yet to come into force at this time. "132 Prisoners in Tibet Given Cut Terms, Parole," *China Daily*, Sept. 12, 1997.

[74] According to Article 45 of the new Criminal Code (a provision unchanged from the previous version) sentences of fixed term imprisonment may be between six months and fifteen years. However, Article 69 stipulates that when individuals are convicted of two or more charges, fixed term imprisonment sentences of up to 20 years may be imposed.

include even speech that is likely to provoke no reaction other than tarnishing the reputation of the state or the Party. Thus neither clause in the new Article 103 requires that any violence, or incitement to violence or other criminal behavior, be involved for the act in question to be an offense.

In Tibet, opposition to Chinese rule in the past twenty years has been overwhelmingly expressed through peaceful resistance, including demonstrations, the chanting of slogans, putting up posters, distributing leaflets and disseminating information abroad. Many individuals have been sent to prison for such acts. Prisoners serving sentences for counter-revolutionary offenses in Tibet make up a much higher proportion of the total inmate population than in mainland China. Minister of Justice Xiao Yang, speaking in 1993, said that in the whole country counter-revolutionaries made up only 0.3 percent of the prison population. But according to a confidential journal for prison officials, in Tibet such prisoners were 6.5 percent of the total number.[75] Other sources put the proportion in Tibet as high as 20 percent, of which the vast majority had been convicted of expression-related crimes.[76]

The clause most likely to be used against dissidents in China proper is Article 105. It combines various concepts from the old law: subversion, counter-revolutionary organization and counter-revolutionary propaganda and incitement,[77] as well as language from the State Security Law. The new article defines the offenses it covers as "organizing, scheming and acting to subvert the political power of the state and overthrow the socialist system" in 105(1) and "incitement to subvert the political power of the state and overthrow the socialist system by means of spreading rumors, slander or other means" in 105(2). Incitement to subversion seems to require little more than communicating dissenting opinions, not provoking violent or criminal acts. Sentences available range from probation to life imprisonment.[78]

If the fact that its precursors accounted for the vast majority of counter-revolution convictions in recent years is any guide – virtually all of the cases known to human rights groups fall into this category – Article 105 will probably be the most frequently used part of this chapter of the new Criminal Code. It codifies the

---

[75] *See* "A Discussion of the Special Characteristics of Ethnic Prisoners in the Tibetan Region and of Measures to Deal With Them," 5 *Research in Crime and Reform* (1991).

[76] This figure is based on the total number of counter-revolutionaries and ordinary prisoners in Tibet given by an official speaking to Western journalists on condition of anonymity in 1995, cited by the Tibet Information Network (TIN). TIN's analysis of a sample set of cases found that the vast majority had been convicted of "counter-revolutionary propaganda and incitement".

[77] Criminal Code of the People's Republic of China (1979), Article 92 ("conspiracy to subvert the government"); Article 98 (organizing and/or participating in a "counter-revolutionary group"); and Article 102 ("counter-revolutionary propaganda and incitement").

[78] In an important change, the death penalty, previously potentially applicable to those convicted of the type of crime now contained in Article 105(1), has been eliminated as an option for this offense. The death penalty was never applicable to Article 102 of the 1979 law.

rationale employed in the cases of Wei Jingsheng and Wang Dan, linking acts of free association and free expression with subversion. In both cases, the courts ignored the defendants' arguments that they had no intention of subverting the government: in essence, the determination that the authorities viewed the two as "endangering state security" was all the "proof" the court needed to convict.[79] This thinking has also been demonstrated in trials of lesser known dissidents. For example, although a group of Guizhou activists who drafted and distributed an open letter to the authorities calling for democratic reform, human rights improvements and the release of political prisoners were charged for counter-revolutionary organizing and propaganda and incitement, the verdict stated that the defendants "aimed to subvert the dictatorship of the proletariat and the socialist system .... [and] the leadership of the CCP".[80] Criticizing the government in a public fashion, such cases show, has thus become synonymous with subversion.

Espionage has always been interpreted extremely broadly in China.[81] Article 110 of the new law essentially covers the same crime of espionage as Article 97 in the 1979 law and maintains the same sentencing range – three years to life imprisonment, or death. The new article includes two main categories of offense: "joining an espionage organization or accepting an assignment from an espionage organization or its representative" in 110(1) and "identifying bombardment targets for an enemy" in 110(2). The text is unclear on whether those who carry out such "assignments" are required to be aware they are doing so for an entity identified by the authorities as a "spy organization".

While of course China may have a legitimate concern about spying by agents of foreign powers on its territory, in practice the actions attributed to people classified as "spies" often have little in common with such activities. Sometimes working for media outside China has been classified as spying, particularly during the 1989 Democracy Movement. A number of minority activists have been convicted of this offense, often on extremely flimsy evidence.

For example, in unconnected cases, Inner Mongolian scholar and activist Hada and Tibetan musicologist Ngawang Choepel were accused of this offense, yet no evidence was ever presented to show that either had access to any privileged information or that they passed anything resembling "intelligence" to any "spy organization". Both are from sensitive ethnic minority regions and were concerned

---

[79] *See* Human Rights in China, *A Travesty of Justice: The Show Trial of Wei Jingsheng* (March 4, 1996); Human Rights Watch/Asia, *China: Slamming the Door on Dissent, Wang Dan's Trial and the New "State Security" Era* (October 29, 1996); and on the conduct of Wang Dan's trial, Wang Lingyun, "A Fair Trial? Or a Farce?," *China Rights Forum*, Spring 1997 (Human Rights in China, eds., 1997).

[80] *See* the cases of Chen Xi, Huang Yanming, Liao Shuangyuan, Lu Yongxiang and Zeng Ning, in *Whose Security?*, *supra* note 2, at 40-49.

[81] During the Cultural Revolution, virtually any unauthorized contact with a foreigner could be labeled "spying".

about the preservation of their respective cultures; both received harsh sentences: fifteen years in prison for Hada, eighteen for Ngawang Choepel. Hada ran a Mongolian Studies book shop and was involved in founding the Southern Mongolia Democracy Alliance, an avowedly separatist organization, which pursued its goals through non-violence. He was said to have had contact with unspecified "Mongolian intelligence organizations".[82] Ngawang Choepel, a Tibetan who lived in exile in India, was collecting material for a film on traditional Tibetan music and dance. The authorities claimed that these activities were a cover for "gathering sensitive intelligence and engaging in illegal separatist activities", but did not make public any evidence.[83] In these two cases the designation "espionage" highlights the authorities' extreme sensitivity about contacts between people in such areas and outsiders.[84]

The new Criminal Code brought together provisions on secrets from various laws and also broadened the scope of the offense and persons to whom it might apply. Article 111 incorporates into the Criminal Code the main principles of the State Secrets Law and 1988 provisions allowing for heavier punishment for giving secret material to parties outside China.[85] Article 111 defines the offense as: "stealing, prying into, purchasing or illegally providing state secrets or intelligence for institutions, organizations and individuals outside the country". While this generally mirrors the formulation in the State Secrets Law, the vague term "intelligence" (*qingbao*) has been added, thus expanding the scope of materials covered beyond information classified in accordance with the formal system that law established. The full range of penalties is available for this crime, from probation to life imprisonment, or death.

Another example of the elastic notion of "secrets" is the case of Chadrel Rinpoche, who until his arrest in May 1995 was one of the most senior Tibetan lamas who cooperated with the authorities in Beijing. Chadrel, who headed the government-appointed search committee for the reincarnation of the Panchen Lama, was detained after he reportedly wrote to the Dalai Lama asking for his approval of the child the committee had identified as the new Panchen. Beijing had authorized such contacts in 1993, but disallowed them due to a shift in policy towards the exiled

---

[82] Inner Mongolian Autonomous Region Higher People's Court, Ruling in a Criminal Case, No.547 (1996)(unpublished document on file with the authors).

[83] For more detail on both these cases, *see Whose Security?, supra* note 2, at 40-49.

[84] This is not to say, however, that ethnic minorities are more likely to be charged with espionage; it merely demonstrates the flexibility with which these terms are used. For more information on the case of Ngawang Choepel, *see* Tibet Information Network, "18 Years for Tibetan `Spy': US Implicated," December 27, 1996.

[85] Supplementary Regulations of the NPC Standing Committee on the Punishment of Crimes Involving Leaking State Secrets, 1988.

Tibetan spiritual leader. Chadrel was tried *in camera* in April 1997, and sentenced to a six-year prison term for "leaking state secrets" and "splitting the country".[86]

A further provision on secrets in the revised Criminal Code, but not contained in the chapter on "Crimes Endangering State Security", removes the presumption that those with access to secrets will be officials, and does not require that the information in question be publicly disclosed for an offense to be committed. "Those who obtain state secrets through stealing, secretly gathering or buying" are subject to penalties of up to seven years in prison. It also adds the new offense, punishable by up to three years imprisonment, of failure to disclose the origins or use of illegally-obtained materials, documents or objects in the categories of "top secret" or "highly secret"

The new law expands the idea of "collusion ... to harm the sovereignty, territorial integrity and security of the PRC" to extend to contact with "foreign institutions, organizations and individuals".[87] Incorporating language from the State Security Law, this change significantly broadens the scope of the law, since it punishes contact with any foreign "forces", including individuals, rather than only with foreign states, as in the old law. Claims of such "collusion" have been a major feature of dissident trials in recent years, with telephone conversations about "the struggle" with friends and associates overseas as well as personal letters on the same subject being presented as examples in the cases of both Wang Dan and Wei Jingsheng. According to Article 106, which did not appear in the old code, persons whose offenses involved such collusion are subject to the heavier penalties in the sentencing ranges in the relevant articles.

Finally, Article 113 stipulates that the offenses specified in the chapter are to be additionally punishable by the death penalty whenever "the harm to the state and the people is especially serious and the circumstances especially odious".[88] This article essentially duplicates a similar provision in the 1979 code, while reducing by a small degree the scope of the death penalty's applicability to the offenses covered in the chapter.[89]

Although the provisions allowing for the criminalization of certain types of expression cover broadly similar ground in both the 1979 and 1997 versions of the

---

[86] *See* "News Update," *China Rights Forum*, (Human Rights in China, eds., 1997) and various publications and releases from the Tibet Information Network. On the shift in central government policy towards the Dalai Lama and the general climate in Tibet, *see Cutting Off the Serpent's Head, supra* note 12.

[87] Criminal Code of the People's Republic of China (1979), Art. 91; Criminal Code of the People's Republic of China (1997), Art. 102(1) (colluding with foreign states) and Art. 102(2) (colluding with foreign institutions, organizations and individuals).

[88] Some exceptions are cited: of the articles examined here, Art. 103(2) and Art. 105 are not punishable by death.

[89] Art. 113 also allows for the confiscation of property as part of the sentence for any of the crimes in the Chapter. As in the 1979 law, there is no requirement that the property be in any way related to the commission of the offense in question.

Criminal Code, the language in the new law is less clearly ideological in nature. Whereas in the old law, offenses of counter-revolution were defined in the chapter's first article as "All acts endangering the PRC committed with the goal of overthrowing the political power of the dictatorship of the proletariat and the socialist system",[90] in the revised version there is only one reference to socialism.[91] There is no definition at all of the central concept, endangering state security, despite the fact that this term has been expanded in a crucial fashion in the revised Criminal Code, as compared with the State Security Law: it now encompasses acts that are purely domestic in character.

The lack of definition, and the use to which the idea of state security has been put so far, do not give grounds for hope that the revised law's provisions will be used in a less arbitrary or more objective way than those they replaced. The very vagueness of the law makes it an effective weapon against the few "chickens" the Party-state selects, as well as a suitably ominous threat to the "monkeys". Indeed, all the signs are that if so selected, those who have dared to exercise their right to free expression could face harsher punishment than even five or six years ago. By linking expression-related offenses inextricably with more serious crimes such as subversion and secession, the new law appears to codify the legal view of pure speech as a form of "action" thus providing for even more severe treatment of such "crimes". Furthermore, the idea first put forward in the State Security Law and now incorporated into the Criminal Code that even contact with individuals outside China's borders can constitute "collusion" with "hostile foreign forces" indicates an attitude that hardly seems in conformity with the official policy of opening up to the outside world.

VIII. Conclusion

It is the people's prerogative, when faced with unreasonable individuals and unacceptable matters, to make criticism. Indeed, it is also their unshirkable duty to do so, and this is a sovereign right with which no individual or government organization has a right to interfere.

Criticism may not always be pretty or pleasant to hear, nor can it always be completely accurate. If one insists on hearing pleasant criticism only and demands its absolute accuracy on pain of punishment, this is as good as forbidding criticism and banning reforms altogether.

– Wei Jingsheng, at his October 1979 trial for counter-revolution[92]

---

[90] Criminal Code of the People's Republic of China (1979), Art. 90.

[91] In Art. 105, as described above.

[92] Quoted in Wei Jingsheng, *supra* note 3, at 225.

The above discussion and cases have shown that the Chinese Party-state uses the justification of protecting state security to restrict both the content and manner of expression of Chinese people. In recent years, Chinese citizens have faced prosecution and imprisonment for a broad range of expressive acts: publishing articles inside and outside China; acting as freelance correspondents for publications in Hong Kong and elsewhere; issuing petitions and open letters; speaking to foreign journalists, diplomats and friends outside China; writing letters to people outside China; making public speeches and chanting slogans; putting up wall posters and distributing leaflets; and publishing independent "illegal" newsletters and magazines.

The offending expression included the following content: criticisms of Government and Party policies on Tibet and other minority regions and advocacy of independence or greater autonomy for them; calls for improvements in human rights, for democratization and for press freedom; discussions of the way the instructions of Party leaders shape government policy; exposés of the nature and scope of repression, such as the crackdown on the 1989 Democracy Movement; discussion of historical questions, such as the role of Mao Zedong; proposals for greater tolerance in political and religious life; advocating free trade unions and freedom of association more generally; and discussion of problems relating to the "dark side" of life in China, such as the abysmal working conditions of migrant workers, poverty, the growing tax burden on peasants, official corruption and so on.

Of course, not all those who expressed themselves on these issues or used one of the forms of expression listed above were arrested and put on trial. The Chinese Party-state has no need to conduct such extensive repression to achieve its desired effect: a few "chickens" chosen at random are sufficient, and if too many people seem to be daring to speak up, the number can be increased whenever necessary.[93] The international outcry against the suppression of the 1989 protests – both the massacre itself and the nationwide arrests and prosecutions which followed – showed the Chinese leadership that there were limits to the tolerance of the international community, and thus this may be an inhibiting factor. But more importantly, the arbitrariness of the implementation of laws on state security and the vague and indeterminate nature of their definitions serve a crucial purpose in their role of controlling expression: no one really knows where the limits of acceptable behavior lie since it depends on the political priorities of those in power at any given moment. Exhortations that all citizens are somehow responsible for preserving these indeterminate entities, state security and state secrets, add to this effect.

---

[93] Between 1992 and early 1994, there was a significant relaxation of political controls on activists, and a number of significant initiatives were launched. However, a crackdown followed in which many of the organizers were arrested. But even during the period of relaxation, prosecutions of dissidents continued. *See* Liu Qing, "Devoted to Democracy and Human Rights: The Development of the Dissident Movement," *China Rights Forum*, (Human Rights in China, eds., 1995).

This means that in the new state security era, everyone must become a censor of his or her own public behavior. As imprisoned dissident Wang Dan foresaw in the commentary he wrote following the 1994 enactment of the Detailed Implementation Regulations for the State Security Law, such laws serve to further narrow the political space available to *all* Chinese citizens. Wang wrote:

> As the contradictions in society accumulate and sharpen, the use of such repressive measures is not only unreasonable but also harmful. When all the channels available for the expression of political opposition in open, legal fashion are closed, such political forces, which already exist, will merely be forced to participate politically in secret and illegal ways. In terms of social stability and progress, the disadvantages of this greatly outweigh any possible benefits.[94]

Dissidents are only the most obvious target of such laws; the repressive effects of the counter-revolution statutes have always been felt far beyond the confines of the community of people recognized internationally as "dissidents". There is no sign that the use of these statutes' successors, the provisions on state security, will be any different.

---

[94] Wang Dan, *supra* note 61.

EGYPT: NATIONAL SECURITY, FREEDOM OF EXPRESSION AND STATE SECRETS

Nagad Mohamed Al-Boray

I. Introduction

Despite the many fine words vaunting freedom of expression in Egypt, a number of detailed and often contradictory laws exist for the purpose of setting restrictions on that same freedom. Speaking out in whatever form constitutes a risk, subject to the whim of the government; if it so wishes, it may apply legal restrictions limiting the exercise of that freedom, or if it so wishes, it may show tolerance.

The series of laws limiting freedom of expression stretches back to 1937, when the Egyptian Penal Code was promulgated (30 July), and continues to the present with the passage on May 28, 1995 of Act 93, which amended provisions of the Penal Code, the Code of Criminal Procedure and, most controversially, the Law on the Press Syndicate.

This chapter reviews the most significant laws in Egypt limiting freedom of expression on national security grounds. The laws in question are discussed in three groups: those which claim to defend national security, those which involve insult to government officials and other public figures, and those which address threats to public security and peace. The chapter then briefly examines Egyptian criminal laws on revealing state secrets.

II. Freedom of Opinion: Constitutional Protections

Article 47 of the Constitution of the Egyptian Arab Republic of September 1971 states:

> Freedom of opinion is guaranteed. Everyone shall have the right to express his opinion, declare it orally or in writing or visual representation or other means of expression within the boundaries of the law and objective criticism, in order to guarantee the soundness of the national structure.[1]

Article 48 continues:

> Freedom of the press, printing, publishing and the media shall be guaranteed. Censorship of newspapers is forbidden; it is forbidden for the authorities to suspend or to cancel them. It is permitted as an exception under emergency law or in times of war that limited censorship may be imposed on newspaper publications and the

---

[1] All translations of the Egyptian Constitution are from Bar Association of Egypt, *The Egyptian Constitution and Main Complementary Laws,* Supplements to the 5th and 6th editions, 60th year of Al-Mohamah magazine (1980).

> media on matters related to public safety or for the purposes of national security, in accordance with the law.

Article 49 reads:

> The state shall guarantee freedom of scientific research, literary, artistic and cultural creativity and shall provide the necessary means to encourage this to be fulfilled.

Articles 207 and 208 provide strong constitutional protections of press freedom:

> Article 207: The press shall practice its message freely and independently in the service of society, reflecting the various trends of public opinion and contributing to shaping public opinion, strengthening the basic foundations of society, preserving public freedoms, rights and duties and respect for the sanctity of the private life of citizens, all in accordance with the law and Constitution.
>
> Article 208. Freedom of the press is guaranteed and censorship of newspapers is banned. Warning, stopping or canceling by government administrators is banned, all of which is in accordance with the Constitution and the law.

There are two general points to be made about the above provisions. First, they favor freedom of expression and opinion, including freedom of publishing, scientific research and artistic expression. Second, they allow these freedoms to be restricted by law and the Constitution.

These articles of the 1971 Constitution did not revoke previously adopted laws that place restrictions on freedom of expression. Moreover, Parliament has continued to adopt new restrictions and penalties on freedom of expression, several of which are discussed below.

Egyptian law grants its citizens complete freedom to *hold* opinions about any issue – political, religious or social – on condition that they do not communicate such opinions to others. An opinion must be overtly expressed to be subject to prosecution.[2]

---

[2] *E.g.*, Article 171 states:

> Any person who tempts another person to commit a felony or offense through talking or shouting in public, or by an act or gesture in public or in writing, by use of symbols or any other means of representation, shall be considered an accomplice in the act. He shall be penalized with the penalty stipulated for the act if the consequence of this provocation is the actual occurrence of the felony or offense. The talking or shouting shall be considered overt if made through any mechanical means in a public gathering or public street or any other frequented place or if made so that it may be heard by anyone who is in the street or if broadcast through the wireless or any other means. Written material, drawings, photographs, symbols and other forms of representation shall be considered overt if

III. Expression of Opinion Which Constitutes a Threat to National Security or the Basic System of the State

Although the phrases "national security" and "the basic system of the state" are not defined in law, there is general agreement among Egyptian jurists that "national security" is anything related to the independence of the state, its sovereignty or higher state interests. The "basic system" is the system established by the first and second chapters of the Constitution under the titles "The State" and "The Basic Foundations of Society".

These definitions tend to change with changes of regime. For example, the first chapter of Book Two of the Penal Code on felonies and offenses harming the security of the government from abroad, including crimes of expression that constitute a threat to national security, was fully amended after the 1952 Revolution (which saw the expulsion of the king and seizure of power by the military, subsequently legitimized through Act 112 of 1952).

A. Expression of Opinion Which Constitutes a Threat to National Security

Expression will be deemed to constitute a threat to national security if the state views it as harmful to the sovereignty of the state or its independence, that is, to its military, political, diplomatic or economic status. These are considered to be the four cornerstones of Egypt's national security.[3]

1. Harm to the country's military status may be caused by any act that affects the country's military power, at the stage of preparation for or during an actual military emergency, whether defensive or offensive, or that aims to disrupt a military alliance, obstruct an agreement to supply arms or demoralize the spirit of soldiers. The Cairo Criminal Court stated in a 1957 case that "to inform about the movements of the armed forces or to state their ability of defense and assault, to reveal information about their armaments, equipment or ammunition, or to give partial information about them, is harmful to the military status of the country and threatens its national security."[4]

2. Harm to the country's political status may be caused by any act or expression that harms the independence of the state and its foreign policy, such as by embarrassing the country in an international political organization or obstructing

---

distributed randomly amongst a number of people or if displayed so that they may be seen by anyone in a public street or any other frequented place or if sold or put up for sale anywhere.

[3] *See, e.g.*, Article 77 of the Penal Code, which makes it a crime to seek the assistance of, or work as spies for, a foreign state and by doing so harm the military, political, diplomatic or economic status of Egypt.

[4] Cairo Criminal Court, Case No. 716, year 1957, *Qasr Al Aini police station*, at 49.

political negotiations or enabling a foreign country to acquire political influence over the state. The Egyptian Parliament stated, in the course of discussions leading to adoption of Article 78 of the Penal Code (replaced by the present Article 77) that "Egypt's political status is its legal entity as an independent sovereign state."

3. Harm to the country's diplomatic status may be caused by any act that "may hinder diplomacy between Egypt and another state in a manner that leads to the termination of political relations or that may obstruct a diplomatic representative in carrying out his duties."[5]

4. Harm to the country's economic status implies anything that "may harm the economic system including the exchange control system and also matters related to agricultural and industrial production, foreign trade and finance."[6] Harm to the country's economic system was added to the concept of national security by Act 112 of 1958.

What are the types of expression which the law states are a threat to national security? Article 80 of the Penal Code makes it a crime to make false statements or report biased news, statements or rumors which may lead to the harming of military preparations or operations, or arouse panic among people or weaken the strength of the nation. The penalty varies from temporary hard labor if the crime involved a neutral foreign state, to hard labor for life if a hostile country was involved.

It is not relevant whether or not the statement has caused harm or aroused panic. A criminal act is committed simply by reporting statements, even if true and even if there is no actual negative consequence. They may be considered biased if they achieve a goal contrary to the government's policy and this may be considered "provocative propaganda" which could cause civil strife. Writes Dr. Abdel Hakim Foda, "an article or a statement that expresses discontent or criticism for the conditions of the standard of living and gross national product or for widespread corruption may be considered according to this article provocative propaganda that weakens the strength of the nation."[7]

Article 80d prohibits any Egyptian from publishing or declaring abroad any news or statements or false or biased rumors about the internal conditions of the country if such reporting might weaken financial confidence in the state or its prestige or harm the national interest of the country. Therefore, to publish an article on, for example, the widespread use of torture in Egypt which goes unpunished, or on the unrestrained spread of corruption, is against the law, even if the report is true, if it harms the prestige or honor of the state.

No consideration is given to whether the published material actually harmed the state's prestige. In fact, even if the report were seen to improve the state's image,

---

[5] Dr. Ahmed Fathi Sorour, *The Intermediary of the Penal Code,* at 44 (1970).

[6] Justice Mahmoud Ibrahim Ismail, ex-deputy chairman of the Court of Cassation, *Crimes against State Security from Abroad,* at 24 (1959, typed copy), study notes for students of the diploma in criminal science at Cairo University.

[7] Dr. Abdul Hakim Foda, *Comment on the Penal Code,* at 314 (1989).

for instance, by demonstrating the state's tolerance of dissent, the crime is still considered to have taken place. Thus, it is not necessary that the criminal goal is achieved.[8]

Article 77 of the Penal Code provides for the death penalty or imprisonment for a range of vaguely defined crimes against the state aimed at harming the state's interests. Article 77b states that "anyone who works for a foreign country, or who carries out intelligence work for it or who works for it in order to undertake hostile acts against Egypt, shall face the death penalty." Article 77c states the same, but replaces the phrase "hostile acts against Egypt" with the phrase "to aid it [a hostile country] in its military operations or harm the military operations of the Egyptian state". Article 77d punishes by imprisonment anyone who works with a foreign country or for its interests, or spies for it, causing harm to the military, political, diplomatic or economic status of Egypt.

A person may be convicted of attempting any of these acts even without having actually carried out any service to a foreign state.[9] The attempted or actual intelligence activity which may be punished by the death sentence does not have to involve contact with a representative of a foreign state. It suffices for the accused to have contact with any organization which a foreign state acknowledges legally even if it does not represent the authority of the state itself. So, contact with a newspaper or other organization, even a non-governmental organization (NGO), if recognized by a foreign state, may be punishable by death if the purpose is deemed to be to carry out "hostile acts against the Republic".[10] As stated by the Higher State Security Court, "a hostile act is any act that harms friendship or good relations between Egypt and a foreign state or harms the existing peace between them."[11]

The above makes clear that contact between any individual and an NGO from a foreign country in order to organize an international campaign against torture in Egypt could make that individual subject to the provisions of Article 77b and, therefore, to the death sentence.

B. Expression Which Threatens the Basic Structure of the State

As stated above, Chapters One and Two of the 1971 Constitution (Articles 1 to 39) establish the "basic structure of the state", including its social, ethical and economic foundations.

Article 98a *bis* of the Penal Code, supplemented by Act 34 of 1970, one of the most restrictive laws on freedom of expression, penalizes expression that allegedly

---

[8] Id. at 315.
[9] Dr. Fathi Sorour, *supra* note 5, at 26.
[10] Dr. Fathi Sorour, *supra* note 5, at 30.
[11] Higher State Security Court, Case No. 87, year 1961, and Case No 315, year 1961, registered on 20 July 1961.

threatens the basic structure of the state. Article 98a *bis* was promulgated during the time of President Nasser to protect the socialist one-party state, whose political organization consisted of a coalition of "the people's work force," including the workers, farmers, intellectuals, soldiers, and nationalist capitalism. This political system has been radically altered; since then, the Egyptian government fully adopted the capitalist system and political plurality. Therefore, logically, Article 98a *bis* should have been repealed.

Nevertheless, Article 98a *bis* continues to make illegal any organization that promotes enmity towards the principles upon which the socialist regime in Egypt is based. This promotion may be through writing, publishing, alluding or acting, as long as, in the government's view, its target is to incite people to hatred of the socialist system or to promote a system that contradicts its goals. Any person who "forms, organizes or manages" such an organization may be punished with imprisonment of up to 25 years and a fine of between 100 and 1,000 pounds. A person who joins such an organization or participates in its activities, knowing its purposes, may be punished with up to five years' imprisonment and a fine of between 50 and 500 pounds. The same penalties are applicable to anyone who "incites hatred and disdain" for the socialist system or the principles upon which it is based; who possesses printed materials or recordings for distribution or broadcast aimed at inciting such hatred or disdain; or who possesses the means used to print or broadcast such materials or recordings.[12]

---

[12] Article 98a *bis* states:

> Anyone who forms, organizes, or manages a society, organization or group whose purpose is to promote, through any means, opposition to the basic principles upon which the socialist system of the state is founded, or which incites hatred or disdain, or acts against the coalition of the people's work force, or incites resistance to the public authorities, or promotes or recommends any such matter, shall be punished by imprisonment [of up to 25 years] and a fine no less than one hundred pounds and no more than one thousand. Anyone who joins these societies, bodies, organizations or groups, or participates in their activities knowing the goal they promote shall be penalized by imprisonment for a period that does not exceed five years and a fine no less than fifty pounds and no more than five hundred. The same penalty applies to anyone who challenges in any manner the basic principles upon which the socialist system of the state is founded, or anyone who incites hate and disdain for these principles, or anyone who promotes matters against the coalition of the people's work force or incites others against the public authorities. The same applies to anyone who possesses, either directly or through an intermediary, publications or printed matter which promote any of the aforementioned goals, if they are prepared for distribution or for others to read, or to anyone who possesses any means of printing, recording or broadcasting used for any of the aforementioned purposes even if only temporarily.

Article 98a *bis* does not require that, for the expression to be criminal, it must involve or advocate force or terrorism since the crime takes place regardless of the means used. A person may be punished for possessing publications, leaflets or books that argue against the socialist system or devalue it or give an explanation of its drawbacks or show a preference for any other system to it. There does not need to be a large circulation, it is enough that the materials are available for others to read. The Court of Cassation stated that, in adopting Article 98a *bis*,

> Parliament aimed at protecting the Constitution and all of the basic structures derived from the Constitution and established pursuant to it ... [from threats to their existence] ranging from incitement to overthrow [them] to hating or disdaining them. And if the law does not require that the phrases of incitement be in a specific form, there is no doubt that for the crime to take place and have both its material and moral elements met, these phrases must lead to the incitement banned by the law. Also, the law's wording means that the criticism which is directed on its face to a specific body or specific people may still be aimed in practice at the regime itself [and so be subject to prosecution], but this can only be concluded from actual phrases used according to the intention behind them.[13]

For example, the Court of Cassation has made clear that a leaflet that "contains advocacy for the Soviet regime and ... communist doctrine, and encouragement to adopt it" violates the law.[14] Moreover, "it is sufficient for the requirements of the law for someone to address one individual in a private assembly or a private place without going public."[15] In another case, the Court of Cassation further explained: "Punishment according to the law falls upon whomever promotes or advocates doctrines which aim at changing the principles and systems of society, even if he does not personally advise using these doctrines or declares that he does not advise others to use them."[16]

In 1992, Parliament adopted another law which restricts freedom of expression on grounds similar to (without, however, repealing) Article 98a *bis*. Article 86 *bis*, promulgated by Act 97 of 1992 and called the anti-terrorism amendment by the media, states:

> Anyone who forms, founds, organizes, or administers a society, body, organization, group or gang in violation of the law with the purpose of promoting in any manner the breakdown of the institutions established by the Constitution or laws; prevents one of the state institutions or one of the public authorities from practicing their work; attacks the personal freedom of citizens; or

---

[13] Cassation session May 13, 1949, Quarter Century Group, part 1, at 319 (1970).
[14] Cassation session May 18, 1954, Quarter Century Group, part 1, at 321 (1970).
[15] Id., at 320, clause 8.
[16] Cassation session December 16, 1935, Quarter Century Group, part 1, at 320, clause 5.

> inflicts harm upon the national unity or social peace shall be punished by imprisonment [of up to 25 years].
> Anyone who undertakes the command or leadership of such an entity, or provides it with material or financial assistance, while knowing the goal it promotes shall be punished by temporary hard labor.

Anyone who joins such an organization or participates in its activities while knowing its goals shall be punished by imprisonment of up to five years. Also punishable by up to five years' imprisonment is anyone who promotes verbally, in writing or by any other means the goals mentioned in the first clause; who possesses (in person or through an intermediary) publications or recordings that promote or encourage such goals if intended for distribution to others; or who possesses any means of printing, recording, or broadcasting that has been used, or is being prepared for use, even if temporarily, for the printing, recording, or broadcasting of any of the above mentioned messages.

During the discussion of this article in Parliament, MP Lotfy Wakid stated:

> The contents of this article may threaten the freedom of the press, the freedom of thought, and the freedom of balanced debates between all parties. To criminalize thoughts which run counter to what we believe to be correct will in practice promote underground thoughts. To counter ideas with ideas is the true confrontation which will lead to convincing the people. To ban a group of people and set restrictions upon them no matter how much we disagree with them will lead to underground work. This article, in this form, will apply more to non-terrorists. For example, the article makes subject to punishment anyone who 'inflicts harm upon ... social peace'. What is likely to inflict harm on social peace is open to debate, and there are several points of view. It is possible that I may write something aiming to promote social peace, while another party may view this same writing as a threat to social peace. Therefore, this article in its present form cannot be justified, and in the end, it will lead to the destruction of all aspects of democracy that exist in the country, from freedom of thought to freedom of the press.

In reply to the above comments, the Chairman of Parliament and the Minister of Justice stated that Article 86 *bis* merely restated Article 98a *bis*, and that its only addition was to make incitement or promotion of some ideas crimes punishable by law.[17] Lawyer Abdallah Khalil commented:

> Article 86 *bis* of the Penal Code has created a dangerous restriction on freedom of opinion and expression. It reflects the habit of

---

[17] Minutes of Parliament, Session 102 of 15 July 1992, at 22-23.

> Egyptian legislators to search for any restrictions in other legislation [in this case, Article 129 of the German Penal Code] and add them to Egypt's Penal Code while not balancing these restrictions with any safeguards or rights for citizens [as contained in the legal system from which the legislation is borrowed]. In fact, these restrictions are matched by an actual reduction of safeguards .... Article 86 *bis* penalizes the promotion of ideas of any sort, even if they are peaceful. But, demanding changes in the Constitution or the abolition of a law bears no relation to terrorist acts, since the Constitution was adopted by people and is subject to amendment. To demand amendment of the Constitution either individually or within a pacifist group is a right of both individuals and groups.[18]

A third law (in addition to Articles 98a *bis* and 86 *bis*) which imposes excessive and vaguely-worded restrictions on freedom of expression is Article 98b. This Article states:

> Anyone who manipulates religion for promoting or encouraging verbally, in writing, or in any other way extremist ideas with the purpose of creating strife or demeaning or disdaining one of the divine religions or the groups that belong to these religions, or for harming national unity and social peace, shall be punished by imprisonment for a period of no less than six months and no more than five years or by a fine of no less than five hundred pounds and no more than a thousand pounds.

This article was added to the Penal Code by Act 29 of 1982 on 22 April 1982.[19] The clarification memorandum on the law states that the article was added to penalize anyone who manipulates religion to promote extremist ideas, incite religious strife or demean one of the divine religions or groups that belong to them. The legislation is aimed at stopping the use of the Islamic religion or Koranic texts to demean the Christian religion, and *vice versa*. Therefore, the accusation of atheism negates the charge of manipulating religion because manipulating religion assumes a belief in it; atheism is a set of ideas.[20]

The judicial implementation of this article has shown the extent to which it may be misused to suppress freedom of expression. In a case known as the case of

---

[18] Abdallah Khalil, *Laws Restricting Civil and Political Rights*, at 88-89 (Egyptian Organization for Human Rights, 1993).

[19] Also added by this law was Article 98a. Article 98a subjects to imprisonment of up to five years and a fine of 50 to 500 pounds anyone who promotes within the Egyptian Republic, by any means, change of the basic principles of the Constitution or the political system or social organization of the state.

[20] Nagad Al-Boray, memorandum to the military governor in Case No. 580, year 1990, published in *Freedom of Opinion and Belief: Restrictions and Dilemmas* (Egyptian Organization for Human Rights, 1994).

Alaa Hamed,[21] the writer Alaa Hamed and his publisher where charged with violations of Article 98 for writing and publishing a book which, in the public prosecutor's view, contained atheistic ideas and apostasy. He charged:

> They have manipulated religion to encourage, through writing and publishing, extremist ideas, namely, atheism, overt apostasy, and the denial of divine religions and their prophets, and generally ridiculing the prophets and Islam and the Prophet Muhammad, God's peace be upon him. Specifically the first [Alaa Hamed] did so by writing the book, *A Distance Within a Man's Mind*, which contains extremist ideas, all of which harm national unity and threaten social peace.

Alaa Hamed was sentenced to five years' imprisonment with labor and a fine of one thousand pounds, and the book was confiscated.[22] In the explanatory memorandum for this ruling (the first time a court had written such a memorandum), the court stated:

> From the papers and documents of the case and the contents of the book in question, *A Distance Within a Man's Mind*, ... it becomes clear that it contains extremist ideas from the imagination of the author, whose sole purpose was to deride and distort religious beliefs in order to harm national unity. ... The book on the whole ridicules all the prophets and states that all the religions, God, good, reward and punishment are only symbols of events that never happened, and ... ridicules the religious beliefs of all levels of people for the purpose of achieving his goal of religious strife and harming national unity.[23]

Although Article 98 was adopted to confront the Islamist fundamentalist current which used Islamic religion to insult and demean other religions, it has been applied to favor Islamic fundamentalists. In particular, it has been used by the Prosecution Bureau against Muslims who convert to Christianity, on the ground that they thereby have shown disdain for the Islamic religion.

---

[21] State Security Emergency Court, Case No. 580, year 1990, judgment issued 25 November 1991.

[22] Alaa Hamed did not serve the prison sentence because the military governor did not ratify the sentence due to public and international criticism. However, on 26 May 1997, he was sentenced to one year's imprisonment for another book, *The Bed*. He spent two weeks in prison for both books. He is appealing the decision in *The Bed* case, and was released pending the appeal.

[23] *Id.*

IV. Expression which Insults the Dignity of the Government, Its Officials, Employees or their Equivalent

The Penal Code defines three forms of expression which may degrade the dignity of the state, its officials or its employees: insult, abuse, and slander. This section focuses on insult because it has been the most broadly construed by the courts and, therefore, poses the greatest threat to freedom of expression.

Article 133 of the Penal Code states that "anyone who insults by hints, words or threats a public employee or one of the law officers or anyone assigned to a public service while on duty or because he is on duty shall be punished by imprisonment for a period that does not exceed six months or pay a fine that does not exceed two hundred pounds."[24]

Whereas the law defines the meaning of slander and abuse, it does not define the meaning of the word "insult". The Court of Cassation defines an insult as "any saying or act which convention declares disdainful and degrading to dignity in the eyes of other people."[25] Courts have stated that an insult may be comprised of non-abusive or polite phrases, if those phrases, regardless of what they may seem, bear an insult in their context.[26] An insult may be in the form of signs or hints, such as a movement made by the offender's body, or any position he takes.

Egyptian law extends the meaning of insult to the point where any expression may be considered an insult even if the maker of that expression did not intend insult. If it is proved that he uttered the insulting expression there is no need to prove whether he intended an insult or not.[27] Also, for the crime to take place it is not necessary that the insult is made publicly; rather it suffices that the insult is directed at the person being insulted, even if it is sent in a sealed letter.[28] An insult may be made in conversation or in a raised voice. For example, someone may tell a public employee, "No, this is not honest; I'm going to make a complaint against you." Or a defendant, upon hearing the verdict against him, may say "this is unjust". Even if he or she says "long live justice", he or she may still be accused of directing an insult, since the Court of Cassation has stated that, "although this phrase generally indicates satisfaction with the justice system, if it were to come from an upset person

---

[24] Any person appointed on a permanent basis to carry out work for one of the public utilities whether that be in the government, a municipal administration, or one of the state authorities is considered a public employee. Dr. Abdul Hakim Foda, *supra* note 7, at 550. *See also* Higher Administrative Court, December 13, 1970, *discussing* Act 126, year 1913, Sixteenth Year Group, at 55. "Persons assigned to public office" are those assigned by the state to carry out a public service for society even though they do not occupy a permanent state office. Cassation session October 7, 1958, Technical Bureau Group, year 8 (1959), at 753 (1971).

[25] Cassation session 1 February 1932, *Group of rules in twenty-five years,* at 301.

[26] Dr. Fathi Sorour, *supra* note 5, at 341.

[27] Cassation session 25 December 1967, Technical Bureau Group, year 18 (1968), at 1271 (1971).

[28] Cassation session 8 June 1942, Quarter Century Group, part 1, at 37.

disappointed by the judge's verdict it would be considered praising in the context of cursing, which is the worst kind of sarcasm."[29]

A special category of this crime is the crime of insulting the President of the Republic, stated in Article 179 of the Penal Code. It is punishable by up to two years' imprisonment. Since the law's enactment in 1957 (by Act 112), there have been no prosecutions under the law. Before 1957, in pre-Republic days, an insult to the royal person was punishable by between six months' and five years' imprisonment. The term was doubled if the crime took place in the presence of the king.

Article 184 makes it a crime to insult Parliament, the army, the courts, or other specified public offices, punishable by a fine of up to two hundred pounds. Article 184 has been considered to include even such expressions as "down with the Egyptian government, down with the Cabinet", which the authorities may view as impolite and malicious expressions intended to breach honor and dignity. Any political criticism of the work of the Cabinet is considered under Article 184 to be an insult. In fact, the Court of Cassation overturned the verdict of a court that permitted the use of fiery expressions in a political debate, stating that "although the ruling that was appealed states that it is customary to use fiery expressions, threats, exaggeration and warnings in the course of debate because one cannot convince others by quiet methods, this is a matter that cannot be approved by the Court of Cassation. In fact, the ruling poses a great danger to the dignity of persons, and encourages abuse and insult."

The courts have set wide parameters for the meaning of the word insult and have condemned political criticisms that, they consider contain an insult. The law of insult effectively grants public officials and employees immunity from public scrutiny, when instead they, and their work, should be subject to careful monitoring to ensure that they perform their public functions properly and well.

V. Expression Which Threatens Public Security

Expression may also be restricted in order to prevent a threat to public security or public peace. The law's use of several terms, including "public security", "public peace" and "social peace", reflects a pervasive concern for order and for preventing turmoil that could lead to clashes between members of society or between members of society and security forces.

The imprecision of the concept of "public peace" caused much debate in the French Senate when it adopted the Press Law of 1881, Article 27 of which is the historical precedent for similar articles in Egyptian law. The debate centered on whether the article could (or should) be applied to a newspaper that published false

[29] Cassation session May 2, 1929, *discussed in* Guindi Bek Abdallah, *The Encyclopedia of Criminology*, part four, at 628 (1941).

news, regardless of the extent of the turmoil created by it. The MPs also debated how close the connection in time and place had to be between the challenged expression and public unrest in order to establish the necessary causal connection. The head of the law committee replied to these concerns saying that "slight unrest such as the breaking of a window of a café is not enough. Disturbing public peace is far more dangerous than that." The French Minister of Justice issued a directive to the prosecutor' s office on 9 November 1881, four months after the French press law was passed, clarifying that "the news item must create a serious disruption of public peace."[30]

Article 176 of the Egyptian Penal Code, amended by Act 29 of 1982, makes it a crime to incite hatred of a group of people, if the incitement leads to public unrest. Article 177 penalizes anyone who incites others not to obey the law or encourages people to commit a felony or other offense. The penalty for these two crimes is imprisonment for up to a year.

Article 188, amended by Act 93 of 1995, makes it a crime to publish false news or statements or aggravating propaganda that disrupt social peace or arouse panic amongst people or inflict harm to the public interest or lead to disdain of the institutions and officials of the state. The penalty is imprisonment for up to one year and a fine of no less than 5,000 pounds and no more than 10,000. However, if the publication has the intention of harming the country's economy or national interest and this harm takes place, the penalty is imprisonment, and the fine between 10,000 to 20,000 pounds.

Article 188 illustrates how Parliament restricted freedom over time. When this article appeared in the Penal Code of 1937, it penalized only the publication of false news, forged papers, or false ascription of statements to others. At the time, the Court of Cassation made clear that, for the crime to be proved, the prosecutor had to establish that the news item was false, and that the publisher knew it was false and published it deliberately.[31]

An amendment made by Act 568 year 1955 placed the burden of proving good intention on the defendant and created the presumption that, as long as the defendant had published the false news item or the forged paper, he intended to disrupt social peace. The clarification memorandum on Act 568 states:

> The freedom of individuals to publish news related to the public interest is not absolute but, like all other personal freedoms, is limited by the right of the social entity to protect its interests. One of these interests is that the correct news gets to the citizens on all public matters. Publishing illusions and lies may mislead public opinion.

---

[30] Dr. Riyad Shams, *Houriyat al Ray'ia wa Garra'im as-Sahafa w'al Nashr* at 527 (1936).

[31] Cassation session May 20, 1992, Technical Bureau Group, year 3, no. 366, at 982 (1971).

Therefore, Parliament decided to require the defendant to prove his innocent intention rather than, as before, requiring the prosecutor to prove the defendant's bad intention.

An even more disturbing amendment was made to Article 188 by Act 93 of 1995 (on 28 May 1995) by which publishing "statements" and "biased and aggravating propaganda" were added to "false news" and "forged papers" as grounds for liability. A news item or statement which is correct may now be punished if the prosecutor considers it "biased" or "aggravating propaganda", intended to arouse public opinion.

Article 188 as amended resembles Article 80 of the Penal Code, discussed in Section IIIA, above. According to both of these articles, publication is presumed to have been with bad intent and the defendant must prove both the truth of a statement and that he did not have any malicious goals. It is especially difficult for a person to prove lack of bad intentions if he criticizes the government or government policies or belongs to one of the opposition parties.

Article 124 of the Penal Code, amended by Act 24 of 1951 and re-amended by Act 29 of 1982, penalizes by imprisonment for a period of three months to one year, any group of three employees or more who stop working by common agreement or with the purpose of achieving a common target. The maximum penalty is doubled if their joint action could jeopardize the life or health of people, or if it causes strife, turmoil or harm to a national interest.

The third and fourth clauses of Article 124 penalize any employee who leaves his work or refuses to carry it out with the purpose of obstructing the course of work or disrupting its order, by imprisonment of up to six months and a fine of up to 500 pounds. The maximum penalty is doubled if the act could jeopardize the life or health of people, or if it causes strife, turmoil or harm to a national interest.

The prohibition of the right to strike violates the International Covenant on Economic, Social and cultural Rights ratified by Egypt through presidential decree 537 of 1981. The Higher State Emergency Security Court in Cairo issued an important judgment in 1986 in a case known as the railway workers strike.[32] Thirty-seven workers were acquitted of the strike charges on the ground that provisions of Articles 124 and 124a had been superseded by Egypt's ratification in 1981 of the International Covenant, which was incorporated into Egyptian law by operation of Article 151 of the Constitution. The military governor refused to ratify this ruling. Nevertheless, it constitutes an important judicial precedent, establishing the status in Egyptian law of international human rights treaties ratified by Egypt, and making clear that laws may be superseded by inconsistent provisions of such treaties.[33] It should be noted that, in 1981, Egypt also ratified the International Covenant on Civil and Political Rights, guaranteeing the rights to freedom of expression and association, which rights are also violated by provisions of Articles 124 and 124a.

---

[32] Higher State Security Emergency Court, Case No. 419, year 1986, El Ezbekeya, *discussed in* Abdallah Khalil, *Laws Restricting Civil and Political Rights*, *supra* note 18, at 8.

[33] *Id.*

VI. Revealing State Secrets

Egyptian laws are quite strict concerning what is considered to be a state secret, and even stricter concerning what is considered to constitute unlawful disclosure of such secrets. Such strictness may be understandable during times of war, or when disclosure is made to agents of a hostile country. However the Egyptian courts, especially the military courts, have extended the concept of what is considered secret to include matters that have already become public.

A secret is a matter that the state decides to keep from people other than those assigned to keep it or use it; if a person is aware that information is secret, he can be found guilty of unlawful disclosure if he reveals the information, even if he was not told to keep it secret.[34]

The Court of Cassation stated that it is possible to deduce whether or not information or documents are confidential "from matters such as the importance spies give to the material and documents handed to them and the reward the offender gets for his work and the precautions taken to keep the information secret."[35] However, the Criminal Court stated that "the external conditions cannot be proof of the secrecy of the information without examining them."[36] Dr. Fathi Sorour has explained:

> Evidence that leads to the conclusion that an incident or issue is secret must lead in mind and logic to this result even if the assumption is incorrect. It is not sufficient to establish the secret nature of information to rely on the concern of the offenders with it. Evidence of the secret nature of information must come from its contents, not simply from external conditions surrounding it.[37]

Courts have ruled that "the competent court has the power to determine whether or not a matter is secret. It may consult the opinion of the competent authority, but is not obliged to follow the opinion made by it."[38]

Article 85 of the Penal Code sets forth a broad, four-part definition of secrets which, if revealed, are considered to threaten national security: (1) military, political, diplomatic, economic and industrial information which by nature is not known to people who are not allowed to have access to the information; (2) objects which have a material aspect (such as weapons, ammunition, and their components), writings, publications, documents, drawings, maps, designs and photographs; (3) news and information related to the armed forces, its formations, movements, arms, supplies, individuals and anything related to military and strategic affairs; and (4) news and

---

[34] Justice Mahmoud Ibrahim Ismail, *supra* note 6, at 49.

[35] Cassation session 13 May 1958, the group of rulings, year 1958 no. 135. Supported by Justice Mahmoud Ibrahim Ismail, *id.*, at 150.

[36] Case No. 716, year 1957, Qasr El-Nil.

[37] Dr. Fathi Sorour, *supra* note 5, at 50.

[38] Higher State Security Court, ruling 20 July 1961, Case No. 87, year 1961.

information related to precautions and procedures taken to discover crimes that harm the security of the government internally or abroad, the investigations conducted into such matters, and the trials of perpetrators.

A fifth category of state secrets is set forth in Article 70b *bis*, added by Act No. 1 of 1989, namely, "all news, information, statements and documents related to the General Intelligence Agency, its activities, methods of work and personnel, and anything related to its affairs and duties in preserving the safety and security of the state and preserving its political system."

Articles 80a and 80b of the Penal Code state five ways in which secret information can be disclosed illegally, each of which is a crime:

(1) "handing over" a secret, which is done by giving it to others, either secretly or by allowing them to review it by leaving it in the open for them to see;

(2) "revealing" a secret, in whole or in part, by showing it to others, even if by mistake or if the information is forged, and whether or not the person who reveals it is the person who had been entrusted with it;[39]

(3) "acquiring" a secret by any means, photographing it, or recording it;

(4) "destroying" a secret, by destroying the document or thing containing the secret, whether fully or partially, or making it useless by partial or full breakdown;[40]

(5) "publicizing" a secret, by revealing it indiscriminately to any random number of persons.

Article 80 of the Penal Code states the penalties for unlawful disclosure or acquisition of state secrets. Disclosure in the interest of, or to anyone working for, a foreign country, is punishable by death. Disclosure or unlawful acquisition without intent to hand the secret over to a foreign state, is punishable by imprisonment for a period of between six months and five years and a fine of 100 to 500 pounds. A public employee, a public representative or a person assigned to a public service who reveals a state secret, even if by mistake, is penalized by imprisonment. If the crime is committed during war-time, the penalty is temporary hard labor.

The courts do not take into consideration whether the secret information has already been revealed. Courts consider information to be secret, even if already revealed, so long as the state still classifies it as secret. In a 1990 ruling, the Higher Military State Security Court sentenced the defendants to six months' imprisonment because it considered that they had revealed secrets about the General Intelligence agency in a book titled *Women in the Court of Salah Nasr*.[41] The defendant based his defense on the fact that the information contained in his book had previously been published in books, newspapers, and court cases between 1967 and the present date, and that he had merely republished the same information. The military court

---

[39] Id.

[40] Dr. Mahmoud Mustafa, *Explanation of the Penal Code*, special section, at 532 (1959).

[41] Higher State Security Military Court, under the chairmanship of Brigadier Wagdy El-Leisy, Case No. 7, year 1990, against journalist Atef El-Nimr.

rejected this defense on the ground that the General Intelligence Agency considered the information still to be secret.[42] In another 1990 case, the Higher Military Court similarly did not consider publication of information in the armed forces magazine to justify republishing that information in a non-military context, even though the armed forces magazine was distributed and sold to the public. The republication was judged a crime and the journalist was sentenced to one year's imprisonment.[43]

VII. Conclusion

The Constitution of 1971 establishes strong protections of freedom of expression and the press and also incorporates international human rights treaties ratified by Egypt into Egyptian law. Before and since adoption of the Constitution, Parliament passed numerous laws that impose penalties on freedom of expression that are inconsistent with the Constitution and international treaties. There should be a complete review of laws, especially those in the Penal Code, that restrict freedom of expression to recommend which ones should be repealed or amended in light of the Constitution's protections, and with a more realistic concern for issues of genuine national security, as narrowly defined.

---

[42] *Id.* The same court ruled similarly in Case No. 2, year 1990, against defendant Etimad Mohammed Roshdy, known as Etimad Khorshed.

[43] Case No. 13, year 1990, against journalist Mohammed Mohammed Amer.

FRANCE: NATIONAL SECURITY, *SECRET-DÉFENSE* AND FREEDOM OF EXPRESSION

Roger Errera

I. Introduction

This chapter examines a number of issues relating to constitutional and administrative law, as well as to criminal law and procedure, concerning the balance to be struck in French law between national security on the one hand, and freedom of expression and access to information, on the other. At the core of the discussion lies the notion in French law of a national defense secret ("*secret de la défense nationale*", in short "*secret-défense*").[1]

The following aspects will be examined in turn:

1. The constitutional status of freedom of expression and general principles concerning permissible limits to it.

2. Access to information, decisions refusing information, and specific bases for refusing access to information on national security grounds.

3. Restrictions imposed on freedom of expression on grounds of protecting national security or national defense secrets.

II. Freedom of Expression: Constitutional Status and General Principles Concerning Permissible Restrictions

Freedom of expression and communication is a constitutional right under French law,[2] entrenched in two provisions of constitutional stature. First Article 11

---

[1] *See* F. Gauvin, *Le secret de la défense nationale en droit français,* doctoral dissertation, Université de Grenoble, 1996; B. Warusfel, *Le secret de la défense nationale: Protection des intérêts de la nation et libertés publiques dans une societé d'information,* doctoral dissertation, Université Paris V, 1994; B. Warusfel, "Le contrôle du secret de la défense nationale: une exigence de l'Etat de droit," *Droit et défense,* 1996, n° 4, at 23; Emmanuel Derieux, "Securité nationale et liberté de communication en France," *Légipresse,* n° 125, Octobre 1995, at 75. *See also* S. Rostein, *Le secret d'Etat et la démocratie* doctoral dissertation, Université Paris II, 1992.

[2] On freedom of expression in French law, *see* J. Robert and J. Duffar, *Droits de l'homme et libertés fondamentales,* 6th ed. (Paris, 1996), at 615 ff. *See also* R. Errera, "Press Law in France", in S. Coliver, ed., *Press Law and Practice: A Comparative Study of Press Freedom in European and Other Democracies* (London: Article 19, 1993), at 57 ff; "Balancing Legitimate Rights: Freedom of the Press and Other Rights in French Law," *Communications Lawyer* (Spring 1991), at 13; "Recent Developments in the French Law on the Press in Comparison with Britain," in D. Kingsford-Smith and D. Oliver, eds., *Economical with the Truth: the Law and the Media in a Democratic Society* (Oxford, 1990), at 67; "The Freedom of the Press: The United States, France

of the 1789 Declaration of the Rights of Man and of the Citizen,[3] incorporated into the Preamble of the 1958 Constitution, provides:

> Free communication of thoughts and opinion is among the most precious rights of man. Thus all men may freely speak, write and publish, provided they be responsible for any abuse of this freedom in cases determined by law.[4]

In addition, freedom of expression and communication is one of the "fundamental principles guaranteed by the laws of the Republic" which, according to the case law of the *Conseil Constitutionnel* (hereafter "C.C.") have constitutional value.[5]

The C.C., in affirming the constitutional status of freedom of expression and freedom of the press, has stated that these freedoms constitute one of the essential safeguards of all the other rights and liberties.[6] Moreover, the C.C. has affirmed that these freedoms apply not only to those who write, edit and publish, but also to those who read the press; the public's right to be able to choose from a diversity of views thus necessitates a degree of pluralism, at least for general dailies. Such pluralism is an aim of constitutional value.[7]

One of the consequences of the fundamental character of freedom of expression is that Parliament may intervene only to make the right more effective (*i.e.*, to reinforce it) or to reconcile it with other constitutional rules or principles.[8]

---

and Other European Countries," in L. Henkin and A.J. Rosenthal, eds., *Constitutionalism and other Rights: The Influence of the United States Constitution Abroad* (New York, 1990), at 63; "Press Law in France," in P. Lahav, ed., *Press Law in Modern Democracies: A Comparative Study* (New York and London, 1985), at 137.

[3] On the Declaration's influence on French constitutional case-law, *see La declaration des droits de l'homme et du citoyen* (Paris,1989).

[4] Art. 11 has frequently been applied by the courts; *see e.g.*, Cour d'appel de Paris, 13 Jan. 1992, X. *et al. v. y,* in a case relating to the criticism of school textbooks. *See also* R. Beauvois, "La liberté d'opinion et d'expression," in *La Cour de Cassation et la Constitution de la Republique* (Aix-en Provence, 1995), at183.

[5] On French constitutional law, *see* J. Bell, *French Constitutional Law* (Oxford, 1992); A. Stone, *The Birth of Judicial Politics in France: The Constitutional Council in Comparative Perspective* (Oxford and New York, 1992). For a commentary on the case-law, *see* L. Favoreu and L. Philip, *Les grandes décisions du Conseil constitutionnel,* 8th ed. (Paris, 1995); B. Genevois, *La jurisprudence du Conseil constitutionnel* (Paris, 1988). The decisions of the *Conseil constitutionnel* can be found in the official *Recueil des décisions du Conseil constitutionnel* as well as in *Recueil de jurisprudence constitutionnelle,* 1959-1993, L. Favoreu, ed. (Paris, 1994, with supplements for the following years).

[6] *See Conseil constitutionnel,*Oct. 10-11, 1984, at 78.

[7] *See, e.g., Conseil constitutionnel.,* July 29, 1986, at 110.

[8] *Id.*

III. Access to Information and Restrictions Based on National Security Considerations

Under French law, access to information may be restricted or refused on national security or related grounds. The law and practice is examined in this Section under three headings:

A. Statutes adopted during the late seventies which have created a right of access to government-held information and documents, subject to a list of limitations and exceptions.

B. The scope of other legislation requiring disclosure of information or public hearings, and restrictions on grounds of national security or national defense.

C. What happens when a court or a judge asks the Government to produce a document and the latter refuses to do so on national security grounds? How is such a decision to be reviewed?

A. Access to Government-held Information and National Security Exceptions: Legislation Adopted During the Late 1970s

Three areas are examined in this Section: (1) access to government-held documents; (2) access to data; and (3) access to archives.

1. Access to Government-held Documents

The Statute of 17 July 1978 created a right of access to "administrative documents". The right belongs to everyone, French citizens and non-citizens, natural and legal persons.[9] The term "administrative document" has a broad meaning. As no definition is possible, the statute contains a fairly long enumeration, which is not exhaustive.[10] The law applies to state and local bodies as well as to any private body, even if subject to private law, entrusted with the management of a public service. The right can only be exercised in respect of documents that do not contain personal information about an individual.[11] However, everyone has the right to know the statements made in an administrative document which are produced against him or her, and to require that his or her observations are annexed to the document.[12]

In 1979, Parliament added to the Statute of 1978 the right of everyone to have access to documents in which he or she is personally named *(Documents*

---

[9] *See* R. Errera, "Access to Administrative Documents in France: Reflections on a Reform," in N. Marsh, ed., *Access to Government-held Information* (London, 1987), at 87.

[10] *See* Statute of July 17, 1978, Art.1, para. 2.

[11] *Id.* Art. 1.

[12] *Id.* Art. 3.

nominatifs). Medical secrecy or commercial or industrial secrecy cannot be made a reason for refusing access to such documents.[13]

Under Article 6 of the Statute of 1978, the Administration is entitled to refuse to communicate, or grant access to, an administrative document if such communication or access could endanger the secrecy of national defense, foreign policy, state security, public security or other secrets protected by law.

If a document is not, upon request, made available (for which written reasons must be given in the decision itself), the person concerned may request the opinion of the *Commission d'accès aux documents administratifs* (C.A.D.A.), an independent body. C.A.D.A. must give its opinion within one month. Within two months of receiving this opinion, the Administration must inform C.A.D.A. as to whether it intends to comply. In addition to this consultative role, C.A.D.A. may be consulted by the Administration on any question relating to the implementation of the law. It may also propose reforms, and publishes an annual report[14]

C.A.D.A.'s opinions relate mainly to national defense and foreign policy. C.A.D.A. has given its opinion that documents could be withheld from disclosure in several cases, including the following:

- The safety report of the nuclear plant of La Hague, near Cherbourg, in Normandy (C.A.D.A. held that an informed reader could infer from the report the country's nuclear capacity, *i.e.,* the quantity of plutonium manufactured for military purposes).[15]
- The list of underground sites which could be used as shelters by the population in times of war.[16]
- A ministerial circular of 12 March 1982 and 4 November 1983, on the protection of national defense secrets.[17]
- Individual files of persons who have asked to be allowed to see documents covered by defense secrecy.[18]

The case law of the *Conseil d'Etat* (the highest court on administrative and public law matters) reflects the same approach. Following are two examples. In 1986, a pilot of the French Air Force crashed. His mother asked the Minister of Defense for access to the sound recording of the words exchanged between her son and

---

[13] *Id.,* Art. 6 bis.

[14] In addition to C.A.D.A's annual reports *(Rapport de la Commission d'accès aux documents administratifs,* La Documentation française, Paris, 1981 ff.), *see C.A.D.A.: Guide d'accès aux documents administratifs,* Paris, 1997 (hereafter "*Guide*").

March 1981, *Lalonde,* in C.A.D.A.'s second annual report, 1982, at 181. *See also* Dec. 13, 1984, *Association des amis de la terre,* in C.A.D.A.'s fourth annual report, 1986, at 113.

[16] *Commission permanente d'étude et de protection des eaux souterraines et des cavernes de Franche-Comté,* July 4, 1985, in C.A.D.A.'s fourth annual report, 1986, at 118.

[17] *Syndicat CFDT des métallurgistes du Nord de la Seine,* Oct. 24, 1985, in C.A.D.A.'s fourth annual report, 1986, at 137.

[18] *Forme,* Sept. 24, 1982, in C.A.D.A.'s third annual report, 1983, at 88.

another officer before and during the accident. The Minister declined to do so on national defense grounds. This decision was upheld by the Paris administrative court and, on appeal, by the *Conseil d'Etat*. The latter held that the recording had been in accordance with the procedures used for communications between Air Force pilots and air controllers and that disclosure of the recording could endanger national defense secrecy. Instead, the pilot's mother was shown a video cassette containing the full commentary of the accident.[19]

In 1989 a company which transported money in armored vans asked the Minister in charge of the post, telegraph and telecommunications to have access to the contract signed between the Ministry and a rival company. The Minister granted access, with the exception of certain clauses relating to tele-surveillance and transport of money. The lower administrative court and the *Conseil d'Etat* upheld the Minister's decision, on the ground that these clauses contained information the communication of which could endanger the security of the State as well as public security.[20]

C.A.D.A.'s opinions on documents relating to the secrecy of foreign policy also are relevant. On this ground, C.A.D.A. has excluded access to documents relating to international negotiations, foreign relations and exchanges of diplomatic correspondence. Information excluded from disclosure has included the following:

- discussions with the government of Guinea on the fate of Guinean civil servants married to French citizens;[21]
- correspondence between the French Embassy in Beirut and the Lebanese police;[22]
- reports and notes criticizing a foreign government;[23]
- documents used for negotiations between France and Zaire relating to compensation to be awarded to French nationals or companies deprived of their property;[24]
- negotiations between France and Cuba on scientific cooperation;[25]
- the general instruction on visas.[26]

---

[19] Oct. 30, 1989, *Mme Dufour*, at 221, reprinted in *Revue française de droit aérien*, July-Sept. 1990, at 365.

[20] *Société Securipost et Ministre des postes, des télécommunications et de l'espace, Societé Libertés - Services*, Feb.3, 1992, at 50.

[21] *Wagnes*, Feb. 3, 1983, *in* C.A.D.A.'s third annual report, 1983, at 144; upheld by the *Conseil d'Etat*, June 6, 1988, *Association des familles de Français prisonniers en Guinée*, at 232.

[22] Oct. 3,1985, *Monod*, cited in *Guide, supra* note 14, at 104.

[23] Dec. 13, 1984, *Bonnet*, in *Guide, supra* note 14, at 104.

[24] April 23, 1988, *Dubois-Africa*, in *Guide, supra* note 14, at 104.

[25] April 2, 1987, *Ratier*, in *Guide, supra* note 14, at 104.

[26] April 30, 1987, *Loschak*, in *Guide, supra* note 14, at 105. According to C.A.D.A., this document relates to the attitude of the government towards foreign citizens and, thus, to the secrecy of foreign policy.

Whenever the Administration refuses access to a document because it is classified as a defense secret, and the information seeker requests an opinion from C.A.D.A., one of C.A.D.A.'s members must be able to see the information. The Administration, after granting a security clearance ("*habilitation secret deféense*") to one of C.A.D.A.'s members, must then make the information available to him or her.[27] The rationale is that the 1981 decree may not restrict the scope of C.A.D.A.'s powers as defined by the Statute of 17 July 1978.

In some cases, an administrative court may ask to see a document without communicating it to the plaintiff. This is permissible, for instance, under the following circumstances: the Administration refuses to grant access to a document, C.A.D.A. issues an opinion upholding the Administration's decision on the ground that the document could properly be withheld under the 1978 Statute, the administrative court of first instance upholds the Administration's refusal and, on appeal, the *Conseil d'Etat*, after its own inspection of the document, upholds the lower court. Under such circumstances, if the courts disclosed the document before the question was ultimately decided on the merits, they would grant full satisfaction to the plaintiff, and the issue would become moot.[28]

2. Access to Data

Under the Statute of 6 January 1978 on data collection and protection, any person has a right to ask any institution using computerized data (there is a public list of such institutions) whether it holds personal (in French, "nominative") information relating to him or her and, if so, to have access to it.[29] The person has a right to have such data corrected, supplemented, clarified, updated or erased if the data are wrong, incomplete, ambiguous or outdated, or the gathering, use, communication or keeping of the data is forbidden.[30] An independent authority, the *Commission nationale de l'informatique et des libertés* (C.N.I.L.) is in charge of such matters.[31] When the use of the data mentioned above relates to the security of the State, defense or public security,[32] access is indirect: C.N.I.L. asks one of its members belonging to the highest courts -- the *Conseil d'Etat*, the *Cour de cassation* (the highest

---

[27] See, *e.g.*, Feb. 20, 1986, *Beau*, in C.A.D.A.'s fifth annual report, 1987, at 99.

[28] See *Conseil d'Etat*, June 16, 1989, *Banque de France c. Uberschwiller*, at 688; concl. Dael in *Revue française de droit administratif*, 1989, at 973. For C.A.D.A.'s opinion, see its fifth annual report, April 2, 1987, at 101.

[29] Statute of Jan. 6, 1978, Art. 34.

[30] Id., at Art. 36.

[31] On C.N.I.L., *see* its yearly reports *(Rapport annuel de la Commission nationale de l'informatique et des libertés)* and its ten-year review, *Dix ans de l'informatique et des libertés*, Paris, 1988.

[32] Such data include data held by the D.S.T. (*Direction de la surveillance du territoire*), in charge of surveillance against hostile foreign activities in France, and the D.G.S.E. (*Direction générale de la sécurité extérieure)*, in charge of activities abroad.

court for civil and criminal matters) or the *Cour des comptes* (the highest court with responsibility for auditing public accounts) -- to investigate the matter and order the necessary changes. The individual will be duly informed of the C.N.I.L.'s investigation and any corrective action taken.[33]

C.N.I.L. has made a distinction between data banks relating directly and exclusively to the three domains mentioned above (security of the State, defense and public security), and data that have been collected for other purposes but which may contain information relating to one of these domains (*e.g.*, data relating to national military service). Access to the former will be indirect; access to the latter will be direct, for all non-confidential information, if the Ministry of the Interior so agrees.[34] The case law of the *Conseil d'Etat* does not seem, so far, to be fully consistent with this approach, and tends to adopt a more restrictive interpretation of Article 39 of the 1978 Statute.[35] In recent years, there has been an increase in the number of applications to have (indirect) access to data under Article 39 (for instance, an increase of 31 per cent in 1996).[36] Many applications are from non-citizens who have been denied a visa to enter France and relate to the Schengen Information System set up under the 1990 Schengen Convention (which made it easier for nationals of European Union countries to travel within the EU, but more difficult for non-EU nationals).

Access to government-held documents and access to data are both regulated by independent authorities, C.A.D.A. and C.N.I.L. respectively. The composition of these bodies and the fact that their members may not be removed during their terms further ensures their independence from the executive. Their members include Members of Parliament appointed by the Speaker of the National Assembly or Senate, and members of the highest courts (the *Conseil d'Etat*, the *Cour de cassation*, and the *Cour des comptes*). Bodies of this nature have also been created in such domains as regulation of the broadcast media,[37] the Stock Exchange,[38] and competition.[39]

C.A.D.A. and C.N.I.L. clearly belong to a domain closely related to individual freedoms.[40] This is also the case of another body, the *Commission nationale de contrôle des interceptions de securité* (C.N.C.I.S.), created by a statute of

[33] Statute of Jan. 6, 1978, at Art. 39.
[34] See C.N.I.L.'s opinions of Oct. 15, 1983 and Dec. 31, 1984, in its *Cinquieme rapport annuel 1984* (Paris 1985), at 86.
[35] *See Conseil d'Etat, Mme Loschak*, April 27, 1988, at 173.
[36] C.N.I.L., *17e rapport annuel 1996* (Paris 1997), at 20-23. See also *Dix ans, supra* note 31, at 143 ff.
[37] *Conseil superieur de l'audiovisuel* (C.S.A.).
[38] *Commission des operations de bourse* (C.O.B.).
[39] *Conseil de la concurrence* (C.C.).
[40] On these independent bodies, *see* M. Gentot, *Les autorités administratives independantes*, Paris, 1991.

10 July 1991, which regulates telephone-tapping ordered on security grounds by the executive.

3. Access to Public Archives

Pursuant to the Statute of 3 January 1979 on archives, the rule is that all government-held archives are to be made accessible to the public after 30 years from the date generated.[41] However, such an apparently liberal clause is severely restricted by Article 7, under which the 30 years mentioned is extended to 60, 100, 120 or even 150 years. The period of 60 years applies to documents relating to the security of the State or national defense.

Such documents are listed in a decree of 3 December 1979. The list, which is *very* long, includes the archives of the President of the Republic and the Prime Minister; those of the Ministry of the Interior relating to State security; national police archives relating to private life, State security or national defense; reports of ministerial inspectorates relating to private life or State security; archives of the tax service containing information about the property of individuals or other information relating to their privacy; public property archives containing information relating to State security or national defense; documents relating to financial, monetary or commercial negotiations with foreign states; documents relating to unsettled litigation with foreign states; war damages files; and, last but not least, national defense archives mentioned in another decree of 3 December 1979.

The 60-year rule applies generally to all classified documents. Under Article 8 of the January 1979 statute, special permission for access may be granted before the expiration of this period.

These laws and decrees, and the way they are implemented, are coming under increasing criticism. A former member of the *Conseil d'Etat* who has written extensively on administrative law made the following comments in a report published in 1996:[42]

- Regarding the 60-year delay, it seems that the decree of 3 December 1979 has exceeded the scope of the permission granted to the government by Article 7 of the 1979 Statute to regulate the matter. For example, the *Conseil d'Etat* held in 1994 that all documents relating to unsettled litigation with foreign states and documents relating to financial, monetary or commercial negotiations with foreign states do not relate necessarily to the security of the State or to national defense.

---

[41] On the law applying to archives in France, *see* H. Bastien, *Droit des archives* (Paris, 1976); G. Braibant, *Les archives en France* (Paris, 1996). The legislation and regulations are contained in *Direction des Archives de France: Principaux textes relatifs aux archives en vigueur au 1er mars 1996* (Paris, 1996).

[42] G. Braibant, *id.*

Accordingly, it quashed a decision of the Minister of Foreign Affairs refusing to authorize access to such documents.[43]

- Many of the reasons that will justify special delays under the 1979 Law are too permissive. For instance, historical research on the Vichy period has been clearly handicapped.
- The 1979 Statute is anterior to the new instruments relating to the classification of documents (1981) and to the present Penal Code, hence the pressing need for its *aggiornamento* (being brought up-to-date to meet current needs).
- More generally the restrictive clauses relating to privacy, national defense and security of the State need to be reevaluated.
- The discretionary power to authorize access to particular documents is not adequately circumscribed. The power is subject to arbitrary application, and could thus create inequalities or inconsistencies.

In 1997, the new Government announced its intent to seek reform of the 1979 Statute.[44] However, as of early 1998, it had not yet proposed a bill to Parliament.

B. Other Legislation Requiring Disclosure of Information, and National Security Exceptions

Various statutes, not explicitly focused on access to government-held information, contain provisions requiring public hearings or publication of information, except in special circumstances including where publicity could harm national defense or security interests. Following are several examples.

1. Parliamentary Committees of Inquiry

Rapporteurs of parliamentary committees have access to all government-held information and documents, except secret documents relating to national defense, foreign affairs or State security.[45]

---

[43] *Conseil d'Etat*, April 8, 1994, *Ministre des affaires etrangeres c. Mme Jobez,* at 178

[44] *See* the Prime Minister's circular of Oct. 2, 1997, recommending a more liberal policy on access to the public archives concerning the 1940-45 period, 14 *Journal officiel,* Oct. 3,1997, at 339.

[45] Statute of Nov. 17, 1958 on the functioning of Parliament, Art. 6.11, para. 2.

2. Eminent Domain and Public Inquiries

No compulsory buying of private property by the State or another public body may take place before a public inquiry has been held.[46] However, secret purchases relating to national defense may be ordered by the government, without such an inquiry, if a special committee has approved them.[47]

3. Public Procurement

Prior publicity is a compulsory rule applying to public procurement procedures. However, for certain types of contracts, the Administration is free to negotiate directly with contractors. This is the case for works, supplies or services relating to the needs of defense, when certain additional conditions are met.[48]

4. Building Regulations

No building may be erected without a building permit delivered by the municipality.[49] Constructions related to defense secrets are exempted from such an obligation.[50]

5. Public Inquiries

A statute of 12 July 1983 regulates the procedure and contents of public inquiries preceding the compulsory buying of private property by the State or a public authority for a public need. A clause of the statute mentions that such inquiries must, while they take place, respect the secrecy of national defense or any other secret protected by law.[51]

Further, according to a decree of 5 July 1985, no public inquiries are to be held on land, buildings or military installations listed by the decree. In all public inquiries elsewhere, no piece of information that could lead to a revelation of national defense secrets may be included in the file or be communicated to the public.

---

[46] *Code de l'expropriation pour cause d'utilité publique*, Art. L. 11-1.

[47] *Id.*, Article L. 11-3. For more on this committee, *see* Art. L. 11-17 of the same Code and the decree of 26 May 1987.

[48] *See Code des marchés publics* (code of public procurement), Arts. 104.1-5 and 6, and 104.11.

[49] *See Code de l'urbanisme,* Art. L. 422-1.

[50] *Id.* Art. L. 422-1.

[51] Art. 2, last para.

6. Patent Law

The relationship between patents, and therefore patent law, and national defense is obvious. Hence, the preoccupation to avoid situations in which inventions of interest for national defense could be published or transmitted to a foreign state. The present law, contained in the Code of Intellectual Property, may be summarized as follows.

Inventions of interest to national defense for which a patent application has been filed may not be made public or freely exploited without an authorization given by the Minister in charge, after consultation with the Minister of Defense. The Defense Minister is to be informed of patent applications sent to the National Institute of Intellectual Property, and is to decide whether or not to grant authorization within a period of five months from the date the application is filed.[52] However, he may decide to extend the five-month waiting period for a renewable length of one year.[53] If he does so, the applicant for a patent is entitled to compensation for any financial loss incurred.[54] Any violation of these rules may be punished by a fine and, if national defense has been harmed, by a jail term.

Under another provision of the Code, the state is empowered to obtain, upon request, either the permission to exploit, for the needs of national defense, an invention relating to a patent application or a patent. If there is a disagreement on the royalties to be paid, the local civil court will decide on them. Proceedings are held *in camera*.[55]

The state may, at any time, purchase compulsorily, for the needs of national defense, inventions relating to patent applications, or patents. If the state does so, it must pay fair compensation.[56]

7. Duty to Give Reasons for Administrative Decisions

Under a statute of 1979, the Administration is under an obligation to give the reasons for any decision affecting adversely the rights or interests of a person.[57] The reasons must be given in writing, with the decision itself and must contain the legal and factual grounds for the decision.[58] However, negative decisions refusing access to information may not contain the reasons whenever the communication of

[52] Code of Intellectual Property, Art. L. 612-8 and L. 612-9.
[53] *Id.* Art. L. 612-10.
[54] *Id.* Art. L. 613-19.
[55] *Id.* Art. L. 613-20.
[56] Statute of 11 July 1979 on the duty to give reasons for administrative decisions, Art.1.
[57] *Id.* Art. 3.
[58] *Id.* Art. 1. The link with the Statute of 17 July 1978 on access to government-held information is explicit.

the latter could endanger, *inter alia*, secrets of national defense or foreign policy, the security of the State or public security.[59]

C. Access of Courts to Documents Covered by the "*Secret-Défense*" Classification

What happens when a court, or a judge, asks the government to produce a document, on its own initiative or because a party has asked it to do so, and the government declines to do so on the ground that it is covered by the "*secret-défense*" category? This scenario could occur in various situations.

1. Litigation Before Administrative Courts

Under French law, administrative courts *(i.e.,* the *Conseil d'Etat*, as a supreme court, lower administrative courts and administrative courts of appeal) adjudicate cases relating to the annulment of an administrative decision or the award of damages by the Administration following an unlawful act or a fault. In such situations, the practice of the courts is as follows.

Administrative courts are empowered, whenever they determine that it would be useful in cases before them, to ask the Administration to produce the file or documents upon which a challenged decision is based.[60] The only limitation on this authority concerns documents the secrecy of which is protected by law, for instance, in order to protect defense secrets.[61] Courts are not empowered to demand the production of such documents, even less may they ask to see them and *not* communicate them to the other party.

Courts do, however, have the right and the duty to demand that the Administration produce all available information which may be useful to them in deciding cases before them, without violating, directly or indirectly, official secrecy. If the Administration refuses to comply, a court may draw the pertinent conclusions from such an attitude.[62]

The Administration has invoked very rarely "*secret-deféńse*" before the *Conseil d'Etat* (less than half a dozen times in 40 years). This is not without good

---

[59] For a naturalization case, *see Conseil d'Etat*, May 27, 1983, *Ministre des affaires sociales c. Epoux Cajarville*, at 219.

[60] *See Conseil d'Etat, Banque de France c. M. Uberschwiller,* quoted *supra* note 28.

[61] *See* March 11, 1955, *Secrétaire d'Etat a la guerre c. Coulon,* at 149; 1955 *Revue de droit public*, at 995, concl. Grevisse; 1955 *Actualité juridique. Droit administratif*, at 181, note Long; May 11, 1962, *Foucher-Creteau,* at 319, concl. Braibant; Oct. 2, 1963, *Houhou,* at 468; May 27, 1983, *Ministre des affaires sociales c. Epoux Cajarville, supra* note 59; Nov. 25,1983, *Ghariani.*

[62] Paris Court of appeal, Oct. 20, 1981. The case is discussed in F. Gauvin, *supra* note 1, at 332-33.

reason: in most, if not all, cases where it did so, its reluctance to send to the court additional information resulted in the quashing of the challenged decision.

2. Litigation Before Civil Courts

Under French civil procedure rules, courts may ask an expert for an opinion on a point of fact requiring the opinion of a specialist.[63] The expert thus appointed by the court may ask the parties or anyone else to produce documents.[64] If they refuse the court may order their production. What happens if the document is covered by the "secret-défense"? The Paris court of appeal had to decide this question in a 1981 case. A company had been selling transmissions material to the Army under a contract. An intermediary, hired to "facilitate" the conclusion of the contract, had been promised a percentage. The company learnt that he had played no part in concluding the contract and consequently stopped paying him. He sued the company before a commercial court, which appointed two arbiters. They asked the company to see its books. The company refused on the ground that the contract was classified *"secret-défense"*. The court ordered it to produce the requested documents, under a levy. The Court of Appeal, after appointing an expert, quashed the judgment: the company could not open its books and its accounts, in view of the nature of the contract, unless authorized to do so by the Administration. Its behavior was not an obstruction of justice.[65]

3. Litigation before Criminal Courts or Investigative Magistrates

While cases before criminal courts or investigating magistrates (*juges d'instruction*) raise many of the same legal issues as those before civil courts,. their scope and political context often are quite different. Several cases have recently exposed problems with the situation in France.

In 1973 several persons were discovered while attempting to plant listening devices in the offices of a satirical weekly (*Le Canard enchaîné*). The head of D.S.T., called by the investigating magistrate to give evidence, denied everything, but refused to tell the magistrate the positions of police officers employed in his service. One of them began to give evidence. The head of D.S.T. then announced that none of his agents would give evidence before the judge nor appear before him. The judge ordered a confrontation of witnesses. His order was appealed and the Court of Appeal upheld the Minister's position.[66]

---

[63] The new Code of Civil Procedure, Art. 223.

[64] *Id.* Art. 243.

[65] Paris Court of appeal, *chambre d'accusation*, May 21, 1975.

[66] Paris Court of appeal, *chambre d'accusation*, May 25, 1987, 1987 *Recueil Dalloz-Sirey*, at 410, note Pradel.

Another case was the following one: during the mid 1980's, a former Minister was being prosecuted for misusing public funds. One of his accomplices fled France, using a false passport delivered by the Ministry of the Interior. The investigating magistrate needed to know why and how such a passport had been delivered to him. A higher police official, acting under instructions, refused to communicate any information, declaring that the latter was covered by "*secret-défense*". The Minister of the Interior upheld his position, as did the Paris Court of Appeal.[67]

The same device was used by the government on many other occasions. One of them related to the Presidency of the Republic. In 1993, following revelations, several persons brought a criminal action against the authors of illegal telephone-tapping performed between 1983 and 1986 by members of the staff of President Mitterrand. The investigating magistrate requested access to the relevant documents and to hear the testimony of former members of the President's staff in charge of unlawful telephone-tapping. Two Prime Ministers, Mssrs. Balladur and Juppe, rejected the magistrate's request. The President of the Commission charged with overseeing telephone-tapping ordered by the executive on national security grounds inquired into the matter and was allowed to inspect classified documents and to hear persons bound by the "*secret-défense*". However, as he himself was bound by a duty of secrecy, he could not give evidence before the investigating magistrate unless specifically authorized by the Prime Minister.

In other cases, too, the Administration invoked the "*secret-défense*", which precluded any production of classified documents and any testimony by individuals in charge.

In 1974 the government asked the *Conseil d'Etat* for its opinion on a general issue. (The government may ask the *Conseil* for its opinion on a general issue so long as the question does not relate to pending litigation. The opinion is not legally binding but, in practice, carries great weight and is very influential.) The opinion, which applies to all cases and all courts, can be summed up as follows.[68] Any person in possession of a defense secret is under an obligation not to communicate it, even to a court. The authority in charge is empowered to decide what may be

[67] "*Secret-défense*" has also been used as a justification for refusal to answer questions asked by parliamentary committees. After the blowing-up of the *Rainbow-Warrior* in Auckland by members of the French secret services, the rapporteur of the Finance Committee of the Senate, in October 1985, asked some questions on the cost and financing of the operation. The Prime Minister refused to answer.

[68] For details on the cases mentioned above, as well as others, see B. Warusfel, *supra* note 1, at 354-367. For an example of a case which was pending for more than twenty years (in relation to the murder of M. Ben Barka, a Moroccan politician, in Paris in 1965), *see* the reply of the Minister of Defense to the question of a member of the National Assembly: *Journal Officiel A.N.,* Dec. 15, 1997, question n° 5754.

communicated and to designate, should the case proceed, the persons who shall give evidence before the court.

This situation came under strong criticism by legal and judicial authorities,[69] on grounds that it amounted to a negation of the principle of separation of powers and was inconsistent with Article 6(1) of the European Convention on Human Rights relating to fair trial. The executive, these experts contended, should not have full and unfettered discretion to hide its hand especially in cases when "*secret-défense*" was used to avoid the revelation, in court, of improper and unlawful behavior.

Since 1996, a change of climate has been perceptible. The winds of change began to blow from several places. In its 1995 yearly report, the *Conseil d'Etat* recommended the creation of an independent body, which could give its opinion in cases such as those mentioned above.[70] It would be an independent administrative authority, on the model of those already mentioned, such as C.N.I.L. and C.N.C.I.S., the members of which may have access to classified information and documents.

In 1996, the commission in charge of controlling telephone-tapping by the executive on security grounds criticized the abuse of the notion of "*secret-défense*".[71]

In November 1997, following these recommendations, the government decided to send a new bill to Parliament to establish an independent administrative authority; this *Commission du secret de la défense nationale* ("C.S.D.N.") would give its opinion whenever a French court asks to see information or documents that have been classified under Article 413-9 of the Penal Code.[72] Its chair would be the chair of C.N.C.I.S., the commission in charge of controlling telephone-tapping by the government on security grounds. As envisioned in the bill, he or she would be assisted by two members of the *Conseil d'Etat*, the *Cour de cassation* or the *Cour des comptes*, chosen by the President of the Republic from a list of six names transmitted by those bodies. All would be appointed for six-year terms.

The procedure would be as follows: the Administration would transmit to the new authority requests from the courts. The C.S.D.N. would study the requests and review the relevant documents. The Administration would be under an obligation to assist it. Within two months of receipt of a request, the C.S.D.N. would give its opinion to the Administration: in favor of transmission of the requested documents; against transmission; or in favor of transmission with reservations. The substance of the opinion would be published. The Administration would then decide on its course of action. Although the opinion of the C.S.D.N. would not be legally binding, it is expected to be very influential, so that the dialogue

---

[69] For a defense of the status quo, *see* M. Guillaume, "Secret de la défense nationale et Etat de droit," in *Mélanges Braibant* (Paris, 1996), at 366.

[70] *Conseil d'Etat, Rapport annuel*, in *Etudes et documents du Conseil d'Etat* (1996, n°47).

[71] C.N.C.I.S., *4e rapport d'activité 1995* (La Documentation française, 1996).

[72] See *Le Monde,* Nov. 28, 1997.

of the deaf between the courts and the government would disappear, the C.S.D.N. acting as a sort of umpire.

The spirit of this important reform began to be implemented even before the bill was examined in Parliament. In June 1996, a few days after the appointment of M. Jospin as Prime Minister, the investigating magistrate in charge of the inquiry relating to unlawful telephone-tapping by members of the Presidential staff during the mid-1980's wrote again to the new Prime Minister, M. Jospin, asking that persons acquainted with these actions be authorized to give evidence before him. On 23 December 1997, M. Jospin officially asked the future president of C.S.D.N. for his opinion on the magistrate's request.[73]

IV. Restrictions on Freedom of Expression Aimed at Protecting National Security or Defense Secrets

Most restrictions imposed on freedom of expression on grounds of protecting national security or defense secrets are contained today in Book 4 of the new Penal Code, in force since 1993.[74] Title 1 of Book 4 concerns the "fundamental interests of the nation".[75] The new Code has led to the removal of a number of restrictions on freedom of expression that existed previously, and to a modernized definition of offenses. Three categories of restrictions are examined here: (a) restrictions aimed at protecting the military forces; (b) restrictions aimed at protecting national defense secrets; and (c) other restrictions.

Cases discussed here belong almost exclusively to the pre-1993 period. Although different from that of the present Penal Code, the wording of the codes and statutes then in force was not so different as to extinguish the explanatory value of the pre-1993 case law. Of particular relevance is the case law developed during the 1920's and 30's and between 1946 and 1962, *i.e.*, during the Indochina and Algerian wars.

---

[73] *Id.* December 28-29, 1997. The chairman of C.N.C.I.S., who has been named to be the first chairman of C.S.D.N., is Mr. Mandelkern, a respected senior member of the *Conseil d'Etat.*

[74] Before 1993 they could be found in a number of other instruments including the Code of Military Justice; Code of National Service; and Law on the Press of 1881.

[75] Art. 410-1 of the Penal Code defines them as follows: "The fundamental interests of the nation are, for the purpose of the present title, its independence, the integrity of its territory, its security, the republican form of its institutions, the means of its defense and of its diplomacy, the safeguard of its population in France and abroad, the equilibrium of its environment and of its natural sphere and the essential elements of its scientific and economic capacity and of its cultural heritage." There is a link between this article and the definition of the crimes of treason and espionage (Arts. 411-1 to 411-11).

A. Restrictions Aimed at Protecting Military Forces

These restrictions pertain primarily to incitement to a number of specific offenses, such as the following:

1. Inciting, in order to disturb national defense, members of French military forces to abandon their duties or serve a foreign power. The offense exists even in time of peace and even if it not public.[76]

2. Inciting, in order to disturb national defense, members of the French military forces to disobedience.[77] This form of incitement may take any form, public or non public (*e.g.* posters, newspapers).[78] The fact that the words or printed materials were or were not specifically addressed to members of the armed forces is irrelevant.[79] During the war in Algeria (1954-1962) many newspapers and journalists were prosecuted on these grounds.[80]

3. Participating in an organized effort to "demoralize" the Army.[81] Under the pre-1993 case law, the accusation must prove the existence of such an organized effort, beyond mere individual acts.[82]

B. Restrictions Aimed at Protecting National Defense Secrets

Two distinct issues are examined: (1) the legal definition of defense secrets; and (2) the two offenses set forth in the Penal Code.

1. Definition of Defense Secrets

Two texts are of primary relevance: Art. 413-9 of the Penal Code, and the Decree of 12 May 1981.

Under Penal Code Art. 413-9, a national defense secret is defined to be any item of information, processes, objects, documents, computerized data or data banks

---

[76] Art. 413-1 of the Penal Code. The maximum penalty is 10 years' imprisonment and a fine of FF 1,000,000.

[77] *Id.*, Art. 413-3. The maximum penalty is five years' imprisonment and/or a fine of FF 500.000.

[78] *See* Cass. civ., 6 May 1922, *Pfefferkorn et Seigneuret,* 1923 *Recueil Dalloz*, 1, at 75; Cass. crim., 30 Nov. 1935, 1936 *Recueil Dalloz hebdomadaire*, at 72; Cass. crim., 30 Jan. 1936, *Ministre public c. Coutant,* 1936 *Recueil Dalloz périodique*,1, at 47.

[79] *See* Cass. crim., May 2, 1956, *Merot, Bull.* n° 339; *id.*, same date, same name, *id*, n° 338.

[80] *For details, see* A. Heymann, *Les libertés publiques et la guerre d'Algerie* (Paris, 1972), at 237 ff.

[81] The French term is "*une entreprise*" (Article 413-4). The maximum penalty is five years' imprisonment and/or a fine of FF 500.000.

[82] *See, e.g.*, Cass. crim., Feb.25, 1958, *Jadean* (et autres), *Bull.* n° 194; Cass. crim., Oct. 27, 1960, *Roussel (et* autres), *Bull.* n° 490. Military courts had jurisdiction. On prosecutions during the war in Algeria, *see* Heymann, *supra* note 81.

(a) that relates to national defense *and* (b) the dissemination of which has been restricted by protective measures. Protective measures may be taken concerning any item of information or data, the revelation of which could hamper national defense or lead to the discovery of a national defense secret. The level of classification of the information mentioned above and the authorities responsible for determining the way the protection is organized are established by decree.

The Decree of 12 May 1981 remains in force. It contains the answers to the following questions: What are the levels of classification? Who is in charge of implementing them? Who may have access to classified information?

a. Levels of Classification

There are three levels of classification: "*Très secret-défense*"; "*secret-défense*"; "*Confidential-défense*". The classification must be indicated on the information or documents.[83] The authorities which classified them may later modify or suppress the classification. The Prime Minister (through a special delegation), the General-Secretary of National Defense, and a body belonging to the Prime Minister's office (hereafter "S.G.D.N.") play a key role in the classification process.

The designation "*très secret-défense*" is reserved for information the revelation of which would hamper national defense and the security of the State, and which relate to governmental priorities in defense matters. The Prime Minister defines the criteria and the ways and means of classifying such information. There are several sub-levels of classification. He determines the authorities responsible for the implementation of such measures of protection.[84]

The category "*secret-défense*" is reserved for information the revelation of which would hamper national defense and the security of the State.

The category "*confidential-défense*" is reserved for pieces of information which do not have, by themselves, a secret character but the knowledge, gathering or exploitation of which could lead to the revelation of a secret relating to national defense or the security of the State.

The Prime Minister determines the conditions in which each Minister will implement the protection of the information classified under the headings "*secret-défense*" and "*confidential-défense*".

There is a fourth category, "*diffusion restreinte*" (restricted), which each Minister is free to use in his or her Ministry. Detailed rules of protection are

---

[83] The expression "security of the State" figures both in the title of the 1981 decree and in its articles, but is not mentioned in Art. 413-9 or any other provision of the Penal Code. "Security of the State" has been replaced by "the fundamental interests of the Nation", mentioned above. The explanation for this difference is that the Penal Code was enacted in 1993 and the decree, enacted in 1981, has not been revised since.

[84] Decree, Art. 4.

contained in an inter-ministerial circular of 12 March 1982, itself a classified document.[85]

b. Conditions and Procedures for Obtaining Access to Classified Information

The Decree of 12 May 1981 regulates the conditions and procedures for obtaining access to classified information. To obtain access, a person must receive prior authorization. He or she must be recognized as needing to know such information in view of his or her functions, and as presenting no risk, should access be granted, for national defense, the security of the State or his own security.

Authorization is granted for a given level (or sub-level) of classification. The Prime Minister determines the procedure of admission and himself makes decisions regarding the top level ("*très secret-défense*"). Each Minister is empowered to make decisions concerning the two other levels. The same applies for declassification.

There are two main legal consequences of this definition of defense secrets. First, if no measure of protection (*i.e.*, classification) has been taken, the notion does not apply and disclosure is not an offense. Second, as long as a document is classified, its disclosure is an offense, even if the information could not harm legitimate security interests or has already been made public. There has not yet been any case law on these two points.

The present definition is better than the previous one[86] in that it is more precise and therefore carries more legal certainty. It is a constitutional requirement under French law that statutes creating offenses must define them as precisely as possible, in order to avoid any arbitrariness in application.[87]

2. Main Penal Code Offenses

In addition to espionage and treason, both beyond the scope of this paper, the two main offenses stated in the Penal Code apply respectively to (a) persons who, by their functions, are holders of national defense secrets, and (b) all other persons.

a) Any holder of a defense secret (by virtue of his or her profession, mission or function, permanent or temporary) who destroys it in whole or in part, diverts or reproduces it, or lets an unauthorized person or the public know it, is guilty of an offense under Article 413-10. The maximum penalty is seven years' imprisonment and a fine of FF 700,000. If the person with access to the secret allows, through negligence or imprudence, someone else to reveal it or otherwise destroy its secrecy, the penalty is three years' imprisonment and a fine of FF 300,000.

---

[85] *See* Art. L. 413-6 of the Penal Code. *See also* the *arrêté (*a ministerial or inter-ministerial regulation) of Feb. 21, 1994.

[86] *Cf.* Statute (*Ordonnance*) of June 4, 1960.

[87] *See Conseil constitutionnel*, Jan. 20, 1981 and Sept. 3, 1986.

b) It is an offense (under Article 413-11 of the Penal Code) for any person not mentioned in Article 413-10 to: (i) act in order to come into possession of a national defense secret; (ii)destroy it in whole or in part, divert, or reproduce it; or (iii) let the public or any unauthorized person know it. The maximum penalty is five years' imprisonment and a fine of FF 500,000.

For both Articles 413-10 and 413-11, the attempt to commit one of the offenses is punishable by the same penalties.

Under Article 412-8 of the Penal Code it is an offense to incite others to take up arms against the authority of the State or against part of the population. The maximum penalty is five years' imprisonment and a fine of FF 500,000 (or 30 years and three months if the incitement has serious consequences). There does not appear to be any case law on this clause.

Under a clause of a statute of 21 January 1995 revising the 1881 statute on the press, it is an offense to reveal, by any means, the identity of members of the national police, the *Gendarmerie nationale* or the customs administration belonging to services or units listed by a decision of the competent minister, and whose missions demand, on security grounds, that they remain anonymous.[88]

V. Conclusion

On the whole, the law and practice in France concerning defense secrets and expression threatening national security strikes a fair balance between two vital, competing interests. Although there are numerous restrictions on access to public documents by the public in general, their implementation by the courts and independent authorities seems to have been reasonable. Recent reforms expanding access by the courts to secret documents are meaningful. Independent authorities exercise significant power in overseeing government secrecy and their decisions are accorded considerable weight. The wording of the new Penal Code is more precise and more liberal than that of the former one, especially in areas relating to freedom of expression. The overall trend gives cause for cautious optimism.

[88] Statute of January 21, 1995, on security, adding a new Article 39 to the 1881 law on the press. The maximum penalty is a fine of FF 100,000. The services and units are listed for the police in an *arrêté* (regulation) of May 5, 1995, revised by another *arrêté* of Dec. 5, 1995; for the *Gendarmerie*, by an *arrêté* of Nov. 20, 1995; and, for the customs office, by an *arrêté* of Sept. 24, 1996.

Freedom of Expression and National Security: The Experience of Germany

Ulrich Karpen

I. Standards and Principles

A. Freedom of Speech, Press and Broadcasting

Paragraphs 1 and 2 of Article 5 of the 1949 Basic Law (BL) of the Federal Republic of Germany guarantee the right to freedom of expression in the following terms:

> (1) Everybody has the right freely to express and disseminate their opinions orally, in writing or visually and to obtain information from generally accessible sources without hindrance. Freedom of the press and freedom of reporting through audiovisual media shall be guaranteed. There shall be no censorship.
>
> (2) These rights are subject to limitations embodied in the provisions of general legislation, statutory provisions for the protection of young persons and by the citizen's right to personal respect.[1]

Freedom of speech is first and foremost a right of everyone; in addition, it is an institutional guarantee of the press and broadcasting.[2] Freedom of speech protects the private sphere of the individual against governmental interference; furthermore, it is a prerequisite of a democratic constitutional order.

In the emphatic language of the leading case, the Federal Constitutional Court (FCC) declared that freedom of speech is a direct expression of human personality in society and a necessary constituent of a free, democratic order.[3] The court explicitly referred to Justice Cardozo's famous statement: "Freedom of thought and speech is the matrix, the indispensable condition of nearly every other form of freedom".[4] In German constitutional doctrine, the controversy over whether the guarantee of freedom of speech is based primarily on (individual) self-determination or (collective) self-government was solved from the very beginning by using both values as justification.

---

[1] Paragraph 3, which is not directly relevant to press freedom, reads: "Art and scholarship, research and teaching shall be free. Freedom of teaching shall not absolve anybody from loyalty to the constitution."

[2] *See infra*, 296.

[3] 7 FCC 198, 207 (1958) *(Lüth* case).

[4] *Palko* v. *Connecticut*, 202 U.S. 319, 327 (1937).

B. Limitations of Freedom of Speech for the Protection of National Security

Freedom of speech is limited by other constitutional provisions and may be limited by "general laws", which are laws that seek to promote a general social value and which may, incidentally, affect, but are not aimed at curtailing, freedom of speech.[5] Freedom of speech, first of all, may be limited by other constitutional provisions which, although rarely or not at all applied, are meant to secure the free democratic order of the state. The general laws that may take precedence over freedom of expression include those which protect youth, public morality, personal honor, the rights and reputations of others, national security and respect for state institutions.

The Basic Law is intended as, and understood to be, a legal order able to defend its principles against abuse of freedom and attempts to undermine the democratic state. Article 21 (2) of the Basic Law states:

> Parties which, by reason of their aims or the behavior of their adherents, seek to impair or abolish the free democratic basic order or to endanger the existence of the Federal Republic of Germany, shall be unconstitutional. The Federal Constitutional Court shall decide on the question of unconstitutionality.

The freedom of political parties is of course protected by freedom of expression in association with others and freedom of association. In two cases in the 1950s the FCC declared unconstitutional a fascist party[6] and the German Communist Party.[7] The FCC acknowledged the almost contradictory tension between the constitutional principles of guaranteeing freedoms and limiting these freedoms in order to protect the free constitutional order. The FCC held that there must be no freedom for the enemies of freedom and that tolerance of intolerance must be limited. These are the only cases in the constitutional history of the Federal Republic of Germany in which the FCC has declared a party unconstitutional. Since these cases, the overwhelming opinion has come to be that one should combat radical parties by free speech, sound arguments and good campaigning.

The same notion applies to Article 18 of the Basic Law:

> Whoever abuses freedom of expression of opinion, in particular freedom of the press (paragraph (1) of Article 5), freedom of teaching (paragraph (3) of Article 5), freedom of assembly (Article 8), freedom of association (Article 9), privacy of letters, posts and telecommunications (Article 10), property (Article 14), or the right of asylum (paragraph (2) of Article 16) in order to combat the free democratic basic order shall forfeit these basic rights. Such

---

[5] Basic Law (BL), Art. 5(2).

[6] 2 FCC 1 (1952) *(Sozialistische Reichspartei).*

[7] 5 FCC 85 (1956) *(Kommunistische Partei Deutschlands).*

> forfeiture and the extent thereof shall be determined by the Federal Constitutional Court.

Forfeiture would occur only in response to acts which the FCC determined were intended and likely to undermine democracy or the rule of law. The FCC has never made such a pronouncement and this provision, therefore, is seen as a "dead letter".

Article 10 (2) of the Basic Law, a third constitutional provision that limits freedom of speech, was added to the Basic Law by the 1968 Amendment on the defense of the State. Article 10 guarantees the privacy of posts and telecommunications. Paragraph 2 reads:

> This right may be restricted only pursuant to a law. Such law may lay down that a person affected shall not be informed of any such restriction if it serves to protect the free democratic order or the existence or security of the Federation or a Land (state), and that recourse to the courts shall be replaced by a review of the case by bodies and auxiliary bodies appointed by Parliament.

This provision arguably is not in accordance with Article 19 of the Basic Law, which states that no law or measure may encroach upon the "essential content of fundamental freedoms" and that "recourse to the courts shall be open to everybody". In a 1970 judgment, however, the FCC held that Article 10 (2) is necessary for an effective protection of constitutional principles and that oversight by a parliamentary body, rather than the courts, suffices to protect the rights of the person subject to government surveillance.[8]

These constitutional limitations on freedom of expression indicate that in German legal tradition the term "national security" is understood and applied so as to provide strong protection for the free, democratic order as the constitutional framework of the State. National security includes protection of the existence of the State and its constitutional institutions, protection against external and internal adversaries, and the guarantee of the free and democratic order of a State bound by the rule of law.[9] This is emphasized by the Law on the Office for the Protection of the Constitution of 1990, section 1 of which reads:

> Protection of the Constitution serves to uphold the free democratic order, secure the existence and safety of the Federation and the Länder.

Section 92 of the Federal Criminal Code describes in greater detail the scope of national security. This section provides that the existence of the Federal Republic is threatened by anyone who abridges its freedom from foreign subordination, destroys its national unity or separates parts of its territory. The fundamental constitutional principles are the right of the people to vote and choose their government, separation of powers, the existence of a parliamentary opposition, the

---

[8] 30 FCC 1, 19 (1970) *(Abhörentscheidung)*.

[9] BL, Art. 20.

government's responsibility to Parliament, independence of the judiciary, and prohibition of arbitrary government.

Freedom of expression, in addition to being limited by the Basic Law itself, may be limited by "general laws". These include the Criminal Code, the Law on Foreigners, the Passport Law and the Law for Civil Servants. Section 2 (2) of the Berlin Press Code, which uses virtually the same wording as the press laws of all other Länder, reads:

> Freedom of the press may be limited only by the Basic Law itself and by laws that are consistent with its framework.

A law intended to protect national security may restrict freedom of expression only if necessary to protect national security in the sense explained above. Protection of "public order", as in police laws or in Section 37 (2) of the Law on Foreigners, does not supply sufficient ground for restricting free speech. In a 1959 case, the FCC declared unconstitutional a provision of a law of North-Rhine Westfalia which authorized the government to forbid individuals from working as journalists if they undermine the constitutional order by disseminating nationalist, racist or militaristic ideas.[10] The FCC held that application of this state law would entail the forfeiture of freedom of speech, a measure that could only be undertaken by the FCC pursuant to Article 18 of the Basic Law.

C. Applying the Proportionality Principle

According to constitutional jurisprudence, freedom of expression and national security are interdependent. Freedom is an essential part of the Basic Law and national security measures may be used, and may only be used, to defend against misuse of freedom.[11] The FCC does not accept that any general law, including one intended to protect national security, provides a legitimate ground for restricting freedom of expression, but rather balances the "pressing social need" in national security against the constitutional interest in protecting freedom of speech.[12] The balancing takes into account the degree to which the protection of national security might pose a danger of stifling freedom of speech. Any restriction must always be proportionate to the threat.

The FCC applies the proportionality principle in a three-part test. It examines whether measures taken to protect national security pursuant to a constitutional provision or general law and that infringe upon freedom of expression are, first, appropriate and, second, necessary. If they are, the third step involves resolving any doubts as to which interest prevails in favor of freedom of speech. The FCC would test whether in the fragile equilibrium of individual freedoms and public

---

[10] 10 FCC 118, 121 (1959 *(Freies Volk* case).

[11] 5 FCC 85, 137 *et seq.* (1956) *(KPD* case).

[12] 7 FCC 198 (1958) *(Lüth);* 30 FCC 173 (1971) *(Mephisto);* 75 FCC 369 (1987) *(Strauss-Karikatur).*

interests the balance is well kept. If it is not, the court would rule the measures unconstitutional. In a leading case, the FCC ruled illegal the seizure of issues of an imported newspaper based on a law intended to protect the democratic constitutional order. The court held that the lower court did not take into adequate account the public's right to freedom of information, which includes the right to receive information from generally accessible sources.[13]

In balancing the conflicting interests, the courts make a determination based on the particular facts and circumstances of a given case. In the *Spiegel/Schmid* case,[14] the FCC established the *Gegenschlag* (counter-attack) principle which holds that a statement made in response to a possibly defamatory statement is entitled to greater latitude than if made in a neutral context. After Judge Schmid was publicly attacked for being a Communist and thus not fit to be a judge, the magazine *Der Spiegel* published a highly critical story about his past political activities that disregarded documents Schmid had given to the magazine in his defense. In response, Schmid stated that *Der Spiegel* was, in the field of politics, as pornography was in the field of morals. The FCC held that highly insulting expressions of opinion are to be tolerated when made, as in this case, in response to a personal attack.

In the *Lüth* case,[15] the Court underlined the importance of freedom of expression for the individual and democracy. If an opinion is given on a highly controversial issue of public debate, any doubts as to which interest prevails are to be resolved in favor of freedom of speech. The FCC is vigilant in ensuring that measures taken to protect public interests, such as national security, do not have a chilling effect on public discussion.

II. Access to and Disclosure of Information

A. Access to Information and Restrictions on National Security Grounds

Article 5(1) of the Basic Law states that "(e)veryone shall have the right freely to express and disseminate his opinion in speech, writing, and pictures and to inform himself from generally accessible sources". Freedom of information includes the right of access to sources that are outside the federal territory.[16] According to a law of 31 May 1961 on the import of printed matter, newspapers and other printed materials may be seized at the border if they violate the laws protecting the free democratic order, international relations or the prohibition of pornography. The

---

[13] 27 FCC 72 (1969) *(Importkontrolle), citing* BL, Art. 5(2), sent. 1.

[14] 12 FCC 113, 118 (1961).

[15] 7 FCC 198, 212 (1958).

[16] 27 FCC 71, 84 (1969) *(Importkontrolle).*

law has not been used for several years. In the *Importkontrolle* case,[17] the FCC ruled that courts, in applying this law, must take into consideration the right of the public to receive information. Accordingly, because the lower court had not accorded proper weight to this public right, the FCC ruled illegal the confiscation of literature imported from the (former) German Democratic Republic which supported the banned West German Communist Party.

Similarly, Section 7(1) of the Passport Law of 1986 must be interpreted narrowly. It authorizes government to refuse to issue a passport to a person if there are suspicions that he or she might endanger the internal or external security or other vital interests of the Republic. According to the Law on Access to Ecological Information of 1994, everybody has a right of access to information concerning the environment.[18] This right, however, is extinguished if publication would affect Germany's international relations, defense interests or secrecy of government negotiations.

There are also sources of information that are not generally accessible. For instance, Section 5(1) of the Federal Archives Law of 1988 states that everybody has the right to use the archival files and documents maintained by a federal authority that concern the scope of federal administration. However, this right may be asserted only after thirty years have passed from the time the document was produced. Section 5(6) of the Federal Archives Law states that even after 30 years have passed, access may be forbidden if the integrity of the Federal Republic or one of its Länder would be endangered by disclosure.

Article 9(2) of the Basic Law and Section 3 of the Law of Associations of 1964 concern freedom of expression in association with others. Unlike Article 21 of the Basic Law, whereby only the FCC may declare political parties hostile to the Basic Law, the Law on Associations empowers the executive to ban and dissolve associations, if their goals and activities are in contradiction to the constitutional order or the idea of international peaceful relations. Freedom of collective expression is protected by both Articles 5 and 8 (freedom of assembly) of the Basic Law. According to these provisions and the Law on Assembly of 1978, the right to assemble freely is denied to persons who support goals of a party or association that is declared illegal according to Articles 21 and 9 of the Basic Law.

B. Disclosures of Government Agents and Employees

Since the leading *Strafgefangene* case in 1972,[19] there can be no doubt that public employees, civil servants and military personal enjoy freedom of expression

---

[17] *Id.*

[18] Law on Access to Ecological Information of 1994, sec. 1.

[19] 33 FCC 1 (1972).

vis à vis their employers, and that public limitations may be imposed only pursuant to laws enacted by parliament.

At the same time, civil servants of both the federal and Länder governments, soldiers and other employees owe a duty of confidentiality to their employers. Without the special permission of an employer a public employee may not disclose information that he or she received in the course of office.[20]

Some information, in particular personal data of citizens and information that serves "state interests", are classified as "confidential", "secret" or some other designation according to federal and Länder Data Protection Laws and parliamentary and governmental regulations. In exercising their control function, parliaments may, however, establish committees of investigation which can ask for the requisite evidence at public hearings.[21] Since they apply the rules of criminal procedure *mutatis mutandis* to the taking of evidence, this provision allows parliament to obtain most information - except strictly personal data - from government agencies.

Given that civil servants, soldiers and other public employees serve "the whole people not a particular party", they are obliged not to express political opinions.[22] In order to secure public confidence in the independence of the courts, the same applies to judges.[23] In a 1970 case, the FCC ruled that officers and non-commissioned officers violate their duties if, in political discussions while in service, they oppose the free democratic order of the country.[24]

Moreover, all civil servants must swear allegiance to and duly uphold the Basic Law and its values. The second sentence of Section 35(1) of the Law on Federal Civil Servants states that a civil servant in all his behavior must act in accordance with, and support, the free democratic order. In fact, several civil servants were dismissed from their positions in the 1970s after they publicly stated their support for extreme right- or left-wing parties. The duty of allegiance applies to probationary civil servants, including lawyers who must pass their practical training after their studies. In a widely discussed case,[25] the FCC held that this law was in accordance with the "due regard for the traditional principles of the professional civil service" required by Article 33(5) of the Basic Law. Loyalty to the State must be manifested not only in words but in deeds as well.

---

[20] Law on Federal Civil Servants of 1985, sec. 39; Law on Soldiers of 1975, sec. 14.
[21] BL, Art. 44.
[22] Law on Federal Civil Servants, sec. 35(1) & (2).
[23] Law on Judges of 1972, sec. 39.
[24] 28 FCC 36, 47 (1970) *(Dienstpflicht von Offizieren)*.
[25] 39 FCC 334 (1975)*(Radikale im öffentlichen Dienst)*.

III. News Media

A. Freedom of Press and Broadcasting

The press and broadcast media are actors in the formation of public opinion in a democracy. Freedom of the press and broadcasting, in addition to being a constitutional right of individuals against the State, is viewed as a guarantor of freedom of speech and informed public debate, and thus as integral to the protection of democracy.[26] In this respect, sentence 2 of Article 5(1) of the Basic Law states: "Freedom of the press and freedom of reporting by means of broadcasts and films are guaranteed". Similarly, Section 1 of the Berlin Press Law reads: "The press is free. It serves the free democratic order" and Section 3 of the Baden-Württemberg Press Law provides: "The press fulfills a public task by gathering and disseminating news concerning matters of public interest, by taking positions, and by criticizing and contributing in other forms to public opinion".

Concerning the role of the broadcasting media, Section 4 of the North-Rhine-Westfalia Law for the West-German-Broadcasting System of 1990 (which applies only to the public broadcasting station) reads: "The broadcasting station produces and disseminates programs as medium and a factor in the process of establishing free public opinion as a matter of public interest." Section 5 of the law continues: "The free democratic order is applicable for the program as well for the new media services, as offered by the West German Broadcasting System". Section 14 of the Baden-Württemberg Media Law of 1987 (applicable to both public and private broadcasters) read as follows: "Private broadcasting, in addition to public broadcasting, serves the free formation of public opinion". Section 15 of the same law reads: "Private broadcasting fulfills a public task when - in matters of public interest - [it] is gathering and disseminating news, is giving opinion and criticizing or in other ways is contributing to public opinion". Section 48 of the same law states: "The program must not be in contradiction to the peaceful understanding of nations and the free democratic order".

B. Restrictions on News-Gathering and Publishing During Peace Time

There are no federal laws addressed exclusively to the press. The Federal Law on Broadcasting establishes and regulates two federal stations. Otherwise, press and broadcasting are regulated by the Länder. All Länder have enacted press and broadcasting laws which, while varying in detail, basically follow the same lines.

---

[26] 7 FCC 198, 208 (1950) *(Lüth)*.

Section 4 of the Berlin Press Law expressly provides for access to information. Public officials must give information to journalists unless barred by secrecy regulations, in particular if disclosure would damage or endanger public interests, or if a fair court procedure or a preeminent private interest would be violated. Section 51 of the Baden-Württemberg Media Law is essentially the same. The press and broadcasting stations may apply to the courts for a ruling in the event of a refusal.

Concerning government-held information about national security, there is no precise definition of "secret" or even "the rules of secrecy". Most of these rules are found in statutes or administrative regulations. According to Section 93 of the Criminal Code, "state secrets" are facts, objects or pieces of information which are accessible only to a limited number of persons and must be kept secret from foreign powers in order to avert serious damage to the external security of the Federal Republic. In addition to these absolute secrets are documents and kinds of information that have been classified by administrative regulation. The legitimacy of a classification is subject to challenge. If the press publishes classified information, the courts will decide whether the information was legitimately classified. A journalist will not be punished if the information should not have been made secret. Clearly, governments are not entitled to classify information simply in order to keep it secret from the press.

Press freedom does not provide a legitimate ground for the illegal collection of information.[27] Publication of information may be excused, however, if the interest in disclosure is strong and outweighs the interest in secrecy.[28] In this case the journalist who gathered information illegally bears responsibility for breach of privacy and has to compensate for any damage caused by his action. This is particularly applicable to information kept secret allegedly in the interest of national security. This doctrine of the FCC is reflected in such statutes as Section 93(2) of the Criminal Code, which states:

> Facts which are in contradiction to the free democratic order or which are kept secret from treaty partners in violation of arms limitation agreements are not state secrets.

Moreover, Section 97 B of the Criminal Code provides that publication of a genuine secret by one who, however erroneously, believed that the information was not entitled to be kept secret, is not a crime if the person acted with the intent to stop an activity that he believed to be illegal. That paragraph is part of a revision of the Criminal Code that followed the controversial *Spiegel* case in 1966.[29] The case concerned *Der Spiegel*'s publication of an article which, in challenging the effectiveness of German and NATO military defense forces, relied on information which the government claimed included military secrets. The prosecution filed

---

[27] 66 FCC 116, 137 (1984) *(Wallraf).*
[28] 61 FCC 1, 11 (1982) *(Christlich Soziale Union).*
[29] 20 FCC 162 (1966).

criminal charges, including accusations of disclosing military secrets, against the publisher and some journalists, and obtained a warrant to search *Der Spiegel*'s offices and seize all documents related to the article. The FCC, by a split vote of 4 to 4, upheld the search but on narrow grounds. In so doing, the FCC affirmed the presumption against searches of newspaper premises and made clear that the suspicion of criminal activity could not be based on *Mosaiktheorie.* That doctrine held that it is illegal to publish non-secret information collected from different sources if, pieced together, they present an overall picture that could threaten national security. The FCC held that it is an essential function of the press to collect pieces of information, arrange them and draw conclusions. The FCC concluded that there was sufficient other evidence to support a reasonable suspicion of criminal activity and, accordingly, that the search was lawful. Public outrage prompted by the article led to the collapse of the coalition government and was a major factor contributing to an amendment of the law on state secrets (Criminal Code Section 97B) to allow a limited defense of good faith belief that disclosure was necessary to stop unlawful activity.

In another spectacular case, the court ruled that a ban on news was found to be in accordance with freedom of the press.[30] The press was ordered by the government to protect the life of a hostage by not publishing anything, even though there was a legitimate public interest in publishing the story. The court ruled that, while the Federal Government was engaged in negotiations with the terrorists who held Mr. Schleyer hostage and finally murdered him, the papers could be prohibited from publishing information about the negotiations.

There are limits on access to matters pending before the courts. According to Section 353D of the Criminal Code, it is illegal to disclose the contents of official papers used in court, in particular, to cite verbatim from the charging sheet. The independence of the court, which may be endangered by public discussion in the press, is an essential part of the free democratic order at the core of national security. The FCC stressed that a total ban on reporting on criminal proceedings, even while they are in progress, would violate freedom of the press.[31] Thus, while upholding the statute that prohibited references to court documents and testimony that had not been made public, the FCC reaffirmed that journalists' reports of trial proceedings must be protected. The distinction was rational because the legislature reasonably could find that reference to official court documents or testimony would have a greater impact on public opinion than mere reports unsupported by such evidence. In the statement of reasons, the court balanced the impartiality of the judges (especially the lay judges) against the high-ranking public interest in this case and the responsibility of the press to control governmental action and to disclose public grievances.

---

[30] *See* Ulf Brühann *et al.* eds., *Archiv für Presserecht* 171-77 (1978).

[31] 71 FCC 206 (1985) *(Flick-Prozess).*

C. Restrictions on News-Gathering and Publishing During Armed Conflicts

During debates in 1968 that led to amendment of the Basic Law on defense issues, the question of restricting access to information under emergency conditions was vigorously discussed. Finally the enactment of legal provisions was prevented by the opposition press. The general opinion was that there was hardly any measure that could damage the public confidence in government more than limiting the free flow of information.

IV. Restraints on Freedom of Expression

A. Advocacy of Conscientious Objection, Desertion or Giving Support to the Enemy

Among the general laws that limit freedom of the media are various criminal provisions to protect national security, the constitution, state organs, government officials and public order. They break down into two categories: (1) provisions to avoid a danger of overthrowing the democratic constitutional order of the state (high treason); and (2) others to protect the external security of the state by prohibiting the dissemination of to state secrets to unauthorized foreign states (treason). Among the first category are Section 80 (preparation of aggressive war), and other provisions against breach of peace, such as Section 81 *et seq.* (crimes against the territorial and constitutional integrity of the country). Sections 84-89 protect the democratic state by sanctioning the continuation of activities of an illegal party or association,[32] unconstitutional influencing of the armed forces, undermining the readiness for action, etc.

Among the provisions for protecting external security[33] are treason, in particular treason by press and broadcasting (Section 95), conspiracy, hate speech (Section 130), advocacy and incitement to crimes. Disclosure of illegal secrets is not a crime; transmission to a foreign power, however, is punished as (quasi-)treason. The FCC, by a split decision of 4 votes to 4, upheld the legality of the search of *Spiegel*'s offices on the ground that the magazine was suspected of disclosing state secrets in violation of the law on treason.[34] It had published an article criticizing the performance of the German Army in NATO maneuvers and revealing plans, allegedly then contemplated, to equip the army with nuclear weapons. The dissenting four judges reasoned that the press enjoyed greater freedom to publish military secrets than private persons, particularly when the supposed secret

[32] 32 BL, Art. 9.
[33] Criminal Code, sec. 93 *et seq.*
[34] 20 FCC 162 (1966) *(Spiegel).*

information was already available elsewhere, as apparently was the case. The dissenters also observed that the lower court had not adequately explored the existence of other options for obtaining the information. The majority rejected these contentions. While it affirmed the importance of press freedom and the presumption against searches of newspaper premises and noted that the proportionality principle places limits on the permissible scope of searches, it ruled that the search was lawful in the light of credible suspicions of the magazine's criminal behavior.

In the Frankfurt Airport Case[35] the court, by a split vote of 4 to 4, upheld the conviction of a city official for breach of public order for having called (in an ironic manner) for the use of violence in protesting against building a new runway at the Frankfurt airport. The four judges in the minority held that speech must not be judged as criminal due to its dramatic use of exaggeration or appeal to emotion. This rule seems not to have impeded either the press or political parties.

B. Criticism of Government or Government Officials

Section 90 of the Criminal Code prohibits defamation of the Federal President in public by spoken or printed word. Section 90A protects the Federal Republic and its symbols (including its colors, flag, insignia and anthem) and Section 90B protects the Federal and Länder legislatures, governments, constitutional courts and their members against public attacks. Sections 103 and 104 forbid insults to the representatives of foreign states as well as to foreign flags and national emblems.

In practice, these provisions are of little importance. The FCC held that, during the struggle for political power in a democratic state, criticism is a necessary element of controlling government.[36] Given the court's statement that vigorous criticism of public officials is an acceptable and necessary part of a democracy, it is not surprising that the court has generally overturned convictions for defamation of government officials.[37] In recent decisions, the FCC has held that attacks against state symbols, such as the flag and anthem, even if harsh and satirical, must be tolerated in view of the constitutional protections of freedom of speech, the press and arts.[38] Similarly, criticisms of Federal policy and politicians, even if sharp and obviously unfair, are entitled to protection unless they amount to defamation. Thus, the general law on defamation concerning politicians has tended to overtake the various specific laws on insult to government officials.

This litigation seems to have reached a critical peak in a 1994 decision.[39] A three-judge screening chamber of the FCC struck down a conviction for defamation

---

[35] 82 FCC 236, 260 (1990) *(Schuberth)*.

[36] 4 FCC 85, 198 (1956) (KPD).

[37] 24 FCC 278, 283 *(Tonjaeger)*; 54 FCC 129, 139 (1980) *(Roemerberg)*.

[38] 81 FCC 278, 294 (1990) *(Bundesflagge)*; 81 FCC 298, 306 (1990) *(Nationalhymne)*.

[39] FCC Neue Juristische Wochenschrift 1994, 2943 *(Soldaten sind Moerder)*.

of soldiers, on grounds of freedom of speech. The accused had shown at the rear window of his car a label stating "Soldiers are murderers" ("Kurt Tucholsky").[40] Most critics, however, hold this to be an extreme and exaggerated opinion.

C. Republication of Statements by Groups Deemed Threatening to National Security

Sections 84 and 85 Criminal Code prohibit support of a party or organization which has been declared unconstitutional by the FCC (Party) or administration (organization). As long as a party, although militating against state and constitution, is not declared unconstitutional by the FCC, it enjoys the protection of the freedom of party guarantee of Article 21 of the BL. Under this "party privilege" it is not illegal to republish statements of a party although they may endanger national security. After the party has been declared unconstitutional by the FCC, Section 84 is applicable. The court, however, held that under the freedom of speech guarantee it is legal to have and disseminate political opinions of the same manner as those of an unconstitutional party.[41] Liable to punishment, however, are opinions that support an organization or an illegal party directly. Printing party programs in large numbers could be an act to support the party organization. The FCC held that disseminating information about a party, which is opposed to the free democratic order, in a report of the Federal Office for the Protection of the Constitution is not a violation of the "party privilege", *i.e.*, that a party has to be treated as legal until the FCC declares it illegal.[42]

As far as associations and groups which are not parties are concerned, even if they are politically active and hostile to state and constitution, it is legal to share their ideas and to disseminate them. After such an organization has been prohibited by an administrative agency of the interior, according to Section 85 of the Criminal Code it becomes illegal to support it.

V. Extraordinary Procedures for Determining National Security Issues

A. Scope of Judicial Review of National Security Determinations

The meaning of terms such as free democratic order, national security, and state secrets is largely addressed in legal definitions, as in Sections 90 and 92 of the

---

[40] The reference is to Kurt Tucholsky and Ignaz Wrobel, "Der bewachte Kriegsschauplatz," *Die Weltbühne*, Vol. 27 (2) at 191 *et. seq*. (1931).
[41] 25 FCC 44, 59 (1969) *(KPD)*.
[42] 40 FCC 287, 292 (1975) *(Nationaldemokratische Partei Deutschlands)*.

Criminal Code. Due to the monopoly of the FCC to declare a party unconstitutional[43] and to authorize forfeiture of basic rights,[44] the "definition competence" in addition rests with this court. Making use of this competence, the decision to declare unconstitutional the German Communist Party[45] covers some 300 pages and is a treatise on virtually all elements of the constitutional order of the law.

The Criminal Code provisions protecting national security are interpreted and applied by the ordinary (penal) courts. According to Sections 74A and 120 of the Court Organization Law of 1975, there are panels to sit in cases of national security. According to Section 142A of the same act, a Federal Prosecutor investigates cases of national security. As far as seizure of press organs for alleged breach of national security provisions is concerned, press panels of ordinary (civil) courts are competent. Cases of breach of official secrecy by public employees are decided by administrative courts. There are no military courts. As far as offenses of the military disciplinary code by soldiers are concerned, they are heard by special panels of the military service in the first and initial appeal instance, and finally by a disciplinary panel of the Federal Administrative Court. Altogether this is a very detailed, although reasonable, allocation of responsibilities to protect constitution and state.

B. Prior Restraint of Publication

Article 5(1) reads, in part: "There shall be no censorship." Freedom of the press, in principle, includes freedom from registration requirements. This is the essence of Section 2 of the Baden-Württemberg press law, which is valid in an almost identical wording in all Länder: "Press activities, including the founding of a publishing house or other establishment, must not be dependent on government authorization." This differs from the private broadcasting sector, where government justifies licensing, among other grounds, on the scarcity of channels and the public interest in balanced programming. The FCC held that freedom of the press would be forfeited only according to Art. 18 of the BL, not by government regulation of press activities.[46]

Exclusion of any kind of prior censorship does not bar seizure of press products on the grounds of violation of laws protecting national security or personal honor.[47] Measures may take the form of injunctions. Seizure may be decreed only by a judge and only under the conditions that it is likely that the copies are subject to confiscation at forfeiture proceedings or that the broadcasting program may not

---

[43] 2 BL, Art. 21, para. 2.

[44] BL, Art. 18.

[45] 5 FCC 85 (1956) *(KPD)*.

[46] 10 FCC 118, 121 (1959) *("Freies Volk")*.

[47] Press Law, sec. 13-19.

be transmitted and that, in addition, seizure is not a disproportionate remedy.[48] Only under urgent circumstances may the public prosecutor, upon request of a person alleging libel, slander or invasion of privacy, or in an *ex officio* capacity regarding claims of treason, insults against state organs or threat to state security, initiate an inquiry and take immediate measures, including seizure. In some Länder, publications that insult the dignity of a national, ethnic or religious group may also be seized without court order.

When determining whether to uphold an immediate measure, such as an interlocutory order against publication, the FCC considers the likelihood of the measure being upheld on the merits; it then balances the likely impact of refusing an injunction if the applicant is successful on the merits against the negative effects which may occur if the injunction is granted and the applicant is unsuccessful on the merits. In doing so, the court determines whether the interference with press freedom is justified. In general, the court considers that restraints on publication may be appropriate to protect state security, confidentiality and other pressing interests. Second, the court examines whether the measure to be taken is necessary to protect an overriding state or private interest. Third, the court considers whether the interference is proportionate in the sense that the damage to the constitutional freedom must not be disproportionate to the enhancement of the countervailing interest.

C. Procedures for Treating Aliens Deemed to Threaten National Security

If aliens have committed crimes threatening national security, there are administrative procedures to reach faster decisions on expulsion. According to Section 7, paragraph 2, of the Foreigner Law of 1990, a non-resident is not entitled to receive a residence permit if his stay would endanger the interests of the country. This is true in particular for political activities. According to Section 37 of the Foreigner Law, foreigners in Germany are entitled to be politically active in the frame of general laws. Political activities may be restricted, *e.g.*, if they endanger the peaceful coexistence of native and foreign citizens, foreign political interests of the country and other preeminent state goals or if foreigners in their political activities use violence. Activities can be limited or forbidden if they are directed against the constitution, the peaceful cooperation of nations or similar interests. In such a case a foreigner may be ordered to leave the country and expulsion can be enforced.[49] The same is true for persons who apply for asylum on grounds of political persecution under Art. 16 of the BL and the Asylum Procedure Law of 1993. If an applicant is not acknowledged as being a persecutee, he must leave the country. In all cases

---

[48] Baden-Württemberg Press Law, sec. 13.

[49] Foreigner Law, sec. 45.

foreigners, prior to being expelled, have access to administrative courts. Under a few instruments, an urgent decision may permit a shortened period for appeal.[50]

VI. Conclusions

Freedom of expression as a private right and as an element of democracy enjoys solid protection in German law. Freedom of expression in German Constitutional litigation and doctrine is primarily based on the notion of individual rights and on liberal freedom of speech, rather than on a vision of a collective notion of a peoples' government or finding the truth in the whole public opinion. The press is considered to best serve its public function by acting as "public watchdog" in matters of public interest.

Public discussion of grievances, in particular in the field of national security, is considered to offer better protection of the people, state and constitutional order than frequent classification of information as secret. German opinion recognizes a close connection between freedom of expression as a key element of a free democratic constitutional order and effective protection of that order. The ridge, however, is narrow between freedom of speech, even for extreme opinions, and the necessity to uphold the principles of the social and political order.

The general laws, including the Länder press laws, include certain restrictions on freedom of expression which are regarded as necessary and which impose some obligation, not unduly cumbersome, on the press. If these limits are applied in the light of freedom of expression and leave a presumption to freedom *(in dubio pro libertate)*, they keep an acceptable balance.

Legitimate constitutional limitations on the freedom of expression on the grounds of national security are dependent on who decides on the danger for security and constitution. As long as the Federal Constitutional Court retains the "definition competence", the rule of law is not seriously imperilled by the German system for assessing threats to security arising from expressive activities.

---

[50] The Asylum Procedure Law of April 23, 1993 (FedGaz I, 1361) was upheld with minor adaption by 94 FCC 115, 131 (*Asylum*).

NATIONAL SECURITY AND FREEDOM OF EXPRESSION IN HONG KONG

Yash Ghai and Jennifer Van Dale

I. Constitutional Framework

Sovereignty over Hong Kong reverted to China on 1 July 1997 when a new constitutional order came into force. Hong Kong enjoys a special status within China, having been established under Article 31 of the Constitution of the People's Republic of China (PRC) as a special administrative region. The National People's Congress of PRC, following the Sino-British agreement on the transfer of sovereignty, enacted an organic law, called the Basic Law of the Special Administrative Region of Hong Kong (Basic Law) which continues largely intact the previous laws and the legal system of Hong Kong (under the principle of One Country Two Systems which preserves Hong Kong's legal and economic systems although they are different from those which operate on the Mainland). However, the broad constitutional framework within which Hong Kong operates has changed, and it is first necessary to set out its principles which govern rights and freedoms.[1]

The Basic Law protects rights through three different modalities. First, it enunciates a number of rights and freedoms (which are contained largely but not entirely in chapter III). Secondly, it guarantees rights which are protected in the International Covenant on Civil and Political Rights (ICCPR), the International Covenant on Economic, Social and Cultural Rights (ICESCR) and international labor conventions "as applied to Hong Kong". It states in effect that restrictions on rights and freedoms enjoyed in Hong Kong should not contravene the provisions of these treaties (art. 39).[2] Thirdly, by preserving previous laws which are not inconsistent with the Basic Law, it continues the protection afforded by previous laws, particularly the Bill of Rights Ordinance (Bill of Rights) passed in 1991 to give effect to the ICCPR, the Disability Discrimination Ordinance, and the Sex Discrimination Ordinance. The common law, with guarantees of various rights and procedures, is also continued.

The right relevant to this book, the freedom of expression, is well protected. The Basic Law assures to all the residents of Hong Kong the "freedom of speech, of the press and of publication; freedom of association, of procession and of

---

[1] Yash Ghai, *Hong Kong's New Constitutional Order: The Resumption of Chinese Sovereignty and the Basic Law* (Hong Kong University Press, 1997).

[2] Doubts about whether China would also agree to the submission of periodic reports to the treaty bodies were removed when it announced in November 1997 that it would do so, following largely the procedure that Britain had used, namely that the reports would be prepared by the Hong Kong government and referred to China for vetting, and that it would be presented to the treaty body by a Chinese delegation in which the chief spokespersons would be Hong Kong officials (*South China Sunday Morning Post* 23 Nov. 1997).

demonstration; and the right and freedom to form and join trade unions, and to strike" (art. 27). It protects their freedom of conscience and the "freedom to preach and to conduct and participate in religious activities in public" (art. 32). Hong Kong residents also have the "freedom to engage in academic research, literary and artistic creation, and other cultural activities" (art. 34). Educational institutions of "all kinds" are promised "their autonomy" and "academic freedom" (art. 137). The government is required to "protect by law the achievements and the lawful interests of authors in their literary and artistic creation" (art. 140). These articles add up to an impressive framework for the freedom of expression. They have not yet been the subject of litigation and their scope has yet to be determined. It is sometimes said that some of these articles are a replication of provisions in the PRC Constitution, where they are not self-enforcing and consequently have no effect unless propped up by legislation. However we would argue that given the tradition of the common law which is applicable in Hong Kong, constitutional provisions, particularly those relating to human rights, are in general self-enforcing. Nor do we think that the scope of these articles is necessarily as restricted as in China. The whole scheme of rights and freedoms is more generous and extensive than on the Mainland; and rights and freedoms have to be construed in the light of previous laws and practices as well as in the context of international instruments listed in article 39 (and other instruments which have been applied in Hong Kong).

Of these instruments, the ICCPR is the most important (mirrored in the domestic Bill of Rights). The most relevant provision is of course Article 19 dealing with the right to hold opinions and to the freedom of expression. The Bill of Rights guarantees this right in identical terms (art. 16). It provides:

(1) Everyone shall have the right to hold opinions without interference.

(2) Everyone shall have the right to freedom of expression: this right shall include freedom to seek, receive and impart information and ideas of all kinds, regardless of frontiers, either orally, in writing or in print, in the form of art, or through any other media of his choice.

(3) The exercise of the rights provided for in paragraph (2) of this Article carries with it special duties and responsibilities. It may therefore be subject to certain restrictions, but these shall only be such as are provided for by law and are necessary

(a) for respect of the rights or reputations of others; or

(b) for the protection of national security or of public order *(ordre public)*, or of public health or morals.

Three other ICCPR rights closely connected with the freedom of expression are also guaranteed in the Bill of Rights. Article 21 of the ICCPR protects the right of peaceful assembly (the corresponding article in the Bill of Rights being 17). Article 22 of the ICCPR protects the right to the freedom of association with others (its counterpart in the Bill of Rights being article 18). Freedom of conscience and religion are protected by art. 18 of the ICCPR (the equivalent article in the Bill of Rights being 15); this includes the right to manifest one's religion or belief in worship, observance, practice and teaching.

If the Basic Law and associated instruments provide a strong framework for the freedom of expression, it also has a sub-text of the imperative of security. The freedom of expression, the freedom of association and the right of assembly in the ICCPR and the Bill of Rights are subject to restrictions on the grounds, *inter alia*, of national security (in the latter two cases, they have also to be necessary in a democratic society). The concern with national security is reflected even more strongly in the Basic Law, although the Basic Law does not state any grounds for restriction on the freedom of expression and connected rights. China had considerable anxieties about the loyalty of the people of Hong Kong and feared their propensity and ability to cause disruption of public order and to threaten the regime in Beijing. These anxieties and fears were reinforced by the support given by the people of Hong Kong to students and other pro-democracy demonstrators in the Tiananmen Square in May and June 1989, at a critical juncture for the drafting of the Basic Law. China's response was to tighten a draft provision which now requires the HKSAR to enact laws prohibiting any act of treason, secession, sedition, subversion against the Central People's Government, or theft of state secrets to prohibit foreign political organizations or bodies from conducting political activities in the Region, and to prohibit political organizations or bodies of the Region from establishing ties with foreign political organizations or bodies.[3]

Chinese concern with security is also reflected in the provision dealing with the application of national law in Hong Kong (art. 18). The general principle is that only those national laws may be extended to Hong Kong which concern defense and foreign affairs and other matters within the responsibility of the Chinese authorities. Even then these laws can only be applied after consultation with the Hong Kong government and the Committee for the Basic Law (consisting of members from both Hong Kong and China). However, this general principle is by-passed in two instances: when the Standing Committee of the National People's Congress declares a state of war or when it declares a state of emergency in Hong Kong due to the inability of the Hong Kong government to control "turmoil" which endangers national security. In these instances the Central People's Government may issue an order applying "the relevant national laws in the Region" (art. 18). What are "relevant national laws" is not specified, but presumably includes Chinese emergency laws which provide for wide scale incursions into rights and freedoms.

---

[3] This is a greatly expanded version of the Article 23 which appeared in the Draft Basic Law published in February 1989, before the Tiananmen massacre. The draft version read simply "The Hong Kong Special Administrative Region shall enact laws on its own to prohibit any act of treason, secession, sedition or theft of state secrets". The 1988 Draft did not even mention treason: "The HKSAR shall prohibit by law any act designed to undermine national unity or subvert the Central People's Government".

Another manifestation of Chinese concern with security arose from dissatisfaction with the manner and extent of the change of various laws crucial to the maintenance of order which the colonial administration undertook in the last few years of its rule. British colonial authorities had also been obsessed about security and had passed numerous restrictive laws. By the 1980s relatively little use was made of these laws, although they remained on the books. The Tiananmen Square massacre prompted moves to liberalize the laws in Hong Kong so as to avoid the abuse of such colonial laws. The first major step in that direction was the enactment of the Bill of Rights in 1991, followed by amendments to several laws following their scrutiny for compatibility with the Bill of Rights. China objected to the Bill and the subsequent amendments on the basis that they seriously weakened the ability of the government to deal with threats to public order or security. China was not consulted on the enactment of these laws and avowed to repeal these laws on the resumption of sovereignty on 1 July 1997. Under the Basic Law the Standing Committee of the National People's Congress had the power to declare which previous laws were repealed for contravention of the Basic Law. On 23 February 1997 the Standing Committee made its Decision and declared certain parts of the Bill of Rights, the Societies Ordinance and the Public Order Ordinances void (see discussion later).

Despite these restrictive provisions or developments, the general legal framework (and even the political disposition) is today more favorable to the freedom of expression than it was during most of colonial rule. Colonial laws did not share this expansive and positive view of the freedom of expression. Rooted in their colonial origins, they tended to equate the freedom of expression with mischief. At best, expression was tolerated rather than encouraged, to be permitted in small doses, vetted and sanitized. Ideas undermine the ideological structures of colonialism and association threatens the stability of its rule. Thus "public security" was given an extended definition eroding rights which are traditionally recognized under the common law. In the case of Hong Kong, colonial imperatives were compounded by its proximity to China (and the ambiguous attitude of China towards British rule). There was first the anxiety that Hong Kong would become a kind of surrogate battlefield for pro-China and pro-Taiwan forces. Secondly, there was the fear that China might use political groups in Hong Kong to undermine the British administration of Hong Kong. Thirdly, Britain was anxious to prevent the media or political groups in Hong Kong from offending China, to fend off its retaliation. The result of these factors was numerous restrictions on the freedom of expression and association. Many of these restrictions are incompatible with the Bill of Rights, and have been declared so by the courts or have been amended legislatively.

It is necessary to say a few words about the restrictive provisions of the Basic Law or the Decision of the Standing Committee. As far as art. 23 is concerned, any restrictions placed on the freedom of expression or association have to be compatible with the ICCPR given the overriding language of art. 39. The present administration has accepted this view.[4] Steps have been taken to implement some of its provisions, but the implementation of the more sensitive provisions dealing with treason, secession, sedition, and subversion has yet to be undertaken. The government decided to leave that further implementation until an elected legislature was in place after May 1998.

The outgoing colonial government attempted to legislate for this article, in an attempt to forestall more restrictive legislation later. For this enterprise Chinese support would have been necessary in order to ensure that the legislation continued after the transfer of sovereignty. The Chinese authorities refused to co-operate and took the position that under the Basic Law it was up to the Hong Kong Special Administrative Region to implement art. 23. However, it agreed to the enactment of legislation to cover the "theft of state secrets". Britain had extended the UK Official Secrets Acts to Hong Kong. China and Britain agreed that this legislation would be enacted as a local Ordinance and would in that form continue after the change of sovereignty. The Official Secrets Ordinance 1997 therefore implements a part of art. 23. Journalists and human rights groups are not happy with its restrictions, particularly at what is regarded as the non-availability of the defense of public interest in the disclosure of official information. But there is little doubt that it is a more carefully drawn legislation than its predecessors and makes an attempt to classify official information by some rational criteria. In any event it is a great improvement on Chinese legislation on this subject, which has acted as a deterrent to the proper discharge of journalistic functions.

The colonial government also sponsored, over Chinese opposition, laws to cover treason, sedition and subversion (Crimes (Amendment) (No.2) Bill 1997). It proposed to create the offenses of subversion and secession and to liberalize the law on treason and sedition. The legislative council were opposed to the creation of the new offenses, arguing that the substance of these offenses was effectively covered by the existing criminal offenses. In the end they were not passed. However, the rules on treason and sedition were liberalized (see below on sedition).

China criticized the law, saying it would not accept the amendments "which are themselves confusing, and we will take necessary action to rectify the situation".[5] The new administration has since stated that the Basic Law requires the government of the HKSAR (and not the previous Hong Kong government) to enact laws on sedition. The Chief Executive, Tung Chee Hwa, has criticized, *inter alia*, the passage of the Crimes (Amendment) Ordinance in June 1997 and warned that it would be

---

[4] In its Consultation Document, *Civil Liberties and Social Order* (April 1997), the office of the Chief Executive-designate stated as a basic principle for the review of laws that the "amendments must be consistent with the Basic Law and the ICCPR as they are applied to Hong Kong" (para 3.8).

[5] *South China Morning Post* 25 June 1997.

reviewed by the Secretary for Justice.[6] The Secretary has stated that intent and motive are what distinguishes seditious remarks from those expressing discontent, but she has not clarified how intent and motive are to be ascertained.[7] It remains to be seen whether the government will take any fresh initiatives after the new legislature is sworn in.

The government of the HKSAR has implemented that part of art. 23 which deals with the right of association through amendments to the Societies Ordinance. It has also restricted the right of demonstration by amending the Public Order Ordinance, although this is not connected to art. 23 but to the Decision of the Standing Committee to repeal reform to the Ordinance after the Bill of Rights was passed.

The amendments which the Standing Committee made to the Bill of Rights are in practice of little significance, and they have been largely disregarded by the courts. The amendments sought to remove what the Chinese authorities assumed gave a status to it superior to other laws. This was a misreading of the situation since the repealed parts did no more than re-state the common law position that laws in existence before the Bill of Rights was passed would be subject to the Bill while subsequent legislation should, when possible, be read to conform to the Bill. The Bill was in fact entrenched not by its own terms but by the Letters Patent (which served as the constitution of colonial Hong Kong). It is now entrenched by article 39 of the Basic Law, which states that:

> [t]he provisions of the International Covenant on Civil and Political Rights... as applied... shall remain in force and shall be implemented through the laws of the Hong Kong Special Administrative Region. The rights and freedoms enjoyed by Hong Kong residents shall not be restricted unless as prescribed by law. Such restrictions shall not contravene the provisions of the preceding paragraph of this Article.

The Hong Kong Special Administrative Region (HKSAR) is required to implement the ICCPR, which is exactly what the Bill of Rights has done. In any event no rights or freedoms guaranteed under the ICCPR may be restricted except as are consistent with it. The courts appear to refer to the Bill or the ICCPR indiscriminately and assume that both prevail over other laws. In this way the Bill of Rights continues to enjoy a special status under the Basic Law. The language of the amendments to the Letters Patent and the scheme of the Ordinance were designed to tie in with the Basic Law in an attempt to ensure the continuity of the Ordinance.[8]

---

[6] See "Tung rejects Legco treason law vote" *South China Morning Post,* 25 June 1997 at 1, and "Secretary for Justice Ponders New Laws", *South China Morning Post,* 4 July 1997.

[7] "Motives 'key to legality' of Li Peng Slogans", *South China Morning Post,* 24 June 1997 at 6.

[8] See Philip Dykes, "The Hong Kong Bill of Rights 1991: Its Origin, Content and Impact" in J. Chan and Y. Ghai (eds.), *The Hong Kong Bill of Rights: A Comoparative Approach* (1993)

With this account of the constitutional framework for the freedom of expression, we turn to some specific issues and restrictions.

II. Laws on the Freedom of Expression

A. The Emergency Regulations Ordinance

The previous Hong Kong Government had extraordinary power to curtail free expression under the Emergency Regulations Ordinance (Cap 241). Section 2(1) reads:

> On any occasion which the Governor in Council may considers to be an occasion of emergency or public danger he may make any regulations whatsoever which he may consider desirable in the public interest.

These powers are specified in s. 2(2)(c), which provides for "censorship, and the control and suppression of publications, writings, maps, plans, photographs, communications and means of communication". Moreover, any enactment may be amended or suspended under s. 2(2)(g).

Until 1995 there was a ready body of law[9] which the Governor could bring into effect merely by publishing an announcement in the Government Gazette. These regulations included wide powers of censorship and search and seizure.[10]

The Governor was empowered to declare an emergency if he believed it to be "in the public interest", but public interest was not defined anywhere in the ordinance. One concern was that the meaning of "public interest" under this law is much wider than Article 5 of the Bill of Rights, under which an emergency may only be declared if the "life of the nation" is threatened. Since 1 July, "the nation" has been the People's Republic of China and it remains unclear if an emergency may be declared in Hong Kong if there is unrelated turmoil in China. Article 18 of the Basic Law, which deals with emergencies, gives some indication: it states that an emergency

---

[9] Emergency (Principal) Regulations (Cap 241 sub. leg. D). These were repealed by the Emergency Regulations (Repeal) Order 1995.

[10] These include, for example, the power to ban any publication which would be prejudicial to the public interest, the right to open and detain all postal packets, to place restrictions on the import and export of certain articles, to shut down newspapers, to pre-censor any matter before publication and prohibit the publisher from disclosing that it has been altered in the censorship process, to search any premises suspected of being used for illegal publications, and the power to convict any person having in his possession any apparatus which can be used for wireless transmission, or who signals to vessels at sea or aircraft in flight. The Governor may also proscribe any organization which in his opinion has spread sedition or disorder in the territory.

may be declared if there is turmoil in Hong Kong which endangers national unity or security and which is beyond the control of the Hong Kong Government.[11]

B. Sedition

One of the earliest restrictions on free speech in Hong Kong, the law against sedition, is still in existence (ss. 9 and 10 of the Crimes Ordinance, cap. 200). Until June 1997 it was an offense to plan or conspire to commit a seditious act; or to utter seditious words; print, publish, sell, offer for sale, distribute, display or reproduce any seditious publication; or import knowingly any seditious publication. Amendments in the last weeks of British administration required an intent to cause "violence or public disorder or a public disturbance". Any person who has in his or her possession a seditious publication without lawful excuse is also guilty of an offence. Seditious intention was very broadly defined, and until June 1997 included the intention to bring into hatred or contempt or to excite disaffection against the British monarch or the government of Hong Kong or of any other British possessions or dominions, to raise discontent or disaffection among the monarch's subjects or the inhabitants of Hong Kong and to counsel disobedience to law or to any lawful order. It was, however, not seditious to show that the government has been misled or is mistaken in any of its measures or to point out errors in administration with a view to the remedying of such errors. Until an amendment in 1992, the test of seditious intent was an objective one. However, it is unlikely that the amendment would have availed a person found in possession of seditious publications, since intention was no part of that offence. The police had increased powers of search and seizure under this ordinance until June 1997.[12] However, the Crimes (Amendment) (No.2) Ordinance 1997 now changes the definition of sedition so that no offense is committed unless the accused had the intention to cause violence or create public disorder or a public disturbance.

Provisions relating to sedition are also scattered throughout the laws of Hong Kong. For example, until June 1997, it was illegal to post, tender for posting or send by post "any seditious publication within the meaning of any enactment relating to sedition" under s. 32(h) of the Post Office Ordinance (Cap. 98). That

[11] The phrase "which endangers national unity or security" was added after the 1989 student protests in China, which were widely supported by Hong Kong people.

[12] Under sec.13, which was repealed in June 1997(89/97 s. 9), police powers went beyond the already wide powers under section 50(7) of the Police Force Ordinance (cap 232). For a discussion of these powers see the 1994 Report of the Hong Kong Journalists Association and *Urgent Business: Hong Kong, Freedom of Expression and 1997*, by the Hong Kong Journalists' Association and Article 19, January 1993 .

section was repealed a few weeks before the change in sovereignty.[13] Under s. 23 the post office is given extraordinarily wide powers of search and seizure "if there is reason to believe that any offence ... has been committed".

IV. News Media

A. Newspapers

Since the passage of the Ordinance, and more particularly since 1993, a number of restrictions have been removed, due principally to a sustained campaign by the Hong Kong Journalists Association. The freest medium is the newspaper. A newspaper has to be registered with the government before it may be published and distributed, but registration is a straightforward matter. The previous requirement that the registrar of newspapers could require a news agency or the publisher or the distributor of a newspaper to provide any information "in his absolute discretion" as a condition of registration was repealed in 1995.[14]

B. Broadcasting

The majority of restrictions can be found in the Telecommunications, Television, and Broadcasting Authority Ordinances, but there are other ordinances which are cause for concern. For example, until December 1994, the Film Censorship Ordinance allowed censorship for political reasons. While not specifically a national security restriction, s. 10(2)(c) of the Film Censorship Ordinance permitted restrictions based on "whether there is a likelihood that the exhibition of the film would seriously damage good relations with other territories". In practice this meant China. Although the censor was required to take Article 19 of the ICCPR into account, this provision did not provide any real safeguard as he was not required to apply it. Section 10(2)(c) was most famously used to censor part of the Taiwanese film "Mainland China 1989", which was scheduled to be shown at the Hong Kong Arts Center in 1989.

Although s. 10(2)(c) was repealed, the previous Hong Kong Government still took Chinese concerns into consideration when deciding whether or not to censor films. It certainly affected the annual Hong Kong International Film Festival which is run by the Urban Council. In 1994 Beijing withdrew seven films from the festival in protest over the showing of two independent films banned by the mainland authorities. In 1995, controversy arose again when a motion to stop the council from

---

[13] Sec. 11, Crimes (Amendment) Ordinance (No. 2)(Ordinance 89/97).

[14] Newspapers Registration and Distribution (Amendment) Regs. 1995 and the News Agencies Registration (Amendment) Regulation 1995.

sending a list of the mainland films to be shown at the festival to Beijing for endorsement was approved.[15]

Many of the most far-reaching restrictions on freedom of expression were repealed or amended in 1993 by the government, but problems remain. For example, s. 18 of the Broadcasting Authority Ordinance (which allowed the Governor to issue binding directives regarding the content of programs) has been repealed, but under s. 13(O) of the Telecommunications Ordinance the Governor (and now the Chief Executive) still retained the power to make regulations for the purpose of setting standards for the programs and advertising material to be broadcast.[16] The Governor appointed the majority of the members of the Broadcasting Authority, and thus controlled the group which administers the Telecommunications Ordinance. Therefore, while the previous government has repealed one part of one law under which the Governor had the explicit power to control the contents of programming, it has not actually taken the power itself away.

Similarly, s. 8(2)(b) of the Television Ordinance provides that the grant of a license may include a condition requiring the licensee to broadcast "such programs, announcements, and other material as the Broadcasting Authority shall require". Although this is clearly incompatible with the Bill of Rights, it is an improvement over the law as it previously stood. The controversial ss. 14(3)(C) and 27, which allowed the Governor to revoke a license if security so required and for political and religious reasons respectively, have been repealed.

One amendment which has actually taken away restrictions is Regulation 5 of the Television (Programs) Regulations.[17] This regulation required news sources to be approved before they could be reported. It has been amended to require that coverage of international and local affairs be presented in an impartial and accurate manner. Regulation 4, which allowed the Broadcasting Authority to censor certain materials that promoted, *inter alia*, the interests of any foreign political party has been repealed. Similarly, powers were taken from the government with the repeal of ss. 35 and 36 of the Television Ordinance, which allowed the Broadcasting Authority to prohibit the broadcast of any program which posed a threat to the order of Hong Kong, and any material gathered or selected by any person it named.

Some new sections have been added to these ordinances which provide a system of checks and balances: s. 32A of the Television Ordinance allows the Governor (and now the Chief Executive) to regulate and exercise some control over

---

[15] *South China Morning Post* 27 May 1995.

[16] Section 13(C)(3) of the Telecommunications Ordinance explains in detail the effect of these regulations: "... a license may include - (a) a condition that the Broadcasting Authority may require the licensee to refrain from broadcasting any program...which in the opinion of the Broadcasting Authority would contravene any direction or any provision of a Code of Practice issued by the Broadcasting Authority under the Broadcasting Authority Ordinance, or any regulation made under section 13(O)..."

[17] Cap 52 sub leg B.

the broadcasting of programs, but subject to the approval of the Legislative Council. Section 33 has been completely replaced, with the promulgation of new guidelines as to what may or may not be broadcast. These include prohibitions on programs which may incite racial, religious, ethnic or gender-based hatred; cause a breakdown of law and order; or gravely damage public health or morals.[18] Pre-publication censorship is still permitted, but now the Chief Secretary (now called the Secretary for Administration) must apply to the Court of First Instance for an order to do so.[19] Requirements of pre-recording (and thus the control of live broadcasts) are no longer valid.

The Telecommunications Ordinance is similar to the Broadcasting Authority Ordinance, in that under it the members of the Telecommunications Authority are appointed by the Chief Executive. The most worrying power of the Chief Executive under this Ordinance is found in s. 33, which allows him to prohibit the transmission of messages if it is in the public interest. This can be a single message or an entire class of messages. Another draconian power still on the books allows the Chief Executive to take control of telecommunication stations if he feels that an emergency has arisen.

While the previous government made amendments to and repealed some legislation, it is clear that many statutes remain on the books which could lead to arbitrary or selective censorship. Although many of the most serious powers have been reduced or eliminated, the problem remains that much of Hong Kong's media-related law is located in several ordinances and administered by different authorities. It would be helpful to consolidate all these statutes, but efforts by the previous administration were unsuccessful.[20]

Various other laws were amended in 1995 to increase the exercise of the freedom of expression. Some of these amendments have however effectively been repealed by the Provisional Legislature/the new administration. For example, the Public Order Ordinance was amended in 1995[21] to remove restrictions on public

---

[18] Section 33(1).

[19] Section 33(2). Previously, the Governor could unilaterally censor material.

[20] While the previous government considered an omnibus bill which would consolidate all of these statutes, {the actual test of which was not released to the public) it never came to fruition. In May 1996 the Secretary for Recreation and Culture disclosed that the bill had been shelved because it did not have China's blessing, but the next day, the acting Chief Secretary announced that the bill was not shelved and would in fact be introduced as soon as was practicable. He did not, however, indicate when that would be. *South China Morning Post*, 26 and 27 May 1995. Similarly, it was also reported that public access television would not be introduced to Hong Kong's cable network due to China's objections. *South China Morning Post* 9 June 1995.

[21] Public Order (Amendment) Ordinance 1995 (77 of 1995).

meetings and processions, but some restrictions were reinstated in July 1997.[22] Prior to 1995, official permission was required, whereas after the amendment it was sufficient to notify the Commissioner of Police a week ahead of the event. Now it is not necessary to get the Commissioner's "permission", but it is necessary to be notified by the Commissioner that he has "no objection".[23] After the 1995 amendments, the Commissioner could have prohibited the meeting "in the interests of public safety or public order" (s. 9(1)), but only if he considered that these interests could not be met by imposing conditions under which the meeting or the procession were held. Under the 1997 amendments, "in the interests of public safety or public order" has been repealed and substituted with "in the interests of national security or public safety, public order (*ordre public*) or the protection of the rights and freedoms of others".[24] Under the interpretation section of the amended Ordinance, "public safety" and "public order" are given the same meaning as under the ICCPR. "National security" means "the safeguarding of the territorial integrity and the independence of the People's Republic of China".[25] After 1995 provision was made for an appeal to a tribunal against the refusal or conditions by the Commissioner (ss. 16, 44 and 4AA) which has remained substantially the same since the 1997 amendment. The offence of using a loudhailer (loudspeaker) without a police permit has been abolished (s. 19).[26]

With respect to public demonstrations, the Public Order (Amendment) Ordinance states that "a public procession may take place if, but only if ... the Commissioner of Police is notified ... [and he] has notified ... the person that he has no objection".[27]

Among other changes made in 1995, the dual licensing procedure under the Places of Public Entertainment Ordinance has been abolished and replaced with a system requiring a license only for the venue.[28] The granting of this license will be based on safety. The amendment is not entirely satisfactory, as the Commissioner for Television and Entertainment Licensing has absolute discretion in granting or

---

[22] The text of the legislation passed by the Provisional Legislature as well as press releases from the Chief Executive was acquired from the Internet homepage of the Chief Executive. See http:\\www.ceoffice.org.hg\bills\pub.htm.

[23] Public Order (Amendment) Ordinance 1997 (119/97) sec. 6.

[24] *Id.* sec. 3.

[25] *Supra* note 22.

[26] In 1990 five members of the Democratic Party (then the United Democrats) were convicted of using loudhailers without permission during a public protest, contrary to s. 4(29) of the Summary Offenses Ordinance (Cap 228). The law was originally enacted as an anti-nuisance measure, not as a tool for suppressing dissent. Because the law had not been used in such a long time their convictions were overturned on appeal. Section 4(29) was repealed by s. 19 of the Public Order (Amendment) Ordinance.

[27] Public Order (Amendment) Ordinance 1997 (119/97) sec. 6.

[28] Public Entertainment and Amusement (Miscellaneous Provisions) Ordinance (72 of 1995) s. 7, which repeals s. 8 of the Places of Public Entertainment Ordinance.

canceling a permit, and the Secretary for Recreation and Culture now has wide powers to make regulations for public safety which could be used to curtail free expression.[29]

Another change[30] allows reporting of court cases involving indecent matter or revolting medical, surgical or physiological information, and also limits a court's power to hold proceedings away from the public.[31] Now, closed door proceedings are only allowed in the interests of justice, public order or security.

IV. Right to Information

A. Official Secrets

The Official Secrets Ordinance, following changes in the UK law, no longer criminalize the unauthorized disclosure of any government information. Instead it identifies six areas for which such disclosure remains an offence.[32] Although the 1989 provisions are an improvement on the previous law since they make an attempt to relate the restrictions on the disclosure of information to specific security interests, in at least one respect they are worse. Under the old Act, a defense of disclosure in the public interest as well as of prior publication was possible, but would seem to be no longer available after the 1989 change.

B. Right to Information

Closely related to the Official Secrets Ordinance is the status of freedom of information. Article 16 of the Basic Law states that freedom of expression:

---

[29] The Governor no longer has power to make regulations: now this authority is in the hands of the Secretary for Recreation and Welfare, Public Entertainment and Amusement (Miscellaneous Provisions) Ordinance (72 of 1995) s. 5, which amends s. 7 of the Places of Public Entertainment Ordinance.

[30] Administration of Justice (Miscellaneous Provisions) (No. 2) Ordinance (68 of 1995) s. 6. This repeals s. 3(1)(a) and the proviso of the Judicial Proceedings (Regulation of Reports) Ordnance (Cap 287).

[31] For more information on the use of judicial chambers in Hong Kong courts, see Godfrey J., "Administration of the Courts – The Open Administration of Justice and the Bill of Rights" in W. Fong, A. Byrnes and G. Edwards (eds.) *Hong Kong's Bill of Rights: Two Years On* (University of Hong Kong Faculty of Law 1994) at 61.

[32] They are: security and intelligence, defense, international relations, information from foreign governments and international organizations, information useful to criminals, and interception of communications.

> shall include freedom to seek, receive and impart information and ideas of all kinds, regardless of frontiers, either orally, in writing or in print, in the form of art, or through any other media of his choice.

Although it is unlikely that this formulation guarantees access to official information, such access would be in the spirit of this provision. Unfortunately, until 1995 there was no government policy on the public's right to seek information nor for government departments' obligations to disclose it. In March 1995 the government adopted and published its *Code of Access to Information*, which applies to nine departments and branches.[33] The government's goal was to extend it throughout the government by the end of 1996. While the Code's stated procedure "authorises and requires civil servants, routinely and on request, to provide information unless there are specific reasons for not doing so",[34] the Code affects neither statutory rights of access to information nor legal restrictions on access to information.[35]

Not unexpectedly, there are numerous reasons for which information may not be disclosed. This includes "information whose disclosure would harm or prejudice Hong Kong's defense" and "information whose disclosure would harm or prejudice Hong Kong's security". In the *Code of Access to Information - Guidelines on Interpretation and Application*, information whose disclosure would harm or prejudice Hong Kong's defense is described as information "whose disclosure would adversely affect the operational effectiveness of the armed forces in Hong Kong and whose disclosure would put at risk servicemen and their civilian support staff, and those under their protection in Hong Kong".

Presumably, "those under their protection" refers to all Hong Kong residents. Information whose disclosure would harm or prejudice Hong Kong's security includes information which could be of assistance to those engaged in espionage, sabotage or terrorism. It also includes the protection of individuals and sites which may be at risk, and the protection of information whose disclosure would prejudice the operations sources and methods of those whose work involves duties connected with Hong Kong's security.

Another category of information to which access may be restricted is information whose disclosure would constitute either a contravention of any law which applies to Hong Kong or a breach of any obligation arising under common law or under any international agreement which applies to Hong Kong.

---

[33] The Architectural Services, Customs and Excise, Government Supplies, Highways, Home Affairs and Social Welfare Departments and the Home Affairs, Recreation and Culture and Works Branches. As of 1 July 1995 it will apply to 16 other departments and branches. *Eastern Express,* 16 June 1995.

[34] Code of Access to Information (Hong Kong: Government Printer, 1995) at 3 .

[35] *Id.* at 4.

Under the government's Code, not only should information be made available upon request, but certain information should routinely be published. This includes details of the departments' organization, information of the services they provide, and their performance pledges and the extent to which they have been met. To make information seekers' searches easier, departments must also publish a list of their records,[36] a list of information that is available, and the procedures and fees for access to information not routinely published.

There is a review procedure for those who feel that a department has not complied with the Code, but it is not entirely satisfactory. The Ombudsman will handle all grievances, but his decisions have no binding effect. There were 111 requests for information in the first two months of the policy, many of which were for routine information.[37]

While the government's Code is a start, it falls far short of a comprehensive attempt to allow access to government information. Because it is a policy and not a law, it does not actually increase the public's right of access; it merely defines which information is protected, and it can be easily changed. It is not known whether the new administration has plans to change this policy. Aside from national security and legal restrictions, there are numerous other reasons for denying access to information.[38] While some may be justified, the restrictions as a whole sweep across the board and it is conceivable that any request for information can be denied based on one of these qualifications. The Code certainly falls short of the internationally accepted standards as represented by various national laws on the right to information.

The previous government rejected calls for legislation on the right to information.[39] It refused permission for the introduction of a bill sponsored by former Legislative Councilor Christine Loh. Its purpose was to "confer on the public a general right of access to information in documentary form in the possession, custody or control of departments of government or other public bodies constituted under the law for any purpose".

---

[36] "Records" is broadly defined in Annex B of the Code, and includes maps, drawings, photographs, video and sound recordings, CD-ROMS, etc.

[37] Report of the Hong Kong Journalists' Association 1995.

[38] These include external affairs; nationality, immigration and consular matters; law enforcement; legal proceedings and public safety; damage to the environment; management of the economy; management and operation of the public service; internal discussion and advice; public employment, public appointments and honors; improper gain or advantage; research statistics and analysis; third party information; privacy of the individual; business affairs; and premature requests.

[39] Former Chief Secretary Sir David Ford rejected calls for such an ordinance by saying that there are other ways "to make Government more accountable". *South China Morning Post*, 27 February 1992, at 1.

VI. Conclusion

The future of the freedom of expression remains uncertain. The British administration belatedly removed some important restrictions, but several still remain. On the other hand, the Chinese are suspicious of removal of restrictions, viewing them as weakening the executive and its ability to maintain law and order. Influential Hong Kong advisers to China have stated that the repealed restrictions will be restored. There has been little dispassionate examination of the guarantees given in the Basic Law for the freedom of expression and the pursuit of inquiry. There is increasing feeling that the law will matter less than politics, and those bold enough to criticize the Chinese government will meet with retribution. This has already produced considerable self-censorship. A great deal of the media is commercially driven, and access to Chinese market is greatly desired. Media giants such as Rupert Murdoch and Ted Turner have already bent their empires to the whims of the Chinese. Academics are likely to succumb to similar pressures. Ironically, the prospects for the freedom of press look particularly grim now that the previous administration has gone about the task of dismantling legal and administrative restrictions on the freedom of expression.

INDIA: NATIONAL SECURITY, FREEDOM OF EXPRESSION AND EMERGENCY POWERS

K. S. Venkateswaran

I. Introduction

National security has, over the decades, been recognized as one of the legitimate grounds for restricting freedom of expression in India. The colonial British administration promulgated a number of laws which sought to preserve the security of the State, often at considerable cost to traditional freedoms, including freedom of the press.[1] Despite the widespread resentment that such laws engendered in the native population at the time, the architects of independent India's 1950 republican Constitution (many of whom were themselves in the vanguard of the nationalist struggle for freedom) thought it necessary to retain security of the State as a ground on which freedom of speech and expression could be restricted. Accordingly, Article 19 of the Indian Constitution, while guaranteeing that "All citizens shall have the right to ... freedom of speech and expression."[2] also provided that nothing in that guarantee shall:

> affect the operation of any existing law in so far as it relates to, or prevents the State from making any law relating to, libel, slander, defamation, contempt of court or any matter which offends against decency or morality or which *undermines the security of, or tends to overthrow, the State.*[3]

Barely had the ink dried on the Constitution than the Supreme Court of India was called on to rule on the application of this restrictive clause to a case involving a journal, *Crossroads*, which had been banned on the ground that its contents were prejudicial to the maintenance of public order.[4] The statute under which the action had been taken allowed the government to impose restrictions for the purposes of "securing public safety" or "maintaining public order."[5] It was argued on behalf of the banned journal that both these purposes were wider than those relating to the security, or overthrow, of the State, and could not therefore be invoked in justification of the ban.

The Court agreed, holding that a strict interpretation had to be given to the restrictive clause, and struck down the offending statute. The judges drew support for their conclusion from the fact that a reference to "sedition" as a possible ground for restricting free speech had been deliberately dropped from an earlier draft of

---

[1] *E.g.*, the Vernacular Press Act (1878), the Indian Press Act (1910), the Indian Press Ordinance (1930) and the Indian Press (Emergency Powers) Act (1931).
[2] Constitution, Art. 19(1)(a).
[3] Constitution, Art. 19(2) (emphasis added).
[4] *Romesh Thapar* v. *State of Madras*: AIR 1950 SC 124.
[5] The Madras Maintenance of Public Order Act (1949).

Article 19(2), thus indicating a clear intent on the part of the constitutional drafters to allow a wide latitude for criticism of the government, including criticism which might excite disaffection or bad feeling.

This judgment led the government immediately to amend Article 19(2) to ensure that its power to curb free speech in the interest of preventing threats to public order was not removed. The amended Article 19(2) consequently saved laws which purported to impose reasonable restrictions "in the interests of the security of the State, friendly relations with foreign States, public order, decency or morality, or in relation to contempt of court, defamation or incitement to an offense."

II. Sedition

The offense of sedition, contained in the Indian Penal Code,[6] featured prominently in several cases decided in pre-independence India. In a number of these, the Privy Council – then the highest court of appeal – held that sedition included any statement which had the effect of causing disaffection against the State, even if it was not accompanied or followed by incitement to violence or rebellion.[7] Following independence, the question as to whether the offense of sedition violated the constitutional guarantee of free speech engaged the attention of the courts. An early view of the Punjab High Court that it did[8] was reversed by the Supreme Court in 1962[9], albeit with a qualification:

> [A]ny acts ... which have the effect of subverting the government by bringing that government into contempt or hatred, or creating disaffection against it, would be within the penal statute because the feeling of disloyalty to the government established by law or enmity to it imports the idea of tendency to public disorder by the use of actual violence . . . . But the section has taken care to indicate clearly that strong words used to express disapprobation of the inclination to cause public disorder by acts of violence would not be penal. In other words, disloyalty to government established by law is not the same thing as commenting in strong terms upon the measures or acts of government or its agencies, so as to ameliorate the condition of the people or to secure the cancellation or alteration of those acts or measures by lawful means, that is to say, without exciting those feelings of enmity and

---

[6] Penal Code, sec. 124A.

[7] *E.g.*, *Bal Gangadhar Tilak* v. *Queen Empress*: (1897) 25 Indian Appeals 1; *Wallace-Johnson* v. *The King*, A.C. 231 (1940); *Emperor* v. *Sadashiv Narayan*, AIR 1947 PC 82.

[8] *Tara Singh Gopichand* v. *The State*, AIR 1951 Punj 27.

[9] *Kedar Nath Singh* v. *Bihar*, AIR 1962 SC 955.

> disloyalty which imply incitement to public disorder or the use of violence.[10]

The essence of sedition, therefore, lies in the potential for incitement to violence, not mere ill-feeling or disaffection towards the State. In this case, the petitioner, who was a member of a radical left-wing group called "Forward Communist Party" had been charged with sedition after he had publicly threatened members of the ruling party and their land-owning supporters with "liquidation" for their indifference to the plight of the poor. His conviction was upheld by the Supreme Court.

The Court took a similar view in another case decided in 1973, in which the appellant, a trade union activist, was charged with inciting employees of the Defense Department to violence against the Minister for Defense.[11] Addressing a public meeting of such employees, the activist was heard threatening the Minister that he would be killed in the same way as some of the repressive members of the colonial British government had been killed by nationalist revolutionaries. He was sent to trial under the Punjab Security of the State Act (1953), which penalized any speech or writing which, *inter alia*, undermined the security of the State or amounted to "incitement to an offense prejudicial to the security of the State or the maintenance of public order" or tended to "overthrow the State". The appellant contended that because the last mentioned act was not expressly included in Article 19(2) of India's Constitution, the 1953 law was inconsistent with, and therefore superseded by, the Constitution. The Supreme Court rejected this argument, holding that, even if the phrase in question had not been specifically mentioned, it would nevertheless fall within the ambit of "reasonable restrictions ... in the interests of ... security of the State", contemplated by the Article, because "anything tending to overthrow the State must necessarily be prejudicial to the security of the State."[12] The appeal therefore failed.

In this case, the court emphasized the need to strike a proper balance between free speech and considerations of national security. It was indisputable, said the Court,

> that there is no such thing as absolute or unrestricted freedom of speech and expression ... for that would amount to uncontrolled license which would tend to lead to disorder and anarchy. The right to freedom of speech and expression is undoubtedly a valuable and cherished right possessed by a citizen in our Republic ... Freedom to think as one likes, and to speak as one thinks, are, as a rule, indispensable to the discovery and spread of truth and without free speech discussion may well be futile. But at the same

[10] *Id.* at 967-68.
[11] *Santokh Singh* v. *Delhi Administration*, AIR 1973 SC 1091.
[12] *Id.* at 1093.

> time we can only ignore at our peril the vital importance of our social interest in, *inter alia*, public order and security of our State.[13]

Since that judgment, only a few cases involving sedition charges have come before the Indian courts.

III. Judicial Review

The Indian courts have the powers, where necessary, to strike down laws or executive acts which impinge excessively on fundamental rights, though, like their counterparts elsewhere in the common law world, they have often been reluctant to second-guess the executive on matters of national security. It would be fair to say that, on the whole, judges have performed the balancing act quite even-handedly, though there have been occasions, especially when dealing with emergency legislation, when they have been viewed as being unduly deferential to the executive. Some cases of this sort will be examined presently.

There are no reported cases of military courts being used to try civilians for national security offenses. Such cases are routinely handled by the ordinary civil courts, with generally satisfactory results.

Cases involving pure questions of national security have been few and far between. As often as not, the restrictions imposed on free speech involve threats to public safety or public order, albeit on a scale that can legitimately raise fears of potential harm to the territorial integrity, and possibly the security, of the State. In *Virendra* v. *Punjab*,[14] for instance, the Supreme Court ruled constitutionally permissible an order issued under the Punjab Special Powers (Press) Act (1956), which prohibited newspapers in the State from publishing any article, news report or comment on an ongoing agitation and which also banned the import from other States of any newspaper which covered the agitation, both for a period of two months. The Court reasoned that, given the delicate law and order situation created by the agitation, especially in a part of the country that bordered a hostile foreign State, *i.e.*, Pakistan, it was not unreasonable to subordinate freedom of speech to the needs of public order, which was essential to the safety of the State.[15]

As to what constituted "security of the State", the Bombay High Court ruled in a 1960 case[16] that the phrase did not mean "merely danger to the security of the entire country, nor can it be restricted to an upheaval or a rebellion endangering the security of the entire country ... [T]he security of the State can be undermined

---

[13] *Id.* at 1094.

[14] AIR 1957 SC 896.

[15] In doing so, the Court was also influenced by the fact that the order was made for a limited duration and the law provided for a right of representation against it.

[16] *Indulal Yagnik* v. *The State*, AIR 1960 Bom 399.

by danger from both within and without the State.[17] Based on this reasoning, the court upheld a provision in a law[18] which made it an offense intentionally to cause, or attempt to cause, disaffection towards the government amongst members of a police force.

IV. Preventive Detention

Given that India has had, since independence, an almost unbroken succession of laws permitting preventive detention in peace time on grounds of national security,[19] the question as to whether these laws infringed upon the right to freedom of speech of the people detained under them has come before the courts on several occasions. In a 1974 case, one such challenge was rejected by the Supreme Court on the ground that once someone was legally detained - whether punitively or preventatively - he would inevitably have to suffer a loss of some of his other rights, such as the right to freedom of speech and expression and the right to freedom of movement.[20] Such loss of rights was, said the Court, not unreasonable under Article 19(2). The Court reiterated this conclusion in several subsequent cases.[21]

A judgment of the Kerala High Court one year earlier had, however, sought to ensure that the detaining authorities did not completely snuff out the free speech rights of those suffering preventive detention.[22] In that case, the detainee, who had been held under the Maintenance of Internal Security Act (1971), was subjected to an order prohibiting him from purchasing or receiving "Mao literature", and had consequently been denied access to three books by or on Mao Tse-tung.[23] Such an order, said the Court, was not only too wide and too vague, but unjust considering that the detainee had been given access to other books containing passages which were no less capable of inciting the reader to violence and thus endangering the security of the State.[24] The impugned order was set aside.

---

[17] *Id.*

[18] The Police (Incitement to Disaffection) Act (1922).

[19] *E.g.*, the Preventive Detention Act (1950) (from 1950-70), the Maintenance of Internal Security Act (1971) (from 1971-78), the National Security Act (1980) (from 1980-present).

[20] *Haradhan Saha* v. *State of West Bengal*, AIR 1974 SC 2154.

[21] *See, e.g.*, *Khudiram Das* v. *State of West Bengal*, AIR 1975 SC 550; and *A.K. Roy* v. *Union of India*, AIR 1982 SC 710.

[22] *K. Narayanan* v. *The State*, AIR 1973 Ker 97.

[23] The books in question were: (1) *Four Essays on Philosophy* by Mao Tse-tung; (2) *Mao Papers* by Jerome Ch'en; and (3) *Mao Tse-tung* by Stuart Sehram.

[24] The judges cited three examples of such books: (1) *The State and Revolution* by V.I. Lenin; (2) *Lenin on War and Peace*; and (3) *National Liberation War in Viet Nam* by Gen. Vo Nguyen Giap.

V. Special Security Legislation and Emergency Powers

As noted above, the courts in India have sometimes been criticized for showing undue deference to the executive in matters of national security, especially when they have interpreted legislation passed under the cover of an emergency or to meet special security needs. India has experienced three formal, or declared, states of emergency, two of them following armed external aggressions in 1962 and 1971,[25] and the third, between 1975 and 1977, on the more controversial ground of "internal disturbance."[26] The Parliament has also adopted a number of special anti-terrorist laws which derogate from both the Indian Constitution's guarantees on fundamental rights and the State's commitments under the International Covenant on Civil and Political Rights.[27] The attitude of the national courts, especially the Supreme Court, in dealing with such laws has often been to allow the executive a large measure of latitude in deciding the scale and intensity of restrictions which may be imposed on civil liberties under such legislation.

The Supreme Court has repeatedly ruled, for example, that judges are not competent to determine independently whether or not the conditions justifying the imposition,[28] or prolongation,[29] of a state of emergency existed, nor to second-guess the executive about the need for particular measures. This "hands-off" attitude reached its apotheosis in a controversial 1976 judgment[30] in which the court held that, as long as a Presidential Order suspending any of the fundamental rights was in force during an emergency, citizens were completely without remedy against executive acts of oppression. The implications of this judgment for freedom of speech were momentous, because under Article 358 of the Constitution (as it then stood), that right was automatically suspended upon declaration of a state of emergency. The situation has since been improved slightly following adoption of an amendment to Article 358 in 1978, by virtue of which the right to freedom of

---

[25] The first followed an attack by China, and the second, an attack by Pakistan. Both these emergencies were allowed to remain in force for much longer than was warranted by the circumstances giving rise to them. For a critical account of these emergencies, *see* International Commission of Jurists, *States of Emergency: Their Impact on Human Rights* 169-91 (1983).

[26] This emergency, whose validity is suspect under international human rights law, was declared soon after the then-Prime Minister, Mrs. Indira Gandhi, had been unseated from Parliament by a High Court judgment which accused her of corrupt electoral practices. The emergency was used to justify the large-scale detention of opposition politicians, sweeping censorship of the press, and suppression of other civil liberties on an unprecedented scale.

[27] *See, e.g., India: Concluding Observations of the Human Rights Committee*, 60th Session, U.N. Doc. CCPR/C/60/IND/3, July 30, 1997.

[28] *E.g., Makhan Singh* v. *State of Punjab*: AIR 1964 SC 331.

[29] *E.g., P.L. Lakhanpal* v. *Union of India*: AIR 1967 SC 243.

[30] *A.D.M. Jabalpur* v. *Shivkant Shukla*: AIR 1976 SC 1207.

expression would now only suffer automatic suspension in the event of a war or armed external aggression, but the threat has not vanished altogether.[31]

The extent of this threat was demonstrated vividly during the 1975-77 state of emergency when a sweeping Censorship Order was imposed on the press which resulted in a near black-out of all independent news and comment for over a year.[32] It is a tribute to the courage and resilience of the Indian judiciary that, such oppression notwithstanding, some judges came bravely to the aid of journalists who had been subjected to intimidation by the censors. A prominent example of such courage was reflected in a 1976 judgment of the Bombay High Court which ruled that the censor had been wrong in preventing *Freedom First*, a liberal monthly, from publishing several articles critical of the government, on national security grounds.[33] The court declared in ringing tones:

> It is not the function of the Censor acting under the Censorship Order to make all newspapers and periodicals trim their sails to one wind or to tow along in a single file or to speak in chorus with one voice. It is not for him to exercise his statutory powers to force public opinion into a single mold or to turn the Press into an instrument for brainwashing the public. Under the Censorship Order the Censor is appointed the nurse-maid of democracy and not its grave-digger.[34]

The Gujarat High Court was no less scathing in its condemnation of mindless censorship. In *C. Vaidya* v. *H. D'Penha*,[35] the court reviewed an order of the Censor to close down a journal which contained voices of dissent against the emergency, on the ground that they amounted to a "prejudicial report", i.e. matter prejudicial to national security. The court stated:

> To peacefully protest against any governmental action with the immediate object of educating public opinion and the ultimate object of getting the ruling party voted out of power at the next general elections is not a prejudicial report at all. Such a public education is the primary need of every democracy.[36]

---

[31] Despite the amendment to Art. 358, it is still possible for the government to suppress freedom of speech during an emergency declared for internal reasons by passing an order under Art. 359 suspending the right of citizens to petition any court to enforce Art. 19.
[32] For a full account of the effects of this order, *see White Paper on the Misuse of Mass Media During the Internal Emergency* (Government of India, 1977).
[33] *Binod Rao* v. *M.R. Masani*, 78 Bom. L.R. 125 (1976) .
[34] *Id.* at 169.
[35] Special Civil Application. No. 141 of 1976, Judgment dated March 22, 1976 (unreported), *cited in* Soli J. Sorabjee, *The Law of Press Censorship in India*, 181-200 (1976).
[36] *Id.* at 193.

One of the most contentious pieces of special security legislation enacted in recent years, the Terrorist and Disruptive Activities (Prevention) Act (1987)[37] made it an offense, *inter alia*, to question, however peacefully, the territorial integrity of India or to support any claim for the secession of any part of the country from the Union.[38] This law featured in a case before the Punjab High Court which ruled in 1993 that a mere demand for secession or for the formation of an independent sovereign State could not be penalized, as long as that demand was made through peaceful and non-violent means.[39] This judgment was seen as a significant victory for free speech, especially in the context of what was until recently an increasingly stringent security climate in India. The constitutional validity of the Act was upheld by the Supreme Court in a landmark judgment the following year, but that judgment did not deal with any challenge on the ground of the right to freedom of speech and expression.[40]

VI. Security Restrictions on Freedom of Expression during Non-Emergencies

Even during periods of relative normalcy, the Indian Government has shown itself to be extremely sensitive to issues of national security. For several years now, access to a large part of the national territory, including such northeastern states as Arunachal Pradesh and Mizoram, has been severely restricted, with even Indian nationals being obliged to obtain special permits to visit those areas. Foreigners are virtually banned from entering such territory. Occasionally, the government creates "no-go" areas for security reasons in other parts of the country as well. For instance, when the Indian army stormed Sikhism's holiest shrine, the Golden Temple in Amritsar, in October 1984, to flush out suspected terrorists hiding there, a comprehensive ban was imposed on foreign journalists from entering the temple

---

[37] This Act, originally intended as a temporary measure to deal with the increasing terrorist violence in Punjab, was based on a 1985 Act of the same name. It was continued in force by two-year extensions until May 1995 when, following growing domestic and international criticism, the government allowed it to lapse.

[38] Sec. 4(2) of the Act defines "disruptive activity" as "any action taken, whether by act or speech or through any media or any other manner whatsoever: (i) which questions, disrupts, or is intended to disrupt, whether directly or indirectly, the sovereignty and territorial integrity of India; or (ii) which is intended to bring about or supports any claim, whether directly or indirectly, for the cession of any part of India or the secession of any part of India from the Union." The punishment for such activity is imprisonment for from five years to life, with or without a fine.

[39] This judgment does not appear to have been reported, but it was publicized in a news item in the *Indian Express*, Bombay, on April 14, 1993. It was delivered in the case of Lt. Col. Pratap Singh by Justice S.S. Grewal. No further details of this judgment are available, nor is it known if it was appealed to the Supreme Court.

[40] *Kartar Singh* v. *State of Punjab*, 3 SCC 569 (1994).

precincts and its neighborhood. There is a permanent ban imposed on photographing certain government buildings, including civilian airports.[41]

The sensitivity of the government has also revealed itself in numerous instances of censorship of books and journals which carry maps of India that are not to the authorities' liking. A recent example is a ban imposed on the distribution of the computer software, Windows 95, which allegedly carried an incorrect map of Kashmir. The ban was only lifted after the manufacturers of the software made certain changes to the map.

VII. Access to State-Held Information and Official Secrets

The lack of a properly coordinated system of data collection and dissemination, combined with a deep-rooted culture of secrecy, makes it extremely difficult to obtain even relatively innocuous information from official sources. The culture of secrecy is legally underpinned by the Official Secrets Act (1923) which makes it an offense for anyone to communicate or receive, without proper authorization, any information or document designated "secret" by the government, although that term has not been defined anywhere in the Act. Modeled on its 1911 British counterpart (which has since been repealed), this Act has been subject to frequent criticism from the media for its "catch-all" character, and for the lack of a "public interest" defense for defendants. The government has repeatedly failed to heed calls for radical reform of the law, but agreed in 1997 to define the phrase "official secret" so as to reduce the scope for ambiguity and "thus remove its omnibus character."[42] Although this has been seen by campaigners as a step in the right direction, the government continues to be criticized for not going far enough.

Among the more controversial uses to which the Official Secrets Act has been put in recent times has been to deny information to environmental activists campaigning against various ecologically doubtful projects initiated by the Central and State governments, such as the Narmada Valley Project in the State of Gujarat. This project, which has attracted considerable international criticism, involves the building of a large dam on the river Narmada which, in the opinion of many environmental experts, would have devastating consequences for the local ecology and population. Earlier, the Act had been used, equally controversially, to suppress

[41] This ban is sanctioned by the Official Secrets Act (1923).

[42] *Government of India Report of the Working Group on Right to Information and Promotion of Open and Transparent Government*, 8-9 (May 1997). This document proposes that "official secret" should be defined as "any information the disclosure of which is likely to prejudicially affect the sovereignty and integrity of India, the security of the State, friendly relations with foreign States, economic, commercial, scientific and technological matters relating to national security and includes any secret code, password, sketch, plan, model, article, note or document in relation to a prohibited place."

information about the health and environmental effects of the massive leakage of toxic gas from the Union Carbide Company's plant in Bhopal in 1984.

Government servants are subjected to severe penalties under their rules of discipline, as well as sanctions under the Official Secrets Act, for unauthorized disclosure of information. In 1988, for instance, a senior scientist, Dr. Buddhi Kota Subbarao, who had been carrying out research on defense-related matters while in the employment of the Indian Navy, was arrested and detained under the Official Secrets Act as he was about to board a plane for the United States a year after he had taken voluntary retirement from the Navy. The basis of the charges against him was the discovery in his luggage of certain documents which the authorities deemed to be "sensitive". These documents, which were, surprisingly, not produced before the magistrate who remanded him to custody, consisted of his (unclassified) Ph.D. thesis and freely available technical literature on marine satellite communications from Japan, the USA, the UK, Germany and Sweden.

Dr. Subbarao was charged with offenses under the Official Secrets Act and the Atomic Energy Act, and was held in detention for nearly two years, during which period he was denied medical treatment for a serious spinal injury caused by ill-treatment while in custody. He eventually managed to get bail after protracted legal proceedings in the course of which the charges against him were quashed. The government appealed, subjecting him to a lengthy, expensive and traumatic appellate process until he was finally cleared of all charges by the Supreme Court in 1993. The manner in which Dr. Subbarao's prosecution was conducted came in for strong criticism from the Bombay High Court and from journalists who observed the case.[43]

In 1997 the Government of India circulated proposals for a Freedom of Information Bill after acknowledging that there was "a broad sweep of change towards openness and transparency [in government] across the world."[44] This move was given a warm, but cautious, welcome by campaigners for free speech, many of whom continue to be skeptical about the government's commitment in this area. The draft Bill requires all public authorities to maintain records in a systematic manner and to accede to reasonable requests for information from the general public. It does, however, exclude a number of types of information from disclosure, including "information which would prejudicially affect ... [the] security of the State.[45] Most observers agree that the success of the measure, if adopted, will depend largely on the spirit in which it is implemented by the government bureaucracy, which will not become clear until several months after the Bill is enacted and brought

---

[43] *See, e.g.*, Judgment of Mr. Justice M.F. Saldhana in Criminal Writ Petition No. 180 of 1991 (unreported), *cited in* Burjor Taraporewalla, "Dr. B.K. Subbarao's Quest for Justice: The epic trial of an innocent man framed as a spy," *in The Lawyers*, 8-46, Bombay (Aug. 1994).

[44] *Report of the Working Group on Right to Information and Open and Transparent Government*, *supra* note 42, at 3.

[45] Freedom of Information Bill 1997, sec. 9(1), reproduced in *Report of the Working Group*, *id.*, at 16.

into force. At the moment, it is the subject of a public consultation exercise which is expected to last until early 1998.

VIII. Conclusion

National security issues have rarely figured with any degree of prominence in Indian public discourse, and then primarily in the context of emergency or special security legislation. There are undoubtedly areas of concern from the civil liberties point of view which need to be addressed. Arguably, the foremost of these is the unsatisfactory state of the law on official secrets. There have also been increasingly vocal calls for allowing greater access to State-held information, and the Government's proposed Freedom of Information Bill is clearly a step in the right direction. Nevertheless, much more needs to be done in terms of law reform, including, for example, a review of the constitutional provisions on emergency powers which currently permit unacceptably wide curbs to be placed on freedom of expression.

Concurrent with these legal reforms must come a fundamental change in the prevailing governmental culture and attitudes of the state bureaucracy which have traditionally been one of unthinking secrecy. This will need a sustained and carefully planned program of re-education and re-orientation. One hopeful prospect is that the impetus provided by the ongoing process of economic liberalization will serve as a vital catalyst for change. Another source of encouragement is the judiciary which has, despite inevitable institutional constraints, frequently struck a blow for freedom in matters involving national security claims.

National Security, Freedom of Expression and Access to Information: The Israeli Situation

Ruth Gavison

I. Introduction

A. General Introduction[1]

Since its inception, Israel has been a Parliamentary democracy. While the original design was for the state to enact a constitution, in 1950 the Knesset (Israel's parliament) decided to enact a series of "basic laws" which together would form a constitution. The basic laws that were enacted dealt primarily with the structure of government. They were not entrenched in any way, with the exception of a few provisions that explicitly specified the requirement of a super-majority for their amendment.

The courts' approach has been dynamic. They accepted the requirement of special majority as binding. Initially, it was accepted by all that the Israeli legal system did not allow judicial review of primary legislation in the absence of explicit authorization. In the mid eighties, there were tentative voices on the Supreme Court suggesting that such review could, in principle, be introduced by adjudication, once the general climate supports such a move.

However, in 1992, the Knesset enacted two basic laws dealing with human rights: The Basic Law: Freedom of Occupation, and the Basic Law: Human Dignity and Freedom. The latter is more central due to the breadth of its title (despite the fact that the rights specifically mentioned in the text relate only to life, freedom of movement, property, privacy and defamation, and freedom from arbitrary arrest or detention). Both laws contain a section specifying that the Knesset cannot violate the rights protected unless this is done for a legitimate purpose, and in a scope not broader than what is required. There is quite a controversy on the status and meaning of these laws. Most constitutional writers agree, however, that the laws open an era of judicial review over post-1992 primary legislation by the Knesset.[2] For

---

[1] There are a number of recent accounts of Israel's legal system, especially the constitutional system. The most systematic comprehensive account of Israel's freedom of expression jurisprudence is still P. Lahav's chapter on Israel's Press Law in Pnina Lahav ed., *Press Law in Modern Democracies: A Comparative Study* (1985) (*hereinafter* Lahav 1985).

[2] For a short description of the new laws see D. Kretzmer, "The New Basic Laws on Human Rights: A Mini-Revolution in Israeli Constitutional Law?," 26 *Isr. L. Rev.* 238-405 (1992). The Basic Law: Human Dignity and Freedom contains a provision expressly "protecting" existing legislation from such review. However, there is now a debate in the Court whether the Basic Law permits, or even requires, a change in the balance struck earlier between conflicting

our purposes it should be said that the basic law does *not* expressly cover freedom of speech. Nonetheless, there have been voices, among them that of the influential Chief Justice Aharon Barak, who have interpreted Dignity and Liberty in this law to mean the whole range of classical human rights, including, of course, freedom of expression.[3]

It is particularly hard to know how (and if) the new laws will affect the extent to which freedom of expression is protected in Israel, however, this was one of the areas in which the Supreme Court has been most active despite the absence of a constitution. As discussed below, Israel has a very impressive free speech jurisprudence, mostly judge-made. In some cases, including areas classically defined as relating to matters of security, the Israeli Supreme Court reached decisions more favorable to free speech than those rendered by courts in many constitutional democracies. On other matters so defined, however, the picture is very different.

The legal regime applicable in Israel itself is substantially different from that applicable in the occupied territories. The latter are controlled by a combination of Jordanian law that applied in 1967 and the additions and modifications introduced by military orders issued by Israel under international occupation law. There is similarity in some of the legal provisions (primarily those contained in the Defense Regulations inherited by both sides of the Green Line from the British Mandate). Moreover, Israel decided to apply its own legal system in Jerusalem and in the Golan Heights. In the following account, I shall deal primarily with freedom of speech under Israeli laws.[4]

Some background facts about Israel are also crucial to the understanding of its free speech/national security jurisprudence. Israel was founded in 1948 in the wake of a United Nations resolution and the withdrawal of the British Mandatory authority. It is a cleavaged society, and the deepest cleavages are the ones between Jews and Arabs (who comprise about 17% of the population) on the one hand, and between religious Jews and non-orthodox Jews. Israel has faced a threat to its existence from the neighboring Arab states since its inception. Its relation to the Arab minority in Israel was greatly influenced by this perceived threat, and the feeling that the Israeli Arabs belonged, in some important sense, to this threat. In addition, there is an intense debate about the "Jewishness" of the state between the

---

interests.

[3] For Barak's views, *see* his monumental *Interpretation in the Law: Constitutional Interpretation* (1994). Others have argued that the consensus in the Knesset was based on the exclusion of the rights not specifically mentioned from the scope of the law, and that this consensus should be respected at least in the short term. *See, e.g.*, Kretzmer, *supra* note 2.

[4] The description is not territorial intentionally. As mentioned above, Israeli law applies in the Golan Heights and, more significantly, in Jerusalem. Since most of the Palestinian press and quite a lot of Palestinian political speech is located in Jerusalem, Israeli laws are the relevant ones. Besides, Jewish settlers in the territories are usually subjected to the jurisdiction of Israeli civil courts and to Israeli laws.

orthodox who tend to see it as related to Jewish religion, and non-orthodox who define their Jewishness as cultural or ethnic. These two tensions are related but distinct: Arab nationality is perceived to threaten all Jewish groups, but for the national-religious Jewish segment of Israeli society, the internal struggle against secularism and the external struggle against Arabs seem to intensify each other.[5]

Finally, the political process of negotiation started by the Oslo agreement in September 1993[6] has heightened the inter-Jewish debate about the future of the territories. The debate was heated from the very beginning, and grew more passionate as the Israeli army agreed to pull out of Palestinian cities. The protest included claims that Prime Minister Rabin, his government and the process they were leading lacked any legitimacy, and culminated in November 1995 with Rabin's assassination by a young religious man, who claimed he was executing a command of Jewish law.[7]

B. Legal Framework for Limitations of Freedom of Expression

There are legal provisions mainly designed to deal with security issues and more general mechanisms which may be used for this purpose. Israel incorporated into its own legal system all the laws valid in the area before the foundation of the State. Among these are the Defense Regulations enacted by the British to handle the deteriorating internal security in the area, as well as the Mandatory Press Ordinance dealing with the regulation of written media.[8] The Defense Regulations impose a general requirement of licensing on all regular or political publications, permit refusal

---

[5] This point was dramatically illustrated by Meir Kahane's party, which combined an ultra-religious standpoint with an explicit, blatant and violent attack against Arabs. Some of Israel's recent limitations on free speech - *e.g.*, the legal prohibition against racial incitement - are due to the emergence of violent Jewish racism. However, Kahane was not usually perceived as a threat to Israel's national security.

[6] The Oslo agreement between Israel and the PLO reflected an agreement between the Rabin government and the Palestinians that the armed conflict will be changed into a negotiated settlement, and envisaged a gradual withdrawal of Israeli forces from all the occupied territories, leaving the more explosive issues of the Jewish settlements and Jerusalem to the last stages of negotiating the permanent arrangement.

[7] This paper was written in the early summer of 1995, before Rabin's assassination and the rise of Netanyahu to power in June 1996. The events surrounding the assassination created a serious re-thinking of the use of law to curb incitement. For a short analysis of this process see Ruth Gavison, "Incitement and the Limits of Law", *in* Robert Post ed., *Censorship and Silencing: Practices of Cultural Regulation* (forthcoming 1998). However, updating the paper would have required major changes throughout, so I have preferred to leave it mostly as written, placing it in the time of writing.

[8] For a detailed study of the Press Ordinance (1933) and the powers it grants the executive, *see* P. Lahav, "Governmental Regulation and the Press: A Study of Israel's Press Ordinance," 13 *Isr. L. Rev.* 230, 489 (1978).

or denial of licenses without the need to provide reasons, and establish a mechanism for military censorship. This mechanism was largely replaced, for the established Jewish press, with a voluntary arrangement.[9] Censorship is applied, however, to the Arab press. In recent years, with the proliferation of local and non-establishment Jewish press, the effectiveness of the arrangement has been eroded somewhat.

The same period generated Ordinances dealing with censorship of films and the theater. The latter were abolished in 1991, and the former are being modified into a rating system.[10]

Israel itself had for a long time a monopoly over the electronic media, which were regulated by a 1969 National Broadcasting Authority Act. In the last decade, broadcasting has become more diversified.[11]

Israel's criminal code includes a number of provisions dealing with speech-related offenses, including a 1988 section against racial incitement. Inciting to use arms against the government is a criminal offense,[12] as is inciting individuals not to enlist to the armed forces or to participate in a military duty.[13] Israel has a 1965 Defamation Law and a 1981 Privacy Law, but these have not been used to curb speech related to security issues.

Finally, Israel enacted a Law against Terrorism in 1949. Initially, it was designed against Right-Wing Jewish groups, but it soon became a major legal tool against Palestinian organizations. In 1980, a section criminalizing expression of support for such an organization was added to the law. For some time it was used to prosecute individuals publicly expressing support of the PLO.[14]

As a general rule we may say that the courts, especially the Supreme Court, developed a very impressive free speech jurisprudence on most matters of vital

---

[9] For an account of the law and the voluntary arrangement, *see* Lahav 1985, *supra* note 1 at 274-277. *See also* M. Negbi, *Freedom of the Press in Israel - The Legal Aspect*, ch. 3 (1995) (in Hebrew).

[10] For a detailed description of the development on this issue, *see* Amnon Rubinstein, *Israel's Constitutional Law*, ch. 29 (4th ed. 1991) (in Hebrew).

[11] In addition to the public radio and TV system governed by law, Israel now has additional TV channels. These are statutory, but based on a complicated system of licensing private bodies. The same applies to radio stations. A major concern is the fact that these licenses are obtained by groups controlled by individuals and companies that control parts of the written press, thus creating semi-monopolies in the media. For details *see* Negbi, *supra* note 9 at ch. 9.

[12] Section 136 of the Criminal Code 1977 defines "incitement" as any conduct generating hate, contempt or disloyalty to the state or its legally constituted organs, seeking to lead residents to use illegal ways to change the law, to provoke indignance or resentment in the population, or to create hostilities between segments of the population. Section 133 makes incitement an offense with a maximum punishment of five years of imprisonment.

[13] Section 109 of the Criminal Code. The maximum punishment for incitement not to enlist is five years, for incitement or aiding in desertion - seven years, and if the incitement or aiding is in a period of active military operations - fifteen years.

[14] It is interesting to note that the PLO is still considered, legally speaking, a terrorist organization, despite the fact that the Oslo process is being slowly implemented, and Arafat is the chairman of the Palestinian Entity. Needless to say, the law is not enforced.

political importance. The record is significantly weaker when security matters are at stake, and when expression by Arabs is concerned. The record is also much weaker on matters of access to information and the right to know.

II. Regulation of Speech Relating to National Security

A. Access to and Disclosure of Information

1. Access to Information

Israel does not, at present, have a Freedom of Information Act. There have been initiatives to legislate such an act over the past fifteen years. Recently, a public committee on the subject was formed, and presented its recommendations to the Minister of Justice. The Committee does recommend the enactment of such an act, with the usual exceptions, including, of course, national security.

Israel repealed its Official Secrets Act (inherited from the British Mandatory regime), but the legal system maintains good legal control over governmental information.[15] Nonetheless, there seem to be quite a lot of informal passages of information from governmental sources to other individuals and to the press, so the feeling often is that it is rather hard to keep secrets in Israel.[16]

Archives are opened after a period of twenty years, while matters of national security, foreign affairs, or personal matters may be kept secret up to fifty years.[17] Access to archives is usually limited. The nuclear and biological possibilities of Israel are seen as top secrets. The Landau Enquiry Commission on methods of investigation by the General Security Services (GSS), for example, added to its public report a secret appendix dealing with its proposals for guidelines on investigation practices. Similarly, the Agranat Commission of Enquiry on the Yom Kippur war had a secret appendix that was very recently made public after twenty years had elapsed.[18]

It seems that data about the state of the economy is accessible and published, with the exception of the exact size and details of the budget of the Ministry of Defense. However, information about leakages from nuclear facilities, or about the

---

[15] *See* 338-339, *infra*, discussing disclosures by employees.

[16] *See, e.g.*, I. Galnoor, "Government Secrecy in Israel," *in* I. Galnoor ed., *Government Secrecy in Democracies* (1977) (noting the paradox between a mentality of secrecy and the fact of extensive disclosure).

[17] Archives Law 1955, Archives Regulations 1966, amended 1979.

[18] Interestingly, there was some initial debate about the question whether the appendix should be made available. However, when it was disclosed, it seemed that it included nothing much that was not known beforehand.

effect of Chernobil in Israel, were not disclosed, and that policy generated some public debate but no legal action.

2. Disclosure by Government Agents or Employees

The law imposes duties of secrecy on civil servants.[19] Those employed in "sensitive" places sign a special secrecy pledge. As mentioned above, there are fora which are defined as secret.

However, if information is leaked by an employee, whether publication is prohibited depends on the nature of the data. Section 113 of the Penal Code establishes the offense of aggravated espionage, defined as the delivery of secret information without being authorized to do so, punishable by a maximum imprisonment of 15 years.[20]

An interesting case arose in June 1995, when the then-head of the opposition, Binyamin Netanyahu, attacked the government in public debate saying that its positions on the Golan compromised Israeli interests. He claimed that he based his allegations on an official document prepared by the IDF before the meetings of Israeli and Syrian chiefs of staff. At the beginning the authenticity of the document was denied, but later it was conceded that it was in fact an internal position paper prepared within the IDF. Clearly, the document was illegally leaked.

The Attorney-General decided that there would be no prosecution for the public disclosure of the document because Netanyahu's disclosure was within his parliamentary immunity. This left open the question as to what would have happened if the document had been published by a journalist.[21] It seems that the legal system in Israel could have allowed a conviction, though its activist court may well have developed something like the Pentagon papers doctrine, allowing

---

[19] Section 117 of the 1977 Penal Code prohibits the disclosure of information received through one's employment to a person not competent to receive it. The prohibition applies to information irrespective of its being classified. The prohibition stays valid, for non-classified information, for 5 years after the civil servant has retired.

[20] The power to prosecute under this section is rarely invoked. For one such case *see* Lahav 1985, *supra* note 1 at 278.

[21] In fact, some MPs challenged the AG's decision in court. They both relied on HC 1843/93 *Pinchassi* v. *Israel Knesset*, PD 49(1) 661, 688, in which Justice Barak said, in an *obiter dictum*, that even speeches in the Knesset are not all necessarily protected. He gives the example of a MP who, during a speech, gets out a pre-written list of secret information, and reads it out loud. Barak distinguished this case from the case in which an MP inadvertently discloses secret information. The AG concluded Netanyahu's case was not a clear exception to the rationale of the immunity, while the legal advisor to the Knesset thought that it was. The court decided that immunity did apply to Netanyahu's disclosure in the Knesset, but that investigation should be made of the leak to Netanyahu. It turned out the investigation was undertaken by the army, and a few officers were reprimanded. HC 5151/95 *Ran Cohen* v. *AG* (not yet published).

publication in the public interest even if the disclosure was in fact both illegal and unjustified.

It is interesting to note that a public debate was conducted in Israel in the wake of the Netanyahu affair about the desirability of disclosure in such circumstances. Most commentators in Israel thought that this was an instance of a justified claim of secrecy on the government's behalf, and that Netanyahu's disclosures could have hurt Israel's negotiating position. The debate revealed the difficulty in reaching a balance between allowing justified secrecy and satisfying the public's right to know and to debate the features of the agreement before it is concluded.[22]

A controversial prosecution for disclosure of information was that concerning Mordechai Vanunu. Vanunu was charged with aiding the enemy and with collecting and disseminating secret information in violation of section 113 of the Penal Code, and received eighteen years imprisonment, for disseminating information concerning Israel's nuclear arms industry to the foreign press.[23] Leaks that are less dramatic are usually dealt with by disciplinary and similar measures.

3. The News Media

Since the foundation of Israel, it has been under an Emergency Situation. Thus, the distinction between armed conflicts and peace does not easily apply. However, there is a distinction between the periods. For example, in Israel the right to demonstrate is recognized very broadly. However, when demonstrations were held against the war in Lebanon during the war, there were some public outcries against this, and some plans to legislate a prohibition on demonstrations during wars. A special section in the penal code, which has not been used, makes it an offense to disseminate "defeatist propaganda . . . at a time of actual fighting".[24]

During war time, physical access to the front may be limited and controlled by the army (as it was in Lebanon). The army in fact used its powers to exclude journalists from certain areas, despite the fact that there was no actual fighting taking place there.

---

[22] This debate is now very central in Israel concerning the negotiations with the PLO and Syria. People supporting the negotiations claim, with justice, that it is impossible to negotiate when details are all the time subject to public debate. Publicity prevents the kind of flexibility in negotiation that is crucial for successful dialogue. Those objecting to the agreements, on the other hand, claim, with justice, that if the government is allowed to strike a bargain and present it, on a take it or leave it basis, it preempts effective public debate. Clearly, the results of these negotiations do affect matters of national security. There has been no legal resolution of this issue, and I expect it will continue to be resolved in the political arena. In August 1995 an initiative, to require that any agreement with the PLO be subject to a referendum prior to signing, was very narrowly defeated in the Knesset.

[23] Cr.App. 172/88 *Vanunu* v. *State of Israel*, PD 44(1) 265.

[24] 1977 Penal Code, sec. 103.

Similarly, military commanders use their powers to close areas when they are not interested in press presence and coverage. This was used at times during the Intifada. The reasons given were that the presence of the press did not serve only or mainly to document what was happening, but that the Palestinians were staging their demonstrations for the press. The exclusion of the press, it was said, was thus a legitimate part of discharging the duty to protect public order. However, these decisions triggered great opposition within Israel, especially when pictures documenting the way Israeli soldiers were treating Palestinians were published.

When Israel's government had a monopoly over the electronic media, the Court made it clear that it would look into decisions made by the board of the statutory National Broadcasting Authority (NBA) on their merits. Two such decisions deserve special mention. First, in a two to one decision, the Court invalidated an NBA decision not to interview people affiliated with the PLO. The Court stressed that the right of the public to know included being exposed to all points of view, and that the NBA was subject to a requirement of fairness. The Court decided a sweeping prohibition on all those affiliated with the PLO was too vague, and did not indicate any threat to legitimate public interest.[25] Later, a unanimous Court overruled as overbroad an internal NBA guideline not to broadcast MP Meir Kahane live unless the item was newsworthy.[26] However, a controversy developed concerning whether the NBA was permitted to prevent broadcasting speech that is a criminal offence (in that case, the 1988 offense of racial incitement). While Barak J. thought this would be an undesirable prior restraint, Bach J. thought that the NBA could clearly prevent usage of its facilities to spread racial incitement prohibited by law.

The willingness of the Court to exert control over the official public channel, and the debate over control of the media by the left, were highlighted by a petition to the High Court to block the regular participation of a journalist known for his left-wing orientation, Amnon Abramovitz, on a prestigious Friday night program. A right-wing group called The Association for the Public's Right to Know brought the petition, which was withdrawn when the State notified the Court that the Fairness Doctrine required it to expose viewers to disparate points of view.[27]

The licensing apparatus of electronic media also creates dangers for free speech. The law states that people operating illegal radio or TV stations can be indicted, and that the stations can be suspended and the equipment seized. Usually,

---

[25] HC 243/82, *Zichroni* v. *NBA*, PD 37(1) 757.

[26] HC 399/85, *Kahane* v. *NBA*, PD 41(3) 255.

[27] While courts and media talk about the fairness doctrine, it was never used in Israeli jurisprudence to justify a judicial interference with a decision of the broadcasting authorities or of the press.

the enforcement of these provisions is of economic significance only.[28] However, for years a station called "The Voice of Peace" was operated without a license, based on a boat just outside Israel's territorial waters. In the last decade, the right-wing settlers have operated in a similar way a political station called "arutz 7". As the dissent against the Oslo process grew, arutz 7 became more and more aggressive, in many instances verging on the illegal. At the end of July 1995, the boat and the equipment were seized when the boat came into Tel-Aviv port for repairs. A public outcry ensued, and the station was allowed to continue its operation.

B. Expression Deemed Threatening to National Security or Territorial Integrity

The provisions granting power to curb speech vary. Many are very general in their language. They refer to national security or public order, or fail to mention any grounds for justifying the limitation on expression. So to see what is really deemed threatening it is necessary to go beyond the legal provisions themselves, and examine actual enforcement.

1. Disclosure or Dissemination of Military Information

Military movements, location and availability of arms, etc., are deemed top military secrets, and their disclosure, either to unauthorized individuals or to the press, is a criminal offense. These types of information are in the core of what is deemed a threat to national security, especially in a country in a constant threat of war. With the exception of the Vanunu case, there is no serious questioning of this situation in Israel. In the Vanunu case, the debate concerned the question of whether all information about Israel's nuclear capacity should be kept secret, and there was a question about whether the information disclosed was not in fact known before.[29]

Beyond this core, there is some tendency to describe as "military" information matters which are not necessarily entitled to similar secrecy. For example, matters that should not be disclosed include facts embarrassing to Israel's foreign relations. While the government's reluctance to see these things published is understandable, it is not clear that they deserve the same level of secrecy as military secrets.

Details about the identity and organization of security service personnel was also regarded as top secret. In *Shnitzer,* the Court showed willingness to look into

---

[28] Recently, illegal radio stations situated near Israel's international airport have occasionally disabled the controls, leading to a preventive strike of a few hours, which ended only after the equipment was seized.

[29] *See* Ruth Gavison, "Freedom of Expression, State Security and Nuclear Capacity," *in* S. Shetreet ed., *Freedom of Speech and State Security* (1991).

such claims and to reject, at times, the government's judgment that secrecy was justified.[30]

2. Advocacy of Refusal to Serve in the Army or to Obey Orders in Military Service

Urging others to avoid army service or to disobey military orders is illegal under Israeli criminal law.[31] However, the discretion to enforce these laws is vested with the Attorney-General, and those who held this position have systematically refused to enforce the law against those who expressed such views. These policies were the subject of public controversy, including some petitions to the high court.[32]

3. Support for Terrorist Organizations

In the 1980s, a number of individuals, both Israelis and Palestinians, were detained, interrogated and at times prosecuted and convicted for supporting the PLO as a partner for negotiations. "Supporting" meant not only making statements supporting or legitimating the PLO, but also carrying its flag. Even members of the Israeli-Palestinian Council, whose sign was the two flags combined, were interrogated.

It should be noted that the 1980 law that permitted this activity was not amended despite the mutual recognition of Israel and the PLO in the Oslo agreement.

For a short period (1988 to 1993), Israel's criminal law made it an offense to meet with PLO officials or affiliates. A number of individuals who met with PLO members were in fact prosecuted and convicted; some of them even received prison sentences. These prison sentences were commuted for those defendants who chose to appeal to the Supreme Court. At least one individual, who decided not to appeal, in fact served a short prison sentence for such a meeting. In addition, Ezer

---

[30] HC 680/88 *Shnitzer* v. *Military Censor*, PD 42(4) 617. This attitude in fact changed, and after Rabin's assassination, it became public policy to identify the heads of the secret security forces. In part, this was the result of the fact that their names had been published on the internet, so the demand of secrecy seemed futile.

[31] One should note, however, that Israeli law also makes it an offense to obey a military order that is "blatantly illegal on its face". This prohibition was invoked when soldiers obeyed orders to kill or harm unarmed individuals.

[32] There seems to be some asymmetry between enforcement against right and left in this context: while no one was indicted for such calls, a leftist group that helped individuals who were imprisoned for refusal to serve in Lebanon and in the West Bank were interrogated, even though they consciously refrained from explicitly encouraging disobedience or draft evasion. When right wing Rabbis announced their halakhic verdict (p'sak halacha) that evacuating camps in the West Bank is prohibited by Jewish law, and that soldiers should not obey orders to do so, the AG announced there will be no interrogation.

Weitzman, now President of Israel, lost his place in the cabinet in 1990, when it was disclosed that he talked to PLO leader Yasir Arafat.

4. Incitement and Seditious Libel

Israel's criminal code includes offenses that prohibit a call to use violence against the government or other groups in the population. Prosecution under these sections requires the consent of the AG. They have been used sparingly, with a bias towards Arab nationalistic expression.

A recent example of such a use of the law is the prosecution of an Arab writer, Jabbarin, for literary texts in which he expressed feelings of empowerment in the wake of the Intifada.[33]

The AG has expressed unwillingness to use the criminal law for expressions, including ones calling for the use of violence, in the context of the public debate about the Arab-Israeli conflict. Some of these decisions were challenged, and to date the Court has upheld all of them.[34]

5. Racial Incitement

Racial incitement became an offense in Israel amidst lively public debate in 1988, to add a legal tool to fight the blatant and extreme statements made by Meir Kahane against Arabs. Indictment requires the consent of the AG, and the power was very sparingly used.

In the summer of 1995 the Jerusalem district court convicted an orthodox Jew, Rabbi Iddo Alba, of this offense, based on a monograph he published after the Hebron massacre. The monograph examines Jewish law concerning the killing of Gentiles, stressing that it is about the law, not a suggestion for action. The book states that the commandment of "Do Not Murder" applies only to Jews, and that when there is a war between Jews and another people, it may be permissible, or even a religious duty, to kill all members of that people.

The district court stated that the combination of the content and the context of publication, and the fact that Alba was also indicted for collecting arms to hurt Arabs, suggested that the required intention to incite to racism obtained.[35]

---

[33] Jabbarin was convicted by the magistrate court, and sentenced to a short term in prison. The Association for Civil Rights in Israel (ACRI) took the case on appeal to the District Court, which upheld the conviction and lowered the punishment. In 1996, the Supreme Court upheld the conviction, but ACRI's request for a further hearing was granted.

[34] As noted above, this is an area of the law that has undergone some change and development in the wake of Rabin's assassination. The picture is not yet clear. *See supra*, note 7.

[35] The Supreme Court started hearing the appeal in a regular panel of three the day after the Rabin assassination. The panel was enlarged, and in 1996 the Supreme Court affirmed the conviction by a split five to two vote. Notably, the dissenting judges were both religious, and

III. Extraordinary Procedures for Assessing National Security Claims

A. Judicial Review

Section 19 of the Press Ordinance empowers the Minister of Interior to suspend the publication of a newspaper if he thinks it is likely to endanger public peace. In 1953, the Supreme Court held that the Minister of Interior could only use this power if there is probable danger that security or public order are seriously damaged.[36] In that case, the newspaper published a blatant critique of an alleged statement by Israel's foreign minister, committing Israel to send troops to Korea. The newspaper in fact urged its readers to refuse to obey such order if it is given. The court found that the requirement of probable danger was not met, among other things because the statement was denied.

Since then, the power under section 19 has been used very sparingly, mainly against the Arab press.[37] The probable danger test was extended to other areas of censorship and limitations on free speech, and in 1988 the Supreme Court declared that the level and scope of judicial review on national security matters was no different than it was for judicial review of all other administrative decisions.[38] The case was in fact a free speech v. national security one: the military censor refused to permit the publication of the outgoing head of the GSS, claiming that publication would threaten both him and the service as a whole. The court was not persuaded.[39]

However, in other cases, the court refuses to take responsibility for making security assessments. The picture is clearest in cases concerning the territories. The Court very rarely invalidates decisions to put individuals in administrative detention, to deport or to demolish houses. In all such cases, military authorities invoke

---

the majority included president Barak, who has developed a consistent pro-speech position.

[36] HC 73/53 *Kol-Ha-am* v. *Minister of Interior*, PD 7 871.

[37] See HC 644/81 *Ommer International Inc. NY* v. *Minister of Interior*, PD 36(1) 227, where a unanimous court found that the use of power was justified since the Al-Fajer, a major Palestinian newspaper, congratulated acts of murder and terrorism which could well endanger public peace. *See also* the reference in Rubinstein, *supra* note 10 at 728 n. 16, to the unpublished HC 3176/90 *Jabbarin* v. *Minister of Interior*, in which the court upheld a three month suspension order under section 19 against an Arabic newspaper published in Um-El-Fahem.

[38] The grounds for judicial review of administrative action in Israel are pretty broad. They include, in addition to *ultra-vires* and illegal motives, a general ground of "unreasonableness". For a general survey, *see* I. Zamir & E. Zysblatt eds., *Public Law in Israel* (1997).

[39] HC 680/88 *Shnitzer* v. *Military Censor*, PD 42(4) 617. The Court, per Barak J., decided that the *Kol-Ha-am* ruling, requiring that limitations of free speech are allowed only if there is probable danger for a substantial damage to state's security, should be applied to the voluntary censorship arrangement as well. *See also supra* note 36.

national security reasons.[40] Before *Shnitzer*, the Supreme Court applied the same unwillingness to look into security determinations in one of the rare censorship cases to reach it.[41]

Similarly, the Court refused to look into the denial of licenses to Arab newspapers allegedly financed by the PLO or other Palestinian groups under the Defense Regulations. The Court said that the issue was not one of free speech at all, since this was a part of a legitimate war against terrorist organizations.[42] The court also refused to question, or even order the disclosure of information justifying the refusal to give an Israeli Arab the license to publish a newspaper.[43] In the wake of the Basic Laws, an opportunity to challenge the *Mahoul* ruling arose when a license to publish was denied without disclosing reasons. ACRI argued that the Basic Law: Freedom of Occupation is not consistent with the denial of a person's right to be a journalist without some showing of probable danger. The authorities granted the license without putting the decision to a judicial test.

B. Prior Restraint of Publication

As mentioned above, the Defense Regulations create a regime of military censorship, which may impose prior constraint on *all* publication. In fact, in the Jewish press, the censor issues a list of topics that must be cleared with him before publication.[44] Requirements of licenses and the power to suspend publication are also forms of prior restraint. I have noted some of their uses in present-day Israel above.

---

[40] For a detailed account of Supreme Court rhetoric on demolition of houses *see* D. Kretzmer, "Judicial Review of Sealing and Demolition of Homes in the Territories," *in Klinghoffer Book on Public Law* 305 (1992) (in Hebrew).

[41] HC 234/84, *Hadashot Inc.* v. *Minister of Defence*, PD 38(2) 477. Hadashot was closed for three days under section 100 of the Defence Regulations because it published information about a subject that was included in the list of subjects requiring prior screening, and about which a specific notice of prohibition to publish was issued. The court was not willing to look at the merits of the claim that the publication, in fact, would not endanger state security in any way.

[42] There have been five such cases in the seventies. *See* Rubinstein, *supra* note 10 at 741 n. 66. In HC 541/83 *Assli* v. *Jerusalem District Supervisor*, PD 37(4) 837, Barak J. states explicitly that the license is not denied because of the content of the publications, but due to the connection between the newspaper and the terrorist organization. Thus, no proof of a probalistic connection between speech and danger is required.

[43] HC 322/81, *Mahoul* v. *Supervisor of the Jerusalem District*, PD 34(1) 505.

[44] The regulations are literally enforced against the Arab press in Jerusalem, and the editors are required to pass everything, including advertisements, for screening before publication.

In a number of decisions the Supreme Court suggested it will not permit the use of censorship powers for the theater and films.[45]

C. Use of Military Courts to Try Cases Involving Civilians

Israel does have a parallel system of military courts under the Defense Regulations, which in principle may have jurisdiction over some actions by civilians. This system was used in the past to try civilians, mainly Arabs, but this practice ceased. The features of the military courts that seemed attractive were their personnel, who enjoy less independence than the usual judiciary, and the fact that in Israel only military courts can impose the death penalty.[46]

D. Summary Deportation and Exclusion Procedures for Aliens Deemed to Threaten National Security

Immigration laws in Israel distinguish between Jews and their families on the one hand, and others. Jews and their families are entitled to enter Israel and to Israeli residence and citizenship under the 1950 Law of Return. These rights may be denied under some circumstances, including a threat to the public interest. In rare cases, Jewish aliens are denied the right to enter Israel and stay in it.[47] I cannot recall a case of deportation under the same grounds.

The discretion the Minister of Interior has on granting visas and permits to enter to people not covered by the Law of Return is extremely broad, and the court has been unwilling to give its exercise close scrutiny. Occasionally, requests for unification of families are denied on the basis of security grounds. Some human

---

[45] The two liberal decisions came after a period of limited review of the power of the censorship board. One is HC 14/86 *Laor* v. *Theater and Movies Board*, PD 41(1) 421, in which the Court overruled the board's decision not to allow public performance of a play dealing with Israeli occupation, drawing an analogy between it and the Nazi occupation. Despite the Court's ruling, the theater decided not to produce the play. Concerning the movies, the Court overruled a decision not to allow the screening of *The Last Temptation of Christ* in HC 806/88 *Universal City*, PD 43(2) 22. In a recent decision the Court undermined the power of the board to cut parts deemed too violent or pornographic, in a case involving the movie *The Empire of the Senses*.

[46] The Japanese terrorist who shot dozens of people in Israel's international airport was indicted in the military court because the state asked for the death penalty. He was not executed, and was later released from prison. It should be noted that some Israeli soldiers prefer being tried in military courts, because the powers of pardon in that system are vested in the chief-of-staff and military personnel.

[47] Around the agreement on withdrawal from Hebron in late 1996, radical right-wing Jews were not allowed into the country.

rights organization claim that security reasons are invoked to cover-up demographic reasons – the wish to limit the size of the non-Jewish component of the population in Israel.

Israel inherited from the mandatory period laws permitting the deportation of citizens for security reasons. In fact, Jewish activists were deported under these laws before the establishment of the state. Israel abolished these laws within Israel, but it claims the right to deport residents of the Occupied Territories. Individuals deported in the past were not directly involved with violent acts, and were often described as inciters. Deportations have not been used since the Supreme Court upheld the controversial deportation of 415 Hamas activists in the end of 1992.

IV. Conclusions and Recommendations

I believe the picture drawn above supports my initial contention that Israel's record is a very mixed one. The legal arsenal on the books, especially from the mandatory period, is extremely ominous. In some areas, this arsenal is used to obtain dangerous results. In many others, the reality is much better than what the law "promises". In part, this is because the responsibility for initiating criminal proceedings lies with the Attorney-General, and the individuals filling that job have been extremely cautious about invoking laws suppressing political speech in the Jewish sector. In part, this is because the laws are so harsh and extreme, that alternative mechanisms were developed (*e.g.*, in the context of censorship). The Court has been very active in striking liberal balances between speech and security. Most importantly, all these institutional developments reflect the fact that Israel does have a vibrant democracy, despite the burden put on freedom and tolerance by the cleavages and the conflicts.

This does not mean that Israel should be proud of its reality and keep its laws. First, the dangerous laws are used in some contexts, in a manner that is discriminatory: Arab speech is censored and curtailed in ways unjustified in a democracy, even when one takes Israel's security needs into account. Second, unjust laws have chilling effects even when they are not used. I noted above that a robust debate about the limits of the duty to participate in active military duty was affected by fears of prosecution. Third, it is not clear that laws that have not been used in the past will never be used in the future. The seditious libel laws are now revived somewhat, after a long period in which many thought they were abolished for all practical purposes.[48]

The cleavages are intense, and the threats are real. The political process starting in 1993 creates a major division within the Jewish community. This illustrates a situation that until now was known only as part of the conflict between

[48] For a short period after Rabin's assassination, there was overzeal in the tendency to prosecute individuals who expressed support for the murder.

Jews and Arabs. It is likely that the intensity of the cleavage and the dissent will create new pressure to suppress dissidents who may be seen as inciters.

The fact that the enforcement of draconian laws was sparse should not mislead us: these laws should be repealed. Israel does not need licensing provisions for newspapers, or administrative powers to suspend them. These should be abolished. Israel's security needs may justify a temporary and limited regime of military censorship. The arrangement should be formulated in a way that will be equally applicable to all media, limiting the powers of the authorities to suppress newspapers and publications they deem undesirable. Access to information of public interest should be made easier, and a general duty on officials to provide information should replace the present sweeping prohibition of disclosure. Expressing support of organizations should not be a crime.

Clearly, striking the right balance between speech and public peace and security will continue to require complicated judgments. The legislature should seek to reformulate the laws so that they will not be as overbroad as they are now. The Attorney-General and all law enforcement agencies should continue to show caution in invoking laws curbing speech, and should be more aware of the need to apply these laws without bias and discrimination. The Court should continue to subject the exercises of these powers, including the power to prosecute, to close scrutiny.

NATIONAL SECURITY AND FREEDOM OF EXPRESSION IN JAPAN

Lawrence W. Beer

I. Introduction

In 1997, in the aftermath of the Cold War, colonialism and the break-up of blocs, many are trying to reframe questions and answers regarding national security and freedom of expression in law and policy throughout the world. In this endeavor, it may help to lay bare even the most obvious of the long-dominant assumptions about national security needs, and then to see whether these assumptions should not be modified, if not for all countries, at least for many. I make no claim to expertise in national security studies; I have a long-term interest in freedom of expression and constitutionalism in Japan.[1] With important results, Japan's operative assumptions regarding national security for five decades have deviated from what most scholars and nation-state leaders would consider normal. Under its "Peace Constitution", Japan has renounced, in theory, law and practice, war and the threat or use of force to settle international disputes. For decades, Japan has almost always limited its defense expenditures to less than 1% of its GNP. Japan (without U.S. assistance) is not militarily competitive with other East Asian nations; but without the unique restraints of Article 9 of the Constitution, Japan would likely be one of the few great military (and, arguably, nuclear) powers, with considerably less concern for freedom of expression than now.

To create a setting for explaining the nature and possible usefulness to other countries of aspects of Japan's model for thinking about freedom and national security, I would begin by setting forth my understanding of the current world context and common security assumptions.

II. The Current World Context and Common Security Assumptions

I take the present world context as defined by such factors as the end of the Cold War, the USSR and colonialism; the rearrangement of ethnic relationships in a number of areas (sometimes peacefully, often with violence); historic continuing growth in mutual understanding among authentic representatives of the major world religions (*e.g.*, Islam, Buddhism, Christianity) and their converging support of universal human rights; the destructive power of nuclear, chemical and biological weapons; multinational needs for sustainable development, employment and environmental protection; explosive growth in communication and transportation technology; the economic might of Japan, other Asian nations, and the G-7 countries; the capacity of predatory capitalism to obstruct the evolution of world

---

[1] Lawrence W. Beer, *Freedom of Expression in Japan: A Study in Comparative Law, Politics and Society* (1984); and "Freedom of Expression in Japan: The Continuing Revolution," in P. Luney & K. Takahashi eds., *Japanese Constitutional Law* 221 (1993).

peace under law; the unmatched barbarism of twentieth-century warring; the flimsy linkages between national security law and protection of freedom of expression; and the unprecedented worldwide attention to constitutional government and human rights. It is a significant advance in world civilization that 181 of 186 nation states now have single-document national constitutions, some 130 of which have been adopted since 1970. Most constitutions contain human rights provisions reflecting what is now broadly respectable around the world. However, imperfect human rights enforcement is seen in all nations; the revolutionary assumption that the inherent dignity and value of each human being demands socio-legal respect is now commonplace. Accordingly, it is a particularly propitious time for thinking to center on "the right to live in peace, free from fear and want", as stated in the Preamble of the Constitution of Japan.[2]

Following are several of the most common assumptions regarding freedom and security in many countries:

1. Leaders of many, if not most, countries consider their countries to be under serious threat of attack. They believe that one or more external and/or internal political enemies *threaten* the existence of the territory of their political and/or economic system (and/or those who currently hold power). For leaders to *motivate* their people to accept the credibility of their national security assessments and the legitimacy of their military policies, it is helpful for them to be able to create the impression that the threat is to the very *existence* of the state, culture or regime, and not simply to a limited national interest such as short-term economic benefit or a temporary wound to national pride. Unfortunately, there is at times a grand canyon between reality and leaders' definitions of threat, as in the unjustified acts of President George Bush against the helpless small state of Panama to get General Manuel Noriega.
2. Maintenance of the ability to respond to such threats with adequate deterrent force – military and/or police – should be the highest priority of the state.
3. To assure effective military and/or police response to threats, special laws, policies and regulations limiting civil rights and expanding government prerogatives are necessary, because freedom of expression may add to the threat and because secrecy of state information may be necessary to respond to the threat.
4. With respect to government budgetary priorities and policy preoccupations, no other public interest should be allowed to challenge effectively military and/or police ascendancy, whether the primary

[2] For the text of the 1947 Constitution of Japan, *see* Lawrence W. Beer & Hiroshi Itoh, *The Constitutional Case Law of Japan, 1970 through 1990* at 653-65 (1996).

perceived threat be internal or external or both, and whether or not the threat actually exists.

5. With historical logic, great power status should be defined in modern times primarily in terms of great military power, including destructive capacity superior to that of other nations. It is inevitable that other civilizational values be radically subordinate to military security, although economic and technological power are beginning to compete with military capacity as the primary foundation of national security.

The above seem to have been the dominant assumptions up to now, and the world has as yet no adequate peace enforcement mechanism under the United Nations. In some states these assumptions exist in tension with democracy, human rights, constitutionalism and/or some other system of belief and thought. On all continents, in politico-legal systems ranging from those allegedly most democratic to those bluntly dictatorial, freedom of the press and other mass media, freedom of social, political and economic speech, the freedoms of assembly and association, and free access to government information about official acts and about oneself have been needlessly suppressed under these assumptions by both official and informal means.

III. Expression and National Security in Japan

A. Japan's Arc: From Isolationist to Militaristic to Non-Military Superpower

Before September 1945, Japan was masterfully repressive in operating under the above assumptions. How did the pre-war system develop? In the 1850s, Western military power forced Japan to open diplomatic and trade relations under unequal treaties. The Tokugawa family regime (1600-1868) rigorously enforced isolation from the outside world for over 200 years as the foundation for Japan's national security. To achieve full independence from the imposed treaties and a place of pride in the world, Japan adopted Western military thought and technology, and engaged in broad-ranging legal, social and economic changes. By 1905 when she defeated Russia in war, Japan had achieved her goals and was a world power.

Critical to Japan's modernizing efforts was the development of a completely new legal and constitutional system.[3] In 1868, Japan's oligarchs transformed the Emperor (*Tenno*), a virtually powerless institution for roughly 1,000 years, into the central legitimizing symbol for a unitary state and the formal repository of sovereign power in the state. Others made decisions in the Emperor's name as hundreds of feudal domains were replaced by a centralized state under a near absolute monarchy.

---

[3] Masami Ito, "The Modern Development of Law and Constitution in Japan," *in* L.W. Beer ed., *Constitutional Systems in Late Twentieth Century Asia* 129-44 (1992); Junji Banno (trans. J.A.A. Stockwin), *The Establishment of the Japanese Constitutional System* (1992).

Over many decades, modern means of universal education, indoctrination, and control created an effective police state enforcing reverence and absolute obedience to the sacred Emperor's government.[4] Well-educated Special High Police (*Tokko*, "thought police") and the dreaded military police (*Kempeitai*) systematically fomented extreme nationalism and personal self-abnegation. From the 1850s until 1945 Japan was for substantial periods in the equivalent of a state of national emergency.

Aggressive militarism, suppression of freedom and other individual rights, and reverence for the Emperor-centered state (*kokutai*) utterly failed with Japan's defeat in the Second World War in 1945. The low point in Japan's long history was 1930 to 1945, what the Japanese call "the dark valley period".[5] The wartime constitutional system was rejected and replaced, with catalytic input from the U.S.-dominated Occupation,[6] by the 1947 Constitution of Japan (*Nihonkoku Kempo*) which renounced war as a national right, established popular sovereignty in place of the Emperor's sacral sovereignty, and protected and promoted rather than denied fundamental human rights. To understand Japanese constitutionalism with respect to national security, it is essential to keep in mind this modern history and the revolution of freedom which began in 1945 and continues today.

In Japan's constitutional culture, the three core elements in the constitutional system have been seen as intimately related: popular sovereignty and a truly powerless Emperor under the Preamble and Article I, renunciation of war under the Preamble and Article 9, and a guarantee of a range of rights under Articles 11 to 40, 44, and 97. In Japan's recurring vigorous debates about the Constitution, tampering with the Article 9 "no war clause" has often been seen as implying a danger to individual freedoms and a portent of a restoration of the Emperor to his status as the center of an authoritarian state. Inadequate attention to human rights has been interpreted as a harbinger of militarism and imperial control. Any show of special respect for the imperial family or *Shinto* ceremonies, as was displayed after the death of Emperor Hirohito (1989) and at the accession of Emperor Akihito, or in judicial decisions, raises in some minds the specter of repression under a mythologized Emperor.[7] Put simply, any hint of militarism or even apparently

---

[4] Beer, *supra* note 1 at 45-71; Gregory J. Kasza, *The State and the Mass Media in Japan, 1918-1945* (1988); Richard H. Mitchell, *Thought Control in Prewar Japan* (1976).

[5] *Id.*

[6] Beer, *supra* note 3 at 175-82; and "Constitutionalism and Rights in Japan and Korea," *in* L. Henkin and A. Rosenthal eds., *Constitutionalism and Rights: The Influence of the United States Constitution Abroad* 225-59 (1990).

[7] Lawrence W. Beer, "Constitutional Revolution in Japanese Law, Society and Politics," 16 *Modern Asian Studies* 33-67 (1982). Related judicial decisions have focused on public funding of *Shinto* shrines to the war dead. The Supreme Court first held such local government support unconstitutional in 1997. *Nikkei Weekly*, April 17, 1997. *See* David M. O'Brien, *To Dream of Dreams: Religious Freedom and Constitutional Politics in Postwar Japan* (1996).

modest emphasis on the needs of the Self Defense Forces (SDF, *Jieitai*) or a sniff of Emperor-*Shinto* nationalism has tended to provoke a vigorous response from civil liberties advocates. Of course, in analogous forms, unbalanced nationalism or ethnocism and excessive preoccupation with military needs rather than other priorities bode ill for freedom of expression in many countries. The strength of Japan's system of protecting and promoting freedom is undoubtedly due in part to the clarity of her renunciation of militarism.

The Constitution of Japan was "imposed" upon a lame-duck Cabinet in 1946, but not on Japan's people. The most representative body in Japan's history to that time was elected in April 1946, with suffrage extended to all men and women of age twenty or above. This House of Representatives thoroughly debated the draft constitution co-authored by Japanese and Occupation personnel, and approved the document with only a few dissenting votes. The Constitution has been welcomed by most Japanese ever since as an appropriate expression of their political ideals and social values.[8] Awareness of the popular consensus of respect and support for the Constitution has constrained the small but powerful political minority which chafes under one or more aspects of the Constitution or the security relationship with the United States.

In short, the Japan of 1997 has broken the old mold of assumptions as a quasi-pacifist, democratic superpower, and her experience over the past fifty years deserves wider study.[9] (The term "superpower" now seems inappropriate in light of the collective and limited nature of the emerging world leadership). Japan's fifty year record of peace with freedom is impressive and is as much a cause as a result of her prosperity. In long range terms, militarism tends to have anti-development effects. Of crucial importance and contrary to internationally common assumptions, most Japanese have not felt militarily threatened by any country near or far; so Japan has not felt a pressing need for a military establishment that is competitive with even her smaller neighbors (the two Koreas and Taiwan), let alone commensurate with her considerable economic and technological power since the 1960s. The only major question marks in Eastern Asian security are the intentions of North Korea and China; the preponderant view among Japanese is that no country has now or is likely to have in the foreseeable future, any persuasive reason to attack Japan. The economic dependence of China and other nations on Japan is a strong deterrent; the U.S.-Japan Mutual Security Treaty is another factor diminishing any sense of

---

[8] Sato Tatsuo, assisted by Sato Isao, *Nihonkoku Kempo Seiritsushi* (The History of the Establishment of the Constitution of Japan), 4 volumes (1994); James S, Marshall, *Japan's Successor Generation* (1985); Beer, *supra* note 6.

[9] On Japan's security thought and system, *see* Peter J. Katzenstein, *Cultural Norms and National Security: Police and Military in Postwar Japan* (1996); Richard J. Samuels, *Rich Nation, Strong Army: National Security and the Technological Transformation of Japan* (1996); Henry Shue, *Basic Rights* (2d ed. 1996); and, on Japanese public opinion, Office of Research, U.S.I.A., *"Global Partnership": Views of the Japanese Public* (1992).

international danger. On the other hand, recurring perceptions by Asian neighbors of Japanese insensitivity to its wartime aggression still trigger vehement responses and alleged fear of reemergent militarism, at home and abroad. This pattern has served the purpose of discouraging militarist nationalism in Japan's politics and society. Only the United Nations and the United States are Japan's security allies, and the U.S. sense of security threat in Asia is much stronger than Japan's. Japan's current SDF are technologically advanced and costly for their numbers, but are geopolitically modest. More important to the present discussion, the SDF are not presumed to be the highest budget priority and they are significantly limited by the Constitution of Japan, by law and policy, and by the quasi-pacifist attitudes of the great majority of Japanese.

B. Japan's Constitutional Principles

The key provisions are the following:[10]

> *The Preamble.* We, the Japanese people [are] resolved that never again shall we be visited with the horrors of war through the action of government. . . We . . . desire peace for all time . . . and an honored place in an international society striving for the preservation of peace . . . free from fear and want.
>
> *Article 9.* 1. Aspiring sincerely to an international peace based on justice and order, the Japanese people forever renounce war as a sovereign right of the nation and the threat or use of force as a means of settling international disputes.
>
> 2. In order to accomplish the aim of the preceding paragraph, land, sea and air forces, as well as other war potential, will never be maintained. The right of belligerency of the State will not be recognized.

The SDF have never been used to fight. Japan stopped shooting in August 1945, and has never begun shooting again. In what other ways has the intent of these provisions been manifested in legal and political practice? What has not been done is as instructive as what has been done. Japan has no national security law system under which freedom of expression may be subjected to special restraints in times of crisis or war. The Constitution of Japan contains no provisions relating to acts of war, such as declaring war or concluding peace; no article touches on martial law declarations or preservation of military secrets. Article 76(2) precludes military courts: "No extraordinary tribunal shall be established, nor shall any organ or agency of the Executive be given final judicial power."

---

[10] Beer and Itoh, *supra* note 2 at 653-55.

The Supreme Court has held that under Article 9 Japan retains the natural law right to self-defense, that the Treaty of Mutual Cooperation and Security between the United States of America and Japan (the Mutual Security Treaty, 1960) is not on its face unconstitutional, and that, although generally the Court must take into account the political nature of such issues, the Court retains the right to determine whether a law or other government action is clearly and obviously in violation of Article 9.[11] The Supreme Court has not directly decided whether the SDF are unconstitutional. The great majority of Japan's constitutional lawyers continue to consider the SDF unconstitutional, as did the 1973 Sapporo District Court in its *Naganuma Nike Missile Site* decision (overturned on appeal on technical grounds).[12] The public, however, accepts the SDF as constitutional as long as they do not fight abroad and are kept to a modest level.

Military interests are not presumed to be a high priority. For example, a Tokyo High Court decision, which was let stand, denied that in peacetime Defense Agency activities involve a higher public interest than those of civilian airports or other government agencies. Noise pollution is a general concern affecting "the public welfare"; the noise of military aircraft violated the personal rights of citizens (Articles 12, 13 and 29 of the Constitution).[13] Even less might one assume that civil liberties and other "rights and freedoms of the spirit" (*seishinteki jiyuken*)[14] may be subordinated to military interests.

C. Relevant Laws

No law provides for special restraints on the rights and freedoms of ordinary citizens for reasons of national emergency or national security; but civil servants and military personnel operating under virtually identical provisions in the National Public Employees Law, the Local Public Employees Law, or the Self-Defense Forces Law must not divulge secrets which have come to their knowledge in the course of performing their duties, whether they are on active duty or retired. In its 1978 *Nishiyama* decisions, the Supreme Court convicted a journalist for inducing a Foreign Ministry employee to give him a cable which suggested the government had lied

---

[11] For translations of the Supreme Court decisions, *see* John M. Maki, *Court and Constitution in Japan: Selected Supreme Court Decisions, 1948-1960*, 198 (1964); Hiroshi Itoh & Lawrence H. Beer, *The Constitutional Case Law of Japan: Selected Supreme Court Decisions, 1961-70*, 103 (1978).

[12] Beer & Itoh, *supra* note 2 at 83 (Cases 3, 4, and 5).

[13] 13 Tokyo High Court, *Asahi Shimbun*, July 15, 1987.

[14] Scholars refer to the following cluster of freedoms in the Constitution as "rights and freedoms of the spirit": the right of petition (Article 16); freedom of thought and conscience (Article 19); freedom of religion (Article 20); "freedom of assembly and association as well as speech, press and all other forms of expression" (Article 21); academic freedom (Article 23).

about financial arrangements attendant to the reversion of Okinawa to Japanese sovereignty in 1972.[15] Japan has no general espionage law or state secrets law; but special legislation implementing Article VI of the U.S.-Japan Mutual Security Treaty protects secrets regarding U.S. military forces in Japan and weapons supplied to Japan by the United States.[16] In the 1980s, the government sought passage in the Diet (Japan's parliament) of "State Secrets Bills", but strong opposition from minority parties, the mass media, the legal community, and citizen groups doomed them to failure. The bills were not well crafted and aroused technical objections as well as alleged fears of authoritarian secretiveness. In 1997 Japan was expected to pass a Freedom of Information Law; forty-three of forty-seven prefectures already have freedom of information and privacy ordinances. Some Diet members contend the Defense Agency has not always been as forthcoming with information to the Diet as is called for by civilian control. Nevertheless, that control is assisted by the prohibition on military persons serving in the Cabinet (Article 66.2 of the Constitution).

D. Limits on Military and Emergency Powers

Due to the wartime abuses of their authoritarian governments, the postwar democratic constitutions of Germany, Japan and Italy carried no provisions on emergencies. This situation continues in Japan, but not in Europe:

> Despite a lot of resistance [emergency rules] were introduced into the German Constitution in 1968. Both the newly established democracies in Spain, Portugal, and Greece in the 1970s and in Central and Eastern Europe in the 1990s have included emergency provisions in their Constitutions.[17]

---

[15] Beer, *supra* note 1 at 304-305; Beer & Itoh, *supra* note 2 at 543 (Case 38). Since the 1995 rape of a twelve-year-old school girl by U.S. military personnel, U.S. facilities on Okinawa, comprising 18% of the land area and 75% of U.S. forces in Japan, have received the political attention long denied them by both the U.S. and Japanese Governments. The inequity of burdens on Okinawans, the post-Cold War base needs, and a stronger Japanese government voice in determining U.S. force levels were among pressing issues in Japan's domestic politics as well as in Japan-U.S. relations in mid-1997. *Christian Science Monitor*, April 10, 1997. *See* the symposium on Okinawa issues *in 23(3) Japan Echo*, 32-55 (Autum, 1996).

[16] Headquarters, United States Forces *Status of Forces Agreement with Related Documents* (1960); Special Criminal Law to Implement the Agreement under Article VI of the Treaty of Mutual Cooperation and Security between the United States of America Regarding Facilities and Areas and the Status of United States Forces in Japan, Law 138 of 1952, as amended. For a translation of the law, *see* The Japan Newspaper Publishers & Editors Association *Press Laws in Japan* 10-11 (1993).

[17] "Conference Report: Human Rights and the Functioning of Democratic Institutions in Emergency Situations," *The Japan Foundation Newsletter*, Vol. 24, No. 5, at 7 (Jan.1997).

The Prime Minister represents the Cabinet and has jurisdiction over the SDF under Article 7 of the SDF Law. There is no independent military command structure as under the prewar system. Article 71 of the Police Law gives the Prime Minister, upon the recommendation of the civilian National Public Safety Commission, the authority to declare a state of "national emergency" and to assume direct control over Japan's police. "National emergency" is understood to cover such events as foreign invasions, a large-scale natural disaster, or internal disturbances. However, in the "Great Hanshin Earthquake Disaster" (Kobe) of 1995, which took 6,300 lives, the central and local governments were criticized for their slow mobilization of the SDF in the absence of an adequate pre-existing system for rapid response. The actual primary function of the SDF since the 1950s has been disaster relief.

The House of Representatives must approve actions taken pursuant to a declaration of emergency. If that House is not in session at the time of the Emergency, the Cabinet may call an emergency session of the House of Councillors, but actions then taken are "provisional and . . . null and void unless agreed to by the House of Representatives" within ten days of the opening of the next Diet session, pursuant to Article 54.2 and 54.3 of the Constitution.[18] It is not clear what measures affecting freedom of expression might be taken provisionally in an emergency.

Article 18 bans "bondage of any kind. Involuntary servitude, except as punishment for crime, is prohibited" also.[19] This is interpreted in the spirit of Article 9 to mean that military conscription would be unconstitutional as "involuntary servitude". The export of weapons is prohibited, to Japan's considerable economic loss; but under 1980s agreements Japan supplies the U.S. with its superior "dual-use" (*i.e.*, civilian and military) technology. Some advocate a formal legal ban on both the import and the export of weapons.[20]

The vigor of freedom of political speech in Japan has allowed the tolerant co-existence of radically diverse views and has also given the time necessary in a factionalized but consensus-oriented society for agreements with strong majority support to emerge which creatively concretize implementation of Article 9. For example, prior to the restoration of Japan's sovereignty over Okinawa in 1972, the Japanese assumed that the United States maintained dreaded nuclear weapons on that island. Representing a multi-party consensus, the Diet established the "three no-nuclear principles" in November 1971, although political parties and factions within the ruling Liberal Democratic Party (LDP) differed among themselves on other security issues. These principles ban Japan's manufacture or possession, or the introduction into Japan, of nuclear weapons even if potentially hostile neighboring countries should develop nuclear weapons (*e.g.*, China, Russia, North Korea), and

---

[18] James Auer, "Article Nine: Renunciation of War," *in* Luney & Takahashi, *supra* note 1 at 69-86; Osamu Nishi, *The Constitution and the National Defense Law System in Japan* (1987).
[19] Beer & Itoh, *supra* note 2 at 656.
[20] *See supra* note 9.

even though Japan's nuclear power technology is of the highest order. Anti-militarist sentiment is strengthened each year by substantial media and social commemoration of the Hiroshima (August 6, 1945) and Nagasaki (August 9, 1945) atom bombings. The popular consensus is that all nuclear weapons testing should cease and that all nuclear weapons should be destroyed.

Japan has almost always limited its defense expenditures to a maximum of 1% of its GNP. Japan (without U.S. assistance) is not militarily competitive with other nations in the region. Its forces in the 1990s rank twenty-sixth in the world in size. In the absence of Article 9, Japan would have likely become one of the few great military (and arguably nuclear) powers. Most important in the present context, it is improbable that a militarized Japan would consider freedom of expression compatible with national security. Militaries tend to exaggerate threats; their business is to foresee and prepare to fight threats, not to engage in peaceful democratic governance. Japan's earlier militarist nationalism was contemptuous of other peoples and of human rights in general. Now, Japanese are much more internationalist and respectful of rights, and assume freedom as part of the natural order of things in Japan. Japan illustrates the possibility of a nation state changing from a thoroughly militarist and repressive government to a country that is free and peaceful, unthreatened and unthreatening.

Japan does not define national security primarily in terms of internal order or military security, but as a "comprehensive security".[21] By this is meant not only national security (secured with the help of the United States and the United Nations), but also security with respect to long-term social and economic needs, protection of human rights and democracy under the Constitution of Japan, and attention to regional and world developmental and ecological concerns. Japan supports the United Nations generously and unequivocally, and continues to place hope idealistically in the further development of its institutions for peace and freedom. In addition, Japan leads the world in non-military development aid to less fortunate countries, under ODA (Official Development Assistance) formulas of the OECD (Organization for Economic Cooperation and Development). On the other hand, even modest SDF participation in UN peace-keeping operations is rigorously limited by law under Article 9 of the Constitution, and roughly 80% of Japanese oppose overseas SDF military action even under UN auspices.[22]

The anti-militarist "Peace Constitution" undergirds Japan's system of national security and freedom of expression, and allows for paradoxes. For example,

---

[21] *Id.*

[22] Japan may participate in overseas peace-keeping operations only if: (1) they are under United Nations auspices; (2) Japan's participation is welcomed by the parties to ceasefire arrangements as a neutral party; (3) Japanese SDF only use small arms and only to prevent injury or death; and (4) it is understood that Japan will withdraw from monitoring the ceasefire if it is broken. Of the many opinion polls on defense issues, *see*, e.g., *Tokyo Shimbun*, July 23, 1994, reporting on the views of 13,723 respondents.

for decades a series of highly controverted court cases (the *Ienaga Textbook* Trials)[23] has revolved around the high school history textbook coverage of modern Japanese militarism and aggression against Asian neighbors before 1945. Some politicians and Ministry of Education officials have wanted to downplay Japanese aggression and atrocities while others have favored repentant honesty and openness. The continuing equivocal stance regarding war responsibility of some politicians and bureaucrats infuriates other Asian countries and many Japanese. Yet, the young have been conditioned to a quasi-pacifism through the education system. A foreigner teaching at a Japanese university may be stunned to find students puzzled at the inability of many foreigners to comprehend Japan's undeviating rejection of war and preference for peaceful means of settling international disputes. After all, war is horror, peace is pleasant and humane. Such students can understand when cadets of Japan's multi-service national academy, the Defense University (*Boei Daiqaku*) quit upon graduation because the SDF might be becoming more "3D" (dirty, difficult, dangerous) with participation in United Nations peace-keeping. Under Articles 9 and 18 of the Constitution, they cannot be forced to serve. Although Japan's social system, like those of all democracies, restricts free speech in certain contexts, law and politics enforce a high degree of tolerance for the expression of diverse ideas, from pacifism to militarism, from Communism to radical economic liberalism, and many views in between.

IV. Conclusion

Japan's (near) absolute renunciation of war and the use of force in international relations, along the lines of the 1928 Kellogg-Briand Pact signed by so many nations, coexists with a refusal to find other countries very threatening. The past fifty years of Japan's international experience show their assumptions to have been quite realistic for Japan, not mindlessly or irresponsibly Utopian. In that same period, trigger-happy leaders in nations large and small have caused untold suffering to many millions, not least in Asia. While Japan's constitutional stance may seem to have been impossibly Utopian for many countries in other geopolitical settings of the past decades, we now live in a new post-colonialist and post-Cold War era when rethinking of assumptions is in order. Whatever the past justifications for restraint of freedom of expression based on perceived threats, internal or external, the number of countries in which military security can be credibly adduced as grounds for limiting free speech seems to have substantially decreased in the past ten years.

As the foundation for national security, Japan's reliance under Article 9 on unequivocal renunciation of war and dependence on peaceful means of dispute resolution and on the United Nations, a strong system of freedom of expression,

---

[23] Beer, *supra* note 1 at 248-80; Beer & Itoh, *supra* note 2 at 516 (Case 36).

increased reliance on economic and technological indispensability to other countries, and heavy investment in cultural interlocking (as through the Japan Foundation and the Japan-U.S. Center for Global Partnership) presents a thought-provoking and useful new model. Leaders of militarized political cultures like that of the United States might well look hard at the geopolitical example of Japan while redefining military roles in the emerging era. Japan illustrates how a country can get over authoritarianism, militarism, and war. Primary dependence for national security on an integrated government-military-industrial complex is needlessly costly and harmful. For many countries, the assumption that foreign nations generally represent a threat necessitating preparation for military response is not empirically credible, nor is the frequently attendant suspicion regarding freedom of expression. Japan's peaceful constitutionalism is not now Utopian, but a major contribution to the world's constitutionalist traditions: military influence on political decisions should be nil; military budgets should not be given privileged consideration in the absence of clear, credible national danger; military action is usually unacceptably barbaric; no special legislation restricting freedom of expression in the name of national security is justified, and legal restraints in times of genuine national emergency should be minimal and subject to review; as basic to international law as the national right to self-defense should be the duty not to resort to arms to settle international disputes. This seems the vision emanating from Japan's law, policy and experience since 1945.

FREEDOM OF EXPRESSION, FREEDOM OF INFORMATION, AND NATIONAL SECURITY: THE CASE OF NORWAY[1]

Nils Petter Gleditsch

I. National Security and Liberal Values

Freedom of expression is among the basic human rights codified in the 1948 Universal Declaration of Human Rights and in the 1950 European Convention for the Protection of Human Rights and Fundamental Freedoms. Nevertheless, the right to impart information and opinions is not absolute. Article 29(2) of the Universal Declaration of Human Rights recognizes limitations "determined by law for the purpose of meeting the just requirements of morality, public order and the general welfare in a democratic society". And among the many exceptions permitted by Article 10(2) of the European Convention are national security and territorial integrity.

National security is a basic value at the societal level, and one that, like religion or, more recently, the environment, often takes on an "absolute" character. If the future of the nation is at stake, then it appears senseless to argue about peacetime norms or liberal values like freedom of expression and information. In democratic societies in peacetime, however, it tends to be recognized that whatever the value attributed to national security there has to be some balancing against other

---

[1] This chapter is a product of a long-standing interest in freedom of information in relation to national security, resulting in a number of publications on Norway, as well as an article with a more general comparative perspective. *See* Nils Petter Gleditsch, "Freedom of Information and National Security in Norway: Legislation and Practice," *PRIO Inform*, no. 10 (1982); "Hemmeligholdets bastion? Hemmelighold og offentlighet i forsvarsspørsmål i Storbritannia," *PRIO Report*, no. 3 (1985); "Look to Scandinavia?," *PRIO Inform*, no. 3 (1985); "Ytringsfrihet i forsvarspolitikken," *in* Mads T. Andenæs & Ragnar Aamodt, eds., *Ytringsfrihet* at 88-102 (1986); "Hemmelighold: Den britiske modellen," *4 Norsk Statsvitenskapelig Tidsskrift* 173 (1988); "Massemediene og sikkerhetspolitikken," *in* Nils Thomsen *et al.*, eds., *Pressens Årbog* at 34-76 (1989); "Freedom of Information and National Security: A Comparative Perspective", *4 Law and Policy Studies* 25 (1995); Nils Petter Gleditsch & Einar Høgetveit: "Freedom of Information and National Security: A Comparative Study of Norway and the United States", *21 Journal of Peace Research* 17 (1984); and `Norway', *in* Frances d'Souza *et al.*, eds., *Information Freedom and Censorship. World Report 1991* (1991). In addition to my earlier collaborator Einar Høgetveit, who has also commented on a draft of this article, I acknowledge my intellectual debt to the late Torstein Eckhoff. Lovdata, the Norwegian legal database, checked court actions relating to the relevant laws. Bjørn Otto Sverdrup and Synnøve Eifring assisted with the literature and Henning Jakhelln commented on an earlier version of the article. None of the above have any responsibility for what follows. Finally, I would not wish to hide my activist role in trying to extend freedom of information in relation to national security, having served as a witness, a court-appointed expert, and a defendant in some of the cases reviewed in Section IV(A)(1) below.

values. This chapter addresses balancing through legislation and legal and administrative practice in Norway. I first review some of the general issues (Section II), before moving on to a specific consideration of the national security issues (Sections III and IV).

II. Basic Principles

Section 100 of the Norwegian Constitution of 1814 guaranteed freedom of expression and freedom of the press in what for its time was remarkably clear language:[2]

> There shall be liberty of the press. No person may be punished for any writing, whatever its content may be, which he has caused to be printed or published .... Everyone shall be free to speak his mind frankly on the administration of the State or on any other subject whatsoever.[3]

However, the Section made exceptions for acts of disobedience to the laws; incitement to disobedience; contempt of religion, morality, or the constitutional powers; and defamation of individuals. These general exceptions have been made more specific over the years through legislation and court interpretations. Moreover, some Norwegian legal experts argue that authorities have a general right to limit freedom of expression, that Section 100 imposes substantial limits on the freedom of expression and the press, and that the "disobedience to the laws" exception is quite broad.[4]

Section 66 of the Norwegian Constitution protects the freedom of expression of Members of Parliament. This is a wider freedom than applies to the general public; no one may be punished for utterances made in Parliament. On the other hand, MPs must respect the parliamentary rules of procedure forbidding improper or defamatory speech. MPs who table questions found to concern matters of national security may find these questions rejected or referred to secret session. For public utterances outside Parliament, MPs are protected only by Section 100.

Norway is a party to the International Covenant on Civil and Political Rights (ICCPR) as well as the European Convention for the Protection of Human Rights and Fundamental Freedoms (ECHR). Although the Courts have been unable

---

[2] The text of the present constitution as well as the original 1814 version can be found in Tønnes Andenæs, ed., *Grunnloven vår. 1814 til 1971* (1971). A more recent commentary on the constitution is found in Mads T. Andenæs & Ingeborg Willberg, *Grunnloven - kommentarutgave* (1983). For a legal discussion of sec. 100, *see* Joachim Benno, *Ytringsfrihet: en konstitusjonell utfordring?* (1994).

[3] Quoted from Amos J. Peaslee, *Constitutions of Nations* (4th ed. 1985). *See also*, *Freedom of Information and Expression in Norway: A Commentary by Article 19 on the Report submitted to the Human Rights Committee by the Government of Norway* (1989).

[4] *See* Benno, *supra* note 2 at 38 *et seq.*

to apply these directly, it has been government policy to work towards incorporating these and other international conventions into Norwegian legislation. In 1993 a public commission recommended to the Ministry of Justice that the Norwegian Constitution be amended to this effect,[5] and this constitutional amendment was passed in 1994. However, the interpretation of the Supreme Court is still that Norwegian law takes precedence whenever there is a conflict. To date, the ICCPR and ECHR have played a minor role in the protection of freedom of expression and information in Norway.

The freedom of expression prescribed by the Constitution encompasses *opinions* as well as *information*. In addition, legal theory usually assumes that freedom of expression cannot truly function without the right to *collect information*, to *possess* it, and to *process* it. To accord citizens freedom of expression is meaningless if other citizens are not at the same time free to receive that information.[6] Conversely, being informed is frequently a precondition for forming and expressing an opinion. A citizen unaware that his or her country has secretly developed nuclear weapons is not in a position to protest. When governments limit information about controversial facts, they also prevent - intentionally or not - critical opinions from being formed. Direct suppression of opinions is in a sense the last line of defense for a government. Preventing the public from even knowing that there is something to protest is a less visible and more efficient repressive strategy. For practical reasons, I have divided the following discussion into two parts, *freedom to express opinions* and *freedom to collect and disseminate information*, even though the two are often intimately related.

III. National Security and the Expression of Opinions

In addition to these constitutional provisions, the expression of opinions is sanctioned in several laws. For instance, the Administrative Procedures Act *(Forvaltningsloven)* specifies that the parties have a right to express their opinions before an administrative decision is reached; various acts stipulate that the parties should be heard in a court case; and the Civil Service Act *(Tjenestemannsloven)* grants civil servants the right of oral explanation before they can be reprimanded or fired.[7]

---

[5] Norwegian Government Publications Office "Lovgivning om menneskerettigheter," *Norges offentlige utredninger* (1993). The current government has promised additional legislation, but the change of government at the time of writing (September 1997) makes it uncertain what form this may take or what priority it will be given.

[6] Eric Barendt, *Freedom of Speech* (1987); Benno, *supra* note 2.

[7] Benno, *supra* note 2 at 43-45.

The most important and controversial limitations to the expression of opinions relate to libel, religious blasphemy, and racial discrimination.[8] These are relatively unlikely to have much bearing on national security issues.

Section 47 in the Norwegian Military Penal Code *(Militær straffelov)* intervenes directly in the freedom of expression in peacetime in that it prohibits "inciting a military man to ill-will against the military service or to hatred against his superiors". The maximum punishment is three years, four if the incitement occurs in written form. This Act applies only to military personnel, but a parallel provision is found in Section 134 in the civilian Penal Code. These provisions date back to World War I.

These measures have been used a number of times. In 1923 the Labour Party youth declared a strike against the military and a number of prominent labor leaders went to jail for inciting refusal to serve in the armed forces. Among those who served time were two later prime ministers. Since the Second World War, four cases have been prosecuted. In 1950, four persons were fined for handing out leaflets claiming that the military alliance with the Americans had made Norwegians into "mercenaries of the United States". In 1971 a former soldier, Lasse Efskind, wrote a "little red book" on organizing soldiers. The author and the publisher were charged but eventually acquitted by the jury.[9] In a third case, a man was convicted for inciting soldiers to refuse to use a shooting-range which the military had built against strong local opposition. Finally, as late as 1986, five left-wing socialists were convicted for attacking the military in abusive terms ("officers have square heads") and advocating soldiers' organization.[10] There have been no similar cases after 1986.

---

[8] The most extensive recent legal survey of limits to freedom of expression in Norway is found in Benno, *supra* note 2. Other general discussions can be found in Johs. Andenæs, *Ordets frihet - ordets ansvar* (1985); Mads Andenæs & Erik Huitfeldt, *Trykkefrihed bør finne sted* (1989); Mads T. Andenæs & Ragnar Aamodt, *Ytringsfrihet* (1987); Toril Brekke *et al.*, *Den farlige ytringsfriheten* (1994); Skjalg Fremo, *Innsynsrett og hemmelighold: En rapport om klagesaker etter offentlighetsloven 1982-87* (1989); Gunne Hammarstrøm, *Bombe i debatten* (1992); Steinar Hansson, ed., *Retten til fri ytring* (1995); Steingrim Wolland & Rolf Øvrum, *Budbringerens dilemma* (1992); Nils Øy, *Start pressen* (1985); *Taushet* (3rd ed. 1994); and *God, kritisk journalistikk skal ikke straffes: Om krenkelser i norske media* (1994). On freedom of expression and racial discrimination, *see* Henning Jakhelln, "Freedom of Speech and the Prohibition of Racial Discrimination," *26 Scandinavian Studies in Law* 97 (1982). On libel *see* Henry Mæland, *Ærekrenkelser* (1986); and on privacy *see* Mads T. Andenæs & Halvor Elvik, *Stopp pressen? Om ytringsfrihet og personvern* (1984). On law and press ethics, *see* Hans Andreas Ihlebæk, *Lov og etikk i journalistikk* (1977) and on the political economy of press freedom *see* Sigurd Allern, *Kildenes makt. Ytringsfrihetens politiske økonomi* (1992).

[9] The author of the "red book" was hardly an average soldier. The son of the King's former personal physician, Efskind held a university degree and was a well-known speed-skater - later even a world record-holder.

[10] These cases are reviewed in greater detail in Gleditsch (1987), *supra* note 1, with references to publications in Norwegian.

Several military men who have been passed over for promotion (resulting in earlier retirement), have not had contracts renewed, or have been denied renewal or upgrading of their security clearances, have charged that the authorities have in fact punished them for expressing critical opinions about the military. Such conflicts of loyalty arise in any public or private service and in the absence of any comprehensive study, it is hard to judge whether the national security establishment tends to penalize opposition more than other bureaucracies.[11]

There have been numerous confrontations between military personnel and conscientious objectors and representatives of peace movements over the right to distribute information about conscientious objection on or near induction centers. Such confrontations are likely to continue as long as Norway maintains conscription. However, such cases are generally resolved before they escalate to fines or court actions. It is clearly permitted to inform draftees that conscientious objection is a legal right for anyone who satisfies the criteria of the law; in fact, the government itself provides such information to the relevant cohorts. Public funds are also used to support the organization for those performing alternative service *(Sivilarbeidernes Hovedsekretariat)*, and thus indirectly the public dissemination of information about the right to object and guidance on how to exercise that right.

IV. National Security and Freedom of Information

Information is controlled through a variety of legal instruments and societal control mechanisms. A comprehensive study of freedom of information and national security must take into account the variety of ways in which access to information may be constrained or enhanced by laws, regulations, and administrative practice.

A basic distinction is between legal instruments and practice designed to *promote access* and those which are designed to *protect secrets*. The Public Access Act (*i.e.*, the Norwegian Freedom of Information Act) is the most important instrument of the first kind, while the Security Instruction and the national security sections of the Penal Code exemplify the second. Within each legal instrument, there may be provisions pointing in the opposite direction: an exemption in the FOIA which

---

[11] A captain in military intelligence in 1974 completed a graduate thesis in political science at the University of Oslo in which he alleged that the government had been misled in certain national security cases by civil servants and military officers. This led to an official investigation, which concluded largely against him. *See* Andreas Schei *et al.*, *Loran C og Omega. Innstilling fra utvalget til undersøkelse av saken om etablering av Loran C og Omega-stasjoner i Norge (Granskingsutvalget Loran C-Omega)* (1977). An English summary is available in Nils Petter Gleditsch, *The Schei Report on Loran-C and Omega* (1978). The officer's career was sidetracked and he later left the armed forces. As a reserve officer he discovered years later that his security clearance had been eliminated without his being told. He lodged a complaint and after considerable publicity his clearance was eventually reinstated.

provides for secrecy, or an exemption in a secrecy clause specifying what cannot legitimately be classified.

Comparative studies of freedom of information generally place the Nordic countries among the most liberal, because they have well-established freedom of information acts. However, a more complete evaluation must also take into account the secrecy legislation. Figure 1 provides an overview of access and secrecy rules.

Figure 1. Norwegian Secrecy and Access Regulations Relevant to National Security

SECRECY	ACCESS
Defense Secrets Act	Public Access Act
Penal Code, national security sections	Law on Administrative Procedures
Military professional secrecy legislation	Archival legislation
Civil service professional secrecy legislation	Declassification provisisons
Security Instruction and Protection Instrution	
Defense-relevant Inventions Act	
Atomic Act	
Arms Export Control Act	
Secrecy exemptions in other legislation	

A. Openness Legislation

1. Freedom of Information

Efforts to introduce information into Norwegian public administration can be traced back at least to 1845.[12] In neighboring Sweden a right of access to public documents formed part of the Freedom of Press Act of 1766. However, the idea failed to take hold in Norway and it was not until 1970 that the Norwegian Parliament (Storting) passed the Public Access Act *(Offentlighetsloven)*. The law took effect on July 1, 1971 and establishes as a general rule that the records of public administration are open to public inspection unless exempted by law. A few years earlier, in 1967, the Administrative Procedures Act *(Forvaltningsloven)* had opened up official records to inspection by parties to an administrative case.[13] The 1970 law built on some of the same principles but considerably broadened access to official documents, particularly by making information available to the general public.

Attitudes to freedom of information were much more favorable among public interest groups and in Parliament than in the executive branch in general and the Ministry of Justice in particular.[14] The administration was mainly concerned about the added burden of work which the law threatened to impose and the arbitrariness of some of the proposed exemptions. It was also feared that civil servants and private parties to government decisions would be reluctant to provide written information which could be revealed later. Finally, it was felt that sufficient legal protection was provided by existing legislation, the Ombudsman institution, and so on. The opposition of the Defense Staff (the Norwegian equivalent to the U.S. Joint Chiefs of Staff) to the idea of freedom of information is particularly relevant:

> The principle of an absolute silence in the line of duty and the principle of 'need to know' is established in the Armed Forces today. Introducing a freedom of information rule will, in the view of the Defense Staff, lead to an unsatisfactory situation, especially perhaps from a pedagogical point of view.[15]

---

[12] Einar Høgetveit, *Hvor hemmelig? Offentlighetsprinsippet i Norge og USA, særlig med henblikk på militærpolitiske spørsmål* at 70 (1981). For the history of freedom of information in Norway *see also* Eric S. Einhorn, "Denmark, Norway, and Sweden," *in* Itzhak Galnoor, ed., *Government Secrecy in Democracies* 255-262 (1977) and Arvid Frihagen, "Norway," *in* Donald C. Rowat, ed., *Administrative Secrecy in Developed Countries* 106-124 (1979).

[13] There have been numerous revisions of the Administrative Procedures Act to date, most recently in 1995.

[14] Høgetveit (1981), *supra* note 12 at 70 *et seq.*

[15] These comments were made in 1958 in connection with a proposal for an access clause in the Administrative Procedures Act. *Id.* at 70.

Since the act took effect, the principle of public access to government records has come to be generally accepted. The law has been amended a number of times, but the changes since 1970 are relatively minor, especially with regard to national security.

Since 1982, the Public Access Act has a specific exemption for "documents which contain information which, if it became public, could harm national security, national defense, or the relations to foreign powers or international organizations". This exemption originally referred to "information significant for national security". This formulation was so broad that it could not be interpreted literally. Whether or not the revised wording is more liberal, is open to debate.

A document does not have to be classified to be exempted from disclosure on grounds of national security. This is a major difference between the Public Access Act and the U.S. Freedom of Information Act and establishes a gray area of secrecy between the domain of the formally classified records and the area of public access. Arbitrary decisions are more likely in this gray area than in the case of documents subject to formal classification procedures. In a study of administrative practice in Norwegian ministries in 1978, Høgetveit[16] found some surprising unclassified documents which had been exempted from release on national security grounds: the application for a port call in Oslo by tall ships participating in a sailing competition, press cuttings on medals awarded in the Kremlin and the reopening of U.S. bases in Turkey, and circulars about the import of hard liquor to the NATO Northern Command Headquarters at Kolsås near Oslo.

Besides national security, important exemptions concern: (a) internal records, (b) commercial records, (c) the Cabinet protocol, (d) documents relevant to hiring in public service (except the list of applicants), (e) documents concerning criminal activity, (f) examination records and public competitions, (g) documents prepared by a ministry for the annual preparation of the budget, and (h) pictures in personnel files. All of these can have implications for freedom of information in the national security area, but they apply with equal force to other areas of public policy.

The Public Access Act does not have retrospective force. However, most public institutions will use the criteria established in the Act as the main guideline to the release or nonrelease of older documents, following the principle of "additional openness" *(meroffentlighet)* also expressed in the law. The general idea is that nothing should be kept from the public even if it may legally be exempted from release, provided no harm will be done by its release.

Other general limitations of the Act are that denials do not require a detailed justification, but simply citation of the claimed exemption; that no time frame is specified for a reply to a request for the release of a document; and that, where other documents in a case are covered by an exemption clause and release of some but not

---

[16] *Id.* at 218.

all documents would give a misleading picture harmful to private or public interests, additional documents may be withheld.[17]

2. Declassification Procedures

The formal procedures for security classification will be dealt with below in Section IV(B)(5). In 1982, provisions for declassification were introduced into the Security Instruction for the first time. These provisions put the onus of verifying that a classification retains its validity on the agency issuing the classified document. The agency is bound to review the classification level when receiving a request for access to the document, when the document is used in the preparation of a current case, when corresponding information is made public in other countries, when the document is transferred to a public archive, or when other reasons so dictate. This change followed an extensive public debate on secrecy at the end of the 1970s, and recommendations made by a public commission on declassification.[18] The commission had recommended automatic declassification procedures on the U.S. model, but this proposal was initially rejected. In 1988, however, a 30-year rule was introduced for all documents of more recent origin than 1955 (older documents already having been declassified *en bloc*), but with exceptions for minutes of the National Defense Council and the Cabinet's Security Committee,[19] material significant for national security or relations to foreign powers and international organizations, documents on defense installations in current use in the "total defense", mobilization plans, and records of the secret services and government security procedures. A national declassification council was appointed at the same time and the various departments are obliged to report annually on their declassification efforts.

3. Archival Legislation

The 30-year rule was introduced in the Archives Act of 1992 which sets strict rules for the transfer of public records to the national archives and prevents excessive weeding and archival destruction. Such rules are particularly relevant in the national security area, where weeding has been very extensive. A public commission

---

[17] More detailed discussions of the Public Access Act can be found in Anders Frihagen, *Offentlighetsloven. Offentlighet, tauhetsplikt og partsinnsyn* (3d ed. 1994); Høgetveit, *supra* note 14; and Torstein Eckhoff, revised by Eivind Smith, *Forvaltningsrett* (5th ed. 1994).

[18] "Nedgradering og offentliggjøring av dokumenter," *Norges offentlige utredninger*, no. 51 (1980).

[19] The Security Committee is a subcommittee of the Cabinet that routinely deals with security matters. Roger Sørdahl & Nils Petter Gleditsch, "Kilder til sikkerhetspolitisk etterkrigshistorie," 65 *Historisk Tidsskrift* 273 (1986).

on the defense archives[20] concluded in 1990 that very extensive destruction of archival material had taken place in the 1980s, frequently in violation of archival regulations adopted as early as 1961. Some of the archives which would be of key importance for the writing of Norwegian national security history – such as the files of the Defense staff and NATO files in the services – had been extensively weeded. For the military intelligence staff, the report found "only insignificant remnants" of their case files for the entire period 1946-69.[21] The Head of the National Archive[22] in 1985 introduced a temporary moratorium on weeding in the defense archives and publicly declared the archival destruction that had taken place "a national catastrophe".

B. Secrecy Legislation

1. The Penal Code

The oldest current security legislation in Norway is found in Sections 90-94 in the Penal Code *(Den borgerlige straffelov* or just *Straffeloven)* of 1902 which prohibit the acquisition, dissemination, revelation, and betrayal to a foreign power of information which should be kept secret because of Norway's security in relation to foreign powers. There were similar formulations in the earlier Penal Code, which was superseded by the 1902 act. The terms dissemination, revelation, and betrayal denote increasing degrees of seriousness of the offense. A secret is disseminated if, for instance, a secret document is given to someone for keeping; it is revealed if it is communicated directly even just to one other person; and it is betrayed if it is revealed to a foreign power.[23]

---

[20] "Forsvarets arkiver," *Norges offentlige utredninger* (Norwegian Government Publications Office 1990, no. 7).

[21] *Id.* at 117 *et seq.*

[22] The Norwegian National Archive is the depository agency for most files of national importance. However, there are also public archives at the regional and local level. The Archives Act of 1992 applies to all of them, except archives generated by Parliament and underlying organs such as the Norwegian Auditing Agency *(Riksrevisjonen).* The regional archives contain some significant older information about the armed forces. The Parliament has its own archive which contains, *inter alia*, the complete stenographic records of the so-called "extended foreign affairs committee", a goldmine for those who write about Norwegian foreign affairs.

[23] Critical legal discussions of the sections on the Penal Code's sections on national security can be found in Høgetveit, *supra* note 14 at part 3.02, and in Henning Jakhelln, "Freedom of Speech Concerning Defence Matters: Illusion or Reality," *31 Scandinavian Studies in Law* 119 (1987). A more detailed discussion (also more favorable to the Supreme Court's interpretations) is Wilhelm Matheson, *Spionasje, Opposisjon og Straff. Om Straffelovens paragraf 90 og 91* (1982).

These sections of the Penal Code have traditionally been applied only to cases of espionage. While the questions of evidence, judging the actual harm done by a spy, and so forth, may be difficult and controversial, such cases are rarely relevant to freedom of expression because spies are unlikely to reveal publicly the secrets they have gathered; rather, they expose them covertly to a foreign power.

In 1954 the Supreme Court for the first time applied what has come to be known as "the combination principle" (or "the puzzle principle") in a case against a Norwegian communist, Asbjørn Sunde. Sunde had been a member of the Wollweber group and was prominent in the communist resistance to the German occupation of Norway during World War II.[24] While the prosecution was convinced that Sunde was a major spy, it was hard to find evidence of any particularly important piece of information he had transmitted to a foreign power. However, the court found that a collection of relatively minor pieces of information added up to a secret within the meaning of the law. A similar principle was applied in 1968, in the conviction of another Norwegian who spied for the Russians (now best known for having spied on the U.S. intelligence aircraft U-2 at Bodø airfield).[25] While these two cases did not raise any issues of freedom of expression, they introduced a legal principle which became very controversial in the late 1970s.

In 1977 an activist from Folkereisning mot krig, the Norwegian branch of War Resisters' International (WRI), and two journalists from the left socialist weekly *Ny Tid* became the first people to be charged with a security violation under the national security sections of the Penal Code, even though they were not accused of spying for a foreign power. Since none of the defendants had access to any classified information, the conviction hinged on the court's application of the combination principle. The chief defendant had combined information from newspaper biographies, car registration numbers, inquiries by telephone, etc., to compile an extensive list of personnel in the secret services. For this reason the case became known as "the lists case". He had also combined information from telephone directories, a trade union directory, and other open sources to produce a list of signals intelligence installations operated by military intelligence.

In a subsequent case, *Ikkevold*, the journal of the Norwegian WRI section, was investigated in 1981-82 for various articles about the NADGE radar chain, military communications stations, and similar topics. The case was eventually shelved. During this time, *Ikkevold* had problems getting documents released according to the Public Access Act, because the military authorities held that the information might be used for a criminal purpose.

A slightly different case was brought against the editor of the Marxist-Leninist daily paper *Klassekampen*, who was charged with publishing internal messages from a military exercise purporting to show that NATO training in Norway addressed the use of nuclear weapons, a contentious issue in a country which

---

[24] Egil Ulateig, *Raud krigar, raud spion* (1989).

[25] Kjell Fjørtoft, *Spionfamilien* (1986); Paul Einar Vatne, *Jeg var russisk spion* (1981).

is nuclear-free in peacetime. The charges were probably brought against the editor because the military failed to catch the insider who leaked the information. The Supreme Court, in a 3-2 opinion, sentenced the editor to a trivial fine; the minority would have rejected the lower court verdict entirely. This case did not involve the combination principle, but was brought on the basis that the exercise messages were properly classified. The Court accepted that the messages contained information detrimental to national security, although not on all the points claimed by the prosecution.[26]

The combination principle was, however, applied to a court case against two researchers (including the present author) who in 1979 published a report on technical intelligence installations in Norway.[27] In addition to the written sources used by the defendants in the "lists case", these researchers had observed the installations from publicly accessible places, made notes on antennas and other observable equipment, and compared their observations to information gleaned from such sources as U.S. Congressional hearings, technical military magazines, and advertising material from defense manufacturers. Like the defendants in the lists case, the two researchers were given suspended prison sentences, fined and ordered to pay court costs. Because the personnel of the listening stations in Norway were locally known as "the rabbits" (presumably because of their "long ears") this case became known as "the rabbits case".

Shortly before the lower court trial the two published a book in Norwegian[28] which included the offending report. While the new material in the book was not found offensive, the Public Prosecutor initiated an investigation of the publishers, which was later dropped. The lower court found the publication of the book to be an aggravating circumstance against the defendants. While the Supreme Court upheld the conviction, it explicitly modified this point, finding that the republication in another language and further dissemination were irrelevant to the national security charges.

The final case of this kind was a second round against *Ikkevold.* Following the dismissal of the earlier case, the journal had published a number of critical articles in 1983 against Norwegian alliance policy, charging that U.S.- and NATO-funded

---

[26] The present author served as a court-appointed expert in this case.

[27] Owen Wilkes & Nils Petter Gleditsch, *Intelligence Installations in Norway: Their Number, Location, Function, and Legality* (1979). For English-language reports on the trial, *see* Nils Petter Gleditsch, "The `National Security Trial' Against Peace Researchers in Norway," 20 International Peace Research Newsletter 19 (1982); Nils Petter Gleditsch, "Norwegian National Security Trials: New Rounds," 23 International Peace Research Newsletter 23 (1985); Nils Petter Gleditsch & Owen Wilkes, eds., *The Oslo Rabbit Trial. A Record of the `National Security Trial' against Owen Wilkes and Nils Petter Gleditsch in the Oslo Town Court* (1981); and Nils Petter Gleditsch, ed., *Round Two. The Norwegian Supreme Courts* v. *Gleditsch and Wilkes* (1982).

[28] Owen Wilkes & Nils Petter Gleditsch, *Onkel Sams kaniner. Teknisk etterretning i Norge* (Pax 1981).

military infrastructure in Norway provided important targets for Soviet attack in wartime, including nuclear attack. In the last of these articles *Ikkevold* identified a SOSUS-type submarine listening station in North Norway. In a highly dramatic action the police searched the office of *Ikkevold* and the workplaces and homes of all the members of the editorial committee (one of whom was the chief defendant in the "lists case") and an extensive indictment was prepared.[29] In four successive verdicts - two in the lower court, two in the Supreme Court - the charges were progressively whittled down until at last they concerned only the location of the building in the alleged SOSUS station. While the first lower court verdict gave the chief defendant an unconditional prison sentence, the final Supreme Court action was to dismiss all charges. Subsequently, no charges of security violations have been laid against journalists or others who aim to enlighten the public rather than the intelligence service of a foreign country.

The combination principle represents an important challenge to journalism and research because combining open sources is precisely what journalism and research is all about. If such activity can produce information which it is illegal to publish, who is going to be the judge? When the issue was raised in connection with the 1954 and 1968 spy cases, the defendants had little public sympathy and the implications for freedom of information and expression were hardly discussed. In the series of court cases from 1977 onwards, this issue was present from the start. Initially, the mass media were skeptical of those who provoked the legal confrontation through their unorthodox activity, but eventually the civil liberties issues occupied a prominent position in the public discussion. This was a dilemma for the courts, as expressed by the Supreme Court in "the rabbits case":

> The defendants have every right to publish the contents of public documents of a military or military-technical kind, to draw conclusions from such publications, and argue on that basis. But considerations of freedom of expression and freedom of research cannot justify that they reveal military secrets to the detriment of national security.

The unresolved issue here is what happens when someone uses his "every right" to obtain "military secrets" on the basis of open sources. In the *Ikkevold* case, the Supreme Court came to the conclusion that it is hard to talk of a secret if "it is a matter of few pieces of information and that combining the information does not involve problems worth mentioning". The "lists case" and the "rabbits case", on the contrary, involved the extensive collection and processing of information.

In a critique of the Supreme Court decision in the "rabbits case" a law professor deplores the courts' tendency to put security first and freedom of

[29] One of the defendants developed serious psychiatric problems and could not stand trial. He subsequently sued the government for damages.

expression second, with no real balancing between the two.[30] However, there is an element of balancing in that the courts have refrained from declaring illegal the combination of only *completely open* sources, particularly written sources. In the lists case, the court concluded that local interviews, telephone conversations, tailing military vehicles, etc., constituted "underhand" means, as did obtaining records from local building councils (on the assumption that they could not be obtained by anyone), and taking pictures from publicly accessible places (on the assumption that they violated the Defense Secrets Act). The first case against *Ikkevold* (in 1981-82) was dropped precisely because the prosecuting authorities could not find anything but written, published sources. Similarly, when the police attempted to confiscate research material held by Owen Wilkes, his defense attorney successfully protested the action and had the confiscation limited to fieldwork not already published. The Supreme Court's first verdict in the *Ikkevold* case stated that the collection of information would more easily be found illegal if the methods were "underhand". In the next round, the lower court went on to say that the methods used by *Ikkevold* were not underhand, but that the journalists had used "considerable cunning" and that their background knowledge was decisive for the paper's exposure of the listening station. The Supreme Court rejected the idea that it was an aggravating circumstance to be a competent journalist. It also rejected the argument of the defense attorneys that the defendants must be acquitted because they had used standard methods of journalism. Instead, the Supreme Court based its acquittal on the judgment that what had been revealed was not sufficiently secret to be protected by the law.

In the earlier cases, the prosecution and the military witnesses applied fairly loose standards with regard to defining exactly what was secret, and different military witnesses did not always agree with one another. In the 1983 *Ikkevold* case, for instance, the Head of Military Intelligence claimed that the only secret information concerned the location of the particular building which housed the submarine listening station, while other military witnesses claimed that even the approximate geographical location of the station was secret. One of the reasons why the Supreme Court overturned the lower court verdict was that this question had not been clarified.

The *Ikkevold* case ended in complete defeat for the prosecution. However, it started out with a bold strike for a much harsher judgment of the security violation. In the "lists case", the first verdict involved an unconditional prison sentence, later changed to suspended sentences or fines for all defendants. In the "rabbits case", the prosecution sought unconditional sentences, rejected in the lower court but only narrowly defeated (2-3) in the Supreme Court. In the *Ikkevold* case the prosecution argued that publishing the information was equivalent to "betraying it to a foreign power". This principle, if accepted, would entail much heavier

---

[30] Henning Jahkelln, "Freedom of Speech Concerning Defence Matters: Illusion or Reality," *Scandinavian Studies in Law* 119 (1987).

punishment, up to several years in jail. The lower court, expressing some doubt, rejected this idea, but nevertheless sentenced the chief defendant to an unconditional prison term. The Supreme Court rejected the principle categorically and overturned the verdict.[31]

While the *Ikkevold* case was making its way through the courts, the Treholt spy case exploded. Treholt, a senior civil servant and former deputy minister, had not published information but furnished it to the KGB and to Iraqi intelligence. However, the prosecution, relying on the evidence of four court-appointed experts, asked the court to apply a very wide conception of security, subsuming political secrets and events in countries outside the NATO alliance under the national security sections of the Penal Code. Such an interpretation had not been attempted in earlier spy cases, which involved military secrets and other information directly related to Norway's own national security. This "extended concept of security" was strongly contested by the defense attorneys, supported by two late-appointed additional court experts. The court's interpretations were very close to those of the new experts, rejecting a number of the specific charges. For instance, an assortment of classified documents found in the defendant's briefcase on his arrest was judged by the court not to be relevant to national security. The verdict probably represents an extension of the concept of security under the Penal Code, but far less than the interpretation sought by the prosecution. The court made a positive reference to the combination principle, but found that it had little relevance to the case. Nevertheless, the defendant was found guilty and sentenced to the maximum penalty.[32] The Treholt case led to a certain amount of soul-searching in the media regarding their own "conviction" of the defendant long before he had gone to trial.

In 1990 the Ministry of Justice appointed a public commission to review the national security legislation. The commission's mandate mostly concerned the need to evaluate whether the present legal formulations were sufficient to deal with the incipient threat of international terrorism, but also mentioned industrial espionage and "similar violations of national security or national interests". Lurking in the background was the possibility of changing the law to secure convictions in future

---

[31] In contrast to the relatively lenient verdicts in the Norwegian courts, neutral Sweden actually did send two journalists to jail for publishing information about a secret intelligence organization, the so-called "IB affair". Denmark, on the other hand, has followed the Norwegian pattern of strict interpretations of security, but lenient punishment. *See* Gleditsch 1986, *supra* note 1.

[32] Treholt appealed the verdict to the Supreme Court but withdrew his appeal after the case had started because of some initial procedural decisions which he claimed to show the court as biassed. Later, he unsuccessfully petitioned for a new review of the case in the lower court, but eventually was pardoned on medical/humanitarian grounds in 1992. There is an enormous literature on the Treholt case, which I have reviewed in detail in Nils Petter Gleditsch, "Treholt-litteraturen: En studie i polarisering," *52 Internasjonal Politikk* 275 (1994) and more briefly in "The Treholt Case - a Review of the Literature," *10 Intelligence and National Security* 529 (1995).

Ikkevold cases. To the Ministry of Justice such considerations, if they were present at all, must have been entirely secondary, and to the commission they appear not to have played any role at all.

A law designed to combat terrorism can also have considerable implications for freedom of speech. Specifically, it is sometimes argued that whereas a secret is no longer a secret in relation to an enemy power once it has been revealed, one terrorist may remain ignorant of a secret revealed to another. Thus a journalist, say, might be convicted for republishing sensitive material that had already been published. Moreover, even seemingly innocuous information, like the Prime Minister's home address, could be construed to be relevant to national security from the perspective of terrorism. However, the commission report[33] did not justify continued secrecy for information which has been released or revealed once. Neither was such a principle enunciated in the later revision of the preparedness legislation.[34]

2. The Defense Secrets Act

The Defense Secrets Act from 1914, enacted in connection with the outbreak of the First World War, sets even narrower limits for the collection and dissemination of national security information. This Act prohibits the collection of several types of information about military installations – such as notes, sketches, and photographs – without explicit reference to national security.

Like the Penal Code, the Defense Secrets Act was extended beyond spy cases when, in the late 1950s, a journalist for a national newspaper was fined for an apparently inadvertent penetration of a military exercise area.[35] In 1979 the law was also invoked in the "rabbits case". The defendants had taken pictures and made sketches of military installations, but the court found this activity to be legal. The prosecutor's reliance on the Defense Secrets Act appeared secondary. However, the law also played an important role in the application of the combination principle. As already noted, the courts had been reluctant to apply the combination principle to a set of easily available open sources. In this case, the violation of the Defense Secrets Act showed that some of the sources were tainted, in the sense of not being completely open, and this became an important link in the application of the combination principle.

A men's magazine *(Alle Menn)* was charged in 1981 with publishing a picture of the signals intelligence station in Vadsø, the largest of the signals intelligence

[33] "Strafferettslige regler i terroristbekjempelsen," *Norges Offentlige Utredninger* (Norwegian Government Publications Office 1993, no. 3).
[34] "Beredskapslovgivningen i lys av endrede forsvars- og sikkerhetspolitiske rammebetingelser. Innstilling fra Beredskapslovutvalget," *Norges offentlige utredninger* (Norwegian Government Publications Office 1995, no. 31).
[35] Gleditsch 1986, *supra* note 1.

stations described by Gleditsch and Wilkes.[36] After the "rabbits case" had run its course in the Supreme Court, the case against the magazine was dropped. In 1984-85 *VG*, Norway's largest newspaper, was charged with a security violation for publishing an article and a picture of a coastal fortress. This case was also dropped eventually.

3. The Duty to Secrecy in Special Positions

The Penal Code and the Defense Secrets Act enforce secrecy for everyone. Other sections in the Penal Code, the Military Penal Code, and other acts dictate secrecy for people in special positions, such as the civil service, military personnel, etc.

In a case in 1973-74 a soldier with Marxist-Leninist leanings was convicted and sentenced to a short suspended prison term for leaking military exercise reports to *Klassekampen*, purporting to show that "the enemy within" was targeted during the exercise.[37]

In a more serious case, Svein Blindheim, a former officer in military intelligence, was charged with revealing espionage and sabotage operations on Soviet territory involving Finnish citizens in the early 1950s. The operations were organized by Norway, but funded and probably initiated by Western intelligence. A highly decorated war veteran, Blindheim had been in charge of training some of the Finns. He revealed this information to a left socialist newspaper which initially did not reveal Blindheim as its source. When the authorities stonewalled, Blindheim decided to go public. He was charged with a violation of the Military Penal Code, and eventually given a suspended sentence. Blindheim's information was confirmed by Christian Christensen, a former officer in the security service and a colleague of Blindheim's who had become a conservative newspaper editor. Unlike Blindheim, Christensen was a strong supporter of NATO and the Norwegian armed forces, but he felt that much of the secrecy was politically inspired. The charges against Christensen were eventually dropped.

In 1983, Christensen published a book in which he aimed to show that Norway had been an "intelligence superpower", for example by using its very extensive merchant marine for intelligence gathering for its allies in places they could not easily access, like China. A massive uproar followed the publication of the book, and Christensen's indictment (based on the Military Penal Code as well as the national security sections of the Penal Code) was widely interpreted as a deterrent against memoir-writing by other officers in the secret services. The charges were dropped eventually, but there were no more memoirs for several years. By this time Christensen had become a vocal critic of the secrecy which he felt was largely

---

[36] *Supra* note 27.

[37] Gleditsch 1986, *supra* note 1 at 100; Narve Trædal, *Soldaten som ikke ville teie. Trædal-saka: norsk våpenmakt - retta mot kven?* (Oct. 1974).

inspired by the Labour Party's desire to avoid internal conflict over controversial aspects of its national security policy.

Finally, two members of Parliament leaked information from the secret "Schei report" on the case of the Loran-C navigation stations, which the US had built in Norway in 1958-60 in support of the Polaris ballistic submarine program.[38] The entire report was published in book form the next day[39] with annotations to show the security deletions in the previously released sanitized version.[40] The Defense Minister, although highly critical of the leak, immediately stated that this was not a violation of national security. Being an accessory to a breach of an oath of secrecy is not a punishable offense in Norway. No charges were laid against the book's publishers, although the book's contents were kept away from the viewers and listeners of the national radio and TV stations - at that time still a public monopoly - and the book was boycotted by a number of public libraries.

Even though no security breach in the sense of the Penal Code was involved, the leak of a confidential report could be construed as a violation of Section 121 of the Penal Code, which prohibits the dissemination of confidential information acquired in the line of official duty. The Storting appointed an *ad hoc* committee to consider whether the two MPs should be the subject of an impeachment trial, but the committee recommended against it and Parliament reprimanded its two members. The Socialist Left party did not accept the reprimand, and voted in favor of an impeachment trial, in a vain hope to get the issue aired and its two MPs acquitted.

4. Other Secrecy Legislation

In 1978 it was estimated that altogether there were about 150 laws containing secrecy provisions.[41] More recently, there has been a process of consolidation of these clauses. In any case, many, perhaps most of them - such as the professional secrecies of medical doctors and social workers - are irrelevant to national security matters. But a number of relevant provisions remain, of which a few examples will be given here.

The Defense-relevant Inventions Act (1953) prohibits the publication of "inventions relating to war materiel or other matters of direct significance to the

---

[38] Owen Wilkes & Nils Petter Gleditsch, *Loran-C and Omega. A Study of the Military Importance of Radio Navigation Aids* (1987).

[39] *See* Schei *et al.*, 1977; Gleditsch 1978, *supra* note 11.

[40] There is only a weak tradition in Norway for sanitizing documents in the American way, where the deletions are clearly visible. Thus when the Schei committee report was released in sanitized form in 1975, it had been edited and retyped so that the deletions could not be spotted.

[41] Asbjørn Kjønstad, "Sosialarbeidernes taushetsplikt," *Lov og Rett* 491 (1978). Extracts of secrecy provisions are given in a handbook for journalists; *see* Øy, *supra* note 8.

nations's defense" and decrees that patents relating to such inventions may be classified. There are no verdicts under the Act.

Atomic secrecy has played in important role in the U.S. debate, both in spy cases and in cases affecting freedom of information. The Norwegian Atomic Energy Act (1972) has a special secrecy provision (Section 53). But since Norway has no nuclear power stations, the nuclear activity has been very limited and I am not aware of any legal action on the basis of this section.

The Export Control Act (1987) was passed after a major political scandal in which the publicly-owned Norwegian munitions firm Kongsberg Våpenfabrikk and the Japanese Toshiba firm were accused of exporting equipment to the Soviet Union that could enable Soviet attack submarines to proceed more quietly through the oceans and thus escape Western surveillance.[42] It was alleged by the Reagan Administration that this was a major setback in the strategic arms race and the U.S. Congress threatened sanctions against Japan and Norway. As part of the political clean-up after this scandal Norway passed stricter legislation to prevent the export of technology. In a country with a moral image, arms exports of any kind have always been controversial.[43] Critics of Norwegian alliance policy and overly close military links to the U.S. have criticized Norwegian institutions who have engaged in contract research for the Pentagon,[44] particularly when the universities have engaged in such research. However, the traditional concern has been export of military hardware.

By the 1980s it had become obvious that military research and development played a crucial role in the strategic arms race. The United States, in particular, was greatly concerned about the export of sensitive technology to the Soviet Union and called for stricter guidelines against exports, actively seeking to prevent the publication of sensitive technologies which could then be copied in other countries. The United States also sought to classify the results of civilian research in cryptography which, if published, might hinder the signals intelligence efforts of the National Security Agency. The position of the U.S. Administration ran into opposition from the research community as well as from civil liberties circles because of its potential implications for the free dissemination of knowledge. A similar debate might have arisen in Norway since the Export Control Act gives the government wide powers to ban the export of "technology which can be of significance for other countries" in the development, production, or use of military products, or which directly help develop a country's military capability (Section 1). However, there has been no debate about what limitations such a law places on the export or publication of information, possibly because the exports of arms and

---

[42] Olav Wicken, "Stille propell i storpolitisk storm," in *Forsvarsstudier* no. 1 (1988).

[43] Olav Wicken, "Moralens vokter eller våpenkremmer? Regulering av norsk våpeneksport 1935-1992," *Forsvarsstudier* no. 3 (1992).

[44] *See* Nils Petter Gleditsch *et al.*, *Norge i atomstrategien* at 109 *et seq.* (1978).

military technology are generally unpopular anyway. To my knowledge there have been no legal confrontations involving the act.

Section 86 in the Planning and Building Act of 1985 *(Plan-og bygningsloven)*, most recently amended in 1993, exempts military agencies from the control of local authorities in the process of obtaining building permits and so forth, provided that an area or a facility has been declared to be secret within the meaning of the Defense Secrets Act. This provision frustrates public debate on the establishment of military installations which are potentially controversial in a local community.

The Administrative Procedures Act has a 60-year limit for personal and business information and the Public Statistics Act a 100-year limit for census data and similar information; these provisions are likely to be more important in other areas than the security area.

5. The Security and Protection Instructions

The rules for the handling of classified information in the select groups that have access to such information is circumscribed by the Security Instruction *(Sikkerhetsinstruksen)* and the Protection Instruction *(Beskyttelsesinstruksen)*. These regulations are given by the Cabinet with no direct foundation in a specific law; they are based on the Cabinet's general right to govern.[45] The first of these - the equivalent of the U.S. Executive Order on Classification – sets rules for the storage and dissemination of information related to national security and Norway's relations to foreign countries. The second is used for documents which need to be protected for other reasons, because disclosure may harm "public or private interests" – a firm, an institution or an individual. Violation of the Security Instruction or the Protection Instruction is in itself a punishable offense only for those who have received information in the line of duty. The current version of these instructions is from 1988, when the provisions for automatic declassification were introduced.

The Security Instruction was first promulgated in its present form in 1972 and has four layers of secrecy (Top Secret, Secret, Confidential, and Restricted), which is fairly standard in NATO countries. NATO documents are classified in four parallel layers (Cosmic Top Secret, NATO Secret, NATO Confidential, NATO Restricted). The Protection Instruction has just two levels, Strictly Confidential and Confidential.[46] Older documents may be classified by other, no longer current terms. Nothing has been revealed, to my knowledge, about other forms of more restricted classification, for especially sensitive areas like information derived from telephone tapping or signals intelligence, but it must be presumed that such systems exist. This type of information would probably be covered by the blanket exemptions in the declassification provisions.

---

[45] Frihagen, *supra* note 17; Matheson, *supra* note 23.

[46] The Security Instruction uses the term *Konfidensielt* and the Protection Instruction *Fortrolig*, but in everyday Norwegian the two terms are equivalent.

Norway had a reputation for being quite secretive, particularly compared to the United States.[47] Since there was no systematic declassification program, and it was difficult even to get documents reviewed for declassification, it was common for historians to rely heavily on the archives of other NATO countries, such as the United States, for the history of Norwegian foreign relations in general and security policy in particular. Following the introduction of the declassification provisions, most historians judge Norway to be considerably more open than its Nordic neighbors and above average for the NATO countries. The extensive weeding of Norwegian defense files will contribute to a heavy reliance on archives in other countries, but more importantly U.S. and U.K. files frequently have to be used in order to understand the context of Norwegian policy and to gauge the reaction of other countries to Norway's policies.

Norwegian historians, including graduate students, routinely work with records from the Foreign Ministry which have not been released to the National Archives. Publications based on such records have to be reviewed for release, the idea being that the Foreign Ministry will only ask the author to delete factual information of a sensitive kind. This system works fairly smoothly, although historians occasionally complain that the archivists do not go out of their way to direct them to the right records, and there have been occasional conflicts over the interpretation of the material. A major history of the Norwegian foreign service is currently being published on the basis of almost complete access up to the present. Until recently, military records had not been used by historians to the same extent, but several historical works on military research and development and military intelligence are now in progress. Although these works, as well as the foreign service history, represent cases of privileged access given to a select group of historians, the new openness is likely to have beneficial consequences for a wider group of historians eventually.

Generally, the further one moves away from the departments which routinely handle requests for access under the freedom of information and declassification provisions, the more legal access rights of the public suffer. Conflicts occur more frequently when journalists request current information affecting Norway's relations to other countries. The press organizations have repeatedly complained that the government does not comply with the provisions of the Freedom of Information Act, for instance by not entering certain documents in the correspondence logs, by late responses to requests for documents, etc. *Aftenposten*, Norway's largest quality daily, has been monitoring the ministries regularly and publishes details of questionable exemptions and failures to log departmental records.

---

[47] For a legal study of secrecy in Norwegian foreign policy decision-making, *see* Per Helset, *Hemmelighold og demokrati i norsk utenriks- og sikkerhetspolitikk* (1981). Comparisons between the United States and Norway with respect to freedom of information are found in Høgetveit, *supra* note 14; and Gleditsch & Høgetveit, *supra* note 1.

V. Freedom of Information and Expression in Wartime

Whereas national security is a relatively minor source of limitations on freedom of expression and information in peacetime, it plays a large role in wartime. Offenses which are punishable in peacetime would be more harshly punishable in wartime, and the enforcement of such provisions would presumably be much stricter.

For instance, Section 86 of the Penal Code specifies that "incitement to treachery, propaganda for the enemy, or misleading information designed to weaken the people's force to resist", a broader formulation than that found in Section 134 (*see* Section III of this chapter *supra*), would be punishable by a maximum of five years in prison. This provision was introduced in 1950, although the government stressed at the time that "even in wartime one must try to maintain as high a degree of freedom of speech as is compatible with the exigencies of war".[48]

In wartime or during states of preparedness there would no longer be any right to conscientious objection. However, those admitted to conscientious objector status in peacetime retain that status and would mostly be called up for service in civil defense. This is under the jurisdiction of the Ministry of Justice rather than the Ministry of Defense, but still considered a part of the overall defense effort ("the Total Defense"). There is no legal provision for conscientious objection to civil defense service and objectors have been fined and have served limited prison sentences for refusing service.

In this century, World War II is the only military conflict in which Norway became involved, although there was fear of war with Sweden after Norway's secession from the Union in 1905, with Germany in World War I, and with the Soviet Union during the Cold War. Given the present situation in Europe, it seems very unlikely that Norway will be involved in any armed conflict on her own territory or that of her immediate neighbors in the short to medium term future, if ever. The only type of armed conflict likely to involve Norway is peacekeeping and peace enforcement actions in conflicts to which Norway is not a party, as in former Yugoslavia. In such conflicts the government is very unlikely to invoke the duty to serve for reluctant military personnel or to dispute the right to publicly debate the pros and cons of Norwegian participation. While peacekeeping missions are viewed as a central part of Norwegian foreign policy (and peace enforcement missions may be similarly viewed in the future), they are not interpreted as relevant to Norwegian national security in a direct sense.[49]

---

[48] Cited from Jakhelln, *supra* note 23 at 124.

[49] In the Norwegian UNIFIL contingent in Lebanon, a freedom of expression issue arose in 1988 when an officer was repatriated by the Norwegian armed forces and subseqently fired from UN service. He had engaged in news reporting critical of Israel during his spare time from service with UNIFIL. The decision to fire him was challenged in the courts, but the Ministry of Defense won the case. *See* Eidsivating Lagmannsrett 647/89 of 30 September 1991.

During World War I extensive press censorship was organized in all the Nordic countries, even though as neutrals they were not directly involved. The Defence Secrets Act was also passed in 1914 as a preparedness measure. During World War II, the German occupation and the establishment of the Quisling regime led to much more direct and drastic repressive measures, including the firing of recalcitrant editors and the closing down of newspapers. But even in the Norwegian administration in exile in London measures were taken which intervened more directly in personal liberties than is common during peacetime, such as extensive censorship of the press and personal correspondence. During this period, Norwegian public administration was strongly influenced by British official secrecy. Such habits extended into the post-war period as well. For instance, it was reported in August 1945, three months after the war had ended in Europe, that about 350 people were engaged full time in monitoring private correspondence.[50]

Apart from wartime, special measures may also be introduced during periods of special preparedness, or "when war threatens". The most important legal instrument here is the preparedness law *(Lov om særlige rådgjerder under krig, krigsfare og liknende forhold)*, passed in 1950 after an extensive and acrimonious national debate. This legislation enables the government to pass emergency legislation without consulting Parliament when there is an urgent need to safeguard national security, public order, etc. While measures directly affecting freedom of expression and information are not specified in the law – instead, it gives the government broad powers to legislate in any relevant area – the public debate focussed to a large extent on such questions, in addition to the question of the detention of opposition elements. In 1994 it was officially admitted for the first time that the authorities had maintained lists of people to be interned in a crisis. Such lists are no longer maintained in peacetime, but it has not been revealed officially when the lists were discarded.[51] Such emergency measures were never put into practice during the Cold War, and it seems unlikely that they will be invoked now, short of a very major setback in interstate relations in Europe. The 1995 report on the revision of the preparedness legislation concluded that although war puts special demands on society, media censorship is becoming increasingly unrealistic, for technical as well as political reasons.[52]

---

[50] Rune Ottosen, *Fra fjærpenn til Internett. Journalister i organisasjon og samfunn* 51 *et seq.* (1996); *Dagbladet,* August 11, 1945.

[51] The official confirmation came in two letters from the Minister of Justice to a left-wing MP in April and June 1994. *See Aftenposten,* July 17, 1994. *Klassekampen,* July 15, 1994, alleges that such lists were maintained up until the 1980s.

[52] *See Beredskapslovgivningen ..., supra* note 34 at 64, 93.

VI. Prior Restraint and Voluntary Secrecy in Peacetime

Section 100 of the Constitution is generally interpreted as prohibiting prior restraint of any printed publication, but not for other forms of expression, such as theatre performances, broadcasting, or public demonstrations. The 1964 law on medicines, which censored medical advertising and was probably in violation of this general rule, was amended in 1992.[53] Of course, by threatening to apply legal sanctions after publication, the authorities may achieve an equivalent restraint. Høgetveit[54] cites an example of a descriptive volume on Norwegian hydroelectric power stations[55] which was censored in this way by the civil defense committee of the national power authority. Other Norwegian publications, from maps to postcards, have also been vetted in advance in close collaboration with military authorities.

During World War I a great deal of secrecy was voluntary rather than imposed by laws and regulations. The same was the case during the Cold War. Following the release of the secret report on Loran-C and Omega at a public meeting in 1977 (*see* Section IV(B)(3) *supra*), few newspapers (and only one of the half-dozen national papers published in Oslo) reported the event. One provincial editor was fired for publishing an extract from the book. "The duty to keep secret" *(taushetsplikten)* was widely assumed as the guiding principle. The Defense Minister stated that national security was not involved, and thus there was no legal obstacle to publishing the information, which in any case had already been disseminated widely in book form. Newspaper editors nevertheless put patriotic silence (or avoidance of assumed legal difficulties) above the duty to inform the public.

The national news agency (NTB) and the national broadcasting company (NRK) also did not report the contents of the report – NRK waited for six months before finally producing a radio program. NTB and NRK were both national monopolies. The Norwegian press was largely tied to the political parties. Controversial information about national security affairs therefore tended to be released by small left-wing opposition papers or by the kind of magazine that publishes bear hunts and soft pornography along with war stories and espionage capers.

When the U-2 intelligence aircraft was shot down near Sverdlovsk on its way to Bodø airfield in 1960, Norway became embroiled in a major international controversy which scuttled the Paris summit meeting and hampered President Eisenhower's conduct of international affairs during the seven remaining months of his presidency. Yet not a single Norwegian newspaper published a story about the U-2 visits to Bodø *before* 1960, even though they were well known in the city and Swedish TV reporters easily uncovered the story twelve years later.

---

[53] Benno, *supra* note 2 at 37.
[54] *Supra* note 14 at 13.
[55] Arne Solem, *Norske kraftverker*, vol. 2 (1966).

Halvard Lange, who was Foreign Minister for the first two decades after World War II, traditionally held confidential and unattributable press briefings. NRK had in its program rules a clause advising caution when national security was involved and would sometimes consult military authorities for advice on what to broadcast. The diary of a Lange advisor reveals that, at the request of the Foreign Minister, the Soviet Union was rarely criticized in the Norwegian press in the "bridge-building" period immediately after World War II.[56] A historical study of Norway's participation in COCOM, the secret organization for strategic embargo of the Soviet Union and its allies,[57] shows that the Norwegian authorities for many years managed to prevent public acknowledgement that COCOM even existed.

It is less surprising that the authorities would try to influence the extent and direction of news in the mass media than that the media cooperated to such an extent. The internal regulation on press ethics, the so-called "be careful" poster *(Vær varsom-plakaten)*, received the following addition in 1956, evocative of the times:

> Be on guard against news items which reveal military or other secrets of significance to national security. Be aware that it is frequently difficult for the non-expert to evaluate the harm done by the release of such information. They may frequently seem harmless, but can still be of great significance to a foreign power's intelligence service. When in doubt, always check with the responsible authorities.

The ethics regulations were revised in 1966, but not until 1975 was this section deleted.[58]

The press organizations had been criticized from within for their passive attitude when the authorities started to use the national security sections of the Penal Code against journalists and political activists. In the *Ikkevold* case, however, a number of senior journalists from mainstream media testified in their behalf and several press organizations also expressed their concern. Apart from contributing to the political atmosphere surrounding the trial (and possibly even the acquittal) this concern eventually led to a tightening of the legislation regulating searches on newspaper premises in 1986.

In the last two decades, most of the ties between the press and the political parties have been severed; the broadcasting monopoly no longer exists; and the journalistic profession is much more aware of the need to form its own judgment when authorities claim that publication will harm important interests - including national security. The end of the Cold War, eliminating credible military threats in Northern Europe, has strengthened the independence of the media in matters of national security.

---

[56] Knut Einar Eriksen, "Norge i det vestlige samarbeidet," in *Vekst og velstand* 166, 183 (Trond Bergh & Helge Pharo, eds. 1977).

[57] Tor Egil Førland, *"Vi sier intet" - Norge i COCOM 1948-53* (1988).

[58] For a discussion of the change in 1975, *see* Liv Hegna, *Forsvaret og pressen* (1975).

In 1957 the authorities established a governmental press service in wartime, which is staffed by civil servants and prominent media representatives and holds preparedness exercises in peacetime. A number of prominent journalists have also attended the Defense College, which includes classified defense national security briefings. Some concern has been expressed that this may decrease the peacetime independence of the media.

The independence of historians, social scientists, and other researchers is also debated. Norwegian research is generally conducted on public funding and researchers might be reluctant to bite the hand that feeds them. However, most of the research on national security takes place in universities, which traditionally have a great deal of autonomy, or in institutions funded by the Ministry of Education, rather than the Ministries of Defense and Foreign Affairs. The Ministry of Education is currently yielding control of many institutes and centers to the Norwegian Research Council, which also provides a buffer between the researchers and the users. Research institutes in the national security area are increasingly dependent on project grants from the Ministries of Defense and Foreign Affairs and it cannot be excluded that this will affect their independence. However, many departmental grants are now also administered by the Research Council, providing the same kind of buffer as for the basic grant.

VII. Controlling the Secret Services

The question of national security restrictions on freedom of expression and information has been closely linked in many countries to the problem of exercising public control over the secret services. This is not only so because the secret services is one of the branches of government most immune to public inquiry, and thus present a particular challenge to freedom of information. Equally important, political surveillance of citizens (or even the belief that opinions and political activities are monitored and registered by the authorities) may intimidate the free expression of opinion. This issue was raised, for instance, in connection with the *Ikkevold* trial, when it was inadvertently revealed that the police had used documents obtained in the search of the editorial office to copy the membership register of the Norwegian section of the pacifist War Resisters' International.[59]

Charges that political opinions have led to surveillance and covert sanctions against political deviants, have been made throughout the post-war period. In a much-debated case, a Norwegian Marxist-Leninist who had been active in solidarity work for Palestine discovered physical evidence of telephone-tapping. He sued the government, which maintained a "neither confirm nor deny" principle and got this

[59] Henning Jakhelln, "`Ikkevold'-saken ex post," *Hefte for kritisk juss* 1988, 10; "Ytringsfrihet om forsvarsforhold. `Ikkevold'-saken ex post," *Jussens venner* 1990, 73.

accepted in the courts.[60] This is an enormous topic which I cannot examine in any detail here. I note, however, that following the end of the Cold War a left/right coalition in the Norwegian Parliament had tired of repeated but increasingly implausible statements from the Labour government denying that political surveillance had taken place during the Cold War. In 1994 Parliament appointed a commission of inquiry with very wide investigative powers and with considerable resources. The 1996 report from this commission[61] demonstrated that massive political surveillance had taken place, frequently with questionable legality. The committee report itself was a unique example of public openness about matters which had previously been held very close. Another outcome of the Norwegian Parliament's more assertive attitude was to set up its own oversight committee to monitor all the secret services, including military intelligence. Previously, only the special branch of the Norwegian police had been monitored (since the end of the 1960s), and that by a government-appointed committee, which was regarded by many as a part of the system.[62]

VIII. Conclusion

Freedom of information and freedom of expression will continue to come under pressure from other societal values, and hardly anyone would argue that they should be totally unrestricted. There is wide acceptance of the view that there are legitimate restraints in terms of libel, privacy, pornography, racially offensive writing, as well as national security. However, it is also generally accepted that such limits will have to be expressed in clear and precise language, and that the media themselves will have to judge whether a piece of writing is offensive or not – and face the consequences in court if their judgment is mistaken.

National security certainly played a role, if not a dominant role, in restricting freedom of expression during the Cold War. With a slight reservation for developments in international terrorism and the way Norway responds to it, national security seems likely to be relegated to the back burner in the discussion of freedom of expression in the next decade. On the other hand, there is increasing concern in the media and among professional writers that concerns for privacy, the prevention of libel, and the reduction of racial, religious and gender discrimination, may unduly restrict freedom of expression. This unease was reflected in 1994 in two reports to

---

[60] Geir Hovland, " Lysestøl-saken - rettssikkerhet eller rikets sikkerhet? En kommentar til telefonavlyttingssaken Rt. 1987 sec. 612", *Hefte for kritisk juss* 1988, 2.

[61] *Rapport til Stortinget fra kommisjonen som ble nedsatt av Stortinget for å granske påstander om ulovlig overvåking av norske borgere (Lund-rapporten). Dokument* no. 15 (1995-96) (Norwegian Parliament 1996).

[62] "Kontrollen med de hemmelige tjenester," *Norges offentlige utredninger* (Norwegian Government Publications Office 1994, no. 4).

the Minister of Culture, one by a Professor of Law[63] and the other by a committee of humanist intellectuals[64]. In 1996 the Ministry of Justice, in response, *inter alia*, to demands from press and writers' organizations as well as the Norwegian Union of Lawyers, appointed a public commission to study current challenges to freedom of information and expression with a view to revising Section 100 of the Constitution. In the debate leading up to the appointment of the Commission the Ministers of Culture and Justice nevertheless decried the somber picture of the state of freedom of expression painted by these organizations.[65] The Commission has a fairly high profile and its report, due in 1999, will undoubtedly stimulate public discussion and legal reform. However, it seems very unlikely that national security will be high on the Commission's agenda.

---

[63] Eivind Smith, "Den konstitusjonelle regulering av ytringsfriheten i de nordiske land," unpublished study for the Ministry of Culture (Department of Public Law, University of Oslo 1995).

[64] *See* Brekke *et al. supra* note 8.

[65] *Aftenposten*, 15 June 1995.

Freedom Of Expression And National Security: The South African Experience

Gilbert Marcus

I. Introduction

Freedom of expression was one of the greatest casualties of apartheid. In order to maintain the system of racial domination, successive South African governments utilized a vast array of security and censorship laws. Direct censorship in the form of banning of publications and newspapers was only one dimension of an all encompassing system which restricted the free flow of information.[1] Censorship in South Africa had a far wider reach, manifesting itself in the banning of organizations,[2] individuals[3] and the prohibition of gatherings,[4] and intruding in less obvious ways such as the system of segregated education[5] and the selection of news by state controlled media.[6] In this way, censorship in its various guises became integral to apartheid.[7]

State security was invoked as the justification for a sustained assault on civil liberties which reached its zenith between 1985 and 1990 when South Africa was

---

[1] For an overview of the system of censorship, *see* Christopher Merrett, *A Culture of Censorship: Secrecy and Intellectual Repression in South Africa* (1994).

[2] Organizations were banned in terms of the Internal Security Act 74 of 1982. Included among those organizations banned until 1990 were the African National Congress, the South African Communist Party and the Pan Africanist Congress.

[3] Individuals were also subject to restriction orders in terms of the Internal Security Act 74 of 1982. These restriction orders could take a variety of forms. Individuals could be confined to particular areas. Individuals could be "listed" in consequence of which they could not be quoted.

[4] The Internal Security Act 74 of 1982 made provision for the prohibition of gatherings except with official permission. Between 1976 and 1990 there was a nationwide prohibition on all outdoor gatherings (*see* GN1125 of 1976, which was repeatedly renewed). In 1985 the Minister of Law and Order, acting under section 46(3) of the Internal Security Act went even further and prohibited gatherings held "in any building" which were organized by 64 named organizations in 30 magisterial districts (GN1433 Government Gazette 9806 of June 28, 1985). This prohibition was imposed for an initial period of six months and was extended for a further six months, with the addition of a further 11 organizations (GN2869 Government Gazette 10055 of December 31, 1985).

[5] Separate education for blacks and whites was effected by the Bantu Education Act 47 of 1953.

[6] The South African Broadcasting Corporation which controlled both television and radio broadcasts was a powerful propaganda medium for the government.

[7] G.J. Marcus, "The Wider Reaches of Censorship," 1 *South African Journal on Human Rights* 69 (1985). In 1990 there were approximately 100 laws which impacted upon the free flow of information. *See* Bell Dewar & Hall, *Kelsey Stuart's Newspapersmen's Guide to the Law* (5th Ed.).

subject to permanent emergency rule. From the time that the minority National Party seized power in 1948 until its ultimate demise in 1994, a security mentality dominated South Africa:

> The partisan nature of apartheid security policy is well known and requires little elaboration. Although the policy purported to be in the 'national interest', its primary goal was to maintain the system of minority rule and safeguard the racially exclusive state and the white community. Security strategy was formulated by a select group of cabinet ministers and security officials, excluding parliament and the public from effective participation.
>
> The strategy was essentially repressive in character and was carried out principally through military and paramilitary means. The political and economic reforms . . . in the early 1980s and the socio-economic black upliftment programs . . . in the mid-1980s did not dilute this emphasis but rather broadened the concept of counter-revolutionary warfare.
>
> While the immediate threats to security were perceived to be the liberation movements and internal anti-apartheid groups, the targets of State repression included large sections of the civilian population in South Africa, Namibia and Angola. . . .
>
> The net results of Pretoria's security policy were devastating. The death of thousands of people; the impoverishment of millions of lives; massive economic waste and damage; a regional arms race; and a greater resolve by the liberation movements and international community to end apartheid. In short, the outcome was perpetual insecurity for the states and inhabitants of South and Southern Africa.[8]

The reforms ushered in by former President FW De Klerk on 2 February 1990[9] leading to the transition to democracy in April 1994 and the adoption of a new Constitution have laid the foundation for a new approach to freedom of expression and state security. While there have been significant steps towards openness, the legacy of secrecy still remains.[10]

---

[8] Laurie Nathan, *The Changing of the Guard: Armed Forces and Defense Policy in a Democratic South Africa* at 10 - 11 (1994).

[9] In a dramatic speech delivered in Parliament on February 2, 1990, then State President F.W. De Klerk announced the unbanning of unlawful organizations, the release of imprisoned leaders, the return of exiled South Africans and the start of negotiations for an inclusive democratic constitution.

[10] The new democracy has undoubtedly ushered in the era of the greatest freedom of expression hitherto enjoyed by South Africa. Significantly, however, many of the laws which directly or indirectly inhibit or prohibit altogether the freedom of expression remain intact. The Internal Security Act 74 of 1982 has been substantially amended to limit the circumstances in which

II. State Security and Censorship: Historical Overview

A. Direct Censorship

In terms of the Publications Act[11] and before its amendment in 1993, thousands of publications and films were banned for being "prejudicial to the safety of the State, the general welfare or the peace and good order".[12] In anticipation of the first democratic elections, this provision of the Publications Act was repealed in obvious recognition of the fact that free and fair elections could not be possible if there were inhibitions on free and open debate.[13] In terms of the procedures prescribed by the Publications Act,[14] decisions as to whether or not a publication was "undesirable" were taken by committees whose deliberations were conducted secretly and before whom affected parties had no right of audience.[15] An appeal from a committee decision went to the Publications Appeal Board. While "any person" had the right to complain about a publication, only a limited class of persons enjoyed the right of appeal. Such classes were essentially confined to those with a direct financial interest in the publication.[16] The Publications Appeal Board was the final arbiter on questions of undesirability and had the power to confirm, set aside or vary a committee's decision. Because of the limitation on the right of appeal, relatively few publications came before the Publications Appeal Board.

A comprehensive review of the decisions of the Publications Appeal Board dealing with State security is beyond the scope of this paper.[17] The attitude of the Publications Appeal Board to matters of State security was inconsistent and

---

organizations may be prohibited and many of its more offensive features have been repealed.

[11] Act 42 of 1974. This Act has been repealed and replaced by the Films and Publications Act 65 of 1996. The new Act, however, has not yet come into operation.

[12] Section 47(2)(e) of Act 42 of 1974.

[13] Section 47(2)(e) of the Publications Act 42 of 1974 (together with other sections of the Act) were repealed by section 1 of the Abolition of Restrictions on Free Political Activity Act 206 of 1993.

[14] For an overview of the workings of the Publications Act, *see* J.C .W. Van Rooyen, *Censorship in South Africa* (1987).

[15] That the operations of these committees violated the principles of natural justice was expressly recognized in *S* v. *Maroney* 1978 (4) SA 389 (A). Once a publication had been declared "undesirable", it could not be distributed. In extreme cases, mere possession of an undesirable publication could be prohibited.

[16] Sec.10(1)(a) and sec. 13(1) of Act 42 of 1974. Others with a right of appeal included the person who submitted the publication for a decision and the Directorate of Publications, the body responsible for administering the statute.

[17] For a substantial review of the decisions up to 1984, *see* Louise Silver, *A Guide to Political Censorship in South Africa* (1984). *See also* G. J. Marcus "Reasonable censorship?" Corder ed., *Essays on Law and Social Practice in South Africa* 349 (1988).

enigmatic. If trends were discernible, it seemed as if the Board was prepared to show a measure of tolerance towards serious academic texts but was generally hostile towards anything directed at a more popular readership. The Board frequently acknowledged the necessity to tolerate criticism. Hence, it recognized that freedom of expression was integral to democratic government and was a right enjoyed by every citizen. Mere criticism of the military or the police, even if false or one-sided, was permissible. The fact that anti-government emotions were evoked was also not sufficient for a finding of undesirability. Nor was mere sympathy with socialism, communism and prohibited organizations.[18]

The rhetoric, while superficially enlightened, was beguiling. The stated commitment to principle frequently crumbled where publications or films challenged the legitimacy of the government. The fear of allowing revolutionary dogma to fall into the hands of the masses was an obvious concern. Dealing with a book containing a number of serious articles, the Board observed:

> Should the book be read by large numbers of blacks, it may well incite many of them to violence. But this is not a book for the masses. In the normal course its likely readers will consist of educated persons, whether black or white, and the sophisticated black will find little in the book that is new to him.[19]

By contrast, an internationally acclaimed periodical, *Newsweek*, fell foul of the censors. The Board was particularly concerned with an article expressing the views of young black activists who espoused violence:

> The views of these radicals are, however, generally well known in South Africa and the article therefore loses much of its informative value for South Africans. In the present situation where the very aspects of stone throwing, sabotage and barbaric killings, highlighted by the article are the main ingredients of the unrest, it becomes problematical to accumulate these radical views in one article and thereby give prominence and, indirectly, glamour, to the cause of the radical. But, in the present sensitive climate the excessive, blatant quoting of these statements which are all pro-violence and pro-revolution is likely to lend credibility to and even justification for the violence.[20]

A diary published by the Congress of South African Trade Unions consisting of some 200 pages was considered so radically undesirable that even its possession was prohibited. Various dates were commemorated in the diary

---

[18] Heartland 43/82 This decision embodies a summary of the Board's general approach. The Board's decisions are published by the Centre for Applied Legal Studies *Digest of Decisions of the Publications Appeal Board* (G. Marcus & L. Morgan, eds.).

[19] Apartheid in Crisis 3/87.

[20] *Newsweek* 187/85.

highlighting events of historical importance and relevance to workers. The Board reasoned thus:

> It is important to bear in mind that a great deal of emotion is connected to many of the events documented in this publication. Many of the events which on the face of it seem quite neutral, become extremely controversial and emotional when read in the context of the whole. The publication is also not just an ordinary diary. It is in fact a readable history of political agitation, subversion and the successes of communism and revolution. Reference is made to general strikes, local strikes and boycotts and obvious clashes with the police are set side by side with successes in revolution, heroes of revolution and communism. References are also made to action taken by the African National Congress. What is innocuous in itself becomes incitation to subversion and sedition against the State, which is likely to contribute to the eruption of political violence. In the Board's view a substantial number of likely readers of this publication are likely to make use of this publication as a timetable to evoke feelings of severe discontent as well as contempt for State authority. For many readers, therefore, the publication would not only be a diary, but a history of the success of subversion and disruption of State authority. And this publication would strengthen their feelings of hatred for the State and thus contribute to a clash with State authority in order to attain their post-revolutionary ideal.[21]

Although the Publications Appeal Board rendered a number of courageous decisions which ran counter to the prevailing security mentality, the impact of these decisions was ultimately minimal given the vast scale of bannings at the committee level.[22]

---

[21]1987 Cosatu's Workers Diary 176/87.

[22]The Publications Appeal Board, particularly under the chairmanship of Professor J.C.W. Van Rooyen, showed a willingness to establish a jurisprudential basis for prohibitions in the name of State security. In several decisions, the Board held itself guided by the American "clear and present danger" test. *See, e.g., Saspu National* 107/84. For a discussion of the way in which the Board applied the "clear and present danger" test, *see* Mary Cheh, "Systems and Slogans: The American Clear and Present Danger Doctrine and South African Publications in Control," 2 *South African Journal on Human Rights* 29 (1986).

B. Official Secrecy and State Security

The banning of publications and films was the most high profile manifestation of censorship. More insidious, however, was the vast range of information which could not be published by reason of the laws governing official secrecy. One of the most far reaching prohibitions is that contained in section 118 of the Defense Act[23] which provides:

> 118 (1) No person shall publish in any newspaper, magazine, book or pamphlet or by radio or any other means -
>
> (a) Any information relating to the composition, movements or disposition of:
>
> (i) The South African Defense Force or any auxiliary or voluntary nursing service established under this Act, or any force of a country which is allied to the Republic; or
>
> (ii) Any South African or Allied ships or aircraft used for naval or military purposes;
>
> (iii) Any engines, rolling stock, vehicles, vessels or aircraft of any railway, road, inland water or sea transport system or air service over which an officer of the South African Defense Force has assumed control ....; or
>
> (b) Any statement, comment or rumor relating to any member of the South African Defense Force or any activity of the South African Defense Force or any Force of a foreign country, calculated to prejudice or embarrass the government in its foreign relations or to alarm or depress members of the public, except where publication thereof has been authorized by the Minister or under his authority. . . .
>
> (2) No person shall publish in any manner whatsoever any secret or confidential information relating to the defense of the Republic, or any information relating to any works proposed, undertaken or completed for or connected with the fortification or defense of the Republic except where the information has been furnished or the publication

[23] Act 44 of 1957.

thereof has been authorized by the Minister or under his authority. . . .

The section creates various presumptions which operate against an accused person in any prosecution. Thus, it is presumed until the contrary is proved "that any information relating to the defense of the Republic is secret or confidential".[24] In addition, information "relating to military equipment" is deemed to be secret or confidential unless publication of such information has been authorized by the Minister or under his authority.[25] In terms of section 101 of the Act, the State President "may during operations in defense of the Republic or for the prevention or suppression of terrorism or for the prevention or suppression of internal disorder in the Republic by proclamation in the Gazette, or in such other manner as he deems expedient in the circumstances, establish and provide for the doing of all things necessary to enforce a censorship over all or any description of postal, telegraphic, telephonic or radio matter or communications passing within, into or from the Republic, and over all or any description of letters, written or printed matter, parcels, pictures, drawings, sketches, photographs or gramophone records (including any article, apparatus or device upon which or by means of which intelligence or sounds of any kind have been recorded and can be reproduced) addressed or intended to be delivered or conveyed to any person". This section has never been invoked.

The full impact of the restrictions on the free flow of information will probably never be known. When the South African Defense Force invaded Angola in 1975, South Africans were among the last to know, notwithstanding the fact that the foreign news media had covered the invasion. Only years after the events is the truth beginning to emerge concerning the role of the South African Defense Force in the destabilization of neighboring countries.

The secrecy provisions of the Defense Act are coupled with extraordinary powers intended to indemnify members of the Defense Force in relation to acts connected with the combating of terrorism. One particularly notorious example demonstrates how pernicious this law was. In 1978 a detachment of the South African Defense Force captured a number of persons near Cassinga in Southern Angola. They were then taken across the border into Namibia and held at a Defense Force base. A number of those captured were kept in detention, first at Oshakati and later in a camp in the Mariental district. In April 1984 an application for release of the thirty-seven prisoners held at the Mariental camp was instituted in the South West Africa division of the Supreme Court. The application was opposed with a defense which is without precedent in any civilized legal system. The Minister of Justice, acting under the authority of the State President, issued a certificate in terms of section 103 *ter* (4) of the Defense Act directing that the judicial proceedings "instituted by reason of an act advised, commanded, ordered, directed or done in

---

[24] Act 44 of 1957, sec. 118(5)(a).
[25] Act 44 of 1957, sec. 118(6).

good faith by the State President, the Minister or a member of the South African Defense Force for the purpose of or in connection with the prevention or suppression of terrorism in an operational area" shall not be continued. The application for the release of the prisoners failed. In neither the Court of first instance[26] nor on appeal[27] is there any suggestion of judicial disquiet at legislation intended to emasculate the authority and integrity of the Supreme Court.[28]

The Defense Act does not stand alone. It is bolstered by a series of other statutes, ostensibly promulgated in the interest of state security, which prevent, on pain of criminal sanction, the publication of information. One of the most far-reaching of these measures is the Protection of Information Act.[29] The provisions of this statute go substantially beyond any legitimate realm of official secrecy.[30]

Other statutes which prohibit the publication of information include the Armaments Development and Production Act,[31] the National Supplies Procurement Act[32] and the National Key Points Act.[33] These and other statutes[34] have had the effect of shrouding matters of security in a veil of secrecy.

---

[26] *Kauluma* v. *Minister of Defense*, 1984 (4) SA 59 (SWA).

[27] *Kauluma en Andere* v. *Minister van Verdediging en Andere*, 1987 (2) SA 833 (A). The Appellate Division of the Supreme Court was South Africa's highest court.

[28] For a discussion of this and other instances in which the legislature has sought to prevent the judiciary from exercising its traditional functions, see G. J. Marcus, "Respect for the Courts: Myth and Reality," 1 *South African Journal on Human Rights* 236 (1985).

[29] Act 84 of 1982. This Act repealed and replaced the Official Secrets Act 16 of 1956.

[30] *See generally* Bell, Dewar & Hall , Kelsey Stuart , *Newspaperman's Guide to the Law* at 149-154 (5th ed.), and G.J. Marcus, "The Veil of Secrecy," 29 *The Review* 56 (1982).

[31] Act 57 of 1968, sec. 11A of which makes it a criminal offense to disclose information "in relation to the acquisition, supply, marketing, importation, export, development, manufacture, maintenance or repair of or research in connection with armaments . . . except on the written authority of the Minister or of a person authorized thereto by the Minister."

[32] Act 89 of 1970, section 8A of which provides that, "No person shall disclose to any person any information in relation to any goods or any service referred to in an arrangement or order made or issued under section 2 or 3(1), or any statement, comment or rumor calculated directly or indirectly to convey such information or anything purporting to be such information" except under specified circumstances.

[33] Act 102 of 1980 which authorizes the Minister of Defense to declare any place or area to be a "national key point". Once an area has been declared a national key point it becomes a criminal offense in terms of section 10(2) of the Act to furnish "any information relating to the security measures applicable at or in respect of any national key point or in respect of any incident that occurred there without being legally obliged or entitled to do so, or without the disclosure or publication of the said information being empowered by or on the authority of the Minister or except as may be strictly necessary for the performance of his functions in regard to his employment in connection with, or his ownership of, or as may be necessary to protect, the place concerned."

[34] *E.g.*, the Petroleum Products Act 120 of 1977, the Nuclear Energy Act 92 of 1982 and the Central Energy Fund Act 38 of 1977.

C. Emergency Powers

During the successive states of emergency declared between 1985 and 1990 a further dimension of censorship was added to existing laws.[35] Regulations promulgated pursuant to emergency powers had a breathtaking sweep. During the emergency period, five newspapers were temporarily closed down[36] and several others faced the threat of closure. Although there were minor variations in the regulations promulgated pursuant to each declared state of emergency, they retained an essential core.[37] There was a general prohibition on the making or publishing of "subversive statements" whether orally or in writing. The definition of "subversive statement" was extensive and framed to include statements "in which members of the public are incited or encouraged or which is calculated to have the effect of inciting or encouraging members of the public" to do various things such as taking part in boycott action, taking part in an act of civil disobedience and participating in an unlawful strike or stayaway. A second category of statement, although not totally prohibited, was subjected to special control. Publications and television, film or sound recordings containing any news or comment or advertisement "on or in connection with" a variety of topics including "any security action", "any deployment of a security force" or the treatment in detention of detainees was prohibited. Such matter could be published, however, if authorized by a government official. Save with official permission, the taking of any photograph or production of any television or film recording "of any unrest or security action or of any incident occurring in the course thereof" was prohibited.

Perhaps the most bizarre provision was the prohibition on the publishing of "any blank space or any obliteration or deletion of part of the text of a report or

---

[35] A state of emergency could be proclaimed in terms of the Public Safety Act 3 of 1953. The Act vested power in the State President to declare a state of emergency if, in his opinion, "any action or threatened action by any persons is of such a nature and of such extent that the safety of the public, or the maintenance of public order is seriously threatened . . . and the ordinary law of the land is inadequate to ... ensure the safety of the public, or to maintain public order." The State President was empowered to promulgate regulations which he considered "necessary or expedient" for safeguarding the public or maintaining public order.

[36] The five newspapers were *New Nation, South, The Weekly Mail, Grassroots* and *New Era*. For a discussion of the closure of *New Nation* and the unsuccessful legal attempts to prevent is closure, *see* G. J. Marcus, "Fanning Revolution, Unrest and Violence: A Case Study of Censorship under the Emergency," 2 Harvard Human Rights Yearbook 125 (1989) and Richard Abel, *"Censorship and the Closure of New Nation" in Politics By Other Means - Law in the Struggle Against Apartheid*, 1980 - 1996, Chapter 8 "Censorship and the Closure of New Nation".

[37] For an overview of emergency powers between 1985 and 1989 *see* the chapter entitled "The Administration of Justice" in *Annual Survey of South African Law between 1985 and 1990.*

of a photograph or part of a photograph" which is stated or appears to be intended to be understood as a reference to the effect of the emergency regulations.[38]

The cumulative effect of the assault on freedom of expression in South Africa has been to foster ignorance, suspicion and intolerance, a legacy bequeathed to the new South Africa.

III. The Constitution

On April 27, 1994 and coinciding with the first democratic elections, South Africa adopted an Interim Constitution.[39] The Interim Constitution was replaced by a Final Constitution ("the Constitution") on 4 February, 1996.[40] The Constitution was intended to be a "ringing and decisive break with the past which perpetuated inequality and irrational discrimination and arbitrary governmental and executive action."[41] The Constitution contains a Bill of Rights and vests the superior courts with the power to strike down laws which violate the Constitution. While none of the rights in the Bill of Rights are absolute, they may only be limited in specified circumstances. Limitation is permitted only in terms of law of general application and to the extent that the limitation is reasonable and justifiable in an open and democratic society based on human dignity, equality and freedom, taking into account all relevant factors, including the nature of the right, the importance of the purpose of the limitation, the nature and extent of the limitation, the relation between the limitation and its purpose and less restrictive means to achieve the

---

[38] *See generally* G. J. Marcus, "Civil Liberties under Emergency Rule" *in* Dugard, Haysom & Marcus, *The Last Years of Apartheid: Civil Liberties in South Africa* at 32 (1992). *See also*, Harvey Tyson, *Editors under Fire* at 275-6 (1993).

[39] The Constitution of the Republic of South Africa (Act 200 of 1993) ("the Interim Constitution"). The Interim Constitution was adopted before democratic elections took place. It was intended as an interim measure pending the finalization of a constitution after elections. The Interim Constitution stipulated a set of "Constitutional Principles" with which the final constitution had to comply. In addition, it required the newly created Constitutional Court to certify that the final constitution complied with the constitutional principles.

[40] The Constitution of the Republic of South Africa, 1996 (Act 106 of 1996). The Constitutional Court initially refused to certify the Final Constitution for want of compliance with the constitutional principles. See Ex parte Chairperson of the Constitutional Assembly: In re Certification of the Constitution of the Republic of South Africa, 1996 (4) S.A. 744 (CC). After identified defects had been remedied, the Constitution was finally certified. See Ex parte Chairperson of the Constitutional Assembly: In re Certification of the Amended Text of the Constitution of the Republic of South Africa, 1996 (2) S.A. 97 (CC).

[41] *S.* v. *Mhlungu & Others* , 995 (3) S.A. 867 (CC) at 873 - para 8.

purpose.[42] Openness and freedom are included in the core values of the newly created constitutional order.[43]

Freedom of expression is enshrined in Section 16 of the Constitution in the following terms :

16 (1) Everyone has the right to freedom of expression, which includes -
(a) freedom of the press and other media;
(b) freedom to receive or impart information or ideas;
(c) freedom of artistic creativity; and
(d) academic freedom and freedom of scientific research.
(2) The right in sub-section (1) does not extend to -
(a) propoganda for war;
(b) incitement of imminent violence; or
(c) advocacy of hatred that is based on race, ethnicity, gender or religion, and that constitutes incitement to cause harm.[44]

The Constitution also creates a right of access to information. Section 32 of the Constitution provides :

32 (1) Everyone has the right of access to -
(a) any information held by the state;
(b) any information that is held by another person and that is required for the exercise or protection of any rights.
(2) National legislation must be enacted to give effect to this right, and may provide for reasonable measures to alleviate the administrative and financial burden on the state.[45]

---

[42] Section 36 of the Constitution.

[43] Section 1 of the Constitution identifies various values which are foundational to the Constitution. These include a "multi-party system of democratic government to ensure accountability, responsiveness and openness." Section 39(1)(a) of the Constitution requires every court, tribunal or forum, when interpreting the Bill of Rights, to "promote the values that underlie an open and democratic society based on human dignity, equality and freedom." Section 36(1) permits the limitation of a right in the Bill of Rights only in terms of law of general application to the extent that the limitation is reasonable and justifiable in an open and democratic society based on human dignity, equality and freedom, taking into account all relevant factors.

[44] For an overview of the guarantee of freedom of expression *see* G. Marcus and D. Spitz, "Expression," *in* Chaskalson, Kentridge, Klaaren, Marcus, Spitz & Woolman, *Constitutional Law of South Africa* Chapter 20 (1966).

[45] By reason of section 241 read with item 23 of Schedule 6 to the Constitution, until the legislation envisaged in section 32(2) has been enacted, the guarantee of access to information must be regarded to read as follows :

Every person has the right of access to all information held by the state or any of its organs in any sphere of government insofar as that information

IV. The Cameron Commission: A Test Case for Openness

It did not take long for the new constitutional guarantees to be tested against the demands of national security. On October 14, 1994, Mr. Justice E. Cameron was appointed to chair a commission of inquiry "into alleged arms transactions between Armscor and one Eli Wazan and other related matters."[46] In order to facilitate the Commission's work, and to overcome the prohibition on disclosure of security related matters contained in the Defense Act,[47] the Armaments Development and Production Act[48] and the Protection of Information Act,[49] ministerial permission for the right to publish or receive evidence relating to the matters which the Commission was investigating was conditionally granted by the Minister of Defense.

The Minister granted conditional exemption from the statutes in question but required hearings to be held *in camera* in the event that the Commission had reason to believe that "the personal life or safety of any individual would be put at risk", or that "the national security of South Africa may be threatened" or "international trade relations between South Africa and any country with which it has international trade relationships may be threatened."[50] During the course of evidence, reference was made to a document known as "Log 17". The South African Defense Force was anxious that the contents of Log 17 not be made public and made application to have its contents protected. In the course of the ruling, Mr. Justice Cameron described Log 17 as follows:

> The "Log pamphlet" sets out a standard course of action to regulate and control armament sales between the then SADF and Armscor. The country list is the first annexure to the log pamphlet. It assigns each of 179 countries respectively to group 1: Countries with no limitation in respect of marketing exports. Group 2: Countries to which only non-sensitive armaments may be exported or group 3: Countries to which no marketing or exports may occur.[51]

The Defense Force led evidence in support of its application to keep Log 17 from public scrutiny. The evidence was summarized by Mr. Justice Cameron as follows:

---

is required for the exercise or protection of any of their rights.

[46] The terms of reference of the Commission are contained in Government Notice R1801, Government Gazette 16035 of October 14, 1994.

[47] Act 44 of 1957, sec. 118.

[48] Act 57 of 1968, sec. 11A.

[49] Act 84 of 1982, sec. 4.

[50] Letter dated November 7, 1994 from the Minister of Defense to the Chairman, Cameron Commission.

[51] Transcript of the Cameron Commission 1426-1427.

> The testimony of Mr. Land and of Colonels Williams and Neethling was to substantially the same effect. Colonel Williams stated that virtually no country provides details of its arms sales. Revelation of details, he explained, may undercut your competitive edge, and lead to commercial rivals stealing your potential customers. Specifically on country listings, he expressed the view that publishing them may problematise your foreign policy in that
>
> (1) Allies could compare equipment and a country's findings that it is excluded from certain sales, could cause considerable disruption and anxiety amongst would-be friends.
>
> (2) Neighbors amongst whom delicate relations are being forged could receive false perceptions, and
>
> (3) Certain countries privileged in terms of the categorization could be targeted by the intelligence agencies of those excluded from specific sales.
>
> Colonel Williams recognized that the log pamphlet had been drawn up before the transition . . . to a democratic order and a new government. . . . As Mr. Land and Colonel Neethling pointed out, the old pre-transition listings could form a basis on which countries could extrapolate their new listings. Moreover, the fact of old adverse listings could embarrass international partners. Disclosure could furthermore, Colonel Williams suggested, deprive South Africa of moral influence, with newborn democracies, we might be embarrassed to be disclosed as the old regime's arms trade partners. . . . Neighboring countries who, under the old dispensation, had been classified as group 3 countries could potentially be insulted with adverse consequences for political, military, multilateral and regional relationships. . . . In addition, countries revealed to have been in the most favorable category, namely group 1, could be inferred to have been trading with South Africa before the lifting of United Nations restrictions. This could result in severe embarrassment to them especially in relation to their domestic politics.[52]

The Cameron Commission was unmoved by these protestations. In ruling that the document could be made public, Mr. Justice Cameron stated:

> Reasonableness as a standard of public conduct in South Africa now requires that decision-makers should have due regard to appropriate constitutional standards and principles. These include

[52] Transcript of Cameron Commission 1428-1431.

> in the present case the value of openness and visibility in government and official processes. In other words, an assessment whether the reasonable justification test has been fulfilled may include in the weighing process, giving consideration to the public's constitutional right to know and the constitutional value of an open society. To put the matter differently, the public's right to know, should not be omitted from an assessment whether the reasonable justification standard has been fulfilled.[53]

The argument that diplomacy in arms transactions requires a measure of secrecy was rejected:

> It is precisely that secrecy that may create the conditions for subterfuge, duplicity, abuse of power, corruption, malpractice and irresponsibility. The right of the public, where reasonable and practicable to know must therefore be asserted."[54]

While acknowledging that the decision to allow disclosure was not "without risk of harm or without anxiety to its consequences", the conclusion was that the risk in the present case was "not sufficient to entitle us to bar from the press and the public their important right to examine our past, including our past armaments dealings, whether or not that examination causes embarrassment and even complexity, whether for other governments or indeed, for the present government of national unity."[55]

Not content with this ruling, the representatives of the Defense Force gave notice of their intention to have the decision reviewed. An application was launched in which orders were sought interdicting and restraining Mr. Justice Cameron from disclosing or publishing the contents of Log 17 pending the finalization of the proposed review. The application was supported by an affidavit from General Meiring, then Chief of the South African National Defense Force. It was contended that the evidence adduced on behalf of the Defense Force established that there was sufficient reason to believe that publication of the document in question would threaten the national security of South Africa and the diplomatic or bilateral relations between South Africa and other countries. It was suggested that the damage would be irreparable once the documents had been released. It was argued that should the review succeed, interested parties as well as the public at large never had any "right" to have sight of the documents. While acknowledging the constraints imposed by the Constitution, it was pointed out that certain statutory provisions were still in force which protected the confidentiality of the document.[56]

---

[53] Transcript of Cameron Commission 1433.
[54] Transcript of Cameron Commission 1440.
[55] Transcript of Cameron Commission 1441.
[56] Affidavit of Armin Kluth in South African National Defense Force v. The Honorable Mr Acting Justice Edwin Cameron N.O. and 3 Others.

The application for review was abandoned shortly after its launch. After the institution of proceedings, the *Weekly Mail*, a local newspaper, published the contents of the 1989 version of Log 17 which apparently contained most of the information in respect of which the restraining order was sought. The information had thereby effectively been projected into the public domain.[57] The application for review was then withdrawn and the press published the contents of Log 17 without restraint.

A number of features of this episode call for comment. Of particular significance was the impact of the new Constitution on the ruling handed down by the Commission. The Constitution plainly imposed special obligations upon the Commission in dealing with the sensitive issues at hand. By contrast, the attitude of the Defense Force was still deeply rooted in an ethos of secrecy and an apparent lack of comprehension of the demands of openness and accountability in a democratic dispensation. Most importantly, however, history has vindicated the Commission's ruling. In the years that have passed since disclosure of Log 17, none of the dire consequences predicted have come to pass. There is an important lesson in this. Professor Emerson has observed:

> The dynamics of reconciling the requirements of national security with the maintenance of constitutional liberties involve a number of . . . considerations. The first is that claims of national security must always be viewed with a high degree of scepticism. Governments always resent criticism or dissent and are prone to suppress such activity in the name of national security. Governments also frequently employ appeals to national security as a method of distracting public attention from other problems with which the nation must deal. The secrecy attached to many national security issues allows the government to invoke national security claims in order to cover up embarrassment, incompetence, corruption, or outright violation of law. Subsequent events almost always demonstrate the asserted dangers to national security have been grossly exaggerated. To put it another way, when national security claims are advanced there may well be a confusion of the interests of the administration in power with the interests of the nation.

The attempt at suppression in front of the Cameron Commission was not the first since the transition to democracy nor has it been the last. On an earlier occasion, the new Minister of Defense threatened interdict proceedings against the Weekly Mail for publishing details of the alleged "dirty tricks" carried out by a unit known as the Directorate of Covert Collection. The threats ultimately came to

---

[57] *Weekly Mail*, December 2, 1994.

nothing, but the fact that they were made at all again illustrated that old habits die hard.[58]

The lessons of the Cameron Commission did nothing to deter the arms manufacturer Denel from attempting to suppress information about a multi-million rand arms deal with what it coyly described as a "middle eastern country". Following reports in various newspapers that Denel was involved in a R7 billion arms deal with a middle eastern country, Denel pursued a two-pronged strategy. First, it laid criminal charges against the newspapers concerned for contravening the Armaments Development and Production Act.[59] Second, it sought an urgent interdict in the High Court to restrain publication of the name of the client state. The grounds upon which the restraining order was sought were not the usual claims of national security. Instead, it was alleged that disclosure of the identity of the client state would jeopardize the very existence of the contract since the mysterious client had insisted on confidentiality. Moreover, if the contract fell through, jobs in the armaments industry would be at risk. On this basis, Denel obtained a temporary interdict against a number of newspapers. From this point onwards, the saga took on the dimensions of a farce. The chairperson of the National Conventional Arms Control Committee, Professor Kader Asmal, who is also the Minister of Water Affairs and Forestry, revealed at a press conference that the client state was Saudi Arabia. This information could not be published by those newspapers who were prohibited from doing so by reason of the temporary interdict. The world, however, now knew that the client was Saudi Arabia. This was published in foreign newspapers and on the Internet. Since disclosure of the name of the client could not longer be suppressed, the interdict was discharged at Denel's request.[60]

Questions of official secrecy emerged in the unexpected setting of what appeared to be a routine criminal prosecution of one Dr. Wouter Basson for various drug related offenses. What made the prosecution unusual was that Dr. Basson had allegedly been involved in South Africa's chemical weapons programed. It was alleged that the department which Dr. Basson had headed produced drugs for assassinating or incapaciting opponents of the State and allegedly also drugs for distribution to the general population to sap their revolutionary zeal. Dr. Basson applied for bail. The prosecutor successfully persuaded the presiding magistrate to hear his evidence in camera. Application was then made to the High Court by various newspapers to gain access to the record of evidence in the bail hearing. This attempt was partially successful. The Court permitted a censored version of the

---

[58] *Weekly Mail*, June 17-23, 1994.

[59] Act 51 of 1968, referred to in footnote 31, *supra*. The charges were not proceeded with.

[60] The case is cited as Denel (Pty.) Ltd. and Another v. Independent Newspaper Holdings Ltd. (Pretoria High Court Case No. 16931/97.) The sequence of events appears in the *Action Alert Update* published by the Freedom of Expression Institute on July 22 and 24, 1997 and August 1, 4, 6, 7, 11 and 20, 1997 and in the *Monthly Bulletin* for August/September 1997.

record to be made available to the public pending argument on those issues which were considered by the State to be secret. The litigation to obtain unhindered access to the record and the relevant documents attracted astonishing resistance from the Attorney-General, the Ministry of Foreign Affairs, the Ministry of Defense, the South African Council for the Non-Proliferation of Weapons of Mass Destruction and the National Intelligence Agency. The matter remains unresolved.[61]

These cases reveal an on-going concern that the security mentality which dominated official thinking under apartheid still persists.

V. Reforming the Culture of Secrecy

A. Amending the Defense Act

There are many statutes in force in South Africa which are entirely at odds with the promises of the Constitution. While they are not actively being enforced, their existence produces a chilling effect on the freedom of expression. There is, however, an apparent awareness that certain laws are incompatible with the new democracy. The Minister of Defense has instituted an investigation into the provisions of the Defense Act and has called for comment from a wide variety of organizations. A discussion document has been prepared dealing, *inter alia*, with the present restrictions contained in the Defense Act.[62]

The discussion document suggests that section 101 of the Defense Act, dealing with the imposition of censorship, be scrapped. As far as section 118 of the Defense Act is concerned, the document suggests "sweeping changes" to make it compatible with the Constitution.[63]

---

[61] For an overview of the saga see *Freedom of Expression Institute Update* March/April 1997. The matter is still pending before the Pretoria High Court in Times Media & Others v. De Vos NO & Others Case No. 2814/97.

[62] Undated discussion document entitled "Input from Chief Directorate Communication: Analysis of the Defense Act With a View to Changing It".

[63] The proposed new text provides:

(1) No person shall publish in any newspaper, magazine, book or pamphlet or by any other means any classified information relating to -

(a) The maintenance and protection of state security and national strategic intelligence;

(b) The general protection of all international interests of a state;

(c) All information pertaining to military operational matters, the disclosure of which may endanger lives or jeopardise national military capabilities;

The discussion document concludes:

It is clear that in times of war or during a state of emergency it is necessary to have exemptions written into the Constitution, in the sense that a person's human rights should, when necessary, be suspended during such times. Such a provision already exists concerning a state of emergency but not with regard to a state of

---

except if in the judgment of the Minister the disclosure of such information is necessary for the exercise of any constitutionally designated human right of any person.

(2) If a dispute should develop about whether such information is needed for the exercise of any persons constitutionally designated human right, the matter should be referred to the Constitutional Court, the judgment of which will be considered final.

(3) The Minister will be obliged to disclose any information which does not fall into the abovementioned categories (a), (b) and (c) except in case of a state of emergency (insofar as these are deemed necessary for the restoration of peace or order) or during a state of national defense as declared by the President.

(4) Any proprietor, printer, publisher or editor of any newspaper, magazine, book or pamphlet in which any such information as aforesaid is published or broadcasted and any person responsible for the publication of such information by such or any other means, shall be guilty of an offence, and proceedings in respect thereof may be taken against all or any of such persons.

(5) Any person who unlawfully discloses to any other person any classified information relating to the defense of the Republic which came to his or her knowledge under all conditions of restriction mentioned in sub-sections (1) and (3) by reason of his membership of the South African National Defense Force or by reason of his employment in the public service of the Republic or in any other office, post, appointment or capacity under the government by reason of any contract relating to the defense of the Republic or any employment by a contract relating to the defense of the Republic or any employment by a contractor under such a contract, or which was given to him in confidence by any person who was authorised or whose duty it was to give him such information, shall be guilty of an offence, unless such disclosure was authorised by the Minister or under his authority under the conditions mentioned in sub-sections (1) and (3), or by order of a competent court under the conditions authorised in sub-sections (1) and (3) or it was the duty of such person in the interests of the state to disclose such information to such other person.

national defense (war). An attempt could be made to negotiate this.

The document also recommends that there be certain categories of information which ought to be protected from disclosure. These include information "that pertains to the maintenance and protection of State security and national strategic intelligence", as well as "all information regarding military operational matters, the disclosure of which may either endanger lives or detract from the SANDF's constitutionally designated responsibility of service in the interest of protecting lives and property" and "all information pertaining to the international interests of a State.

Whether or not the envisaged changes to the Defense Act are compatible with the demands of the Constitution is doubtful. The central philosophy underlying the proposed amendments is still one of official secrecy subject to discretionary disclosure. What is significant, however, is the apparent willingness of the government to openly discuss issues which were previously simply kept from public view.[64] Amendments to the Defense Act in isolation will not be sufficient to meet the demands of openness required by the Constitution. A complete review of the many statutes containing limitations on the freedom of expression is required.

---

[64] The government has recently released a White Paper on national defense in which proposals for a new defense policy are discussed. ("Defense in a Democracy," *White Paper on National Defense for the Republic of South Africa* May 1996). The document acknowledges that transformation of the Defense Force is essential due to the advent of democracy. It suggests that "defense policy and military activities shall be sufficiently transparent to enable meaningful parliamentary and public scrutiny and debate insofar as this does not endanger the lives of military personnel or jeopardize the success of military operations." As far as secrecy is concerned, it states : "Parliamentary and public scrutiny and debate will only be meaningful if there is sufficient transparency on military matters. A measure of secrecy will undoubtedly be necessary in order to safeguard national security interests, the lives of military personnel and the integrity of military operations. However, the governing constitutional principle is 'freedom of information'. Exceptions to this principle will be limited, specific and justifiable in a democratic society, and will be dealt with in legislation." The White Paper further states that the Department of Defense "recognizes that it has a positive duty to provide sufficient information to ensure adequate parliamentary and public scrutiny and debate on defense matters.".

B. Censorship

A Task Group appointed to investigate the system of censorship expressly recommended that there should be no provision in any new statute to facilitate the banning of publications on grounds of state security. The report stated:

> In spite of a substantially liberal approach by the structures under the Publications Act up to 2 February 1990, and the constant unbanning of publications by committees after that date, we believe that criminal law, applied with sensitivity and understanding for freedom of political speech, is the only measure which should be applicable when the State proves beyond a reasonable doubt that there exists a clear and present danger that State security would be endangered by a publication or film distributed with the purpose of endangering that security.
> A survey of judgments of the Publications Appeal Board during the 1980s also reveals that there was seldom, if ever, evidence beyond a reasonable doubt that a film or publication would lead or contribute to, for example, a riot or terrorism. ... Political speech lies at the very heart of democracy and to stifle it under a new Act would conflict with the idea of a symbolic and 'historical bridge' between the past and a 'future founded on the recognition of human rights' as expressed in the coda to the Constitution of the Republic of South Africa.[65]

The Task Group's recommendations concerning censorship on grounds of national security were accepted.[66]

C. Access to Information

There are currently proposals for a statute intended to facilitate access to official information.[67] While the proposed measure recognizes exemptions in the interests of state security, its central philosophy is one of access to information and

---

[65] Report of the Task Group: Film and Publication Control, 63-64 para 8.4.8 (Dec. 1994). The statement in the report is particularly remarkable given the fact that the Chairman of the Task Group, Professor J. C. W. Van Rooyen, was the chairman of the Publications Appeal Board between 1980 and 1990. Although under his chairmanship, the approach of the Publications Appeal Board was considered to be liberal, there were nevertheless instances in which he confirmed the prohibition of publications on grounds of State security.

[66] The principal recommendations are embodied in the new Films and Publications Act 65 of 1996. The new Act has not yet come into operation.

[67] The proposals are contained in the Draft Open Democracy Bill published in Government Gazette 18381 of 18 October, 1997.

not secrecy.[68] The recommendations contained in the draft bill are extremely far-reaching. If enacted, radical amendments to a wide range of existing statutes which restrict access to information would have to be effected.

---

[68] In section 37 of the draft Bill, the exemption in the interests of defense and security is framed as follows:

34(1) The information officer of a governmental body may refuse a request for access to a record of the body if its disclosure would be likely substantially to harm the national defense or security of the Republic by -

(a) frustrating any measure for the prevention, detection or suppression of -

(i) aggression against the Republic;

(ii) sabotage or terrorism aimed at the people of the Republic or a strategic asset of the Republic, whether inside or outside the Republic; or

(iii) an activity aimed at changing the constitutional order of the Republic by the use of force or violence; or

(iv) a foreign or hostile intelligence operation;

(b) Jeopardizing the effectiveness of a governmental body, branch of that body or person responsible for the prevention, detection or suppression of an activity contemplated in sub-paragraph (a) (i), (ii), (iii) or (iv) of paragraph (a) by disclosing its or his or her capabilities, deployment or performance;

(c) jeopardizing the effectiveness of -

(i) arms; or

(ii) other equipment, including communication or cryptographic systems,

used or intended to be used or being developed, designed, produced or investigated for preventing, detecting or suppressing an activity contemplated in sub-paragraph (a) (i), (ii), (iii) or (iv) of paragraph (a) by disclosing their or its capabilities, quantity, deployment or performance; or

(d) jeopardizing the effectiveness of methods or equipment for collecting, assessing or handling information used for the prevention, detection or suppression of an activity contemplated in sub-paragraph (i), (ii) or (iii) of paragraph (a) (i), (ii), (iii) or (iv), or disclosing the identity of a confidential source of information used for that purpose.

D. Accounting for the Past

The Promotion of National Unity and Reconciliation Act[69] has as its object, "the investigation and the establishment of as complete a picture as possible of the nature, causes and extent of gross violations of human rights committed during the period from 1 March 1960 to the cut-off date contemplated in the Constitution, within or outside the Republic, emanating from the conflicts of the past, and the fate or whereabouts of the victims of such violations."[70] Although the Truth and Reconciliation Commission established by the Act has been concerned primarily with events of the past, it has already succeeded in bringing to light some of the covert activities of the security forces.[71]

VI. Conclusion

Legislative reform is essential if South African is to transcend its long history of official secrecy. Legislative reform, however, will not itself be sufficient. A political commitment to openness and accountability is also required. The judiciary

---

[69] Act 34 of 1995.

[70] This statute was passed pursuant to the obligations in the postscript to the interim Constitution entitled "National Unity and Reconciliation" which provides that, "in order to advance such reconciliation and reconstruction, amnesty shall be granted in respect of acts, omissions and offences associated with political objectives and committed in the course of the conflicts of the past. To this end, Parliament under this Constitution shall adopt a law determining a firm cut-off date, which shall be a date after October 8, 1990 and before December 6, 1993 and providing for the mechanisms, criteria and procedures, including tribunals, if any, through which such amnesty shall be dealt with at any time after the law has been passed."

[71] The evidence emerging from the hearings before the Truth and Reconciliation Commission presents a horrifying picture of State sanctioned "hit squads" which conducted a campaign of murder, torture and terrorism against anti-apartheid activitists. The Truth and Reconciliation Commission will present its findings in a written report during the course of 1998.

will also have to play its part. There are some signs that the Courts, now the guardians of the Constitution, will give full effect to the guarantee of freedom of expression and access to information.[72]

[72] In the realm of freedom of expression, there have already been some significant judgments. *See, in particular*, Government of the Republic of South Africa v. Sunday Times Newspaper & Ano. 1995 (2) SA 221 (T) in which the court declared a regulation promulgated in terms of the Commissions Act 8 of 1947 to be unconstitutional as a violation of the guarantee of freedom of expression in that it impermissibly prohibited publication of the report of an official Commission of Inquiry. The Court was influenced in its reasoning by the United States jurisprudence on prior restraint in cases such as New York Times Co v. United States 29 L Ed (2d) 822 and Near v. Minnesota 75 L Ed 1357. *See also*, Holomisa v. Argus Newspapers Ltd. 1996 (2) S.A. 588 (W) in which Cameron J. articulates the importance of freedom of expression in a democracy. There are, however, decisions dealing with the common law of defamation in which the courts have held that the guarantee of freedom of expression has not brought about any change to this area of law. *See* Bogoshi v. National Media Ltd. & Others 1996 (3) SA. 78 (W) and Potgieter v. Kilian 1996 (2) S.A. 276 (N).

FREEDOM OF EXPRESSION AND NATIONAL SECURITY IN SOUTH KOREA

Kyo Ho Youm

I. Introduction

The uniqueness of South Korea as a divided nation confronting the ever belligerent North Korean communists across the Demilitarized Zone (DMZ) explains in part why national security has been a primary interest in the hierarchy of sociopolitical values in the country since the Korean War of 1950-53.[1] Not surprisingly, the Korean government has in varying degrees restricted freedom of expression on the ground that it should be reconciled with the national security emergencies facing the Asian country.

Nevertheless, national security cannot be used as a *carte blanche* for the Korean government in limiting the constitutionally guaranteed freedom of speech and the press at the slightest threat — real or imagined. Given that "[t]he true condition of a country's freedom can best be seen by stripping away the legal jargon and focusing on the actual balance it has struck between liberty and security,"[2] the national security interests of the Korean government should be strictly scrutinized whenever they are presented as a possible justification for restricting freedom of expression.

In balancing national security with freedom of expression in a democracy, the role of the independent judiciary is crucial. As journalism scholar Dennis Wilcox stated: "[A] national press is free, not necessarily because of constitutional guarantees, but because an unintimidated judiciary protects the press against government encroachment."[3] This observation, of course, presupposes a functioning checks-and-balances structure of government, which ensures the independence of the judicial branch from the other two branches — executive and legislative.

On the premise that "[t]he establishment of an institution is one thing, yet its efficient operation is another,"[4] this chapter examines the statutory and judicial framework on freedom of expression and national security in South Korea.

---

[1] Rodney P. Katz, "National Security," *in* Andrea Matles Savada & William Shaw eds., *South Korea: A Country Study*, 303 (4th ed. 1992).
[2] Alan M. Dershowitz, "The Role of Law During Times of Crisis: Would Liberty Be Suspended?", *in Criminal Law Theory and Process* 1207 (Joseph Goldstein et al. eds. 1974).
[3] Dennis L. Wilcox, "Black African States," *in Press Control Around the World* 222 (Jane Leftwich Curry & Joan R. Dassin eds. 1982).
[4] Dae-Kyu Yoon, *Law and Political Authority in South Korea* at170 (1990).

II. Access to and Disclosure of Information

A. Access to Information and Restrictions on National Security Grounds.

The Constitution Court addressed the question of access to information as a right in a 1989 case. That case had resulted from the refusal of a county office to grant the petitioner access to public records relating to the title to a forest and other real estate.[5] The Court, while conceding that the right to know was not absolute and might be regulated in the public interest,[6] held that there should be a concrete legal standard to balance the public interest against individual harm caused by such a regulation.[7] The Court enunciated the following standard for access to government information:

> The right to know should be broadly accepted if the requester is concerned with the requested information and the release of the information is not harmful to public interests. We are of the opinion that it is indisputable that public information must be mandatorily released to those who have a direct interest in it.[8]

In applying this standard to the case, the Court held that the documents in question should have been made available to the petitioner, for they were not classified secrets. The disclosure of the documents would not invade the privacy rights of others. Furthermore, no other law barred the release of the documents.[9]

In May 1991, the Constitution Court again ruled on the right to know. This case arose when a prosecutor's office refused to allow a petitioner in a defamation trial to copy the court records in his case.[10] The petitioner claimed that the refusal violated his right to know as guaranteed by the Constitution.[11] In response, the Constitution Court stated that freedom of speech and the press is made possible by a sufficient guarantee of access to information. The Court drew upon the United Nations Universal Declaration of Human Rights of 1948[12] as well as the

---

[5] 88 Honma 22, Constitution Court, Sept. 4, 1989, *Official Gazette* (Korean), Oct. 6, 1989, at 50 (*hereinafter* Right to Know Judgment).
[6] *Id.* at 55.
[7] *Id.*
[8] *Id.*
[9] *Id.*
[10] 90 Honma 133, Constitution Court, May 13, 1991, 3 *Constitution Court Case Report* (Korean) 234, 237-38 (1992).
[11] *Id.* at 238.
[12] *Id.* The United Nations Universal Declaration of Human Rights states: "Everyone has the right to freedom of opinion and expression; this right includes freedom to hold opinions without interference and to seek, receive and impart information and ideas through any media and regardless of frontiers." Universal Declaration of Human Rights, G.A. Res. 2174 (III) U.N. GAOR, art. 19, U.N. Doc.A/810 (1948).

Constitution for its conclusion that the right to know is "naturally included in the freedom of expression."[13] And under the Court's analysis, the essence of the right to know lies in the "people's right to know about information in the possession of the government."[14]

The Court also considered the "right to liberty" and a "right to petition" under the Constitution as aspects of the right to know. The "liberty" aspect, the Court said, meant "not to be impeded by the government in obtaining access to, collecting, and using information."[15] The "petition" aspect, the Court continued, is the right to petition the government to eliminate restrictions on informational access.[16]

The Court held that, if release of the requested documents "would not conflict with the fundamental rights of those concerned or violate the national security, maintenance of law and order, and public welfare interest," disclosure of the documents would be a "faithful" execution of the government's duty to guarantee this basic right of its citizens.[17] The Court also brought the right to know within the sphere of "the right of life" as modern society changes to a "high-information society."[18] The Court based the right to know on the premise that the quality of life in an information-oriented society would be greatly diminished without access to information.

In February 1992, the Constitution Court reviewed the Military Secrets Protection Act of 1972.[19] The Military Secrets Protection Act[20] was being challenged as overly vague. Those questioning the validity of the Act had been charged with violating the law by releasing a classified report on national defense.[21] They claimed that the statute, which proscribed the unauthorized gathering and the intentional and negligent disclosure of military secrets, infringed upon their constitutional right to free speech and free press.

The Court upheld the Act insofar as its application is confined to the disclosure of unpublicized military secrets "which are duly marked as classified

---

[13] *Id.* at 246.
[14] *Id.*
[15] *Id.*
[16] *Id.*
[17] *Id.* at 249. The Constitution Court reasoned that the duty of the State to comply with the request for access to governmental information by way of freedom of expression, i.e., right to know, was derived from Article 10 of the Constitution, which states in part: "It shall be the duty of the State to confirm and guarantee the fundamental and inviolable human rights of individuals."
[18] *Id.*
[19] 98 Honga 104, Constitution Court, Feb. 25, 1992, *Domestic & Foreign Legal News* (Korean), July 15, 1992, at 5 (hereinafter Military Secrets Protection Act Judgment).
[20] Law No. 2387 (1972), revised by Law No. 3492 (1981), *reprinted in Compendium of Codes* (Korean) 2265-66 (1991).
[21] Military Secrets Protection Act Judgment, *supra* note 19 at 5.

military information in accordance with a legal procedure and which are substantially valuable enough to create a clear danger to national security, if disclosed."[22] The Court declared that dissemination of information known to ordinary people with average knowledge and experience could not be a violation of the Act.[23]

In balancing the public's right to know against national security interests, the Constitution Court noted that "national security, the maintenance of law and order or . . . public welfare" may form the basis for exceptions to basic freedoms and rights unless the restrictions violate the "essential aspect" of these freedoms or rights.[24] The Court went on to recognize the inhibitive effect of ill-defined military secrets protections on press and academic freedom.[25] The overzealous protection of military secrets, the Court warned, would contravene the right to know, which the Court had recognized as an element of speech and press freedom in earlier cases.[26]

The right to know, the Court proclaimed, is necessary to a democratic society for the promotion of individual and social values such as self-fulfillment, the search for truth, participation in political decision-making, and balancing between stability and change.[27] Further, the Court called attention to the "checking value" of the right to know in making the government responsive to people.[28] These higher values of freedom of the press and speech led the Court to conclude that "the boundary of military secrets should be as minimal as necessary to extend the parameters of people's freedom of expression or 'right to know' to a maximum possible degree."[29]

The Military Secrets Protection Act was completely revised by the National Assembly in December 1993.[30] The new statute is a significant improvement of the old one in that it defines military secrets in less broad terms and newly recognizes the

---

[22] *Id.* at 12.
[23] *Id.*
[24] *Id.* at 9.
[25] *Id.* at 10.
[26] *See* Right to Know Judgment, *supra* at note 50.
[27] Military Secrets Protection Act Judgment, *supra* note 19 at 11. While the Constitution Court provides no citation, its discussion of the right-to-know related values, i.e., freedom of the press and speech, is strikingly identical to the values that the late Professor Thomas Emerson of Yale Law School identified with the freedom of expression. *See* Thomas I. Emerson, *Toward a General Theory of the First Amendment* 3-15 (1966).
[28] *Id.* Although Vincent Blasi looked at the "checking value" theory on freedom of the press in the United States as an institutional concept, *see* Vincent Blasi, "The Checking Value in First Amendment Theory," *American Bar Foundation Journal* 521-649 (1977), the Constitution Court is broader than Blasi's in its view of the right to know in Korea. The Court has noted the individual and social value of the right to know, in addition to the institutional "watchdog" notion.
[29] *Id.*
[30] *See* Military Secrets Protection Act, Law No. 4616 (1993), *reprinted in Compendium of Codes* (Korean) 2552-53 (1994).

public interest in getting access to military secrets. For example, Article 2 of the revised statute defines "military secrets" as "military documents, books, electronic records . . . which are unknown to the public and whose contents, if disclosed, would bring about a clear danger to the security of the State, and which have been marked or known as military secrets and for whose protection special measures have been taken."[31] The public's right to know about the military secrets is stipulated by the law. Individuals may request the Minister of Defense in writing for release of military secrets.[32] Military secrets may be disclosed "when it is needed to inform the public or when it is deemed to be clearly in the interest of national security."[33] They may also be provided or explained to research institutes if requested for technological development and academic research.[34]

B. Disclosures by Government Agents or Employees

A Seoul district court in September 1993 recognized the "people's right to know" as a possible justification for blowing the whistle on government wrongdoing. In *State* v. *Yi Mun-ok*,[35] an inspector of the Board of Audit and Inspection of the Korean government was accused of violating the Criminal Code[36] by revealing to a Korean newspaper a secret internal report on real estate owned by business conglomerates.[37]

The Seoul Criminal District Court asserted that the report released by Yi Mun-ok was neither classified as secret by law nor treated as a secret for political, military, or economic purposes.[38] The court noted that a document, which has never been classified as secret and whose contents do not fall within the boundaries of "substantial secrets," cannot become an official secret under the Criminal Code

---

[31] *Id.*, art. 2. *Compare with* Military Secrets Act, art. 2 (1981) (defining "military secrets" as information "which, if disclosed, will create a harmful consequence for the national security").
[32] *Id.* at art. 9.
[33] *Id.* at art. 7.
[34] *Id.* at art. 8.
[35] 90 Kodan 3615, Seoul Criminal District Court, Sept. 6, 1993, *slip opinion* (Korean).
[36] The Criminal Code prohibits disclosure of official secrets. Article 127 states: "A public official or former public official who divulges official secrets obtained in the course of performing his duties and classified by law as secret shall be punished by penal servitude or imprisonment for not more than two years or suspension of qualifications for not more than five years." Criminal Code, Law No. 293 (1953), revised by Law No. 4040 (1988), art. 127, *translated in* 2 *Current Laws of the Republic of Korea* 761-812 (1995) (hereinafter *ROK Current Laws*).
[37] *Yi Mun-ok*, *supra* note 35 at 2-3.
[38] *Id.* at 3-4.

merely because the document is being internally processed by an administrative agency.[39]

The Seoul district court stated that Yi's disclosure of the report did not affect public confidence in the government, nor did it undermine the credibility of the business groups involved. The court reasoned:

> Judging from the *people's right to know*, the alleged state interest in keeping the report from the public did not stem from the objective and general interest of the government, administrative agencies, or the public. Rather, it was derived from the subjective and peculiar perspectives of the banking supervisor or the businesses on the report.[40]

The Seoul court's ruling on "whistleblowing" in the context of the right to know constitutes an expansive reading of press freedom, especially given the fact that Korea provides no legal protection for "whistleblowers" as does the United States.[41]

III. News Media

A. Restrictions on News Gathering and Publishing During Peacetime.

South Korea has emerged as one of the most democratic Asian nations in the sense of participatory politics since 1987,[42] when the Korean government launched a series of sweeping sociopolitical and legal reforms. One Korean newspaper publisher argued: "Before democracy was restored in 1987, newspapers were suppressed by authoritarian regimes. Freedom of the press was almost completely lost. Today, the Korean press enjoys an unprecedented amount of freedom, which is the most crucial element of democracy."[43]

---

[39] *Id.* at 3. The Seoul district court gave the following definition of "official secrets":

> Official secrets under law are not necessarily limited to those statutorily designated secrets. Also included among the secrets is the information that is kept secret for political, military, economic, or social necessities, and also the information the government, administrative offices, or the general public has a considerable interest in keeping confidential from an objective and general perspective.

Id. (citing 89 To 2822, Supreme Court, June 22, 1982).

[40] *Id.* at 5 (emphasis added).

[41] *See, e.g.*, 5 U.S.C. sec. 2302(b)(8)(1993).

[42] Charles Graybow, "Asia: Democracy or Development . . . or both?," *Freedom Review* 58 (1995).

[43] Sang Hoon Bang, The Korean Press: New Challenges in a Changing World (1992) (speech delivered at the International Press Institute convention in Budapest, Hungary) (text on file with author).

Freedom of the press in a democratized Korea, however, is restricted for actual or perceived national security interests. The 1995 human rights report of the U.S. Department of State pointed out the South Korean government's limitation of the expression of ideas that the government views as communist or pro-North Korea.[44]

The Korean Constitution contains a provision that empowers the government to restrict all constitutional guarantees including freedom of the press. Article 37 states: "The freedoms and rights of citizens may be restricted by law only when necessary for national security, the maintenance of law and order or of public welfare."[45] In accordance with the constitutional provision for the legislative power of the government, the Korean government has enacted and enforced a number of laws and regulations restrictive of freedom of speech and the press.[46] Some of the laws and regulations have directly dealt with freedom of the press. The Act on Registration of Periodical (Periodicals Act),[47] the Broadcast Act,[48] and the Act on Import and Distribution of Foreign Periodicals (Foreign Periodicals Act)[49] are cases in point. Others bear on the press in an indirect way.

The Periodicals Act enumerates several conditions for which the Ministry of Public Information (MOPI) can use its suspending authority,[50] but none of them directly relates to national security interests. The statute, however, prohibits anyone who is subject to punishment under the National Security Act and other specified laws from being a publisher or editor of a periodical. The broadcast law is identical to the Periodicals Act in its disqualification provisions which enumerate certain individuals who are not eligible to be the "head or person in charge of programming" of a broadcasting station.[51]

Under the Foreign Periodicals Act, the Ministry of Culture and Sports can take comprehensive measures against foreign periodicals which the Korean government finds may "subvert the constitutional system of the State or undermine

---

[44] U.S. Department of State,"South Korea," *in Country Reports on Human Rights Practices for 1994*, at 624 (1995).

[45] Constitution, amended in 1987, art. 37(2), *translated in* 1 *ROK Current Laws*, *supra* note 36 at 1-24.

[46] *S ee Complete Collection of Korean Press Laws, 1945-1981* (Korean) 2-3 (Chong Chin-sok ed., 1982) (noting that more than 360 laws and regulations relating to the Korean press were enforced between 1945, when Korea was liberated from its Japanese colonial rule, and 1982) (hereinafter *Korean Press Laws*).

[47] Law No. 3979 (1987), revised by Law No. 5145 (1995), *translated in The Korean Press 1997*, at 139-52 (1997).

[48] Law No. 3978 (1987) revised by Law No. 5145 (1995), *translated in The Korean Press 1997*, *supra* note 47 at 178-91.

[49] Law No. 4688 (1993), *reprinted in Compendium of Codes* (Korean) 2941-42 (1994).

[50] *See* Periodicals Act, art. 12(1), (2).

[51] Broadcast Act, art. 9.

the public security and customs" of Korea.[52] The government can order them suspended from sale or their contents deleted,[53] and retract the permit for distribution of the periodicals.[54]

Numerous restrictive special laws and regulations combined with the traditionally authoritarian political culture had undoubtedly contributed to constraining press freedom in South Korea until recent years. Before 1987, the ruling authorities had long employed the repressive laws to perpetuate a cowed press. Typical of the special laws are the National Security Act[55] and the now abolished Anti-Communist Act.[56]

When the National Security Act was first enacted in 1948,[57] it was directed at "anti-State activities" posing a danger to the national security of Korea and thus was intended to ensure the security of the State and the freedom of citizens. The law, however, was used by the Korean government "not only against espionage or sabotage, but also to control and punish domestic dissent, such as the publication of unorthodox political commentary, art, or literature, on the ground that such expressions benefitted an 'antistate organization.'"[58] More often than not, the law had been employed by past governments to protect "political security" interests.[59]

The Anti-Communist Act, another special law relating to national security in Korea, was enacted shortly after the military coup d'etat led by General Park Chung Hee in 1961. It was "[p]erhaps the single most important law in terms of its widespread political effect" and "perhaps the greatest articulated threat to the educated groups."[60] The law provided for hard labor for up to seven years for any person who praised, encouraged or sided with or "through other means" the activities

---

[52] Foreign Periodicals Act, arts. 7, 8.
[53] *Id.*, art. 7.
[54] *Id.*, art. 8.
[55] Law No. 3318 (1980), revised by Law No. 4373 (1991), *translated in* 3 *Laws of the Republic of Korea* X-64 to X-70-1 (4th ed. 1995) (hereinafter *ROK Laws*).
[56] Law No. 643 (1961), revised by Law No. 1997 (1968), *translated in Laws of the Republic of Korea* 776-80 (3d ed. 1975). The Anti-Communist Act was repealed by the National Security Act in 1980.
[57] Law No. 10 (1948), *reprinted in* Pak Won-sun, 1 *Study of National Security Laws* (Korean) at 227 (1989).
[58] William Shaw, "Government and Politics," *in South Korea: A Country Study*, *supra* note 1 at 245. For an excellent discussion of the National Security Act, *see* Kuk Cho, "Tension Between the National Security Act and Constitutionalism in South Korea: Security for What?", 15 *B.U.Int'l L.J.* 125 (1997).
[59] *See* Yi Pom-yol, "National Security Act Abused for Political Security," *Shin Dong-A* (Korean) 262-68, March 1988. *See also* Jerome Alan Cohen & Edward J. Baker, "U.S. Foreign Policy and Human Rights in South Korea," *in* William Shaw ed., *Human Rights in Korea: Historical and Policy Perspectives* 184-85 (1991).
[60] David I. Steinberg, "Law, Development and Korean Society," *in* Sang Hyun Song ed., *Introduction to the Law and Legal System of Korea* 61 (1983).

of anti-State organizations or their members or foreign communist organizations.[61] "The only requirement for conviction under the Anti-Communist Law," U.S. critics asserted, "was that the conduct in question be deemed to have benefitted an anti-state organization. No subjective intention on the part of the actor to aid such an organization need be proved."[62]

As compared with pre-1980 cases, only a few National Security Act cases have involved the Korean press since 1980. Noting the chilling impact of the National Security Act on the Korean press over the years, *Chosun Ilbo* publisher Sang Hoon Bang stated:

> [T]he existence of the National Security Law can still restrict the freedom of thought and press in Korea. The National Security Law is a product of the Cold War, when South Korean communists were punished by that Law. In recent years, however, the National Security Law has been severely criticized for being abused to limit individual freedom. Accordingly, the Law was revised after the democratization [of 1987] and does not have its restrictive power as before.[63]

Yi Yong-hi, an editorial advisor to the left-of-center *Han-Kyoreh Shinmun* (One-Nation Newspaper) was arrested for attempting a secret visit to North Korea to interview President Kim Il Sung in April 1989, and was charged with a criminal act under the National Security Act of 1980.[64] A single-judge Seoul criminal district court in *State* v. *Yi Yong-hi*[65] in September 1989 had sentenced Yi to a suspended prison term. Yi, in an appeal to the three-judge appellate panel of the Seoul criminal district court, claimed that the government had infringed on press freedom, adding that his attempt to visit North Korea for a journalistic purpose did not constitute a violation of the National Security Act.[66] In February 1993, the appellate panel rejected Yi's argument, reasoning that freedom of the press, though constitutionally protected, must be balanced against other constitutional provisions.[67] In affirming the initial ruling, the panel stated: "The accused's planned trip (to North Korea) might have jeopardized our national security if it had been exploited by the North

---

[61] Anti-Communist Act, art. 4(1).

[62] Cohen & Baker, *supra* note 59 at 184.

[63] Bang, *supra* note 43. *See also* Yoon, *supra* note 4 at 172 (noting that the Anti-Communist Act and the National Security Act "have inevitably placed some restriction on civil liberties, especially freedom of expression. Alleging that the government authorities have reacted excessively to violations of these laws, their constitutionality has been repeatedly challenged").

[64] *See Human Rights in Korea: Facts and Fiction*, *supra* note 59 at 32-33.

[65] 89 Kodan 3509, Seoul Criminal District Court, Sept. 25, 1989, *slip opinion* (Korean). Yi had already spent 160 days in jail since his arrest. Chin Sok Chong, "The South Korean Press," *in* Donald N. Clark ed., *Korea Briefing, 1992*, at 139 (1992).

[66] *Yi Yong-hi* v. *State*, 89 No 5990, Seoul Criminal District Court, Feb. 2, 1993, *slip opinion* (Korean).

[67] *Id.* at 3-4.

Korean government as an opportunity to publicize its position (on South Korea) abroad or if it had created chaos in our North Korea policy by causing disorderly visits to North Korea."[68]

Another press freedom case was *State* v. *Kim Tae-hong*,[69] widely known as the *Mahl* (Word) case. The *Mahl* case, which attracted considerable attention from both in Korea and abroad, resulted from the 1986 publication of *Mahl* magazine of Korean government's detailed press guidelines.[70] The underground magazine, published by the Council for Democratic Press Movement (CDPM) in Seoul, an association of banned journalists in Korea, published the texts of hundreds of daily press guidelines issued by the Ministry of Culture and Information between Oct. 19, 1985, and Aug. 8, 1986. In December 1986, three months after the publication in *Mahl* of the politically embarrassing press guidelines, the authorities arrested two CDPM officials alleged to have been involved in the publication and also a journalist said to have leaked the guidelines to the CDPM for violating the National Security Act of 1980.

On June 3, 1987, Judge Pak Tae-bom of the Seoul Criminal District Court sentenced the two of the defendants to suspended prison terms and set aside a penalty for the third. In finding two defendants guilty of violating the National Security Act, Judge Pak held that they knowingly possessed the prohibited "subversive" books espousing the revolutionary ideology of North Korea.[71] The judge stated, however, that the defendants were motivated by their "interest in the reality and development" of the South Korean press and thus deserved another opportunity to contribute to society.[72]

The three-judge appellate panel of the Seoul Criminal District Court in July 1994 reversed Judge Pak's decision.[73] The appellate panel relied on the "clear and present danger" doctrine for rejecting application of the National Security Act of 1980. The Court stated: "In order to punish the defendants under the National Security Act, the books in the possession of the defendants must create a *clear danger* that their contents will threaten the existence and security of the State and will bring about a substantive harm to the basic order of free democracy."[74] The court continued that "if the contents of the books do not cause a substantive harm to the existence and security of the State or to the basic order of free democracy, or if it is

---

[68] *Id.* at 4.

[69] 87 Kodan 503, Seoul Criminal District Court, June 3, 1987, *Press Guidelines* (Korean) 230-39 (Council for Democratic Press Movement ed., 1988).

[70] For a detailed discussion of the press guidelines issued by the Korean government under President Chun Doo Hwan in 1980-87, *see* Kyu Ho Youm, *Press Law in South Korea* (1996).

[71] *Kim Tae-hong*, Seoul Criminal District Court, *Press Guidelines* (Korean), *supra* note 69 at 237.

[72] *Id.* at 229.

[73] *Kim Tae-hong* v. *State*, 88 No. 781, Seoul Criminal District, July 5, 1994, *slip opinion* (Korean).

[74] *Id.* at 8 (emphasis added).

not clear whether they are doing the harm, the defendants cannot be punished" under the law.[75] The court argued that it was "difficult to conclude that the books, read as a whole, create the kind of 'clear danger' as defined previously."[76]

B. Restrictions During Armed Conflicts

Military censorship is imposed on the Korean press in time of war, as it was during the Korean War in 1950-53. The Korean Constitution accords the President the power to take necessary measures to maintain national security "in times of internal turmoil, external menace."[77] Article 77 of the Constitution provides the President with the power to proclaim martial law, when it is necessary to "maintain the public safety and order by mobilization of the military forces in time of war, armed conflict or similar national emergency."[78] Under extraordinary martial law, special measures may be taken to restrict freedom of expression. The special law authorizes the martial law commander, who is appointed by the President, "to take special measures with regard to . . . the press."[79]

The martial law clause of the Constitution had been frequently used by the Korean government prior to 1987 to suppress both political freedoms and civil liberties. For example, during the 1970s, the Park Chung Hee regime often resorted to emergency measures and martial law as all-purpose weapons to prevent the press from criticizing the government or reporting any dissidence.[80]

Just before Park initiated the much criticized "Revitalizing Reforms" in October 1972, the government issued Martial Law Decree No. 1, which banned "all indoor and outdoor demonstrations for the purpose of political activities" and made

---

[75] *Id.* at 9. *See also Choe Un-yong* v. *State*, 92 No 633, Seoul Criminal District Court, Aug. 5, 1992, 2 *Lower Court Decisions* (Korean) 449-60 (1992).
[76] *Id.* at 10.
[77] Constitution, art. 76.
[78] *Id.* art. 77(1).
[79] Martial Law, Law No. 3442 (1981), art. 9(1), *translated in* 1 *ROK Laws*, *supra* note 55 at II-154 to II-156. The Martial Law describes the circumstances under which the President shall enforce the extraordinary measure of martial law:

> [E]ither to cope with the military needs or to maintain the public safety and order, in time of war, state of siege, or similar national emergency under which the functioning of the Administrative and Judiciary branches of the government is deemed conspicuously difficult under the state of either armed conflict with the enemy or the extreme disturbance of social order.

Id. art. 2(2).
[80] For a discussion of the emergency measures and martial law enforced by President Park Chung Hee, *see* Hak-Kyu Sohn, *Authoritarianism and Opposition in South Korea* (1989).

"speeches, publications, press and broadcasts" subject to censorship.[81] The policy guidelines of the government under this decree were more draconian. Under the guidelines, a news blackout was forced on:

1. Any article that distorts, defames or instigates against the purpose of the Declaration of the State of National Emergency of Oct. 17, 1972;
2. Any article that misleads the public by inciting on the public opinion and sentiments;
3. Any article that is detrimental to ensuring the security of society;
4. Any article that deals with military information;
5. Any article that undermines the morale of the military forces;
6 Any article that relates to the duties of the martial law authorities;
7. Any article that is harmful to the national interests.[82]

IV. Expression Deemed Threatening to National Security or Territorial Integrity

A. Advocacy of Conscientious Objection, Desertion or Giving Support to the Enemy.

The 1980 National Security Act, which incorporated various provisions of the Anti-Communist Act, provided:

> Any person who has benefitted the anti-State organization by praising, encouraging, or siding with or through other means the activities of the anti-State organizations or, their members or the person who had been under instruction from such organization, shall be punished by penal servitude for not more than seven years; Any person who has, for the purpose of committing (the above actions), produced, imported, duplicated, kept in custody, transported, disseminated, sold or acquired documents, drawings and any other similar means of expression shall be punished by the same penalty as set forth in each paragraph.[83]

The National Security Act was revised in May 1991 to "control anti-State activities which endanger the national security, so that the safety of the State as well as the existence and freedom of the citizens may be secured."[84] The 1991 revision of

---

[81] Martial Law Decree No. 1 (1972), *translated in Korea Times*, Oct. 18, 1972, at 1.

[82] "Matters Prohibited from Publicity Notice," *reprinted in Korean Press Laws*, *supra* note 46, at 787.

[83] National Security Act, Law No. 3318 (1980), art. 7(1), (5), *translated in* 3 ROK Laws, supra note 55, at X-64 to X-70.

[84] National Security Act (1991), art. 1(1).

the National Security Act was the Korean government's legislative action subsequent to the Constitution Court's qualified ruling[85] of 1990 on the constitutionality of Article 7 of the Act.[86] The revised National Security Act is designed to curb governmental abuse by requiring that the law's interpretation and application "be done within the necessary minimum for the accomplishment of the (law's) purpose . . . ."[87] Stipulating that the law "should not be interpreted excessively or should not limit unreasonably the human rights of citizens secured by the constitutional law,"[88] the Act mandates a narrow judicial interpretation.

Under the new National Security Act, "anti-State organization" is defined as "an association or group within the territory of the Republic of Korea or outside, organized for the purpose of assuming a title of the government or disturbing the State."[89] The revised provision does not penalize contact with communist organizations or governments in countries other than North Korea. The National Security Act of 1980 was also revised so that acts of praising, encouraging, publicizing, or showing sympathy for an anti-State organization will be punished only when committed with the knowledge that it will endanger national security and survival and the free and democratic basic order. Article 7 of the revised statute stipulates:

> (1) Any person who has, *with the knowledge* that he might endanger the existence, security of the State or the basic order of free democracy, praised or encouraged or propagandized or sided with the activities of an anti-State organization, its member or a person who had been under instruction from such organization, or who has propagandized or instigated a disturbance of the State, shall be punished by penal servitude for a term not exceeding seven years;
> (2) Deleted;
> (3) Any person who has organized an association which purports to commit the actions as stipulated in Paragraph 1 or has participated in such an association, shall be punished by penal servitude for not less than one year;
> (4) Any person who has, as a member of the association as mentioned in Paragraph 3, fabricated or disseminated false facts concerning such matters that might cause social disorder shall be punished by penal servitude for not less than two years;

---

[85] *See* Honga 113, Constitution Court, *Official Gazette* (Korean), May 1, 1990, at 27.

[86] "Reasons for Revision of the National Security Act," *Official Gazette* (Korean), May 31, 1991, at 20.

[87] National Security Act (1991), art. 1(2). For a discussion of several major provisions of the National Security Act, as revised in 1991, *see* Amnesty International, *South Korea: Prisoners Held for National Security Reasons* 6-8 (1991).

[88] National Security Act (1991), art. 1(2).

[89] *Id.*

> (5) Any person who has, for the purpose of committing the actions as stipulated in Paragraph 1, 3 or 4, produced, imported, duplicated, kept in custody, transported, disseminated, sold or acquired documents, drawings and other similar means of expression shall be punished by the same penalty as set forth in each paragraph.[90]

The current National Security Act further requires that punishment of acts of giving or receiving goods or money to or from a member of an anti-State organization, or communicating with a member of an anti-State organization or someone acting under its instructions, or escaping from or to the territory of an anti-State organization be based on proof of such knowledge.[91]

Before 1980, the Anti-Communist Act was often applied in national security cases. In *Chong Chae-in* v. *State*,[92] the Supreme Court refused to find the defendant's statement illegal under the Anti-Communist Act. In *Chong Chae-in*, the defendant, then a member of the opposition New Democratic party, denounced the ruling class in South Korea in the same way as a North Korean communist would do. He claimed that the government under President Park Chung Hee was characterized by three criminal elements — injustice and corruption, an attempt at establishing the generalissimo, and a scheme to destroy democracy once and for all. While admitting that some phrases used by the defendant were those frequently adopted by North Koreans in attacking South Korea, the Supreme Court held that this did not necessarily mean that the opposition politician attempted to serve the interests of the enemy in the North. The Court rejected the prosecutor's argument that the defendant advocated communism through his vociferous criticism of President Park and his government. The Court considered the defendant's purpose in making the criticism. The defendant wanted to emphasize the weaknesses of the ruling Democratic Republic party from the perspective of his opposition party, according to the Court.[93]

The Seoul Criminal District Court in *State* v. *So Min-ho*,[94] a 1972 Anti-Communist Act case, considered whether freedom of the press and speech would protect the campaign speech of a presidential candidate arguably beyond the established constitutional boundaries. At issue in the case was a speech by So, who proposed that the armed forces of North and South Korea be reduced in proportion to the population of the North and the South to lighten the enormous financial burden of military expenditures placed upon the people of the two Koreas. Given

---

[90] *Id.* at art 7(1) (emphasis added).

[91] *Id.* arts. 6, 8.

[92] 72 To 1730, Supreme Court, Sept. 26, 1972, 26(3) *Supreme Court Decisions* (Korean) 16-18 (1972).

[93] *Id.* at 17.

[94] 67 Ko 10961, Seoul Criminal District Court, Apr. 17, 1972, *Law Times* (Korean), May 1, 1972, at 6.

that North Korea participated in the armistice conference at Panmunjom and in the International Olympic Game, So also argued: "North Korea is recognized as a legitimate political entity by the world community. Thus, we have to recognize North Korea as such."[95]

The Seoul district court first related the Anti-Communist Act to the "clear and present danger" in applying the law:

> The freedom of speech clause of the Constitution does not allow an unlimited liberty. When . . . the contents of a statement pose a clear and present danger to our social order and public welfare, the freedom can be restricted by law. Article 4(1) of the Anti-Communist Act is one of those revised statutes to restrict a statement when it brings about a clear and present danger to the social order and public welfare.[96]

The Seoul district court then concluded:

> Although the speech in question was made by So in the capacity of a presidential candidate to express his political views, it creates a clear and present danger to social order in that it suggests that North Korea should be recognized as a legitimate sovereignty . . . . This apparently contributes to enhancing the international prestige of the puppet regime of North Korea.[97]

Korean courts often took into account the context of various anti-State statements in distinguishing illegal anti-State expressions from innocuous insults, epithets, name-calling, rhetorical hyperbole, invective or other verbal abuse. The Supreme Court in *State* v. *Chong Chae-yong*[98] examined the situation in which the defendant asserted that the law of South Korea was "worse than that of the communists." Noting that the statement was an intemperate comment by the outraged defendant on the way police treated him on suspicion of a traffic violation, the Court held:

> It might be far-fetched to conclude that the defendant made the statement as a way to mean, "The Commies' laws are really good." Assuming that they are the worst of its kind, the defendant made the statement in the course of expressing his strong feeling about the treatment he received from the police.[99]

In several cases, the Supreme Court held that the Anti-Communist Act would not apply to statements made under the influence of alcohol. *Chong Ui-yong*

---

[95] *Id.*
[96] *Id.*
[97] *Id.*
[98] 71 To 2022, Supreme Court, Dec. 28, 1971, 19(3) *Supreme Court Decisions* (Korean) 78-80 (1971).
[99] *Id.*, at 79.

v. *State*[100] involved a statement: "Our government does not do a job governing people as well as the North Korean government does." The Supreme Court said the statement was not meant to praise North Korea, since it was made by the defendant while arguing with other people at a drinking party. In a similar vein, the Court rejected the government assertion that the Anti-Communist Act would proscribe such statements as: "The Commies will not kill all of us (South Koreans) even when another Korean War breaks out"[101] and "It is impossible to make ends meet in South Korea no matter how hard you may work. Let's defect to North Korea, where your hard work pays well."[102] The Court stated that the defendants were drunken at the time of making the statements.[103]

While heated arguments and similar mitigating circumstances justified otherwise criminal statements under the Anti-Communist Act, several Supreme Court cases indicate that favorably reasoned comments on communism could be punishable as a violation of the act. The defendant in *State* v. *Yu Kap-chong*[104] claimed: "The Korean War resulted from the combined efforts of the Soviet Union and the United States." The Court, characterizing the defendant's remark as helpful to North Korea, ruled that the statement would benefit the propaganda of North Korea against the United States and South Korea.[105] In *Song Su-yong* v. *State*,[106] the defendant was alleged to have stated:

> The purpose of communism is bad. But its means are not bad. My Japanese books say so. Contrary to the general understanding that the scientific management technique discussed in the study of public administration originated from the United States, the truth is that it was first developed by the Soviet Union. The communists' scientific management technique has a great deal for us to learn.[107]

---

[100] 76 To 3603, Supreme Court, Dec. 14, 1974, *Monthly Court Case Report* (Korean, May 1975, at 84-85.

[101] *See State* v. *Paek Sang-ki*, 75 To 982, Supreme Court, Nov. 25, 1975, *Monthly Court Case Report*, Feb. 1976, at 70-72.

[102] *See Yi Che-bong* v. *State*, 76 No 11699, Seoul Criminal District Court, Feb. 16, 1977, *Law Times* (Korean), Mar. 7, 1977, at 9.

[103] *See State* v. *Kim Chong-ho*, 76 To 2045, Supreme Court, Feb. 12, 1974, *Monthly Court Case Report* (Korean), May 1974, at 78-79; *Yon Hak-hum* v. *State*, 76 to 2671, Supreme Court, Sept. 28, 1976, *Law Times* (Korean), Oct. 18, 1976, at 4.

[104] 70 To 1325, Supreme Court, Sept. 29, 1970, *Monthly Court Case Report* (Korean), Dec. 1970, at 80-81.

[105] *Id.* at 80.

[106] 73 To 166, Supreme Court, Mar. 13, 1973, *Monthly Court Case Report* (Korean), May 1973, at 78.

[107] *Id.*

The Court held that the defendant's statement to his colleagues at work would foster communism outside South Korea, which the defendant was fully aware of.[108]

B. Advocacy of Self-Determination

Advocacy of self-determination is a nonissue in South Korea where "ethnic, religious, linguistic or cultural minorities do not exist."[109]

C. Criticism of Government or Government Officials

The Korean government in March 1975 revised the Criminal Code and made it a crime to defame the State.[110] Article 104-2 of the Criminal Code read:

> 1. Any Korean national, who endangers or is assumed to endanger the security, interests, or the prestige of the Republic of Korea by defaming or insulting the Republic of Korea or the governmental bodies established under the Constitution, or by distorting the facts about them or by circulating false facts or in any other way, outside of the country, shall be punished by penal servitude or imprisonment for not more than seven years;
> 2. Any Korean national, who commits such acts as prescribed in the preceding paragraph by use of foreigners or foreign organizations inside of the country, shall be punished in the same way as in the preceding paragraph.[111]

During the 1975-1988 period, when anti-State defamation was a crime under the Criminal Code, two cases involved alleged violation of Article 104-2. *Kim Chol-gi v. State*[112] was the first decision in which the Supreme Court interpreted the Criminal Code on anti-State libel. The case began on July 23, 1982, when Kim Chol-gi, the executive director of the Korean Ecumenical Youth Council, circulated 300 anti-government leaflets to about 10 Korean and foreign correspondents in Seoul.[113]

---

[108] *Id.*
[109] Republic of Korea, *Consideration of Reports Submitted by States parties Under Article 40 of the Covenant: Initial Reports of States parties Due in 1991*, at 70 (1991).
[110] Law No. 239 (1953), revised by Law No. 2745 (1975), art. 104-2, *translated in* 3 *ROK Laws*, *supra* note 55 at X-1 to X-44 (4th ed. 1983).
[111] Criminal Code, art. 104-2.
[112] 83 To 515, Supreme Court (en banc), June 14, 1983, 2 *Supreme Court Decisions* (Korean) 440-55 (1978-87).
[113] "Re-Appeal of Defamation of the State, Prosecutor Recommending Three Years in Prison," *Choongang Ilbo* (Korean), Nov. 25, 1983, at 11.

A Seoul district court found Kim guilty of violating the Criminal Code and sentenced him to an 18-month prison term. In his appeal to the Seoul Criminal District Court, Appellate Division, Kim argued: "What was criticized in the leaflets was the ruling authorities of Korea, not the Republic of Korea or the governmental bodies established by the Constitution. Further, the criticism of the governmental policy was an exercise of Kim's basic right as a citizen and was not an act which endangered or was deemed to endanger the prestige of the Republic of Korea."[114]

The appellate division of the Seoul Criminal District Court in February 1983 held that paragraph 2 of Article 104-2 of the Criminal Code was designed to prevent foreign disturbance by punishing Korean nationals for using foreigners within Korea to endanger the security, interests, and the prestige of Korea by defaming Korea and its constitutional bodies.[115] The appellate court stated: "In order for an act to constitute a crime of anti-State defamation, it is required that a Korean national use a foreigner in Korea and the foreigner defame Korea and its constitutional bodies in foreign countries."[116] The court concluded that Kim did not violate the law because there was no proof that the foreign correspondents who received the seditious material from Kim did commit the proscribed act of defaming Korea abroad.[117]

In reversing the lower court's ruling, the Supreme Court, sitting en banc in July 1983, concluded that notwithstanding the language of the revised Code: "[I]t is clear that Article 104-2 of the Criminal Code was designed to forbid the stipulated acts (committed by Koreans) to foreigners or foreign governments."[118] In its 11-2 opinion, the Supreme Court held that Kim's distribution of the anti-government leaflets to foreign journalists constituted the kind of activities proscribed by the law. The Court noted that the print material was to defame the State.[119]

Strongly dissenting from the majority, however, Justice Yi Il-gyu argued that the crime of defamation against the State required three elements: (1) The violator of the Code should be a Korean national; (2) The location of the crime should be outside of Korea; and that (3) The interests to be protected by the Code should be the public opinion and credibility of Korea and its constitutional bodies in foreign countries. Justice Yi concluded that although Kim defamed the State by taking advantage of foreign correspondents in Korea, he could not be punished under the Criminal Code so long as the correspondents did not commit the acts outside of Korea, which endangered or were assumed to damage the security, interest, and the prestige of Korea.[120]

---

[114] *Kim Chol-gi*, Supreme Court, *supra* note 110, at 454.

[115] *Id.*

[116] *Id.*

[117] *Id.*

[118] *Id.* at 445-46.

[119] *Id.*

[120] *Id.* at 447-48.

Another dissent was filed by Justice Yi Hoe-chang, who criticized the majority of the Court for its "carelessly overextended interpretation" of the law.[121] Justice Yi, focusing on the meaning of the "by use of" foreigners or foreign organizations, stated that it should be viewed as "aiding or abetting" foreigners to defame the State.[122] Under the law, according to him, a Korean national's libel against the State could not be penalized, but Koreans' act of aiding and abetting foreigners to defame the State within Korea might be prohibited under Article 104-2(2) "because foreigners' defamatory acts will have a serious danger of affecting the public opinion and trust toward the State abroad."[123]

Justice Yi Hoe-chang claimed that the majority's holding that using foreigners to commit the proscribed acts under Article 104-2(2) meant doing the acts to the foreigners might make the clause inapplicable to a Korean national, who, as an indirect principal offender, aids a foreigner in defaming the State within Korea.[124] He doubted that punishing Korean nationals for defaming the State to foreigners would be more important than punishing Korean nationals for persuading foreigners to libel the State.[125]

The ruling in *Kim Chol-gi* was followed by the Supreme Court in *Kim Pyong-gon* v. *State*.[126] This 1986 anti-State defamation case resulted from Kim Pyong-gon's alleged distribution to a foreign correspondent in Seoul of a written statement on President Chun Doo Hwan's planned visit to the United States in April 1985.[127] The Seoul Criminal District Court, Appellate Division, affirming the single-judge decision of the same court, held that Article 104-2 (2) provided not for a crime of aiding and abetting but for the act of committing a crime.[128] The court ruled that the defendant's distribution of the statement at issue to a foreign correspondent endangered the prestige of Korea and was assumed to harm the interests of Korea by insulting or defaming the President or by distorting the facts and disseminating false facts about the president.[129]

Kim appealed the decision of the Seoul Criminal District Court to the Supreme Court, arguing that the statement was a political expression to be protected

---

[121] *Id.* at 450.
[122] *Id.* at 448-49.
[123] *Id.* at 449.
[124] *Id.* at 450.
[125] *Id.*
[126] 86 To 1209, Supreme Court, Aug. 19, 1986, 34(2) *Supreme Court Decisions* (Korean) 486-89 (1986).
[127] *Kim Pyong-gon* v. *State*, 86 No 973, Seoul Criminal District Court, May 14, 1986, 2 Lower Court Decisions (Korean) 434 (1986).
[128] *Id.* at 430, *citing Kim Chol-gi*, Supreme Court, *supra* note 112.
[129] *Id.*

by the Constitution.[130] The four-justice panel of the Supreme Court, dismissing the appeal, held:

> A mere expression of political opinions does not constitute the crime. We, however, disagree with the defendant that his statement was an expression of his political beliefs as a citizen in that it was to protest the U.S. government's invitation to the President of Korea and that his statement did not target a particular constitutional agency. Indeed, it is clear that the defendant's statement exceeded far and above the boundaries of the political freedom of citizens and thus constituted a criminal act of violating the legal interests of protecting the security, interests, and the prestige of the State.[131]

D. Republication of Statements by Groups Deemed Threatening to National Security.

Under the Anti-Communist Act, it was a crime to listen to North Korean broadcasts and read leaflets disseminated by North Korean authorities. In adjudicating such cases, Korean courts considered the intention of the listeners or readers in getting exposed to the North Korean propaganda onslaught. The Supreme Court in *Nam Tuk-u* v. *State*[132] held that accidental listening to the North Korean broadcasting denouncing the Park Chung Hee regime of South Korea was not a violation of the Anti-Communist Act. The case grew out of an allegation that the defendant heard the broadcast from North Korea in a coffee shop and he prevented an employee of the coffee shop from turning off the radio. He was indicted for violating the Anti-Communist Act in assisting the activities of anti-State organizations by getting other people in the coffee shop to hear the broadcast from North Korea. The lower court ruled the defendant guilty. On appeal, the Supreme Court remanded the judgment to the original court, stating that the defendant "inadvertently heard the broadcast in question, which indicates that he did not intend to violate the law."[133]

In December 1976, however, the Supreme Court in *Paek Kwang-ok* v. *State*,[134] held that the defendant had violated the Anti-Communist Act when he took notes of what he heard from North Korean broadcasts. The Court observed that the

---

[130] 86 To 1209, Supreme Court, Aug. 19, 1986, 34(2) *Supreme Court Decisions* (Korean) 486 (1986).

[131] *Id.* at 487-88.

[132] 68 To 1118, Supreme Court, Oct. 22, 1968, *slip opinion* (Korean); Supreme Court Ruling Card no. 3412.

[133] *Id.*

[134] 76 To 3097, Supreme Court, Dec. 14, 1976, *Law Times* (Korean), Dec. 27, 1976, at 4-5.

defendant, who had been already won over by an anti-State organization, listened purposely to the North Korean radio and kept notes of the broadcasts. Note-taking of the broadcast was clearly tantamount to serving the interests of the enemy, the Court held.[135]

The Anti-Communist Act punished possession of documents, drawing, and other similar means of expression in support of the activities of an anti-State organization. The Seoul Criminal District Court in *Hwang Chong-guk* v. *State*[136] sentenced to six months in prison a defendant who acquired allegedly seditious literature from North Korea and passed it around without notifying authorities. The court ruled that the defendant's dissemination of leaflets and books on a South Korean soldier who defected to North Korea was to encourage the subversive activities of the enemy against South Korea.[137]

The possession or purchase of books on socialism or communism was subject to punishment under the Anti-Communist Act, although the criminal intent of defendants was required to be proved by the government. In applying the Anti-Communist Act to the purchase or sale of books on communism and similar ideologies, Korean courts determined whether the defendant knew that the books would contribute to North Korea's efforts to "brainwash" South Koreans into following communism. The Supreme Court in *Yi Yong-su* v. *State*[138] ruled the law inapplicable to a college student who bought or checked out the books in question from his school library for the sole purpose of doing academic research, not for anti-State organizations or communist followers abroad.[139] The Court stated that the defendant gathered his research materials primarily because it related to the ideology and value system advocated by communist organizations outside South Korea.

In September 1994, the Supreme Court affirmed the ruling of the Kwangju High Court for two college students who were charged with violating the National Security Act with possession of pro-communist books on communism or sociology.[140] The Court agreed with the lower court that the students kept the books for academic work as political and sociology majors. The Court, however, disagreed with the lower court's reasoning that there was no criminal act on the part of the students because they did not possess, read or discuss the books to side with North

---

[135] *Id.* at 5.

[136] 68 To 1080, Seoul Criminal District Court, Feb. 6, 1969, *Law Times* (Korean), Feb. 24, 1969, at 6.

[137] *Id.*

[138] 82 To 716, Supreme Court, May 25, 1982, 20(2) *Supreme Court Decisions* (Korean) 20-27 (1982); *Law Times* (Korean), June 21, 1982, at 6.

[139] *But cf. Chong Chae-hong* v. *State*, 82 To 269, Supreme Court, June 8, 1982, *Monthly Court Case Report* (Korean), Nov. 1982, at 128-29.

[140] *State* v. *Yi* _____ *(appellee's full name not provided)*, 94 To 135, Supreme Court, Oct. 20, 1994, *Law Times* (Korean), Oct. 20, 1994, at 10.

Korea or with a view to benefitting the North.[141] The Court stated that the criminal act of possessing prohibited books under the law did not require proof of the defendants' "purposeful" intent of benefitting an anti-State organization.[142]

Publication of a Korean-language translation of *Dialogue with 800 Million People*, a collection of essays about life in China, originally written by John K. Galbraith, Harrison Salisbury, Edgar Snow, and other noted Americans, was ruled a violation of the Anti-Communist Act in 1979. In *Yi Yong-hi* v. *State*,[143] Yi Yong-hi, professor of mass communication in Hanyang University in Seoul, argued in his appeal to the Supreme Court that in finding criminality of a challenged statement, the statement should be read as a whole and in the context relating to its main theme.[144] Nevertheless, the Court's approach was non-contextual and selective in reading the statement under the Act. The Court, affirming the judgment of the Seoul Criminal District Court, held:

> If a person uses a word or phrase that cannot be interpreted in any possible way as praising, encouraging, or siding with the activities of an anti-State organization under the Anti-Communist Act, his statement does not constitute a crime. On the other hand, if he uses a word or phrase in his statement in praising, encouraging or agreeing with the activities of an anti-State organization, knowing that his statement impresses readers favorably on the anti-State organization, his statement is a crime. It does not matter whether his conclusion may be contradictory and the statement describes the anti-State organization as it is.[145]

In 1992, the Supreme Court applied the "other similar means of expression" provision of the National Security Act in upholding a lower court's decision against a student dissident. The Court in *Ho Tong-jun* v. *State*[146] held that the defendant's act of communicating with a students organization in North Korea through interviews with Korean and foreign reporters fell within the prohibited "other similar means of expression" under the statute. The Court rejected the defendant's argument that his freedom of correspondence under the Constitution should protect his expression and he was not aware of the response from the North Korean students organization to his interview.[147]

---

[141] *Id.*
[142] *Id.*
[143] 78 To 2706, Supreme Court, Jan. 16, 1979, 21(1) *Supreme Court Decisions* (Korean) 1-6 (1979).
[144] *Id.*, at 6.
[145] *Id.*, at 3.
[146] 92 To 1211, Supreme Court, Aug. 14, 1992, 40(2) *Supreme Court Decisions* (Korean) 717-26 (192).
[147] *Id.* at 725-26.

A 1993 decision of the Seoul Criminal District Court, Appellate Division, raised an issue of whether a magazine editor violated the National Security Act in publishing dissident novelist Hwang Sok-yong's travelogue on his visit to North Korea. In *Yi Si-yong* v. *State*,[148] the defendant, editor-in-chief of *Changjak Kwa Pipyong* (Creation and Criticism) magazine, appealed the judgment of a one-judge trial court. He claimed that Hwang's writings did not benefit North Korea. He further asserted that he was not aware that it would benefit North Korea and that he did not intend to benefit North Korean with publication of Hwang's articles.[149] The appellate panel of the Seoul Criminal District Court disagreed, stating that North Korea would benefit from the contents of the travelogue. The court reasoned:

> The writings went beyond the author's real-life description of what he saw during his trip to North Korea. Following the writer's subjective intentions, it defames the democratic society of the South. It emphasizes the relative superiority of the North Korean system, ideology, and life, and praises the leadership and self-reliance ideology of President Kim Il Sung of North Korea.[150]

The court concluded that the defendant's publication of Hwang's articles on North Korea endangered the security and free democratic system of South Korea and benefitted North Korea with "forceful and aggressive expressions."[151]

V. Extraordinary Procedures For Determining National Security Issues.

A. Scope of Judicial Review of National Security Determinations.

The constitutionality of the National Security Act of 1980 was questioned in *Ko Chin-hwa* v. *State* in October 1987.[152] The Supreme Court ruled that the law was constitutional as a legal means for South Korea to protect its security and the liberties of its citizens while thwarting North Korea's engagement in subversive activities aimed at communizing the South.[153] The Court defined "benefitting anti-State organizations" under Article 7(1) of the Act: "It is an action whose contents, viewed objectively, may benefit an anti-State organization. The law does not require that the actor should be conscious of a purpose of benefitting the anti-State organization. The criminality requirement under the law is met if a person's act was

---

[148] 92 No 6354, Seoul Criminal District Court, Jan. 20, 1993, 1 *Lower Court Decisions* (Korean) 412-20 (1993).
[149] *Id.* at 414.
[150] *Id.* at 415.
[151] *Id.*
[152] 86 To 1784, Supreme Court, *Official Gazette of Courts* (Korean), Dec. 15, 1986, at 84-87.
[153] *Id.* at 85.

known to benefit the anti-State organization."[154] The Court found that the defendant violated the law in possessing books which contained contents bearing a similarity with North Korea's propaganda against the South because he was aware that the books would aid North Korea.[155] Dismissing the fact that the books were translated for publication in South Korea, the Court stressed that the defendant possessed the books "not for a purely academic purpose."[156]

The Constitution Court in 1990, in reviewing the National Security Act of 1980,[157] ruled that the Act was "constitutional on condition of proper interpretation."[158] The Act was challenged for the vagueness of Article 7. In an 8-1 decision, the Constitution Court, defining the proper application of the statute, upheld the National Security Act. The Court ruled that the Act would not violate the Constitution if applied only to "the clear danger of bringing about substantive evils to the State," not to actions unharmful to the security of the State or to the basic order of a liberal democracy.[159] Consequently, so long as there is no substantive evil conferred on the State from conduct or speech, the law has no application. Nor can the security law be enforced under circumstances in which the evil is not clear.[160]

The restriction on the interpretation of the law, the Court argued, was "a natural demand evolving from the preferred position of freedom of expression" under the Constitution.[161] In applying the statute to the specific facts, the Court suggested that courts consider "the proximity between a conduct and its danger to society" and "especially the gravity of the evil" resulting from the dangerous conduct.[162]

In dissent, Justice Pyon Chong-su argued that the National Security Act violated the speech and press guarantees of the Constitution. Because freedom of expression is the "institutional foundation of democracy" and a "singularly important basic right" of citizens under the Constitution, he rejected what he perceived to be the "bad tendency" test of the majority for restriction on expression.[163] Pyon asserted

---

[154] *Id.*

[155] *Id.* at 86. *See also Yi Pu-yong* v. *State*, 90 To 450, Supreme Court, Jan. 29, 1993, 41 (1) *Supreme Court Decisions* (Korean) 639-53 (1993).

[156] *Id.*

[157] For the Korean government's position on the National Security Act, *see Human Rights in Korea: Facts and Fiction* 25-51 (1990). For a criticism of the National Security Act, see Marcia Greenberg & Helet Merkling, *Broken Promises, Unfulfilled Dreams: Human Rights and Democracy in South Korea* 11-18 (Kerry Kennedy Cuomo et al. eds., 1992).

[158] 89 Honga 113, Constitution Court, Apr. 2, 1990, 2 *Constitution Court Case Report* (Korean) 49 (1990) (*hereinafter* National Security Act Judgment).

[159] *Id.* at 62-63, 65.

[160] *Id.* at 65-66.

[161] *Id.* at 63.

[162] *Id.*

[163] *Id.* at 67 (Pyon Chong-su, J., dissenting). Though Justice Pyon cites no sources for his version of the "bad tendency" test, he was probably influenced by U.S. constitutional theory on freedom of expression. This is also evident from his discussion of "clear and present

that a criminal law punishing expressions of opinion required the highest degree of definitional precision.[164] The mere tendency of a statement to cause harmful consequences to the State could not be a sufficient ground for invoking the law against the speech. Instead, he stated that the law could be invoked "only when it is proved that the statement may create a clear and present danger of incurring the evils defined by the law (the clear and present danger doctrine)."[165]

Two months later, the Constitution Court affirmed this ruling in a second decision on the National Security Act. In that case, the Court addressed the question of whether the statute could be constitutionally applied to punish possession of books written "for the purpose of helping an anti-State organization."[166] The Court's categorical affirmation of the limited application of the National Security Act indicates that the Court is especially vigilant against the possible abuse by the authorities of the statute's broad and vague restrictions on freedom of the press and speech.

B. Prior Restraint of Publication

The Constitution of Korea prohibits prior restraint of expression. Article 21 stipulates: "All citizens shall enjoy freedom of speech and the press, and freedom of assembly and association; Licensing or censorship of speech and the press, and licensing of assembly and association shall not be recognized.:[167] The Constitution Court held that to censor or interfere with the contents of news reports would violate the "essential aspect" of press freedom, while to require registration of periodicals with the MOPI under the Periodicals Act would not.[168]

A Taegu district court in 1967 adopted the "clear and present danger" test in upholding the press in an Anti-Communist Act case. In *Yi Sang-kwan* v. *State*,[169] Judge Han Pyong-Chae ruled that the defendants, who published a news story on an espionage search operation, should be justified in reporting the operation, for their

---

danger." The "bad tendency" test, also known as the "reasonable tendency" test, is no longer recognized as a First Amendment principle in the United States.

164 *Id.* at 63.

165 *Id.* (parentheses in original). The "clear and present danger" test was developed by the U.S. Supreme Court in 1919 as a replacement for the bad tendency test. *See Schenck* v. *United States*, 249 U.S. 47 (1919).

166 90 Honga 11, Constitution Court, June 25, 1990, *Official Gazette* (Korean), July 26, 1990, at 20-21.

167 Constitution, art. 21(1), (2).

168 90 Honga 23, Constitution Court, June 26, 1992, 4 *Constitution Court Case Report* (Korean) 300, 307 (1993). The Constitution Court upheld the constitutionality of the registration provision of the Periodicals Act, which requires that periodicals, as defined by the statute, be registered with the MOPI before they can be published. *See* Periodicals Act, art. 7.

169 65 Ko 8762, Taegu District Court, Oct. 18, 1967, *Law Times* (Korean), Nov. 6, 1967, at 6.

story "did not pose the kind of *present and clear danger* that would irreparably jeopardize" the spy operation under way.[170] Judge Han, who stressed that press freedom could not be curtailed merely on the ground that anti-communism happened to be a national policy of Korea, stated:

> Freedom of the press is most important for survival of a political democracy. Only press freedom can ensure an ideal national consensus for us. It can also protect civil rights from being infringed upon by the government. It contributes to our playing a creative role in our overall national development through its criticism and factual reporting. Indeed, press freedom is a *life and death issue* for our democracy.[171]

The *Yi Sang-kwan* case arose from a newspaper article, which said that Yongdok County police began a search for North Korean espionage agents after being alerted to the discovery of several spying devices. *Taegu Maeil Shinmun* published the story notwithstanding the request from the police for a news blackout on the espionage operation. The government argued that the publication assisted North Korea by helping the communist agents to flee. In rejecting the government's arguments, Judge Han observed that first, in spite of the "news blackout" request, the newspaper received no "official written request" from those in a responsible position; second, the information published in the newspaper had been already known to almost every one in the area for a week prior to the publication; and third, there was no evidence indicating that publication of the story was intended to aid North Korea. The ruling of the single-judge district court of Taegu was appealed by the government to the three-judge appellate panel of the same district court. The appellate panel of the Taegu District Court affirmed the decision of Judge Han, without expressing its views on Judge Han's application of the clear and present danger test.[172]

The Seoul Criminal District Court in *Kim Che-yol* v. *State*[173] declared in 1970 that "Once classified military information is discussed in public, it can no longer be categorized as secret. The publication of now unclassified information is not subject to punishment under the Anti-Communist Act and the Military Secrets Act."[174] The *Kim Che-yol* case involved Tongyang News Agency, which reported a three-year combat preparation plan debated at an open meeting of the National Defense Committee of the National Assembly of Korea. The court held that the government's request for a news embargo on the plan was no more than a cooperative understanding between the government and the press. So, the court

---

[170] *Id.* (emphasis added).
[171] *Id.* (emphasis in original).
[172] *See State* v. *Yi Sang-gwan*, 68 No 451, Taegu District Court, Nov. 7, 1969, *Journalists Association of Korea Newsletter* (Korean), Nov. 21, 1969, at 2.
[173] 68 Ko 21972, Seoul Criminal District Court, June 15, 1970, *Law Times* (Korean), Aug. 17, 1970, at 6; Aug. 24, 1970, at 6.
[174] *Id.*, *Law Times* (Korean), Aug. 24, 1970, at 6.

ruled, "even though the press did not comply with the embargo request, it could not be criminally punished."[175] On appeal, the Supreme Court affirmed the lower court's ruling, stating that the story on the defense budget plan did not establish the reporters' positive intent to serve the interests of North Korea.[176]

In 1972, however, the Supreme Court defined classified state secrets broadly enough to cover virtually everything. The Court in *Yim Chong-jo* v. *State*[177] held that although it was already published in newspapers or broadcast over radio and TV, the information, when known to North Korea and found useful to it, was protected as a classified state secret under the National Security Act. The *Yim Chong-jo* decision supports Professor Pnina Lahav's proposition that "if the history of governmental suppression teaches anything, it is that the concept of national security has been quite elastic, and has been used by governments to shelter information that was politically embarrassing or that for some political reason the government did not wish the people to know."[178]

C. Use of Military Courts to Try Cases Involving Civilians

Military court is provided for as a special court under the Constitution of Korea. The Supreme Court has the final appellate jurisdiction over military court.[179] Military courts are rarely used in national security cases involving civilians. Under the Martial Law, however, civilians in connection with national security crimes may be tried in military courts. Article 10 of the Martial Law states:

> (1) [i]n the area of enforcement of an extraordinary martial law, a person who commits such crime as prescribed in Article 14 or as set forth in one of the following items shall be tried at a court-martial, provided that the Martial Law Commander may, when necessary, entrust the competent judiciary court with the trial:
> [. . .] 11. Crimes stipulated in the National Security Act.
> (2) In the area of enforcement of an extraordinary martial law, where there is no judiciary court in existence or communication to and from the competent judiciary court is interrupted, all the criminal cases shall be tried by the Court-Martial, notwithstanding the foregoing Paragraph 1.[180]

---

[175] *Id.*
[176] 71 To 2264, Supreme Court, Feb. 29, 1972, *Law Times* (Korean), Mar. 20, 1972, at 4.
[177] 72 To 1514, Supreme Court, Sept. 12, 1972, *Monthly Court Case Report* (Korean), November 1972, at 76-77.
[178] Pnina LaHav, "The Press and National Security," *in* Avner Yaniv ed., *National Security and Democracy in Israel* 180 (1993).
[179] Constitution, art. 110. For a discussion of the military court system in South Korea, *see* Jang-Han Lee, "The Korean Military Justice System," *The Army Lawyer* 37-40 , Oct. 1986.
[180] Martial Law, Law 3442 (1981), revised by Law No. 3933 (1987), art. 10.

D. Summary Deportation and Exclusion Procedures for Aliens Deemed to Threaten National Security.

The Minister of Justice is authorized to regulate foreigners' entry into and exit from South Korea. The Immigration Control Act of 1992 provides for the Minister's authority to "control . . . the immigration of all nationals and aliens who enter into, or depart from, the Republic of Korea, and [to] control . . . the sojourn of aliens who stay in the Republic of Korea."[181]

The Korean government prohibits foreigners from visiting Korea on national security or public order grounds. Article 7 of the Immigration Control Act states in pertinent part:

> The Minister of Justice may prohibit the entry of an alien who falls under any of the following Subparagraphs: [. . .]
>
> 3. Person who is deemed to have a considerable reason to commit any act detrimental to the interest of the Republic of Korea or security of the public;
> 4. Person who is deemed to have a considerable reason to commit any act detrimental to the economic or social order or the good morals.[182]

The Minister of Justice may deport foreigners from Korea when they fall within the prescribed categories of Article 7. Further, foreigners may be barred from leaving Korea if they undermine the security and social order of Korea or if they are suspected of committing "a grave crime" and are under investigation.[183]

The Immigration Control Act has been used by the Korean government to deport or exclude foreigners who it considered to be a threat to its national security interests. Among those foreigners who were subject to deportation from Korea was Satoshi Shinohara. The 39-year-old Japanese businessman was deported back to Japan one hour after he arrived in Seoul's Kimpo International Airport on June 1, 1988. He had been on a South Korean anti-terrorist list for his involvement in a student movement in Japan in 1974.[184] Shinohara reportedly came to Korea for business talks with electronic companies including Hyundai Electronic Industry Co.[185]

---

[181] Law No. 4522 (1992), art. 345, *translated in* 1 *ROK Current Laws*, *supra*, note 55 at 345-75.
[182] *Id.* at art. 11(1).
[183] *Id.* at art. 29.
[184] "Japanese on Korean Police List Refused Entry to Seoul," Kyodo News Service, June 2, 1988, *available in* LEXIS, Nexis Library, Asia/Pacific News/Analysis File; "Japanese 'Terrorist' Deported from South Korea," British Broadcasting Corp., June 4, 1988, *available in* LEXIS, Nexis Library, Asia/Pacific News/Analysis File.
[185] "Japanese on Korean Police List Refused Entry to Seoul," *supra* note184.

More recently, Masatoshi Shinohara, the Seoul bureau chief of Japan's Fuji Television, was deported from South Korea after he was sentenced to a suspended prison term of two years for a criminal violation in April 1994.[186] He was also banned from visiting Korea for five years.[187] In December 1993, Shinohara, who received military secrets from a Korean naval intelligence officer and turned them over to the Japanese embassy, was convicted by a Seoul district court for violation of the Military Secrets Protection Act. The Seoul High Court affirmed the district court's ruling against Shinohara. The high court disagreed with Shinohara that the military secrets he obtained were not the type of information that was classified for protection by the Military Secrets Protection Act and that he did not engage in the criminal act of "gathering" the documented information for an espionage purpose because the Korean military officer, whom he had long been acquainted with, voluntarily provided him the information "with no prior notice."[188] Shinohara did not appeal the Seoul High Court's decision to the supreme Court of Korea.[189]

The Immigration Control Act also disallows foreigners from engaging in "political activities" during their stay in Korea.[190] The Korean government in August 1988 was reported to deport two American peace activists from South Korea on the ground that they participated in a political rally in Seoul to mark an aborted meeting between North and South Korean university students in the truce village of Panmunjom.[191] Charles Scheiner of the War Resisters League and the National Mobilization for Survival and Susan Bailey of the Washington-based People's Anti-War Mobilization spoke at the rally in support of the 2,000 South Korean students before they started a march to Panmunjom to talk to North Korean students about reunification of the Korean peninsula.[192] Bailey was quoted as telling the South Korean students: "Students and workers all over the United States are watching you."[193]

---

186 "Convicted Japanese Correspondent Deported from South Korea," Xinhua News Agency, May 4, 1994, *available in* LEXIS, Nexis Library, Asia/Pacific News/Analysis File.
187 *Id.* (quoting a justice ministry official of the Korean government).
188 *Shinohara Masato* v. *State*, 94 No 166, Seoul High Court, April 22, 1994, *slip opinion*.
189 "Convicted Japanese Correspondent Deported from South Korea," *supra* note 186.
190 *Immigration Control Act*, art. 17(3).
191 Sonya Hepinstall, "South Korea to Deport Two American Peace Activists," Reuters, Aug. 22, 1998, *available in* LEXIS, Nexis Library, Asia/Pacific News/Analysis file.
192 *Id.*
193 *Id.*

VI. Conclusions and Recommendations

In interpreting freedom of expression under national security law, Korean courts have failed to establish consistent reasoning in their rulings. Consequently, court decisions have confounded the problem of defining the extent to which Koreans could expect to be statutorily protected by the courts in exercising their freedom. It is noteworthy, however, that in at least half a dozen cases, Korean courts clearly recognized the affirmative function of the press, while the courts in general have tended to be narrow in interpreting the constitutional clause on freedom of expression.

As compared with the Supreme Court, lower courts have been bolder in experimenting with various free speech or free press theories in ruling on national security restrictions. Several lower courts have been remarkably libertarian in their views on the role and function of the Korean press. The Seoul and Taegu district courts' applications of the "clear and present danger" test in the 1960s are a good example. In recent years, lower courts frequently utilized the test and also the "preferred position" concept in national security cases.

The Supreme Court often engages in *ad hoc* balancing in ruling on freedom of expression issues. As a result, the Court to date has established few constitutional standards of its own. Moreover, the Court has not yet seriously considered adopting the "clear and present danger" test or its variations, as established in the First Amendment law of the United States. Most significantly, however, the three dissenting justices in a 1992 case set forth what they termed the "concrete and probable danger" doctrine as a standard for balancing national security with freedom of expression under the National Security Act.[194] If it is accepted by the Supreme Court in the future, the doctrine, which seems to have its conceptual genesis in the clear and present danger theory, is expected to alter the way the National Security Act has been interpreted over the years.

On the other hand, the Constitution Court has played an increasingly significant role in shaping the contours of freedom of expression since 1988. First, the "gravity of the evil" test is used to apply the National Security Act. Second, access to public information is a constitutional right as part of freedom of expression. Third, censorship of speech and the press is a constitutional violation of the "essential aspect" of speech and press freedom.

---

[194] *See Kim Sang-myong* v. *State*, 90 To 2033, Supreme Court, Mar. 31, 1992, 40(1) *Supreme Court Decisions* (Korean) 702 (1992) (Yi Hoe-chang, Yi Chae-song and Pae Man-un, dissenting). The "concrete and probable danger" test is comparable to U.S. Judge Learned Hand's test on freedom of expression under the First Amendment, i.e., "whether the gravity of the 'evil,' discounted by its improbability, justifies such invasion of free speech as is necessary to avoid the danger." The "gravity of evil" test was adopted by the U.S. Supreme Court in *Dennis* v. *United States*, 341 U.S. 494 (1951).

While the National Security Act has been less of a direct threat to freedom of expression in South Korea since 1987, the still persisting "ideological confrontation" between North and South Korea makes it likely that the controversy over the law will continue.

Turkey: Protection of National Interests and the Indivisible Unity of the State

Kerim Yildiz

I. Introduction

Since 1984, the Government of Turkey has been engaged in an armed conflict with the Kurdistan Workers' Party (PKK), which seeks an independent Kurdish State in southeastern Turkey. Over 15 million Kurdish people live in Turkey, of whom 10 million live in the Southeast. More than 21,000 people have been killed, over 3 million civilians have been displaced, and over 2,785 Kurdish villages have been evacuated and in many cases destroyed as a result of the fighting.[1]

The Turkish Government declared a state of emergency in 1987 in ten southeastern provinces where the PKK had engaged in substantial terrorist violence. Under the Turkish Constitution a state of emergency may be introduced in times of declared war, natural disaster, serious economic crisis, widespread acts of violence or other serious deterioration of public order. A regional governor has retained authority over the ten provinces and three adjacent ones covered by the state of emergency decree. The state of emergency allows the governor to exercise certain quasi-martial law powers, including restrictions on the press and removal from the area of people whose activities were deemed hostile to public order. The government renewed the state of emergency decree in 1994.[2] More recently, the Turkish government has begun a process of lifting the state of emergency in the Southeast. Whether such a change will result in an improvement of the human rights situation of the people living in the region remains to be seen.

Turkey has received considerable criticism, from both domestic and international sources, for its human rights record. Concern has focused on the following: (1) torture and suspicious deaths of detainees; (2) disappearances and extra-judicial killings of politicians, human rights activists, journalists and Kurdish nationalists; (3) government infringements on freedom of speech, press, and association; (4) denial of due process to those under the jurisdiction of State Security Courts and in the emergency region; (5) the killing of Kurdish civilians and the destruction of Kurdish villages in the Southeast by the military; and (6) the suppression of Kurdish cultural expression.[3]

Police and security forces continue to harass, intimidate, torture and even kill human rights monitors, journalists, lawyers and academics for publicly expressed ideas. Yet, the government rarely prosecutes police or security officers for any

---

[1] U.S. House of Representatives, Congressional Resolution 136, 104th Congress, 2d Sess. (1996).
[2] U.S. Department of State, "Dispatch: Turkey Human Rights Practices" (Wash. DC, 1994).
[3] Helsinki Watch, *Paying the Price: Freedom of Expression in Turkey* (1989).

offenses. In the few cases in which security personnel have been prosecuted, sentences have been lenient.

While the PKK is widely considered to be responsible for a substantial number of disappearances and murders in the southeast region, this of course cannot justify the government's excesses. PKK guerrillas have targeted village officials, teachers and other noncombatants in an effort to intimidate the populace.[4]

The PKK once again offered to lay down their weapons in December 1995.[5] However this offer was viewed skeptically by the Turkish government in light of previous failed cease-fire attempts. The most recent such attempt occurred in 1993 when the PKK declared a unilateral cease-fire. The cease fire ended several months later when PKK guerrillas attacked and killed 30 soldiers.[6] The climate of hostility and distrust remains the single largest obstacle to reducing unlawful killing, torture and other human rights abuses.

II. Legal Framework

A. Turkey's International Obligations

In 1954 Turkey ratified the European Convention on Human Rights (ECHR), and in 1987 it accepted the right of individual petition. The Turkish government has accepted the binding nature of all of the articles of the ECHR except for Article 5 (concerning deprivation of liberty), from which it derogated.[7] Pursuant to Article 90 of the Turkish Constitution, the ECHR is binding as the domestic law of Turkey and enjoys constitutional status. The Constitutional Court declared in 1963 that the fundamental rights set forth in the 1961 Constitution corresponded to the rights contained in the ECHR. The Constitutional Court has neither reaffirmed nor repudiated this declaration in interpreting the Constitution of 1982.[8]

Turkey is a party to a number of other human rights treaties, including the European Convention Against Torture, the European Social Charter, and the U.N. Convention on the Rights of the Child.[9] The Turkish government established a Parliamentary Human Rights Commission and a Human Rights Ministry to promote

---

[4] Human Rights Foundation of Turkey, *Turkey Human Rights Report* (1994).
[5] H.R. Con. Res. 136, *supra* note 1. The cease-fire was officially called off in Aug. 1996.
[6] Kurdish Human Rights Project (KHRP), *Lawyers in Fear, Law in Jeopardy* (1993).
[7] KHRP, *Advocacy and the Rule of Law in Turkey* (1995).
[8] Article 19 and International Human Rights Law Group, *Political Speech in Turkey* (Wash. DC, 1995).
[9] U.S. Commission on Security and Cooperation in Europe (USCSCE), *Briefing: Human Rights in Turkey*, 9 (Apr. 1993).

Turkey's compliance with these treaties.[10] Turkey is not a party to the International Covenant on Civil and Political Rights.[11]

B. Constitution of 1982

The Turkish Constitution of 1982 was adopted under the military regime of the National Security Council (*Milli Guvenlik Konseyei*, or MGK).[12] Three provisions amply illustrate the overarching priority given to the protection of state interests and security. Individual rights may be limited or withdrawn when the state determines there is a threat.

First, the eighth paragraph of the preamble says that the Constitution should be read with due loyalty to its "determination that no protection shall be afforded to thoughts or opinions contrary to Turkish national interests, the principle of the existence of Turkey as an indivisible entity with its state and territory, Turkish historical and moral values, or the nationalism, principles, reforms and modernism of Ataturk."[13]

Second, Article 13 of the Constitution states that "Fundamental rights and freedoms may be restricted by law, in conformity with the letter and spirit of the Constitution, with the aim of safeguarding the indivisible integrity of the state with its territory and nation, national sovereignty, the Republic, national security, public order, general peace, the public interest, public morals and public health."[14]

The third provision emphasizing the supremacy of state security over individual rights is Article 14 of the Constitution, which reads in part:

> None of the rights and freedoms embodied in the Constitution shall be exercised with the aim of violating the indivisible integrity of the state with its territory and nation . . . .[15]

These restrictions are far broader than permitted by the ECHR, which requires that any restrictions on a fundamental right or freedom must be "necessary in a democratic society" and must be directed at protecting one of a short list of permissible interests.[16] The above provisions demonstrate that the state, through the

---

[10] KHRP, *Advocacy, supra* note 7.

[11] U.N. Human Rights Center, *International Instruments: Chart of Ratifications as at 30 June 1997* (New York and Geneva, 1997).

[12] Murat Belge, "Trapped in Its Own History," *Index on Censorship*, at 135 (1995).

[13] *Constitution of Turkey*, pream. para. 8.

[14] *Id.* art. 13.

[15] *Id.* art. 14.

[16] *See, e.g., Sunday Times* v. *United Kingdom*, Series A, no. 30 (Judgment of April 26, 1979). Article 10 of the ECHR permits restrictions on freedom of expression only if "necessary in a democratic society, in the interests of national security, territorial integrity or public safety, for the prevention of disorder or crime, for the protection of health or morals, for the protection of the reputation or rights of others, for preventing the disclosure of information

government in power, is charged with closely directing the country's society, culture and morals. There is no room for a strong "opposition". Anchored in this constitutional mandate, the governing elite shows little tolerance for criticism and opposition. Many journalists, for example, have been tried and sentenced under the country's very broad Anti-Terrorism law for offenses such as criticizing or insulting the president, public officials, Ataturk (founder of the modern Turkish nation), or for printing anti-military propaganda.[17]

The Constitution reflects the long cherished ideal of an indivisible, unified state based on one people and one language. The state, via leaders from Ataturk to the present, has tried to convert ethnically heterogeneous peoples into a homogenous population of Turks. The process has involved suppressing the cultural identity and expression of non-Turkish peoples. The security interests and national ideals entrenched in the Constitution have had serious consequences for human rights.

C. The National Security Council

The National Security Council (*Milli Guvenlik Konseyi*, or MGK) is a multi-member advisory body set up by the Constitution for the purpose of formulating, coordinating and implementing security policy.[18] The MGK is composed of the Prime Minister, the Chief of General Staff, the Ministers of National Defense, Internal Affairs and Foreign Affairs, the commanders of the respective armed forces, and the General Commander of the Gendarmerie. The President of the Republic serves as chairman.[19]

The MGK meets monthly and submits to the Council of Ministers its views on the formulation, establishment and implementation of measures it deems appropriate for the preservation and security of the state. In practice, almost all of the suggestions made by the MGK are translated into the policy of the Turkish government.[20] In essence, the MGK has assumed an executive function rather than the advisory role set forth in the Constitution. Specific policy recommendations have focused on repressing freedom of expression of political opponents of the state.

Examples of laws drafted at the request of the MGK include the Law on Assembly and Demonstrations and the Law of Associations. The Law on Assembly and Demonstrations states that protests must be authorized by the provincial governor, and penalizes violations with imprisonment for six months to three years.[21] The Law of Associations prohibits any form of political statement or activity by an

---

received in confidence, or for maintaining the authority and impartiality of the judiciary."

[17] USCSCE, *supra* note 9. *See also* Section III, *infra* 184-197.

[18] Murat Belge, *supra* note 12.

[19] *Id.*

[20] Yasar Kemal, "The Dark Cloud Over Turkey," *Index on Censorship*, 141 (1995).

[21] Law No. 2911: Law on Assembly and Demonstrations.

organization other than a legal political party, and penalizes violations by one to three years of imprisonment.[22]

III. Restrictions on Freedom of Expression

A. The Anti-Terrorism Law

The offenses which most seriously restrict political activities, and which are tried by State Security Courts, are those set forth in the Anti-Terrorism Law. Article 1(1) defines terrorism as:

> [A]ny kind of act done by one or more persons belonging to an organization with the aim of changing the characteristics of the Republic as specified in the Constitution, its political, legal, social, secular and economic system, [or] damaging the indivisible unity of the State with its territory and nation . . . by means of pressure, force and violence, terror, intimidation, oppression or threat.

This definition poses a threat to freedom of expression because the term "pressure" is vague and has been widely used to criminalize statements that do not constitute threats or advocacy of violence. They are therefore entitled to protection. A terrorist is defined in Article 2:

> [A]ny member of an organization, founded to attain the aims defined in Article 1, who commits a crime in furtherance of these aims, . . . or any member of such an organization, even if he does not commit such a crime, shall be deemed to be a terrorist offender. Persons who are not members of a terrorist organization, but who commit a crime in the name of the organization, are also deemed to be terrorist offenders.

The danger of this definition is that State Security Court prosecutors too frequently accuse persons of being terrorists who share some of the cultural and political goals of terrorist groups. People who do not, however, share terrorists methods.

Article 8 of the Anti-Terrorism Law penalizes the publication of propaganda which threatens "the indivisible unity of the state".[23] Attempts to limit the definition of separatist propaganda in 1994 failed.[24] In 1995, however, Article 8 was amended

---

[22] Law No. 2098: Law of Associations.

[23] Anti-Terrorism Law, Art. 8: stating the definition of propaganda as "[w]ritten and oral propaganda and assemblies, meetings and demonstrations aimed at damaging the indivisible unity of the State. . . . If the offense of propaganda as mentioned . . . is committed by a periodical according to Article 3 of the Press Law No. 5680, the publishers are to be punished additionally . . . ."

[24] Committee to Project Journalists, *Attacks on the Press in 1994* (1995).

to require proof of "motive" or "intention" to disrupt the integrity of the country. In addition, the upper and lower terms of imprisonment were reduced.

As discussed below, Turkish authorities have indicted parliamentarians, journalists and writers under the Anti-Terrorism Law for statements calling for increased local self-government or cultural autonomy for the southeastern, predominantly Kurdish region.

B. Restrictions on Peaceful Advocacy of Kurdish Rights

On March 2, 1994, the Turkish Parliament voted to strip six Kurdish deputies of their parliamentary immunity to allow an investigation into their alleged separatist activities. Five were members of the pro-Kurdish Democracy Party (DEP). The deputies were arrested and jailed while the Ankara State Security Court prosecutors prepared their indictments alleging treasonous activities under Article 168 (2) of the Penal Code. Article 168 (2) of the Penal Code provides for the imposition of severe prison sentences for anyone found guilty of aiding or abetting the PKK. In June 1994, the Constitutional Court banned the Democracy Party, stripping its thirteen deputies of parliamentary membership. Two more DEP members were arrested and accused of acting as part of the political wing of the banned PKK. The former deputies maintained that the DEP had no connections with the PKK and was a legal organization pursuing change through democratic and peaceful means. The trial of the two former DEP deputies was later merged with that of the original six defendants.[25]

In December 1994, the eight defendants were convicted of various charges, including: dissemination of separatist propaganda; being a member of an armed society or band; and knowingly supporting such a band. The sentences ranged from three years and six months (suspended) for two of the deputies to 15 years for the remaining six deputies. Both the defense and prosecution appealed the decision.[26] In October 1995, the Turkish Supreme Court released two of the imprisoned parliamentarians, although four deputies (Leyla Zana, Hatip Dicle, Selim Sadal and Orhan Dogan) remain in prison. The European Commission and Court of Human Rights have considered several applications made in regard to their case; the Court on November 26, 1997 found that the detention of Leyla Zana for twelve days without judicial supervision was improper and therefore in contravention of Article 5 of the European Convention on Human Rights.

The Parliamentary Assembly of the Council of Europe, in April 1994, adopted Resolution 1030, concluding that the deputies had not exceeded their right to freedom of expression guaranteed by Article 10 of the ECHR and the provisions

---

[25] Article 19 and the Law Group, *supra* note 8. The statement of facts represents the result of a May 1994 fact-finding trip by a Law Group delegation.
[26] *Id.*

of the Turkish Constitution and calling on the Government of Turkey to withdraw the charges.[27] In 1995 and again in 1996, the Parliamentary Assembly of the Council of Europe issued resolutions calling for the release of the parliamentarians.[28] The 1996 Resolution (No. 1298), although commending the Turkish government for progress made in the field of human rights, states that "the continuing imprisonment of the other four (DEP deputies)remains a serious violation of human rights and negates the very essence of parliamentary democracy".

C. Restrictions on the Media

1. Use of the Anti-Terrorism Law against Publications

The Anti-Terrorism Law has been used against journalists and some publications -- in particular, Ozgur Gundem, Ozgur Ulke and Yeni Politika – for publication of statements made by PKK leaders. No distinction is made between commentary and news.

Ozgur Gundem was a left-wing Turkish language newspaper sympathetic to claims for Kurdish minority rights. By covering human rights abuses in southeast Turkey, it became a main source of information for local, regional and international human rights organizations. In April 1994, an appeals court issued orders to close the paper permanently. The reasons cited in the order included promotion of separatism and printing the views of the banned PKK.[29] Most of Ozgur Gundem's staff moved to Ozgur Ulke, which opened shortly after its predecessor's closure. Ozgur Ulke also has been constantly harassed by the government for publishing the views of Kurdish nationalists and editorials by PKK leaders.[30] Eventually, Ozgur Ulke was banned by the authorities only to be succeeded by the daily Yeni Politika. To illustrate the difficulties faced by this most recent pro-Kurdish daily it should be noted that over a period of three months in 1996, 93 out of 103 issues of the paper were confiscated by the authorities.

2. Detention of Journalists

The Committee to Protect Journalists (CPJ) has for years documented numerous cases involving arbitrary detention, harassment, and imprisonment of

---

[27] Council of Europe, Res. 1030, "On the Arrest and Detention of Six Members of the Turkish Grand National Assembly," WP 1403-12/41/94-12-E para. 5, (adopted April 13, 1994).

[28] Parliamentary Assembly, Res. 1266 (1995) and Res. 1298 (1996).

[29] Kurdish Human Rights Project (KHRP), *Freedom of the Press in Turkey: the Case of Ozgur Gundem* (1993).

[30] Nicole Pope, "Letting Go - Turkey has a Choice: More Democracy? More Army?" *Index on Censorship* 154 (1995).

journalists. According to C.P.J.'s 1996 annual report, at least seventy-eight journalists remained in prison at the end of 1996, the highest number of any country in the world.[31]

3. Confiscation of Publications

The Turkish government may restrict the printing and distribution of newspapers under the Press Law of 1950.[32] Supplementary Article 1 to the Press Law enables a prosecutor, if he believes a publication committed a criminal offense, to stop distribution of the publication and confiscate printed materials without a court order. Any decisions to halt distribution or confiscate materials must be reviewed by a magistrate. State Security Court prosecutors have ordered the confiscation of numerous issues of leftist and pro-Kurdish periodicals, including *Aydinlik, Emegin Bayragi, Denge Azadi, Ozgur Gelecek, Gercek, Newroz, Hedef, Ozgur Gundem, Ozgur Ulke* and *Yeni Politika.*[33]

4. Broadcasting

Broadcasting freedom is addressed in Act 3984 and in the 1950 Press Law. These laws state generally that broadcasting is not to be censored. However, in direct contravention of this statement, the Prime Minister or an official authorized by him may halt a broadcast whenever he or she believes that it might threaten national security or public order.[34]

D. Persecution of Defense Lawyers and Human Rights Defenders

In late 1993 and early 1994, the government arrested 20 Turkish and Kurdish attorneys in Diyarbakir and charged them with political crimes under the Penal Code and the Anti-Terrorism Law. All had been involved in defending suspected members of the PKK. Seven of the lawyers, all members of the Diyarbakir branch of the Human Rights Association in Turkey, were eventually tried in February 1995. On February 27th, the police arrested four more members of the Human Rights Association in Diyarbakir, without warrants. Three were allegedly beaten and threatened by the police before being taken into detention. There is substantial concern that the attorneys were targeted by the government because of their

---

[31] C.P.J., *Attacks on the Press in 1996* (N.Y. 1997).
[32] Anti-Terror Law, Art. 8.
[33] U.S. Dept. of State, *Turkey, Human Rights Country Reports, 1992* (Wash. D.C. 1993).
[34] C.P.J., *supra* note 31.

involvement in bringing human rights cases to the European Commission.[35] The year 1997 saw a hitherto unsurpassed level of persecution of human rights activists, the temporary closure of several offices of IHD (*Insan Haklari Dernegi* - The Turkish Human Rights Association) and the imprisonment of IHD members.

E. Restrictions on the Kurdish Language and Culture

Many of the government's actions against Kurdish culture and language are premised on the allegation that any organization or material connected with the Kurds is threatening to the indivisibility of the Turkish state. In 1991, amidst much international pressure, the Turkish government repealed a law prohibiting publications or communication in Kurdish. The repeal legalized some spoken and printed Kurdish communications. Under the political parties law, however, all discussion that takes place at political meetings must be in Turkish. Kurdish may not be spoken in court proceedings or in other official government settings. Moreover, materials dealing with Kurdish history, culture and ethnic identity continue to be subject to confiscation and prosecution under the Anti-Terrorism Law.[36]

Even purely cultural efforts by Turkey's Kurds have been thwarted by application of the law. In 1992, the Kurdish Cultural Foundation applied to a court for registration as a foundation. The organization's stated purpose was to promote research and publication on Kurdish language, literature, history and folklore. The court subsequently denied registration to the organization claiming it was based on race and thereby violated the Constitution's prohibition of racial discrimination.[37]

One of the most notorious cases is that of cultural anthropologist Ismail Bescliski. Bescliski researched and wrote on Kurdish culture, society, and history. He served a total of ten years in prison between 1971 and 1987 for his writings which a court ruled were separatist propaganda.[38] In 1993 he was again indicted on two counts of disseminating separatist propaganda based on two of his recent books. He was tried and convicted in a State Security Court under the Anti-Terrorism Law, sentenced to 20 months, and fined 42 million Turkish Lira ($ 100) on each count.

---

[35] The Bar Human Rights Committee [of England], Kurdish Human Rights Project, and the Law Society [of England], *The Law: Freedom of Expression and Human Rights Advocacy in Turkey* (1995).

[36] *See* International Helsinki Federation for Human Rights, chapter on Turkey, *Annual Report 1996* (Vienna, 1997).

[37] U.S. Department of State, *"Turkey" Country Reports 1992*, *supra* note 33.

[38] Michael M. Gunter, *The Kurds of Turkey* (1990), at 6-7.

IV. Reduced Protections of Due Process to Decide National Security Issues

In 1992, the Turkish Parliament passed special legislation to bring Turkey's criminal procedures into line with its obligations under the European Convention on Human Rights. The Turkish government claimed that this legislation (known as the CMUK) brought "the Turkish law into conformity with international standards in the vital areas of detention periods, arrest procedures and interrogation practices."[39] CMUK was the subject of additional reform in 1996 and 1997, further limiting pre-trial detention periods and making explicit the right of a detainee to have access to a lawyer.

Article 12 of the CMUK requires police to inform anyone taken into custody of the crime with which he or she will be charged and of the right to remain silent and have a lawyer present during all interrogations. Article 13 prohibits torture, force, violence, ill-treatment, false promises or administration of drugs during interrogation or detention. The Article also establishes an exclusionary rule. Any statements extracted by unlawful means may not be considered evidence for a conviction even if the defendant confesses. Article 20 states that a defendant has a right to meet privately, and communicate freely, with a lawyer. Article 22 requires the local bar association to provide counsel to an indigent defendant who requests one.[40]

Article 31, however, contains a loophole by means of which the government has circumvented the procedural protections of the CMUK. The loophole is that the provisions, other than Article 13, do not apply to crimes falling under the jurisdiction of State Security Courts.[41] State Security Courts have jurisdiction over cases involving acts prohibited by the Anti-Terrorism Law, drug smuggling, membership in illegal organizations, and the dissemination of ideas damaging the unity of the state. These courts may hold closed hearings. Persons accused of crimes falling under the jurisdiction of these courts may be detained twice as long before arraignment as defendants under other court jurisdictions. Whereas defense attorneys generally have access to the prosecutors' files after arraignment, in cases involving the Anti-Terrorism Law, insults to the president or defamation of the Turkish nation, defense counsel may be denied access on national security grounds.[42] Until the 1997 amendments to CMUK, people, who were tried by State Security Courts had no right to counsel. The decision concerning access to counsel was left to the prosecutor who generally denied access on the ground that the opportunity to consult an attorney could prejudice an ongoing investigation.[43]

---

[39] T. C. Resmi Gazete (Turkish Republic Official Gazette), No. 21422, 1 Dec. 1992.
[40] "Torture is an Everyday Occurrence in Police Life," *Die Woche* [English Translation], May 5, 1994.
[41] Human Rights Foundation of Turkey, *500-Day Report* (1993).
[42] *Id.*
[43] *Id.*

The Turkish Constitution specifies the right to request a speedy arraignment and trial. However, judges have ordered indefinite detention in a number of cases, and people accused of nonviolent political crimes are commonly held in custody until the conclusion of their trials.[44]

V. State of Emergency Region

Since 1987, the provinces of the Southeast with the heaviest concentration of Kurdish people have been placed under a state of emergency. The legal bases for the imposition of the state of emergency are the Turkish Constitution and the State of Emergency/ Emergency Regional Governance laws.[45] The State of Emergency legislation is currently under review and it is anticipated that it may be lifted altogether within the next year or two, although whether this will result in improvement in the general human rights situation in the region is difficult to foretell.

The State of Emergency Law empowers the Council of Ministers assembled under the chairmanship of the President to declare a state of emergency when widespread violence threatens to destroy rights and freedoms or causes the deterioration of public order. The Turkish Constitution allows the Council to issue decrees during a state of emergency having the force and effect of law. A special governor oversees implementation of the decrees. There can be no judicial review of the decrees by the courts.[46]

Measures which authorities may take in a state of emergency include prohibition of any kind of assembly or procession or movement of vehicles in certain places or within certain hours; prohibition of the publication, importation or distribution of books, magazines or newspapers; restriction or prohibition of every kind of broadcasting; and the restriction or prohibition of all plays and films.[47]

In addition, courts are not permitted to enjoin measures taken by a governor under the authority of an emergency law, even if the measures violate human rights. The 1987 decree issued by the Council of Ministers gave the governor immunity from legal liability. The immunity runs counter to Turkey's obligations under the European Convention for Human Rights, which states that "everyone whose rights or freedoms . . . are violated shall have an effective remedy before a national authority notwithstanding that the violation has been committed by persons acting in an official capacity."[48]

---

[44] *Id.*

[45] David A. Korn, "Turkey's Kurdish Rebellion," *Freedom Review*, May-June 1995, at 33-35.

[46] Amnesty International, "Turkey: A Policy of Denial" (1995).

[47] Korn, *supra* note 45.

[48] Amnesty International, *supra* note 46.

VI. Conclusions and Recommendations

1. The State's actions described above have served to generate support for the PKK. While there is no doubt that the PKK is a terrorist organization, it is equally true that such anti-state movements feed on unemployment, poor living conditions and human rights violations by the authorities. The Turkish government should address the underlying political, economic, and cultural conditions that have made many Kurdish citizens sympathetic to the PKK's initial goal of establishing a separate Kurdish state.

2. The Turkish government is unduly inclined to seek a military solution to the Kurdish issue rather than a negotiated political one. This is evidenced by the Turkish Parliament's vote to strip the six Kurdish deputies of their immunity and the government's determination to prosecute and imprison them despite widespread international protest, including from the Council of Europe. The military is alleged to have pressured the Parliament to vote as it did. The government as a whole must resist pressure from powerful interest groups such as the military. The military of course gains in power and authority the longer the hostilities continue or escalate. The continued closure of democratically minded political parties does not bode well for the future of Turkish parliamentary democracy and should be considered carefully by the Turkish Constitutional Court in light of Turkey's international obligations.

3. Allegations of unfair prosecutions in the State Security Courts have caused a fundamental loss of confidence in the judicial system. Reforms enacted under the CMUK included reduction of the periods of permissible detention and recognition of a suspect's right to proper access to a lawyer in confidence. The loopholes by which the state may circumvent these rights should be eliminated. The recent reductions in the period of detention before a detainee is brought before a judge should be further amended and a system should be implemented to ensure that non-observance of the rule of law is punished.

4. Lawyers who defend human rights activists or accused terrorists are at grave risk of physical attack and legal harassment. They are vital to the success of the rule of law in Turkey and to the government's compliance with international human rights norms. The government should establish an independent commission to inquire into, and formulate ways to stop, the intimidation, harassment and legal impediments that lawyers face in trying to provide effective legal counsel. The independent inquiry should involve representatives of the international community to avoid allegations of bias.

5. The government must ensure that all prosecutions are instituted in accordance with the law and that the conduct of the proceedings be in accordance with internationally recognized principles governing fair trials. The Turkish courts must apply the provisions contained in the European Convention on Human Rights.

FREEDOM OF EXPRESSION, DISSENT, AND NATIONAL SECURITY IN THE UNITED KINGDOM

Laurence Lustgarten

I. Introduction

The United Kingdom's[1] record in protecting freedom of expression in the face of claims of "national security," or other allegedly paramount state interests, is mixed. Legal and political developments over centuries have produced an odd pattern in which genuine progress in curtailing long-standing methods of suppression of expression has been partly offset by the creation of new and ingenious forms of suppression by different, more subtle means.

This history yields several important practical lessons and also one general warning: while it is essential to propose remedies for specific laws or procedures that curtail freedom of expression and dissent, it may never be assumed that the war against suppression of expression has been won. Governments quickly regroup their forces and marshal them on new and different terrain, chosen when possible to be most favorable to themselves.

We need therefore to look beyond present problems and consider ways in which presently unexploited legal procedures might be used for speech curtailing purposes, in order to pre-empt such possibilities. We should also look to strengthen institutions which have been shown to be effective in curbing authoritarian measures taken by governments. A judiciary formally and in reality independent of the executive is one, but as the United Kingdom experience will show, equally and sometimes more important is institution of trial by jury.

II. Certain Current Forms of Censorship Not Present in UK

Though this chapter contains strong criticism of various ways in which the British government has misused its powers against political opponents, certain mechanisms of repression commonly employed against political opposition elsewhere have not been featured in the UK. One such mechanism is the invocation of emergency laws against critics of the regime.

In Northern Ireland, the long-running and many-sided political violence has led to serious restrictions on the legal protections available to people in the hands of the police and before the courts. Though broadcasters seeking to report the conflict have been subject to certain restrictions, these have been imposed under ordinary

---

[1] Throughout this chapter the terms "United Kingdom", "Britain" and "England" are used interchangeably. Technically, I shall be talking about the law of England (and Wales), although Scotts law is not materially different in relation to the issues under discussion.

regulations, and not under emergency law. This has been something of a mixed blessing, because while the Government's actions have been subject to judicial review, when challenged these restrictions have almost invariably received the blessing of the courts. The Press, which, unlike broadcasting, is not subject to general statutory controls, has not been directly curbed in any way. Bias, disinformation and in some cases self-censorship have been far more important in determining what has, and has not, appeared in British newspapers on the subject of Northern Ireland.

Nor has it been the practice in Britain for the state to use the libel laws for political purposes. Criminal libel is virtually dormant; having been briefly revived in some private disputes in the 1970s, it was greeted with strong disapproval in the House of Lords.[2] The civil law of defamation remains a serious problem for the media when faced with rich and ruthless private individuals who may use the threat to sue to keep information about their improper or unlawful conduct out of public knowledge. The best known example was Robert Maxwell, but there remain others of his kind. However, politicians very seldom sue when allegations of misbehavior concern their conduct in office (as opposed to sexual or other escapades), and in two recent spectacular examples, former Conservative ministers who had sued the liberal *Guardian* newspaper each abandoned their actions in humiliating circumstances.[3]

Moreover, the House of Lords has commendably held that a local authority which had been criticized by a newspaper could not sue in defamation for damage to its reputation as a governing body.[4] Libel as a hindrance to criticism of the state and its leaders should be seen as largely a non-issue in Britain.

III. The History of Suppression of Speech in the United Kingdom

There is a notable trajectory in the history of repression of criticism and dissent in Britain. It begins with common law offences (with the sole statutory addition of the Treason Acts) aimed directly at speech and writing critical either of government policy or eminent individuals. The latter targets were if anything considered more important, for political rule was personalized in the Monarch along with key advisers and courtiers, and criticism of their probity or character was regarded (to use modern terms) as attacking the legitimacy of the state. Hence the criminalization of *scandalum magnatum* – scandalizing (that is, mocking) the great. The parallel with practice in contemporary dictatorships is striking.

---

[2] *See Gleaves* v. *Deakin*, A.C. 477, 483 (1980) (Lord Diplock).

[3] Both Mps, Jonathan Aitken and Neil Hamilton, had been implicated in various forms of corruption, and had founded their actions, at least in part, on evidence shown to be false. The latter was defeated for re-election by a non-party "anti-sleaze' candidate in the 1997 General Election.

[4] *Derbyshire County Council* v. *Times Newspapers*, A.C. 543 (1993).

At the same time, in England as in the rest of Europe until at least the 19th century, the state was inextricably bound up with religion. Divine authority (whether of the Church of Rome or of national churches established under state patronage after the Reformation) conferred legitimacy on secular power. Attacks on religious doctrine, practices and authority were therefore equally attacks on the legitimacy of royal power: politics and religion were inseparable. Thus, when the ecclesiastical courts and the Court of the Star Chamber had been abolished, the common law courts quick stepped into the breach and proclaimed blasphemy an offense within their jurisdiction. The judges who asserted this power knew well what they were about: "to say, Religion is a Cheat, is to dissolve all those Obligations whereby Civil societies are preserved, and that Christianity is a parcel of the Laws of England; and therefore to reproach the Christian religion is to speak in subversion of the Law".[5]

The political thrust of this reasoning is clear: if the bonds of "Obligation" were thrown off, deference and obedience to the ruling elite might be threatened. Respect for the established church, its religious dogmas and its moral precepts would be enforced by criminal law in a manner exactly parallel to prohibitions on questioning the fitness of the rulers to rule and the propriety of their actions.[6]

Blasphemy has long ago lost its political importance throughout the common law world, and it is not necessary here to explore the history of how that occurred. However, it is worth bearing that history in mind, for it casts light on one serious present-day threat to freedom of expression. In many Islamic countries, blasphemy remains a serious offence, used particularly against artists and intellectuals who offer cultural critiques of the regime in power. Yet this is not simply the oppression of one political group by another which has been more successful in the competition for political power. Islamic society, like all of Europe two centuries ago and most of Europe much more recently, does not recognize the separation of law, morality, religion, and culture into discrete spheres of life. Nor does it regard these as matters of personal choice, or what has irritatingly become known as 'life style' in the West. This integration of spheres of life which have become fragmented elsewhere means that anything which appears as a significant threat to one aspect is treated as a threat to the totality. Empirically, this view may well be correct: hereditary rule of Christian monarchs in Europe was sapped as much by religious and cultural disaffection as by enthusiasm for the principles of democracy or socialism. The struggle for freedom of expression therefore confronts a far more deeply rooted and determined ideological opposition in Muslim countries than in those which have come within the Western cultural sphere.

---

[5] *R.* v. *Taylor*, 1 Vent. 293, 86 ER 189 (1676).

[6] *See further*, L. Lustgarten and I. Leigh, *In From the Cold: National Security and Parliamentary Democracy*, [hereafter *In From The Cold*], at 203-05 and sources cited in n.44 therein (Oxford, 1994).

The second, and even more important, common law offense used to curb dissent was sedition.[7] In view of its continued importance as a tool of suppression in Commonwealth states today -- one of the inglorious legacies of Empire -- it is worth detailing its rise and decline in England in some detail.

Sedition, like blasphemy, was a creation of the judiciary, developed at the behest of the Crown.[8] At the end of the 17th century, Parliament grew alarmed at the use of the Treason Acts against pamphleteers and publishers, for the possibility of its application to those who chose the wrong side in the faction-ridden court politics of the time threatened all politicians. The resulting legislation, which made convictions for treason based on printed criticism almost impossible, led to a search for a suitable replacement. Sedition, previously a subcategory of the law of defamation, was developed into a distinct branch of criminal law. The judges enlarged the range of prohibited conduct, and circumscribed the jury's role in deciding the relevant issues. Hence, the resemblance to treason grew increasingly stronger, as exemplified by the direction to the jury in one of the last cases in which the old law prevailed:

> Sedition is a crime against society, nearly allied to that of treason, and it frequently precedes treason by a short interval . . . The objects of seditions generally are to induce discontent and insurrection, and stir up opposition to the Government . . . the very tendency of sedition is to incite people to insurrection and rebellion. Sedition has been described as disloyalty in action.[9]

From the prosecuting government's point of view, sedition was an ideal weapon because its breadth and vagueness could encompass almost anything. As one commentator notes,

> The sources of the decisions on sedition in the first half of the nineteenth century include broad notions. They cover the illegality of conspiracies, unlawful societies, 'combinations against the government', incitement as a misdemeanor, and cases regarded as examples of unlawful assembly by reason of a seditious intent. This last group was seen in general political terms rather than the likelihood of breaches of the peace.[10]

The charge was most readily employed against speakers and writers, and hence the modern history of sedition throughout the common law word is tightly intertwined with freedom of speech and the ability to criticize governments. As the British political elite became more secure in its position, and mid-Victorian Britain

---

[7] The discussion here draws heavily upon *In From the Cold*, *supra* at 205-10.

[8] This paragraph is based on P. Hamburger, "The Development of the Law of Seditious Libel and the Control of the Press", 37 Stan.L.Rev. 661 (1985).

[9] *R.* v. *Sullivan* 11 Cox CC 44, 45 (1868).

[10] M. Supperstone, *Brownlie's Law of Public Order and National Security*, at 235-36 (footnotes omitted) (London, 2d ed. 1981).

developed a self-confidence in liberal institutions that led to greater tolerance, sedition prosecutions diminished and the offense itself was narrowed by the courts. In a famous trial in 1886, the jury (which acquitted the defendant) were instructed that sedition requires

> an intention to bring into hatred or contempt or incite disaffection against the person of Her Majesty ... or to excite Her Majesty's subjects to attempt, otherwise than by lawful means, the alteration of any matter in Church or State by law established, or to raise discontent or disaffection amongst Her Majesty's subjects, or to promote feelings of ill-will and hostility between different classes of such subjects.[11]

Sedition in Britain soon fell into abeyance, though not complete disuse. They remained a potent force throughout the Empire, particularly when combating independence movements. Speeches by independence leaders of colonial populations urging freedom and independence, were regarded by the colonial authorities as inflammatory and dangerous. Sedition laws, a mechanism designed to control the masses at home were readily adapted for use against subject peoples overseas.

Sedition charges were also used against left wing labor activists, particularly Communists, in the white Dominions. However, such prosecutions against religious minorities in Canada produced a major curtailment of the offense. In *Boucher* v. *The King*,[12] the Supreme Court of Canada held that in order for sedition to be established, there must exist "an intention to incite violence or create public disturbance or disorder against the institutions of government . . . there must be violence or defiance for the purpose of disturbing constituted authority." This decision in turn has had a benign influence in Britain; described by the English Law Commission as 'the most careful analysis which has been given to the law of sedition in recent years',[13] *Boucher* was cited by the Divisional Court as the leading authority for its rejection of the attempt by a Muslim cleric to revive the offense by instituting proceedings against Salman Rushdie for publishing *The Satanic Verses*.[14]

The decline of sedition in Britain is one of the relatively rare examples of progress in relation to freedom of dissent. The idea that any form of expression can *of itself* constitute a threat to the security of the nation cannot be squared with even the most rudimentary conception of liberty or democracy. This is true regardless of the content of the expression, including advocacy of violent revolution or overthrow of an elected government. There is less reason for toleration when speech begins to merge in time and place with other forms of prohibited, and especially violent, actions. However, this becomes a matter of public order, protection of the safety of

---

[11] *R.* v. *Burns*, 16 Cox CC 355, 360 (1886).
[12] *Boucher* v. *R.*, 2 D.I.R. 369 (1951).
[13] Law Commission (England), Working Paper No. 72, *Treason, Sedition and Allied Offenses* (1976).
[14] *R.* v. *Chief London Stipendiary Magistrate, ex p. Choudhury*, 1 Q.B. 429, 452-53 (1991).

individuals, or possibly both. The virtue of the *Boucher* test is that any seditious speech would also amount to incitement or conspiracy to commit a substantive offense of some seriousness, such as an offense against the person or criminal damage. The English Law Commission recognized this and therefore considered sedition to be otiose, and recommended its abolition.[15] The basic principle that the criminal law restrict its scope to criminal acts alone, and never to ideas is a paramount principle which it is essential to defend, above all when national security is proclaimed as the reason for curbing freedom of expression.

One other element, common to the history of both sedition and blasphemy, deserves to be highlighted. Technically, both were species of libel, in the 18th-century usage of the term meaning a small writing. In libel cases, jurors were required to answer only two narrow questions of fact: did the accused publish the alleged libel, and did the publication carry the meaning claimed in the indictment? The key question of whether the publication was seditious was left to the judge – one reason why late 18th century judges, and Lord Mansfield, the Lord Chief Justice, in particular, were subject to invecture and decision. The judges were seen as government stooges or placemen, and their interpretations of the law regarded as entirely political.

After years of agitation for reform, Charles James Fox finally carried his Libel Act in 1792, which laid down the principle, never since disturbed, that jurors alone would decide the question of sedition. Taking what is undeniably a legal decision away from the judge and allocating it to laypersons may seem inappropriate, even irrational, but the reform was deliberately designed as a check on abuse of the power of prosecution. It should be seen too as directly connected to the fact that juries are never required to give reasons for their verdicts. This allows full scope for what is known as 'jury nullification': the refusal to convict, not because the accused is factually innocent, but to thwart what representatives of the wider community regard as a politically biased or oppressive prosecution.

It should be a guiding precept in designing protections for freedom of expression within the machinery of justice. The power of decision making should in all possible instances be given to the jury, not to judges, however formally independent of the prosecuting authorities.

---

[15] *R.* v. *Burns*, note 12, *supra*, at para. 77. Even more compelling is the case for abolition of the offense of seditious conspiracy, which combines all the vices of sedition with the procedural advantages the government gains when it can employ conspiracy laws. *See In From The Cold*, at 210-16.

IV. The Ascendancy of the Official Secrets Act

A. Criminal Sanctions.

Direct punishment of writers, publishers and speakers through criminal prosecution has come in recent decades to have a decidedly anachronistic flavor. This is not solely because the technology of communications has been transformed so radically, with the heavily regulated medium of television becoming the primary means through which news and opinions reach most members of the public. This development *is* important, but of greater consequence has been the profound change of political context.

The use of offenses like sedition reflected the vulnerability and concerns of the political elite in an earlier era. Up to the mid-nineteenth century, when virtually no one had the right to vote, the majority of people were illiterate and police forces rudimentary, the great fear was of "the rabble" inflamed by pamphleteers or soap-box orators lampooning ministers and their policies.

The modern Western state has far greater legitimacy in the eyes of its subjects. It provides both elaborate trappings and sufficient substance of democracy to create an identification between the ruled and their rulers in order to ensure loyalty and obedience. Now the state is quite capable of withstanding the traditional form of generalized and highly emotive criticism, which in any case seems to have lost its audience in an audio-visual culture of mass consumerism.

However, mass literacy and widened access to education, coupled with an astounding combination of scandals and incompetence shown by successive governments over 40 years, have produced widespread disillusionment and the virtual evaporation of the deference that outsiders used to regard as peculiarly British, or at any rate English. The result is that the battleground of dissent has shifted. The government is much less secretive than it was 40 years ago, but the public and the press no longer content with accepting the official version, demand to know much more.

From the viewpoint of officialdom, one of the main virtues of secrecy is the ability to deflect or dismiss criticism by pretending to possess more complete and more accurate information. If critics can be portrayed as ill- informed, they can more readily be dismissed. Nowhere is this control over information more rigorously defended than in relation to foreign affairs, "defense" and "national security". Hence, in Britain successive Official Secrets Acts are the direct descendants of blasphemy and sedition, and conflicts over official secrecy have moved to centre stage.[16]

One initial point should be noted. For many years Britain stood virtually alone in the West in its refusal to enact any sort of freedom of information

---

16 The Official Secrets Act of 1911 was exported throughout the Empire, and remains (quiescent) on the statute book in both Canada and Australia.

legislation. This has now changed dramatically: a White Paper in December 1997[17] set out the basic structure for a statute which has been much praised by F.O.I. campaign groups for its progressive approach. The Bill should be enacted with little alteration by the end of 1998, (though its implementation will be phased in thereafter) and may well make major incursions into the excessive secrecy that has surrounded British government generally. In relation to national security, its likely impact is less clear. The White Paper, alluding to practice in comparable countries, proposes that information relating to the interests of "national security," "defence" and "international relations" (one portmanteau category) may be withheld from the public if the government can show that its disclosure would cause "substantial harm" to those interests. Experience elsewhere has shown that such access exemptions tend to be widely interpreted by governments, and are supplemented by other legislative and executive prohibitions on release of information. Judges have shown themselves consistently impervious to pleas for narrow interpretation of these exemptions and related powers.[18] Nor have constitutional provisions on freedom of speech been interpreted as requiring positive rights of access to official information, however useful they may be in striking down restrictions on speech or publication by citizens or the media.

Britain thus seems belatedly to have joined the mainstream of democratic practice in relation to access laws, but these have had little effect in making available information about current controversial policies and operations in the hyper-sensitive "national security" area. Where Britain has stood out, however, is in the use of official secrets legislation to deter and punish those who have sought to make public information withheld by the executive, purportedly in the interests of national security though actually as protection against embarrassment or justified criticism.

In 1911, a prohibition on unauthorized disclosure, section 2 of the Official Secrets Act, came into force on the back of a statute, rammed through a half-empty Parliament on a Friday afternoon, whose main provision was concerned with espionage.[19] Governments had long been awaiting the opportunity to deal with "leaking" through criminal penalties,[20] and the statute was remarkable for its almost unlimited breadth. Moreover, whenever its vague language fell to be construed by the courts, they *always* chose the wider interpretation. A reading of these cases

---

[17] A White Paper is a statement of government policy which sets out, often with considerable specificity, proposals for legislation in a particular area. Most Bills of any significance are usually preceded by a White Paper. The one of freedom of information is 'Your Right to Know, Cm3918 (1997).

[18] For the judicial record in Canada and Australia, *see* Lustgarten & Leigh, 116-26; for the United States, P. Birkinshaw, *Reforming the Secret State* 54-62 (Milton Keynes, 1990).

[19] This espionage has remained in force virtually unamended since 1911 and has been relatively uncontroversial. It is not considered further in this paper.

[20] *For background on the 1911 Act, see* D.G.T. Williams, *Not in the Public Interest* ch. 1 (London, 1965).

shows the idea that the judiciary act would restrain potential abuses of the Acts by applying the maxim of strict construction of penal statutes to be a complete myth.[21]

In general terms, section 2 made it unlawful for any person who had obtained any official information (in any form) as a result of his present or former position as the holder of an office under the Crown or as a government contractor to reveal that material without "authorization." This prohibition, enforced by the possibility of up to 2 years imprisonment, applied indiscriminately to *all* government material, regardless of antiquity, subject or triviality. Although prior approval of the Attorney General was required before any prosecution could be mounted, that purported safeguard did not prevent the launch of over fifty prosecutions between 1955 and 1985. Many, perhaps most of these were excessive or unnecessary: they involved either negligence, or other forms of incompetence, by those in the public service or the armed forces, or conduct that should have been prosecuted as theft or corruption. Beginning in the late 1960s, section 2 began to be subject to an increasingly loud and insistent crescendo of criticism, some of which came from within the judiciary itself.[22]

The most controversial prosecution under section 2 was also the last. A senior civil servant in the Ministry of Defense called Clive Ponting had reason to know that answers given by Ministers to questions raised by Opposition MPs about the sinking of an Argentine ship during the Falklands War were misleading if not false. He therefore (covertly) supplied the most persistent parliamentary critic with some material indicating that he was not being told the truth. Ponting's only conceivable statutory defense was to invoke an exclusion in section 2, which did not apply where the defendant communicated the information "in the interest of the State." Ponting argued that since the responsibility of Ministers to Parliament is the fundamental principle of the unwritten British constitution, disclosure which upheld that principle by unmasking duplicity was in the highest "interest of the State." The trial judge, who was extremely hostile to Ponting, rejected this emphatically and directed the jury that the interest of the State was to be equated with the policies of the government of the day. The jury, however, showed its mettle and, fully appreciating the authoritarian implications of the judge's direction, exercised its historic right of "nullification" and acquitted Ponting.

Taking the issues into the highest realms of constitutional principle and political philosophy made the trial into a major news event. The jury's verdict was the death knell for section 2, the Government taking the view that the Act was so discredited that convictions under it could no longer be expected. However, its response was not to let the matter rest, but to introduce new legislation. Before that decision was taken, however, it began to deploy new and in some ways more dangerous weapons.

---

[21] *See* Lustgarten & Leigh at 240-41.

[22] For an excellent popular history, which also provides a summary description of numerous cases, *see* D. Hooper, *Official Secrets* (London, 1987).

B. The Civil Route

In 1986, the year following the Ponting trial, a totally unknown official who had retired from MI 5, Britain's security service, published a book which was partly about his experiences in the job, but mostly about his obsessions with Russian "moles." His name was Peter Wright, and the book was called *Spycatcher* – both of which were to become famous round the world in a remarkably short period of time.

Wright's book was first published in Australia, where he was living in retirement. It is overly long, excessively technical in places and turgid in others, but contains material fascinating for what it reveals about the conduct of government in Britain.[23] Most importantly, it is based almost entirely on Wright's experiences in the Security Service. Partly due to the shock of having so much of MI5's operations brought to light, and partly to stave off the prospect of other ex-agents and officials revealing more, and more recent, material it wished to keep secret, the Thatcher government moved swiftly and relentlessly to suppress not merely its publication, but all comment upon it. Thus began a three-year world-wide battle which, though ending in a victory for freedom of expression, did so almost by accident and only after a long period of suppression.

The legal mechanism by which the government pursued its aim was breach of confidence. This is a well-recognized action in private law, going back to the successful effort of the husband of Queen Victoria to prevent a public exhibition of sketches he and the Queen had drawn of their family, which had been pirated by a printer's assistant.[24] It had, however, been extended to matters of state in the 1970s,[25] emerging as a newly-fashioned weapon of suppression that successive governments were not slow to exploit. Its history stands as a warning of the dangers of allowing governments to make use of legal principles designed to protect private interests. Another way to say this is that the government as litigant should be restricted by principles of public law, and not be treated as though it had the characteristics of a private citizen -- in particular, that of inherent liberty.. This conception may be slowly entering the thinking of English judges,[26] but there is a long road to travel before its acceptance can be regarded as beyond question, and it was even less well established at the time of the *Spycatcher* litigation. After all, less than a decade earlier, one of England's most senior judges had rejected a challenge to the legality of telephone tapping, which had been undertaken with no statutory authorization at

---

[23] For a detailed assessment of the value of the book (quite different from what Wright himself intended to achieve by publishing it), *see* Lustgarten, *Learning From Peter Wright*, 60 Pol.Q. 222 (1989).

[24] *Prince Albert* v. *Strange*, 1 Mac & G 25 (1849).

[25] In the Crossman Diaries case, *Attorney-General* v. *Jonathan Cape Ltd.*, Q.B. 752 (1976).

[26] *See* especially the *Derbyshire County Council* case, *see supra* note 3, which overruled precedent and held that a public body could not sue for defamation of its governing reputation in response to newspaper criticism.

all, in part on the grounds that government officials, like any citizen, could do anything they liked so long as it was not explicitly forbidden.[27]

Compared with criminal proceedings under official secrets legislation, taking the civil route had extraordinary advantages for the government. As plaintiff, rather than prosecutor, it could prevail by satisfying the much lower standard of proof. In many instances, the defendant has not even the opportunity to be heard in the initial round of the litigation. This is because the procedural law of injunctive relief permits an *ex parte* application, which has been exploited for decades by employers seeking to curtail strikes. However, government lawyers have taken this a step further and have often applied either over the telephone or late at night at a judge's home[28] for injunctions, which were granted subject to an undertaking that a writ would subsequently be filed and the defendant given notice to appear at a hearing. Of course, once the injunction is granted publication has been prevented and the government has achieved its initial goal. The government then enters the courtroom with several advantages, not least that if the material is of a character that would be politically discreditable to the government, it will have avoided justified criticism and been able to keep the public in ignorance and the Opposition at bay, while being able to use the time gained to assemble its own public relations armory and begin a counter-attack.

Because ordinary civil litigation principles apply in such litigation, the courts apply the standard test when an injunction is sought. Enunciated in a commercial dispute between two multinational companies,[29] it is heavily weighted towards any plaintiff who seeks to preserve the status quo. It does this by accepting that the litigation may be divided into two stages, "interlocutory" and final. The plaintiff therefore has only to meet a lower standard at the first stage for an injunction to be granted; it is perfectly possible (as indeed happened in the *Spycatcher* case) to succeed at the interlocutory stage and lose at the full trial.

However, since the point of the injunction is to prohibit publication at the time it is first sought to put the material in the public domain and popular interest would be at its highest, the interlocutory stage is much the most important. At this point, all the government need show is that it has an arguable case in law, that damages would be an inadequate or inappropriate remedy and, if not, that the "balance of convenience" lies in granting the injunction. Since the first two hurdles are cleared very easily, the decision whether to grant an interlocutory injunction almost always hinges on this last issue.

It is only here that the notion of a public interest in freedom of the press and open debate is even considered, and the vague parameters of the question to be decided are an open invitation for judges to write their personal values into law. Indeed, the judgment requires weighing considerations so qualitatively different that

---

[27] *Malone* v. *Metropolitan Police Commissioner*, Ch. 344 (1979) (Megarry V-C).
[28] This became known during the Spycatcher affair as "pyjama justice".
[29] *American Cyanamid Co.* v. *Ethicon Ltd.*, A.C. 396 (1975).

it is a bit like comparing the taste of strawberries and lobster. Moreover, even judges who take democratic values seriously and give due weight to press freedom find it very difficult to resist statements by the government that national security requires that it prevail.[30] The government has an insidious advantage here, because although the basis of its claim is breach of confidence, when the subject matter of that confidence has overtones of national security, judges tend to be very deferential to its assertions.[31] Governments can thus avoid criticisms that they are invoking national security when their real purpose is to prevent political embarrassment,[32] yet still benefit from judicial deference to win the case. The result in the 1980s was that in at least a dozen applications for interim injunctions concerning a range of articles, radio and television programs (none of which reached the Law Reports), the Crown succeeded in every instance bar one, and that was lost only because it would have required encroaching upon ancient parliamentary privileges.

One important matter that is never adequately specified is the precise public interest in suppression of information. In Round 1 of the *Spycatcher* saga, no dominant reason appears, the majority judgments rather loosely combining anger at the prospect of someone outside the jurisdiction flouting the power of British courts to make their orders effective, with concern that if one Security Service official was allowed to "get away with" unauthorized publication, others would be stimulated to follow.[33] Even the final judgments more than two years later, in which after a full trial on the merits the injunctions were discharged, insist upon the paramount importance of the principle that members of the Security Service (and perhaps by parity of reasoning others with access to similar information) are bound by a life-long duty of confidence to the Crown -- which means silence in respect of the public.[34]

---

[30] The reluctant acceptance of this argument by Lord Justice Bingham in the *Spycatcher* litigation is an example of this, *see infra* note 34. This phenomenon must be seen in the context of the general approach that British courts take when the government plays the national security card in judicial review litigation: they will look to satisfy themselves that national security is genuinely at issue, but will then refuse to question the government's view that it require the action taken in the case before it. This approach was laid down by the House of Lords in the famous GCHQ case, *Council of Civil Service Unions* v. *Minister for the Civil Service*, A.C. 374 (1985).

[31] For a general analysis of judicial approaches to national security cases in a wide range of contexts, *see In From The Cold*, ch. 12, 330-59.

[32] As happened in *Sec. of State* v. *Guardian Newspapers*, A.C. 339 (1984), where two of the five Law Lords dissented and showed themselves markedly unimpressed by the Government's claims. This was nonetheless a passing irritation, since the majority upheld its claim for the return of documents leaked to a newspaper.

[33] *A-G* v. *Guardian Newspapers*, 3 All E.R. 316, 356-57 (Lord Templeman), 363 (Lord Ackner) (1987).

[34] This is stated most explicitly in the leading judgment of Lord Keith, *A-G* v. *Guardian Newspapers* (No. 2), 3 All E.R. 545, 646, (Lord Keith) (1988).

This leaves entirely up in the air the obvious problem of how those who are best placed to know of illegal or improper activities are to get the abuses stopped when their superiors may have authorized or indeed be directly involved in them . Only the Judge at first instance was prepared to say unequivocally that in such circumstances the duty of confidence is discharged and that the Press would be a proper recipient of the information.[35] Most of the judgments in the House of Lords do not address this issue, and those which do touch upon it are nothing like as robust in this respect.[36] Thus the public interest in correction of official misconduct is given much less weight than the internal discipline of the Security Service, a preference that can be defended, but not by arguments which sit comfortably with the values of a healthy democracy.

However, the greatest advantage to the government of taking the civil route was political. It was inconceivable that even a government headed by Margaret Thatcher would have haled editors of leading national newspapers into the dock: the costs of making such powerful enemies would simply have been too great. A criminal trial of such matters generates a blaze of unfavorable publicity, spread over an extended period. By contrast, the technicalities of injunction proceedings are well beyond the understanding of the general public, and once the order is made, any attempt at publication becomes no longer the use of a controversial statute, but a contempt of court. Though perhaps the most arbitrary form of criminal jurisdiction in existence, this carries very different moral and political connotations of "upholding the rule of law". Moreover, and very conveniently, it is enforced by judicial penalties without the possibility of a jury trial. No possible nullification of judicial arbitrariness is permitted.[37]

The final result of the *Spycatcher* cases was simply the triumph of pragmatism. Every British judge who either directly considered or commented on the initial injunctions, which forbade virtually all Press commentary on the issues involved, took the view that they were correctly issued.[38] These were in force for more than a year, after which the widespread sale of the book in the United States, coupled with the failure of the British government's action in Australia, led to attempts by the newspapers subject to the injunctions to have them discharged. This was eventually rejected by a sharply-divided House of Lord.[39] The matter then

---

[35] Scott J., 3 All E.R. 545, 588-89 (1988).

[36] Indeed they are only prepared to accept the propriety of disclosure to the media in the most extraordinary circumstances, *e.g.* Lord Goff, 3 All E.R. at 659-60 (1988).

[37] Compare the position in the United States where the constitutional guarantee of trial by jury has been extended to all but 'petty' contempt cases: C.J. Miller, *Contempt of Court* at 93-96 (2d ed. 1990).

[38] There was much greater dissent when the issue reached the European Court of Human Rights, were these injunctions were upheld only by 14 votes to 10: *Observer and Guardian* v. *United Kingdom*, (14 E.H.H.R. 153)(1991) and *Sunday Times* v. *United Kingdom*, (14 E.H.H.R. 229) (1991).

[39] *See supra* note 33.

received a lengthy trial, which the government lost, as it did the appeals which again ended in the Lords.[40]

The primary ground on which it failed, however, was not freedom of the press or the democratic requirement of full information for scrutiny of government. It was the pointlessness of trying to staunch the flow of information once it had been breached by publication in the United States (where the First Amendment would have made the government's whole legal campaign impossible at the outset). This ineradicable fact was treated as a matter of great regret, with most of the judges clinging obstinately to a statist view of the public interest.[41] Media commentary on the issues was suppressed by the judiciary for over two years.

V. The New Official Secrets Act

The second strand of the Thatcher government's approach was to try to revive criminal prohibitions on disclosure. Its strategy was cunningly gauged: the potential reach of the law was greatly narrowed, though mostly by excluding the sort of material that would never have led to a prosecution.[42] Six categories of information are covered by the Official Secrets Act 1989; those most relevant here are "defense", "international relations", and "security and intelligence." Discussion can be relatively brief, because there has not been a prosecution under the Act in its five years of existence.[43]

For liability to be established, the disclosure must be "damaging," a concept that is defined so as to be tailored to the particular category of information. This specificity is a welcome change from the vague catch-all provisions that have operated in the past, but it has been achieved at a price.

First, there is no longer any scope for the "Ponting defense," in that the "interests of the State" language does not appear in the 1989 Act.

Second, the definition of "damage" is in some instances rigged so as to be almost impossible to establish. For example, where the information relates to international relations, disclosure is declared to be damaging if, among other things,

---

[40] *See supra* note 34

[41] Having decided reluctantly that the injunctions could not be supported, Lord Keith concluded with ruminations on the "possibility of some international agreement aimed at reducing the risks to collective security involved in the present state of affairs": 3 All E.R. 646 (1988).

[42] Here one sees the political importance of discretion granted the Attorney-General by the old and new Acts: prosecutions that could be expected to bring the legislation into disrepute because the subject matter of the disclosure would be regarded by juries and the wider public as inappropriate for criminal penalties can be quietly prevented. The old section 2 was never applied to the full range of disclosures that, on its bare language, could have supported prosecutions.

[43] For fuller analysis, *see* Lustgarten and Leigh, at 224, 228-48.

"it endangers the interests of the United Kingdom abroad [or] seriously obstructs the promotion or protection of . . . those interests," or the unauthorized disclosure is "likely" to have any of those effects.[44] Those "interests" have been left carefully undefined – do they include, for example, furthering arms sales, one of Britain's great export trades? There must be a real concern that a statement by a government witness asserting what those interests are in the context of the particular prosecution will be treated by the court as unimpeachable evidence. This was the approach taken in a famous and controversial Official Secrets Act trial of the 1960s, and was approved by the House of Lords.[45]

The old section 2 was only rarely used against journalists who published disclosures, its main target being their sources, who were usually civil servants or other officials. However, those who made the actual disclosure were in formal terms within its reach, and the same is true of the current law. Section 5 prohibits any "damaging" disclosure of information by any person who has received it as a result of a communication which was itself without lawful authority. It remains very unlikely however that any government would want to provoke a head-on confrontation with the Press by prosecuting journalists under this section. In this respect the situation remains unchanged despite the passage of the new law: in the words of David Leigh, one of Britain's most experienced investigative journalists, "the Act is what the political situation at the moment says it is."[46]

Much the most draconian provision, however, is a direct response to the government's ultimate defeat in the *Spycatcher* litigation. Any past or serving members of the intelligence or security services are simply and absolutely prohibited from revealing without authorization any information gained as a result of their work. There are *no* defenses, and the maximum penalty, as with all offenses under the statute, is two years imprisonment.[47] Thus far this section has been used only once, against an officer of SIS (the overseas intelligence service) who threatened to publish a book revealing secret information when the courts refused to hear his complaint of unfair dismissal at the behest of a certificate issued by the relevant Minister stating that national security was involved. There were no wider political overtones and no public outcry, but the defendant pleaded guilty and hence there was no occasion to see how a jury would react to the terms of the law.

Given that the main target of official secrets laws are the sources of leaks, namely civil servants, it is worth remembering that criminal penalties are by no means the most important means by which governments prevent release of

---

[44] OSA sec. 3(2) (a) (b) (1989).
[45] *Chandler* v. *DPP*, AC 763 (1964).
[46] *In From The Cold*, at 267.
[47] OSA sec. 1 (1989). Technically there is a defense, which is that the accused did not know that the material in question related to security or intelligence matters. Given that the statute applies only to people who have worked in the field for many years, anyone who could avail himself of it would probably have to be mentally incompetent to stand trial.

information they wish for their own reasons to keep from the public. Most individuals are reasonably ambitious, and would like to advance their careers, or at least to maintain them. It requires no heavy arsenal of penalties, merely the certainty of blighted prospects, to produce obedience to rules of secrecy. For those for whom carrots do not work, there are also sticks.

Public officials everywhere are subject to employment regulations. In Britain this takes the form of the Civil Service Management Code, which reinforces the normal rules about employee confidentiality with sanctions ranging from warning to reprimand through to dismissal. It takes an unusually forthright person to ignore the prospect of these sanctions. Indeed the real problem is protecting those whose sense of higher public duty leads them to reveal improper or illegal conduct, and who then are victimized in their work. Such "whistleblowers" should be protected, indeed encouraged, because they are usually the only people with access to the information necessary to make credible accusations of official misconduct.[48] While in opposition, the Labour Party had supported freedom of information proposals which included prohibitions on job-related sanctions against whistleblowers. Regrettably, their generally admirable blueprint for legislation issued when in government omits any mention of this issue.

VI. Controls on Broadcasting

Broadcasting is heavily regulated in Britain, a tradition going back to the elaborate licensing conditions imposed on the BBC at its birth in 1926.[49] In addition, there is a history of politicians exerting behind the scenes pressures on the BBC at times of crises, as well as internal censorship by management over the work of journalists.[50] This was intensified in the mid-1980s, when a television documentary including an interview with a leader of Sinn Fein was temporarily shelved after pressure from the Home Secretary, and the government successfully 'leaned on' the BBC to ban a six-part radio program about issues concerning governance and accountability of security services world-wide.[51]

---

[48] For a brief discussion of the issues, *see In From The Cold*, at 257-60.

[49] The regulatory regime has altered in a number of ways since the matters discussed in the text occurred. However, in relation to those issues there has been little change: Section 10 (3) of the Broadcasting Act 1990 is virtually equivalent.

[50] *See* the sources cited in *In From The Cold*, at 266 note 74.

[51] The quoted phrase is that of Lord Lawson, Chancellor of the Exchequer, *The View From No. 11*, 314 (London, 1992). *See also In From The Cold*, at 266-68.

These and other informal political pressures[52] are probably the most influential levers available to government that wish to prevent criticism and maintain secrecy. However, there is in addition the power of direct prohibition on broadcasting certain material upon command of the Home Secretary. This was invoked in 1988 when the latter ordered all broadcasters to refrain from broadcasting the direct spoken words of any person representing certain organizations, or words spoken by anyone which support or solicit support for such organizations. Although when this was challenged in court the judges expressed surprise at how narrowly focused the ban was, in fact, for several months it was operated far more pervasively than the bare language would suggest, as managers imposed a panicky censorship on journalists.

Neither the BBC nor the Independent Broadcasting Authority had the courage to challenge the ban, but a number of political journalists did. They met with unremitting failure at every level of the courts, and fared no better at Strasbourg.[53] Essentially the judges held that the ban was a reasonable exercise of the Home Secretary's discretion, and that no other principles recognized in English administrative law would serve to invalidate it.

Although this episode was quite unusual, it does illustrate that it is idle to look solely to principles of judicial review of administrative discretion as support for freedom of expression. In its wider context, it also illustrates an even more important point. The Republic of Ireland had an even more severe broadcasting ban in force for many years.[54] It also has a written constitution with an entrenched Bill of Rights which includes a guarantee of freedom of expression. Nonetheless the Irish Supreme Court had no difficulty in upholding the ban, on the grounds that this freedom is stated in the Constitution to be "subject to public order and morality," which it thought plainly encompassed countering threats to the authority of the state and preventing commission of crime.[55] Nor did the European Commission on Human Rights, which dismissed complaints filed from both countries as "manifestly ill-founded," *i.e.*, not raising serious issues of fact or law.[56] It seems quite clear that whenever there is a direct confrontation between freedom of expression and national security, judges everywhere will almost automatically uphold government claims.

---

[52] Most importantly by influencing the allocation of commercial television licenses and packing the BBC Board of Governors with its supporters. Lurking in the background is that the government sets the BBC's license fee, its primary source of income.

[53] *R.* v. *Home Sec., ex p. Brind*, 1 All E.R. 469 (Ct of App.) (1991) A.C. 696 (H.L.). *See also Brind* v. *United Kingdom*, App. No. 18714/91, 18 EHHR (Supp.) CD76 (May, 1994).

[54] Both countries lifted their bans after the cease-fire in autumn 1994.

[55] *The State (Lynch)* v. *Cooney*, I.R. 337 (1982), construing Art. 40.6.1 of the Constitution.

[56] *Purcell* v. *Ireland*, App. No. 15404/89, 70 D & R 262 (1991), and the *Brind* case, note 56, *supra*.

VII. Conclusions

When looking at ways to strengthen freedom of expression against attempts at suppression by the Executive in the name of national security, it is essential that many different avenues be pursued simultaneously. One of the most important is strengthening the independent critical role of Parliament as against the Executive. Since this will require upsetting a century of development whereby the Executive has turned constitutional norms of parliamentary sovereignty and ministerial responsibility on their heads, it is a major project of political institution-building. A subject so vast and complex cannot be addressed in this paper, nor indeed is it part of the creation of legal norms as such. Nonetheless it is fundamental to the enterprise.

A second line of attack is at the level of formal legal principles. Here the most important is to press for adoption of prohibition on "prior restraint," executive or judicial. As found in the interpretation of the First Amendment in the United States, this is not an absolutist doctrine in the sense that it forbids pre-publication censorship under any circumstances. To cite what seems to have been the view that commanded greatest support in the *Pentagon Papers* litigation, for an injunction to be issued, the government must show that publication *would* (not could) cause direct, immediate and irreparable harm to the nation.[57] These criteria are extremely difficult but not impossible for any government to satisfy, which gets the balance right.

As the *Spycatcher* saga showed, in the real world of global communications and multi-national publishing companies, many governments are in this context limited by American constitutional norms, and there are powerful reasons of comity as well as merit for elevating them to international status.

As well as substantive laws curbing publication directly, of equal if not greater importance are protections for those who divulge information. The two key issues here are 1) protection of "whistleblowers" from both criminal prosecution and employment victimization; and 2) protection of the anonymity of media sources.[58] In this respect, a provision of the Swedish Freedom of the Press Act, (which enjoys constitutional status) provides an excellent model to follow. It imposes a positive obligation on journalists and editors not to reveal the identity of any person who has communicated information to him.[59] This goes further than the standard journalist's privilege,[60] in that it cannot be waived even if the journalist wishes to name the source. Journalists have gone to prison in Britain for refusing to reveal sources to

---

[57] *See New York Times* v. *United States*, 403 US 713 (1971) and the discussion in E. Barendt, *Freedom of Speech* at chap. 4, 135-37 (Oxford, 1985).
[58] For more detailed discussion, *see In From The Cold*, at 252-57.
[59] Freedom of the Press Act, Chap.3, Art. 3, although this too is subject to certain (narrow) qualifications.
[60] *See* Korthals Altes, *Protecting Journalists' Sources--a Dutch Proposal for Legislation* (1992) Pub.L. 73 (1992).

tribunals investigating security matters,[61] and the threat of imprisonment for contempt of court in such circumstances continues to hang over their heads today.

The question of punishment returns us to the basic theme which has recurred throughout this essay. It should be a fundamental principal that all decisions leading to imposition of restrictions or penalties on freedom of expression be taken by juries, not by judges and, of course, never by state officials alone. In some instances, this may require giving jurors rather than judges the power to decide questions of law. This is precisely what Fox's Libel Act, just over two centuries ago, did for the purposes of checking the oppressive use of sedition charges.

Nor is this practice limited to common law jurisdictions in the West. The same Swedish legislation discussed above contains a provision mandating a trial by jury in any prosecution in which freedom of the press is in issue. This is the sole occasion in Swedish penal law in which a jury is used; and the qualities specified for jurors clearly envisage their role as protectors of freedom of expression: 'They shall be known for their soundness of judgment, independence and fairmindedness. Different social groups and currents of opinion . . . shall be represented among the jurors.[62] This recognition that the paramount importance of freedom of expression uniquely demands public participation in any attempt at judicial punishment demonstrates that use of the jury need not be limited to the Anglo-Saxon countries.

Jury determination would be of great benefit, both in relation to punishment for contempt and to the issuance of injunctions. Declaring an issue to be a question of law – and therefore to be decided by judges – does not involve the application of an uncontroversial standard or criterion. Still less is it a simple statement of fact. It is either a claim of institutional competence, or an assertion of political power. It is thus a question of judgment about the wider public benefit; and it seems clear from the record that where claims of national security are involved, judges are not to be trusted to protect freedom of expression.

---

[61] *A-G* v. *Mulholland and Foster*, [1963] 2 Q.B. 447 (1990), and *A-G* v. *Clough*, 1 Q.B. 773 (1963).
[62] Swedish Freedom of the Press Act, Ch. 12, Arts. 2-5. This provision applies in any prosecution relating to press freedom, not only in the context of national security. The Act, and the provisions of the Fundamental Law on Freedom of Expression underpinning it, is published in English by the Swedish Riksdag (Parliament). I am most grateful to Mr. Peter Danowsky, of Danowsky & Partners, Stockholm, for making a copy available to me.

SAFEGUARDING LIBERTY: NATIONAL SECURITY, FREEDOM OF EXPRESSION AND ACCESS TO INFORMATION: UNITED STATES OF AMERICA

Paul Hoffman and Kate Martin

I. Expression Deemed Threatening to National Security or Territorial Integrity

A. Advocacy of Conscientious Objection, Desertion, Giving Support to the Enemy, Lowering the Morale of the Military

In the fifty-year period from the decision in *Schenck* v. *United States*[1] to the decision in *Brandenburg* v. *Ohio*,[2] the United States Supreme Court struggled to resolve the tension between claims of "national security" or threats to public order and the First Amendment's free expression guarantees. By 1969, the Court settled on the important principle that speech was protected from government regulation unless it was *directed* to inciting *imminent* lawless action and was *likely* to incite that action.[3] The "*Brandenburg* test" is the First Amendment test applicable to attempts by government to prohibit the advocacy of all forms of unlawful conduct. The requirements of "imminence" and the "likelihood of incitement" have offered sturdier protections for speech than previous formulations of the "clear and present danger" doctrine in American constitutional jurisprudence.

The road to *Brandenburg* began with almost complete deference to Congressional attempts to silence speech critical of the government's efforts to wage war in Europe in World War I. Shortly after the United States entered the war Congress passed the Espionage Act of 1917, which made it a crime, among other things, to "cause or attempt to cause insubordination, disloyalty, mutiny, or refusal of duty, in the military or naval forces."

In *Schenck* v. *United States*,[4] the Supreme Court unanimously affirmed the conviction of a socialist party leader convicted for sending leaflets to men who passed their draft board examinations arguing that conscription was "despotism" and urging them to "ASSERT YOUR RIGHTS!" and not to "submit to intimidation."[5] Justice Oliver Wendell Holmes announced the "clear and present danger" test in rejecting Schenck's First Amendment arguments: "[T]he question in every case is whether the words used are used in such circumstances and are of such a nature as to create a clear

---

[1] 249 U.S. 47 (1919).
[2] 395 U.S. 444 (1969).
[3] *Id.* at 447 (emphasis added). For a useful summary of these developments, *see* Rodney Smolla, *Smolla and Nimmer on Freedom of Speech* at ch. 4 (1994).
[4] 249 U.S. 47 (1919).
[5] *Id.* at 50-51.

and present danger that they will bring about the substantive evils that Congress has a right to prevent."[6] In *Schenck* and other cases arising out of World War I protest, the Court applied the "clear and present danger" test in a manner that enabled the government to sustain prosecutions based on the possibility that the "natural and intended effect" of the words used "would be to obstruct recruiting" for the war effort.[7] In the *Debs* case famed Socialist Party leader and labor leader Eugene Debs was convicted for an anti-war speech in June 1918 and received two concurrent twenty year sentences under the Espionage Act. The Supreme Court affirmed these sentences because the speech might obstruct recruiting.[8]

A crucial turning point on the road to *Brandenburg* was Justice Holmes' sudden change of heart starting with his eloquent dissenting opinion in *Abrams* v. *United States*.[9] Abrams was one of five Espionage defendants sentenced to between three and twenty years in prison for protesting the combination of "German militarism" and "allied capitalism" to "crush the Russian revolution."[10] The Supreme Court affirmed the convictions, but for the first time Holmes dissented.[11] In one of the most important passages of First Amendment jurisprudence Justice Holmes laid out a theory of free expression that has become part of the fabric of First Amendment law in the United States:

> [W]hen men have realized that time has upset many fighting faiths, they may come to believe even more than they believe the very foundations of their own conduct that the ultimate good desired is better reached by free trade in ideas – that the best test of truth is the power of the thought to get itself accepted in the competition of the market, and that truth is the only ground upon which their wishes safely can be carried out. That at any rate is the theory of our Constitution. It is an experiment, as all life is an experiment. Every year if not every day we have to wager our salvation upon some prophecy based upon imperfect knowledge. While that experiment is part of our system I think that we should be eternally vigilant against attempts to check the expression of opinions that we loathe and believe to be fraught with death, unless they so imminently threaten immediate interference with the lawful and pressing purposes of the law that an immediate check is required to save the country. I wholly disagree with the argument of the Government that the First Amendment left the common law as to seditious libel in force. History seems to me against the

---

[6] *Id.* at 52.
[7] *Debs* v. *United States*, 249 U.S. 211, 215 (1919).
[8] *Id.*
[9] 250 U.S. 616, 624 (1919) (Holmes, dissenting).
[10] *Id.*
[11] *Id.*

> notion. I had conceived that the United States through many years had shown its repentance for the Sedition Act of 1798, by repaying fines that it imposed. Only the emergency that makes it immediately dangerous to leave the correction of evil counsels to time warrants making any exception to the sweeping command, "Congress shall make no law . . . abridging the freedom of speech."[12]

In *Gitlow* v. *New York*,[13] the Supreme Court affirmed the conviction of an advocate of "revolutionary Socialism" under a state criminal syndicalism law with Justices Holmes and Brandeis dissenting. The Court found that state legislatures could prohibit entire categories of speech that might incite unlawful conduct without meeting the "clear and present danger" test regarding the particular speech in question.[14] The Supreme Court began to place some limits on the suppression of dissenters in the 1930s in cases like *DeJonge* v. *Oregon*[15] and *Herndon* v. *Lowry*.[16] In particular, the Court required state legislatures to justify the suppression of speech on proof of particular abuses of speech.

These positive developments were derailed during the 1950s as the United States was enveloped by McCarthyism and a hunt for "subversives." Doctrinally, the main event was the Supreme Court's decision in *Dennis* v. *United States*,[17] involving prosecutions under the Smith Act. The convictions of the eleven leaders of the Communist Party in *Dennis* were affirmed by a Supreme Court who adopted a new version of the "clear and present danger" doctrine less protective of free expression in that it did not require the imminence of harm to justify government repression. The Court adopted a test proposed by Chief Justice Learned Hand in the Court of Appeals in which he asked "whether the gravity of the 'evil,' discounted by its improbability, justifies such invasion of free speech as is necessary to avoid the danger."[18] Thus, under this test the gravity of the evil - the overthrow of the government - justified suppression of speech and association even in the absence of evidence of imminence of any actual danger.

In a series of decisions at the end of the 1950s the Supreme Court appeared to retreat from the full implications of *Dennis*.[19] These cases suggested that the Court

---

[12] *Id.* at 630-31.
[13] 268 U.S. 652 (1925).
[14] *Id.* at 670.
[15] 299 U.S. 353 (1937).
[16] 301 U.S. 242 (1937).
[17] 341 U.S. 494 (1951).
[18] 341 U.S. at 510 (citing *Dennis* v. *United States*, 183 F. 2d 201, 212 (2d Cir. 1950)).
[19] These decisions are *Yates* v. *United States*, 354 U.S. 298 (1957). *Scales* v. *United States*, 367 U.S. 203 (1961) and *Noto* v. *United States*, 367 U.S. 290 (1961), involving prosecutions of lower level members of the Communist Party. The distinction drawn in these cases was between "mere advocacy" and the "present" call for "future action." Thus, in *Scales* the Court affirmed the conviction of an "active member" of the Party who advocated the overthrow of the

was following the country in putting the excesses of the McCarthy era behind it and set the stage for the next steps toward *Brandenburg*. In *Bond* v. *Floyd*,[20] the Court overturned the refusal of the Georgia Legislature to seat State Senator Julian Bond when the legislature determined that he could not take his oath of office in good conscience in light of his stated opposition to the Vietnam War. The Court reasoned that Bond's statements of conscience were protected by the First Amendment and could not be construed as a call to unlawful refusal to be drafted.[21] In *Watts* v. *United States*,[22] the Court reversed a conviction for threatening the life of the President of a man who, while announcing at a public demonstration that he would not report for his draft physical, stated, "[i]f they ever make me carry a rifle the first man I want to get in my sights is L.B.J. They are not going to make me kill my black brothers."[23] The Court considered these statements to be "political hyperbole" and not really incitements to violence.[24]

In the *Brandenburg* case itself the Court overturned the conviction of a Ku Klux Klan member under a state criminal syndicalism law because in the circumstances of the case the Klansmen posed no immediate threat to anyone and were guilty only of the "abstract teaching" of racist violence.[25] In *Hess* v. *Indiana*,[26] the Court applied *Brandenburg* in reversing a conviction for disorderly conduct during a campus protest against the Cambodia invasion where the defendant had said, "[w]e'll take the fucking street later." The Court found that the remarks were not directed at anyone in particular, so they were not intended as an incitement, nor was there any evidence that they were likely to produce any imminent disorder.[27]

---

government "as speedily as circumstances would allow" while in *Noto*, the Court overturned the conviction of a "mere member" of the Party where the record in the case failed to demonstrate the "advocacy of action" required by *Scales*. *Compare* 367 U.S. at 251-253 *with* 367 U.S. at 297-299.

[20] 385 U.S. 116 (1966).

[21] *Id.* at 133-35.

[22] 394 U.S. 705 (1969).

[23] *Id.* at 706.

[24] *Id.* at 708.

[25] 395 U.S. 444 (1969). In *Terminiello* v. *City of Chicago*, 337 U.S. 1 (1949), the Court overturned a conviction for a race-baiting speech under a breach of the peace statute that punished speech that "stirs the public to anger or invites dispute." The Court emphasized that the fact that speech stirs listeners to anger or unrest is not enough of a justification for censorship or punishment of the speech involved.

[26] 414 U.S. 105 (1973).

[27] *Id.* In *NAACP* v. *Claiborne Hardware Co.*, 458 U.S. 886 (1982), the Court unanimously reversed a civil judgment against the NAACP and several of its members for damages arising out of a boycott of white-owned businesses. Charles Evers, the leader of the boycott, said in a speech that "necks would be broken" and the Court recognized that the speeches supporting the boycott "might have been understood as inviting an unlawful form of discipline or, at least, as intending to create a fear of violence." In fact, some violence did follow Evers' speeches; however, the Court found that the violence occurred at a sufficient remove in time from the

Since *Brandenburg* invalidated state criminal syndicalism laws and a variety of other laws prohibiting the advocacy of unlawful action, the Supreme Court has not had occasion to consider criminal sanctions or other penalties for advocacy or affiliation of the type prohibited in the Espionage Act of 1917[28] or the Smith Act.[29]

II. Hate Speech

One of the best known cases in recent years relating to hate speech concerned a march by members of the American Nazi Party through the village of Skokie, Illinois.[30] Skokie was the home of many Holocaust survivors and the question was whether the emotional distress that would be suffered by the Jewish inhabitants of the village justified restrictions on the ability of the Nazis to march.[31] Though the Supreme Court never ruled on this issue, the lower federal courts upheld the First Amendment right of the Nazis to march.[32] This principle is well established in American law today.

In *Beauharnais* v. *Illinois*,[33] the Supreme Court upheld the conviction of the President of the White Circle League, a racist organization in Chicago, for distributing racist leaflets. This distribution violated an Illinois group libel statute that prohibited publications that portrayed "depravity, criminality, unchastity, or lack of virtue of a class of citizens, of any race, color, creed or religion" which exposed them to "contempt, derision, or obloquy or which is productive of breach of the peace or riots."[34] Justice Frankfurter's opinion for the Court found a distinction between political speech and restrictions relating to race, color or religion.[35]

The continuing validity of *Beauharnais* is open to substantial question. The *Brandenburg* decision itself concerned racist and offensive speech and in the absence of a direct threat of imminent unlawful conduct, the Supreme Court held that racist speech cannot be subjected to criminal penalties.[36] There is no apparent reason why this result would be different if the charge was based on the kind of criminal libel statute at issue in *Beauharnais*.

---

speeches that they were protected by the First Amendment from civil sanctions.

[28] *Supra* note 7.

[29] *Supra* note 17.

[30] *Infra* note 32.

[31] *Id.*

[32] *Collin* v. *Smith*, 447 F. Supp. 676 (N.D. Ill.), *aff'd* 578 F.2d 1197 (7th Cir.), *cert. den.* 439 U.S. 916 (1978).

[33] 343 U.S. 250 (1952).

[34] *Id.*

[35] *Id.* at 264, n. 18.

[36] *Supra* note 25.

Any doubts on this question appear to be put to rest in the Supreme Court's decision in *R.A.V.* v. *City of St. Paul*.[37] In *R.A.V.* the Court appears to have disregarded the "categorical" approach to the First Amendment in which certain categories of speech received no First Amendment scrutiny at all.[38] The *R.A.V.* case itself involved a prosecution of a minor under a St. Paul, Minnesota, cross-burning ordinance for burning a cross in the yard of a black neighbor.[39] The ordinance did not prohibit all cross-burning but only cross-burnings "which one knows or has reasonable grounds to know arouses anger, alarm, or resentment in others on the basis of race, color, creed, religion or gender. . ."[40] The Supreme Court found that, although all cross-burning could be prohibited, the ordinance violated the First Amendment by singling out racist cross-burning because of the content and viewpoint of the racist message being communicated.[41] Such discrimination based on content, even in the context of a cross-burning, was found to violate the First Amendment.[42]

III. Criticism of Government or Government Officials

At the time the First Amendment was added to the United States Constitution in 1791 the American legal system still featured seditious libel laws and prosecutions for criticism of the government and government officials. However, American political and legal culture also included the 1735 acquittal of printer John Peter Zenger on charges of seditious libel despite laws that precluded the defense of truth and left to the jury only the issue of publication. Thus, there was an unresolved tension between freedom of expression and seditious libel laws from the beginning of the Constitution.

This tension was also displayed in the controversy over the Sedition Act of 1798. Passed by a Federalist-controlled Congress and opposed by the Republicans led by Vice President Thomas Jefferson, the Act prohibited the uttering or publishing of "any false and scandalous and malicious writings against the government of the United States or either house of Congress of the United States or the President of the United States with intent to defame . . . or to bring them . . . into contempt, or disrepute, or to excite against them . . . the hatred of the good people of the United States..." There were a number of prosecutions and convictions under the Act but it expired by its own terms in 1801. Then-President Jefferson pardoned all those who had been convicted so the Act's validity under the First Amendment was never tested

---

[37] 505 U.S. 377 (1992).

[38] *Id.* at 383.

[39] *Id.*

[40] *Id.* at 380.

[41] *Id.*

[42] *Id.* at 393-94.

in the Supreme Court. Congress has never passed another federal seditious libel law since and in its landmark decision in *New York Times* v. *Sullivan*,[43] the Supreme Court found that "although the Sedition Act was never tested in this Court, the attack on its validity has carried the day in the court of history."[44]

The *New York Times* case is one of the most important First Amendment decisions in American history. The case arose out of an advertisement placed in the *New York Times* in 1960 by civil rights advocates who supported the activities of Dr. Martin Luther King in Alabama at the height of the civil rights struggle. The advertisement criticized police misconduct and other actions taken against Dr. King and other civil rights activists and solicited contributions to support this cause. There were several, though minor, factual errors in the advertisement and these errors were used as the basis for a civil libel action filed by Sullivan, one of three elected Commissioners of the City of Montgomery, Alabama, and the Commissioner responsible for the police department. An Alabama jury had little difficulty reaching a verdict against the *Times* and several of the individuals who signed the advertisement and imposing an award of $500,000 in damages.[45]

In a ringing endorsement of the right to criticize public officials, the Court found that the First Amendment limited the reach of state libel laws.[46] This constitutional protection "does not turn upon 'the truth, popularity, or social utility of the ideas and beliefs which are offered.' "[47] The Court emphasized that freedom of expression requires "breathing space" to survive and that the First Amendment had to shield even some false speech from sanction in order to ensure First Amendment freedoms.[48] The test the Court applied was "actual malice," or what has come to be known as "constitutional malice," *i.e.*, that a public official must prove by clear and convincing evidence that an allegedly libelous statement made about them was published with actual knowledge that it was false or with reckless disregard for the truth of the statement.[49]

Since *New York Times* v. *Sullivan* an enormous body of case law has developed applying this standard in a wide array of circumstances. One of the first steps was to apply the "constitutional malice" standard to state seditious libel laws, thus, as a practical matter, essentially ending the possibility of seditious libel prosecutions in the United States.[50] The Court also applied the constitutional malice standard beyond public officials to "public figures."[51] Public figures are either people

---

[43] 376 U.S. 254 (1964).

[44] *Id.* at 276.

[45] *Id.* at 256.

[46] *Id.*

[47] *Id.* at 271 (citing *N.A.A.C.P.* v. *Button*, 371 U.S. 415, 445 (1963)).

[48] *Id.* at 271-72.

[49] *Id.* at 279-80.

[50] *Garrison* v. *Louisiana*, 379 U.S. 64 (1964).

[51] *Id.*

who are widely known in the community at large or who have thrust themselves into the vortex of a particular public controversy so that they invite public comment and therefore must also meet the stringent "constitutional malice" standards of *New York Times* v. *Sullivan* in order to prevail in a defamation case.[52]

Apart from the threat of defamation actions, limited as they are by *New York Times* v. *Sullivan* and its progeny, as a general proposition the First Amendment protects all forms of criticism of public officials or the government from sanction. Indeed, the Court has stressed that the vociferous criticism of government and government officials lies at the heart of First Amendment freedoms.

IV. Flag-Burning

During the Vietnam War era, the Supreme Court struggled with the First Amendment implications of the symbolic desecration of the American flag in the context of political protest.[53] In *Texas* v. *Johnson*[54] and *United States* v. *Eichman*,[55] the Court found flag desecration laws unconstitutional under the First Amendment.

In *Texas* v. *Johnson* the Court was faced with a state criminal conviction under a Texas law prohibiting burning or encouraging the burning of the flag.[56] The Court found that the conviction was based on the content of the message conveyed by the flag burning and thus subject to the most exacting First Amendment scrutiny.[57] The Court held that the state could not restrict the message of contempt for the flag because onlookers would find it offensive or disagreeable.[58] As the Court emphasized, "a bedrock principle underlying the First Amendment . . . is that the Government may not prohibit the expression of an idea simply because society finds the idea itself offensive or disagreeable."[59]

The *Johnson* decision set off a firestorm of public opposition and debate. The furor led the Congress, urged on by President Bush, to pass the "Flag Protection Act of 1989" by large margins.[60] It was not long before the Court was faced with a

---

[52] *Curtis Publishing Co.* v. *Butts*, 388 U.S. 130 (1967).
[53] *See, e.g.*, *Street* v. *New York*, 394 U.S. 576 (1969) (reversing a malicious mischief conviction for flag burning) and *Spence* v. *Washington*, 418 U.S. 405 (1974) (invalidating conviction under statute concerning proper display of flag).
[54] 491 U.S. 397 (1989).
[55] 496 U.S. 310 (1990).
[56] *Supra* note 54.
[57] 491 U.S. at 412.
[58] *Id.*
[59] *Id.* at 414.
[60] Pub.L. 101-131, 103 Stat. 777 as codified at 18 U.S.C. § 700 (Supp. 1990). The Act provided, "[w]hoever knowingly mutilates, defaces, physically defiles, burns, maintains on the ground or floor, or tramples upon any flag of the United States shall be fined under this title or imprisoned for not more than one year, or both."

test of the constitutionality of this new federal flag-desecration statute. As soon as the law became effective in October 1989 two groups of protesters in Seattle and Washington, D.C. burned the flag in defiance of the new law. In June 1990, in *United States* v. *Eichman* , the Court declared the new law unconstitutional based on the same reasoning as *Texas* v. *Johnson*.[61] Based on the reasoning in *Johnson* and *Eichman* it is unlikely that a valid flag-desecration statute can be passed consistent with the First Amendment. Such laws will always be subjected to exacting judicial scrutiny and abstract government interests like national unity or the protection of the patriotic feelings of the majority will not be sufficient to justify such laws.

V. Re-Publication of Statements by Groups Deemed Threatening to National Security

No statute prohibits re-publication of threats made by groups, and the Supreme Court has not addressed the constitutionality of such efforts. But there seems little doubt that news media reports of threats of violence would be protected by the First Amendment under the *Brandenburg* standard requiring both an intent to incite imminent violence and the likelihood of such effect. It is difficult to imagine that a statute banning reporting of threats of violence could meet the *Brandenburg* standard.

VI. Access to and Disclosure of Information

The citizens' right to information about their government has always been recognized in the United States as an essential requirement of democratic government. As James Madison said:

> Knowledge will forever govern ignorance, and a people who mean to be their own governors, must arm themselves with the power knowledge gives. A popular government without popular information or the means of acquiring it, is but a prologue to a farce or a tragedy or perhaps both.[62]

The public's right to know is secured in two ways: first, by affirmative obligations imposed on the government to release information in response to requests from individuals or their representatives in the Congress, and second, by restrictions on the means the government may employ to keep secrets. Moreover, the purpose of the "constitutional guarantee of a free press" has been described as "to create a fourth institution outside the Government as an additional check on the three official

---

[61] 496 U.S. at 317-18.

[62] James Madison, Letter to W.T. Barry, August 4, 1822.

branches. . . . The press is free to do battle against secrecy and deception. . . . But the press cannot expect from the Constitution any guarantee that it will succeed. . . ."[63]

Resolution of some of the most important questions faced by a democracy, concerning war and peace, for example, depends upon information relating to military, diplomatic, or other national security matters. Accordingly, the affirmative right to obtain government information must include information relating to national security matters, although some specific kinds of information may legitimately be kept secret. Similarly, the power of the government to restrict access to even sensitive national security information is limited, depending on the means the government seeks to use, the harm that would result from disclosure of the information, and the public interest in knowing the information.

There have been numerous instances over the past thirty years when information has been published over the protests of the government for fear that its disclosure would harm the national security. But no persuasive case has been made that such publication in fact caused any substantial and long-term harm to the security of the nation. And the government's objections to publication, even when based on legitimate security concerns, are always mired in domestic political considerations. That was certainly true of publication of the Pentagon Papers, a secret government study of the Vietnam War. Erwin Griswold, who as Solicitor General sought to enjoin publication of the Papers in 1971, wrote in 1989 that he had "never seen any trace of a threat to national security" from the publication of the Papers.[64] There is widespread agreement with his view that there is "massive overclassification and that the principal concern of the classifiers is not with national security, but rather with governmental embarrassment of one sort or another."[65] As Griswold pointed out, aside from details of weapons systems, "there is very rarely any real risk to current national security from the publication of facts relating to transactions in the past, even the fairly recent past."[66] It is also clear that the Nixon administration was concerned about the effect of publication of the Papers on the domestic political situation, as well as on the national defense and foreign policy.

The U.S. experience confirms that the dangers posed by possible publication of national security information are slight. Whatever dangers to legitimate interests are posed by publication are far outweighed by the value of public disclosure and the dangers of permitting censorship.

---

[63] Justice Potter Stewart, *Or of the Press*, 26 *Hastings L.J.* 631, 631-36 (1975).
[64] "Ex-Solicitor General Shifts View of 'Pentagon papers,'" *Wash. Post*, Feb. 16, 1989, at. A52.
[65] *Id.*
[66] *Id.*

A. Access to Information and Restrictions on National Security Grounds

1. Constitutional and Common Law Right of Access to Government Information.

The little case law that exists indicates that there is no enforceable right of access to government information directly under the First Amendment. However, many constitutional scholars believe that the First Amendment does in fact protect the right to know government information.[67]

The Supreme Court has recognized a common law right to inspect and copy public records and documents, but the right is rarely invoked and its contours have not been delineated with any precision.[68]

2. Freedom of Information Act.

As a practical matter, there has been no judicial development of constitutionally based claims for access to government information, because a Freedom of Information Act (FOIA) was passed in 1966 to implement the constitutional right to know.[69] The Act is intended to let the people know "what their government is up to," and applies to all recorded information, including computer and electronic records, in the possession or control of the executive branch of the federal government.

The Freedom of Information Act starts with the presumption that all government information must be made public, either through publication by the government or by furnishing copies of specific information to individuals who request it. While the Act provides that certain records are exempt from these disclosure requirements, individuals are entitled to seek judicial review of executive branch decisions to withhold records and, if they "substantially prevail," are entitled to recover attorneys' fees from the government.[70]

The FOIA's publication requirement applies to executive branch agency rules of procedure, substantive rules of general applicability, and statements of general policy, etc., and is designed to ensure that there is no secret "law" being

---

[67] Thomas Emerson, *Legal Foundation of the Right to Know*, 1976 Wash. U.L.Q. 1; Mary Cheh, *Judicial Supervision of Executive Secrecy: Rethinking Freedom of Expression for Government Employees and the Public Right to Access to Government Information*, 69 Cornell L. Rev. 690, 719-734 (1984). The Supreme Court has recognized the right to know. For example, in *Lamont* v. *Postmaster General*, 381 U.S. 301 (1965), the Court upheld the right of citizens to receive "foreign communist propaganda" from abroad without notifying the government.

[68] *Nixon* v. *Warner Communications*, 435 U.S. 589 (1978) (right of access to judicial records); a right of access to congressional records was affirmed in *Schwartz* v. *Dept. of Justice*, 435 F. Supp. 1203, *aff'd* 595 F.2d 888 (D.C. Cir. 1979).

[69] Pub.L. 89-554, 80 Stat. 383 as amended and codified at 5 U.S.C. § 552.

[70] 5 U.S.C. § 552 (a)(4)(B) & (E).

applied by the executive branch.[71] Nevertheless, some intelligence agencies, such as the CIA, do have secret regulations, although the legality of that practice is unsettled.

Certain national security-related information is exempted from the requirement that specific information be disclosed to individuals who request it.[72] Information properly classified secret in the interest of national defense or foreign policy pursuant to presidential order may be withheld.[73] Because the Act requires more than a general claim of national security harm to avoid the disclosure requirements and provides for judicial review, much information originally classified on national security grounds is released under the FOIA. For example, in 1997, two public interest groups successfully forced the CIA to disclose the overall amount of the intelligence budget by suing under the FOIA.[74]

3. Classification Standards.

The current executive order signed by President Clinton in April 1995 provides that in order for information to be classified, its disclosure must reasonably be expected to result in harm to the national defense or foreign relations of the United States and the official making that determination must be "able to identify or describe the damage."[75] The executive order directs that "if there is significant doubt about the need to classify information, it shall not be classified."[76] Information may not be considered for classification unless it concerns specific designated subjects, including military plans, weapons systems or operations, foreign government information, or intelligence activities.[77] Most information must be declassified within 10 years of its original classification marking and all information is to be automatically declassified after 25 years unless the head of the agency, *e.g.*, the Secretary of Defense, determines that its release would cause specific kinds of listed harm.[78]

Sometimes, the mere fact that an agency has information on a subject may itself be classified. In that case, the intelligence agencies may refuse to confirm or deny that records exist. For example, the CIA will refuse to admit or deny that it has records on certain subjects, because if it did so, it would reveal an otherwise secret interest of the CIA in collecting information on that subject.

In connection with adoption of the current classification order, there was a great debate over whether classification and declassification decisions should

---

[71] 5 U.S.C. § 552 (a)(1).
[72] *Id.*
[73] *Id.*
[74] "For First Time, U.S. Discloses Spying Budget" *New York Times*, Oct. 16, 1997, at 27.
[75] E.O. 12958, Sec. 1.2(A).
[76] Sec. 1.2(b).
[77] Sec. 1.5.
[78] Sec. 3.4.

explicitly weigh the potential national security harm from disclosure against the public interest in knowing the information. President Carter's Executive Order 12065 had required such consideration in making declassification decisions[79] and many public interest groups urged the adoption of such a standard as the only meaningful way to insure protection of the public's right to know and to curb the excessive secrecy that had arisen during the Cold War. While President Clinton's order refers to consideration of the public interest in disclosure when deciding whether to declassify documents, it nowhere requires such consideration.[80] This important requirement was omitted from the final order (although contained in an earlier draft) because the executive branch wanted to avoid having the courts balance national security harm and the public interest when deciding whether information was properly classified. Nevertheless, as detailed below, there still exists significant independent judicial review of agency decisions to claim the national security exemption from the FOIA's disclosure requirement. And in 1997, legislation was introduced in Congress to amend the FOIA to require the courts to weigh the public interest in disclosure.[81]

In addition to the exemption for information classified under presidential order, the Congress has legislated additional exemptions for specific categories of national security information. Intelligence sources and methods are exempt,[82] and organizational information concerning certain agencies, such as the National Security Agency, is exempt.[83]

4. Procedural Protections.

There are a number of significant substantive and procedural hurdles which the government must cross in order to claim the national security exemption from FOIA's disclosure requirement. First, information claimed to be exempt on national security grounds is *not* exempt from the Act's search and processing requirements, except in very limited circumstances. Thus, agencies must search for and index requested documents even if their contents may be withheld. Second, non-exempt information must be segregated from exempt information in a particular document and released.[84] Most significantly, the Act provides for independent judicial review of claims by executive branch agencies that information is exempt on national security grounds.[85]

---

[79] *Id.*
[80] E.O. 12958, § 3.2(b).
[81] Government Secrecy Act of 1997, S. 712 § 4 (c) and (f), Cong. Rec., May 7, 1997, at 4111-12.
[82] 50 U.S.C. § 403-3 (c)(6), (Supp. 1997).
[83] 50 U.S.C. § 402 note.
[84] 5 U.S.C. § 552 (b).
[85] 5 U.S.C. § 552 (a)(4)(B).

In 1974, the FOIA was amended to explicitly provide, first, that courts should have the final say as to whether documents are properly classified pursuant to the terms of an executive order and therefore exempt from disclosure and, second, that the government has the burden of proving that information is exempt from disclosure.[86] Before the 1974 amendment, the Supreme Court had previously ruled that the only role of the courts under the Act was to determine whether the executive branch had classified the document, not whether it had done so properly.[87] In the wake of the Watergate scandal, Congress amended the Act to explicitly provide for *de novo* review by the courts. President Ford vetoed the amendment on the grounds that such judicial review violated the constitutional separation of powers by infringing on his national security responsibilities, but the Congress overrode his veto.[88]

Under the 1974 amendment, the government is required to give detailed justifications of why information is classified and the courts may examine the documents, without showing them to the requester's lawyer.[89] The government must submit sworn statements by appropriate officials that the disclosure of the information would in fact cause harm to the national security and the statements must address each item of classified information separately and in detail.[90] However, the courts have decided to give "substantial weight" to an agency's determination that records are classified.[91] If the courts are unpersuaded by the government's affidavits, they have the authority to order disclosure of classified information.[92] However, as the judiciary has become more conservative, it is extremely rare for courts to order disclosure of national security information over the objection of the government. At the same time, the FOIA process, including the filing of a lawsuit, regularly results in agencies releasing tens of thousands of pages of previously classified documents.

Judicial review of government claims that certain national security information may be withheld because it comes within a specific statutory exemption, *e.g.*, for intelligence sources and methods, is usually more limited than review of claims for exemption based on classification. Such review may consist only of verifying that the information does fall within the category exempted by Congress.

The Congress oversees executive branch compliance with the Freedom of Information Act. It may request information from the agencies concerning their

---

[86] Pub L. 93-502, 88 Stat. 1561 as codified at 5 U.S.C. § 552 (a)(4)(B).

[87] *EPA* v. *Mink*, 410 U.S. 73 (1973).

[88] Freedom of Information Act Source Book: Legislative Materials, Cases, Articles, S. Doc. 93-82, 93d Cong., 2d Sess. (Comm. Print 1974) at 484-85.

[89] 5 U.S.C. § 552 (a)(4)(B).

[90] *Vaughn* v. *Rosen*, 484 F.2d 820 (D.C. Cir. 1973), *cert. denied*, 415 U.S. 977 (1974).

[91] *Ray* v. *Turner*, 587 F.2d 1187 (D.C. Cir. 1978).

[92] *Id.*

responses to FOIA requests and hold public hearings with witnesses from the executive branch or the public.

5. Individuals' Access to Government Files on Themselves.

Individuals also have a direct right of access to information about themselves contained in federal government records, under the Privacy Act of 1974.[93] That Act limits the kind of information about individuals that the federal government may collect or maintain and provides procedures for obtaining access to files about oneself similar to those provided under the Freedom of Information Act, including the right to sue in federal court to compel disclosure of such files. This right of access provided under the Privacy Act belongs only to U. S. citizens and permanent residents, while any individual or group is entitled to information under the FOIA.

Information contained in an individual's files, which is properly classified on national security grounds under a presidential order and therefore exempt from disclosure under the FOIA, is also exempt from disclosure under the Privacy Act. [94] In addition, the FBI has specific statutory authority to refuse to acknowledge the existence of classified records on an individual pertaining to foreign intelligence, counterintelligence or international terrorism to the extent the existence of such files is itself classified.[95]

6. Other Access Laws.

In addition to the Freedom of Information and Privacy Acts, there are a number of other laws and internal executive branch procedures affording the public a right of access to some kinds of national security-related information. These include a procedure for executive branch declassification review of information; the Presidential Records Act, requiring preservation of all historically significant records of the President, including all records relating to national security matters; and the State Department Historical Records Act and the John F. Kennedy Assassination Records Collection Act, which require public disclosure of previously classified national security information about the history of U.S. foreign policy and the investigation of the assassination of President Kennedy respectively.[96] In the last two instances, Congress exempted narrow and specific categories of information from the

---

[93] 5 U.S.C. § 552a.

[94] 5 U.S.C. § 552a(k).

[95] 5 U.S.C. § 552 (c)(3).

[96] E.O. 12958, § 3.6; Presidential Records Act of 1978, Pub. L. 95-591, 92 Stat. 2523 as codified and amended at 44 U.S.C. § 2201 et seq.; Foreign Relations Authorization Act, Fiscal Years 1992 and 1993, § 198 Pub. L. 102-138, 105 Stat. 647, 685 as codified and amended at 22 U.S.C. §§ 4351 et seq.; President John F. Kennedy Assassination Records Collection Act of 1992, Pub.L. 102-526, 106 Stat. 3443 as codified and amended at 44 U.S.C. § 2107 note.

disclosure requirements, which exemptions, when enacted, were more narrow than the then-current executive order on classification.

7. Congressional Access to National Security Information.

Finally, the public's right to know is also ensured through congressional access to executive branch information, which it receives as the agent of the citizens, considers, and on occasion, may disclose to the public even over the objection of the Executive Branch. Congress' authority to obtain information from the executive Branch is not explicitly established in the Constitution. Rather, it stems from the constitutional grants of authority to Congress, such as the authority to make all laws.[97] The Supreme Court has never addressed the precise extent of the President's authority to withhold information from Congress on executive privilege grounds.

The Court, however, has affirmed Congress' joint responsibility with the President for national security information when it said that Congress has authority to set classification standards.[98] Congress has enacted classification standards for information related to nuclear energy and has also set declassification standards for other limited kinds of information.

Many laws specifically require executive branch agencies to provide national security information to the Congress. For example, the Intelligence Oversight Act requires the President to ensure that the intelligence oversight committees of Congress "are kept fully and currently informed of the intelligence activities of the United States, including any significant anticipated intelligence activity . . . ."[99] The Act goes on to detail specific disclosure responsibilities of the intelligence agencies.[100] The law is unsettled on when, if ever, the President could resist congressional requests for national security information on the grounds of executive privilege, because in practice such disputes are worked out through mutual accommodation.

In 1996, the executive branch for the first time punished an executive branch employee for disclosing classified information to a member of the House Intelligence Committee without authorization from his superiors to do so. While the Congress has objected, the controversy has not been resolved at the time of this writing.[101]

In general, secret national security information supplied to the Congress is only available to members and their staff and is not made public. However, the rules of each House of Congress provide for procedures whereby the committees and the House as a whole may vote to make such information public, even over the objection

[97] U.S. Const., Art. I, sec. 1.
[98] *EPA* v. *Mink*, 410 U.S. 73, 83 (1973).
[99] 50 U.S.C. § 413 (a)(1) (Supp. 1997).
[100] 50 U.S.C. § 413a (Supp. 1997).
[101] Intelligence Authorization Act, Fiscal Year 1998, Pub. L. 105-107, 111 Stat. 2248, § 306; Conf. Rep. 105-350, Oct. 28, 1997 at 21-22.

of the President.[102] In addition, individual members do on occasion disclose such information. For example, while a court injunction barred publication of the Pentagon Papers, a Senator read them into the record of a committee hearing. The Supreme Court held that the Speech and Debate clause of the Constitution provided him immunity for doing so, even if publication of the Papers otherwise would have been a crime.[103]

While Congress itself enacts legislation in public, not in secret, the Constitution also provides that: "[E]ach house shall keep a journal of its proceedings, and from time to time publish the same, excepting such parts as may in their judgment require secrecy." [104] Congressional committees usually meet in public to hold hearings or consider legislation, although there are exceptions to this general practice based on national security justifications. The most significant one is that the amounts authorized for specific intelligence agencies and activities, as well as some weapons, are kept secret. The constitutionality of this practice has never been decided by the Supreme Court. The legal authorities for and restrictions on intelligence agencies are, however, set forth in public laws. The National Security Act, for example, outlines the duties of the CIA.[105]

VII. Disclosures by Government Agents or Employees

The United States has no "Official Secrets Act" making it a crime to disclose classified information to the press or the public, and many constitutional scholars believe that the First Amendment prohibits enactment of such a law. There is ongoing debate about what legal restrictions may be placed on disclosures of national security-related information by government employees and no definitive Supreme Court rulings.

An enormous amount of currently classified information is in fact leaked to the press. Recent examples include a CIA report on assessing responsibility for atrocities in Bosnia, leaked to the *New York Times*.[106] A member of Congress recently leaked that the CIA was hiding information that one of its paid agents in Guatemala was involved in the murders of an American and a Guatemalan married to an American. The Congressman avoided any formal censure for the leak, and the news stories led to changes in CIA policies regarding recruitment of agents and public acknowledgment and discussion by the CIA of its role in connection with the murders. From time to time, such leaks occasion calls for preventive and punitive

---

[102] Senate Res. 400 § 8(a), 94th Congress; House Rule XLVIII § 7, 104th Cong.
[103] *Gravel* v. *United States*, 408 U.S. 606 (1972).
[104] U.S. Const. Art. 1., cl. 5.
[105] 50 U.S.C. § 403-3 (d)(1) (Supp. 1997).
[106] "CIA Report on Bosnia Blames Serbs for 90% of the War Crimes," *New York Times*, Mar. 9, 1995, at 1.

actions - from using lie detector tests to identify the leaker to imposing criminal penalties for leaking - but many government officials call such measures useless, because it is so difficult to locate the source of a leak.

Many journalists and editors who learn classified information frequently inform the government before publishing the information. Where the government asks them not to publish the information in order to prevent some concrete harm, many journalists and others have said that they may well decide not to publish.

A. Criminal Penalties for Public Disclosures of Information by Government Employees

Congress has consistently refused to enact an "Official Secrets Act" to criminalize the release of nonpublic government information. Many believe that any such law would in any event run afoul of the "right to know" embodied in the First Amendment. Because a "central purpose of the first amendment is to protect and sustain the process of representative democracy by maintaining an informed electorate,"[107] the First Amendment includes the "right of the public to obtain information from the government."[108] "If democracy is to work, the public, as sovereign, must have all information available in order to instruct its servants, the government."[109] Thus, whatever powers the President may have to classify information, the Constitution limits the methods he may employ to maintain secrecy. An Official Secrets Act is too heavy a tool, because its cost to the public's right to know is too great.

Congress has, however, criminalized the release of certain narrow categories of information, taking into account the public's interest in knowing such information as well as the potential harm from disclosure. For example, the Intelligence Identities Protection Act of 1982 makes it a crime for persons with authorized access to classified information identifying intelligence agents to disclose publicly the names of such agents.[110] That statute was supported by civil liberties groups because it was deemed appropriately narrowly drawn, provided adequate notice to government employees of what information was covered, and applied only to information whose disclosure would be likely to cause concrete harm without being important to public policy debates. In general, such statutes criminalize only release by government employees, not subsequent publication by others.[111]

---

[107] *Emerson*, *supra*, note 67, at 14.
[108] *Id.*
[109] *Id.*
[110] Pub. L. 97-200, 96 Stat. 122, 50 U.S.C. § 421.
[111] *See, e.g.*, Atomic Energy Act, 42 U.S.C. §§ 2274 & 2277. (The Intelligence Identities Protection Act, however, does criminalize publication of agents' names in the limited circumstances where publication is part of a pattern of activities intended to expose covert

Despite the lack of an Official Secrets Act, the government has on occasion sought over the years to use the general espionage statute and the theft of government property statute as if those statutes constituted an Official Secrets Act.[112] Most scholars believe that the general espionage statute was only aimed at classic espionage – the covert transmission of information to foreign agents with the knowledge that the United States would be harmed thereby.

The government first used the general espionage law to prosecute Daniel Ellsberg for giving the Pentagon Papers to the *Washington Post* and the *New York Times* in 1971, but that prosecution was dismissed for government misconduct. The government did not again attempt to prosecute leakers under that statute until the mid-1980s, when President Reagan's Justice Department prosecuted a Navy employee for leaking a classified photograph of a Russian submarine to *Jane's Defense Weekly*.[113] The employee was convicted despite demonstrating that publication of the photograph did not reveal any secret information and did not harm the national security of the United States. Although both press and civil liberties groups filed court briefs objecting that the espionage statute was not intended to apply to press leaks, and was unconstitutional if it did, the Supreme Court refused to hear the case.

In the *Morison* case, the government also relied on the general theft of government property statute,[114] even though the Justice Department under President Carter had interpreted the statute as not applying to leaks of government information to the press.[115]

B. Civil and Administrative Penalties for Public Disclosures of Information by Government Employees

There is widespread agreement among both government officials and civil liberties advocates that government officials who publicly disclose information learned through their official duties, and which is supposed to be kept closely held, may be administratively disciplined, including being fired from their jobs, for leaking such information. Most government employees with access to classified information are required to sign secrecy agreements pledging not to disclose information marked classified to unauthorized persons.

---

agents and is done with knowledge that such activities would impair U.S. foreign intelligence activities. 50 U.S.C. § 421 (c).)

[112] These issues are extensively analyzed in Harold Edgar and Benno L. Schmidt, Jr., *The Espionage Statutes and the Publication of Defense Information*, 73 Colum. L. Rev. 929 (1973).

[113] *United States* v. *Morison*, 844 F.2d 1057 (4th Cir.), *cert. denied*, 488 U.S. 908 (1988).

[114] 18 U.S.C. § 641.

[115] 844 F.2d at 1076-1077. For a statement of the Department of Justice's view under President Carter, see United States Attorneys' Manual, Title 9 – Criminal Division, Ch. 2, at 3, Oct. 20, 1978.

In addition, employees who work for the CIA and a few other intelligence agencies are also required to sign agreements that they will never write about anything related to their employment or intelligence activities without submitting their manuscripts to the government before publication and deleting anything the government considers classified. The Supreme Court, without discussion, upheld the constitutionality of such prepublication review agreements for intelligence agency employees and approved the forfeiture of any profits from any writings which were not submitted for review.[116] Three Justices dissented, objecting that the Court was fashioning a "drastic new remedy . . . to enforce a species of prior restraint on a citizen's right to criticize his government."[117]

A subsequent court of appeals decision upheld the constitutionality of the CIA's "classification and censorship scheme."[118] It found that the First Amendment interests in public disclosure of former agents' writings were outweighed by the government's substantial interest in assuring secrecy in the conduct of foreign intelligence operations and found that the classification criteria at issue in that case were neither overbroad nor excessively vague.[119] In doing so, it noted that the agent's secrecy agreement applied only to publication of classified information that came to his attention by virtue of his connection with the CIA and that the state has interests as an employer in regulating the speech of employees that differ significantly from those it possesses in connection with regulation of the speech of the citizenry in general.[120]

In the early 1980s, the Reagan administration sought to extend lifetime prepublication review requirements to all government employees who had ever had access to classified information, but congressional opposition stopped the plan.[121]

In a controversial case in the early 1970s, a federal court entered an injunction against a former CIA employee prohibiting him from speaking or writing about intelligence matters in violation of the secrecy agreement which he had signed.[122] The constitutionality of such prior restraints has not been directly ruled upon by the Supreme Court, but has been much criticized.[123]

---

[116] *Snepp* v. *United States*, 444 U.S. 507 (1980).
[117] *Id.* at 526.
[118] *McGehee* v. *Casey*, 718 F.2d 1137 (D.C. Cir. 1983).
[119] 718 F.2d 1143-46.
[120] 718 F.2d at 1141-42.
[121] See Dycus, Berney, Bonks & Ravenhansen, National Security Law, (1997) at 872-89.
[122] *United States* v. *Marchetti*, 466 F.2d 1309 (4th Cir.), *cert. den.* 409 U.S. 1063 (1972).
[123] Mary Cheh, Judicial Supervision of Executive Secrecy: Rethinking Freedom of Expression for Government Employees and the Right to Access to Government Information, 69 Cornell L. Rev. 690 (1984).

C. Protections for Public Disclosures of Information

The Whistle-Blower Protection Act of 1989 specifically protects government employees from reprisals for publicly disclosing evidence of government waste, fraud or abuse.[124] However, the Act does not protect public disclosure of such information if the information is classified; in that case, to claim legal protection, the employee would have to disclose the information in confidence either to the inspector general of her agency or to a member of Congress.

Former government officials may also use certain internal executive branch procedures to expedite declassification of historical materials that they wish to use in writing or speaking about their government experience.[125]

VIII. News Media

A. Restrictions on News-Gathering and Publishing During Peacetime

1. Media Access Issues.

The Supreme Court has held that the news media has the same right of access to public facilities and proceedings as any member of the public. In recognizing a First Amendment right of access to criminal trials, the Court explained: "[t]he First Amendment . . . prohibit[s] government from limiting the stock of information from which members of the public may draw."[126] The Supreme Court has conditioned this right of access on three considerations: (1) the existence of a "tradition of accessibility," that is, whether "the place and process have historically been open to the press and general public"; (2) whether "public access plays a significant positive role in the functioning of the particular process"; and (3) whether there is a showing that "closure is essential to preserve higher values and is narrowly tailored to serve that interest."[127] Thus, the press has been denied any right to obtain a judicial order that it be permitted to enter military bases or prisons. [128]

The Supreme Court has never approved restricting access to facilities or proceedings on national security grounds. Before the Supreme Court ruled on the First Amendment right of access to trials, some lower courts had closed court rooms to the public and media to avoid the disclosure of certain confidential government

---

[124] Pub. L. 101-12, 103 Stat. 16, 5 U.S.C. §§ 1212 and 1213.

[125] Executive Order 12958 § 3.6.

[126] *Richmond Newspapers* v. *Virginia*, 448 U.S. 555, 575-76 (1980).

[127] *Press-Enterprises Co.* v. *Superior Court*, 478 U.S. 1, 8-9 (1986).

[128] *Saxbe* v. *Washington Post*; 417 U.S. 843 (1974); *JB Pictures, Inc.* v. *Dep't of Defense*, 86 F.3d 236 (1996) (no right of access to military base).

information. In *United States ex rel. Lloyd* v. *Vincent*,[129] the Court of Appeals upheld a limited trial closure during the testimony of an active undercover narcotics agent. In *United States* v. *Bell*,[130] the Court of Appeals allowed closed testimony about a "hijacking profile" developed by the airlines and the government to combat hijacking. Since these cases, the Congress enacted the Classified Information Procedures Act, the premise of which is that all evidence admitted in a criminal trial must be made public.[131] The Act sets out pretrial procedures in criminal trials to determine what classified information will be admitted as evidence at trial and provides for closing such pretrial proceedings.

2. Prior Restraints.

In general, the news media may publish any information it wishes free from any prior restraint.[132] Although the Supreme Court has not said that prior restraints are always unconstitutional, the Court has repeatedly stated that prior restraints are presumptively unconstitutional.[133]

Though *Near* v. *Minnesota* has been enormously influential in establishing First Amendment restrictions on the use of prior restraints, it also created the possibility of an exception to this principle. In dictum, the Court stated, "[n]o one would question but that a government might prevent actual obstruction to its recruiting service or the publication of the sailing dates of transports or the number and location of troops."[134]

The most prominent case to address these issues since *Near* is *New York Times Co.* v. *United States*,[135] commonly referred to as the Pentagon Papers case. In 1971, the *New York Times* and the *Washington Post* came into possession of a 47-volume Pentagon study entitled "History of U.S. Decision-Making Process on Vietnam Policy." The study was commissioned in 1967 by then Secretary of Defense Robert McNamara. The study was classified "Top Secret - Sensitive." The *New York Times* began publishing excerpts from the study on Sunday, June 13, 1971. At first the government asked the *Times* to agree not to publish more excerpts voluntarily but the *Times* refused and the government went into federal court in New York to enjoin further publication. Although the lower court refused to enjoin publication of excerpts, the Court of Appeals reversed and granted the government's request

---

[129] 520 F. 2d 1272, 1274 (2d Cir.) *cert. denied*, 423 U.S. 937 (1975).
[130] 464 F. 2d 667 (2d Cir.), *cert. denied*, 409 U.S. 901 (1972).
[131] Pub. L. 96-456 (1980), 94 Stat. 2025, as codified and amended at 18 App. U.S.C. §§ 1 et seq. (1985).
[132] *Near* v. *Minnesota*, 283 U.S. 697 (1931).
[133] *Organization for a Better Austin* v. *Keefe*, 402 U.S. 415, 419 (1971).
[134] 283 U.S. at 716.
[135] 403 U.S. 713 (1971).

pending a full trial on the merits.[136] The *Washington Post* began to publish its own excerpts of the study on June 18, 1971, and the government went to federal court in Washington, D.C. to enjoin the *Post*. After the courts in Washington refused to enjoin publication of the excerpts by the *Post*, the Supreme Court agreed, on June 25, 1971, to hear both cases the following day, Saturday, June 26, 1971, and prohibited the newspapers from further publication until the Court issued its opinion.[137]

On June 30, 1971, the Supreme Court issued a three paragraph *per curiam* decision finding that the government had failed to meet its heavy burden of justifying its request for a prior restraint against publication of the Pentagon Papers and dissolved the stays against publication.[138] There were six separate opinions issued by the Justices in the majority.

The opinions of Justices Black and Douglas took an absolutist view of First Amendment prohibitions against prior restraints, suggesting that there were virtually no situations in which a prior restraint could be justified.[139] Justice Brennan recognized that there might be a case in which a "national security" exception to the rule against prior restraints would be justified but that this exception could only be justified when the nation was at war. In response to the argument that the reality of nuclear weapons made the modern era analogous to a time of war, Justice Brennan found that the government had not presented any showing that an "event of that nature" might occur if the Pentagon Papers were published.[140]

The opinions of Justices White, Stewart and Marshall all focused on the absence of a congressional statute authorizing the government to seek a prior restraint in these circumstances. In the absence of such a statute and given the showing in this case, these Justices agreed that the government had not met its burden of justification.[141] Justice Stewart described that burden as requiring proof that publication "will surely result in direct, immediate, and irreparable damage to our Nation or its people."[142]

In a subsequent lower court case, *The Progressive* magazine attempted to publish an article entitled "The H-Bomb Secret: How We Got It, Why We're Telling It" in its April 1979 issue.[143] In this article, the author tried to demonstrate how much an untrained layman could piece together about how to build a hydrogen bomb from publicly available information. Unlike the Pentagon Papers case, here a specific statute prohibited disclosure of some of the data in the article and

---

[136] *Id.* at 714.
[137] *Id.*
[138] *Id.*
[139] *Id.* at 715-19, 720.
[140] *Id.* at 726.
[141] *Id.* at 730, 732-33, 742-47.
[142] *Id.* at 730.
[143] *United States* v. *Progressive, Inc.*, 467 F. Supp. 990 (W.D. Wis.), *dismissed without opinion*, 610 F. 2d 819 (7th Cir. 1979).

authorized the government to seek a court order enjoining public dissemination of such material.

The district court judge found that, although the article was not a "do-it-yourself" manual about how to build a bomb, the article could speed the development of thermo-nuclear bombs by some countries, thus presenting the choice between the preservation of life and freedom of expression. Having framed the question in this way, the judge granted the government's request for an injunction against publication and urged the parties to settle the case.[144] While the appeal was pending, the information was published elsewhere. The government gave up and dismissed its case against *The Progressive* because the prior restraint issued by the district court had been rendered useless.

The government has not sought an injunction against publication of national security information since the *Progressive* case. Not only are there formidable legal barriers to obtaining any such order, but practical difficulties also make such prior restraints unlikely. The government is very unlikely to know about publication in advance unless a publisher voluntarily informs officials, and even then it is likely that the information will end up being published in more than one place.

The Pentagon Papers case is an extraordinary affirmation of freedom of expression, even in the midst of a war. The Court rejected the government's evidence as insufficient to justify restraining speech even in the face of lengthy affidavits that publication would damage the war effort, threaten lives, jeopardize intelligence sources and interfere with diplomatic efforts to end the war. The Court made the judgment that the risks to freedom of expression were even greater and history has proved them correct.[145]

B. Restrictions on News-Gathering during Armed Conflicts

In the past 15 years, the U.S. Department of Defense increasingly has sought to limit media access to information about armed conflicts. The Pentagon has done so primarily by limiting journalists' access to conflict zones.

The trend began during the 1983 U.S. invasion of the Caribbean island of Grenada. Pentagon personnel barred journalists from the island during the first two days of fighting. Reporters who tried to reach the island by private boat were detained and held incommunicado. Journalists who tried to fly into the island by private plane were forced to turn back.[146]

---

[144] 467 F. Supp. at 993, 995-97.

[145] *See* David Rudenstine, The Day the Presses Stopped, A History of the Pentagon Papers Case (1996).

[146] Jacqueline Sharkey, Under Fire: U.S. Military Restrictions on the Media from Grenada to the Persian Gulf, 72-75 (1991). For an additional critique of press restrictions during the Grenada operation, see Ted Carpenter, the Captive Press: Foreign Policy Crises and the First

Media criticism of the Pentagon's restriction of access to the Grenada invasion led to the establishment of a "pool system." The system was designed to ensure that reporters would be present during the initial stages of military operations. Under the system, the Defense Department is supposed to provide a group or "pool" of reporters representing print and broadcast media access to military units from the outset of an operation. These journalists then share their information with colleagues who remain behind the lines.

In practice, the pool arrangement has turned out to be a further constraint on the press. During the invasion of Panama in 1989, the Department of Defense ensured that the media pool was activated too late to cover the early hours of the invasion. When the pool reporters did arrive, their movements were restricted.

In the Persian Gulf War, a pool system was used at the beginning of the allied buildup and was reinstated in January 1991 after the air war began. Pools were accompanied by military escort. All written work, photographs and video were subject to security review before being released.

The media complained about the restrictions and the Pentagon promised to correct any problems. Nonetheless, the ad hoc nature of the access rules made it difficult to challenge them. A number of smaller media and individual writers brought a lawsuit against the Pentagon, but it was dismissed. The judge stated, "[T]he Court should not now be evaluating a set of regulations that are currently being reviewed for probable revision, to determine their reasonableness in the context of a conflict that does not exist and the precise contours of which are unknown and unknowable."[147]

Meanwhile, the military provided journalists with its own videotapes showing bombing success; these tapes were broadcast by the media, along with oral briefings in which Defense Department personnel made statements that exaggerated the success of U. S. weapons.[148] The military did not voluntarily offer information about unsuccessful aspects of its operations. However, when the press did eventually obtain and publish information about military failures, the Pentagon made no legal effort to block such reports, and undoubtedly would have been unsuccessful if it had tried.

On the other hand, the courts refused to require the military to allow the media to cover the arrival of caskets carrying the remains of military personnel killed in the war.[149] Since the events at Dover Air Force Base had nothing to do with operational security or troop safety, a group of journalists filed suit challenging the exclusion on First Amendment grounds. The court rejected the challenge, not on national security grounds, but based on the line of cases holding that the First

---

Amnendment, 198-99 (1995).

[147] *Nation Magazine* v. *United States Dep't of Defense*, 762 F. Supp. 1558, 1575 (S.D.N.Y. 1991).

[148] Sharkey, *supra* note 140 at 145-52.

[149] *JB Pictures, Inc.* v. *Department of Defense*, 86 F.3d 236, 238-39 (D.C. Cir. 1996).

Amendment does not mandate a right of access to government information or sources of information within the government's control.

Thus, the media are effectively free to publish whatever they obtain on their own, but no court has held that they have a right under the First Amendment to insist that the government supply information on military matters or grant access to war zones.

IX. Extraordinary Procedures for Determining National Security Issues

The Supreme Court said in *Marbury* v. *Madison*: "[T]he very essence of civil liberty certainly consists in the right of every individual to claim the protection of the laws, whenever he receives an injury."[150] As explained by Professor Choper: "[A]lthough there has been less than universal agreement that the security of individual liberty is the central function of judicial review, the argument that it constitutes a paramount justification has been made frequently and consistently throughout America's history by its foremost constitutional leaders."[151]

In a series of decisions beginning in the late 1950s and culminating in the Pentagon Papers case, the Supreme Court struck down restrictions on individual rights imposed in the name of national security. The Supreme Court required first a clear statement by the Congress and the President authorizing the restriction in order to be sure that both the legislative and executive branches had specifically decided that the restriction was necessary and warranted to protect national security interests.[152] But such a judgment by the Executive and/or Congress was only the beginning, not the end of the judicial inquiry. The Court then independently determined whether the restriction on freedom of expression violated the First Amendment. In doing so, the Court did not simply defer to government assertions concerning the national security interests at stake, but made its own evaluation of the evidence. The most striking example of this is the Pentagon Papers case, where the Supreme Court found that the government's affidavits did not prove the requisite immediate and grave harm to the nation.[153]

Only this kind of searching and independent inquiry by the judiciary will adequately protect freedom of speech. Otherwise, when such rights are most threatened by the almost irresistible claims of national security, whether legitimate or not, there will be no check on government power and no protection against abuse.

Nevertheless, since the Pentagon Papers case, the Supreme Court, while not expressly overruling earlier precedents, has retreated from its vigorous review of

---

[150] 5 U.S. (1 Cranch) 137, 163 (1803).

[151] Jesse Choper, *Judicial Review and the National Political Process: A Functional Reconsideration of the Role of the Supreme Court* at 66, 69 (1980).

[152] *Kent* v. *Dulles*, 357 U.S. 116 (1958); *Greene* v. *McElroy*, 360 U.S. 474 (1959).

[153] *New York Times Co.* v. *United States*, 403 U.S. 713 (1971).

government restrictions on individual rights in cases involving foreign policy, defense or intelligence considerations. Instead, the Supreme Court has upheld government actions without engaging in any close scrutiny of the government's assertions of harm or determining whether more narrow alternatives exist to protect the national security interest. It has done so, either by relying on various doctrines of nonjusticiability or simply on the basis that the President is due great deference in foreign affairs.[154] The Court's opinions focus not on First Amendment questions, but on presidential power in foreign affairs.[155]

While the Court has become less likely to analyze the issue in First Amendment terms, the Congress has enacted specific legislation to protect freedom of speech and provide for independent judicial review. The prime example of this is the Freedom of Information Act, discussed above, in which the Congress specifically directed the courts to review *de novo* executive branch claims of harm to the national security.[156]

X. Use of Military Courts to Try Cases Involving Civilians

In 1866, the Supreme Court ruled that the military had no jurisdiction, even in time of war, to try civilians in the United States in areas that were not under military control as a result of the collapse of civilian society.[157] "The laws and usages of war can never be applied to citizens in states which have upheld the authority of the government, and where the courts are open and their processes unobstructed."[158] The Supreme Court has been quite strict in recent years in not recognizing any exceptions to this rule, holding that military courts could not try cases involving ex-servicemembers,[159] dependents of servicemembers,[160] or civilian employees of the military.[161] It has not, however, had a case involving civilians in areas under military

---

[154] *See Haig* v. *Agee*, 453 U.S. 280 (1981); *Regan* v. *Wald*, 468 U.S. 222 (1984); *Dames & Moore* v. *Regan*, 453 U.S. 654 (1981). None of these cases, however, include any in-depth discussion of the role of the courts in reviewing direct government restrictions on freedom of expression in the name of national security. The Supreme Court either sidestepped the issue altogether by disposing of it in a footnote, without oral argument or briefing on the issue, *United States* v. *Snepp*, 444 U.S. 507 (1980); or its opinions primarily discuss issues of statutory construction or executive branch power.
[155] Harold Koh, *The National Security Constitution* (1990).
[156] *Supra* note 67.
[157] *Ex parte Milligan*, 71 U.S. 2 (1866).
[158] *Id.* at 127.
[159] *United States ex. Rel. Toth* v. *Quarles*, 350 U.S. 11 (1955).
[160] *Kinsella* v. *United States ex rel. Singleton*, 361 U.S. 234 (1960).
[161] *McElroy* v. *United States ex rel. Gnagliardo*, 361 U.S. 281 (1960).

control during wartime when there was no functioning civilian system of justice, the only possible exception to the rule outlined in the 1866 Supreme Court case.

XI. Conclusions and Recommendations

1. The First Amendment protects speech advocating illegal acts, including the violent overthrow of the government, unless the speech is directed to inciting imminent violence and is likely to incite such violence. Such protection extends to association with groups advocating such violence and it extends to hate speech. There is no national security exception to this rule or to that outlined in the next paragraph.

2. Criticism of government officials and other public figures is a valued part of public discourse and protected by the First Amendment, which requires a heavy showing of falsity and reckless disregard of falsity before such speech may be subject to civil penalties.

3. The public has a right to know about government activities, including information related to national security matters.

4. The government may classify only those specific and narrow categories of information that must be kept secret in order to protect a legitimate national security interest. The standards for classification must be public.

While statements of these principles are not found in judicial opinions, they are universally accepted in U.S. practice. The principle that information may only be classified if its disclosure would cause identifiable harm to the national security, which is not outweighed by the public interest in knowing the information, should be recognized in the law.

5. The Freedom of Information Act implements the constitutional right to know, by establishing affirmative disclosure requirements for government information and by providing for independent judicial review of decisions to withhold information on national security grounds.

6. Congress has an equal right of access to national security information as the President, subject only to the executive privilege protecting the President's deliberations, to enable it to carry out its constitutional oversight responsibilities and as a proxy for the people's right to know about their government.

7. The government bears such a heavy burden in seeking a prior restraint against publication that it is unlikely to ever be able to meet it.

8. Public disclosures of classified information by individuals who did not learn such information by virtue of their government employment are not a crime, except in one very narrowly defined and unusual circumstance.

9. In order to protect the public's right to know and the free speech rights of government employees, there is no wholesale criminal prohibition on leaking classified information to the press, although administrative sanctions may be imposed for such disclosures. First Amendment advocates believe that the Congress has only criminalized public disclosures of a specific and narrow category of classified

information, whose disclosure would be likely to cause concrete harm without being important to public policy debates. However, the Justice Department and one court of appeals have disagreed about the applicability of general statutes to leaks of information and this unsettled law casts a cloud over First Amendment rights.

10. The existence of independent judicial review is especially important to protect freedom of speech in cases involving claims of harm to national security.

THE FEDERAL REPUBLIC OF YUGOSLAVIA: SUPPRESSION OF DISSENT TO PROTECT "THE NATIONAL INTEREST"

Branislav Milinkovic

In examining the relationship between national security, freedom of expression and access to information in the Federal Republic of Yugoslavia ("FRY" or "FR Yugoslavia", comprised of Serbia and Montenegro),[1] it is not enough to look at the laws and the ways they have been applied. There are several reasons for this.

First, in almost all court proceedings that have involved serious political implications, the judiciary in Serbia and Montenegro have not demonstrated an independent approach to their responsibilities.[2] Therefore, it is very difficult to expect that any court in FRY would reject executive claims of national security.

Second, since its transformation from the national branch of the now-defunct ruling League of Communists of Yugoslavia in 1990, the ruling Socialist Party of Serbia (SPS) has continued to exercise full control over all top positions in the state, society and economy.[3] Therefore, its policies towards the media and political opposition generally have considerably greater impact on freedom of expression than do the infrequent, and far less consequential, court judgments.

Finally, the state and ruling party employ a variety of indirect methods to restrict freedom of expression and information. These methods include economic pressures on the independent media, withholding of public information, arbitrary procedures for allocating broadcast frequencies, and use of conflicting legal provisions at the Federal and Republican levels concerning the legal status of broadcasters to keep them beholden to government officials.

Beginning in the late 1980s, the charismatic Serbian leader Slobodan Milosevic used the media to inflame nationalist passions. State media under his control broadcast biased, misleading, chauvinistic and hate-mongering reports. He silenced dissenting views in Belgrade primarily through economic pressures on the independent media and mass dismissals of journalists from state-controlled radio and television. The claimed justification for these actions, especially during the wars in Croatia and Bosnia-Hercegovina, was to protect the "national interest". What the national interest was never precisely defined, but what it amounted to was Milosevic's view of what was best for the Serb nation and for his own political fortunes.

---

[1] *The Constitution of the Federal Republic of Yugoslavia* ("FRY"), promulgated on April 27, 1992, established a federation of Serbia and Montenegro. *Sluzbeni glasnik SR Jugoslavije*, Year I, number 1.

[2] The most recent and well-known examples are the numerous judgments of the courts during December 1996 which nullified the second round of the local elections in Serbia after the victory of the opposition parties and, without any legal basis, ordered new elections.

[3] V. Goati, ed., *Challenges of Parliamentarism: The Case of Serbia in the Early Nineties* (Belgrade: Institute of Social Sciences, 1995).

Consequently, all journalists had to pursue the "national interest", as the former Serbian Minister of Information, Ratomir Vico, tried to explain:

> Every journalist must serve his nation and his state. He is doing so if he performs his job in a professional and responsible way, with a feeling to make a difference between the national interest and some other political interests.[4]

Former director of state-controlled Radio-Television Serbia and leader of the SPS group in Serbia's Parliament, Milorad Vucelic, accused Serbian journalists from the independent media of harming Serbia in the eyes of the world by "inventing lies about Serbs" and by "serving the purpose of providing sources for the foreign press."[5]

Leaders of the Yugoslav United Left (JUL), the influential coalition partner of the ruling SPS, have stated that foreign assistance to the Serbian media amounts to a form of special warfare against the country. In its party program, JUL claims that such money is "invested in restricting the freedoms and independence of Yugoslav citizens", for "bribing dishonest people" and for "denunciation".

In his speech to Parliament upon becoming the new President of FR Yugoslavia in July 1997, Slobodan Milosevic complained that "a great part of the [domestic] media is in the service of spiritual and moral destruction, and is frequently financially, politically and morally supported from abroad".[6]

As a result of such strong and clear political messages from people in power, the most influential media in FR Yugoslavia do not report or analyze anything that could be understood as questioning the "official line" or "undermining national security". Nevertheless, a group of independent media (television station *NTV Studio B*, radio station *B-92*, daily *Nasa Borba*, weeklies *Vreme*, *Nin* and *Monitor*) offer different views and examine various topics. Authorities tolerate these media because they have limited audiences, almost exclusively in Belgrade and some of the bigger towns.

---

[4] Interview in the daily *Politika*, February 3, 1995.
[5] Humanitarian Law Center, *Spotlight on Human Rights Violations in Times of Armed Conflict*, at 132 (Belgrade, 1995).
[6] Milosevic's speech to the Federal Parliament, July 23, 1997.

I. Expression Deemed Threatening to National Security

A. The Legal Framework

Press freedom and freedom of expression are guaranteed by the Constitutions of FR Yugoslavia,[7] Serbia[8] and Montenegro.[9] Serbia and Montenegro also have Public Information Acts, and Serbia has a special law on radio and television. The procedure for establishing a private newspaper is very liberal, but it is difficult to obtain a license for the electronic media (radio and television) owing to arbitrary procedures for allocating frequencies and conflicting legal provisions at the Federal and Republican levels.

As a successor state to the former Yugoslavia,[10] which ratified the International Covenant on Civil and Political Rights ("ICCPR") in 1971, FRY is a party to the ICCPR. However, it has not accepted the ICCPR's First Optional Protocol (which provides a procedure by which individuals may bring complaints against the country to the UN Human Rights Committee). According to the Federal Constitution (Article 16) all ratified international treaties are an integral part of the domestic legal order, but the practical value of this provision has, to date, been very limited.

Neither the Federal, nor either of the two Republican Constitutions mentions "national security" or "national interests" as permissible grounds for restricting freedom of expression. Relevant constitutional provisions forbidding censorship of the press and other media enumerate only four permissible grounds; namely, to prevent:(1) violent destruction of the constitutional order, (2) jeopardy to territorial integrity, (3) violation of guaranteed freedoms and human rights of others, and (4) incitement to national, racial or religious hatred and intolerance.[11]

The Federal Criminal Code, however, contains a whole chapter on criminal offenses against the constitutional order and security of FR Yugoslavia.[12] The most significant article restricting freedom of expression in the name of national security and related interests is Article 133, which prohibits incitement to violent changes of the constitutional order (*pozivanje na nasilnu promenu ustavnog uredjenja*). Under the Federal, Serbian and Montenegrian Criminal Codes, it is also punishable to insult or

---

[7] *FRY Constitution*, *supra* note 1, Art. 36.
[8] *Const. of Serbia*, Art. 46, *Sluzbeni glasnik Republike Srbije*, No.1, September 28, 1990.
[9] *Const. of Montenegro*, Art. 35, *Sluzbeni list Republike Crne Gore*, No.48, October 12, 1992.
[10] Although the U.N. rejected FRY's claim to be entitled automatically to succeed to the seat of the former Socialist Federal Republic of Yugoslavia in the General Asembly, it did accept its special application to be bound by the ICCPR as a successor state (though not necessarily the only one).
[11] *Federal Const.*, Art. 38; *Const. of Serbia.*, Art. 47; *Const. of Montenegro*, Art. 37.
[12] Chapter XV, Articles 114-139.

ridicule (*izlaganje poruzi*) the state, national symbols or the top-ranking state officials such as the President, Prime Minister and President of Parliament.[13]

B. Advocacy of Minority Rights

Some one third of FR Yugoslavia's total population of 10.5 million are neither Serbs nor Montenegrians. The three largest minority groups are the Albanians (1.7 million, 16.5 per cent of the population), concentrated in the province of Kosovo where they constitute 90 per cent of the population; Moslems (336,000 or 3.2 per cent of the population,) who live in the Sandzak (or Raska) region; and Hungarians (344,000 or 3.3 per cent of the population), who live in the northern Serbian province of Vojvodina, close to the Hungarian border.

1. Kosovo

Kosovo is a well-known flash point for instability in the Balkans because of conflicting claims over its sovereignty. Serbs regard it as the historic "cradle" of their state, while it is populated by Albanians. Albanians do not take part in Serbian public and political life. They have boycotted all multi-party elections since 1990. At the same time, they have created a network of parallel institutions: parliament, government, schools and professional organizations. Systematic police repression and segregation against the Albanian population in Kosovo has been well documented.[14]

Kosovo Albanians complain about the serious human rights situation in Kosovo, while Belgrade officials maintain that "the problem of the Albanian minority in Serbia is a problem of separatism par excellence".[15] Indeed, the final political objective of the Democratic League of Kosovo (LDK), a leading political party of Kosovo Albanians, is an independent and sovereign Kosovo. LDK is a legally registered political party, but it is often treated by Serbian police as an illegal organization; meetings of its branches are regularly interrupted and its members, arrested.

Members of the LDK are most frequently accused of and convicted for subversion and jeopardizing the territorial integrity of the country. During one of these trials,[16] state prosecutor Miladin Popovic openly emphasized before the District Court of Pec (a city in Kosovo) that "it is not just the defendants who are on trial

---

[13] Federal Crim. Code, Art. 157; Serbia's Crim. Code, Art. 98; Montenegro's Crim. Code, Art. 82.
[14] *See* Humanitarian Law Center, *Spotlight on Human Rights in Serbia and Montenegro*, No. 16 at 15-71 (Belgrade, 1996).
[15] Letter from the FRY Government to the UN Commission on Human Rights, U.N. Doc. E/CN.4/1995/153, (February 23, 1995).
[16] Judgment K. num. 90/93 (February 16, 1994).

here today, but also an insane policy led by the heads of the political parties comprised of Albanians who are brainwashed by ruthless propaganda from within the country and abroad and by false promises of help from the United Nations and the Atlantic Pact for the achievement of a Kosovo Republic."[17]

Serbia's Parliament abolished the Parliament and Government of Kosovo on July 5, 1990.[18] This meant the end of the limited autonomy which Kosovo until then enjoyed. On the same day, in order to suppress dissemination of speech advocating Kosovo's independence, Serbia's Parliament adopted two decisions restricting Kosovo's most influential media, *Radio-Television Pristina* and the newspaper *Rilindija.*[19]

Both decisions imposed "provisional measures of social protection against the self-management rights and social property" of the two media organs. Parliament gave as reasons for these measures that the station and paper were beset by "disturbed self-management"; "had endangered social interests"; "had failed to comply with their legal obligations"; and "had broadcast messages, including false and alarming information, against the policy of the Parliament of Serbia, used television to separate Albanians from other ethnic groups in Kosovo, aimed to build support among the Albanian population for the platform of Albanian nationalists and separatists, advocated constitutional changes in Serbia, and demanded a new constitution and the status of a republic for Kosovo, in order to secede from the Socialist Federal Republic Of Yugoslavia."[20]

One month later, Serbia's Parliament decided to "cease the work of the newspaper *Rilindija*",[21] which had been owned by the Parliament of Kosovo. After abolishing Kosovo's Parliament, Serbia's Parliament took over *Rilindija*. It based this decision on Article 38 of the Public Information Act which regulates ownership of the media. Reasons given were similar to those given above to support imposition of the provisional measures:

> [The newspaper] contributed to the negative national homogenization of the Albanians, its reports and comments incited hatred and anti-Serb feelings, and it called for granting Kosovo Albanians the status of "a people" [instead of a national minority, as under the 1974 Federal Constitution], including the right to have their own republic and to secede. [22]

---

[17] *Spotlight Report No.16*, *supra* note 14.

[18] Law of July 5, 1990. The first article of this Law states: "The Kosovo Parliament does not act in accordance with the Constitution, while its delegates endanger sovereignty, territorial integrity and constitutional order of the Socialist Republic of Serbia." (Translation by the author.) *Sluzbeni Glasnik Socijalisticke Republike Srbije*, No. 33/90, July 5, 1990.

[19] *Sluzbeni Glasnik Socijalisticke Republike Srbije*, No. 34/90, July 5, 1990.

[20] *Id.*

[21] *Sluzbeni Glasnik Socijalisticke Republike Srbije*, No. 44/90, August 7, 1990.

[22] *Id.*

During July and August 1990, approximately 1,300 journalists, technicians and other staff of *Radio-Television Pristina* were dismissed; editors and directors first, all others later. Now, virtually the entire staff are Serb; almost all Albanians were forced out. Since summer 1990, on *TV Pristina* there has been only one hour daily of programs in the Albanian language. However, television programs from Tirana, Albania (including special programs for Kosovo) are not jammed and many houses in Kosovo have a satellite antenna to receive the Albanian channel.

In 1991 and 1992, all editors-in-chief of the Albanian press in Kosovo were punished with 15 to 60 days of prison because of articles and opinions they had published. B. Salja, who was an editor-in-chief of the weekly *Zeri*, was sentenced because he had published an ethnic map of Albanians in the Balkans. By doing so, according to the regional court, he had "disturbed the public and insulted patriotic and socialist feelings of the citizens".[23]

2. The Sandzak

The Party of Democratic Action (SDA) is the strongest political party of Moslems in the Sandzak. The political platform of SDA calls for a "special status" (high degree of autonomy) for this region, part of which lies in Serbia and part in Montenegro. Its representatives were Members of Serbia'a Parliament during 1991 and 1992; it boycotted the 1993 elections; and, since the November 1997 Federal elections, it is once again in Parliament.

By the end of 1994, a group of 45 SDA members (24 in Serbia and 21 in Montenegro) were sentenced to prison terms ranging from two to seven years for "attempting to undermine the territorial integrity of the State". Courts in Novi Pazar (Serbia)[24] and Bijelo Polje (Montenegro)[25] concluded that the SDA members had organized arms deliveries to the Sandzak and prepared military plans for secession of the region. Their lawyers, on the other hand, claimed that they had possessed only a few guns in order to protect themselves from Serbian paramilitary groups.

Human rights monitors reported flagrant breaches of criminal procedure in these two trials, including arbitrary detention, torture, delays in filing formal charges, investigation conducted by the state security service instead of by judges, and restriction of the activities of defense counsel.[26] The courts did not single out any specific act of freedom of expression allegedly committed by the defendants which

---

[23] Violeta Oroshi, *Information on Kosovo*, The Right to Pictures & Words, No.4, Belgrade, at 11-13 (June 1994).
[24] Novi Pazar Court judgment K-63/93, Oct. 12, 1994.
[25] Bijelo Polje Court judgment K-25/94, Dec. 28 1994.
[26] *Spotlight*, *supra* note 5, at 118.

threatened national security.[27] Defense counsel and human rights groups argued that the courts in essence outlawed a political opinion (autonomy for the Sandzak) which is a legitimate issue in the public debate and thus entitled to protection.[28]

C. Criticism of Government

After the opposition Serbian Renewal Movement (SPO) organized anti-government demonstrations on the streets of Belgrade on June 1-2, 1993, the Office of the Public Prosecutor of Serbia urged that the SPO should be banned. In a message faxed to the SPO's office, the prosecutor cited "national interests and state interests".[29] There was no trial following this fax-message and the SPO was not banned, but its leader, Vuk Draskovic, was arrested and ill-treated. He was released only after several days of a hunger strike.

Zoran Djindjic, leader of the opposition Democratic Party, was sentenced to four months in prison (which sentence was suspended, and he was placed on probation for two years) on October 23, 1996, for criticizing Serbia's Prime Minister Mirko Marjanovic in the newspapers. Djindjic published an article claiming that Marjanovic had used his political position to enrich his company and himself personally. The public prosecutor indicted him for "insulting the state" and "ridiculing high state officials"; the court convicted him despite the efforts of his defense lawyers to prove that he had "reasonable grounds" to believe that the Prime Minister had abused his office.

D. Conscientious Objection

The right to conscientious objection was recognized for the first time in FR Yugoslavia under the 1992 Federal Constitution. Conscripts who do not want to

---

[27] However, in a series of articles about the events in the Sandzak, the pro-government *Politika Ekspres* called the *Sandzak* journal "the fist of the separatist movements", thus effectively accusing it of inciting secession. *See* Milutin Niciforovic, "How Serbia stopped secession of Raska and war in the Sandzak," *Politika Ekspres*, 14-28 December 1993.

[28] *See* Council of Europe, Parliamentary Assembly, Res. 1030 (1994), ¶ 6, text adopted by the Assembly on Apr. 13, 1994 (13th Sitting), in which the Parliamentary Assembly condemned the detention and prosecution of six members of the Turkish Grand National Assembly for advocating autonomy for the Kurdish region, and declared its view that peaceful advocacy of some degree of autonomy is entitled to the protection of Article 10 of the European Convention. *See also* Principle 7(a)(i) of the Johannesburg Principles on National Security, Freedom of Expression and Access to Information, and the Commentary thereto, elsewhere in this volume.

[29] *Spotlight*, *supra* note 5, at 40.

perform 12 months of military service because of "religious or other reasons" may instead perform 24 months of civil service.

The Federal Constitutional Court clarified that this new provision could be used only by new conscripts, and not by those members of the reserve forces who had already performed their military service before the 1992 Constitution's entry into force.[30] This is an important limitation of the new rule. Many people who were in the reserve forces were mobilized for the war in Croatia in 1991. If drafted again, they will not be able to resist conscription by choosing alternative service.

Legislation in force during military operations of the former Yugoslav People's Army in Croatia in 1991, did not allow conscientious objection. This was one of the reasons why some 300,000 mainly young men from Serbia and Montenegro, who did not want to be drafted for the war left the country.[31]

The Center for Anti-War Action (CAA) in Belgrade, which had advocated conscientious objection in 1991, was attacked and damaged by some militant groups a few times. Police investigations yielded no suspects. Activities of the CAA were regularly criticized in the official media. However, no legal proceedings against the Center, for instance, on the basis of possible threats to national security, were initiated.

II. Access to and Disclosure of Information

A. Constitutional and Statutory Provisions

There is no special legislation such as a "freedom of information act" in FR Yugoslavia. Still, according to Article 122 of the Federal Constitution and Article 10 of Serbia's Constitution, "activities of the state organs are accessible to the public" and this accessibility can be limited or excluded only "in cases determined by law". Similar provisions are also embodied in the Federal and Serbian Public Information Acts.[32]

Journalists from independent media were dissatisfied because of the difficulties they faced in attempting to obtain various kinds of information from governmental sources. Accordingly, an opposition Member of Serbia's Parliament asked the Ministry of Information in March 1995 for an explanation of how these constitutional and legal provisions had been implemented in practice. The Ministry's response provides a good illustration of the Government's policy of withholding information. The Ministry stated that it distributes information on the "same

[30] Federal Constitutional Court, decision number 51/94, May 25, 1994.
[31] The great majority of this huge group of "draft evaders" is still abroad. So far, there have been no reports of those who returned to FR Yugoslavia being prosecuted.
[32] *Federal Public Info. Act*, Art. 2; *Serbian Public Info. Act.*, Art. 11.

principles" which are "equal for everybody" and that it issues statements after all meetings of the Government. The Ministry concluded by explaining that "information about activities of the Government and its organs is disseminated in accordance with the program of the Government and the plan of the Ministry of Information."[33]

B. Difficulties in the Parliament

On the initiative of the ruling Socialist Party of Serbia, Serbia's Parliament decided to cancel direct broadcasting of its parliamentary sessions on July 26, 1995. At the same time, the Parliament established a new rule: that it would vote before every session to decide whether the session would or would not be broadcast. President of the Parliament Dragan Tomic explained that this was done to stop "violence in the Parliament" and because "Parliament was abused for purposes of the media".

This decision prompted almost all of the opposition parties to walk out of Parliament. Because of the Government's strong control over the most influential media, especially state television, opposition parties regarded the broadcast of parliamentary sessions on television as their main, and virtually only, opportunity to publicize their political ideas country-wide. A similar situation has prevailed in the Federal Parliament.

III. The News Media

The Government's firm control over the most influential media in Serbia, including state-run radio and television, is well documented.[34] The news is restricted or distorted in order to serve official political lines. National security is not understood as the security of the state or even the nation, but rather as the security of the regime in power.

---

[33] *Politika*, March 1, 1995, at 12.

[34] *See, e.g.*, U.N. Special Rapporteur for Human Rights in Former Yugoslavia, *Report on the Media*, U.N. Doc. E/CN.4/1995/54, December 13, 1994; Mark Thompson, *Forging War* (London: Article 19, May 1994); Marjan Malesic, ed., *The Role of the Mass Media in the Serbian-Croatian Conflict* (Stockholm, May 1993); International Organization of Journalists, *Reporters and Media in ex-Yugoslavia* (Prague, 1992).

A. Restrictions on News-Gathering During Peace Time

One clear example of restrictions justified on national security grounds was the 36-hour blackout in March 1991 of transmission by the independent television station *NTV Studio B* and radio station *B-92,* to prevent them from broadcasting opposition demonstrations in Belgrade. There was no subtlety in the police action. While the opposition demonstrations were still going on, a group of ten police officers entered *NTV Studio B* and demanded immediate cessation of the program. The-then director of *NTV Studio B,* Dragan Kojadinovic, negotiated to be able to continue broadcasting on condition that he not present any new information about the demonstrations. Nonetheless, editors managed to broadcast a written message on the screen that the program had been censored. After this message, many citizens protested. Finally, the stations were permitted to continue their news broadcasts.

The Public Prosecutor's ban against *NTV Studio B* was based on accusations against director Kojadinovic that he had "invited the population to resist the authorities" in his news. The station lodged a challenge against the ban, but the Public Prosecutor failed to respond to it.[35]

The most striking recent example of media manipulation came in reaction to the mass protests all over Serbia after the nullification of the opposition's victory in the November 1996 local elections. The Government-controlled media either ignored the protests altogether or labeled protesters as "traitors" who were destroying Serbia. During the three months of peaceful protests, the Serbian police used excessive force not only against protesters but also against many domestic and foreign journalists. Most of these beatings occurred when members of the press were filming, photographing or otherwise covering acts of police brutality against demonstrators.[36]

B. Restrictions During Armed Conflict

No information has been made public concerning possible instructions on reporting about war operations during the armed conflicts in Croatia and Bosnia-Herzegovina. However, the fact that hundreds of journalists were dismissed from Radio and Television Serbia in 1992 and 1993 for political reasons shows that objective information was indirectly restricted.

An order issued by the Federal Defense Ministry in April 1994 prohibiting radio amateurs from transmitting messages to Bosnia is one example of restrictions placed on freedom of expression on national security grounds. Military officials accused radio operators of espionage and passing militarily relevant messages to the (primarily Moslem) Army of the Republic of Bosnia-Herzegovina. Radio amateurs

---

[35] Mark Thompson, *supra* note 34, at 59.

[36] These cases are well documented in the report by the Humanitarian Law Center, *Political Use of Police Violence During the 1996-1997 Potests in Serbia* (Belgrade, 1997).

strenuously denied these accusations and pointed out that they provided the only way for many refugees from Bosnia to talk to their relatives or friends. Nevertheless, they were compelled to stop transmitting any messages.[37]

C. Action against Foreign Correspondents

In April 1994, the Federal Ministry of Information withdrew the accreditation of fifteen foreign correspondents and removed their names from the registry of foreign correspondents. These journalists, who had mainly worked for the French and U.S. media, lost the right "to engage in the gathering of news and information about events in Yugoslavia". In the official orders, signed by the Federal Minister of Information, Slobodan Ignjatovic, it was stated that "accreditation may be withdrawn if a correspondent does not observe the law or ethical standards of news and information gathering". No more concrete explanations for each individual case were given.

Minister Ignjatovic stated that the orders were intended to punish journalists who had not been "professional" and who had "demonized the entire Serb nation". This explanation, together with the subsequent campaign against foreign journalists in the official press, suggests that withdrawal of accreditation had something to do with the Government's view of its national security interests. The action had a "chilling effect" both on other foreign correspondents (specially those having Yugoslav nationality) as well as local journalists.

IV. Extraordinary Procedures

A. Prior Restraint of Publication

Prior censorship is unconstitutional. Indirect methods to force some publishing houses not to publish some books or journals do exist. Although the result of these indirect methods could perhaps best be described as self-censorship, the impact is the same as if mechanisms of prior restraint had been formally employed.

B. Military Courts and Cases Involving Civilians

The jurisdiction of the military courts in FR Yugoslavia is extremely wide. They have jurisdiction over criminal prosecutions of all offenses committed by

---

[37] *See also Spotlight, supra* note 5, at 135-142.

military personnel regardless of whether or not the act alleged was committed while on military duty or whether or not it was in any way connected with military service. They also have jurisdiction over charges of crimes committed by prisoners of war. In addition, military courts have jurisdiction over civilians for all acts constituting crimes against the armed forces and for certain serious offenses against the constitutional order. This means that civilians are subject to two standards of due process and justice.

The military judges are far more isolated from public opinion than their civilian counterparts. Moreover, their independence is seriously comprised by the fact that they have to obey the same rules and regulations of military service as other military personnel.[38]

V. Conclusion

The pursuit of "national interests" was invoked by Serbian authorities to inflame ethnic passions and justify Serbian military actions during the war in ex-Yugoslavia. Some of the worst atrocities committed in Europe since World War II were made possible, to a large extent, by total control of the most influential media and suppression of dissent. The national institutions, including the courts, were not sufficiently strong or independent to challenge this control. Had the international community taken firm action early on to counter the gross violation of freedom of expression, perhaps many of the worst atrocities could have been prevented.

[38] Law on Military Courts, Arts. 41 and 42.

APPENDIX A:

Notes on Editors

Sandra Coliver has been working in Bosnia since May 1996, as a UN human rights expert and Legal Advisor to the International Crisis Group. She previously served as Law Program Director of Article 19, the International Center Against Censorship, headquartered in London. She has authored several reports, journal articles, and one book on freedom of expression themes, and has edited three books, on press law and practice, hate speech, and access to health information. She received a BA from Yale University and a JD from the University of California, Berkeley. She has taught at UC Berkeley and American University law schools, and served as a Council of Europe expert on media freedom issues. She was a trial and appellate lawyer for several years.

Stephen Bowen is a barrister specializing in international human rights, criminal and administrative law. He holds academic degrees from Oxford University, the Polytechnic of Central London and the London School of Economics. He has held various posts with the United Nations, most recently in former Yugoslavia where he served as Chief of Staff of the UN Special Coordinator for Sarajevo, and as an expert member of the Field Operation of the UN High Commissioner for Human Rights. He also acted as Chief Counsel to the Election Appeals Sub-Commission, the OSCE body responsible for supervising elections in Bosnia and Herzegovina. Between 1993 and 1995 he was Legal Officer at the Palestinian Center for Human Rights. He is currently Program Director of the International Human Rights Law Group.

Joan Fitzpatrick is Professor of Law and Foundation Scholar at the University of Washington School of Law in Seattle. She is the author of "Human Rights in Crisis: The International System for Protecting Rights During States of Emergency" (University of Pennsylvania Press 1994). She served as rapporteur for the International Law Association during its study of human rights and states of emergency. She is the author of numerous articles concerning human rights, refugees, and the death penalty.

Paul Hoffman is a civil rights lawyer in Santa Monica, California. He is the Chair of the Board of Amnesty International-USA and the former legal director of the ACLU Foundation of Southern California. He is also a member of the international Board of Article 19. He has litigated many cases involving issues of freedom of expression and national security.

APPENDIX B:

Notes on Authors

Nagad Mohamed Al-Boray is a Cairo attorney with a distinguished background in the Egyptian human rights movement and expertise in the field of freedom of expression. A law graduate of Cairo University, he spent ten years with the Egyptian Organization for Human Rights (EOHR) serving as its Secretary General from 1994 until 1996. In May of 1996, Mr. Al-Boray and others established the Group for Democratic Development, a non-partisan organization dedicated to the support and development of democracy in Egypt. He has, among other cases, defended Professor Hamed Abu Zaid, novelist Alaa Hamed and feminist Nawwal Saadawi, and sued the government for refusing to register the EOHR.

Lawrence W. Beer is Fred Morgan Kirby Professor of Civil Rights, Emeritus, Lafayette College, Pennsylvania. His specialties are Japan's constitutional law and human rights law in Asia. Major works include "Freedom of Expression in Japan" (1984); "Constitutionalism in Asia: Asian Views of the American Influence" (1979, 1988); "Constitutional Systems in Late Twentieth Century Asia" (1992); and with Hiroshi Itoh, "The Constitutional Case Law of Japan: Selected Supreme Court Decisions, 1961-70"(1978); and "The Constitutional Case Law of Japan, 1971 through 1990" (1996). He held positions at the University of Colorado (Boulder), Denver University, Sophia University (Tokyo), Hokkaido University (Sapporo, Japan), University of Washington, Oxford University, University of Kansas, Lewis & Clark Northwestern School of Law, University of Melbourne, Australian National University, and Lehigh University.

Lawrence Early holds law degrees from Queens University, Belfast (LLB) and the University of Exeter (LLM). He has also been admitted to the Bar of Northern Ireland. He joined the Council of Europe in 1982 having previously been a Lecturer in the Faculty of Law of the University of Sheffield specializing in public law and EEC law. He worked in the Council's Legal Directorate between 1982 and 1990 in areas including data protection and refugee and asylum law before becoming Head of Media Section in the Directorate of Human Rights. During that time he was Secretary to the Steering Committee on the Mass Media, the Standing Committee on Transfrontier Television and the European Ministerial Conference on Mass Media Policy. Since the end of 1997 he has been working as Head of Section in the registry of the European Court of Human Rights.

Roger Errera is a member of the Conseil d'Etat, France's highest court of administrative law and a former member of the Board of Governors of the Ecole nationale de la magistrature (at which most French judges are trained). He is Professor of Law at the Central European University in Budapest, and was a Visiting

Professor of French Law at University College, London, as well as a Senior Research Fellow at the Institute of Advanced Legal Studies. He serves on the editorial committee of several legal journals, such as "Public Law" (London), "Revue trimestrielle des droits de l' homme" (Brussels), and the "International Human Rights Journal" (Strasbourg).

Elizabeth Evatt, AC, has been a Member of the UN Human Rights Committee since 1993. She has been the Chair (1989-91) and a member (1984-92) of the UN Committee on the Elimination of Discrimination Against Women; the President (1988-93) and a member (1993-94) of the Australian Law Reform Commission; a Deputy President of the Australian Industrial Relations Commission (1989-94); and Chief Judge of the Family Court of Australia (1976-88). She is a Barrister-at-Law (Inner Temple, London), and received her law degree from the University of Sydney (1955) and an LLM from Harvard (1956).

Ruth Gavison is Haim Cohn Professor of Human Rights at the Faculty of Law, and the Chair of the Academic Committee of the Center for Human Rights, Hebrew University in Jerusalem. She received a BA in philosophy and economics (1970), LLB (1968) and an LLM (1970) from the Hebrew University and PhD in legal philosophy (1975) from Oxford University. She has been a visiting professor at the Yale Law School (1978-80) and at the Law Center of the University of Southern California (1990-91). She was a founder and chairperson of the Association for Civil Rights in Israel.

Yash Ghai is from Kenya and currently the Sir YK Pao Professor of Public Law at the University of Hong Kong. He has taught at the University of East Africa, Uppsala University, the University of Warwick (UK) and has been a visiting professor at the Yale Law School, Toronto University, Melbourne University, the National University of Singapore and Harvard Law School. He has published extensively on public law; his books include Public Law and Political Change in Kenya (1970, with Patrick McAuslan) Law in the Political Economy of Public Enterprise (1977), The Political Economy of Law: Third World Perspectives (1987, edited jointly with Robin Luckham and Francis Snyder), Law, Politics and Government in Pacific Island States (1988), Heads of States in the Pacific: A Legal and Constitutional Analysis (1990, with Jill Cottrell), The Law Politics and Administration of Decentralization in Papua New Guinea (1992, with Anthony Regan) and The Hong Kong Bill of Rights: A Comparative Perspective (1993, edited with Johannes Chan). He has advised various governments and political parties on constitutional matters and was a consultant on the independence constitutions of Papua New Guinea, Solomon Islands and Vanuatu. In 1996 and 1997, he advised opposition parties in Fiji on the drafting of its new constitution which was adopted in mid-1997. In recent years, his research and publications have focused on ethnicity and human rights, globalization and human rights, and the transfer of Hong Kong's sovereignty to China (on which subject he published a book in May 1997, Hong Kong's New Constitutional Order: The Resumption of Chinese Sovereignty and the Basic Law).

Nils Petter Gleditsch, born 1942, mag.art. in Sociology (University of Oslo, 1968), is Senior Research Fellow at the International Peace Research Institute, Oslo (PRIO), Editor of the Journal of Peace Research, and Professor of International Studies at the Norwegian University of Science and Technology in Trondheim. His most recent books in English are "The Peace Dividend" (co-edited, North-Holland, 1996) and "Conflict and the Environment" (edited, Kluwer Academic, 1997).

Felipe Gonzalez is the Representative for Latin America for the International Human Rights Law Group. He is also an Associate Professor of International Human Rights Law and Jurisprudence at Diego Portales University Law School in Santiago de Chile. He is the author of the book "Protección Democrática de la Seguridad Interior" (1991) and editor and co-author of "Las acciones de interés público" (1997).

Ulrich Karpen is Professor of Constitutional and Administrative Law at the University of Hamburg School of Law, a Member of the Hamburg State Parliament and Chairman of the European Association of Legislation. He has written extensively on the German Constitution in general and freedom of expression in particular, including a chapter in English in a book that he edited, titled "The Constitution of the Federal Republic of Germany: Essays on the Basic Rights and Principles of the Basic Law" (1988).

Louise Krabbe is a Danish jurist and is currently working with the Danish Center for Human Rights. She has previously worked with several organizations on issues relating to freedom of expression and information including Article 19, The Baltic Media Center and the Commissioner of the Council of the Baltic Sea States.

Viviana Krsticevic, Harvard Law School LLM (1993), Stanford University MA (1992), is co-executive director of the Center for Justice and International Law (CEJIL), a human rights organization that litigates the majority of cases pending before the Inter-American Commission and Court on Human Rights on behalf of victims. She has taught an Advanced Human Rights Seminar at American University, published several articles on international human rights law, including "The Development and Implementation of Legal Standards Relating to Impunity in the Inter-American System of Human Rights Protection" (1996); and "La denuncia individual ante la Chymosin Interamericana de Derechos Humanos en el sistema interamericano de protecciosn de los derechos humanos", in: Protecciosn internacional de los derechos humanos de las mujeres (Instituto Interamericano de Derechos Humanos (IIDH), Costa Rica 1996).

Lawrence Lustgarten is a Professor of Law at the University of Southampton. He has written extensively on national security issues, constitutional law, criminal justice and racial discrimination. He is author of "The Governance of Police" (1986) and co-author of "In From the Cold: National Security and Parliamentary Democracy" (Oxford University Press 1994). He is active in constitutional reform and civil liberties organizations and has taught or researched at universities in Australia, Canada and Tanzania.

Paul Mahoney obtained Honors BA in jurisprudence from University of London in 1969 and was lecturer in law at University College London from 1967-73. He was called to the Bar of England and Wales in 1971. As a barrister, he practiced in London from 1972-74. He was Legal Officer in the registry of the European Court of Human Rights from 1974-90 and 1993-95. From 1990-93 he was Head of Personnel of the Council of Europe. In June 1995, he was elected Deputy Registrar of the European Court of Human Rights. In 1988, he was Ariel Sallows (Visiting) Professor of Human Rights at the University of Saskatchewan, Saskatoon, Canada. He is Associate Editor of the Human Rights Law Journal. He has been author member of articles on the European Court of Human Rights and co-editor with Professor Kathleen E. Mahoney of "Human Rights in the Twenty-First Century: A Global Challenge" (Martinus Nijhoff, 1993).

Gilbert Marcus is a senior advocate of the High Court of South Africa and one of the leading free speech and media lawyers in Johannesburg. He was an associate professor of law with the Center for Applied Legal Studies at the University of Witwatersrand. He received his BA and LLB from the University of Witwatersrand and an LLM from the University of Cambridge. He has written extensively in the field of media law.

Kate Martin is Director of the Center for National Security Studies and general counsel to the National Security Archive. Since 1988, Ms. Martin has worked on the entire range of issues at the intersection of freedom of speech and information and national security. She has testified before Congress on numerous issues, including classification standards. She has also successfully sued both the CIA for the disclosure of the intelligence budget and the White House for preservation of National Security Council e-mail. With the Helsinki Foundation in Warsaw, she co-directs an international project to establish oversight and accountability of security and intelligence agencies in emerging democracies. Ms. Martin teaches national security law at Georgetown University Law School. She graduated from the University of Virginia Law School in 1977, where she was a member of the Law Review, and from Pomona College in 1973 with a BA in Philosophy.

Cecilia Medina is the Vice-Chairperson of the UN Human Rights Committee. She is a Professor of International Human Rights Law at Diego Portales University Law

School in Santiago de Chile and a researcher at the Netherlands Institute of Human Rights, University of Utrecht. She is author of the book "The Battle of Human Rights: Gross, Systematic Violations and the Inter-American System" (1988) and editor and co-author of "Sistema Jurídico y Derechos Humanos" (1996).

Juan E. Méndez has been the Executive Director of the Inter-American Institute on Human Rights in San José, Costa Rica since 1996. From 1982 to 1994, he held the position of General Counsel of the Human Rights Watch-Americas in Washington, DC. He was Professor of Law at Georgetown University from 1992-1996 and at the University of Notre Dame in 1996. He was visiting faculty in the Oxford University Summer Program on International Human Rights Law, 1997-1998 and visiting fellow of the Kellogg Institute at the University of Notre Dame in 1996. Mr. Méndez is the author of several articles and book sections on accountability for past human rights violations, right to truth, and relativism and universality of human rights.

Branislav Milinkovic is a Research Fellow at the Institute of International Politics and Economics in Belgrade and Secretary General of the Federal Republic of Yugoslavia's Branch of the International Law Association. He is also an adviser at the Humanitarian Law Center, a Belgrade based non-governmental organization focusing on human rights monitoring, and an international editor of "Helsinki Monitor", the Dutch Quarterly on Security and Cooperation. He has published many articles in the Federal Republic of Yugoslavia and abroad (The Netherlands, Sweden, Germany) mainly on freedom of expression and the OSCE. He wrote a book on media freedoms (1996) and edited a book on hate speech in Serbian media (1994).

Andrew Nicol is a barrister at Doughty Street Chambers, London, specializing in media and public law, including immigration. He became a Queen's Counsel in 1995. He was educated at Cambridge, studied at Harvard and Berkeley as a Harkness Fellow, worked for the State of California and a solicitors' firm in Sydney, and taught law at the London School of Economics for ten years. He is co-author of "Media Law" (Longmans/Penguin), and has written extensively on the topic. He has been consulted by the Council of Europe as an expert on media law particularly in the context of changes in Eastern and Central Europe.

Drew Porter is an Associate with the law firm of McDermott, Will & Emery in New York. He attended Columbia University's School of International and Public Affairs and Columbia Law School, where he was Notes Editor for the Journal of East European Law.

K.S. Venkateswaran, a member of the Indian Bar, is currently a lecturer in law at the University of Ulster in Jordanstown, Northern Ireland where he teaches constitutional and administrative law. He has previously been involved in establishing an international database on states of emergency at the Queen's

University of Belfast. A former Nuffield Press Fellow at Cambridge University, Mr. Venkateswaran has written extensively on media-related issues. His publications include "Mass Media Laws and Regulations in India", "Media Monitors in Asia", and a forthcoming study of emergency regimes in the Asia-Pacific region. Mr. Venkateswaran has undertaken a number of research projects for leading international NGOs.

Jose Miguel Vivanco received a JD from the University of Chile in 1983 and from Salamanca Law School (Spain) in 1986, and a LLM from Harvard Law School in 1990. He was a legal advisor and attorney for the Inter-American Commission on Human Rights (1987-89). In 1990, he founded the Center for Justice and International Law (CEJIL) an NGO composed of ten organizations from the Americas that file complaints before international human rights bodies, and functioned as its executive director until August 1994. In September 1994, he became Executive Director of the Americas division of Human Rights Watch. He is an Adjunct Professor of Law at Georgetown University Law Center and the John Hopkins University School of Advanced International Studies. He has received several scholarships and fellowships in the field of human rights, and has written numerous publications and presentations.

Claude E. Welch, Jr. is Distinguished Service Professor in the Department of Political Science and co-Director of the Human Rights Center at the State University of New York at Buffalo. His books include "Protecting Human Rights in Africa: Strategies and Roles of Non-Governmental Organizations" (University of Pennsylvania Press, 1995); "Asian Perspectives on Human Rights" (Westview, 1990); and "Human Rights and Development in Africa" (State University of New York Press, 1984). The 1984 and 1995 books were both cited by the American Library Association as "outstanding" academic books of the year. Several of his articles have appeared in the Human Rights Quarterly. Professor Welch is currently at work on a book-length study of the impact and effectiveness of major international human rights NGOs.

Sophia Woodman is the Hong Kong Representative for Human Rights in China (HRIC) and the Editor of HRIC's quarterly journal, China Rights Forum. She is a member of HRIC's Executive Committee and has an MSc in politics from the School of Oriental and Africa Studies, London.

Kerim Yildiz is the Executive Director of the Kurdish Human Rights Project, an independent, non-partisan organization based in London that is committed to the protection of the human rights of all Kurds. He received a post-graduate degree in international human rights law from the Human Rights Center of the University of Essex and is involved in more than 100 cases against Turkey that are pending before the European Commission on Human Rights.

Kyo Ho Youm is an Associate Professor at the Cronkite School of Journalism and Telecommunication at Arizona State University (USA). He specializes in press-government relations, media law and international communication. Since 1985, he has published more than 60 articles in scholarly journals and one book , "Press Law in South Korea" (Iowa State University Press 1995). He has served as Law Division head of the Association for Education in Journalism and Mass Communication and serves on the editorial boards of eight journalism and communication law journals.

Yu Ping is a PhD candidate at the University of Washington School of Law, and a former member of the law faculty of Fudan University, Shanghai. He is a Legal Consultant of the organization Human Rights in China (HRIC) and a member of HRIC's Executive Committee.

APPENDIX C:

List of Participants at the Johannesburg Conference

The following experts participated in the Consultation that drafted these Principles in their personal capacity. Organizations and affiliations are listed for purposes of identification only.

Laurel Angus, Executive Director, Centre for Applied Legal Studies, University of the Witwatersrand, South Africa
Lawrence W Beer, Professor of Civil Rights, Department of Government and Law, Lafayette College, USA
Geoffrey Bindman, solicitor, Bindman and Partners, London, UK
Dana Briskman, Legal Director, Association for Civil Rights, Israel
Richard Carver, Africa Programme Consultant, ARTICLE 19, London, UK
Yong-Whan Cho, Duksu Law Offices, Seoul, South Korea
Sandra Coliver, Law Programme Director, ARTICLE 19, Washington DC, USA
Peter Danowsky, Danowsky & Partners, Stockholm, Sweden
Emmanuel Derieux, Professor of Media Law, University of Paris 2, and Co-editor, *Legipresse*, Paris, France
Frances D'Souza, Executive Director, ARTICLE 19, London, UK
Elizabeth Evatt AC, member, UN Human Rights Committee and legal consultant, Sydney, Australia
Felipe Gonzalez, Professor of Law, Diego Portales University, Santiago, Chile and Legal Officer for Latin America, International Human Rights Law Group, Washington DC
Paul Hoffman (Conference Chair), media lawyer, Los Angeles, USA
Gitobu Imanyara, Advocate of the High Court of Kenya, and Editor-in-Chief, *Nairobi Law Monthly*, Kenya
Lene Johannessen, Media Project, Center for Applied Legal Studies, University of the Witwatersrand, Johannesburg, South Africa
Raymond Louw, Chairman, Freedom of Expression Institute, Johannesburg, South Africa
Laurence Lustgarten, Professor of Law, University of Southampton, UK
Paul Mahoney, Deputy Registrar, European Court of Human Rights, Council of Europe[1]
Gilbert Marcus, Advocate of the Supreme Court of South Africa, Johannesburg, South Africa
Kate Martin, Executive Director, Center for National Security Studies, Washington DC, USA

---

[1] Because of his position as an international civil servant, Mr. Mahoney did not take any position on these Principles.

Juan E Mendez, General Counsel, Human Rights Watch, New York, USA
Branislav Milinkovic, editor, *Review of International Affairs*, Belgrade, Federal Republic of Yugoslavia
Etienne Mureinik, Professor of Law, University of the Witwatersrand, Johannesburg, South Africa
Ann Naughton, Publications Director, ARTICLE 19, London, UK
Mamadou N'Dao, human rights lawyer and consultant, Panos Institute, Dakar, Senegal
Andrew Nicol, QC, Doughty Street Chambers, London, UK
David Petrasek, Mandate and Legal Policy Adviser, Amnesty International, London, UK
Laura Pollecut, Executive Director, Lawyers for Human Rights, Pretoria, South Africa
John Sangwa, Simeza, Sangwa & Associates, Lusaka, and member, Faculty of Law, University of Zambia
Sergei Sirotkin, Human Rights Commission, Moscow, Russia
Malcolm Smart, Deputy Executive Director, ARTICLE 19, London, UK
Tanya Smith, UN Centre for Human Rights, Geneva, Switzerland
Soli Sorabjee, Senior Advocate, Supreme Court of India, New Delhi, India
K. S. Venkateswaran, advocate, Indian Bar, and member, Law Faculty, University of Ulster, Northern Ireland
Kerim Yildiz, Executive Director, Kurdish Human Rights Project, London, UK
Kyu Ho Youm, Professor, Cronkite School of Journalism and Telecommunication, Arizona State University, USA

APPENDIX D:

Relevant Provisions of International Instruments

UNITED NATIONS

UNIVERSAL DECLARATION OF HUMAN RIGHTS

Adopted and proclaimed by General Assembly Resolution 217 A(m) of 10 December 1948.

Article 19

Everyone has the right to freedom of opinion and expression; this right includes freedom to hold opinions without interference and to seek, receive and impart information and ideas through any media and regardless of frontiers.

Article 20

1. Everyone has the right to freedom of peaceful assembly and association.

2. No one may be compelled to belong to an association.

Article 29

1. Everyone has duties to the community in which alone the free and full development of his personality is possible.

2. In the exercise of his rights and freedoms, everyone shall be subject only to such limitations as are determined by law solely for the purpose of securing due recognition and respect for the rights and freedoms of others and of meeting the just requirements of morality, public order and the general welfare in a democratic society.

INTERNATIONAL COVENANT ON CIVIL AND POLITICAL RIGHTS

Adopted and opened for signature, ratification and accession by General Assembly Resolution 2200 A(XXI) of 16 December 1966. Entered into force 23 March 1976.

Article 2

2. Where not already provided for by existing legislative or other measures, each State Party to the present Covenant undertakes to take the necessary steps, in

accordance with its constitutional processes and with the provisions of the present Covenant, to adopt such legislative or other measures as may be necessary to give effect to the rights recognized in the present Covenant.

3. Each State Party to the present Covenant undertakes:

(a) To ensure that any person whose rights or freedoms as herein recognized are violated shall have an effective remedy, notwithstanding that the violation has been committed by persons acting in an official capacity;

(b) To ensure that any person claiming such a remedy shall have his right thereto determined by competent judicial, administrative or legislative authorities, or by any other competent authority provided for by the legal system of the State, and to develop the possibilities of judicial remedy;

(c) To ensure that the competent authorities shall enforce such remedies when granted.

Article 5

1. Nothing in the present Covenant may be interpreted as implying for any State, group or person any right to engage in any activity or perform any act aimed at the destruction of any of the rights and freedoms recognized herein or at their limitation to a greater extent than is provided for in the present Covenant.

Article 14

1. All persons shall be equal before the courts and tribunals. In determination of any criminal charge against him, or of his rights and obligations in a suit at law, everyone shall be entitled to a fair and public hearing by a competent, independent and impartial tribunal established by law. The Press and the public may be excluded from all or part of a trial for reasons of morals, public order (*ordre public*) or national security in a democratic society, or when the interest of the private lives of the Parties so requires, or to the extent strictly necessary in the opinion of the court in special circumstances where publicity would prejudice the interests of justice; but nay judgment rendered in a criminal case or in a suit at law shall be made public except where the interest of juvenile persons otherwise requires or the proceedings concern matrimonial disputes or the guardianship of children.

Article 17

1. No one shall be subjected to arbitrary or unlawful interference with his privacy, family, home or correspondence, nor to unlawful attacks on his honor and reputation. Everyone has the right to the protection of the law against such interference or attacks.

2. Everyone has the right to the protection of the law against such interference or attacks.

Article 19

1. Everyone shall have the right to hold opinions without interference.

2. Everyone shall have the right to freedom of expression; this right shall include freedom to seek, receive and impart information and ideas of all kinds, regardless of frontiers, either orally, in writing or in print, in the form of art, or through any other media of his choice.

3. The exercise of the rights provided for in paragraph 2 of this article carries with it special duties and responsibilities. It may therefore be subject to certain restrictions, but these shall only be such as are provided by law and are necessary:

   (a) For respect of the rights or reputations of others;

   (b) For the protection of national security or of public order *(ordre public)*, or of public health or morals.

Article 20

1. Any propaganda for war shall be prohibited by law.

2. Any advocacy of national, racial or religious hatred that constitutes incitement to discrimination, hostility or violence shall be prohibited by law.

Article 21

The right of peaceful assembly shall be recognized. No restrictions may be placed on the exercise of this right other than those imposed in conformity with the law and which are necessary in a democratic society in the interests of national security or public safety, public order *(ordre public)*, the protection of public health or morals or the protection of the rights and freedoms of others.

Article 22

1. Everyone shall have the right to freedom of association with others, including the right to form and join trade unions for the protection of his interests.

2. No restrictions may be placed on the exercise of this right other than those which are prescribed by law and which are necessary in a democratic society in the interests of national security or public safety, public order (*ordre public*), the protection of public health or morals or the protection of the rights and freedoms of others. This article shall not prevent the imposition of lawful restriction on members of the armed forces and of the police in their exercise of right.

INTERNATIONAL CONVENTION ON THE ELIMINATION OF ALL FORMS OF RACIAL DISCRIMINATION

Adopted and opened for signature, ratification and accession by General Assembly Resolution 2106 A(XX) of 21 December 1965. Entered into force 4 January 1969.

Article 4

States Parties condemn all propaganda and all organizations which are based on ideas or theories of superiority of one race or group of persons of one color or ethnic origin, or which attempt to justify or promote racial hatred and discrimination in any form, and undertake to adopt immediate and positive measures designed to eradicate all incitement to, or acts of, such discrimination and, to this end, with due regard to the principles embodied in the Universal Declaration of Human Rights and the rights expressly set forth in article 5 of this Convention, *infer alla:*

(a) Shall declare an offense publishable by law all dissemination of ideas based on racial superiority or hatred, incitement to racial discrimination, as well as all acts of violence or incitement to such acts against any race or group of persons of another color or ethnic origin, and also the provision of any assistance to racist activities, including the financing thereof;

(b) Shall declare illegal and prohibit organizations, and also organized and all other propaganda activities, which promote and incite racial discrimination, and shall recognize participation in such organizations or activities as an offense punishable by law;

(c) Shall not permit public authorities or public institutions, national or local, to promote or incite racial discrimination.

ORGANIZATION OF AFRICAN UNITY

AFRICAN CHARTER ON HUMAN AND PEOPLES' RIGHTS

Adopted by the OAU on 27 June 1981. Entered into force in October 1986.

Article 1

The Member States of the Organization of African Unity parties to the present Charter shall recognize the rights, duties and freedoms enshrined in this Charter and shall undertake to adopt legislative or other measures to give effect to them.

Article 2

Every individual shall be entitled to the enjoyment of the rights and freedoms recognized and guaranteed in the present Charter without distinction of any kind such as race, ethnic group, color, sex, language, religion, political or any other opinion, national and social origin, fortune, birth or other status.

Article 9

1. Every individual shall have the right to receive information.

2. Every individual shall have the right to express and disseminate his opinions within the law.

Article 10

1. Every individual shall have the right to free association provided that he abides by the law.

2. Subject to the obligation of solidarity provided for in Article 29, no one may be compelled to join an association.

Article 11

Every individual shall have the right to assemble freely with others. The exercise of this right shad be subject only to necessary restrictions provided for by law in particular those enacted in the interest of national security, the safety, health, ethics and rights and freedoms of others.

Article 25

States parties to the present Charter shall have the duty to promote and ensure through teaching, education and publication, the respect of the rights and freedoms contained in the present Charter and to see to it that these freedoms and rights as wed as corresponding obligations and duties are understood.

Article 27

1. Every individual shall have duties towards his family and society, the State and other legally recognized communities and the international community.

2. The rights and freedoms of each individual shall be exercised with due regard to the rights of others collective security, morality and common interest.

Article 28

Every individual shah have the duty to respect and consider his fellow beings without discrimination, and to maintain relations aimed at promoting, safeguarding and reinforcing mutual respect and tolerance.

ORGANIZATION OF AMERICAN STATES

AMERICAN CONVENTION ON HUMAN RIGHTS

Adopted by the OAS on 22 November 1969. Entered into force 18 July 1978.

Article 1: Obligation to Respect Rights

The States Parties to this Convention undertake to respect the rights and freedoms recognized herein and to ensure to all persons subject to their jurisdiction the free and full exercise of those rights and freedoms, without any discrimination for reasons of race, color, sex, language, religion, political or other opinion, national or social origin, economic status, birth, or any other social condition.

Article 2: Domestic Legal Effects

Where the exercise of any of the rights or freedoms referred to in Article 1 is not already ensured by legislative or other provisions, the States Parties undertake to adopt, in accordance with their constitutional processes and the provisions of this

Convention, such legislative or other measures as may be necessary to give effect to those rights or freedoms.

Article 8: Right to a Fair Trial

1. Every person has the right to a hearing, with due guarantees and within a reasonable time, by a competent, independent and impartial tribunal, previously established by law, in the substantiation of any accusation of a criminal nature made against him or for the determination of his rights and obligations of a civil, labor, fiscal, or any other nature.

5. Criminal proceedings shall be public, except insofar as may be necessary to protect the interests of justice.

Article 11: Right to Privacy

1. Everyone has the right to have his honor respected and his dignity recognized.

2. No one may be the object of arbitrary or abusive interference with his private life, his family, his home, or his correspondence, or of unlawful attacks on his honor or reputation.

3. Everyone has the right to the protection of the law against such interference or attacks.

Article 13: Freedom of Thought and Expression

1. Everyone has the right to freedom of thought and expression. This right includes freedom to seek, receive, and impart information and ideas of all kinds, regardless of frontier either orally, in writing, in print, in the form of art, or through any other medium of one's choice.
2. The exercise of the right provided for in the foregoing paragraph shall not be subject to prior censorship but shall be subject to subsequent imposition of liability, which shall be expressly established by law to the extent necessary to ensure:

   (a) respect for the rights or reputations of others; or

   (b) the protection of national security, public order, or public health or morals.

3. The right of expression may not be restricted by indirect methods or means, such as the abuse of government or private controls over newsprint, radio broadcasting frequencies, or equipment used in the dissemination of information, or by any

other means tending to impede the communication and circulation of ideas and opinions.

4 Notwithstanding the provisions of paragraph 2 above, public entertainments may be subject by law to prior censorship for the sole purpose of regulating access to them for the moral protection of childhood and adolescence.

5. Any propaganda for war and any advocacy of national, racial, or religious hatred that constitute incitements to lawless violence or to any other similar illegal action against any person or group of persons on any grounds including those of race, color, religion, language, or national origin shall be considered as offenses punishable by law.

Article 14: Right of Reply

1. Anyone injured by inaccurate or offensive statements or ideas disseminated to the public in general by a legally regulated medium of communication has the right to reply or to make correction using the same communications outlet, under such conditions as the law may establish.

2. The correction or reply shall not in any case remit other legal liabilities that may have been incurred.

3. For the effective protection of honor and reputation, every publisher, and every newspaper, motion picture, radio, and television company, shall have a person responsible who is not protected by immunities or special privileges.

Article 15: Right of Assembly

The right of peaceful assembly, without arms, is recognized. No restrictions may be placed on the exercise of this right other than those imposed in conformity with the law and necessary in a democratic society in the interest of national security, public safety or public order, or to protect public health or morals or the rights or freedoms of others.

Article 16: Freedom of Association

1. Everyone has the right to associate freely for ideological, religious, political, economic, labor, social, cultural, sports, or other purposes.

2. The exercise of this right shall be subject only to such restrictions established by law as may be necessary in a democratic society, in the interest of national

security, public safety or public order, or to protect public health or morals or the rights and freedoms of others.

Article 29: Restrictions Regarding Interpretation

No provision of this Convention shall be interpreted as:

(a) permitting any State Party, group, or person to suppress the enjoyment or exercise of the rights and freedoms recognized in this Convention or to restrict them to a greater extent than is provided for herein;

(b) restricting the enjoyment or exercise of any right or freedom recognized by virtue of the laws of any State Party or by virtue of another convention to which one of the said states is a party;

(c) precluding other rights or guarantees that are inherent in the human personality or derived from representative democracy as a form of government; or

(d) excluding or limiting the effect that the American Declaration of the Rights and Duties of Man and other international acts of the same nature may have.

AMERICAN DECLARATION OF THE RIGHTS AND DUTIES OF MAN

Approved by the Ninth International Conference of American States on 2 May 1948.

Article 4

Every person has the right to freedom of investigation, of opinion, and of the expression and dissemination of ideas, by any medium whatsoever.

Article 5

Every person has the right to the protection of the law against abusive attacks upon his honor, his reputation, and his private family life.

Article 21

Every person has the right to assemble peaceably with others in a formal public meeting or an informal gathering, in connection with matters of common interest of any nature.

Article 22

Every person has the right to associate with others to promote, exercise and protect his legitimate interests of a political, economic, religious, social, cultural, professional, labor union or other nature.

COUNCIL OF EUROPE

EUROPEAN CONVENTION ON HUMAN RIGHTS

(Convention for the Protection of Human Rights and Fundamental Freedoms)
Signed by Contracting States of the Council of Europe on 4 November 1950. Entered into force 3 September 1953.

Article 6

1. In the determination of his civil rights and obligations or of any criminal charge against him, everyone is entitled to a fair and public hearing within a reasonable time by an independent and impartial tribunal established by law. Judgment shall be pronounced publicly but the press and public may be excluded from all or part of the trial in the interests of morals, public order or national security in a democratic society, where the interests of juveniles or the protection of the private life of the parties so require, or to the extent strictly necessary in the opinion of the court in special circumstances where publicity would prejudice the interests of justice.

Article 8

1. Everyone has the right to respect for his private and family life, his home and his correspondence.

2. There shall be no interference by a public authority with the exercise of this right except such as is in accordance with the law and is necessary in a democratic society in the interests of national security, public safety or the economic well being of the country, for the prevention of disorder or crime, for the protection of health or morals, or for the protection of the rights and freedoms of others.

Article 10

1. Everyone has the right to freedom of expression. This right shall include freedom to hold opinions and to receive and impart information and ideas without interference by public authority and regardless of frontiers. This Article shall not

prevent States from requiring the licensing of broadcasting, television or cinema enterprises.

2. The exercise of these freedoms, since it carries with it duties and responsibilities, may be subject to such formalities, conditions, restrictions or penalties as are prescribed by law and are necessary in a democratic society, in the interests of national security, territorial integrity of public safety, for the prevention of disorder or crime, for the protection of health or morals, for the protection of the reputation or rights of others, for preventing the disclosure of information received in confidence, or for maintaining the authority and impartiality of the judiciary.

Article 11

1. Everyone has the right to freedom of peaceful assembly and to freedom of association with others, including the right to form and to join trade unions for the protection of his interests.

2. No restrictions shall be placed on the exercise of these rights other than such as are prescribed by law and are necessary in a democratic society in the interests of national security or public safety, for the prevention of disorder or crime, for the protection of health or morals or for the protection of the rights and freedoms of others. This Article shall not prevent the imposition of lawful restrictions on the exercise of these rights by members of the armed forces, of the police or of the administration of the State.

Article 14

The enjoyment of the rights and freedoms set forth in this Convention shall be secured without discrimination on any ground such as sex, race, color, language, religion, political or other opinion, national or social origin, association with a national minority, property, birth or other status.

Article 16

Nothing in Articles 10, 11 and 14 shall be regarded as preventing the High Contracting Parties from imposing restrictions on the political activity of aliens.

Article 17

Nothing in this Convention may be interpreted as implying for any State, group or person any right to engage in any activity or perform any act aimed at the destruction of any of the rights and freedoms set forth herein or at their limitation to a greater extent than is provided for in the Convention.

ORGANIZATION ON SECURITY AND COOPERATION IN EUROPE

1989 VIENNA CONCLUDING DOCUMENT

(34) The participating States will make further efforts to facilitate the freer and wider dissemination of information of all kinds, to encourage cooperation in the field of information and to improve the working conditions for journalists

In this connection and in accordance with the International Covenant on Civil and Political Rights, the Universal Declaration of Human Rights and their relevant international commitments concerning seeking, receiving and imparting information of all kinds, they will ensure that individuals can freely choose their sources of information."

DOCUMENT OF THE COPENHAGEN MEETING OF THE CONFERENCE ON THE HUMAN DIMENSION

June 5 - 29, 1990

(9) The participating States reaffirm that

(9.1) everyone will have the right to freedom of expression including the right to communication. This right will include freedom to hold opinions and to receive and impart information and ideas without interference by public authority and regardless of frontiers. The exercise of this right may be subject only to such restrictions as are prescribed by law and are consistent with international standards. In particular, no limitation will be imposed on access to, and use of, means of reproducing documents of any kind, while respecting, however, rights relating to intellectual property, including copyright.

(24) The participating States will ensure that the exercise of all the human rights and fundamental freedoms set out above will not be subject to any restrictions except those which are provided by law and are consistent with their obligations under international law, in particular the International Covenant on Civil and Political Rights, and with their international commitments, in particular the Universal Declaration of Human Rights.

These restrictions have the character of exceptions. The participating States will ensure that these restrictions are not abused and are not applied in an arbitrary manner, but in such a way that the effective exercise of these rights is ensured.

Any restrictions on rights and freedoms must, in a democratic society, relate to one of the objectives of the applicable law and be strictly proportionate to the aim of that law.

(28) The participating States recognize the important expertise of the Council of Europe in the field of human rights and fundamental freedoms and agree to consider further ways and means to enable the Council of Europe to make a contribution to the human dimension of the CSCE. They agree that the nature of this contribution could be examined further in a future CSCE forum.

DOCUMENT OF THE MOSCOW MEETING OF THE CONFERENCE ON THE HUMAN DIMENSION

Sept. 10 - Oct. 4, 1991

(26) The participating States reaffirm the right to freedom of expression, including the right to communication and the right of the media to collect, report and disseminate information, news and opinion. Any restriction in the exercise of this right will be prescribed by law and in accordance with international standards.

EUROPEAN UNION

TREATY OF ROME

Article 30

Quantitative restrictions on imports and all measures having equivalent effect shall, without prejudice to the following provisions, be prohibited between member states.

Article 34

1. Quantitative restrictions on exports, and all measures having equivalent effect, shall be prohibited between member States.

2. Member States shall, by the end of the first stage at the latest, abolish all quantitative restrictions on exports and any measures having equivalent effect which are in existence when this Treaty enters into force.

Article 36

The provisions of Articles 30 to 34 shall not preclude prohibitions or restrictions on imports, exports or goods in transit justified on grounds of public morality, public policy or public security; the protection of health and life of humans, animals or plants; the protection of national treasures possessing artistic, historic or archaeological value; or the protection of industrial and commercial property. Such prohibitions or restrictions shall not, however, constitute a means of arbitrary discrimination or a disguised restriction on trade between Member States.

Article 59

Within the framework of the provisions set out below, restrictions on freedom to provide services within the Community shall be progressively abolished during the transitional period in respect of nationals of Member States who are established in a State of the Community other than that of the person for whom the services are intended.

The Council may, acting by a qualified majority on a proposal from the Commission, extend the provisions of the Chapter to nationals of a third country who provide services and who are established within the Community.

APPENDIX E:

Selected Bibliography

INTERNATIONAL AND COMPARATIVE LAW

W.F. Korthals Altes et al. eds., *Information Law Towards the 21st Century* (1992).

ARTICLE 19 ed., *Secrecy and Liberty: National Security, Freedom of Expression and Access to Information* (1995).

E. Barendt, *Broadcasting Law: A Study of Regulation in Europe and the United States* (Oxford University Press, 1993).

E. Barendt, *Freedom of Speech* (Oxford University Press, 1985).

A. Bayefsky & J. Fitzpatrick, "International Human Rights Law in United States Courts: A Comparative Perspective", 14 *Mich. J. Int'l L.* 1 (1993).

T. Buergenthal, "The American and European Conventions on Human Rights: Similarities and Differences", 30 *Am. U. L. Rev.* 155 (1981).

S. Coliver ed., *The Article 19 Freedom of Expression Handbook: International and Comparative Law, Standards and Procedures* (1993).

S. Coliver ed., *Press Law and Practice: A Comparative Study of Press Freedom in European and Other Democracies* (London: ARTICLE 19, 1993).

S. Coliver ed., *Striking a Balance: Hate Speech, Freedom of Expression and Non-Discrimination* (London: ARTICLE 19/University of Essex, 1992).

Committee to Protect Journalists, *Attacks on the Press, Annual Reports, 1988- Present* (New York).

Commonwealth Secretariat and Interights, *Developing Human Rights Jurisprudence-The Domestic Application of International Human Rights Norms:* Vol. 1, Judicial Colloquium in Bangalore, Feb. 24-26, 1988; Vol. 2, Judicial Colloquium in Harare, April 19-22, 1989; Vol. 3, Judicial Colloquium in Banjul, The Gambia, Nov. 7-9, 1990 (London).

J. Fitzpatrick, *Human Rights in Crisis: The International System for Protecting Rights During States of Emergency* (Philadelphia: University of Pennsylvania Press, 1994).

J. Fitzpatrick Hartman, "Symposium on the Siracusa Principles: Working Paper for the Committee of Experts on the Limitation Provisions", 7 *Hum. Rts. Q.* 15 (1985).

G. Fox & G. Nolte, "Intolerant Democracies", 36 *Harv. Int'l L.J.* 1 (1995).

I. Galnoor ed., *Government Secrecy in Democracies* (New York: Harper & Row, 1977).

N.P. Gleditsch, "Freedom of Information and National Security: A Comparative Perspective", 4 *Law & Policy Studies* 25 (1995).

N.P. Gleditsch & E. Hogetveit, "Freedom of Information in National Security Affairs: A Comparative Study of Norway and the United States", 21 *J. of Peace Research* 17 (April 1984).

R. Hazell, *Freedom of Information: Lessons from Canada, Australia and New Zealand.*

International Law Association, Committee on the Enforcement of Human Rights Law, Interim Report of the Committee, Seoul Conference (1986).

International Law Association, Final Report (Queensland 1990).

F.G. Jacobs & S. Roberts, *The Effect of Treaties in Domestic Law* (London: Sweet & Maxwell, 1987).

A.C. Kiss, "Symposium on the Siracusa Principles: Commentary by the Rapporteur on the Limitation Provisions", 7 *Hum. Rts. Q.* 15 (1985).

A.C. Kiss, "Permissible Limitations on Rights", *in* L. Henkin ed., *The International Bill of Rights* (1991).

P. Lahav ed., *Press Law in Modern Democracies: A Comparative Study* (New York & London, 1985).

A. Lester, "The Overseas Trade in the American Bill of Rights", 88 *Columbia L. Rev.* 537 (1988).

B. Lockwood, Jr., et al., "Symposium on the Siracusa Principles: Working Paper for the Committee of Experts on he Limitation Provisions", 7 *Hum. Rts. Q.* 15 (1985).

S. Marks, "Principles and Norms of Human Rights Applicable in Emergency Situations: Underdevelopment, Catastrophes and Armed Conflicts", *in* K. Vasek & P. Alston eds., *The International Dimensions of Human Rights* 175 (Paris: UNESCO, 1982).

T. Meron ed., *Human Rights in International Law: Legal and Policy Issues* (1984).

D. McGoldrick, *The Human Rights Committee* (Oxford University Press, 1991).

F. Newman & D. Weissbrodt, *International Human Rights* (Cincinnati: Anderson Pub. Co., 1990).

D. Nimmo & M.W. Mansfield, *Government and the News Media: Comparative Dimensions* (Waco, TX: Baylor University Press, 1982).

Note, "Balancing the Interest of National Security and Free Speech: A Proposed Modification of the English Approach Suitable for Adoption in the United States", 4 *Touro J. of Transnat'l L.* 217 (1993).

M. Nowak, *International Covenant on Civil and Political Rights: A Commentary* (Strasbourg: Engel Publishing, 1993).

A. Plamondon, "A Comparison of Official Secrets and Access to Information in Great Britain and the United States", *in* 16 *Communications & the Law* 51 (1994).

K. Ramjattan, "Freedom of Expression: A Comparative Analysis", 2 *J. of Human Rights L. & Practice* 53 (1992).

S.A. Riesenfeld & F.M. Abbot eds., "Symposium on Parliamentary Participation in the Making and Operation of Treaties", 67 *Chicago-Kent L. Rev.* 293 (1991).

D. Rowat, *Administrative Secrecy in Developed Countries* (London & Basingstoke: Macmillan, 1979).

G. Scuttrups, *International Freedom of Information Acts* (Washington, DC: The National Security Archive, Oct. 1994).

S. Shetreet, *Free Speech and National Security* (Dordrecht/Boston/London: Martinus Nijhoff Pubs., 1991).

R. Smolla, *Free Speech in an Open Society* (1992).

C. Tomuschat, "Universal and Regional Protection of Human Rights: Complementary or Conflicting Issues", *in* Duncker & Humblot eds., *Strengthening the World Order: Universalism v. Regionalism* (West Berlin, 1990).

S. Walker, "Freedom of Speech and Contempt of Court: the English and Australian Approaches Compared", 40 *Int'l & Comp. L.Q.* 583 (1991).

P. Wilhelm, *Protection of Sources* (Fredrikstad, Norway: The Norwegian Institute of Journalism, 1988).

INTERNATIONAL PROCEDURES

P. Alston ed., *The United Nations and Human Rights: A Critical Appraisal* (Oxford Clarendon Press, 1992), including:
- P. Alston, "The Commission on Human Rights";
- A. Eide, "The Sub-Commission on Prevention of Discrimination and Protection of Minorities";
- T. Opsahl, "The Human Rights Committee".

C.F. Amerasinghe, *Local Remedies in International Law* (Cambridge: Grotius Publications Ltd., 1990).

Amnesty International, *Summary of Selected International Procedures and Bodies Dealing with Human Rights Matters*, AI Index: IOR 30/01/89 (London, 1989).

De Zayas, Moller, & Opsahl, "Application of the International Covenant on Civil and Political Rights Under the Optional Protocol by the Human Rights Committee", 28 *German Yearbook of Int'l L.* 55 (1985).

C. Gray, *Judicial Remedies in International Law* (Oxford University Press, 1990).

H. Hannum ed., *Guide to International Human Rights Practice*, 2d ed. (Philadelphia: University of Pennsylvania Press, 1992), including:
- K. Boyle, "Europe: The Council of Europe, the CSCE, and the European Community";
- C. Flinterman & E. Ankumah, "The African Charter on Human and Peoples' Rights";
- S. Lewis-Anthony, "Treaty-Based Procedures for Making Human Rights Complaints Within the UN System";
- S. Marks, "The Complaint Procedure of UNESCO";
- D. Shelton, "The Inter-American Human Rights System";
- D. Vincent-Daviss, "Bibliographic Essay".

J.F. Hartman, "Working Paper for the Committee of Experts on the Article 4 Derogation Provision", 7 *Hum. Rts. Q.* 89 (1985).

International Commission of Jurists, *States of Emergency: Their Impact on Human Rights* (Geneva, 1983).

J.A. Jolowicz ed., *International Enforcement of Human Rights* (Berlin: Springer, 1987).

A. Lester, "*Amici Curiae*: Third Party Interventions Before the European Court of Human Rights", *in* C.H. Verlay ed., *Protecting Human Rights: The European Dimension* (1988).

M. Nowak, *UN Covenant on Civil and Political Rights: CCPR Commentary* (1993).

A. Trindade, *The Application of the Rule of Exhaustion of Local Remedies in International Law* (Cambridge/London/New York: Cambridge University Press, 1983).

UNITED NATIONS DOCUMENTS & PUBLICATIONS

D.P. Cumaraswamy, Special Rapporteur on the Independence of Judges and Lawyers, *Question of the Human Rights of All Persons Subjected to Any Form of Detention or Imprisonment*, U.N. Doc. E/CN.4/1996/37 (1996).

L. Despouy, Sub-Commission Rapporteur on States of Emergencies, *8th Annual Report*, UN Doc. E/CN.4/Sub.2/1995/20 (June 26, 1995).

Draft Declaration on Freedom and Non-Discrimination in Respect of the Right of Everyone to Leave Any Country, Including His Own, and To Return to His Country, UN Doc. E/CN.4/Sub.2/1991/45.

General Comment 10, Report of the Human Rights Committee to the General Assembly, 38th Session, Supp. No. 40 (1983), A/38/40, Annex V.

A. Hussain, Special Rapporteur on Freedom of Expression, *Promotion and Protection of the Right to Freedom of Opinion and Expression*, U.N. Doc. E/CN.4/1996/39 (1996).

Johannesburg Principles on National Security, Freedom of Expression and Access to Information, *adopted* Oct. 1, 1995, Article 19.

The Siracusa Principles on the Limitation and Derogation Provisions in the International Covenant on Civil and Political Rights, U.N. Doc. E/CN.4/1985/4, Annex, 30 (1985), *reprinted in* 7 *Hum. Rts. Q.* 3 (1985).

D. Turk & L. Joinet, Special Rapporteurs, *The Right to Freedom of Opinion and Expression: Update of the Preliminary Report*, submitted to the UN Commission on Human Rights, UN Doc. E/CN.4/Sub.2/1991/9 (July 16, 1991) and *Update of the Preliminary Report*, UN Doc. E/CN.4/Sub.2/1991/9 (1991).

D. Turk & L. Joinet, Special Rapporteurs, *The Right to Freedom of Opinion and Expression: Final Report*, submitted to the UN Commission on Human Rights, UN Doc. E/CN.4/Sub.2/1992/9 (July 14, 1992).

UN Centre for Human Rights & UN Institute for Training and Research, *Manual on Human Rights Reporting* [HR/Pub./91/1] (New York: United Nations, 1991).

UN Centre for Human Rights & UN Institute for Training and Research, *UN Action in the Field of Human Rights*, UN Doc. ST/HR/2/Rev. 3 (1988).

Universal Declaration of Human Rights, G.A. Res. 217A(III), U.N. GAOR, 3rd Session (Resolutions, part 1), U.N. Doc. A/810 (1948), *reprinted in* 43 *Am. J. Int'l L. Supp.* 127 (1949).

AFRICA

J. Bayart, *The State in Africa: The Politics of the Belly* (London: Longman, 1993) (originally published as *L'Etat en Afrique: la politique du ventre* (1989)).

E. Bello, "The African Charter on Human and Peoples' Rights: A Legal Analysis", 104(5) *Hague Recueil* 161 (1985).

R. Carver, *Truth From Below: The Emergent Press in Africa* (London: ARTICLE 19, 1991).

Cobbah, "African Values and the Human Rights Debate: An African Perspective", 9 *Human Rights Q.* 309 (1987).

G. Faringer, *Press Freedom in Africa* (New York: Praeger, 1991).

W.J. Foltz, "Building the Newest Nations: Short-Run Strategies and Long-Run Problems", *in* K.W. Deutsch & W.J. Foltz eds., *National-Building* 117 (New York: Atherton, 1965).

R. Gittleman, "The African Charter on Human and Peoples' Rights: A Legal Analysis", 22 *Virginia J. Int'l L.* 692 (1982).

R. Gittleman, "The Banjul Charter on Human and Peoples' Rights: A Legal Analysis", *in* C.E. Welch, Jr. & R.I. Meltzer eds., *Human Rights and Development in Africa* 152 (Albany: State University of New York Press, 1984).

M. Hamalengwa, C. Flinterman & E. Dankwa, *The International Law of Human Rights in Africa: Basic Documents and Annotated Bibliography* (1988).

R. Howard, *Human Rights in Commonwealth Africa* (Totowa, NJ: Rowman & Littlefield, 1986).

K. Mbaye, "Human Rights in Africa", *in* K. Vasak & P. Alston eds., *The International Dimensions of Human Rights* (Paris: UNESCO, 1982).

R.C. Moore, *The Political Reality of Freedom of the Press in Zambia* (Lanham, MD: University Press of America, 1992).

Z. Motala, "Human Rights in Africa: A Cultural, Ideological and Legal Examination", 12 *Hastings Int'l & Comp. L. Rev.* 373 (1989).

B. Okere, "The Protection of Human Rights in Africa and the African Charter on Human Rights and Peoples' Rights: A Comparative Analysis with the European and American Systems", 6 *Human Rights Q.* 147 (1984).

C.E. Welch, Jr., *Protecting Human Rights in Africa: Strategies and Roles of Non-Governmental Organizations* (Philadelphia: University of Pennsylvania Press, 1995).

C. Young, *The African Colonial State in Comparative Perspective* (New Haven: Yale University Press, 1994).

Nigeria

G. Fawehinmi, *The Law of Contempt in Nigeria* (1980).

G. Fawehinmi, *Nigerian Law of Libel and the Press* (1987).

G. Fawehinmi, *Nigerian Law of the Press Under the Constitution and the Criminal Law* (1987).

B.O. Okere, "Freedom of the Press in Nigeria", 4 *Human Rights L.J.* 149 (1983).

South Africa

L. Johannessen & T. Cohen, "South Africa", *in* ARTICLE 19, *Media Law and Practice in Southern Africa* (vol. 1) (1996).

F.E. Kanyongolo, "National Security and Legal Protection of Media Freedom", *in* ARTICLE 19, *Media Law and Practice in Southern Africa* (vol. 4) (1996).

J.O. Manyarara, "Protection of Sources", *in* ARTICLE 19, *Media Law and Practice in Southern Africa* (vol. 2) (1996).

G. Marcus, "Fine Distinctions: Scientific Censorship and the Courts", 4 *South Africa J. Human Rights* 82 (1988).

G. Marcus, "Freedom of Expression Under the Constitution", 10 *South Africa J. Human Rights* 140 (1994).

C. Merrett, *A Culture of Censorship: Secrecy and Intellectual Repression in South Africa* (1994).

J.C.W. van Rooyen, *Censorship in South Africa* (Juta & Co. Ltd., 1987).

AMERICAS

T. Buergenthal, "The American and European Conventions on Human Rights: Similarities and Differences", 30 *Am. U. L. Rev.* 155 (1981).

T. Buergenthal & R. Norris, *Human Rights: The Inter-American System* (Dobbs Ferry, NY: Oceana Pubs., 1982-1990), 5 Binders.

T. Buergenthal, R. Norris & D. Shelton, *Protecting Human Rights in the Americas: Selected Problems,* 3rd rev. edition (Strasbourg: N.P. Engel, 1990).

Inter-American Commission on Human Rights, *Report on the Compatability of "Desacato" Laws with the American Convention on Human Rights (Annual Report, 1994),* OEA/Ser.L/V/II.88, Doc. 9 rev. 1, Feb. 17, 1995.

Justicia Penal y Libertad de Prensa (San Jose, Costa Rica: Commission of the European Communities & ILANUD, 1992), including essays on press freedom and freedom of information in Argentina, Brazil, Costa Rica, El Salvador, Guatemala, Honduras, Nicaragua, and Panama.

J. Mendez et al., *Freedom of Expression and National Security in the Inter-American System of Human Rights Protection* 9 (Sept. 1995).

A.L. Sung, "Freedom of the Press: Costa Rican Journalist Licensing Law Violates American Convention on Human Rights", 27 *Harv. Int'l L.J.* 679 (1986).

Canada

P. Anisman & A. Linden eds., *The Media, the Courts and the Charter* (Toronto: Carswell, 1986).

R.G. Atkey, "Reconciling Freedom of Expression and National Security", 41 *U. of Toronto L.J.* 38 (1991).

J. Bauer, "Press Law in Canada", *in* ARTICLE 19 ed., *Press Law and Practice* (op. cit.).

A. Bayefsky, *International Human Rights Law: Use In Canadian Charter of Rights and Freedoms Litigation* (Toronto & Vancouver: Butterworths, 1992).

Canadian Government, *On Course: National Security for the 1990s* (Sept. 1990). (The government's response to the House of Commons Special Committee Report below.)

House of Commons Special Committee, *In Flux But Not in Crisis: Report on the Review of the Canadian Security Intelligence Service Act and the Security Offences Act* (Sept. 1990).

R. Martin & G. Adam eds., *A Sourcebook of Canadian Media Law* (Carleton University Press, 1991).

United States

ACLU, memorandum on Free Trade in Ideas, re: travel to Cuba (Jan. 1996).

A. Adler ed., *Litigation Under the Federal Freedom of Information Act and Privacy Act*, 1993 ed. & 1994 Supp. (Washington, DC: Center for National Security Studies).

Center for Strategic and International Studies (CSIS), *Congressional Oversight of National Security: A Mandate for Change* (1992).

H. Chang, *National Security v. First Amendment Freedoms, U.S. Supreme Court Decisions on Anti-Communist Regulations, 1919-1974*, Diss. (1993).

M.M. Cheh, "Judicial Supervision of Executive Secrecy: Rethinking Freedom of Expression for Government Employees and the Public Right of Access to Government Information", 69 *Cornell L. Rev.* 690 (1984).

P. Chevigny, "Information, the Executive and the Politics of Information", *in* S. Shetreet ed., *Free Speech and National Security* (Dordrecht/Boston/London: Martinus Nijhoff Pubs., 1991).

S. Coliver & F. Newman, "Using International Human Rights Law to Influence US Foreign Population Policy", 20 *N.Y.U. J. Int'l L. & Politics* 53 (1987).

Congressional Oversight of National Security: A Mandate for Change, Final Report on Congressional Oversight of Defense (Oct. 1992).

T. Emerson, *The System of Freedom of Expression* (Random House, 1970).

T.M. Franck & E. Weisband eds., *Secrecy and Foreign Policy* (New York and London: Oxford University Press, 1974).

D. Frenznick, "The First Amendment on the Battlefield: A Constitutional Analysis of Press Access to Military Operations in Grenada, Panama, and the Persian Gulf", 23 *Pacific L.J.* 315 (1992).

J.H. Garvey & F. Schauer eds., *The First Amendment: A Reader* (West Publishing Co., 1992).

S.S. Gonzalez, "The American Pattern of Freedom of the Press", *in Press, Politics, Public Policy*, The Joan Shorenstein Barone Center, Discussion Paper D-14 (1992).

J. Gora, D. Goldberger, G. Stern & M. Halperin, *The Right to Protest: The Basic American Civil Liberties Union Guide to Freedom of Expression* (Carbondale, Ill.: Southern Illinois University Press, 1991).

F.S. Haiman, *Speech and Law in a Free Society* (University of Chicago, 1981).

M.H. Halperin & D.N. Hoffman, *Freedom vs. National Security: Secrecy and Surveillance* (New York & London: Chelsea House, 1977).

M. Halperin & D. Hoffman, *Top Secret: National Security and the Right to Know* (New Republic Books, 1977).

E. Hendricks, T. Hayden & J. Novik, *Your Right to Privacy: The Basic American Civil Liberties Union Guide to Legal Rights in an Information Society* (Carbondale, Ill.: Southern Illinois University Press, 1990).

L. Henkin, "International Law as Law in the United States", 82 *Mich. L. Rev.* 1555 (1984).

M. Jacobs, "Assessing the Constitutionality of Press Restrictions in the Persian Gulf War", 44 *Stanford L. Rev.* 675 (1992).

R. Jazayerli, "War and the First Amendment: A Call for Legislation to Protect a Press' Right of Access to Military Operations", 35 *Colum. J. Transnat'l L.* 131 (1997).

K.P. Kenealey, "The Persian Gulf War and the Press: Is There a Constitutional Right of Access to Military Operations?", 87 *Northwestern U. L. Rev.* 287 (1992).

R. Lillich, "The US Constitution and International Human Rights Law", 3 *Harv. Human Rights J.* 53 (1990).

B. Neubourne, *Free Speech-Free Markets-Free Choice: An Essay on Commercial Speech* (New York: Association of National Advertisers, 1987).

R. Parker, "Freedom of Expression vs. National Security: the Pivotal Role of the Freedom of Information Act", *in* 28 *Free Speech Yearbook* 132 (1990).

F. Schauer, "Parsing the Pentagon Papers", *Harvard University J.F. Kennedy School of Government* (May 1991).

N. Strossen, "Recent US and International Judicial Protection of Individual Rights: A Comparative Legal Process Analysis and Proposed Synthesis", 41 *Hasting L.J.* 805 (1990).

N. Strossen, "Press Law in the United States", *in* ARTICLE 19 ed., *Press Law and Practice* (op. cit.).

L.H. Tribe, *American Constitutional Law*, 2d ed. (Foundation Press, 1988).

ASIA

Australia

Australian Human Rights Commission (now the Australian Human Rights and Equal Opportunities Commission), *Occasional Paper No. 8: The Right of Peaceful Assembly in the Australian Capital Territory* (1985) (includes discussion of the rights of expression and peaceful assembly as set forth in the ICCPR).
Australian Press Council, Annual Reports.
D. Flint, "Press Law in Australia", *in* ARTICLE 19 ed., *Press Law and Practice* (op. cit.).

China

H.L. Fu & R. Cullen, "National Security Law in China", 34 *Columbia J. Transnat'l L.* 449 (1996).
T.A. Gelatt, "Recent Development: The New Chinese State Secrets Law", 22 *Cornell Int'l L.J.* 255 (1989).

Hong Kong

K. Boyle, "Freedom of Expression", *in* Chen & Ghai eds., *The Hong Kong Bill of Rights* (Hong Kong: Butterworth, 1993).
Y. Ghai, "Freedom of Expression", *in* R. Wackes ed., *Human Rights in Hong Kong* (Oxford University Press, 1992).

India

B.S. Loitongbam, *Armed Forces Special Powers Act: A Study in National Security Tyranny*.
S. Sorabjee, *The Law of Press Censorship in India* (Tripathi, 1976).

Japan

L. Beer, "Freedom of Expression: The Continuing Revolution", 53 *Law & Contemporary Problems* 39 (1990).
H. Itoh & L. Beer, *The Constitutional Case Law of Japan* (1978).
H. Itoh & L. Beer, *The Constitutional Case Law of Japan: Selected Supreme Court Decisions (1961-1970)*.
P.J. Katzenstein, *Cultural Norms and National Security: Police and Military in Postwar Japan* (Cornell University Press, 1996).

Korea

J.M. West & D. Yoon, "The Constitutional Court of the Republic of Korea", 40 *Amer. J. Int'l L.* 71 (1992).

North Korea

K.H. Youm, "Press Laws in North Korea", 2 *Asian J. of Communication* 70 (1991).

South Korea

K. Cho, "Tension Between the National Security Act and Constitutionalism in South Korea: Security for What?", 15 *B.U. Int'l L.J.* 125 (1997).
K.H. Youm, "The Press and National Security: Judicial Balancing in South Korea", 21 *Asian Profile* 291 (1993).
K.H. Youm, "Human Rights in South Korea- Freedom of Expression Examined", 15 *Media Law & Practice* 1 (1994).

Tibet

Human Rights Watch/Asia & Tibet Information Network, *Cutting Off the Serpent's Head: Tightening Control in Tibet 1994-1995* (March 1996).

CARIBBEAN

A. Byre & B. Byfield eds., *International Human Rights Law in the Commonwealth Caribbean* (Dordrecht/Boston/London: Martinus Nijhoff, 1991).
M. DeMerieux, *Fundamental Rights in Commonwealth Caribbean Constitutions* (Barbados: University of the West Indies, 1992).

EUROPE

W.F. Korthals Altes, "European Law: A Case Study of Changes in National Broadcasting", *Cardozo Arts & Entertainment L.J.* (1992).
A. Bloed ed., *From Helsinki to Vienna: Basic Documents of the Helsinki Process* (Dordrecht: Martinus Nijhoff, 1990).
A. Bloed, "Institutional Aspects of the Helsinki Process After the Follow-up Meeting of Vienna", 36 *Netherlands Int'l L. Rev.* 342 (1989).
A. Bloed & P. van Dijk, *Essays on Human Rights in the Helsinki Process* (Dordrecht: Martinus Nijhoff, 1985).
T. Buergenthal ed., *Human Rights, International Law and the Helsinki Accord* (New York: Monclair, 1977).

M. Bullinger, *Report on Freedom of Expression and Information: An Essential Element of Democracy.*

S. Coliver, "Defamation Jurisprudence of the European Court of Human Rights", 13 *J. of Media Law & Practice* (1992).

M. Delmas-Marty, *The European Convention for the Protection of Human Rights: International Protection versus National Restrictions* (Dordrecht, 1992).

V. Dimitrijevic, "Human Rights in the Constitutional Systems of Socialist States", 8 *Neth. Q. Human Rights* 5 (1990).

D. Driscoll, "Freedom of Expression Under Article 10 of the European Convention on Human Rights", *in Proceedings of the Sixth International Colloquium on the European Convention on Human Rights* 278 (Dordrecht: Martinus Nijhoff, 1988).

A.Z. Drzemczewski, *European Human Rights Convention in Domestic Law: A Comparative Study* (Oxford University Press, 1983).

A.Z. Drzemczewski, *The right to respect for private and family life, home and correspondence as guaranteed by Article 8 of the European Convention on Human Rights* (Strasbourg: Council of Europe, 1984).

M.A. Eissen, "La liberte d'expression dans la jurisprudence de la Cour europeenee des droits de l'homme", *in* A. Cassese & A. Clapham eds., *Transfrontier Television in Europe: The Human Rights Dimension* (Florence: European University Institute, 1990).

V. Evans, "The Practice of European Countries Where Direct Effect is Given to the European Convention on Human Rights in Internal Law", *in Proceedings of the Colloquy About the European Convention on Human Rights*: Athens: Sept. 21-22, 1978 (Strasbourg: Council of Europe, 1979).

J.E.S. Fawcett, *The Application of the European Convention on Human Rights* (Oxford University Press, 1987).

J.A. Frowein, "The Interrelationship Between the Helsinki Final Act, the International Covenants on Human Rights and the European Convention on Human Rights", *in* T. Buergenthal ed., *Human Rights, International Law and the Helsinki Accord* (New York: Monclair, 1977).

W.J. Ganshof van der Meersch, "Reliance, in the Case-Law of the European Court of Human Rights, on the Domestic Law of the States", 1 *Human Rights L.J.* 13 (1980).

N.P. Gleditsch, "National Security and Freedom of Expression: The Scandinavian Legal Battles", *J. of Media Law and Practice* (1987).

D. Gomien, *Short Guide to the European Convention on Human Rights* (Strasbourg: Council of Europe, Directorate of Human Rights, 1991).

R. Higgins, "The European Convention on Human Rights", *in* T. Meron ed., *Human Rights in International Law: Legal and Policy Issues* 495 (1985).

F.G. Jacobs, "The Impact of the European Convention on Human Rights on Judicial Decisions in the United Kingdom", *in Perspectives Canadiennes et Europeennes des Droits de la Personne* (Cowansville: Blais, 1986).

M.W. Janis & R.S. Kay, *European Human Rights Law* (University of Connecticut Law School Foundation Press, 1990).

P. Juvelier, "Guaranteeing Human Rights in the Soviet Context", 28 *Columbia J. Transnat'l L.* 3 (1990).

A. Lester, "Freedom of Expression", *in* R. Macdonald, F. Matcher & H. Petzold eds., *The European System for the Protection of Human Rights* (The Hague, 1993).

A. Lester & D. Pannick, *Advertising and Freedom of Expression in Europe* (Marketing Commission of the International Chamber of Commerce, 1984).

S. Lewis-Anthony, "Article 11 and the Rights to Freedom of Peaceful Assembly and Association", Council of Europe, H (92) 11 (1992).

R.J. Macdonald, "The Margin of Appreciation in the Jurisprudence of the European Court of Human Rights", *in International Law and the Time of Its Codification: Essays in Honour of Roberto Ago* 187 (Milan, 1987).

I. Maier ed., *Protection of Human Rights in Europe* (1982).

P. Malanczuk, "Freedom of Information and Communication: Recent Developments in the Helsinki Process", *in* 3 *Hague Yearbook of Int'l L.* 89 (1990).

G. Malinverni, "Freedom of Information in the European Convention on Human Rights and in the International Covenant on Civil and Political Rights", *Human Rights L.J.* 443 (1983).

J.G. Merills, *The Development of International Law by the European Court of Human Rights* (Manchester University Press, 1988).

A. Nicol, *National Security, Freedom of Expression and Access to Information: The European Union.*

M. O'Boyle, "The Right to Speak and Associate under Strasbourg Case-Law with Reference to Central and Eastern Europe", *Connecticut J. of Int'l L.* (1993).

F. Ost, "Le concept de *democratie* dans la jurisprudence de la Cour europeenne des droits de l'homme", *Journal des proces* 13 (1988).

J. Paust, "Transnational Freedom of Speech: Legal Aspects of the Helsinki Final Act", 45 *L. & Contemporary Problems* 53 (1982).

H. Petzold & F. Matscher eds., *Protecting Human Rights: The European Dimension, Studies in Honour of Gerard J. Wiarda* (Cologne: Carl Heymanns Verlag, 1988).

J. Polakiewicz & V. Jacob-Foltzer, "The European Human Rights Convention in Domestic Law: The Impact of Strasbourg Case-Law in States where Direct Effect is Given to the Convention", Parts I and II, 12 *Human Rights L.J.* 65 (1991).

R. Ryssdal, "The Limits of Freedom of Expression in a Democratic Society: Examples from the Jurisprudence of the Court", *Proceedings of the Session on Human Rights and Journalism* (Strasbourg: Council of Europe, 1987).

D. Spielmann, "Abuse of Rights and Equivalent Concepts: The Principle and its Present Day Application", *in XIXe Colloque de Droit europeen a Luxembourg*, Nov. 6-9, 1989 (Strasbourg: Council of Europe, 1990).

P. van Dijk, "The Final Act of Helsinki- Basis for a Pan-European System?", 11 *N.Y. Int'l L.* 97 (1980).

P. van Dijk & G.J.H. van Hoof, *Theory and Practice of the European Convention on Human Rights*, 2d edition (Deventer: Kluwer Publishers, 1990).

D. Voorhoof, "Defamation and Libel Laws in Europe", 13 *J. of Media Law and Practice* (1992).

S. Weber, "Environmental Information and the European Convention on Human Rights", 12(5) *Hum. Rts. L.J.* 177 (1991).

Austria

W. Berka, "Press Law in Austria", *in* ARTICLE 19 ed., *Press Law in Practice* (op. cit.).

W. Berka, *The Law on the Mass Media (Das Recht der Massenmedien)* (Wien, Graz: Bohlau Verlag, 1989).

Bosnia

M. Malesic ed., *The Role of the Mass Media in the Serbian-Croatian Conflict* (Stockholm: May 1993).

Finland

Manninen Sami, "Freedom of Speech in Finland", *in* Maija Sakslin ed., *The Finnish Constitution in Transition.*

France

R. Errera, "Balancing Legitimate Rights: Freedom of the Press and Other Rights in French Law", *Communications Lawyer* (Spring 1991).

R. Errera, "Press Law in France", *in* ARTICLE 19 ed., *Press Law and Practice* (op. cit.).

R. Errera, "Recent Developments in the French Law of the Press in Comparison with Britain", *in* D. Kingsford-Smith & D. Oliver eds., *Economical with the Truth: the Law and the Media in a Democratic Society* (Oxford: ESC Pub. Ltd., 1990).

Germany

R. Herzog, "The Hierarchy of Constitutional Norms in Germany and Its Function in Protecting Human Rights: Reports to the 8th Conference of the European Constitutional Courts", 13 *Human Rights L.J.* 90 (1992).

U. Karpen, "Freedom of Expression", *in* U. Karpen ed., *The Constitution of the Federal Republic of Germany, Essays on the Basic Rights and Principles of the Basic Law with a Translation of the Basic Law* (Baden-Baden, 1988).

U. Karpen, "Press Law in Germany", *in* ARTICLE 19 ed., *Press Law and Practice* (op. cit.).

H. Kohl, "Press Law in the Federal Republic of Germany", *in* P. Lahave ed., *Press Law in Modern Democracies: A Comparative Study* (1985).

Luxembourg

A. Spielmann, A. Weitzel & D. Spielmann, *La Convention europeene des droits de l'homme et le droit luxembourgeois* (Brussels: Nemesis, 1991).

D. Spielmann, "Human Rights and Freedom of Expression in Luxembourg", 2 *Annales du droit luxembourgeois* 209 (1992).

Netherlands

W.F. Korthals Altes, "Protecting Journalists' Sources: A Dutch Proposal for Legislation", *Public Law* 73 (Spring 1992).

F. van Lenthe & I. Boerefijn, "Press Law in the Netherlands", *in* ARTICLE 19 ed., *Press Law and Practice* (op. cit.).

H. Lubberdink, "The Hierarchy of Constitutional Norms in the Netherlands and Its Function in Protecting Human Rights: Reports to the 8th Conference of the European Constitutional Courts", 13 *Human Rights L.J.* 93 (1992).

J. Vervaele, "Application of the European Convention Restrictions in the Dutch Legal Order", *in* Delmas-Marty (op. cit.).

Norway

E. Sandene, "The Hierarchy of Constitutional Norms in Norway and Its Function in Protecting Human Rights: Reports to the 8th Conference of the European Constitutional Courts", 13 *Human Rights L.J.* 97 (1992).

S. Wolland, "Press Law in Norway", *in* ARTICLE 19 ed., *Press Law in Practice* (op. cit.).

Poland

K. Dzialocha, "The Hierarchy of Constitutional Norms in Poland and Its Function in Protecting Human Rights: Reports to the 8th Conference of the European Constitutional Courts", 13 *Human Rights L.J.* 100 (1992).

Russia

Gusev, "The International Instruments on the Protection of Human Rights in the USSR and Their Interpretation in USSR Judicial Practice", 89 *Bull Human Rights* 48 (1990).

Spain

B. Rodriguez Ruiz, "Press Law in Spain", *in* ARTICLE 19 ed., *Press Law and Practice* (op. cit.).

Sweden

H-G. Axberger, "Press Law in Sweden", *in* ARTICLE 19 ed., *Press Law and Practice* (op. cit.).

Switzerland

A. Haefliger, "The Hierarchy of Constitutional Norms in Switzerland and its Function in Protecting Human Rights", 13 *Human Rights L.J.* 81 (1992).

Turkey

Helsinki Watch, *Paying the Price: Freedom of Expression in Turkey* (1989).
K. Yildiz, *National Security and Freedom of Expression in Turkey* (1995).

United Kingdom

Barendt, "Spycatcher and Freedom of Speech", *in Public Law* 204 (1992).
B. Gorlick, "National Security, the Security Service and Accountability: A Critical Survey of the British System" (LLM Paper, 1991).
J. Griffith, "The Official Secrets Act 1989", 16 *J. of Law & Society* 273 (1989).
I. Leigh, "Spycatcher in Strasbourg", *in Public Law* 200 (1992).
L. Lustgarten, *Freedom of Expression and National Security in the United Kingdom*.
L. Lustgarten & I. Leigh, *In From the Cold: National Security and Parliamentary Democracy* (Oxford: Oxford University Press, 1984).
A. Nicol & C. Bowman, "Press Law in the United Kingdom", *in* ARTICLE 19 ed., *Press Law and Practice* (op. cit.).
G. Robertson & A. Nicol, *Media Law*, 3rd edition (London: Penguin, 1992).
K.G. Robertson, *Public Secrets: A Study in the Development of Government Secrecy* (London: Macmillan, 1982).
G. Zellick, "Spies, Subversives, Terrorists and the British Government: Free Speech and Other Casualties", 31 *Wm. & Mary L. Rev.* 773 (1990).

MIDDLE EAST

K. Kenealey, "The Persian Gulf War and the Press: Is There a Constitutional Right of Access to Military Operations?", 87 *Northwestern U. L. Rev.* 287 (1992).

B. Korany, P. Noble & R. Brynen eds., *The Many Faces of National Security in the Arab World* (London: MacMillan).

D. Little, J. Kelsay & A. Sachedina, *Human Rights and the Conflict of Cultures: Western and Islamic Perspectives on Religious Liberty* (1988).

E. Said, "Human Rights in Islamic Perspectives", *in* A. Pollis & P. Schwab eds., *Human Rights: Culture and Ideological Perspectives* (1979).

Israel

R. Gavison, "Atomic Secrets and Free Speech", *in* S. Shetreet, *Free Speech and National Security* (Dordrecht/Boston/London: Martinus Nijhoff Pubs., 1991).

M. Kremnitzer, "Free Speech and the Criminal Code Provisions for the Protection of State Security: The Israeli Case", *in* S. Shetreet, *supra.*

P. Lahav, "Governmental Regulation and the Press: A Study of Israel's Press Ordinance", 13 *Isr. L. Rev.* 230 (1978).

M. Negbi, *Freedom of the Press in Israel- The Legal Aspect* (The Jerusalem Institute For Israel Studies, 1995) (in Hebrew).

INDEX

A

B

C

D

E

F

G

H

I

J

K

O

P

R

S

T

U

V

W

X

Y

Z

International Studies in Human Rights

20. A. Bloed and P. van Dijk (eds.): *The Human Dimension of the Helsinki Process.* The Vienna Follow-up Meeting and its Aftermath. 1991 ISBN 0-7923-1337-2
21. L.S. Sunga: *Individual Responsibility in International Law for Serious Human Rights Violations.* 1992 ISBN 0-7923-1453-0
22. S. Frankowski and D. Shelton (eds.): *Preventive Detention.* A Comparative and International Law Perspective. 1992 ISBN 0-7923-1465-4
23. M. Freeman and P. Veerman (eds.): *The Ideologies of Children's Rights.* 1992 ISBN 0-7923-1800-5
24. S. Stavros: *The Guarantees for Accused Persons Under Article 6 of the European Convention on Human Rights.* An Analysis of the Application of the Convention and a Comparison with Other Instruments. 1993 ISBN 0-7923-1897-8
25. A. Rosas and J. Helgesen (eds.): *The Strength of Diversity.* Human Rights and Pluralist Democracy. 1992 ISBN 0-7923-1987-7
26. K. Waaldijk and A. Clapham (eds.): *Homosexuality: A European Community Issue.* Essays on Lesbian and Gay Rights in European Law and Policy. 1993 ISBN 0-7923-2038-7; Pb: 0-7923-2240-1
27. Y.K. Tyagi: *The Law and Practice of the UN Human Rights Committee.* 1993 ISBN 0-7923-2040-9
28. H.Ch. Yourow: *The Margin of Appreciation Doctrine in the Dynamics of European Human Rights Jurisprudence.* 1996 ISBN 0-7923-3338-1
29. L.A. Rehof: *Guide to the* Travaux PrÇparatoires *of the United Nations Convention on the Elimination of All Forms of Discrimination against Women.* 1993 ISBN 0-7923-2222-3
30. A. Bloed, L. Leicht, M. Novak and A. Rosas (eds.): *Monitoring Human Rights in Europe.* Comparing International Procedures and Mechanisms. 1993 ISBN 0-7923-2383-1
31. A. Harding and J. Hatchard (eds.): *Preventive Detention and Security Law.* A Comparative Survey. 1993 ISBN 0-7923-2432-3
32. Y. Beigbeder: *International Monitoring of Plebiscites, Referenda and National Elections.* Self-determination and Transition to Democracy. 1994 ISBN 0-7923-2563-X
33. T.D. Jones: *Human Rights: Group Defamation, Freedom of Expression and the Law of Nations.* 1997 ISBN 90-411-0265-5
34. D.M. Beatty (ed.): *Human Rights and Judicial Review.* A Comparative Perspective. 1994 ISBN 0-7923-2968-6
35. G. Van Bueren, *The International Law on the Rights of the Child.* 1995 ISBN 0-7923-2687-3
36. T. Zwart: *The Admissibility of Human Rights Petitions.* The Case Law of the European Commission of Human Rights and the Human Rights Committee. 1994 ISBN 0-7923-3146-X; Pb: 0-7923-3147-8
37. H. Lambert: *Seeking Asylum.* Comparative Law and Practice in Selected European Countries. 1995 ISBN 0-7923-3152-4

International Studies in Human Rights

38. E. Lijnzaad: *Reservations to UN-Human Rights Treaties*. Ratify and Ruin? 1994 ISBN 0-7923-3256-3
39. L.G. Loucaides: *Essays on the Developing Law of Human Rights*. 1995 ISBN 0-7923-3276-8
40. T. Degener and Y. Koster-Dreese (eds.): *Human Rights and Disabled Persons*. Essays and Relevant Human Rights Instruments. 1995 ISBN 0-7923-3298-9
41. J.-M. Henckaerts: *Mass Expulsion in Modern International Law and Practice*. 1995 ISBN 90-411-0072-5
42. N.A. Neuwahl and A. Rosas (eds.): *The European Union and Human Rights*. 1995 ISBN 90-411-0124-1
43. H. Hey: *Gross Human Rights Violations: A Search for Causes*. A Study of Guatemala and Costa Rica. 1995 ISBN 90-411-0146-2
44. B.G. Tahzib: *Freedom of Religion or Belief*. Ensuring Effective International Legal Protection. 1996 ISBN 90-411-0159-4
45. F. de Varennes: *Language, Minorities and Human Rights*. 1996 ISBN 90-411-0206-X
46. J. RÎikkÎ (ed.): *Do We Need Minority Rights?* Conceptual Issues. 1996 ISBN 90-411-0309-0
47. J. Brhmer: *State Immunity and the Violation of Human Rights*. 1997 ISBN 90-411-0322-8
48. C.A. Gearty (ed.): *European Civil Liberties and the European Convention on Human Rights*. A Comparative Study. 1997 ISBN 90-411-0253-1
49. B. Conforti and F. Francioni (eds.): *Enforcing International Human Rights in Domestic Courts*. 1997 ISBN 90-411-0393-7
50. A. Spiliopoulou Åkermark: *Justifications of Minority Protection in International Law*. 1997 ISBN 90-411-0424-0
51. A. Boulesbaa: *The U.N. Convention on Torture and the Prospects for Enforcement*. 1997 ISBN 90-411-0457-7
52. S. Bowen (ed.): *Human Rights, Self-Determination and Political Change in the Occupied Palestinian Territories*. 1997 ISBN 90-411-0502-6
53. M. O'Flaherty and G. Gisvold (eds.): *Post-War Protection of Human Rights in Bosnia and Herzegovina*. 1998 ISBN 90-411-1020-8
54. A.-L. Svensson-McCarthy: *The International Law of Human Rights and States of Exception*. With Special Reference to the *Travaux Préparatoires* and Case-Law of the International Monitoring Organs. 1998 ISBN 90-411-1021-6
55. G. Gilbert: *Transnational Fugitive Offenders in International Law*. Extradition and Other Mechanisms. 1998 ISBN 90-411-1040-2